Shooter's Bible

ABOUT OUR COVER

The two scoped Sako rifles featured on our front cover this year are the PPC Benchrest/Varmint (top) and the PPC Deluxe (bottom). The cartridges illustrated represent factory-loaded ammunition and factory unprimed brass produced by Sako at the company's plant in Finland. Since their introduction, these components have together set virtually every world record in national and international benchrest competition. Now, they are fast becoming popular among small-game and varmint hunters as well. Readers who would like to know more about the PPC story are invited to read Wilf Pyle's interesting and informative article, ''The 6 PPC: From Shooting Range to Hunting Field,'' which begins on page 26.

Shooter's Bible

STOEGER PUBLISHING COMPANY

Published by Stoeger Publishing Company
55 Ruta Court
South Hackensack, New Jersey 07606

Library of Congress Catalog Card No.: 63-6200

International Standard Book No.: 0-88317-152-X

Manufactured in the United States of America

Distributed to the book trade and to the sporting goods trade by Stoeger Industries, 55 Ruta Court, South Hackensack, New Jersey 07606

In Canada, distributed to the book trade and to the sporting goods trade by Stoeger Canada Ltd., Unit 16/1801 Wentworth St. P.O. Box 445, Whitby, Ontario, L1N 5S4, Canada

NO. 81
1990 EDITION

EDITOR:
William S. Jarrett

PRODUCTION EDITOR:
Charlene Cruson Step

FIREARMS CONSULTANTS:
Jim Lagiss, Bill Meade,
Vincent A. Pestilli, and
Robert A. Scanlon

COVER PHOTOGRAPHER:
Ray Wells

DESIGN AND PRODUCTION:
Publishers Graphics
Bethel, Connecticut

PUBLISHER:
Paul G. Emberley

Shooter's Bible

Contents

FOREWORD

As we head on into the last decade of the 20th century, this 81st edition of *Shooter's Bible* continues down some well-traveled paths, but it also blazes a few new trails of its own. Our popular feature on "50 Years Ago in Shooter's Bible" runs its course this year in a final 18-page installment on *handguns*, reprinted from the 1940 edition. There you'll find an account of Colt's Bicentennial celebration (1836-1936), along with several pages of Colt handguns that were produced at the time. There's also a cartoon-type history of Smith & Wesson, plus several pages devoted to S&W handguns. Iver Johnson, High Standard and Harrington & Richardson are also featured in this section. If you're interested in knowing what was going on in the handgun field half a century ago, we recommend that you turn to p. 8 and enjoy.

Immediately following is the first of several illustrated articles by prominent writers in the gun field, starting off with Wilf Pyle, who writes on the subject of this year's front cover: the 6 PPC. Other articles cover such diverse topics as Compensators, Jack O'Connor, Chamber Pressure, Deer Hunting, Sporting Clays and the .357 Magnum. It's all in keeping with our continuing desire to provide readers with up-to-date information along with a few nostalgic glimpses of the past.

The catalog section includes as many specifications and illustrations as we could find and fit into the confines of this 576-page annual. Our usual coverage of handguns, rifles, shotguns, black powder, sights and scopes remains intact and even expanded. New manufacturers (to these pages, at least) include Raven Arms and Wildey (handguns), Silma, Laurona and Chapuis (shotguns), McMillan (rifles), Pentax and Nikon (scopes & sights), and more.

As always, the reference section has been completely revised and overhauled. If you're looking for a book on your favorite gun-related subject, or you're searching for a certain caliber or model, turn to the Caliberfinder and Gunfinder sections. Whatever your interests and needs may be, we hope they're satisfied with this 81st edition of *Shooter's Bible*. We look forward to your comments and suggestions.

William S. Jarrett
Editor

Articles

50 YEARS AGO IN SHOOTER'S BIBLE

EDITOR'S NOTE

In last year's edition (Volume 80, 1989), we continued our series of reprints from A.F. Stoeger's catalog of half a century ago. This feature has become so popular with our readers that we've decided to go around one more time. The response has been so favorable, in fact, that we've even reprinted the entire 1940 edition of ''Shooter's Bible.'' It's available now in bookstores and sporting goods stores throughout the country. Priced at $16.95, this 512-page, 50th anniversary edition can also be purchased direct from the publisher (Stoeger Publishing Co., 55 Ruta Court, S. Hackensack, NJ 07606).

Our special reprint this year covers *handguns*. The following pages have been taken directly from Stoeger's 1940 catalog, and here you'll find what was happening at Colt (which celebrated its centennial in 1936), Smith & Wesson, Iver Johnson, Harrington & Richardson, and the other fine pistol and revolver makers of their day. We hope you've enjoyed these glimpses of the past and that you've learned a few interesting facts about pre-World War II guns. We certainly have.

A CENTURY OF ACHIEVEMENT
1836—COLT—1936

The Colt's Patent Fire Arms Mfg. Co., can proudly look back to a century of achievements outstanding in the fire arms industry of this country. Samuel Colt, the founder, was born in Hartford, Conn., July 18, 1814. As a youngster on board a sailing ship bound for Calcutta he completed a working model of the revolving Colt pistol. In the year of 1835 he patented his revolving arm in England and received his first patent in this country in February 1836, and immediately plans were laid for what proved to be the beginning of one of America's industrial giants.

In the same year a small factory was established at Paterson, N. J., for the manufacture of the first Colt revolvers. Frontier conditions in Texas and the Seminole Indian wars in Florida did much to test the value of the Colt revolvers used for the first time in the defense of United States territory. The so-called "Texas-Pistol" used in these wars showed its superiority over the regular clumsy old-fashioned regulation ordnance and the young officers of the army particularly demanded the Colt to be supplied for their troops. Through the influence of General Zachary Taylor the first order for one thousand Colt's was placed with the young concern, and his revolving pistol was now firmly established.

In addition to revolvers, the Paterson plant produced revolving rifles and shotguns in various calibers and models. One of the most debated subjects is the "Walker" Model. This was a heavy .44 caliber six-shooter provided with an attached lever for ramming the bullets into the chamber of the cylinders.

In 1848 Samuel Colt produced a new .31 caliber model and others. The cylinder was removable for loading and later a rammer was added. Among them was the noted "Wells Fargo" model. Other models followed such as the Dragoon Models, adapted officially by the U. S. Government for both mounted and unmounted troops. In 1855 Colt had established mass production methods. In May, 1855, the Colt's Patent Fire Arms Co., was chartered and he established contact with every foreign nation.

Shortly thereafter a new design in revolver construction was developed. This was the jointless frame with top straps to which the barrel was firmly attached and in which the cylinder was inclosed. New models of revolvers and rifles followed in quick succession right up to the outbreak of the Civil War. During this period Colt produced in 1861–69655; in 1862–111676; in 1863–136579 and during 1864 and 1865–69107 pieces. After a hard struggle and achieving great success Samuel Colt passed away on January 10th, 1862.

However, the great business he had established was kept up under the leadership of his faithful associates. With the invention of the metallic cartridge the reloading problem was solved and "rapid fire" made possible. This revolutionized the making of firearms and a full line of new Colt revolvers was produced. In 1873 the famous "Peacemaker" was introduced. This same six-shooter was also produced in .44 and .44-40 calibers and became famous as the Colt "Frontier" revolver.

A unique type of gun introduced in this period was known as the Deringer. The first Deringer introduced by Colt's and National were short, all-metal, single-barreled pistols using .41 caliber, rim-fire cartridges. A second type known as the "No. 2" Deringer using the same caliber cartridge and with wood stocks was later produced by both Colt's and National, which was followed by the third Deringers often referred to as the New Type Deringer. These third Deringers were introduced by Colt's in the late "Seventies" and were furnished with two types of stocks. They used .41 caliber, rim-fire cartridges and were manufactured until about 1912 when the models were discontinued.

During this period (1870–1872) the Colt Company manufactured 40,000 .42 caliber Berdan Breech-loading Military rifles for the Russian Government using for the first time a metallic cartridge having a "Bottle-necked" case, reducing the diameter of the bullet and increasing the powder space. These arms were produced in both musket and carbine types.

The year of 1877 marks the advent of the Double Action revolver. Another advancement was made in 1887, the lateral swinging cylinder with simultaneous ejection. The Bisley model was introduced in 1897, followed shortly by the Bisley Target model. With the turn of the century a new idea in pistols was conceived, a .38 automatic magazine pistol operated by the recoil. During the decade of 1900–1910 automatics of various styles, weights and calibers were made. In 1909 the Army adopted the .45 caliber New Service revolver and in 1911 the U. S. War Department adopted the Colt Automatic pistol as its official arm.

Each year has ushered in some improvement to enchance the efficiency or accuracy and safety of the Colt. Scientific invention marches on. You may obtain a copy of the Colt's book "A Century of Achievement" from us at the price of 25 cents or a de Luxe edition at the price of $1.00.

COLT AUTOMATIC PISTOLS

ACE .22 AUTOMATIC PISTOL CAL. .22 LONG RIFLE

The ACE is designed especially for shooters of the Government Model and Super .38 Automatic Pistols—and has also been in demand by shooters for all around service. Built on the same frame as the Government Model and has the same safety features. Special super-precisioned barrel and hand finished target action. Exceptionally smooth operation and unusually accurate. Rear sight is of target design with adjustments for both elevation and windage. Allows economical target practice for military men, using .22 caliber ammunition in an arm of the same design as the regular military model. For Regular and High Speed Greased Cartridges.

Price $50.25

SPECIFICATIONS

Ammunition: .22 Long Rifle Greased cartridges. Regular or High Speed.
Magazine Capacity: 10 cartridges.
  Length of Barrel: 4¾ inches.
  Length Over All: 8¼ inches.

Action: Hand finished.
Weight: 38 ounces.
Sights: Front sight fixed. Rear sight adjustable for both elevation and windage.

Trigger and Hammer Spur: Checked.
Arched Housing: Checked.
Stocks: Checked Walnut.
Finish: Blued.

Price $41.75

SUPER .38 AUTOMATIC PISTOL CALIBER .38

For the big game hunter, and the lover of the outdoors, the Super .38 offers an arm of unsurpassed power and efficiency. It is built on the same frame as the Government Model and has all of the safety features found in this famous gun. It is especially popular because of the powerful Super .38 cartridges which it handles—having a muzzle velocity of approximately 1300 foot seconds. Will stop any animal on the American continent and is a favorite for use as an auxiliary arm for big game hunting trips. Magazine holds 9 cartridges.

SPECIFICATIONS

Sights: Fixed Patridge type.
Trigger and Hammer Spur: Checked.
Arched Housing: Checked.
Stocks: Checked Walnut.
Finish: Blued. Nickel Finish at extra cost of $5.00.

Ammunition: .38 Automatic cartridges.
Magazine Capacity: 9 cartridges.
Length of Barrel: 5 inches.
Length Over All: 8½ inches.
Weight: 39 ounces.

The Colt Arched Housing is illustrated above— used on all heavy frame Colt models. It provides a more secure and more comfortable grip.

GOVERNMENT MODEL AUTOMATIC PISTOL CAL. .45

The Colt Government Model is the most famous Automatic Pistol in the world. It has for years been the Official side arm of the United States Army, Navy and Marine Corps, as well as the military organizations of many foreign countries. Extremely powerful and absolutely dependable. Magazine holds seven cartridges and magazines can be replaced with great speed. Rugged and simple, it has withstood the most rigorous tests by the United States Government and proved itself unsurpassed in reliability and efficiency.

Price $41.75

SPECIFICATIONS

Ammunition: .45 Automatic cartridges.
Magazine Capacity: 7 cartridges.
Length of Barrel: 5 inches.
Length Over All: 8½ inches.
Sights: Fixed Patridge type.
Weight: 39 ounces.

Trigger and Hammer Spur: Checked.
Arched Housing: Checked.
Stocks: Checked Walnut.
Finish: Blued. Nickel Finish $5.00 extra.

Price $50.00

COLT NATIONAL MATCH CALIBER .45

The regulation Government Model side arm perfected for match competition. Identical in size and operation, but with super-precisioned match barrel. Full grip, fine balance, three safety features. Now with adjustable rear sight and ramp type front sight, Colt's National Match brings you accuracy, power and smoothness never before equalled in a caliber .45 automatic pistol.

COLT SUPER MATCH CALIBER .38

With the exception that it is chambered for the high-powered .38 automatic cartridge, the Super Match Automatic Pistol is identical in every way with the National Match Model. It has the same velvet-smooth action, precision match barrel, same dependable safety features, same checked arched housing, same firm non-slipping grip. Accuracy, of course, is further increased by the new sights now available; ramp type front and adjustable rear. The Colt Super Match answers every demand in a caliber .38 automatic for competitive shooting—and possesses tremendous power for the big game hunter.

Prices: National Match and Super Match with adjustable sight..................$50.25
        National Match and Super Match with fixed sights 45.25

DOUBLE ADJUSTABLE REAR SIGHT AND A RAMP TYPE FIXED FRONT SIGHT WITH SERRATED FACE

Here is a beautiful and efficient new rear sight for the Colt National Match and Super Match Automatic Pistols. It is designed especially for these two arms, constructed with precision, and adjustable for both windage and elevation. Take a close look at the illustration. Note the simplicity of this new sight, how extremely easy it is to adjust and to set accurately. It's just the finest hand gun sight ever made. And we mean just that. A host of shooters are going to like the new ramp type rugged sight out front, too. All of which means cleaner definition, higher and more consistent scoring.

SPECIFICATIONS

Ammunition: .38 Automatic cartridges.
Magazine Capacity: 9 cartridges.
Length of Barrel: 5 inches.
Length Over All: 8½ inches.
Weight: 39 ounces.

Action: Hand honed, velvet-smooth.
Stocks: Checked Walnut.
Sights: Adjustable rear, with Adjustments for elevation and windage. Ramp front sight.

Trigger and Hammer Spur: Checked.
Arched Housing: Checked.
Finish: Blued. Can be furnished in nickel finish at extra cost of $5.00.

ADJUSTABLE SIGHTS ON OLDER PISTOLS

You don't have to buy a new gun to enjoy the truly remarkable advantages of this new rear sight. For seven dollars and seventy-five cents, we will equip your Government Model and Super .38, as well as your National Match Model, or your Super Match, with this new sight combination. This includes the cost of the sight, recutting the sight slide cut, labor and targeting. It's a lot of value for $7.75.

COLT AUTOMATIC PISTOLS

In every part of the world Colt Automatic Pistols are known and used. The speed with which they may be fired, their power and dependability, have made them popular for every type of service requiring an arm of absolute dependability and complete safety. Colt Automatic Pistols are equipped with both manual and automatic safety features—they are the safest automatic pistols that can be purchased. There is a Colt model for every purpose.

WOODSMAN TARGET MODEL

CALIBER: .22 Long Rifle
6½ Inch Barrel

The Colt Woodsman Model is the most popular .22 Caliber automatic pistol ever produced. Thousands of shooters have found it ideal for all around shooting—and for target shooting. Graceful in appearance and beautifully finished. It is furnished with an unusually comfortable grip that fits the hand snugly and securely. Checked walnut stocks make slipping impossible. Fast and certain action—a trigger pull that is smooth and crisp. Ten shot magazine, and slide lock safety. Target sights, either Bead or Patridge.

Price $32.75

SPECIFICATIONS

Ammunition: .22 Long Rifle Greased cartridges. Regular or High Speed.
Magazine Capacity: 10 cartridges.
Length of Barrel: 6½ inches.
Length Over All: 10½ inches.
Distance Between Sights: 9 inches.
Weight: 29 ounces.
Sights: Adjustable, Bead or Patridge. Stippled.
Trigger: Grooved, set-back type.
Stocks: Checked Walnut. Finish: Blued.

Price $32.75

SPECIFICATIONS

Ammunition: .22 Long Rifle Greased cartridges. Regular or High Speed.
Magazine Capacity: 10 cartridges.
Length of Barrel: 4½ inches.
Length Over All: 8½ inches.
Distance Between Sights: Fixed Front sight—7½ inches. Adjustable front sight—7 inches.
Weight: 27 ounces.
Stocks: Checked Walnut.
Sights: Front sight fixed, ramp type with serrated face, or adjustable front sight. Rear sight adjustable for windage. Both stippled.
Trigger: Grooved, set-back type. Finish: Blued.

WOODSMAN SPORT MODEL

CALIBER: .22 Long Rifle
4½ Inch Barrel

The same as the standard model described above, except for length of barrel. It can now be furnished with either fixed or adjustable front sight. Ramp type front sight is sturdy and rugged, built to stand up under hard service and abuse. Adjustable type front sight is same as on target model. Rear sight is adjustable for windage. This model was produced for use in the woods and on the trail, where compactness is essential. Unusually accurate and a thoroughbred Colt in every way. Uses either Regular or High Speed cartridges, including hollow point type. Ten shot magazine.

WOODSMAN HIGH SPEED MAIN SPRING HOUSING

The new Main Spring Housing, built of hardened steel and adapting the Woodsman for use with the new High Speed Cartridges.

Those who may wish to change over their present Woodsman to handle the High Speed Cartridges need simply replace their old housing with the new type.

Price $2.00

POCKET MODEL AUTOMATIC PISTOL

CALIBER: .25

The .25 Caliber Colt Automatic Pistol is designed for personal protection. Because of its small size and light weight it can be easily carried in vest pocket or ladies hand bag. Shoots the hard-hitting .25 Automatic cartridge, with magazine having six shot capacity. Makes a beautiful gift when finished in nickel with pearl or ivory stocks. Three safety features make it absolutely safe to handle.

SPECIFICATIONS

Ammunition: 25 Automatic cartridge. Magazine Capacity: 6 cartridges. Length of Barrel: 2 inches. Length Over All: 4½ inches. Weight: 13 ounces. Stocks: Checked Walnut. Finish: Blued or Nickel.

Price $20.75

Colt Grip Safety and Magazine Disconnector

To doubly insure absolute safety in handling Colt Automatic Pistols, all models (with the exception of the Woodsman Model) are fitted with the world famed Colt Grip Safety—in addition to the Slide Lock Safety. The Colt Grip Safety operates automatically and requires the grip safety to be squeezed simultaneously with pulling the trigger in order to discharge the Arm. The arm cannot be fired by simply pulling the trigger.

Colt Automatic Pistol models in calibers .32, .380 and .25 are also equipped with the Colt Magazine Safety Disconnector.

Price $24.25

This is the favorite model for personal and home protection. Ready always for instant action.

POCKET MODEL AUTOMATIC PISTOL

CALIBERS: .32 and .380

This pocket model Automatic Pistol can be furnished in either .32 or .380 caliber. Large magazine capacity, powerful, rugged and dependable. Flat construction takes up minimum room in pocket, bag or dresser drawer. Three safety features, both manual and automatic.

SPECIFICATIONS

Ammunition: .32 Automatic cartridge. .380 Automatic cartridge.
Magazine Capacity: .32 caliber, 8 cartridges. .380 caliber, 7 cartridges.
Length of Barrel: 3¾ inches. Length Over All: 6¾ inches.
Weight: 24 ounces. Stocks: Checked Walnut.
Finish: Blued or Nickel.

NEW STYLE ARCHED MAIN SPRING HOUSING

For Colt Automatic Caliber .45.
Price $1.50

NEW STYLE SHORT CHECKERED TRIGGER

For Colt Automatic .45 or .38.
Price $1.50
Old Style Trigger, Colt Automatic Caliber .45 or .38.
Price . . . . each $1.50

STOEGER'S 25-SHOT MAGAZINE

Made for the Government Model .45 Automatic Pistol. Fits this model pistol without any alterations. Can be easily loaded by hand. Invaluable for Police, Riot Duty.

This item discontinued

COLT REVOLVERS

The name "Colt" has for nearly a century been the symbol of quality, efficiency and dependability in firearms. Colt Revolvers and Automatic Pistols have been selected by thousands of shooters in every part of the world, for personal protection, police and military service, target shooting and for use in the outdoors. Their ruggedness, accuracy and absolute dependability have stamped them as the standard by which all other firearms are measured. There is nothing finer than a COLT.

POLICE REVOLVERS

The most important item in the equipment of a police officer, sheriff or guard is his service revolver. It must be dependable beyond the shadow of a doubt—and ready for efficient and effective action on a moment's notice. These rigid requirements explain in large measure why Colts have been selected by so many thousands of officers throughout the country—hundreds of whom have told us that the Colt, ready at their side for instant duty, makes it easier to face the dangers so common to the modern peace officer.

OFFICIAL POLICE REVOLVER

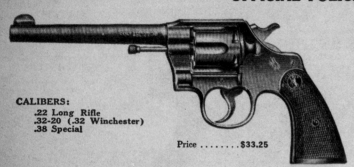

CALIBERS:
.22 Long Rifle
.32-20 (.32 Winchester)
.38 Special

Price $33.25

SPECIFICATIONS: Calibers .38 and .32-20

Ammunition: .32-20 (.32 Winchester)
.38 Short Colt; .38 Long Colt; .38 Colt Special; .38 S. & W. Special (full and mid-range loads); .38 Colt Special High Speed; .38 S. & W. Special High Speed and .38-44 S. & W. Special cartridges in .385 special model.
Lengths of Barrel: 2, 4, 5, 6 inches.
Length Over All: With 6 inch barrel, 11¼ inches.
Weight: With 6 inch barrel, 34 ounces.
Sights: Fixed type, stippled
Trigger and Hammer Spur: Checked. Stocks: Checked Walnut.
Finish: Blued or Nickel. Top of frame matted to prevent light reflection.

The COLT Official Police Revolver is without any question the world's outstanding police arm. This popular service model is famous for its ruggedness, and its ability to stand up under the severe abuse it receives at the sides of police officers the world over. Built on the .41 caliber frame it has ample strength to meet any requirements—and the .38 Special cartridges for which it is chambered offer sufficient power to meet any emergency. The Official Police is furnished with the Colt Positive Safety Lock—which makes accidental discharge impossible. Full size grip, perfect balance, special matted top. Also chambered for .22 Long Rifle cartridges to allow police officers, economical target practice with a small caliber model that is otherwise identical with their regular service arm.

SPECIFICATIONS: Caliber .22

Ammunition: .22 Long Rifle cartridges. Regular or High Speed.
Length of Barrel: 6 inches only.
Length Over All: 11¼ inches.
Weight: 38 ounces.
Sights: Fixed type, stippled.
Cylinder: Embedded Head Type.
Stocks: Checked Walnut.
Finish: Blued only.
Top of frame matted to prevent light reflection.
Trigger and Hammer Spur: Checked.

Colt "Two Point" Hand

You have possibly often wondered what device was used in Colt Revolvers to hold the cylinder chamber and the barrel so rigidly and so perfectly in line. This result is obtained through the use of the Colt "Two Point" Hand found only in Colt Revolvers.

POLICE POSITIVE SPECIAL REVOLVER

The Police Positive Special Model is a medium weight police arm—the standard service revolver of many large police departments in this country and abroad. It is chambered for the powerful .38 Special cartridges and furnished with a grip that is secure and comfortable. The Colt Positive Safety Lock is a feature that prevents accidental discharge. *Colt Police Revolvers cannot be fired unless the trigger is intentionally pulled.* This model is ideal for unmounted police officers, as well as for personal and home protection.

CALIBERS:
.32-20 (.32 Winchester)
.38 Special

Price $31.75

The patented Colt matted frame top. Prevents light reflection and aids in sighting.

Ammunition: .32-20 (.32 Winchester).
.38 Short Colt; .38 Long Colt; .38 Colt Special; .38 S. & W. Special (full and mid-range loads); .38 Colt Special High Speed; .38 S. & W. Special High Speed and .38-44 S. & W. Special cartridges.
Lengths of Barrel: 4, 5, 6 inches.
Length Over All: With 4 inch barrel, 8¾ inches.

SPECIFICATIONS

Weight: With 4 inch barrel, 22 ounces.
Sights: Fixed type, stippled.
Trigger and Hammer Spur: Checked.
Stocks: Checked Walnut.
Finish: Blued or nickel. Top of frame matted to prevent light reflection.

SEE PAGE 8 "HOW TO ORDER"

COLT REVOLVERS

The Colt Positive Safety Lock makes accidental discharge of a Colt Police Revolver absolutely impossible. The illustration above shows the solid bar of steel, 1/10 of an inch thick, which rests between the hammer and frame at all times except when trigger is intentionally pulled.

DETECTIVE SPECIAL

The Detective Special is exactly the same as the Police Positive Special Revolver, except that it has been finished with the short 2 inch barrel. This model is designed especially for pocket use, and has been adopted by large police departments for use by detectives, special investigators and plain clothes men. It handles the same ammunition as the Official Police Model, making it the most powerful arm of its size and weight available. Unusually accurate at short range, and absolutely reliable. Equipped with Colt Positive Safety Lock. Weighs only 21 ounces.

CALIBER:
.38 Special

Price $31.75

SPECIFICATIONS

Ammunition: .38 Short Colt; .38 Long Colt; .38 Colt Special. .38 S. & W. Special (full and mid-range loads); .38 Colt Special High Speed; .38 S. & W. Special High Speed and .38-44 S. & W. Special cartridges.

Length of Barrel: 2 inches.

Length Over All: 6¾ inches.

Weight: 21 ounces.
Sights: Fixed type, stippled.
Trigger and Hammer Spur: Checked.
Stocks: Rounded, checked Walnut.
Finish: Blued or nickel. Top of frame matted to prevent light reflection.

POLICE POSITIVE REVOLVER

The Colt Rearward action, safety type cylinder latch guards against the possibility of the cylinder being accidentally opened by forward pressure from the thumb. The Colt latch can only be operated by a deliberate rearward motion.

Price $30.75

CALIBERS:

.32 Police Positive (New Police)

.38 Police Positive (New Police)

For police officers, bank guards and messengers who require a powerful arm, yet one that can be easily concealed, the Colt Police Positive Revolver is recommended. This model is smaller and lighter than the Police Positive Special Revolver, but otherwise has the same characteristics. Chambered for both the .32 and .38 Police Positive (New Police) Cartridges, which are popular for police and guard service in all parts of the country. This model is also adapted for home protection and can be easily and safely carried in pocket, holster or car. Furnished with the Colt Positive Safety Lock.

SPECIFICATIONS

Ammunition: .32 Police Positive (New Police) .32 S. & W. Short; .32 S. & W. Long (Regular and Sharp Shoulder) in .32 Caliber model.
.38 Police Positive (New Police) and .38 S. & W. cartridges in .38 caliber model.
Lengths of Barrel: .32 caliber, 2½, 4, 5, 6 inches; .38 caliber, 4, 5, 6 inches.
Length Over All: With 4-inch barrel, 8½ inches.
Weight: With 4-inch barrel, .38 cal. 20 ounces; 32 cal. 22 ounces.
Sights: Fixed type, stippled.
Trigger and Hammer Spur: Checked.
Stocks: Checked Walnut.
Finish: Blued or Nickel. Top of frame matted to prevent light reflection.

BANKERS' SPECIAL REVOLVER

CALIBERS:

.22 Long Rifle   .38 Police Positive (New Police)

The .38 caliber Colt Bankers' Special Model has been a great favorite for use by bank messengers, tellers, guards and plain clothes men. It is compact, absolutely dependable and powerful. Easily carried and concealed in pocket or shoulder holster. The new .22 Caliber model uses the regular or high speed .22 Long Rifle cartridges—including the hard-hitting, hollow point. It is in great demand as an arm to be carried at all times, ready for any emergency. Except for caliber, both guns are identical. Both models have COLT POSITIVE SAFETY LOCK.

Price $30.75

Price $30.75

SPECIFICATIONS

.22 Caliber Model

Ammunition: .22 Long Rifle cartridges, Regular or High Speed, including Hollow Point.
Length of Barrel: 2 inches.
Length Over All: 6½ inches.
Sights: Fixed type, stippled.
Cylinder: Embedded Head Type.
Stocks: Rounded, checked Walnut.
Weight: 23 ounces.
Finish: Blued or Nickel. Top of frame matted to prevent light reflection.
Trigger and Hammer Spur: Checked.

SPECIFICATIONS

.38 Caliber Model

Ammunition: .38 Police Positive (New Police) and .38 S. & W. cartridges.
Length of Barrel: 2 inches.
Length Over All: 6½ inches.
Sights: Fixed type, stippled.
Weight: 19 ounces.
Stocks: Rounded, checked Walnut.
Finish: Blued or Nickel. Top of frame matted to prevent light reflection.
Trigger and Hammer Spur: Checked.

© **EVERYTHING IN GUNS UNDER ONE COVER**

COLT REVOLVERS

POCKET POSITIVE REVOLVER

Price $28.75

This model is furnished with the COLT POSITIVE SAFETY LOCK — making it absolutely safe for use by ladies and those not accustomed to handling firearms.

CALIBER: .32 Police Positive (New Police)

The Pocket Positive is an unusually compact revolver, small in size and light in weight. Designed to be carried in pocket or small hand bag and having ample power to make it an ideal arm for personal protection. Small, snug grip with checked rubber stocks. Popular for home protection.

SPECIFICATIONS

Ammunition: .32 Police Positive (New Police); .32 S. W. Short; .32 S. & W. Long (Regular and Sharp Shoulder)

Lengths of Barrel 2, 2½, 3½, 6 inches.

Length Over All: With 2½ inch barrel, 6½ inches.

Weight: With 2½ inch barrel, 16 ounces.

Sights: Fixed type, stippled.

Hammer Spur: Checked.

Stocks: Checked black rubber.

Finish: Blued or Nickel. Top of frame matted to prevent light reflection.

The checked hammer spur used on Colt Revolvers makes possible a firm, sure grip and speeds up cocking for rapid firing.

NEW SERVICE REVOLVER

CALIBERS: .38 Special
   .357 Magnum
   .38-40 (.38 Winchester)
   .44 Special
   .44-40 (.44 Winchester)
   .45 Colt
   .45 Automatic
   .455 Eley

Price $37.75

SPECIFICATIONS

Ammunition: .38 Short Colt; .38 Long Colt; .38 Colt Special; .38 S. & W. Special (full and midrange loads); .38 Colt Special High Speed; .38 S. & W. Special High Speed and .38-44 S. & W. Special cartridges in .38 caliber model.
.357 Magnum.
.38-40 (.38 Winchester).
.44 Special. .44-40 (.44 Winchester).
.45 Colt.
.45 Automatic. .455 Eley (English).
Lengths of Barrel Calibers .38 and .357 Magnum, 4, 5, 6 inches. Other calibers, 4½, 5½, 7½ inches.
Length Over All: With 4½-inch barrel, 9¾ inches. .38 caliber with 6-inch barrel, 11¼ inches.
Weight: 45 caliber, with 4½-inch barrel, 39 ounces. .38 caliber, with 6-inch barrel, 43 ounces.
Sights: Fixed type, stippled.
Trigger and Hammer Spur: Checked.
Stocks: Checked Walnut. Either Round or Square. Specify type desired. Lanyard Loop can be furnished for .38 and .357 caliber models at no extra cost. Standard in other calibers.
Finish: Blued or nickel. Top of frame matted to prevent light reflection.

This is the heaviest service revolver made and has been adopted by many large police departments who require a service arm chambered for heavy caliber ammunition. Chambered for a wide variety of cartridges. Either square or round type butt can be furnished for this model on request, at no extra cost. Perfectly balanced, and extremely rugged. This is the standard arm of the Royal Canadian Mounted Police. A favorite for big game hunting. Has Colt Positive Safety Lock.

SINGLE ACTION ARMY REVOLVER

This is the Colt that played so famous a part in the winning of the West and is still extremely popular in many sections of the country. Its dependability and ruggedness have earned the confidence of shooters for over sixty years. It is popularly known as the "Colt Frontier Model," or Colt Six Shooter. The shape and size of the grip adapt this model to the largest and brawniest hands. Single action, with rod ejection.

CALIBERS: .32-20 (.32 Winchester)
   .357 Magnum
   .38 Special
   .38-40 (.38 Winchester)
   .44 Special
   .44-40 (.44 Winchester)
   .45 Colt

"Frontier" Six Shooter Model

Price $37.75

Ammunition: .32-20 (.32 Winchester). .38 Short Colt; .38 Long Colt; .38 Colt Special; .38 S. & W. Special (full and mid-range loads); .38 Colt Special High Speed; .38 S. & W. Special High Speed and .38-44 S. & W. Special cartridges in .38 caliber model.
.357 Magnum
.38-40 (.38 Winchester).
.44 Special .44-40 (.44 Winchester).
.45 Colt.

SPECIFICATIONS

Lengths of Barrel: 4¾, 5½, 7½ inches.
Length Over All: With 4¾ inch barrel, 10¼ inches.
Weight: .45 Caliber, with 4¾ inch barrel, 36 ounces.
Sights: Fixed type.
Hammer Spur: Checked.
Stocks: Checked black rubber.
Finish: Blued, with case hardened frame, or Nickel.

A NEW GUN CARRIES A FACTORY GUARANTEE

HISTORY OF SMITH & WESSON

Daniel Baird Wesson and Horace Smith began manufacture of the famous Volcanic Action repeating pistol in Norwich, Conn., 1854. In 1856 patents were released to Oliver Winchester and others, resulting in the formation of the Winchester Repeating Arms. Co. Manufacture of the first revolver to employ self-contained ammunition began in a Market Street livery stable at Springfield, Mass. with 25 employees. In 1859 the first building in the present plant location was erected.

With the advent of the Civil War, Government orders expanded the business to 600 employees, and hundreds of thousands of arms were produced.

In 1870 Smith & Wesson designed the famous .44 Russian Model for the Russian Imperial Army and delivered huge numbers of them.

In 1875 the .45 Schofield Model was adopted by the United States Cavalry. It is reliably reported that General Custer used this model in his historic "Last Stand", at the Battle of Little Bighorn.

In 1880 the double action type of revolvers were introduced and the .44 caliber became immensely popular with Western peace officers.

In 1887 the Safety Hammerless was brought out. This arm was and is distinguished by its absolute safety from accidental discharge.

The Military & Police swingout cylinder solid frame model followed in 1902, and with refinements, continues to the present time.

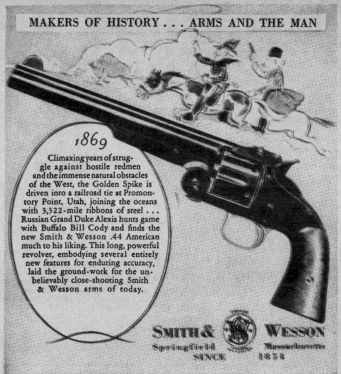

MAKERS OF HISTORY . . . ARMS AND THE MAN

1869

Climaxing years of struggle against hostile redmen and the immense natural obstacles of the West, the Golden Spike is driven into a railroad tie at Promontory Point, Utah, joining the oceans with 3,322-mile ribbons of steel . . . Russian Grand Duke Alexis hunts game with Buffalo Bill Cody and finds the new Smith & Wesson .44 American much to his liking. This long, powerful revolver, embodying several entirely new features for enduring accuracy, laid the ground-work for the unbelievably close-shooting Smith & Wesson arms of today.

SMITH & WESSON
Springfield   Massachusetts
SINCE   1854

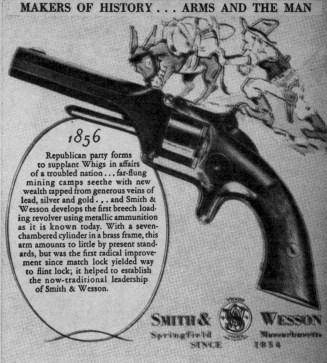

MAKERS OF HISTORY . . . ARMS AND THE MAN

1856

Republican party forms to supplant Whigs in affairs of a troubled nation . . . far-flung mining camps seethe with new wealth tapped from generous veins of lead, silver and gold . . . and Smith & Wesson develops the first breech loading revolver using metallic ammunition as it is known today. With a seven-chambered cylinder in a brass frame, this arm amounts to little by present standards, but was the first radical improvement since match lock yielded way to flint lock; it helped to establish the now-traditional leadership of Smith & Wesson.

SMITH & WESSON
Springfield   Massachusetts
SINCE   1854

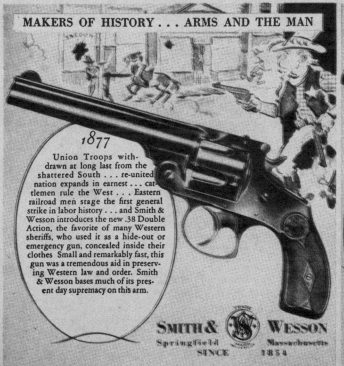

MAKERS OF HISTORY . . . ARMS AND THE MAN

1877

Union Troops withdrawn at long last from the shattered South . . . re-united nation expands in earnest . . . cattlemen rule the West . . . Eastern railroad men stage the first general strike in labor history . . . and Smith & Wesson introduces the new .38 Double Action, the favorite of many Western sheriffs, who used it as a hide-out or emergency gun, concealed inside their clothes Small and remarkably fast, this gun was a tremendous aid in preserving Western law and order. Smith & Wesson bases much of its present day supremacy on this arm.

SMITH & WESSON
Springfield   Massachusetts
SINCE   1854

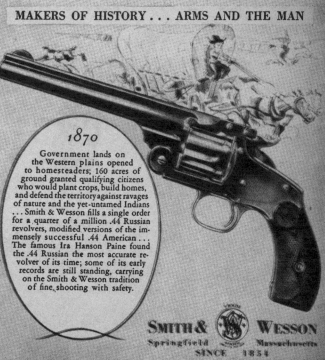

MAKERS OF HISTORY . . . ARMS AND THE MAN

1870

Government lands on the Western plains opened to homesteaders; 160 acres of ground granted qualifying citizens who would plant crops, build homes, and defend the territory against ravages of nature and the yet-untamed Indians . . . Smith & Wesson fills a single order for a quarter of a million .44 Russian revolvers, modified versions of the immensely successful .44 American . . . The famous Ira Hanson Paine found the .44 Russian the most accurate revolver of its time; some of its early records are still standing, carrying on the Smith & Wesson tradition of fine shooting with safety.

SMITH & WESSON
Springfield   Massachusetts
SINCE   1854

© **No Guns Nor Parts Thereof Illustrated Above Now Available**

SMITH & WESSON

The .32 Hand Ejector

$30.00

Here is the revolver for the man who wants a small, light gun with round handle, which has all the features that were first worked out so successfully in the Military and Police Model.

The .32 Hand Ejector has the same kind of action and sights as the large gun.

Up to 50 yards, the little arm gives very accurate results and is extremely pleasant to shoot. The round handle makes the arm less bulky, so that it may easily be carried without a holster.

SPECIFICATIONS

CALIBER: .32 S & W
NUMBER OF SHOTS: 6
BARREL: 3¼, 4¼ or 6 inches
LENGTH OVER ALL: With 4¼-inch barrel, 8¼ inches
WEIGHT: With 3¼-inch barrel, 18 oz.; 4¼-inch barrel, 18½ oz.; 6-inch barrel, 19¼ oz.
SIGHTS: Fixed, 1/10-inch service type front; square notch rear
STOCKS: Black rubber with S & W Monograms
FINISH: S & W Blue or Nickel
This model is not made with adjustable target sights
AMMUNITION
.32 S & W   .32 S & W Long
.32 Colt New Police

The S & W .38/32
2 inch

$30.00

This revolver, the lightest and smallest of the short barreled type, is chambered for the .38 S. & W. cartridge which, while having ample power and shock at close range (745 ft. sec., 180 ft. lbs., with 146 grain bullet), is comfortable to shoot and does not produce an excessive recoil. It has all the features of workmanship, material, and finish that distinguish Smith & Wesson arms; while small it has a most comfortable grip and allows ample room between the trigger guard and front strap of the stock.

SPECIFICATIONS

CALIBER: .38 S & W
NUMBER OF SHOTS: 5
BARREL: 2 inches
LENGTH OVER ALL: 6¼ inches
WEIGHT: 17 ounces
SIGHTS: Fixed, 1/10-inch service type front; square notch rear
STOCKS: Checked walnut with S & W monograms (or hard rubber)
FINISH: S & W Blue or Nickel
AMMUNITION
.38 S & W   .38 S & W Super Police

.32 and .38 Safety Hammerless

.32 CAL.
$28.00

.38 CAL.
$31.00

The .32 and .38 Safety has for years been the favorite arm of the greatest detective agencies and plain clothes men; it is always dependable and cannot jam.

A distinct pause occurs when the hammer has reached full cock position, and before it is released to fire the cartridge.

SPECIFICATIONS

.32 Cal.

LENGTH OF BARREL: 2" or 3"
FINISH: Blue or Nickel
WEIGHT: 14¼ ounces.
LENGTH OVER ALL: 6¾ inches
STOCK: Black rubber with monogram, also Pearl at $4.95 extra
NUMBER OF SHOTS: 5
SIGHTS: Fixed, part of barrel and barrel catch forgings
AMMUNITION
.32 S & W

.38 Cal.

CALIBER: .38 S & W
NUMBER OF SHOTS: 5
BARREL: 2, 3¼ or 4 inches
LENGTH OVER ALL: With 3¼-inch barrel, 7½ inches
WEIGHT: With 3¼-inch barrel, 18¼ oz.; 4-inch barrel, 18¾ oz.
SIGHTS: Fixed, part of barrel and barrel catch forgings
STOCKS: Black rubber with S & W monograms
FINISH: S & W Blue or Nickel
AMMUNITION
.38 S & W   .38 Colt New Police

The .38 Military and Police

$32.50

Round Butt

Patridge type sights (square section front and flat top square notch rear).

The rebounding hammer is locked in half cock position by two steel blocks which make forward motion of hammer impossible, except when trigger is pulled fully.

Drop forged frame, barrel and working parts. Swing-out, heat treated chrome nickel steel cylinder, locked in perfect alignment in firing position by hardened steel bearings at both front and rear.

SPECIFICATIONS

CALIBER: .38 S & W Special
NUMBER OF SHOTS: 6
BARREL: 2, 4, 5 or 6 inches
LENGTH OVER ALL: With 6-inch barrel, 10⅞ inches
WEIGHT: With 4-inch barrel, 28¾ oz.; 5-inch barrel, 29½ oz.; 6-inch barrel, 30½ oz.
SIGHTS: Fixed, 1/10-inch service type front; square notch rear
STOCKS: Black rubber with S & W monograms
FINISH: S & W Blue or Nickel
This model is not made with adjustable target sights

© **THE SHOOTER'S FAVORITE**

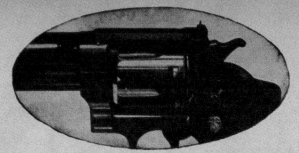

SMITH & WESSON

TRADE MARK REG. U.S. PAT. OFF.

The ".357" Magnum*

$60.00

1512 foot-seconds muzzle velocity! Faster by far than the speed heretofore attained by even the fastest of the small caliber, light weight bullets shot from foreign automatic pistols. *802 foot-pounds muzzle energy!* No hand arm cartridge ever manufactured has developed within hundreds of pounds of this terrific impact. And with this speed and power, *accuracy.* Never, but for those made by other Smith & Wesson revolvers, have there been published machine rest groups made by a large caliber hand arm that can in any way compare with those made with the S. & W. ".357" Magnum* cartridge. While its square-shouldered Sharpe-type lead bullet will shoot through steel plates that are but dented by other cartridges that have heretofore been considered powerful, the S. & W. ".357" Magnum* bullet will upset to .50 caliber in 8 inches of soft paraffin; other bullets pass through practically unchanged in form. Its penetration

in boards is but slightly greater than the .38/44 S. & W. Special, but here again the blasted wood and the condition of the recovered bullet tells of the power actually delivered. THE S. & W. ".357" MAGNUM* HAS FAR GREATER SHOCK POWER THAN ANY .38, .44 or .45 EVER TESTED. And with this power it produces machine rest groups at 20 yards (the standard indoor target range) of less than 1 inch! At 100, 200, 500 yards, and even beyond, the inherent power and accuracy continues to exist.

While this revolver is chambered especially for the long S. & W. ".357" Magnum* cartridge, it accuracy and effectiveness with all the various loads for the .38/44 and .38 S. & W. Special is actually amazing, which makes it the greatest all-purpose hand arm ever to be developed. It must be remembered the extremes in muzzle velocity are the greatest ever tested in one revolver; a complete tri-

umph for the Smith & Wesson system of chambering and rifling. A most interesting fact disclosed by the machine rest groups at 50 to 75 yards is that at these distances the size of the groups does not increase in proportion to the range; the groups actually averaging at 50 yards 1.83 inches and at 75, 2.59 inches.

SPECIFICATIONS

CALIBER: ".357" (Actual bullet diameter .38 S & W Spec.)
NUMBER OF SHOTS: 6
BARREL: 3½, 5, 6, 6½, 8⅝ inches
LENGTH OVER ALL: With 6-inch barrel, 11¼ inches
WEIGHT: With 8⅝-inch barrel 47 oz.; 6½-inch barrel, 44½ oz.; 6-inch barrel, 44 oz.; 5-inch barrel, 42½ oz.; 3½-inch barrel, 41 oz.
CYLINDER: Heat-treated chrome-nickel steel. Recessed head space and patented burnished chamber walls

STOCKS: Choice of S & W Magna or square stocks
FINISH: S & W Blue or Nickel
FRAME: ".357" Magnum, with finely checked top strap matching barrel rib. Front and rear straps, S & W grooving
HAMMER: Full surface of thumb piece checked to prevent slipping in rapid fire. Concentric relief cuts on sides. Hammer fall weighed and timed for uniform ignition and least disturbance of arm

SIGHTS: Choice of any standard target sights
TRIGGER: S & W grooving. Glass-hard point engaging hammer notch
TRIGGER PULL: Single action, 3 to 4 lbs. Double action, 10 lbs.
    AMMUNITION
      S & W .357 Magnum
.38/44   S & W Special
.38   S & W Special Hi-Velocity
.38   S & W Special
.38   S & W Special Super Police
.38   S & W Special Mid Range

The .38/44 Outdoorsman
With Reinforced Frame

Due to the weight and balance of the .38/44 OUTDOORSMAN'S Revolver, it will be found that the high velocity obtained with this new ammunition is accompanied with practically as little recoil as that of the .38 S. & W. Special Cartridge when shot in the revolvers for which it is designed, and is, in fact, less noticeable than the standard 44's or 45's.

A most convenient feature of these two cartridges is that at twenty yards no readjustment of sights is required when changing from one to the other. At longer ranges, however, it will be found that decidedly less elevation is needed when using the .38/44 S. & W. Special due to its tremendous velocity.

SPECIFICATIONS

CALIBER: .38 S & W Special
NUMBER OF SHOTS: 6
BARREL: 6½ inches only
LENGTH OVER ALL: 11¾ inches
WEIGHT: 41¾ ounces
SIGHTS: 1/10 or ⅛-inch Patridge front; square notch rear adjustable for windage and elevation
STOCKS: Magna checked walnut with S & W monograms (or regular S & W checked walnut) Grooved tangs and trigger
FINISH: S & W Blue only
    AMMUNITION
.38 S & W Special Mid Range
.38 S & W Special
.38 S & W Special Super Police
.38/44 S & W Special or Hi-Speed

$45.00

EVERYTHING IN GUNS UNDER ONE COVER

SMITH & WESSON

The K-22 Masterpiece

This .22 caliber, heavy frame revolver makes its bow to the hand gun fraternity as a worthy successor to the world famous S & W K-22 Target revolver. A replica of that favorite the .38 M & P Target Revolver, the S & W Masterpiece embodies all the time-proved, sure-shooting features of the K-22 plus unique improvements that make for greater accuracy, speed and ease of handling.

SPECIFICATIONS

CALIBER: .22
NUMBER OF SHOTS: 6
BARREL: 6 inches only
LENGTH OVERALL: 11⅛ inches
WEIGHT: 35 ounces
SIGHTS: ⅒ or ⅛ inch Patridge front; S & W Micrometer rear (patents pending) adjustable for windage and elevation. Other types of target sights available.
STOCKS: Checked walnut with S & W monograms (or Magna stocks at no extra charge) Grooved tangs and trigger
FINISH: S & W Blue only
FRAME: .38 M & P target

$40.00

The .22/32 Target

The .22/32 is a man's gun, the stock fills the hand, and permits the loose yet firm grip so necessary for good shooting, the 6 inch barrel and full size Patridge sights make sighting easy, while the weight makes the gun hang steadily.

For the fancy shot, sportsman or target marksman, the .22/32 is without an equal. Its accuracy is proven by the fact that the "Any Revolver" Match of the United States Revolver Association has been won with it several times as well as making the record high score.

SPECIFICATIONS

CALIBER: .22
NUMBER OF SHOTS: 6
BARREL: 6 inches
LENGTH OVER ALL: 10½ inches
WEIGHT: 23 ounces
SIGHTS: ⅒ or ⅛-inch Partidge front; square notch rear adjustable for windage and elevation
STOCKS: Special Target model, checked walnut with S & W monograms
FINISH: S & W Blue only
AMMUNITION: Any .22 caliber R. F. cartridge

$35.00

The .22/32 Kit Gun

The Kit Gun is designed for the man who loves the woods and streams. While compact for easy carrying in the pocket or kit bag, the barrel is long enough to give ample sight base for accurate shooting and to develop effective speed with the modern cartridges.

The adjustable target sights permit the use of different cartridges without the necessity of holding off the mark to compensate for varying points of impact.

In the illustration we show the round butt stock, as this is the most compact, and yet allows a comfortable hold with sufficient room between the front of the stock and rear of the trigger guard for the middle finger.

SPECIFICATIONS

CALIBER: .22
NUMBER OF SHOTS: 6
BARREL: 4 inches
LENGTH OVER ALL: With round butt stocks, 8 inches
WEIGHT: 21 ounces
SIGHTS: Adjustable target, rear; ⅒-inch Patridge or U.S.R.A. Pocket Revolver, front
STOCKS: Checked walnut with S & W monograms (round butt, as illustrated, small square butt, or large square butt target)
FINISH: S & W Blue or Nickel
AMMUNITION: Any .22 caliber R. F. cartridge

$35.00

Accessories

WESSON GRIP ADAPTER
for Better Hold

The Adapter is of simple construction: two plates, two screws, and a rubber filler block. The installation takes but a moment and requires no change or alteration of the arm. Fits the .38 M&P, .38/44, .45 caliber Hand Ejector Models; also the K-22, K-23 and the Magnum. Includes longer stock screw to allow for the extra thickness.
Price $2.50

S & W "HUMP BACK" HAMMER
for Rapid Fire Speed

Affords a constant or increasing leverage as the spring tension increases and the power of the thumb lessens. Renders cocking far easier than the conventional hammer. The "Hump Back" Hammer is supplied on the larger models on request at no extra charge. It will be installed on used arms only when sent into us for fitting.
Price, including installation $3.50

A FINE GUN IS A GOOD INVESTMENT

SMITH & WESSON

.38 Military and Police

This arm has established a reputation in all parts of the world for quality, accuracy, and dependability. It is used by the police departments too numerous to mention, and due to its extraordinary accuracy it is also the favorite arm of target experts.

Except for the shape of the handle, it is exactly like the round butt model, uses the same cartridges and has the same smooth action and safety devices.

Made throughout from drop forgings, with chrome nickel steel heat treated cylinder, and ground and polished working parts. It has a fine full grip, beautifully tapered barrel and is finished in heavy nickel or deep blue black.

Square Butt

$33.00

SPECIFICATIONS

CALIBER: .38 S & W Special
NUMBER OF SHOTS: 6
BARREL: 2, 4, 5 or 6 inches
LENGTH OVER ALL: With 6-inch barrel, 11⅛ inches
WEIGHT: With 6-inch barrel, 31 ounces
SIGHTS: Fixed, 1/10-inch service type front; square notch rear
STOCKS: Checked walnut with S & W monograms (or Magna stocks at no extra charge)
FINISH: S & W Blue or Nickel

AMMUNITION
.38 S & W Special
.38 Short Colt
.38 Special Super Police
.38 Colt Special

The .32 Regulation Police

This arm was brought out to meet the demands of one of the greatest police departments for the lightest, absolutely dependable revolver that would shoot the powerful .38 S & W Cartridges accurately. (Does not take the .38 S & W Special Cartridge.)

The practical value of the strength of drop forged parts and a heat treated alloy steel cylinder is shown in this model, as, while having a large surplus strength, it weighs 18 ounces.

Being designed principally for police work, this arm has several features that are of especial interest to anyone needing an arm for personal protection.

SPECIFICATIONS

CALIBER: .38 S & W
NUMBER OF SHOTS: 5
BARREL: 4 inches only
LENGTH OVER ALL: 8¼ inches
WEIGHT: 18 ounces
SIGHTS: Fixed, 1/10-inch service type front; square notch rear
STOCKS: Checked walnut with S & W monograms
FINISH: S & W Blue or Nickel

AMMUNITION:
.38 S & W
.38 S & W Super Police
.38 Colt New Police

$32.00

The .38 Regulation Police

This is a finely proportioned and exceedingly beautiful arm.

Like the Military and Police, this arm is made from drop forgings, has a heat treated alloy steel cylinder held in perfect alignment by front and rear bearings, while gas leakage is reduced to a minimum by close fitting and the elimination of end play of the cylinder by non-wearing hardened steel collars.

The barrel is taper bored to exceedingly close limits, which, with the close chambering, accurate alignment and minimum of space between barrel and cylinder, produces an accuracy which is entirely satisfactory to the most expert.

SPECIFICATIONS

CALIBER: .32 S & W
NUMBER OF SHOTS: 6
BARREL: 3¼, 4¼ or 6 inches
LENGTH OVER ALL: With 4¼-inch barrel, 8½ inches
WEIGHT: With 3¼-inch barrel, 19 oz.; 4¼-inch barrel, 18½ oz.; 6-inch barrel, 19¼ oz.
SIGHTS: Fixed, 1/10-inch service type front; square notch rear
STOCKS: Checked walnut with S & W monograms
FINISH: S & W Blue or Nickel

AMMUNITION:
.32 S & W
.32 S & W Long
.32 Colt New Police

$32.00

SEE STOEGER FOR THE BEST IN GUNS

HIGH STANDARD AUTOMATIC PISTOLS

GENERAL SPECIFICATIONS

The High Standard .22 calibre Automatic Pistol is of modern construction and design. It has all the features desired by the target shooter and sportsman. This pistol comes now in 6 different styles giving the shooter a selection never had before. This pistol can be taken down for cleaning very easily without using any tool whatsoever. All models will take low pressure as well as all standard makes of high speed ammunition.

Manufactured by gun mechanics who have had a lifetime of experience in producing firearms. Carefully inspected and tested. Guaranteed to be reliable and accurate.

These new models are, undoubtedly, the last word in modern construction and design of a .22 automatic. Features never before given to the shooters are now available at a remarkably low price.

HAMMERLESS

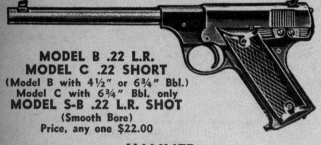

MODEL B .22 L.R.
MODEL C .22 SHORT
(Model B with 4½" or 6¾" Bbl.)
Model C with 6¾" Bbl. only
MODEL S-B .22 L.R. SHOT
(Smooth Bore)
Price, any one $22.00

HAMMER

MODEL H-B .22 L.R.
Barrel 4½" or 6¾"
Price $22.00

HAMMER MODELS "H"

There are some shooters who have always handled a revolver that have become used to an outside hammer and who would have changed to an automatic pistol except that all .22 caliber automatic pistols have formerly been of the hammerless type. With this in view we have brought out a line of visible hammer pistols. There is a little shorter hammer fall and a trigger pull that will show less variation with continued shooting. This is brought out by the fact that one of the most prominent shooters in the country states that in five thousand rounds his trigger pull has not changed more than 4 ounces which he considers is remarkable by comparison with some of the other pistols on the market. These new models with the exception of changes made necessary by the outside hammer follows closely the appearance, weight and balance of our popular hammerless models. We believe that the Models H-D and H-E are the last word in fine target pistols.

MODELS B, H-B, C, AND S-B

There is not a pistol on the market that can equal the High Standard Model "B" at the same price. The reputation of the manufacturers has been built up on the workmanship and quality of material that goes into this fine pistol plus accuracy excelled by none. An automatic for $22 that will handle both low pressure and high speed ammunition. Buy one, and see for yourself the pleasure and enjoyment you can get with this fine pistol using the inexpensive .22 caliber long rifle rimfire cartridges. Powerful enough for small game and sufficiently accurate for fine target work.

Model C is identical to model B, but for .22 shot only; Model S-B is identical to Model B but has smooth bore and intended for use with .22 L.R. shot cartridges.

SPECIFICATIONS

Calibre .22 Long Rifle, barrel 6¾" or 4½", with fixed Patridge sights, magazine capacity 10 shot. Comes with black hard rubber grips, checkered. Comes with heavy barrel, small bore, deep rifling for extreme accuracy penetration and long wear. Weight: 31 oz.

Model B with 6¾" barrel, cal. .22 L.R., price $22.00
Model B with 4½" barrel, cal. .22 L.R., price 22.00
Model C with 6¾" barrel, cal. .22 short 22.00
Model H-B with 6¾" barrel, cal. .22 L.R., price 22.00
Model H-B with 4½" barrel, cal. .22 L.R., price 22.00
Model S-B with 6¾" barrel, cal. .22 L.R., shot, price 22.00

MODELS A AND H-A

The High Standard Manufacturing Company were the first to bring out the new .22 caliber automatic long handle pistols. Realizing that the grip on the .22 automatic was too short for the average hand we spent a great deal of time and money in developing our new long handle models and at the same time added new features such as the automatic slide lock, adjustable rear sight and walnut grips. The Model "A" is practically the same as the Model "B" with the exception of the features mentioned above. It has the same barrel. The automatic slide lock holds the action open when the last cartridge has been fired from the magazine. The adjustable rear sight is positively locked in position and cannot shoot loose. This pistol is recommended to the shooters who want something a little better than the Model "B" and with additional features.

SPECIFICATIONS

Barrel—Small bore deep rifling for extreme accuracy, penetration, and long wear.

Sights—Patridge front with wide blade and special adjustable rear.

Safety—Positive.

Grips—Walnut, finely checkered.

Finish—Blued.

Takedown—Slide removed without the use of any tools for inspection and cleaning of barrel from the breech end. No loose parts, pins or screws to fall out.

Weight of pistol—Model A 36 oz.

HAMMERLESS

MODEL A .22 L.R.
with adjustable
Rear Sight
Price $28.50

HAMMER

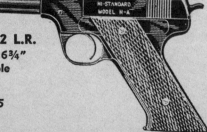

MODEL H-A .22 L.R.
Barrel 4½" or 6¾"
with adjustable
Rear Sight
Price $28.65

©   **STOEGEROL KEEPS YOUR GUN IN CONDITION**

HIGH STANDARD AUTOMATIC PISTOLS

SPECIAL FEATURES OF MODELS A, D & E
New Long Handle

We have felt that the shooter wants more room for the grip on an automatic, and have developed a longer grip that provides more room for the hand. The grips are of walnut, nicely shaped, and finely checked.

NEW AUTOMATIC SLIDE LOCK
A Double Feature

We have provided an automatic lock to lock the action open when the last cartridge has been fired from the magazine. This also operates as a lock on the action when the magazine is empty, and holds the slide open when the pistol is used at the target as a single shot.

HAMMERLESS

MODEL D .22 L.R.
Barrel 4½" or 6¾"
With extra heavy Barrel and adjustable Rear Sight
Price $35.35

HAMMER

MODEL H-D .22 L.R.
Barrel 4½" or 6¾"
With extra heavy Barrel and adjustable Rear Sight
Price $35.35

MODELS D AND H-D

The target shooters have long wanted a heavier barrel on a pistol and in designing our new long handle we had particularly in view the fact that we would need additional weight in the handle to balance the additional weight of the barrel. We therefore have gone to the extra expense of getting out new forging dies so that the metal in the handle would come all the way to the bottom, instead of making a long handle by building a hollow shell of wood that could not put the weight where it belonged. The result was most gratifying and we have plenty of weight in the handle to balance the heavier barrel. The Model "D" has a barrel of medium weight, an adjustable rear sight, automatic slide lock, and trigger pull that undoubtedly will satisfy the most exacting requirements. Regular model has straight grip but can be fitted with thumb rest for the target shooter on special order and at an extra cost.

SPECIFICATIONS

Barrel—Heavy barrel weighing 4 ounces more than on the model A.

Sights—Patridge front with wide blade and special adjustable rear sight.

Safety—Positive.

Grips—Walnut, finely checkered.

Finish—Blued.

Takedown—Slide removed without the use of any tools for inspection and cleaning of barrel from the breech end. No loose parts, pins or screws to fall out.

Weight of Pistol—40 oz.

MODELS E AND H-E

With the same qualifications as to smoothness of operation and trigger pull as the Model "D" but with an extra heavy barrel, this Model "E" is built to meet the demand from that class of shooters who want all the weight possible in a pistol. Here again the long metal handle, extending all of the way to the bottom of the grip provides the necessary weight for a perfect balance. The Model "E" as well as the Model "D" is highly recommended by experts and its users number some of the best nationally known shooters. Regularly furnished with thumb rest grip that is said to be one of the best ever designed for average shooters.

SPECIFICATIONS

Barrel—Extra heavy, barrel, slide and frame giving a straight line effect along the entire top of the pistol.

Sights—Patridge front with wide blade and special adjustable rear sight.

Safety—Positive.

Grips—Full walnut grips with thumb rest, finely checkered.

Finish—Blued.

Takedown—The same as model A or D.

Weight of Pistol—42 oz.

HAMMERLESS

MODEL E .22 L.R.
Barrel 4½" or 6¾"
with extra heavy Barrel and Target Grips with Thumb Rest
Price $40.40

HAMMER

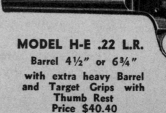

MODEL H-E .22 L.R.
Barrel 4½" or 6¾"
with extra heavy Barrel and Target Grips with Thumb Rest
Price $40.40

FOR HUNTING AND TARGET SHOOTING

HARRINGTON
AND
RICHARDSON

Look for the

target trade-mark

H & R .22 "Special"
Heavy Frame

No. 944 $17.55

The .22 Special is a heavy frame, 9 shot, fixed sight revolver for which any one of the 11 Sportsman stocks can be supplied. The H & R Safety Cylinder is used, making the arm safe with either high speed or regular ammunition.

Break open type—automatic extractor. Ammunition: .22 Short, Long or Long Rifle.

SPECIFICATIONS
BARREL LENGTH: 6 inches
OVERALL LENGTH: 11 inches
WEIGHT: 23 oz.
FINISH: Blue
SIGHTS: Notched rear and gold front
CYLINDER CAPACITY: 9 shots
AMMUNITION
.22 Short, Long or Long Rifle

Look for the

target trade-mark

H & R 9 SHOT 22 CALIBER
Large Frame

No. 922 $11.10

The "922" Model is a medium weight solid frame revolver with a safety cylinder permitting the use of high speed ammunition. The cylinder holds 9 cartridges.

The front sight and lettering on the barrel are in gold. A special stock of checked walnut permits a correct high position of the hand. This is a most satisfactory though low priced revolver.

SPECIFICATIONS
LENGTH OF BARREL: 6 inches
WEIGHT: 21¾ oz.
OVERALL LENGTH: 10½ inch
FINISH: Blue
SIGHTS: Notched rear and gold front
CYLINDER CAPACITY: 9 shots
AMMUNITION
.22 Short, Long or Long Rifle

H & R MEANS QUALITY AND VALUE

HARRINGTON & RICHARDSON REVOLVERS

EUREKA
No. 196
PRICE
$30.50

HAMMER
Easy Cocking.
Extra wide cocking spur makes cock-
ing easy.

CYLINDER
Minimum bullet jump.
Cartridge same length as cylinder.

The New EUREKA No. 196 brings us still nearer the aim of producing a Perfect Target Revolver. It embodies improvements on the justly famous H & R Sportsman and is the latest and best thought as to what a Perfect Target Revolver should be.

The New EUREKA No. 196 is equipped with a short cylinder, just long enough to carry the 22 cal. long rifle cartridge thus eliminating any "wandering" of bullet between cylinder and barrel.

The New EUREKA No. 196 has a short and very fast hammer throw.

The New EUREKA No. 196 carries six 22 cal. Long Rifle, Long or Short cartridges and safely handles any standard factory loaded ammunition.

The New EUREKA No. 196 has an entirely new action—very smooth and fast and will give the shooter years of excellent service.

The New EUREKA No. 196 may be had equipped with different size and shaped stocks to perfectly fit the individual shooters hand.

SPECIFICATIONS
Barrel Length—6¼ inch
Overall Length—11 inch
Weight—32 oz.
Finish—Blue
Sights—Patridge, adjustable front and rear
Cylinder Capacity—9 Shots
Ammunition—.22 Short, Long or Long Rifle

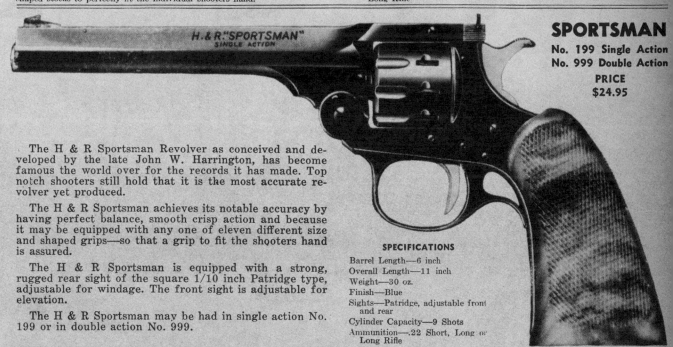

SPORTSMAN
No. 199 Single Action
No. 999 Double Action
PRICE
$24.95

The H & R Sportsman Revolver as conceived and developed by the late John W. Harrington, has become famous the world over for the records it has made. Top notch shooters still hold that it is the most accurate revolver yet produced.

The H & R Sportsman achieves its notable accuracy by having perfect balance, smooth crisp action and because it may be equipped with any one of eleven different size and shaped grips—so that a grip to fit the shooters hand is assured.

The H & R Sportsman is equipped with a strong, rugged rear sight of the square 1/10 inch Patridge type, adjustable for windage. The front sight is adjustable for elevation.

The H & R Sportsman may be had in single action No. 199 or in double action No. 999.

SPECIFICATIONS
Barrel Length—6 inch
Overall Length—11 inch
Weight—30 oz.
Finish—Blue
Sights—Patridge, adjustable front and rear
Cylinder Capacity—9 Shots
Ammunition—.22 Short, Long or Long Rifle

| No. 1—For small or thin hands. | No. 2—Like No. 1 except thicker and more rounding. | No. 3 — Same as No. 2, but with lip at top. | No. 4—Frontier type. No. 4-O—Same shape but thicker. | No. 4TR Thumb Rest. | No. 5—Free Pistol type. No. 5-O—Same shape but thicker. |

No. 4, 4-O 5, 5-O may be had with Thumb rest Feature.

Choice of any of above stocks on Eureka, Sportsman, .22 "Special," and U. S. R. A. Single shot. Price of any stock, when purchased separately $2.20

IVER JOHNSON REVOLVERS

.22 PROTECTOR SEALED EIGHT

HI-HOLD POCKET GRIP

22 SUPERSHOT SEALED EIGHT

HI-HOLD GRIP

WITH ADJUSTABLE FINGER REST

SPECIFICATIONS: Counterbored chambers and extractor; 6 inch barrel with special target sights as above. Gold lettering. Blued finish. De Flex rib for better sighting. Scored trigger. One-piece walnut Hi-Hold grip, hand checkered. Shoots all .22 long rifle, .22 long and .22 short rim fire cartridges. Length over all 10¾ inches. Weight 24 ounces. Cellophane wrapped.

No. 834 ....$20.60

.22 Supershot Sealed Eight: Same as above, but without special sights and finger rest. No. 88 ....$17.45

.22 Supershot 9 Shots: This model does not have the special cylinder with the Counterbored Chambers, and is made in 9 shots. The specifications otherwise are similar to No. 88.
No. 90 ....$16.60

Suitable for home protection. Eight shots; walnut checkered grip; length over all 7¼ inches; weight 20 ounces; shoots high speed or ordinary .22 short, long or long rifle cartridges.

Price $17.45

IVER JOHNSON — SAFETY HAMMER AUTOMATIC REVOLVER

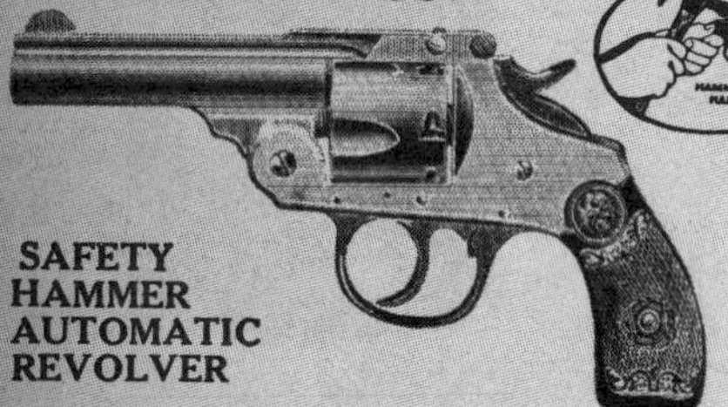

Regular Rubber Grips

Nickel No.	Blued No.	Caliber	Barrel	Weight	Price
100	101	.22 R. F.	3 in.	14 oz.	$15.60
102	103	.22 R. F.	4 in	15 oz.	15.85
104	105	.22 R. F.	5 in	16 oz.	16.10
106	107	.22 R. F.	6 in	16½ oz.	16.35
108	109	.32 S. & W.	3 in	14 oz.	15.60
110	111	.32 S. & W.	4 in	15 oz.	15.85
112	113	.32 S. & W.	5 in	15½ oz.	16.10
114	115	.32 S. & W.	6 in	16½ oz.	16.35
116	117	.32 Special	3¼ in.	19 oz.	15.60
118	119	.32 Special	4 in	19½ oz.	15.85
120	121	.32 Special	5 in	20½ oz.	16.10
122	123	.32 Special	6 in	21 oz.	16.35
124	125	.38 S. & W.	3¼ in.	17½ oz.	15.60
126	127	.38 S. & W.	4 in	19 oz.	15.85
128	129	.38 S. & W.	5 in	20 oz.	16.10
130	131	.38 S. & W.	6 in	21 oz.	16.35

IVER JOHNSON — SAFETY HAMMER AUTOMATIC REVOLVER

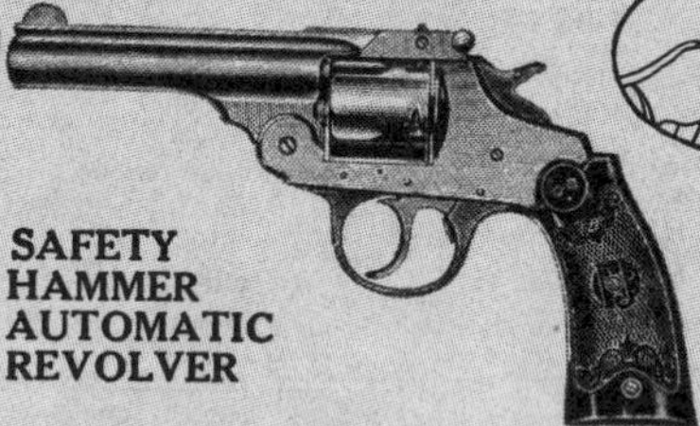

Perfect Rubber Grips

Nickel No.	Blued No.	Caliber	Barrel	Weight	Price
200	201	.22 R. F.	3 in.	15 oz.	$16.40
202	203	.22 R. F.	4 in	16 oz.	16.65
204	205	.22 R. F.	5 in	17 oz.	16.95
206	207	.22 R. F.	6 in	17½ oz.	17.15
208	209	.32 S. & W.	3 in	15 oz.	16.40
210	211	.32 S. & W.	4 in	16 oz.	16.65
212	213	.32 S. & W.	5 in	16½ oz.	16.95
214	215	.32 S. & W.	6 in	17½ oz.	17.15
216	217	.32 Special	3¼ in.	20 oz.	16.40
218	219	.32 Special	4 in	20½ oz.	16.65
220	221	.32 Special	5 in	21½ oz.	16.95
222	223	.32 Special	6 in	22 oz.	17.15
224	225	.38 S. & W.	3¼ in.	18½ oz.	16.40
226	227	.38 S. & W.	4 in	20 oz.	16.65
228	229	.38 S. & W.	5 in	21 oz.	16.95
230	231	.38 S. & W.	6 in	22 oz.	17.15

IVER JOHNSON — SAFETY HAMMER AUTOMATIC REVOLVER

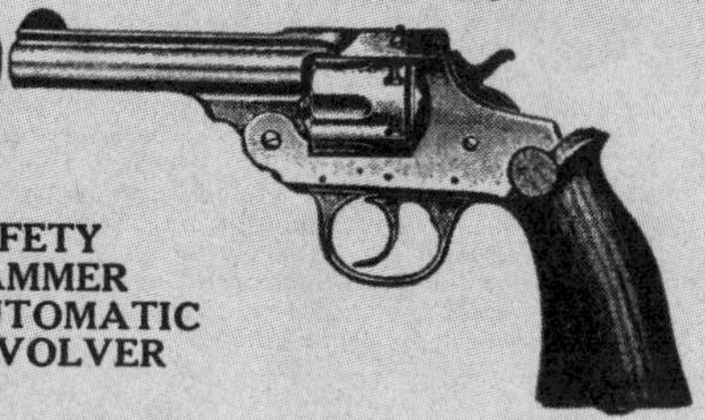

Western Walnut Grip

Nickel No.	Blued No.	Caliber	Barrel	Weight	Price
300	301	.22 R. F.	3 in.	15 oz.	$16.40
302	303	.22 R. F.	4 in	16 oz.	16.65
304	305	.22 R. F.	5 in	17 oz.	16.95
306	307	.22 R. F.	6 in	17½ oz.	17.15
308	309	.32 S. & W.	3 in	15 oz.	16.40
310	311	.32 S. & W.	4 in	16 oz.	16.65
312	313	.32 S. & W.	5 in	16½ oz.	16.95
314	315	.32 S. & W.	6 in	17½ oz.	17.15
316	317	.32 Special	3¼ in.	20 oz.	16.40
318	319	.32 Special	4 in	20½ oz.	16.65
320	321	.32 Special	5 in	21½ oz.	16.95
322	323	.32 Special	6 in	22 oz.	17.15
324	325	.38 S. & W.	3¼ in.	18½ oz.	16.40
326	327	.38 S. & W.	4 in	20 oz.	16.65
328	329	.38 S. & W.	5 in	21 oz.	16.95
330	331	.38 S. & W.	6 in	22 oz.	17.15

(.38 cal. and .32 Special have Hi-Hold Grip uncheckered.)

All Iver Johnson Safety Revolvers both Hammer and Hammerless, are equipped throughout with finest heat-treated open wound piano wire springs and the Iver Johnson patented Safety Device, which makes accidental discharge impossible. The .22 caliber is 7 shots, rim fire, and takes the .22 Short, Long, and Long Rifle cartridges. The .32 caliber is 5 shots, center fire, and takes the .32 S. & W. cartridges. The .32 Special is 6 shots, center fire, built on heavy frame, and takes the .32 S. & W., .32 S. & W. Long and .32 Colt New Police cartridges. The .38 caliber is 5 shots, center fire, and takes the .38 S. & W. cartridges. Always use greased bullets.

Note—ALL IVER JOHNSON REVOLVERS can be furnished with 2 inch barrels at same price as the 3 inch and 3¼ inch.

IVER JOHNSON — SAFETY HAMMERLESS AUTOMATIC REVOLVER

Regular Rubber Grips

Nickel No.	Blued No.	Caliber	Barrel	Weight	Price
400	401	.22 R. F.	3 in.	15 oz.	$15.60
402	403	.22 R. F.	4 in	16 oz.	15.85
404	405	.22 R. F.	5 in	16½ oz.	16.10
406	407	.22 R. F.	6 in	17 oz.	16.35
408	409	.32 S. & W.	3 in	14 oz.	15.60
410	411	.32 S. & W.	4 in	15 oz.	15.85
412	413	.32 S. & W.	5 in	15½ oz.	16.10
414	415	.32 S. & W.	6 in	16 oz.	16.35
416	417	.32 Special	3¼ in.	20 oz.	15.60
418	419	.32 Special	4 in	20½ oz.	15.85
420	421	.32 Special	5 in	21½ oz.	16.10
422	423	.32 Special	6 in	22 oz.	16.35
424	425	.38 S. & W.	3¼ in.	19 oz.	15.60
426	427	.38 S. & W.	4 in	20 oz.	15.85
428	429	.38 S. & W.	5 in	21 oz.	16.10
430	431	.38 S. & W.	6 in	21½ oz.	16.35

IVER JOHNSON — SAFETY HAMMERLESS AUTOMATIC REVOLVER

Perfect Rubber Grips

Nickel No.	Blued No.	Caliber	Barrel	Weight	Price
500	501	.22 R. F.	3 in.	16 oz.	$16.40
502	503	.22 R. F.	4 in	17 oz.	16.65
504	505	.22 R. F.	5 in	17½ oz.	16.95
506	507	.22 R. F.	6 in	18 oz.	17.15
508	509	.32 S. & W.	3 in	15 oz.	16.40
510	511	.32 S. & W.	5 in	10½ oz.	16.95
514	515	.32 S. & W.	6 in	17 oz.	17.15
516	517	.32 Special	3¼ in.	21 oz.	16.40
518	519	.32 Special	4 in	21½ oz.	16.65
520	521	.32 Special	5 in	22½ oz.	16.95
522	523	.32 Special	6 in	23 oz.	17.15
524	525	.38 S. & W.	3¼ in.	20 oz.	16.40
526	527	.38 S. & W.	4 in	21 oz.	16.65
528	529	.38 S. & W.	5 in	22 oz.	16.95
530	531	.38 S. & W.	6 in	22½ oz.	17.15

IVER JOHNSON — SAFETY HAMMERLESS AUTOMATIC REVOLVER

Western Walnut Grip

Nickel No.	Blued No.	Caliber	Barrel	Weight	Price
600	601	.22 R. F.	3 in.	15 oz.	$16.40
602	603	.22 R. F.	4 in	16 oz.	16.65
604	605	.22 R. F.	5 in	17 oz.	16.95
606	607	.22 R. F.	6 in	17½ oz.	17.15
608	609	.32 S. & W.	3 in	15 oz.	16.40
610	611	.32 S. & W.	4 in	16 oz.	16.65
612	613	.32 S. & W.	5 in	16½ oz.	16.95
614	615	.32 S. & W.	6 in	17½ oz.	17.15
616	617	.32 Special	3¼ in.	20 oz.	16.40
618	619	.32 Special	4 in	20½ oz.	16.65
620	621	.32 Special	5 in	21½ oz.	16.95
622	623	.32 Special	6 in	22 oz.	17.15
624	625	.38 S. & W.	3¼ in.	18½ oz.	16.40
626	627	.38 S. & W.	4 in	20 oz.	16.65
628	629	.38 S. & W.	5 in	21 oz.	16.95
630	631	.38 S. & W.	6 in	22 oz.	17.15

(.38 cal. and .32 Special have Hi-Hold Grip uncheckered.)

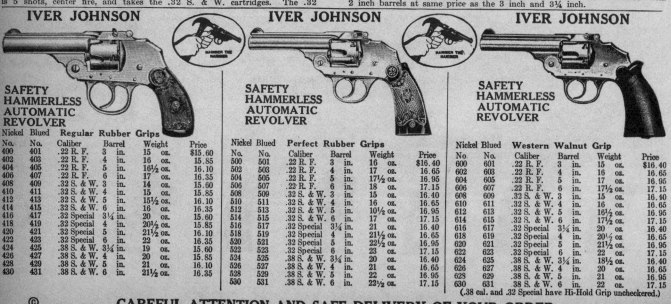

MAUSER AUTOMATIC POCKET PISTOLS

THE ORIGINAL MAUSER SELF LOADING AUTOMATIC POCKET PISTOL

COMPACT, ACCURATE, SAFE, AND TRUE WEAPONS OF DEFENSE
Pocket Models—25 cal. (6.35 MM), 10 shot; 32 cal. (765 MM), 9 shots

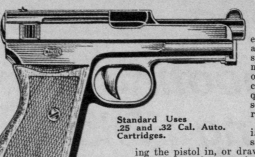

Standard Uses
.25 and .32 Cal. Auto.
Cartridges.

PRINCIPAL FEATURES

1. Ten, nine and eight shots respectively.
2. Solidity and simplicity of construction.
3. Perfect workmanship.
4. Great accuracy, increased by special length of barrel.
5. Reliability and safety.
6. The state of the pistol, viz., cocked or not, is apparent externally.
7. Considerable penetrative power.
8. Substantial grip and good balance.
9. Ease of taking apart for cleaning.
10. Attractive appearance, absence of projecting parts, flat shape and consequent absence of bulge when carried in the pocket.

The component parts of the Mauser pistols are simple and strong and only the highest quality of materials and best workmanship are used in their manufacture which is based on the same methods and principles to which Mauser constructions owe their world wide reputation.

Magazine Capacity. As the magazine of the 6.35 MM pistol holds nine and that of the 7.65 MM holds eight cartridges, the pistol can be made to hold ten and nine shots respectively.

Security in Handling. The shooter can tell when aiming or in the dark by touch, whether the pistol is cocked or not—when cocked, the rear end of the striker is visible at the back of the breech. This is a most valuable feature, as the absence on other pistols of devices clearly showing the state of the weapon, has led to fatal accidents.

The pistol cannot be fired when the magazine is wholly or partly withdrawn. Accidents due to presumption that there was no cartridge in the barrel after withdrawing the magazine are thus made impossible.

The breech remains open after firing the last cartridge, but closes automatically as long as there is a cartridge in the magazine. This gives greater security in handling.

The Safety, which can be operated with ease by the thumb of the right hand when aiming, allows the weapon to be made safe when cocked or not cocked, loaded or not loaded, and as the breech cannot be opened when the pistol is safe, danger in carrying is obviated, nor can those unacquainted with the mechanism, such as servants or children, make the pistol ready for fire.

The system employed for unlocking, i. e., releasing the safety, prevents the safety from being unlocked while carrying the pistol in, or drawing it out of, the pocket. The involuntary firing of more shots than intended, commonly known as "Maximing" is absolutely prevented by the interceptor which disconnects the trigger from the sear while the breech is in motion and makes it necessary to pull the trigger for each shot. No firing can take place unless the breech is entirely closed, even though one should forget to release the trigger after firing.

The Pistol is perfectly balanced, and its substantial and comfortable grip contributes greatly to the accuracy of shooting which is further increased by the comparatively great length of the barrel, and line of sight.

No. 700—Cal. 25, Ten Shot...............Price $25.00
No. 701—Cal. 32, Nine Shot...............Price $28.00

THE NEW MAUSER VEST POCKET PISTOL

This is one of the smallest serviceable pistols in the world, ruggedly constructed and designed for hard use. In construction it is similar to the earlier model Vest Pocket Pistol which has been discontinued, but smaller in size, and particularly designed to lie comfortably in the hand. Holds six shots in the magazine in addition to one in the chamber. Total length, 4.08 inches; depth, 2¾ inches; weight, 9½ ounces.
Price....................$22.50

COMPONENT PARTS LIST OF MAUSER POCKET MODEL

No.	Article	Price
1.	Barrel	$6.00
2.	Barrel Holder	2.25
3.	Barrel Holder Catch	1.25
4.	Striker (Firing Pin)	2.75
5.	Striker Spring	1.25
6.	Barrel Holder Guide	1.25
7.	Interceptor	1.00
8.	Rear Sight	1.25
9.	Extractor	2.50
10.	Breech	7.50
11.	Recoil Spring	1.25
12.	Ejector	3.00
13.	Double Action Spring	.75
14.	Grip Cover Plate	2.75
15.	Frame	7.50
16.	Magazine	3.50
17.	Trigger Complete	3.00
18.	Trigger Spring	.75
19.	Grip Cover Plate Screw, left	.50
20.	Grip Cover Plate Screw, right	.50
21.	Safety Locking Spring	1.50
22.	Trigger Catch Spring	.65
23.	Trigger Catch Pin	.50
24.	Trigger Catch	1.50
25.	Magazine Platform	.75
26.	Safety	3.00
27.	Sear	3.00
28.	Magazine Bottom Plate	.50
29.	Magazine Holder	2.50
30.	Magazine Spring	1.25
31.	Side Plate	3.00

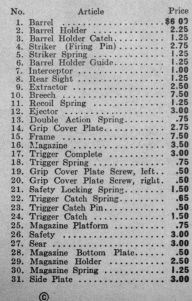

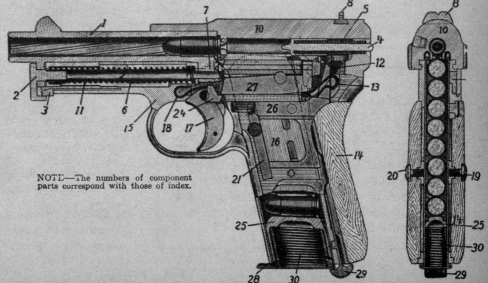

NOTE—The numbers of component parts correspond with those of index.

©

ALL SHIPMENTS ARE INSURED

The 6 PPC: From Shooting Range to Hunting Field

by Wilf E. Pyle

Among present-day benchrest shooters, no single cartridge has garnered more respect, established more records, and brought home more trophies than the 6 PPC. It's a rare benchrest shooter who doesn't use a 6 PPC today, and those who don't probably wish they did. In the wake of the 6 PPC's inherent accuracy, records keep falling and new ones are made, proof that the performance offered by this cartridge is the stuff of which shooting legends are made.

Not only is the benchrest community the traditional testing ground for countless wildcat car-

Wilf E. Pyle, an avid outdoorsman who has hunted nearly all species of game, large and small, is a well known authority in the U.S. and Canada on sporting firearms. He is also an enthusiastic reloader and ballistician. Pyle used the 6 PPC extensively while preparing his third book, Small Game & Varmint Hunting (Stoeger Publishing Co., 1989). His previous works are Hunter's Book of the Pronghorn Antelope (New Century Publishers) and Hunting Predators for Hides and Profit (Stoeger).

The history of benchrest shooting has produced some excellent cartridges. These include (left to right) the .219 Donaldson, .222 Remington, and 6 Pindell-Palmisan cartridge (PPC).

tridges, it's frequently the source of new product development as well. The firearms industry has always kept a close eye on the benchrest circuit

The first commercial 6 PPC rifle to hit the field was the Sako A1. This sleek bolt repeater is built on the time-proven Vixen L461 action.

for new products with a broader market application to hunters and other shooters. Yet, for all the innovation displayed by dedicated benchresters, few products make the transition from target range to hunting fields successfully. Fewer still are ever accepted as hunting cartridges by the general shooting public.

Some wildcats have contributed to improved sporting cartridge design, while others have become viable hunting cartridges. The .219 Donaldson was highly regarded as a varmint cartridge, while at the same time it performed well on the range. Perhaps the most successful commercial cartridge to evolve out of benchrest shooting, however, is the .222 Remington. Developed by

Remington's own Mike Walker, it held benchrest attention until about 1980, when the 6 PPC began making inroads. It also spawned an entire family of related cartridges, such as the .223 and .222 Remington Magnum.

Thanks to its success on the target range, the 6 PPC is now in a state of transition, a position similar to that held by the .222 Remington back in 1950. We know it performs well in bull barreled bench rifles, but how does it do in a sporting rifle? And what can a hunter expect in the fields and pastures of rural America? Where exactly does the 6 PPC fit in a menu already crowded with choices? And why should a hunter or shooter pick this cartridge over any others?

What It Is, and How It Works

To begin, Sako has taken the lead by making available to the general shooting public commercial 6 PPC ammunition. It's loaded with a European extruded-type powder and an American hollow point boattail bullet held together in a Finnish case. All regions of the U.S. have received the new ammo and brass and it is slowly developing a reputation as an accurate commercial cartridge.

In moving the 6 PPC from the target range to the hunting fields of North America, shooters must first be assured of certain advantages, including ease of reloading, good accuracy, acceptable report, and mild recoil. But the shift from target to sporting cartridge involves more than placing great products before the shooting public. The long run success of any cartridge is determined by field performance. Until now, few shooters have had an opportunity to use the 6 PPC for any kind of hunting. But now, according to scattered reports and range talk, some truly dedicated benchrest shooters have adapted their sporting weight rifles to 6 PPC and taken game with it up to and including deer-sized animals.

Physically, the 6 PPC differs markedly from both traditional and modern cartridge designs. Every dimension is scaled down, the result of the designer's wish to seek a wholly efficient case capacity. As a result, the 6 PPC is squat and fat, with a short neck, and the bullet appears out of proportion to the case length. The loaded cartridge measures just over 1½ inches long and weighs a fraction of an ounce, allowing a great number of them to be carried with ease in one's pocket or ammo pouch. Technically, the case has a 30° shoulder, bears a capacity of 2.19 cc's of water, and takes a small rifle primer. It also has a smaller than standard flash hole of .066 inches in diameter. Cartridges obtained from local benchrest shooters or at gun shows, by the way, are often stamped ".220 Russian," because most early cases were formed by expanding the .220 Russian to .243 caliber. Newly manufactured cases should all be head-stamped "6 PPC USA."

Factory ammunition originates from the Sako factory in Finland. Through a contract with Sierra,

Fully configured, this Sako comes in at 7.3 lbs (3.3 kg) with a four-round loaded magazine.

70 grain HPBT bullets are used. The hollow point ensures rapid expansion, while the boattail provides an extra measure of long range stability necessary for accurate shooting. By offering the hollow point style, Sako is tactfully suggesting that this is, after all, a small game cartridge, and not one designed for big game. The powder is a fine grain European type that weighs in around 25.4 grains.

Finding a Rifle to Fit the Cartridge

The first commercial 6 PPC rifle to hit the market was the Sako A1, which became generally available in late 1987. This sleek, lightweight bolt repeater, built on the proven L461 action, is generally known as the Vixen. Sako has long displayed leadership in developing such zephyr-like arms, so it's little wonder that, having committed itself to a commercial grade 6 PPC, the company came up with a product that must have caused American gun makers to shake their heads in frustration.

Sako's Vixen embodies the functional needs and aesthetic values of today's shooters. Because small caliber barrels need not be as heavy as those found on larger caliber models, the Sako barrel is very light. Its contours are pleasing to the eye, tapering from about 1.36 inches at the action to a pencil-thin .592 inches at the muzzle. Barrel length is a handy 22¾ inches. The result: a rifle that is light and quick to get on target, but with enough heft to see the shooter through extended plinking sessions at prairie dogs and gophers. After all, modern hunters are not interested in roaming the countryside carrying rifles that weigh 11 pounds or more (loaded and outfitted with scope and sling). Sako's model weighs 7.3 pounds (3.3 kg) with a 4-round magazine (loaded), Conetrol mounts, a Leupold M8-4X Compact scope, and a lightweight IMMI StrapAid one-inch sling in place. Dressed this way, a shooter can pursue rabbits or ground squirrels all day long without suffering undo fatigue.

Weight is important for another reason not often made clear in the shooting press: lightweight, mild-kicking rifles are needed to attract and hold the next generation of shooters. Young people—and women of all ages—are not interested in handling heavy guns with punishing recoils and loud reports. The Sako A1 and the 6 PPC form a package that goes a long way toward satisfying their demands.

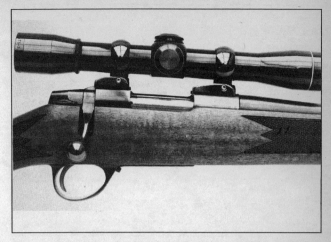

This Conetrol mount hardware was used for testing on a Sako A1 rifle. These mounts fit in nicely with the trim lines of the Sako Hunter.

A Look at the Finer Details

Sako stocks have long held a reputation as things of beauty and function. Three grades of walnut, each differing in pattern and grain, are available (with higher degrees of checkering and wood carving offered on the upgraded models). The standard grade, called Hunter, provides ample checkering that is functional and good-looking. Several years ago, Sako increased the height, decreased the weight, and expanded the size of the roll-over on its stock models. Today's stocks sport palm swells, thick red rubber butt plates, and hand-fitting forestocks. Length of pull remains at 13⅞ inches.

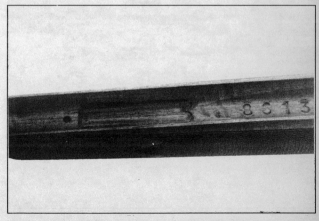

Sako's top-quality stock is sealed and finished on the inside, an essential feature for any sporting rifle that is used under conditions of changing humidity.

The Sako barrel, which is free floating, touches the stock just behind the forend.

The Hunter also features sealed inletting, a critical element in any sporting rifle—especially one that will be used in humid weather conditions. It's not enough for a manufacturer to select good wood that cures properly; the completed stock must also be sealed against moisture with stains and finishes. Most manufacturers seal only the exterior of their stocks. However, the barrel channel, action inletting, and inside walls of each stock must also be sealed to help reduce the chances of harmful moisture penetrating the wood. Such moisture can cause a shift in the point of impact

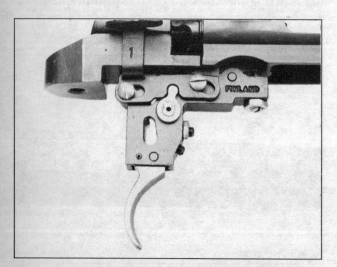

The trigger is fully adjustable for weight and backlash. Sear engagement and weight (approx. 4 lbs.) are set at the factory.

by creating pressure on the action screws and pushing the forend against the barrel. That explains why a rifle often shoots in a different manner from one season to the next. Sako's barrel is free floating, too, which helps to ensure greater accuracy. A thin piece of paper could slide easily between barrel and forend were it not for the fact that the barrel lightly touches the stock $1^{1/2}$ inches to the rear of the forend tip.

The trigger, which is fully adjustable for weight and backlash, is set at the factory at about four pounds (but is easily adjusted down to two pounds or so). A trigger pull weight of $2^{1/4}$ pounds is the minimum recommended for any sporting rifle. Trigger tension is adjusted by first removing the action from the stock and loosening a hexagonal locknut located next to the trigger, then backing off the set screw until the desired weight is obtained. When doing this, however, proceed with caution; it doesn't take much turning to reduce pull, and if the screw is turned too far the rifle won't fire. Retighten the hex locknut, replace the stock, and the rifle is ready to go.

Backlash (also known as "trigger over-travel") is likewise adjustable. Backlash is defined as the continuing rearward travel of the trigger after the firing pin has been released. It's important to understand that after the trigger is squeezed and the firing pin is on its way toward the primer, there is still a potential danger of having the rifle pulled off target. A tight (or zero) backlash helps prevent this movement. It may seem insignificant, but even a gentle push can translate into a long range miss. Every sporting rifle should be set for minimal over-travel; fortunately, Sako's adjustment is crisp and easy to set.

Aesthetically, Sako's A1 Hunter features a well finished trigger guard that is both handsome and functional. The trigger, which is wide and grooved, provides good feel and helps reduce shooter fatigue during long shooting sessions. One-inch detachable sling swivels are included as standard equipment. The magazine floor plate is latched on the front of the trigger guard with a dot plunger and is hinged just behind the forward receiver screw. The plunger locks the plate securely, holds it tight to the bottom of the action, and is easy to use. The plate drops down for quick, muddle-free release of the 6 PPC cartridge. The magazine holds four cartridges and, with one in the chamber, supplies five quick shots as fast as you can work the bolt.

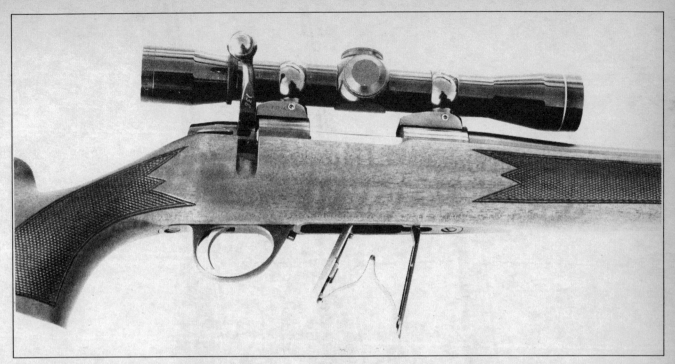

The magazine floor plate is latched on the front of the trigger guard with a dot plunger and hinged behind the forward receiver screw. The plate drops down out of the way for quick, muddle-free release of the 6 PPC cartridges.

As with any sporting rifle, checkering is effective only when the diamond cuts are sharp and clearly defined. Sako's checkering is well executed and functional. Its forend checkering acts as a gripping surface designed to help control the fore-stock during recoil. Additional checkering on the pistol grip helps to draw the butt stock more firmly into the shoulder.

A few years ago, heavily lacquered stocks were common on Sako rifles, with oil finish an optional, special-order feature. But now, in response to public demand, a dull oil finish is available off the shelf. For the predator hunter, a dull stock is a must. Light reflecting off a highly polished stock can act as a signal mirror, tipping off prairie-wise predators at considerable distances. So where there's a choice, a dull finish is recommended for all sport shooting. It doesn't show wear and scratches the way lacquered stocks do, and it won't bounce errant light waves about the countryside. The new matte lacquer finish on the repeater rifle certainly satisfies the need for both beauty and function.

No discussion of rifles would be complete without a review of the wood-to-metal fit. Proper fit between action and stock is critical to accuracy. Sako has excelled at this for several years, and its new 6 PPC is no exception. The trigger guard is precisely inletted and the action fits tightly into the stock, precluding the need for glass bedding.

Accuracy is the Name of the Game

In combination, the 6 PPC and the little Sako A1 make a lightweight, powerful package that is difficult to resist. And yet, even for this extraordinary combo to succeed and prosper it must shoot accurately, perform reliably, and deliver the individual advantages of both cartridge and rifle with consistency.

One excellent scope for Sako's package is a Leupold Compact 4X held in place with Conetrol mounts and Conetrol Gunnur rings. Mounting and ring hardware don't often receive enough attention, and their contribution to accuracy is thereby ignored. Mount hardware must fit within very close tolerances, and Conetrol mounts fit Sako dovetails especially well. The rings are streamlined and have no projections, mounting screws or

In line with the needs of most hunters, the stocks on these Sako rifles have all been oil-finished.

Straight out of the box and without any adjustments, Sako's compact rifle consistently prints one-inch groups at 100 yards.

ridges. Using this combo, an initial sighting-in was conducted at 100 yards from a concrete benchrest using factory Sako 6 PPC USA ammunition (factory ammunition was used to determine how well the products performed before proceeding on to handloads). Three shot groups were fired, allowing time in between for the rifle to cool. Right out of the box, with no adjustments needed, this little rifle printed one-inch groups at 100 yards. A few subsequent 1¼-inch groups shifted the average for 10 groups to a fraction over one inch. Bear in mind that these groups came from a sporting grade rifle, not a custom-designed benchrest model or a varmint rifle. Whereas a benchrest shooter would find one-inch groups at 100 yards unacceptable, they are more than adequate for 90 percent of all field shooting situations. Lightweight rifles also have a reputation for poor shooting because of their thin barrels and springy actions; moreover, many traditionalists claim lightweight rifles are difficult to

hold on target. So a one-inch group using Sako's out-of-the-box, lightweight rifle has to be impressive.

Several reloads were put through the rifle. One typical benchrest load consisted of 26 grains of H4895 and a 70 grain McCracken bullet. Reloads using a 70 grain Hornady spire point, a 75 grain Hornady hollow point, and a 90 grain Speer full metal jacket were also tried with different powders. These bullets represent three specific applications: general plinking, varmint shooting, and predator hunting. The results were interesting and impressive. While there were no visible or measurable pressure signs, this particular load was obviously too hot for the Sako. Accordingly, subsequent reloads were developed well below recommended maximums. Many shooters recognize that maximum loads don't always produce the tightest groups. They also follow the practice of starting below the maximum and increasing the powder charge gradually, all the while checking for signs of pressure. The Hornady 70 grain spire point, using 24 grains of IMR 4198, produced one-inch groups consistently at 100 yards and turned up several ⅞-inch groups. This powder is a proven performer in .222 Remington. The Hornady 75 grain hollow point did best with Winchester 748, leaving behind one-inch groups (but few fell below that mark). Speer's 90 grain full metal jacket, using 24 grains of IMR 4895, averaged just under one inch. This is acceptable performance in a predator load and offers potential as an intermediate range coyote cartridge.

In fact, the commercial bullet now available—a boattailed hollow point—is designed especially for small game. Lightweight hollow points are made to expand rapidly and explosively as they strike the target. They also disintegrate upon hitting the ground. While this safety feature helps reduce ricochet, it makes penetration of tough bone and muscles unlikely, if not impossible.

In terms of energy and downrange ballistics, the commercial 6 PPC develops enough energy to take any small game. It leaves the barrel at 3145 fps, traveling 2433 fps at 200 yards, and delivers an impressive 920 foot pounds. At 300 yards, velocity drops to 2116 fps and energy is reduced to 696 foot pounds. The inherent accuracy of the cartridge, based on its good velocity and the excellent ballistic coefficient of the bullets, translates into a fine trajectory for distant small game targets.

A Look at the Competition

Wildcat riflemen have enjoyed a heyday with the .243 caliber, but sporting riflemen have not always shared their enthusiasm for it. The first American-made 6mm cartridge was the Lee Navy, which was developed for the straight pull, bolt action 6mm Lee Navy rifle. Winchester produced a commercial sporting rifle based on the Lee action between 1898 and 1903. Unfortunately, it lacked visual appeal, was not particularly accurate, and offered no striking advantages when compared to the powerful lever guns available at the time. Not until Warren Page (Field & Stream's editor) experimented with the caliber in the late 1940s and early 1950s did interest grow among long range woodchuck shooters.

The 6 PPC's closest competitors today are the .243 Winchester and the 6mm Remington. Both are dual-purpose cartridges capable of taking on all game up to deer and antelope. Early on, the .243 was highly touted as an antelope cartridge, while the 6mm Remington was promoted as a high-intensity varmint round. Introduced in 1955, the .243 Remington remains little more than a .308 Winchester necked down to .243 inches. Back then, the military 7.62mm × 51mm cartridge was quite popular, so Winchester decided to preempt the competition by announcing its .308 Winchester (which was really an unaltered version of the military 7.62). This short round, so necessary in the military M14 semiautomatic rifle, proved popular. Experimenters quickly saw the advantages of moving the .243 caliber bullet (which was used in the

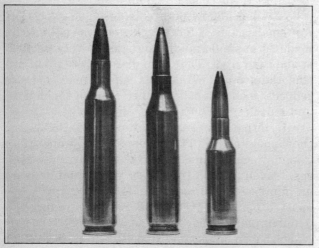

The .243 caliber is represented by the 6mm Remington, .243 Winchester, and now the 6 PPC.

wildcat .240 Page) onto the case of a necked-down .308.

The .243 Winchester was available at first in Winchester's Model 70 bolt action and its Model 88 lever rifles. Spurred on by favorable publicity in the shooting press, other firms, including Savage and Sako, soon added to the popularity of the cartridge. A factory 80 grain bullet leaves the muzzle of a 24-inch barrel at 3350 fps and travels very flat. Sighted-in for two inches high at 100 yards, the bullet is 5.4 inches low at 300 yards and is still traveling at 2259 fps. The .243 caliber bullet displays good ballistic coefficients, too, which means it bucks wind well and provides good downrange ballistics. This kind of performance, along with a reputation for accuracy with mild recoil, left a favorable impression with riflemen all over the world.

The 6mm Remington didn't enjoy the early success of the .243 Winchester, however. Known as the .244 Remington in 1955, the cartridge was hampered by the slow 1 turn in 12 twist of the Remington 722 rifle barrels then in use. This twist failed to impart enough spin to stabilize spitzer or spire point bullets in the 90-plus grain category, or any other projectile measuring more than one inch in length. As a result, this rifle and cartridge combination was soon judged by the shooting public as useful for shooting varmints only when 75 to 90 grain bullets were used. Sales fell quickly as shooters and hunters flocked to the .243 Winchester.

Remington reacted in 1963 by renaming its cartridge the 6mm Remington and increasing the twist on its barrels to 1 turn in 9 inches. This change provided stability to all weights of bullets and neatly sidestepped the bad reputation acquired by the now defunct .244 Remington. The cartridge does well in today's market, producing an acceptable 3470 fps muzzle velocity; and when sighted in for two inches high at 100 yards, it strikes the target 4.5 inches low at 300 yards. At that distance, an 80 grain bullet still has 982 foot pounds of striking energy, enough for any deer-sized animal.

The .243 Remington and 6mm Remington have been slugging it out for years. Neither has emerged as the universally accepted cartridge, and it's a safe bet that in most shooters' minds both cartridges are still considered "deer only" cartridges. Indeed, no modern cartridge can lay claim to being

The 6 PPC has become famous among benchrest shooters. Here a champion shooter zeroes in on the target.

THE choice for small game hunting. The .32-20 and .25-20 were probably the last cartridges recognized as true small game cartridges. The .32-20, which was arguably the best small game cartridge ever made, gave shooters a muzzle velocity of 2100 fps, pushing 80 grain flat-nosed bullets at 225 foot pounds of energy at 100 yards. It remains popular with backwoodsmen who use old guns and newly produced cartridges to take game at close range. Modern factory .32-20 cartridges with 100 grain bullets leave the muzzle at 1210 fps and produce 230 foot pounds of energy at 100 yards. On the down side, the .32-20 produces low velocity and therefore offers poor long-range trajectory. At 200 yards, it will be some 30 inches low, which is not good enough to meet today's standards for a small game cartridge.

To sum up: for shooters in search of a handy sporting rifle capable of taking small game and digesting a broad range of reloads, the 6 PPC in the Sako A1 is highly recommended. Compared to older cartridges, the 6 PPC offers updated velocity, finer trajectory, and better bullets. Compared to modern-day .243's, it produces no recoil to speak of and yet boasts similar trajectory and equal bullet design. Will the 6 PPC make the transition from target cartridge to beloved sporting round? It's only a matter of time.

The Comp Gun—
A Pistol Shooter's
Dream

by Charles E. Petty

A new word has entered the pistol shooter's vocabulary. The word is *comp* (short for *compensator*) and it has taken the action shooting sports world by storm. Whether you're into practical shooting (IPSC), NRA Action Shooting (Bianchi Cup), bowling pins, or such speed events as the Steel Challenge, you just aren't competitive these days unless you have a comp gun.

In broad terms, a comp is a device that reduces recoil and muzzle rise. Comps are hung on the muzzles of Government Model automatics, or one of the many copies now available. This new handgun phenomenon began back in 1978 with a Louisiana gunsmith named Jim Clark. He built his first "bowling pin" gun that year by fitting a barrel about one inch longer than the standard five-inch

Government Model. He was then able to thread the extra length and install a round piece of steel weighing three to four ounces. This extra weight had a dramatic effect on the way the gun behaved under recoil. And since muzzle rise was reduced as well, shooters could now get their guns back on target faster.

Clark's improvement was followed quickly by another innovation developed by Arkansas gunsmith J. Michael Plaxco, who cut a series of ports in the weight. Plaxco's porting produced an even greater reduction in muzzle jump, so that now virtually all compensators include ports in one form or another. Current styles use either a single slot or a series of slots (or holes) cut into the compensator, but both work the same way. The action is not unlike muzzle brakes, which vent a portion of the powder gases upward. The laws of physics then take over, with the upward action of the gas producing a downward force on the barrel. It is this combination of weight and gas action that makes comps work.

At first, some serious doubts were expressed by handgun experts about the effects of hanging something like a compensator on the muzzle of a gun. Would it cause a loss of accuracy? To check this out, the author built his own comp gun and

Charles E. Petty is a lifelong hunter, reloader, competitor and collector. As such, he is actively involved in almost every aspect of shooting. His articles appear regularly in The American Rifleman, American Handgunner, Guns, Shooting Industry, and more. He is the author of a book, "High Standard Automatic Pistols," published in 1976.

Colt's MKIV Government Model in .45 caliber with compensator.

then tested it by firing the gun in a machine rest. Although comps are not meant to be removed, it wasn't hard to fire a series of groups with the comp in place and then, without removing the gun from the rest, take off the comp and repeat the series using the same ammunition. Instead of experiencing a loss of accuracy, which previous experience with muzzle brakes on other target pistols had led me to expect, the reverse was true. Test results showed convincingly that accuracy was slightly better with the comp in place than with it off. The difference was not great—about 2.3 inches at 50 yards with the comp in place and 2.5 inches with the comp removed—but it was im-

pressive when coupled with the very real reduction in recoil.

The newfound popularity of comps in action events has spawned a whole new generation of gunsmiths who now specialize in the custom work that is required, almost without exception, for comp guns. A thriving industry has also developed in the manufacture of the longer barrels and myriad other accessories that must be custom-installed. It all amounts to a minor revolution. Gunsmithing and metalworking skills that once were fast disappearing have been resurrected, and gunsmiths throughout the country have added their own versions of comps. In short, it has been one of the

This photo shows properly fitted barrel lugs from an accurized gun. Note the burnished appearance of the flat surface on top, where the slide stop pin mates with the lugs.

best things to happen to shooting in years, with demand for new products and services frequently outpacing the supply or the gunsmiths' abilities to turn out the work.

That work, by the way, can prove expensive. Prices can run as high as $3,000 for a top-of-the-line gun made by a "name" gunsmith. One obvious factor at work here is the effect that champion shooters have on such equipment and services. Should one of the stars in IPSC, for example, win a major event with a new type of comp, you can bet that gunsmith's phones will be ringing off their hooks the next day with requests for similar work. This demand naturally drives prices up and lengthens the waiting time (it's not unusual for a good gunsmith to have orders backed up for two years or more). It also creates work for newcomers in the gunsmithing business, and it's certainly possible to get as good (or better) quality work from a craftsman who hasn't yet earned a big—and costly—reputation.

The ABC's of Modification

Modifications performed on the Government Model, as a prime example, fall basically into two categories: *necessary* and *cosmetic*. The former includes those things that must be done to make the gun accurate, such as fitting slide to frame for a smooth, tight fit. There's also the three-point fitting of the barrel, as follows: (1) the fit of the barrel lugs to the slide stop pin; (2) the fit of the barrel to the bushing; and (3) the fit of the headspace extension to the slide.

In terms of accuracy, fitting the barrel lugs to the slide stop pin is by far the most important job. A snug fit between these two components is absolutely essential to ensure that the barrel locks up the same way in the slide with each and every shot. That's the only way to ensure the gilt-edged accuracy one expects (and pays for) in a custom-made barrel.

Next in importance is the fit at the front end. Browning's barrel bushing is made deliberately loose, so that the front of the barrel is free to move. Some accurized guns use bushings that are oversized in relation to the slide, and undersized in relation to the barrel. That makes it possible to fit the bushing to the slide (and explains why you sometimes need a special wrench to remove the bushing). It also ensures that the barrel will fit snug within the bushing once everything is locked up. This creates a difficult situation, though, because it is hard to judge whether a bushing is too tight, too loose, or just right.

Fortunately, the evolution of the comp gun has given us another answer to the problem of front end fit. Jim Clark was probably the first to use a tapered sleeve on the barrel to replace the bushing. The sleeve fits right into the slide and eliminates the bushing altogether. Claims for the sleeve are that it promotes reliability and better accuracy. Since one method does not appear to be clearly superior to the other, it usually boils down to which method is preferred by the designated gunsmith.

Assuming the first two jobs have been done properly, the fit of the headspace extension on the barrel to the recess in the slide becomes less important. But it also presents an opportunity to judge quickly the craftsmanship of a gunsmith. With the slide off and the barrel in place, all one has to do is hold the slide up to the light and look at the area where the headspace extension fits the slide. If little or no daylight shows, but the slide moves freely in and out of lockup, you know the smith took extra pains with it. If, on the other hand, there's a lot of daylight showing, or the extension has a lopsided look, the smith may not have taken those extra steps. Guns that have been properly or poorly fitted in this area may shoot equally well, so it's really not something to lose sleep over—but it's still a useful point to check.

Once the basic accuracy job has been completed, most of the remaining work becomes either cosmetic or functional in nature, but none will make the gun shoot any better. Action shooting has given us beavertail grip safeties, melted sights, checkering, ambidextrous safeties, and a host of lesser features that may make the gun look or feel better (and, of course, drive up the cost). Melted sights, by the way, refers to the method of installation, wherein the slide is milled down to allow the rear sight to be mounted much lower than is ordinarily possible. Not only does this look good, it also helps avoid snagging in the holster and permits the use of a much lower front sight as well.

Choosing the Right Caliber and Bullet Weight

The key to the whole system, of course, is the comp itself, which comes in only two basic types: either it has a single port or a series of smaller ones. Almost all of them now include an expansion chamber that allows the gas (as it leaves the bar-

The three most popular cartridges for practical shooting (left to right): .45 ACP, 10mm Auto, and .38 Super. All are handloads with the popular and economical cast bullets.

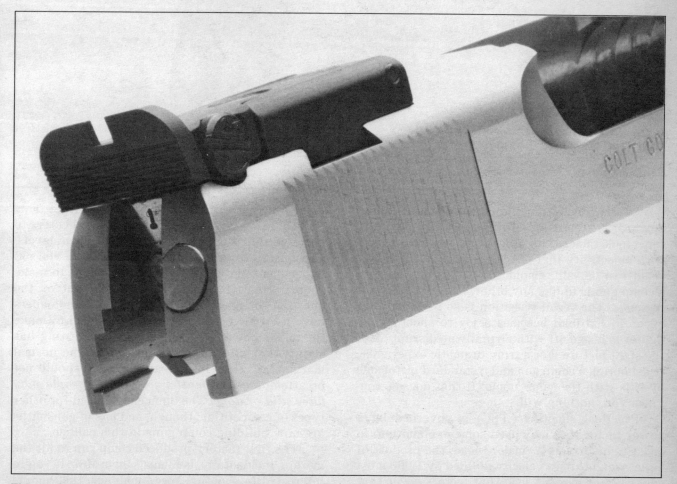

This example of a "melted" sight installation on a Colt Government Model features a Wichita adjustable sight. It has rounded corners to avoid snagging, and the slide has been milled for the lowest possible installation.

Llama's 9mm M87, the first factory-produced comp gun.

rel) to expand within the comp before escaping upward. There are variations on both themes, and some look racier than others, but it's hard to say with objectivity that one is better than the other. What can be said, emphatically, is that shooting a comp gun is unlike any other pistol shooting experience. The recoil sensation is so modified that even .45 hardball becomes a joy to shoot, while lighter loads go off with virtually no disruption of the sight picture. For a truly dramatic experience; try shooting a comp gun and a standard pistol side by side with the same ammo. If that doesn't convince you, nothing will.

Practical shooting (IPSC) is governed by a power factor that may need some explanation. In order to qualify as a "major" load, the product of bullet weight times velocity divided by 1,000 must equal 175 or more. A load that factors *below* that level is scored "minor," which carries a lower point value for hits outside the center of the target. This penalty can be serious and forces most shooters to make certain their loads reach the major levels. These rules strongly favor the .45 ACP. The .38 Super has to be loaded close to the limit to make major, while the 9mm is absolutely out of the question for reasons of safety. Some handloaders have used heavier bullets with the 9mm to make the major power factor; but pressure testing has shown that all such loads far exceed the normal margins of safety in the cartridge and should not be attempted—*no matter what some people may have said or done.* The 9mm can be used for other types of competition, though, and lots of gunsmiths are now building comp guns in this caliber.

The first factory-produced comp gun to hit the market, incidentally, is Llama's 9mm M87. If you're interested in shooting speed matches, the 9mm is no handicap, and the M87 is ready to go right out

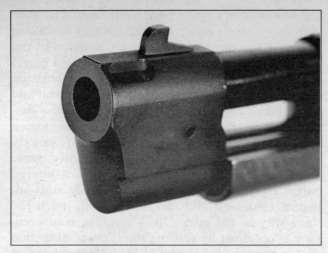

A closeup view of Llama's M87 compensator.

of the box. Its only drawback is the minor caliber scoring involved in shooting IPSC, but that doesn't dilute the fact that this is one of the most fun guns to shoot. The light recoil of the 9mm cartridge is reduced even further by the M87's comp, making it seem hardly more than a .22. It's also one of the most accurate 9mm's around, capable of sub-2" groups at 25 yards with good ammo. Coming straight from the factory, it includes all the standard features found in good comp guns, and the retail price tag ($1,450) is well below what you'd pay for a custom gun. Even IPSC's minor caliber scoring handicap is avoidable, because the M87's accuracy and light recoil make it easier to hit the "A" zone, which, under the rules, means that no penalties can be assessed (for using a minor caliber).

By far the most popular caliber among comp gun shooters, though, is the .45 ACP, and there's no doubt that it is the most versatile cartridge. Loaded to near maximum, it becomes the IPSC major of choice; and loaded down somewhat, it's great for steel and pure speed as well. The .38 Super, on the other hand, is extremely popular among the top guns because it has less recoil, due primarily to the lighter bullets used in that caliber. Many shooters believe they must own a super simply because that's what most of the stars use. The .38 Super can be a finicky beast, though, and it has to be handloaded—and loaded *hot*—to make the major power factor. Unless you're a serious handloader and are already proficient in the basic skills of the action events, the .38 Super is not the best choice for a first comp gun.

The 10mm is another good candidate for practical shooting because of its power potential. In fact, the 10mm can be loaded *down* to major levels with cast bullets and still produce only a bit more recoil than a .38 Super that's loaded up to the maximum. Until recently, guns and components for the 10mm were scarce, but that situation is changing rapidly. The .41 Action Express has also received a lot of press as a potential comp gun cartridge, but only time will tell.

Finding the Right Comp Gun for You

In addition to buying a used model, there are three ways to obtain comp guns. First, and most expensive, is simply to order one from a custom gunsmith. Depending on how many fancy extras you want, including the gunsmith's own reputation, expect to pay between $1,500 and $3,000, not to mention a waiting period of as much as two years or more. There's a lot of work involved and you'll just have to wait your turn.

Fortunately, there are other, less expensive options. If you already own a Government Model, or one of the copies, you can buy a kit or a "drop in" replacement barrel with a comp. Kits are built around custom barrels that require all the fitting outlined earlier. Unless you are already skilled in the art required to fit one of these models, you could be making a costly mistake. This is not exactly a home gunsmithing project. One bad swipe with a file can turn a $300 or $400 comp kit into so much useless metal. A good alternative for those who want a comp gun but aren't prepared to spend the kind of money we've been talking about is a

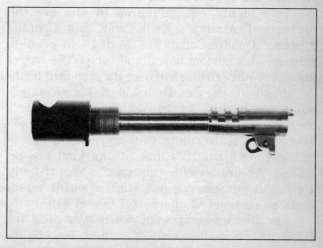

Springfield Armory's Kwik-Comp .45 kit includes a custom barrel and comp.

This Springfield Armory handgun is equipped with the company's Kwik-Comp drop in kit.

drop in comp, which replaces the standard barrel with little or no fitting. The accuracy of drop-ins may not be quite as good as the custom-fitted barrels, but they'll provide all the benefits of a comp for only $200 or so. It's a great way to find out whether comp guns are for you.

Two highly regarded drop in kits are the Springfield Armory's Kwik-Comp and Centaur Systems' Quadra-Comp. The Springfield product consists of a custom barrel and comp. The barrel doesn't require fitting and uses the standard bushing already on the gun. To install the barrel, simply adjust the position of the comp so that it doesn't hit the slide. Once this position is established, Lok-Tite is applied to the threads and a set screw is tightened. No modifications of any kind are required. Accuracy with this unit is surprisingly good, and for someone just starting out it represents an economical alternative (about $195).

The Quadra-Comp unit, which also sells for around $195, isn't exactly a drop-in, but the installation is equally simple. The heart of the system is a replacement slide stop, which allows adjustment for a more positive lockup. The slide stop has a small roller bearing, and by installing shims of various thicknesses it's possible to duplicate the lockup found in carefully fitted barrel lugs. All it takes to find the proper combination of shims (which are furnished) is a little trial and error. Since the barrel design eliminates the conventional barrel bushing, the kit also includes a replacement recoil spring and guide. It isn't exactly like the tapered sleeves used on some custom guns, but it works basically the same way. After the barrel has been installed and the slide stop adjusted, the comp gun can be fitted in much the same way as the Springfield unit. Superior accuracy is obtained by finding the right combination of shims to produce a snug fit of slide stop to barrel lugs.

And finally, as discussed earlier, there is Llama's factory-produced 9mm M87, which is beginning to appear on the market. There will be more in the future, so keep an eye out for them as well in your search for the "perfect" comp gun.

The Wave of the Future

There's no doubt that the practical shooting sports have revitalized gunsmithing (or pistolsmithing, if you prefer) and brought craftsmanship back into the picture. In only 10 years, the comp has evolved from a simple hunk of metal hung on the muzzle to something that looks like it came straight out of Buck Rogers. The process is unfin-

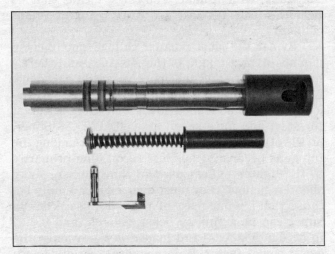

In Centaur System's Quadra-Comp kit, the roller bearing in the slide stop is the key to accuracy. Note also the single-unit, captive recoil spring and guide, along with the T-shaped port on the compensator.

ished, of course, but further vast improvements in comps are not likely. Still, that doesn't stop gunsmiths from trying out new ideas and designs. After all, when the difference between success and failure is measured in hundredths of a second, small improvements often become quite meaningful. There may not be any more quantum leaps in the comp gun field, but the sport will continue to change, which promises that the 1990s should prove as interesting and innovative as were the 1980s.

If a comp gun sounds like something you might want to try, it's wise to do a little homework before making any serious decisions or investments. Comp guns are highly specialized pieces of gear and are definitely not meant for everyone. The best way to watch them in action is to visit any IPSC match.

Check with a local gun shop to find out about locations, or write to the U.S. Practical Shooting Association, P.O. Box 811, Sedro Woolley, WA 98284. IPSC shooters are a friendly lot and they welcome newcomers. Most have programs to help ease your introduction to the sport, and chances are good they'll let you test out a member's comp gun if you ask. Another good idea is to read *American Handgunner*, which is THE magazine of the action shooting sports. In it, you'll also find plenty of ads from gunsmiths and dealers offering a multitude of specialty products and services to go along with the guns themselves. So spend some time learning about comp guns and the practical shooting sports before taking the plunge. Then, if you do decide to go ahead, be prepared to have the time of your shooting life.

This #130 Master Grade Accu-Comp "LE" features checkering and Hogue grips.

The Fascinating World of Sporting Clays

by Ralph F. Quinn

Since their inception in the late 1800s, clay target sports—namely, trapshooting and skeet—have enjoyed phenomenal growth and increased stature among scatter-gunners throughout the United States. Initially, this burst of popularity stemmed from the informal nature and simplicity of the sport itself. Such shoots typically took place in the back lots and byways across America, with their participants tossing targets with hand traps or small portable units. This enabled hunters to practice for upland game on a year-round basis.

To hunters, creating a sport that duplicates the flight of live game birds made great sense, and devotees flocked to both skeet and trapshooting

Ralph Quinn has been a full-time freelance writer specializing in shooting and outdoor subjects for more than a decade. As a lecturer, video/film producer and book author, he travels frequently throughout the U.S. and abroad in search of new material. A longtime A Class skeet and trap shooter, he contributes regularly to upland shooting publications and enthusiastically supports sporting clays for hunters everywhere.

with unbridled enthusiasm. As organized matches grew in number, however, shooters became mere technicians in their attempts to break the magical "100 target" mark. The original idea of using clays for hunting practice soon took a back seat to competition for competition's sake, and it didn't take long before the average gunner lost interest. As a result, untold thousands of potential clay sport addicts from the hunting ranks were passed over simply because they had neither the time and money nor dedication to excel in a shooting event that had little or no application to actual field gunning.

Fortunately, all that has changed. Today, across the U.S. and Canada, there is renewed interest in the shotgun game of "Hunters' Clays," or, as Continentals call it, "Sporting Clays." Originally developed in England at the turn of the century to simulate game bird and waterfowl hunting, the sport has caught fire and now promises to become the premiere shooting sport of the 1990s and beyond.

Given the natural settings in which clay events are held, along with the informal nature of competition rules, it's easy to see why hunters are jumping for joy. Gone are the carefully manicured concrete layouts, pre-mounted guns and intense competition normally associated with trap and

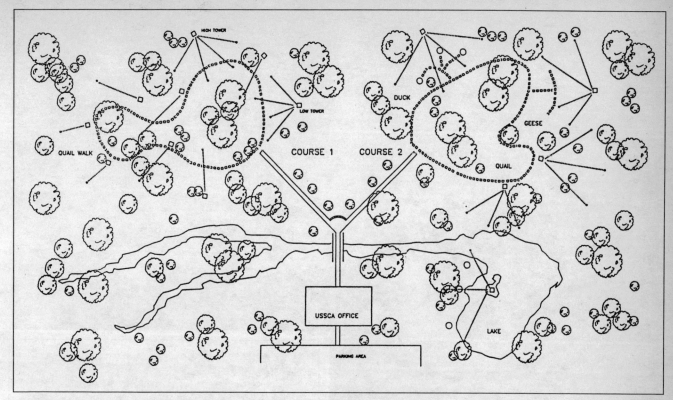

This course at the U.S. Sporting Clays Assn. Headquarters (Houston, Texas) is a good example of a good range layout.

This sporting clays participant is gunning on a "chance to double" stand. By centering the pattern, both targets can be broken with one shot. Note the tape barrier used to restrict shotgunners.

skeet. Instead, sporting clays participants and observers can stroll through picturesque woodlots and rolling fields, taking targets as they would on an actual upland hunt—crossing, outgoing, incoming, high overhead—with ease and pleasure. There's the added thrill of connecting on a particularly tough target. Competition still exists, but it's now internal. Often there is a free exchange of tips and gunning advice among competitors, and even some judicious cheerleading. Practicing such shooting heresies at regulation trap or skeet events would be considered strictly taboo.

Laying Out the Course

Another big plus sporting clays offers is the minimal time and expense needed to lay out a shooting course. Under normal circumstances, most sporting clays courses consist of 5 to 10 stations, requiring 25 to 50 targets launched over four requisite fields, such as flushing, tower, duck blind targets, chance-to-double, and the like. Yet, if a group of hunting buddies wishes to lay out a spe-

Simultaneous doubles launched behind the gunner simulate fast-rising grouse or pheasants. Wide target separation makes scoring more difficult.

cial, limited course of four stations simulating grouse and woodcock targets, time and dollar factors can be reduced considerably. By using highly portable and affordable ground traps by Trius, Outers and Hoppe, or the more expensive and durable Farey traps, equipment expense can be held to a fraction of what a normal trap and skeet setup costs. Also, since foot traps can be placed almost anywhere and quickly adjusted to throw targets in any number of "safe" directions, a challenging clays course can be put together on just a few acres of land.

Although every clays setup has a distinct regional personality, usually tied to a local style of hunting or the types of game birds found in that area, certain targets have become standard fare on sporting clays courses. In most cases, each stand is tagged or labeled according to the upland bird

Simultaneous doubles are just one kind of target available to clays participants. Portable traps keep shooters from "grooving in."

it is designed to imitate. For instance, the "Covey Rise" is a series of 4 to 6 targets that rise simultaneously, low in trajectory and straight ahead, just as a covey of quail might do. A "Springing Teal" or "Vaulting Woodcock" stand is a single target thrown nearly vertical; or, in some instances, targets may be launched in pairs over water or through dense tree cover.

Partridge (or "Pat") targets are incoming singles or doubles launched over a hedge, the crest of a hill, or a rise. Traditionally, these targets are fast and low, requiring shooters to fire directly in front of their stands or at an angle. The "Pigeon" is usually a tough crossing target launched at long distances (35 to 40 or more yards). Another challenging target is the "High Pheasant." Here, standard clays are launched from towers or hillsides to simulate driven pheasants. Because pheasant drives are unique to European gunning, most U.S. shotgunners find this target impossible

Sporting clays offers shotgunners realistic upland game targets in natural surroundings. Scorer and participants follow each course as a team, beginning and ending together.

to lead. Finally, there is the "Hare" or "Rabbit" target, which is thrown from a foot trap mounted perpendicularly. These so-called "Bolting Hares" are unpredictable, causing many a top gun to drop a point when the target unexpectedly "jumps."

The list of target possibilities is virtually endless, limited only by one's imagination and the amount of land available. Typically, a sporting clays layout consists of 10 stands, with five shots fired at each location. At a recent USSCA-sanctioned shoot, participants fired 10 shots at five stands for a total of 50 rounds. And the 1988 Eastern Shotgun Sports SKATs tourney in Ipswich, New Hampshire, featured 10 shots at 10 stands over a period of two days, but that is an exception. The basic philosophy in sporting clays tourneys is to get as many difficult targets as possible in the four fields of play, thereby creating an authentic hunting atmosphere.

As in trap and skeet events, a sporting clays squad consists of five shooters, plus a referee or scorer. Participants pass from stand to stand, rotating and firing in sequence until the course is complete. As each gunner takes his position, he (or she) may load and call for a target. A low gun position, with the toe of the stock visible beneath the armpit, is required throughout. British and European shooters typically use the International Skeet position, with the stock at hip level; but in the U.S., clays devotees use something in between. Since upland gunning requires a low gun position, the rule makes sense.

U.S. sporting clays participants use a modified low gun position, with the butt held even with the elbow and below the armpit.

After a target has been called for, launch can be immediate or delayed up to three seconds. The time lapse often throws off the best, especially shooters who've gunned only one or two courses or who consistently "groove in" at trap or skeet events. Targets are released singly or in doubles, simultaneously or separately, or as a trailing double involving a delay between targets. Another favorite is the report double: once the first target has been fired on, a second target is launched. Again, this is much like field shooting, where so often a second bird gets up before you're ready. An interesting variation of the report double is the "poison" (or white) target to simulate a hen pheasant. If the shooter mounts his scattergun, it's scored as a lost bird. Just as in upland gunning, this tactic helps keep shooters honest.

Unlike trap and skeet, sporting clays uses several targets of different sizes, ranging from the tiny 60mm mini, which is so popular in Europe and England, to the 90mm midi and the 110mm standard clay. The midi target is another reason why the sport has become so challenging and popular. Midis are usually launched as low, incoming targets, with the added restriction of shooting stands (blind-like cages used to limit a shooter's gun movements). Their smaller size makes these targets appear faster and farther away than they really are, and plus-side shooting results.

Minis are easier to recognize when launched against an open sky, but in dense cover they are tough! The Rabbit (or battue) clay is similar in size to standard targets but quite thin (about 3/8" wide). Limestone content, plus a heavy rim, make these clays extremely durable. Launched from a perpendicular trap, they roll along at high speed, making unpredictable vertical hops.

Picking the Right Gun

What gun works best for sporting clays? A simplistic answer would be: the gun you handle and shoot best in upland situations. For the average novice, any lightweight, smooth-swinging shotgun bored IC/M with 28″ barrels is a good choice. Since sporting clay rules allow shooters to change barrels or chokes to suit a particular stand, screw-in choke models have become quite popular both here and abroad—especially over/unders and semiautomatics. The side-by-side still has a following in England but is fast losing ground to the stacked barrel guns. This may be due to the band-

Women shooters enjoy clays competition using light recoil over/unders in 20 gauge. Note the international low gun position.

wagon effect, or perhaps it's because the side-by-side's broad sighting plane tends to obscure fast-rising targets. Of the winners who participated in the Eastern Shotgun Sports SKATs tourney (September 1988), all shooters used over/unders with interchangeable choke tubes.

With such a variety of incoming and outgoing targets, speed and manipulation are essential. It follows that any open-bored shotgun (improved cylinder or improved modified) with moderately long barrels (28 inches or more) works best. On crossing shots, however, a longer sighting radius may be better. Some shotgunners find extended tubes overwhelming at first, but once a smooth swing has been mastered the percentage of hits on passing targets will definitely increase. Top British shooters recognized this long ago; as a result, the

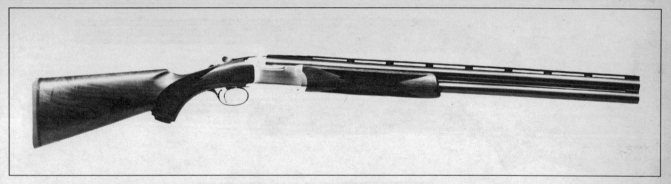

Sturm, Ruger offers the only American-made over/unders for sporting clays events. The company's screw-in choke system combines versatility with economy.

best in the field there use improved cylinder borings in a 30-inch barrel.

Shooters who become seriously involved in sporting clays will no doubt purchase one of several fine 12 gauge over/unders that have been designed specifically for these events. Because of this, most of the world's leading gun makers are working overtime to meet the increased demand. For example, Sturm, Ruger is offering its slick, stainless Red Label O/U in both 26- and 28-inch barrels, fitted with a four-tube system (full, modified, improved cylinder and skeet). Dollar for dollar, this gun is an exceptional value—a quality-crafted shotgun with design features usually reserved for pieces costing four times as much.

For shooters who demand good performance at modest price, a number of Spanish and Italian over/unders are also available. American Arms offers its Sterling model in 28-inch tubes with the multi-choke feature. Ellett Brothers markets the Regent VII Competition with 28-inch tubes and screw-in chokes. A notch up in price are Valmet's 412 ST, SKB's 885, Browning's Citori Invector, and Classic Doubles' 101. Weatherby's Athena, Rott-

weil's American Skeet, and Beretta's 682, 686 and 687S models are all excellent choices. For those who can afford them, Perazzi, Krieghoff and Merkel offer sporting clays models that are literally in a class by themselves.

Even though over/unders still dominate modern clay tourney circles, there is a strong move toward autoloaders, both here and in England. The Remington 1100, long a favorite among trap and skeet fans in the U.S. (especially when fitted with Rem-Choke) is at the top of the list. Beretta's Model 302 is a big hit in Europe, as is Benelli's Super 90, another Italian self-loader. Browning's gas-operated B-80 model with Invector choke is another fine gun for shooters who are recoil-conscious. If you presently own a repeater, use it in good health—and remember that sporting clays was designed *by* hunters *for* hunters.

On Choosing the Right Ammo

When it comes to choosing ammo, the standard $1\frac{1}{8}$-ounce trap or skeet load, No. $7\frac{1}{2}$ or 8 shot, does the job nicely for nearly all stands (USSCA rules permit shot sizes $7\frac{1}{2}$ to 9). Later, shooters

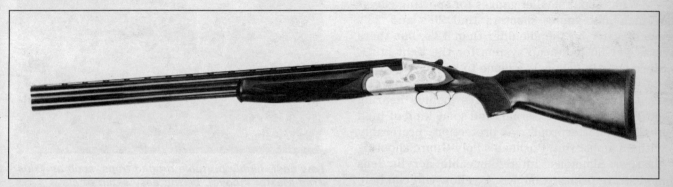

American Arms' Bristol model is offered in 12 gauge with 28" barrels and choke tubes.

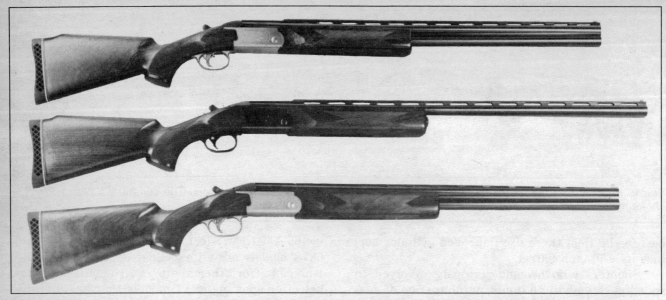

Valmet's line of 412ST shotguns includes (from top to bottom): Grade II Trap O/U, Grade I Trap Side-by-Side, and Grade II Skeet.

can manipulate shot in relation to distance, choke and stand. Emory "Red" Ball, a top-flight sporting clays instructor, offers these words of wisdom for beginners: "Use the No. 8 shot with the hardest coat you can find, load to 1,145 feet per second, and you're well on your way to success. Ninety-nine percent of the time, you'll be shooting at the soft belly of a clay target, which is easily broken."

If you are an ammo experimenter and would like to try hulls created specifically for the clays market, Federal offers its T122 load, and Dan Arms has its Max Trap. In addition, Rottweil is pushing its nickle-plated trap load, and Remington has its' Premier Pigeon and International Shotshells. Most are heavy on recoil, but performance is outstanding.

What about smaller gauges for sporting clays? Women and young shooters find 20's and 28's much easier on the shoulder than 12's, but there is as yet no handicap system for the light stuff. Since sporting clays is a game to be enjoyed, why not use whatever feels best for you?

Other gear needed for clays include hearing muffs (internal or external) and some kind of high quality, shatterproof eye protection, preferably with an amber tint. Bushnell's Poly-Guard shooting glass or Simmons' interchangeable acrylic lens models are prime examples. A yellow tint can help separate speeding targets from leafy backdrops

Low cost, highly portable ground traps, such as Trius Trap Master (above), permit easy setup of clays courses with minimal investments in time and land.

Tools of the sporting clays trade include a shell bag and screw-in chokes (over/under). Targets used include (left to right) 90mm Midi, Rabbit and Standard 110mm clay. A "white poison" target (on far right) is used to keep the gunners "honest."

quickly, a feature which by itself can spell the difference between a scored point and a lost bird.

Since you'll be lugging 50 to 100 hulls per round, a shell bag is a must for serious competitors. European shooters prefer leather bags similar to those marketed by Dunn's (Grand Junction, Tenn.). Orvis and Remington both sell fine shooting bags for quality-minded sportsmen. If the unit you choose has outside pockets, so much the better for carrying choke tubes or a quick-energy snack.

And in Conclusion. . . .

Two clays organizations currently offer information to inquiring parties in the U.S. They are the National Skeet Shooting Association (FM 417 at Paft Road, San Antonio, Texas 78253), which runs its own program and is fast attracting new members nationwide; and the U.S. Sporting Clays Association (50 Briar Hollow, S. 490 East, Houston, Texas 77027), which operates more than 100 affiliated courses in 30 states. The USSCA has sample shooting fields and range layouts available, and an up-to-date list of its member clubs worldwide. It also conducts training courses for the development of qualified instructors.

If growth is any indication of future success, the sporting clays sports are definitely here to stay. With hunting lands and game supplies dwindling, and interest in shooting and shotgun sports on the wane, these events can—and do—offer upland gunners a viable alternative to year-round gunning. If there's no course near your home, it's easy to gather a few traps and design your own. Once you've experienced the hunting-style atmosphere of a fast-crossing Pigeon, Vaulting Woodcock, or exploding Covey Rise, there's no turning back. You'll be hooked.

The .357 Magnum And The Men Who Made It

by Stanley W. Trzoniec

Question: Is it possible to shoot a gun in the 1990s using a classic cartridge that is guaranteed to remain popular into the distant future? Answer: Yes. And that legendary cartridge is none other than the familiar .357 Magnum. Sired in the mid-1930s, it has lived through some lively times and still rides high on the list of modern shooters who demand the utmost in variety without the unnerving feeling that a stick of dynamite is about to go off in their hands.

This classic trapped in modern times should, first of all, be taken for what she is. Her opponents constantly complain that she is no marvel in the ballistic department. Comparing the .357 Magnum to the .44 or even the .41 Magnum is foolhardy—

Stanley Trzoniec is a veteran firearms writer and photographer who has long specialized in the reporting of all modern weapons. An accomplished handloader, he has written on that subject for virtually every major firearms journal. Currently Special Projects Editor for Harris Publications, he is also the author of several books and has written over 500 articles on firearms and the outdoors.

and probably unfair. Proponents of this venerable cartridge rank the .357 right where it should be: middle of the line. For that is where she really shines.

How the .357 Was Born

Being first in line to carry the *Magnum* label rates at least a few lines of history. Colt first introduced a .38 caliber cartridge way back in 1874. Stuffed with black powder, it utilized bullets from 145 to 160 grains, reaching a velocity of almost 800 feet per second (fps). Called the Long Colt, she was fair in accuracy only because groove and bore diameters in weapons at that time ran the gamut from .363 to .369 inches. With a bullet whose outside diameter was, say, .359 inches, this cartridge fairly bounced its way down the bore. Taking note of the situation, Smith & Wesson, along with Remington Arms, decided there must be a better way, and in 1899 they released jointly a cartridge using about 18.0 grains of black powder. A year later, the switch was made to smokeless propellant, and catalog information now called the new cartridge a ".38 Special."

Not to be outdone—or outgunned—Colt followed suit with its introduction of a .38 Colt Spe-

Still recognized as the "flagship" of the .357 line, Smith & Wesson's Model 27 is available in a variety of barrel lengths and finishes.

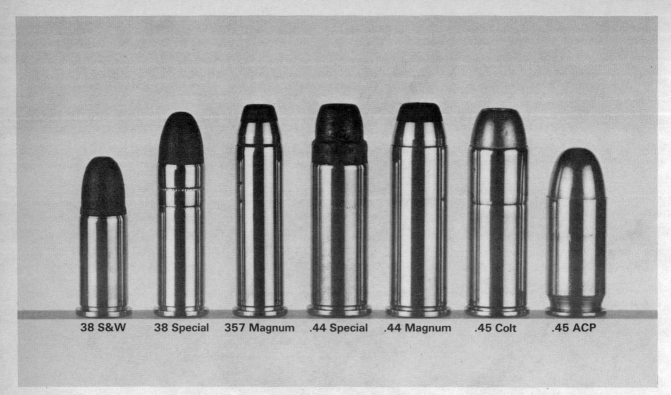

In today's cartridge lineup (see above), the .357 remains one impressive round.

| 38 S&W | 38 Special | 357 Magnum | .44 Special | .44 Magnum | .45 Colt | .45 ACP |

cial. It was identical on almost all counts with the Smith & Wesson "Special," except in overall cartridge length and bullet shape. The Colt measured 1.51 inches, the Smith & Wesson 1.55. As for projectile design, the edge in effective stopping power went to Colt. Whereas Smith & Wesson chose the traditional round nose configuration, Colt in all its wisdom went the way of a flat nose design in an obvious ploy to woo law enforcement to its side.

Up until the 1930s, the ever popular .38 Special remained all that law enforcement personnel could turn to for general firepower. A group of police officers might have a chance with the .38, but one-against-one it was practically useless. Attempts were made to upgrade the .38 Special into more formidable armament, but the results were feeble compared to what the .357 Magnum offered a few short years later. Still, the .38 Special maintained its popularity right into the 1930s. By then, arms companies were so eager to please that many new and innovative loads began to see the light of day. For police use, a 110 metal grain penetrating (not piercing) load came on line with a zinc alloy bullet complete with an advertised velocity of

"over 1,300 fps." A 150 grain "metal-piercing" load was also introduced, as was a controversial load dubbed by its maker (Western Cartridge Company) the ".38 Special SUPER Police." To make their new product saleable, Western Cartridge topped off four grains of Infallible with a 200 grain blunt nose bullet. Velocity dropped to 671 fps, slightly under the company's claim of 725 fps. At least one law enforcement agency—the St. Louis (Mo.) Police Department—used this offering in quantities large enough to gauge its effectiveness. As a result, during one month alone three felons met their demise without undue cost to the taxpayer of St. Louis.

Still, something was lacking. In the background, development of still another high-performance round—the .38/44 Special—was in the works. Elmer Keith, working with Remington Arms, had proved that a higher velocity round with a 158 grain bullet could be fired safely in a larger gun (a .38/44 Hand Ejector) at unheard of velocities approaching 1,115 fps. And yet, as impressive as that seemed at the time, the .38/44 soon fell by the wayside.

Elmer Keith vs. Phil Sharpe

In all, this particular period—from 1930 to 1935—was a very busy time for experimenters within the .38 caliber world. The gut feeling—that this .38 caliber could be made even more powerful by the use of the right propellant, bullet and gun—seemed to grow day by day. Finally, in April of 1935, the .357 Magnum cartridge was unveiled. How that actually came about is a story in itself, revolving around two greats of that period: handgun expert Elmer Keith and handloading and ballistic authority Phil Sharpe.

The central character behind all this, however, was Major Douglas Wesson, head man of the company that still bears his name. Seeking a more powerful gun in Smith & Wesson's lineup, he contacted both Keith and Sharpe and asked for their input. Keith began at once to experiment with a heavier 173 grain bullet over charges of #80 powder (but still in .38 Special cases). This charge, incidentally, followed current thinking by another handloading expert, J. R. Mattern, who had used the 160 grain bullet to attain velocities up to 1,200 fps. To prove its usefulness, Keith poured 1,000 rounds or more through a large frame gun without ill effects. Confirmation by Peters Cartridge Company showed an incredible pressure range approaching 42,000 pounds per square inch.

While test results proved there was indeed room for a more powerful cartridge, opinions about how strong the .38/44 series of handguns really were began to waver. Literally thousands of .38 Special handguns were out in the field now, most of them having been manufactured years before without the structural strength made possible by modern manufacturing methods. According to Major Wesson at the time, two new events took place as a result of Keith's experiments. One was a brand new, state-of-the-art handgun; and the other was a modification of the case, making it one-tenth of an inch longer so as to eliminate all possibilities of its being chambered (and shot) in a weaker or older weapon.

Elmer Keith was so deep into the project now that he even began designing bullets, casting them and forwarding boxes of them to Wesson, urging him to load or, better yet, adapt them for commercial use. Much to Keith's chagrin, Wesson did neither. In deciding not to load Keith's bullets into factory cases, Wesson doubtless considered liability to be a major factor even then. As for Keith's

bullet design, Winchester made some modifications, redesigning the crimping groove and making it into simply another lubrication groove. This was not at all satisfactory to Keith, who claimed a loss in accuracy over his previously tested projectile. But he seemed to quiet down once the first results came in. Carrying a payload of 15.3 grains of 2400 powder, his new load reached over 1,500 fps from a .357 barrel measuring 8¾ inches in length.

Meanwhile, in another part of the country, Phil Sharpe was hard at work on the same cartridge, thereby causing serious conflicts over who should get credit for the .357 Magnum. In his book, *Complete Guide to Handloading*, Sharpe had this to say: "The .357 Magnum cartridge was born in the mind of this author [Sharpe] several years ago." Since his book was published in 1937, that placed him within the same time frame as Keith. Sharpe continued: "On a hunting trip, D. B. Wesson used a pair of heavy framed Outdoorsmen revolvers to shoot a large assortment of handloads previously tested by the author." Again, in line with Keith's thinking, Wesson was already showing some concern about possible failures relating to the guns themselves; thus, a stronger handgun and a better balanced cartridge were beginning to take on higher priorities in Wesson's thinking.

This photograph of Phil Sharpe (right) appears in his book, "Complete Guide to Handloading." Sharpe is talking to veteran sharpshooter Harry Pope.

Quoting again from his book, Sharpe states, "This author is not connected with any arms or ammunition maker and desires this fact clearly understood. He [Sharpe] did not design the gun or the cartridge, although he cooperated and collaborated in a minor way." The key word to remember here is *minor*, which appears to lose its impact in light of further developments.

For handloaders, there are enough components here to fill every possible .357 situation.

For those licensed to carry big bore handguns, this 6" .357 is ideal.

While Keith was experimenting with a single load using a heavy bullet, Sharpe was busy contacting Winchester, Remington, DuPont and Hercules in an effort to secure the "perfect" combination of bullet and propellant. As he stated, "Over 100 different Magnum loads with assorted bullets, including 146 and 156 grain Sharpe-inspired bullets, were tested. . . ." Ten different powders found little favor with the author, so Winchester took over the development in this touchy area. Numerous case designs were also tried, using normal to extra-thick walls, as were various bullets by both Sharpe and Keith.

Clearly, there was an overlap of ideas at work. Sharpe admits that his bullet was based on a Keith design, however lighter in weight it may have been. Being closer to the source, Sharpe designed the projectile so as to be engineered more closely to .357 Magnum specifications. Whereas Keith's style had to be greatly resized to fit the lifestyle of new Magnum revolvers, Sharpe's product performed the same function with less work involved. In the end, Winchester rejected both Sharpe and Keith designs—probably in an attempt to give itself a pat on the back for all research—but later admitted that Sharpe and his engineering ideas had led them down the right path. Final bullet design called for a "Sharpe-type contour" in preference to Keith's suggestion. In the final analysis, though, Keith's bullet, with its longer bearing surface, was (and remains) one of the best on the market.

Smith & Wesson Introduces Its .357 Magnum

Let's turn our attention now to the gun itself. As mentioned earlier, because of pressure factors

So-called "heavy barrel" guns are nothing more than handguns with full-length barrel underlugs. They do add weight, however, and tend to reduce recoil. Shown here, from top to bottom, are a Dan Wesson, a Colt Python, and Smith & Wesson's Model 586.

cluding specified barrel lengths, sights and a finely checkered top strap. To complete the picture, a certificate of ownership was prepared at the factory and shipped with each gun. Now known as Model 27, it remains a fine-tuned handgun capable of delivering the best accuracy possible from host .357 Magnum ammunition.

The .357 Magnum is now widely considered the most popular cartridge around for beginning and advanced shooters. Since guns made to chamber the .357 will also shoot .38 Specials with equal safety, it's easy for beginners to make the transition from .38 to .357 without having to buy a second gun. All gun makers—from Astra to Dan Wesson—chamber this round in their revolvers, and recently even some semiautomatic .357 pistols have gone on the market. Still, even with the advancement of the 9mm pistol, new guns keep coming on line. Take, for example, Smith & Wesson's Model 686. Complete with a new frame size (L), it adds a bit more strength and heft compared to the company's sister gun, Model 19. Ruger has re-designed its Security-Six model, and now we see the stainless GP-100 taking over. Colt's Python has become the toast of handguns for its lockwork, good looks and expert workmanship.

For handloaders (according to RCBS die sales), the .38/357 has ranked first for the last six years running, never dropping much below second or third, depending on what the "fad" cartridges happened to be doing. Combine all this with the large array of bullets, powders, primers, cases and other components available, and you can spend a

and the new round itself Smith & Wesson decided to enter the Magnum age with style, touting the new round as the most powerful yet devised by man. In his book, *History of Smith & Wesson*, Roy Jinks writes: "The development of the Smith & Wesson .357 Magnum began with the well known arms and ammunition writer of the 1930's, Philip B. Sharpe. Sharpe had spent a great deal of time developing heavy loads that could be successfully used in Smith & Wesson .38/44 revolvers. He had been communicating with the factory throughout the 1930's, urging them to develop a special handgun that would handle loads beyond that which could be loaded in the .38 Special revolver." Again, we find Sharpe's name mentioned in a more positive way than Keith's.

As it was marketed, Smith & Wesson's .357 Magnum became the best one could buy. It had the finest heat treated steels, a protected ejector rod, and a cylinder that enclosed the case heads. It was a custom gun, made to each customer's desires, in-

Thanks to the invention of the speedloader, law enforcement officers can now load a Smith & Wesson Model 19 .357 with six rounds at a time.

Two new guns have been added to the .357 fold: Ruger's GP-100 (top) and Colt's King Cobra (bottom). Both are stainless, heavy-duty revolvers.

lifetime searching for the "perfect" load for your .357 pistol. In *Handloader's Guide* (written by the author and published by Stoeger Publishing Co.), a whole gamut of .357 possibilities is covered, including the new .357 Remington Maximum. While longer in case length and more powerful, the "R-Max" is undeniably a .357. In factory ammunition, dozens of combinations in bullet weights, velocities and applications exist, enough to satisfy law enforcement, self-defense, sportsmen and handgun hunters alike.

To sum up, while Elmer Keith deserves credit for the .41 and .44 Magnums, he comes up a shade shy on the .357. Phil Sharpe clearly takes the honors. As for metallurgy and ballistics, Smith & Wesson and Winchester both deserve pats on the back. Some question whether the .357 Magnum will continue its great success in years to come. In times past, a first-time shooter and buyer would almost certainly purchase a .38 caliber weapon; better yet, word soon spread that you could shoot both the .38 and .357 in the larger caliber gun. But now,

with the onset of high-volume automatics in 9mm, one must pause and wonder if the .357 era will eventually come to an end. With all its colorful history and popularity, this writer thinks not. After all, the .357 is more than an American tradition. It's a classic.

Dramatic effects can be observed by firing various cartridges in sand. Note the bullet expansion in the photo above. A .38 Special is on the left, and a .357 on the right.

Jack O'Connor: America's Greatest Gun Writer

by Jim Casada

Without question, Jack O'Connor ranks #1 among America's top gun writers of the 20th century. During a long and extraordinarily productive career, he became a household name to three generations of sportsmen. Much of his fame derived from the steady stream of informative columns he produced during his 33-year tenure as Arms & Ammunition Editor at *Outdoor Life*. He was also the author of more than a dozen books (see a complete listing at the end of this article), and in his later years he served as Executive Editor of *Petersen's Hunting Magazine*. For all his notoriety, however, surprisingly little is known about the sensitive, caring person who lurked behind the mask of a gruff gun scribe.

Who exactly was Jack O'Connor? He entered this world on January 22, 1902, in Nogales, Arizona, and by the time he was 12 he had already shot his first trophy, a fine mule deer. From then on, he knew that hunting and the outdoors would play a major role in his life. Thanks in large measure to his doting grandfather, James Wiley Woolf, young Jack spent a great part of his boyhood afield, experiencing all the joys of a sporting apprenticeship.

O'Connor's childhood had more than its share of problems and pain, though, and later on he went

Jim Casada teaches history at Winthrop College (Rock Hill, SC) and contributes regularly to outdoor publications on a variety of subjects. He is currently editor-at-large for Sporting Classics magazine and contributing editor for Fly Fishing Heritage, The Flyfisher, Flyfishing News & Reviews and N.C. Outdoorsman. He also writes three weekly newspaper columns, is working on a manuscript on "Great Hunters/ Writers in Africa," and preparing a history of the South Carolina Wildlife Department.

through a great personal tragedy in the death of a son, Jerry. Anyone who reads between the lines of his autobiographical book, *Horse and Buggy West: A Childhood on the Last Frontier*, will appreciate the troubles that haunted O'Connor, especially in his younger days. The same holds true for *The Last Book: Confessions of a Gun Editor*, which was published posthumously because its contents were so brutally frank that the publisher, Jim Rikhoff of Amwell Press, a longtime friend of O'Connor's, felt it was the only way the book could appear.

O'Connor's stubborn determination to speak

O'Connor was always a natty dresser, as this photo from the mid-1970s suggests.

Jack O'Connor examines an AYA shotgun made especially for him by the famous Spanish firm.

the truth, no matter what the cost or situation, was actually one of the man's most engaging characteristics. His son, Bradford, recalls the time a bigwig from the U.S. Army Corps of Engineers addressed an audience of Idaho outdoorsmen, trying to reassure them that the Corps had no intention of building a dam in their area, one that could very well destroy their sport. After listening to the man with growing vexation, O'Connor, who was in the audience, stood up abruptly and growled: "That is a goddamned lie, soldier boy, and you know it!" He then read a clipping from an Oregon newspaper, quoting the same official as saying the dam would indeed be built.

That kind of irreverent outspokenness was an integral part of Jack O'Connor's character, and he could no more control it than he could stifle his fiery temper. By the same token, the man was generous to a fault and his honesty was transparent. These endearing qualities, together with his exceptional intellect and a rare knack for writing and speaking, served him well with his admiring audiences. They always knew that O'Connor could be relied upon to call the shots as he saw them. If he felt a new gun was a piece of trash, he said so in no uncertain terms.

A Career is Born

After serving with the U.S. Army's 158th Infantry at the end of World War I, O'Connor studied for a while at Arizona State Teachers College, then spent a year at the University of Arizona before receiving his bachelor's degree at the University of Arkansas in 1925. Two years later, he got his master's degree in English from the University of Missouri. Shortly after that, he met and married Eleanor Bradford Barry, and theirs became a life-long relationship marked by strong mutual devotion, the rearing of four children, and countless days spent afield together. Meanwhile, Jack completed his studies and began working as a newspaper reporter. From 1927 to 1930, he worked concurrently for the Associated Press, taught college, and wrote for several Texas dailies.

Without doubt, the rigid routine of newspaper writing gave O'Connor a discipline and working ethic that lasted throughout his career. During the depths of the Depression, he taught English and journalism. He also had his first book published, a novel called *Conquest*. The book failed to attract a wide audience and even forced O'Connor to leave his teaching position because one of his characters in the novel had called another a "son of a bitch."

It was then that O'Connor turned to magazine writing to supplement his meager income. Since he was an avid hunter, the outdoor magazines offered him a logical outlet, and it was from this point on that his career began to come into focus. He sold his first piece to *Sports Afield* and sales to *Field & Stream* and *Outdoor Life* soon followed. His second novel, *Boom Town*, appeared in 1938, and that was followed by his first book on the outdoors—*Game in the Desert*—which was based largely on articles he had written for *Field & Stream*. Issued in a limited, numbered edition of 950 copies, the book was a thing of rare beauty, featuring a binding made of a green, shiny cloth simulating snake skin. Today, copies of that book are valued at $500 to $1,000, depending on their condition. The book was later reissued under a new title, *Hunting in the Southwest*, and it is still available in the Amwell Press edition, *Game in the Desert Revisited* (1984).

Bolstered by the success of this book, along with a steady stream of published articles, O'Connor's stature as an outdoor writer grew rapidly. He was incredibly industrious, and in the midst of all this feverish activity there came a real watershed in his career. It happened in 1939, when Captain E. C. Crossman, the gun columnist for *Outdoor Life*, committed suicide. Ray Brown, the magazine's editor at the time, asked O'Connor if he'd be interested in writing a monthly column. Jack accepted, and within a year he was promoted to Arms & Ammunition Editor. Thus began a career that spanned more than three decades. During his long tenure with the magazine, O'Connor built up a devoted following, and there is little doubt that he played a significant role in the magazine's steadily rising circulation.

The Books Take Over

Even as he became firmly entrenched in the magazine world, O'Connor kept on producing books at a steady pace. The sheer magnitude of his productivity over an extended period of time tells us several things about him as a writer: he wrote fast and well, he worked exceptionally hard, and he had an almost compulsive desire to convey the joys of hunting to his readers. His approach was one that any outdoor communicator should strive to emulate. He always tried to take his audience along with him—to carry them, if only in their imaginations, to the settings he described. Whether it was hunting quail in the sagebrush of his beloved Southwest or tracking lions in the African veldt, he was a master at this. He made the tang of gunpowder, the camaraderie of evening campfires, the thrill of a difficult stalk so tangible as to seem almost real.

He also knew his field inside and out, and few writers have ever approached his expertise with guns. A great advocate of avoiding overkill, he eschewed powerful weapons when he felt lesser calibers could do the job. He also was adamant in his opposition to "freebies." He bought his guns at the normal discount offered to outdoor writers and politely refused to accept gifts that might be at all construed as attempts to curry favor. In the long run, this policy served him well, because the gunmakers knew they could count on him for honest opinions.

While O'Connor kept in constant touch with his readers through his monthly magazine pieces, he will likely be remembered more for his books. *Hunting in the Rockies* appeared in 1947, and two years later, in what many feel was his finest effort, he made his first real break-through in the field of outdoor books with *The Rifle Book*. It became a bestseller in its field, and 15 years after its original appearance a revised edition appeared. The same thing happened with two other O'Connor volumes—*The Shotgun Book* and *The Complete Book of Rifles and Shotguns*—both of which attracted wide audiences and enjoyed considerable longevity. During O'Connor's lifetime, more than

Jack O'Connor wearing his medal-bedecked hat, one of his favorites.

500,000 copies appeared in print. Another useful index of O'Connor's continuing popularity is the fact that various posthumous collections of his articles and reprints of his books continue to appear.

One of O'Connor's favorite book editors was Angus Cameron, who for many years presided (with what many have described as rare genius) over all outdoor publications at Knopf, long considered one of the country's most prestigious publishing firms. Cameron recalls O'Connor with great fondness, describing him laughingly as "a reactionary old curmudgeon [who was] somewhere to the right of Ghengis Khan" in his political outlook. O'Connor gave as good as he got, often chiding Cameron for his own leanings in their monthly telephone conversations. One of Cameron's favorite anecdotes concerns the time he worked on O'Connor's manuscript of *The Rifle Book*, which the author had left with his editor before leaving on an African safari. After some time in Africa, O'Connor hunted in Spain for a few days before returning home. While in Spain, he visited the premises of AYA, the noted Spanish gunmaker. There he asked AYA's craftsmen to make him a custom-made shotgun, which in due time he presented to Cameron. No bill was attached stating the cost of this unique weapon of singular beauty, however, and several letters to O'Connor on the subject produced nothing but evasive answers and a strange unwillingness to discuss the matter.

Finally, Cameron called O'Connor and told him in no uncertain terms that he wanted to pay for the shotgun. At that point, Jack informed his long-time friend and editor that the rifle was a gift from him "for past kindnesses." When Cameron protested, O'Connor cut him off with typical abruptness: "Angus, you've got to learn to receive as graciously as you give" (referring to Cameron's careful editing of his books over the years).

Generosity of this kind was often experienced by those whose friendship O'Connor cherished. Jim Rikhoff, another close friend and publisher (Amwell Press), recalls his own fond memories of O'Connor's generous nature. He remembers too what a powerful and agile mind O'Connor possessed, one which Rikhoff felt placed Jack above the ordinary run of gun writers. Reminded of the near unfathomable nature of O'Connor's character, Rikhoff likes to point out all manner of contradictions, such as the Brooks Brothers suits and the sartorial splendor which seemed so much at odds with O'Connor's western roots. As Rikhoff puts it,

"He was an extremely talented but equally complex man . . . a mixture of the sensitive and sensible, of the ribald and reflective, of insight and inspiration, of instinct and intellect."

Beneath the bravado and carefully cultivated image, though, one always returns to the same conclusion: Jack O'Connor was a man of many talents. Chief among these, perhaps, was his understanding of the importance of friendship. His life was full of friends and adventures, the kind that most people can only dream about. He was, for example, one of only a handful of men who ever scored a double grand slam on all four varieties of North American sheep. He made six safaris to Africa, hunted tigers in India, and made two trips to Iran—in addition, of course, to hunting every species of game North America had to offer.

Active to the last, Jack O'Connor died of a heart attack on January 20, 1978, while on a cruise aboard the *S. S. Mariposa* en route from Hawaii to San Francisco. The funeral was held in the town he had called home for many years: Lewiston, Idaho. His remains were cremated and scattered by his son, Bradford, over a mountain range inhabited by his favorite hunting quarry: sheep. With this request, O'Connor showed in death, as he had done so consistently in life, what can perhaps be best described as *style*. As an author, he was unquestionably a masterful stylist; but the same held true in the way he dressed, his feel for sportsmanship, and so many other aspects of his life. This is a part of his legacy, as is the substantial body of outdoor writing he left behind. It places him squarely in the very forefront of America's rich literature of the outdoors.

The Published Works of Jack O'Connor

The following list covers Jack O'Connor's books in order of their first publication. Included are works for which he was a major contributor as well as anthologies and various posthumous publications. Many remain in print, but first editions of all his books are now prized collectors' items.

Conquest (Harper, 1930). A novel.
Boom Town (Knopf, 1931). A novel.
Game in the Desert (Derrydale, 1939). Originally limited to 950 numbered copies, this work was published in a trade edition by Knopf in 1945 with a new title: *Hunting in the Southwest*. The only difference in the contents

A deskful of books by Jack O'Connor and other memorabilia attest to a lifetime of outdoor labors and loves.

of the two books was a new preface. In 1977, Amwell Press issued a new edition of 950 copies, with new artwork and a foreword by Jim Rikhoff, entitled *Game in the Desert Revisited*. The book includes a substantial introduction by O'Connor and updated postscripts to chapters 19 and 20. It was first issued in a limited edition to members of the National Sporting Fraternity, then released to the general public by Amwell Press. This edition and other Amwell publications can still be obtained by writing to Amwell Press, P.O. Box 5385, Clinton, NJ 08809-9990.

Hunting in the Rockies (Knopf, 1947)

Sporting Guns (Franklin Watts, 1947).

The Sportsman's Encyclopedia (Outdoor Life, 1948; revised edition, 1956). This work featured contributions from America's foremost authorities on the great outdoors, with O'Connor as a major contributor.

The Rifle Book (Knopf, 1949; 2d edition, revised, 1973). A third revised edition was distributed in 1978 by Random House.

Sportsman's Arms and Ammunition Manual (Outdoor Life, 1952).

The Big Game Rifle (Knopf, 1952).

The Outdoor Life Shooting Book (Outdoor Life, 1957).

The Complete Book of Rifles and Shotguns (Outdoor Life, 1961; 2d edition, revised and updated, Popular Science, 1965). This book was a true bestseller (by 1966 it had gone through 13 printings). It also appeared in a boxed edition, along with *The Complete Book of Shooting* (see below), as a selection of the Outdoor Life Book Club.

The Big Game Animals of North America (Outdoor Life, 1961; 2d edition, revised, 1977).

Jack O'Connor's Big Game Hunts (Dutton,

1963). Consists of 26 stories reprinted from *Outdoor Life*.

The Complete Book of Shooting (Harper & Row, 1965; 2d edition, revised and updated, 1982; the latter was distributed to the book trade by Stackpole Books).

The Shotgun Book (Knopf, 1965; 2d edition, revised, 1978).

The Art of Hunting Big Game in North America (Knopf, 1967; 2d edition, revised, 1977).

Horse and Buggy West (Knopf, 1969).

The Hunting Rifle (Winchester, 1970). This work later appeared as a paperback volume in Stoeger's Sportsman's Library.

Sheep and Sheep Hunting (Winchester, 1974; memorial edition, 1983).

The Best of Jack O'Connor (Amwell Press, 1977). The first edition was limited to 1,000 copies, with subsequent printings made available to the book trade.

The Last Book (Amwell Press, 1984). This title appeared as a boxed volume, including a foreword by Bradford O'Connor and an introduction by Jim Rikhoff.

Hunting on Three Continents with Jack O'Connor (Safari Press, 1987). A collection of 30 stories written between 1973 and 1977, with an introduction by John Batten.

Bullet Performance on Deer

by Norman E. Johnson

Do you want to know how to get a deer hunter's blood pressure up fast? Try making a few disparaging remarks about his favorite cartridge or load. Unfortunately, when it comes to the cartridges and bullets they use, most hunters hold fast to long cherished, but often flawed, convictions.

Granted this is a controversial subject. And true, the field of ballistics is not an exact science. Still, there are enough established principles and supporting data available to remove most of the hidden mysteries on the subject. In order to make a valid distinction between sentiment and fact, however, we should first clarify some of the most frequently misunderstood terms used by experts and laymen alike. Perhaps then all parties concerned will have a better understanding of what

Norman Johnson has been writing for most of the major shooting and hunting publications for more than 20 years and currently serves as Shooting Editor for Outdoor Sports & Recreation Magazine. He also owns and operates the Plum City Ballistics Range (Plum City, Wisconsin), which covers testing and research of firearms, ammunition and related subjects.

bullet performance is all about, particularly as it applies to deer hunting.

A close look at the vast array of bullets available to the average shooter shows clearly that most of them are designed for specific purposes. When a company devotes countless hours to bullet research, design and testing, it stands to reason that the shooter will get maximum performance by using the right bullet—one that performs the task for which it was especially designed. So let's take a look at some of the important functions a bullet performs, and then note how these functions are made possible through style and design.

Accuracy Comes First

For the .30-.30 shooter, accuracy is less important than it is to the deer hunter who prides himself on his ability to kill a deer at long range with a scoped .270 or .30-06 rifle. In most hunting situations, bullet accuracy is most important, simply because it largely determines whether—and where—the bullet will hit the target. Bullet accuracy can be controlled in several ways. First, each bullet must be of uniform weight. Second, each bullet must be uniform in diameter and must conform to the bore diameter of the gun from which it is fired. Not all bullets perform well in all guns; it's not uncommon to discover one bullet

Accuracy is a prime consideration when choosing a bullet for deer. These two 100-yard groups (five-shot), using Speer 100 grain .25 caliber bullets, indicate excellent accuracy.

that will shoot sub-minute-of-angle, while another proves totally unacceptable.

Target bullets are made differently than bullets meant for hunting, even though many bullets intended for target shooting will kill deer. Target bullets are usually held to closer overall tolerance, but that doesn't mean good hunting bullets don't produce good accuracy, because they do. Modern hunting bullets can be depended upon to perform as advertised; and the more you learn about and use these bullets, the greater advantage you'll create as a hunter.

These sectioned bullets, each showing its internal construction, are identified as follows: (A) 7mm Nosler full partition PSP (B) .30 caliber Nosler semi-partition PSP bullet (C) .30 caliber Remington bronze point (D) .270 caliber Winchester silver tip.

Vital to all shooters is bullet mass in proportion to its cross-section diameter—i.e., its sectional density. A bullet's sectional density is determined by dividing the weight of the bullet in pounds (7,000 grains equals one pound) by its cross-sectional area in square inches. Especially important to the deer hunter is the fact that sectional density must be great enough to maintain both velocity and bullet penetration after impact. A bullet that won't maintain velocity benefits neither the hunter nor the target shooter. The hunter will find such a bullet dropping too fast at longer ranges; moreover, it won't produce the penetration needed for quick kills. Shooters will find bullets with low sectional density undesirable from the standpoint of

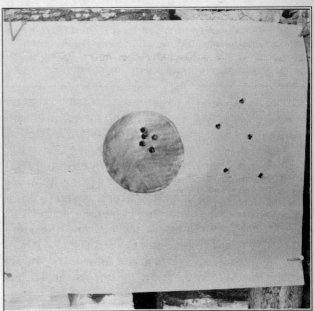

Tests show that no two rifles will shoot the same bullet with equal accuracy. These two .30-06 groups were shot using the same bullet and load in different, slightly used rifles.

wind-drift as well. To the deer hunter, even a .22 caliber bullet (63 gr./.179 S.D.) may have a greater sectional density than a .30 caliber bullet (110 gr./ .166 S.D.).

In addition to sectional density, bullet configuration and point form are important—and that brings up the subject of *ballistic coefficiency*, which takes into account the overall efficiency of a projectile to overcome air resistance and wind drift. The higher the coefficient of form the more will a bullet perform aerodynamically (all other things being equal, of course). This should not be

These sectioned bullets are all excellent for deer. (A) .270 caliber Winchester silver tip (B) 7mm Nosler full partition 160 grain PSP (C) .30 caliber Nosler semi-partition PSP (D) .270 caliber Remington PSP (E) .30 caliber Remington bronze point.

confused with a bullet's potential to kill, however, even though it may fly better and maintain its energy longer than a bullet with a lower coefficient number.

When a bullet is fired, it is immediately affected by gravity and air resistance as it leaves the muzzle, causing it to slow down gradually until it comes to a complete stop. Common sense tells us that the faster a bullet travels, and the more efficiently it moves through the air, the less it will slow down or drop over a given time span. Muzzle velocity is therefore extremely important. Unfor-

Some bullets have near-fragmented jacket expansion. Sometimes, where velocity is too high and jacket too thin, the lead core will leave the jacket of a bullet, as shown here.

tunately, initial velocity does not decide overall *bullet trajectory*. Both sectional density and bullet point form make up the coefficiency of form which enables a bullet to maintain the flat trajectory necessary for hunting purposes. In other words, a long, thin, pointed bullet of equal velocity and weight will travel on a flatter trajectory and with less wind drift than a larger caliber bullet with a more blunted point. A glance at any ballistics table indicates how a bullet's coefficiency of form relates to hunting, especially in long range shooting common to deer hunters.

Bullet Penetration and Expansion

The final keys to bullet effectiveness are penetration, expansion, and delivered energy. Bullet

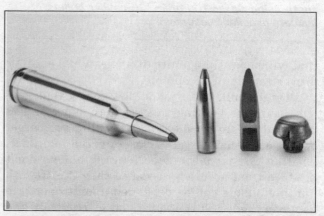

This cartridge and bullet combination—a Nosler 140 grain partition in Remington 7mm Magnum—is ideal for long range deer hunting. The expansion back to the partition (extreme right) indicates optimal control.

energy simply means the ability of a bullet to do a certain amount of work as a direct result of its velocity and weight (as defined in foot pounds of kinetic energy). One effective formula for determining bullet energy goes as follows: multiply the weight of the bullet in grains by its velocity (in foot seconds) squared. Then multiply that figure by .000002218 to arrive at bullet energy in foot pounds. For example, a 100 grain bullet at 3000 fps works out this way:

$$100 \times 3000 \times 3000 \times .000002218 = 1996 \text{ fpe}$$

In practical terms, this formula enables one to make energy comparisons of various bullets, an important attribute indeed for any hunter who is in the process of selecting a cartridge or bullet for use on deer.

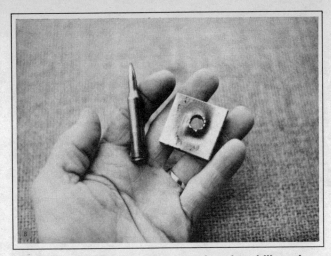

This .220 Swift is a super, one-shot deer killer when used with a good bullet. Note how easily a 55 grain bullet zipped through this half-inch boiler plate.

A bullet's killing power, then, is the direct result of its applied energy as the bullet penetrates, followed by expansion and continued penetration. Among the factors that control the killing power of a big game bullet are bullet jacket thickness and hardness, bullet design, core hardness, and point type (including its shape and the material used). For a bullet to be most effective in killing game, it must produce adequate initial expansion without flattening out; otherwise, it will lose velocity, causing insufficient penetration. To keep on penetrating, a bullet must have enough controlled expansion so that it can retain most of its original base diameter and weight thrust. All bullets on impact shed velocity at a fast rate, even though expansion may be little or nonexistent. Ideally, a bullet will continue to penetrate even after it has expanded. No two shooting situations are ever exactly alike, of course, and so these important factors—expansion and penetration—can vary considerably, leaving the hunter often bewildered when his favorite bullet fails to kill.

In general, the lead-tipped, pointed, soft point bullet with proper jacket thickness will produce excellent kills on deer of any size with cartridges and bullets of recommended velocity and energy. This type of bullet expands readily (but not excessively) and continues to penetrate effectively—assuming the deer has been hit where it should be. These same bullets with jacketed lead core construction seem to perform best with rifle velocities ranging from about 2000 fps to 3200 fps.

Regardless of bullet weight, shape or construction, the cartridge must provide the velocity. Among those that are better suited for deer, note the following examples:

OVER-KILL CARTRIDGES
.375 H&H Magnum
.300 H&H Magnum
.338 Winchester Magnum
.300 Winchester Magnum
7mm Remington Magnum
.264 Winchester Magnum
.257 Weatherby Magnum
7mm Weatherby Magnum

IDEAL DEER CARTRIDGES
.243 Winchester
6mm Remington
.250 Savage
.257 Roberts
.25-06 Remington
.270 Winchester
7×57 Mauser
.280 Remington
.30-06 Springfield
8mm Mann
.30-40 Krag
.308 Winchester
.300 Savage
.32 Winchester Special
.30-30 Winchester

UNDER-POWERED CARTRIDGES
.17 Remington
.22 Hornet
.218 Bee
.25-20 W.C.F.
.222 Remington
.223 Remington
.222 Remington Magnum
.256 Winchester Magnum
.30 carbine
.220 Swift
.22-250 Remington
.225 Winchester

The rifled shotgun slug can be accurate and effective on deer as well. A good shotgun should hold three-inch, five-shot groups at 50 yards, as in this example.

Bullets that do not fall within this range may fail to expand and kill properly, even though penetration is adequate. Attempting shots that fall outside this bullet velocity/expansion range may well result in lost animals.

How Bullets Stop Game

Too many deer hunters go into the field with little or no thought as to why an animal drops from a lethal hit. A bullet can wound, stop or kill game in several ways. It can result in a major shock to the central nervous system, bring about vital organ dysfunction, cause severe hemorrhaging, and do heavy damage to muscle or connective tissue. In any case, hydrostatic shock and/or cavitation of soft tissue must be present in order to induce sudden death. A high velocity, expanding bullet will produce a massive amount of tissue cavitation and resulting trauma to surrounding organs, blood vessels, and important functional muscles of locomotion.

At least three dozen different cartridges are commonly used to kill deer, and perhaps only a dozen of these are ideally suited for the job when used with good bullets. Among the most popular combinations for whitetails (as selected by a group of surveyed hunters) are the following:

.243 Win/100 gr.	.280 Rem/140 gr.
6mm Rem/100 gr.	7mm Mauser/140 gr.
.25-06 Rem/100 gr.	.30-30 Win/150 gr.
.257 Roberts/100 gr.	.30-06 Spfd/150 gr.
.270 Win/130 gr.	.300 Savage/150 gr.
7mm-08 Rem/140 gr.	.308 Win/150 gr.

Among those combinations rated in the over-kill category are some of the belted magnums, such as the 7mm Rem. Mag., .270 and .300 Weatherby Magnums, and .300 Win. Mag. At the other extreme, there are the poor to marginal cartridges for deer, those with under-kill velocity/energy levels. Some states limit cartridges to caliber designation irrespective of energy, while others use bullet energy as their governing criteria for taking deer. According to the Wisconsin Department of Natural Resources, handgun cartridges claiming a muzzle energy of 1000 fps or greater are legal for use on deer. Using a .30 carbine with its 110 grain bullet at 965 pounds of energy would, at best, be considered borderline based on this criteria. And yet, when placed in the right hands, that same combination has taken many a deer.

This subject would not be complete without mentioning the high velocity centerfire .22 caliber cartridges for use on deer, specifically the .220 Swift (followed closely by the .22-250, .225 Winchester and a few others). Whereas killing power is the primary function of bullet penetration, expansion and delivered energy, it follows that a good .22 caliber bullet can be very effective in killing deer-sized animals. When a standard pointed soft point bullet shot from a .220 Swift can zip through 1/2-inch of boiler plate, you know that pure energy is at work. This same high velocity .22 centerfire cartridge may be a marginal performer on deer, however, when placed in the hands of a hunter who simply hits the animal

The soft lead rifled shotgun slug features high sectional density, high energy, and adequate expansion. In many areas, the shotgun and slug are the only legal means of taking deer.

Where legal, the .357 Magnum handgun loaded with good bullets, as shown in the illustration above, can be effective on deer. Bullet expansion is critical, however.

wherever he can. Most cartridges tend to fail—and usually do—under these circumstances.

As we have seen, a number of variables are involved in making a killing shot, and correct bullet placement ranks high among them. Indeed, many a rifle hunter could take a lesson from the bowhunter who must carefully assess all of the variables before he makes a shot. That's one of the secrets, for sure, to killing humanely. Selecting the best cartridge with optimal velocity and using a near perfect bullet represents only part of the story of good deer hunting. The hunter must still perform well to make any bullet effective.

Chamber Pressure: Is It Your Friend or Your Enemy?

by Don Lewis

Anyone who has experienced near disastrous episodes involving excessive chamber pressure will not soon forget it. It may be a cartridge that has been improperly reloaded, causing hot gases to sear one's face; it could be a detachable magazine bouncing off your workbench like a rubber ball; or it may be a cartridge in a bolt action rifle that has ruptured, ripping the floorplate off, opening the bolt partially and splitting the stock in back of the receiver. The results in any case are similar: faces badly burned by gases, tingling hands, a badly shaken nervous system, or worse. In each instance, the person who was reloading the shells in an attempt to increase velocity gave little or no thought to the expanding gases, or what we call *chamber pressure*.

A retired corporate credit manager, Don Lewis now spends most of his time testing and evaluating guns and scopes in his own well-equipped shop in Kittanning, Pennsylvania. In addition to contributing regularly to Shooter's Bible, Lewis writes about gun-related subjects for Pennsylvania Game News, Pennsylvania Woods & Waters, and other prominent periodicals in the field.

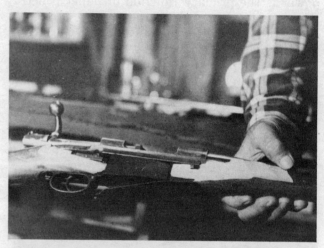

Here is dramatic evidence of what can happen to a rifle action that cannot withstand a super-hot load.

Of all the various aspects of internal ballistics, chamber pressure is probably the least understood, because few handloaders, local gunsmiths and rifle makers have any way of measuring it accurately, if at all. Pressure-recording devices are so complex and costly that the only method left is to accept the pressure readings shown in the manuals as being within the safe limits of the rifle. But this can be misleading. Most pressure readings are

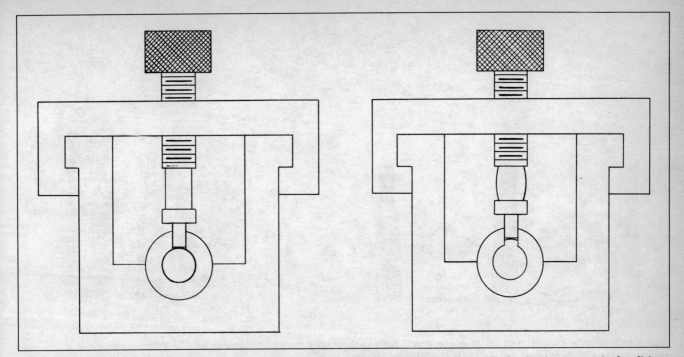

In the copper crusher gauge system for measuring chamber pressure, a copper cylinder is shown ready for firing (left). After firing, note that the case wall of the cylinder (right) has been punched out.

taken with loads fired in special pressure barrels, not in average hunting rifle barrels. This means the pressure readings for given loads shown in reloading manuals must be used *only as guides*. The handloader who works with a variety of rifles can never be absolutely sure if the pressures listed will be the same in his rifles.

The subject of chamber (or breech) pressure has always been somewhat mystifying, due mostly to a lack of concrete data. Pressure is obviously a necessity in a firearm. It's the force that drives the bullet through the barrel and onto the target. And it must do so in a very short working time in order to generate sufficient force to finish the job. For one thing, smokeless powder does not explode; it burns progressively from the rear to the front of the case. When the powder charge is ignited by the primer, gases begin to build pressure inside the cartridge case, which explains why it's so imperative that the case not rupture. The growing pressure expands the case wall against the chamber wall, pushing the shell head tight against the bolt face. With no further room for expansion, the only alternative left is for the bullet to move forward.

In an exceedingly short time, internal pressures build to as high as 60,000 psi in some high

This illustration shows what happens to a case after numerous firings with hot loads have stretched and weakened it beyond safety limits.

velocity rifles. While many rifles can handle that much pressure, an excessive amount becomes not only a safety hazard but can detract from accuracy as well. Over the years, pressures of 50,000 to 55,000 psi have become acceptable in strong bolt action rifles—but not so in rifles like the old Krag, or many of the early pump and lever action rifles. These older rifles were designed for much lower pressures.

Pressure-Measuring Devices, Old & New

For many years, the standard procedure in obtaining chamber pressure involved the use of the

Reloaders who wildcat cases must often work with unknown pressures. Here a 30-30 Winchester case is progressively transformed into a .219 Donaldson Wasp.

crusher gauge. With this method, a special pressure barrel for each caliber is fitted into a Universal-Bond receiver. The barrel has a hole of exact dimensions drilled into the chamber. A precision-machined steel piston is then fitted into the hole and an arbor with an adjustable anvil is fastened around the barrel. A copper cylinder of known dimensions is placed between the piston and the anvil. When the cartridge is fired, a brass disc is punched out of the case wall, forcing the steel piston against the copper cylinder with the same force that is generated against the base of the bullet, thereby compressing the cylinder. By comparing the compressed length of the cylinder with its original length, the pressure rating (in "pounds per square inch," or *psi*) is determined by means of a tarage table supplied with the copper cylinders. Each batch (or lot) of cylinders is checked on a special machine that provides controlled pressures, and a tarage table is then made for that lot.

The crusher system may seem foolproof, but it has its drawbacks. For one thing, the special barrel that's used is most likely not identical to the one the handloader might use, so the results cannot be the same. If it's true that uniform readings require that each batch of cylinders must meet uniformity tolerances dictated by the Sporting Arms & Ammunition Manufacturers' Institute (SAAMI), then a batch of off-standard cylinders will doubtless produce false readings.

Some critics of the crusher system question its accuracy, claiming that the results it provides are not stated in true pounds-per-square-inch. That's because the calibration of each copper cylinder is made with dead, or *static*, weights, while in actual firing the application of force is *dynamic* and registered in micro-seconds. This kind of analysis, say the critics, does not allow enough time for the cylinder to compress exactly as it should for a given pressure, especially at the higher stages.

With the crusher system so clearly susceptible to a variety of factors that influence pressure readings, it's not unreasonable to question its accuracy. The fact is, though, that the copper crusher system has over the years produced sufficient data to show how various loads compare at acceptable levels, and so it remains in use. All things being equal in each cartridge case—such as neck thickness, flash hole diameter and case capacity—the copper crusher system does indicate that a given primer, powder or bullet combination compresses a number of uniform copper cylinders to an *average* degree.

Another method for measuring chamber pres-

In using the York-Cantrell Breech Pressure Measurement System, when the test button (foreground) is depressed, the pressure reading will appear immediately on the meter.

sure—known as the *strain gauge* system—does not require a special barrel or any drilling or modification of the barrel and action. A fine wire is embedded in a thin material and both are then cemented tightly around the barrel. Chamber pressure causes the barrel to expand. While this expansion is very slight, it's enough to stretch the wire and reduce its cross-sectional area. This reduction in turn causes a change in the wire's electrical resistance, which is proportional to the pressure. The strain gauge, like the copper crusher system, is complex. It is also very expensive.

The *piezo-electric gauge* system utilizes a crystal that produces a measurable electric charge when subjected to pressure. In operation, a small steel stud is placed against the crystal. As the pressure rises in the firearm, equal pressure is exerted on the stud, which transfers the pressure to the crystal. The minute electric waves produced by this method can, when passed through an amplifier, be read on a cathode-ray oscilloscope.

In the late 1960s, the author tested a *York/Cantrell Breech Pressure Measurement System,* which works on the cartridge case with factory-altered primer pockets and can be used with any rifle. It's an electrical pressure-sensing device in which a thin metallic pressure sensor, equipped with a small tab, is placed in the primer pocket (which has been slightly enlarged) of the cartridge case. A shallow indentation is drilled next to the primer pocket. The small tab on the sensor fits into this indentation to prevent the bolt face from shearing off. Once the sensor has been subjected to pressure generated in the chamber, its electrical properties are changed as the pressure changes. The York/Cantrell system measures these differences and gives a true reading in absolute pounds per square inch.

After a series of test rounds have been fired, each case is placed in the measuring instrument. The sensor's tab is touched—once only—with a needle contact and the pressure reading is indi-

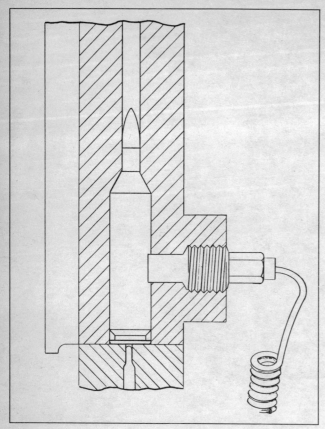

Another good method for measuring chamber pressure is the ballistic transducer, a quartz-type device that conforms to the case. Note the wire coil leading to an oscilliscope.

cated on a large calibrated dial. No special tools are needed. The only requirement is to wait long enough for the cases to cool completely. In one test using this method, considerable variations were noted from shot to shot using the same rifle, despite great efforts to load the ammunition with as much precision as possible. Using selected cases, bullets from the same box were checked on a scale and powder charges were weighed to 1/10-grain of accuracy. The result: pressures that varied as much as 5,000 to 8,000 psi. Results from other methods—including copper crusher devices, piezos, and strain gauges—all record similar differences. But since routine ballistic reports give only *average* pressures for a given load, these extremes are not mentioned. That's why it's unwise (and possibly dangerous) to go beyond the suggested maximum powder charges shown in reloading manuals. It's also important to discard cases that are old or show signs of fatigue or weakness. A

significant rise in pressure in an old or weak case could spell real trouble.

A more modern system is the *ballistic transducer,* which is a quartz-type device. It develops a voltage proportional to the pressure placed on it and, like the piezo-electric system, is used in conjunction with an oscilloscope.

The Pros and Cons of High Chamber Pressure

While there's a natural tendency to think of high chamber pressure as a bad thing, remember that many of today's high velocity cartridges work efficiently at chamber pressures once considered dangerous. For instance, the 30-40 Krag operates safely at around 40,000 psi, and the 30-06 is safe with pressures touching the 50,000 psi level. A large magnum rifle cartridge may require 60,000 psi to operate effectively. So high pressures are not necessarily bad. Modern cartridges are more efficient than the black powder jobs of the gaslight era, in fact, because they *do* work at higher chamber pressures.

Pressures in shotshells and handgun cartridges are much lower than in centerfire rifle cartridges. Chamber pressure must be lower in shotguns for several reasons, but primarily because paper or plastic cases are involved. High pressures in shotguns also have a tendency to disrupt shot charge patterns. Consequently, pressure levels run ideally between 6,800 psi and 11,000 psi.

Handgun pressure for conventional cartridges start around 15,000 psi, reach 20,000 psi in some semiautomatics, and climb further up the pressure ladder with magnum handgun cartridges. These handgun figures are comparable to black powder rifle pressures of the gaslight era.

Chamber pressure figures vary in reloading manuals because there can be such wide variations in the components—including the case itself. Temperature and humidity alone can cause pressure readings to vary. And it is not just the primer, powder or bullet that can cause drastic changes in chamber pressure, as many handloaders think. Insufficient neck clearance can cause pressures to rise dramatically as well, simply because there's not enough space for the bullet to escape. A large bearing surface on a bullet will increase pressure, too, as will an oversized flash hole.

The primer may be the tiniest component, but it can play a major role in chamber pressure. That's

The author chronographs a series of reloads for a Ruger M-77 heavy barrel 220 Swift. After range testing, each empty case is tested (with a York-Cantrell sensor) for chamber pressure.

because primers, even from the same lot, may have different burning temperature rates. A rifle primer must be hotter and have a longer burning rate than a pistol primer; conversely, a rifle primer will be too hot for fast-burning pistol powder. Magnum rifle primers have even hotter and more sustained burning rates in order to ignite larger powder charges. So be sure never to interchange or mix pistol and rifle primers.

Several telltale signs will indicate excessive chamber pressure, the most common being stiff extraction. When the bolt handle is too tight or too hard to lift, chamber pressure in that rifle is probably too high. A flat, cratered primer is another danger sign. Excessive pressure causes the case head to slam against the bolt face, flattening the primer. At the same time, the primer metal flows around the firing pin to form a miniature crater. Crater forming is not always a sure sign of excessive chamber pressure, however, since a worn or oversized firing pin hole in the bolt face can also produce premature primer cratering. The primer will not be completely flat, though, nor squeezed to the very limits of the diameter of the primer pocket. In other words, the primer will still show some radius.

Much emphasis is placed on the strength of the barrel and action. This is important, true, but first consideration must be given the shell case. *It must hold.* If a case ruptures and loose gas enters

Proper tools and lots of experience are required to cut a chamber in a barrel properly. Note the chamber reamer and GO and NO GO headspace gauges.

the action, the consequences can be severe, regardless of how strong the action may be.

Another mistake is in thinking that some actions are beyond breaking. Each time metal is subjected to stress, it actually weakens and eventually will fail. This failure may take years to develop, but when actions are pressed repeatedly to above normal limits the end can come quickly.

With black powder guns becoming more popular among the hunting and shooting fraternity, some new converts have come to believe that these thick-barreled muzzleloaders cannot be overloaded. Not so. Black powder produces lower pressures than smokeless—approximately 7,000 psi in flintlocks compared to 60,000 in magnum centerfire rifle cartridges—but it still generates pressure. The more powder, the more pressure. Prior to the Civil War, hunters kept increasing their powder charges until unburned powder came out of the barrel. This was supposed to indicate when they had attained a maximum powder charge, but it surely had its shortcomings. Pressure continues to build and doesn't level off at a certain point, as some black powder enthusiasts insist. Long before the pressure reaches its highest point, a loose-fitting breech plug could let go with dire consequences.

The ballistic ramifications of chamber pressure are myriad and mind-boggling. For instance, the same carefully weighed powder charge ignited by the same brand and type of primer will give different average pressures with bullets of the same weight but of different makes and designs.

This is due largely to jacket thickness and hardness, different bearing surfaces, different core hardnesses, or the relationship between jacket and core. Also, when cartridges loaded with double base powders (nitroglycerin and nitrocellulose) are exposed to extreme cold (−20 F. or more) for a considerable length of time, chamber pressure may rise to a dangerous level. Under such abnormal conditions, shells should be kept in thick containers or in pockets where they can absorb body heat.

It's easy to see why the chamber pressure subject can become so complicated, because there's no easy way to tell how much pressure will develop using any given combination of primer, powder and bullet. A certain brand and number of primer purchased today may not give the same pressure results as the same brand and number of primer that worked so perfectly five years earlier. In fact, each time the handloader uses a different load combination, he is stepping into the unknown in terms of pressure.

As shown in the accompanying chart, pressure rises in a fairly predictable curve so long as the loads fall within what can be considered the normal working range of a powder. When a certain point is reached, the addition of more powder can cause abnormal increases in pressure with little or no accompanying velocity increases.

So a word to the wise: Always start with the lowest suggested load and work your way up gradually. Pressure may be an absolute necessity for a firearm to work, but it must never be taken for granted. It can be the shooter's best friend, true—but it can also be his worst enemy.

The shooter here is chronographing reloads, making sure that velocity does not drive pressure beyond safe limits.

The following tables are provided as information only and are not necessarily recommended as loads for any rifles. The considerable spread between minimum and maximum pressures with given loads in given guns illustrates the impossibility of predicting accurately what these, or other, loads will produce.

22-250 Remington

Rifle: M700 Remington **Cartridge Case: Winchester** **Powder: 4895**
Bullet: 53-gr. Hornady Match H.P.

	30-gr.	32-gr.	34-gr.	36-gr.
Maximum Pressure*	40,000 psi	46,500 psi	57,000 psi	61,500 psi
Minimum Pressure*	35,500	40,500	45,000	59,500
Average Absolute	36,800	43,000	52,100	61,000
Approx. Crusher	36,000	39,500	46,000	53,000
Approx. Velocity	3,225 fps	3,375 fps	3,550 fps	3,800 fps

30-06

Rifle: 1903 Springfield **Cartridge Case: Remington** **Powder: Reloader 21**
Bullet: 165-gr. Speer Spitzer

	51-gr.	53-gr.	55-gr.
Maximum Pressure*	52,500 psi	59,000 psi	60,000 psi
Minimum Pressure*	36,000	51,000	52,000
Average Absolute	43,750	53,000	55,000
Approx. Crusher	39,000	47,800	49,000
Approx. Velocity	2,650 fps	2,775 fps	2,850 fps

300 Winchester Magnum

Rifle: Custom M 1917 Enfield **Cartridge Case: Remington** **Powder: 4831**
Bullet: 190-gr. Sierra Match King

	72-gr.	74-gr.	76-gr.
Maximum Pressure*	58,000 psi	59,000 psi	65,000 psi
Minimum Pressure*	56,000	54,000	59,000
Average Absolute	56,500	58,000	63,000
Approx. Crusher	50,000	52,000	53,500
Approx. Velocity	2,775 fps	2,825 fps	2,900 fps

* York-Cantrell system used to obtain Maximum and Minimum Pressure readings.

Big Bores for Small Game

by Wilf E. Pyle

Imagine that you've just completed a successful mule deer hunt with your trusty .300 Winchester Magnum and you have a whole day to spend in camp. You notice that the area abounds in jack rabbits, and so you decide to give your rifle a real workout. Or perhaps you're in Wyoming hunting antelope, and you seize an opportunity to bring down some black-tailed prairie dogs.

Many hunters can relate stories of similar opportunities they've been able to take advantage of simply by having a rifle and load combination capable of doing such double duty. The fact is, large bore hunting rifles can be used successfully on small game targets—whether rabbits, squirrels, gophers or prairie dogs—without hesitation. The problem is, too many hunters are unfamiliar with the bullets, loads and techniques needed to squeeze added versatility from their favorite big game guns. With good load development, smart bullet selection, and proper powder consideration, any hunter can take small game accurately and reliably with his big bore out to ranges equalling those for big game.

In the olden days, it was common for one gun to see duty on every kind of game. But today, most hunters own more than one rifle, or at least they aspire to. They prefer to have one rifle for deer hunting, another for large game, like moose or elk, and still another for the big bears. That may be fine (if you can afford it), but situations often arise where it's impractical to carry two or more specialized rifles into the field. Trips to distant hunting grounds, frequently accessed only by air travel, make it difficult to carry a rifle for every application. Pack trips also preclude traveling with more than one gun.

Developing small game loads for big game rifles is hardly a new discovery. As early as 1927, the late Colonel Townsend Whelan strongly advocated reduced loads for small game taken with the 30.06 and other .30 caliber cartridges. On his trips through northern Canada, Whelan used what he called "squib loads" to take the heads off spruce

Rarely does Shooter's Bible feature more than one article by a writer in the same edition, but in Wilf Pyle's case we've made an exception. His articles on the 6 PPC (p. 26) and "Big Bores for Small Game" were too inviting to pass up. Fellow admirers of the author's work will be delighted to learn that his new book, "Small Game & Varmint Hunting" (Stoeger Pub. Co.) is now available.

With smart reloading, highly specialized big game rifle-cartridge combinations, such as this Sako Mannlicher in .308 Winchester, can do excellent double duty as small game rifles.

grouse and rabbits destined for pot meat. Even for the colonel, though, mastering the art of reduced loading was a difficult task. He encountered problems caused by differing points of impact between full and reduced loads, bullets of differing weights, problems with lead bullets, and the improper mixing of reduced loads with full-house hunting kinds.

Fortunately, a great selection of lightweight bullets is now available for hunters who seek varmint-quality bullets for their big game rifles. A new selection of powders allows hunters to match bullet and powder closely for best performance in big game rifles. Commercial ammunition makers are also increasing varmint load offerings in their fac-

tory lineups. And each year these options increase as new products enter the market.

Colonel Whelan didn't have these choices, but he did have the right idea on how to gain extra versatility from a .30 caliber (or larger) rifle. He knew that a selection of properly constructed reloads covering a variety of field situations—from small to large game—gave him some real advantages. In the end, he brought home more game, became a better marksman, experimented with more cartridges, and derived greater enjoyment from the outdoors. And not so coincidentally, he also went down in shooting history as a highly respected rifleman.

With proper bullet selection, big game rifles, like the one being fired here, can be used for many different kinds of shooting—from small game and varmints to targets and plinking.

The Advent of Modern Bullets

Increased versatility of the rifle and load combination tells only part of the story. Because they are designed to come apart and fragment upon impact, the modern lightweight bullet greatly reduces the chances for uncontrolled ricochet, making shooting along the urban-rural fringe a much safer proposition. It also produces correspondingly less recoil, thus allowing the hunter to shoot more and broaden his shooting enjoyment.

There's another added dimension to the big gun-small game equation, one that old Colonel Whelan missed out on. Today's lightweight bullets are designed to allow reduced velocity shooting and are target-marketed specifically at hide and fur hunters. The ideal fur hunter's bullet is one that leaves all of its energy within the animal; it doesn't shoot through the carcass, leaving a large, torn exit hole in the valuable hide. These bullets are good performers on edible small game as well, ensuring minimal damage to the meat portion— but allowing enough penetration and expansion to anchor large-sized rabbits and other game. The Speer 100 grain plinker and the Hornady 100 grain Short Jacket are fine examples of this kind of bullet.

Full metal jacketed bullets provide the ultimate in penetration and reduced expansion, especially when driven at slow velocities. Hornady and Speer both offer 110 grain .308 bullets of this type, and Hornady also has a 150 grain full metal jacket. Many hunters have long held a mistaken belief that 110 grain bullets of any type are poor performers in high-powered .30 caliber rifles. In fact, for straight-up varmint shooting at ranges just over 200 yards, any of these bullets will work well in standard sporting grade rifles. While they may drop sharply in velocity due to poor ballistic coefficients, the loss goes unnoticed by black-tailed prairie dogs or gophers taken from the opposite side of the colony.

Hollow point bullets, while not preferred by most big game hunters, shift the versatility of larger caliber rifles toward small game, especially where wholesale tissue destruction is not important. Pot hunters and fur takers would not likely choose a hollow point, at least not without considerable previous load experimentation; but these same hollow point bullets can have tremendous application on such pests as ground squirrels and prairie dogs.

Still, impact velocity is critical. No bullet nearing the end of its trajectory and moving ever slower can be expected to provide dependable penetration and expansion. Hollow point bullets will usually open up, even at relatively low ve-

The Hornady products shown here represent only a few of the more than 60 bullet types that are available in .30 caliber.

locities, making penetration highly variable. Good impact velocity is needed to ensure adequate penetration and to provide as well the terminal energy necessary for radical expansion. Hollow point bullets become failures when the bullet explodes on the target surface. Traditionally, this occurs mostly on big game animals, but the same thing can happen with small game.

Some hunters feel that when lightweight bullets are loaded in .30 (and larger) caliber cartridges, performance must compete favorably with cartridges like the .243 and 6 mm. While it's true that the so-called dual-purpose cartridges have a firm hold on the versatility myth, a 110 grain bullet loaded in a .30-06 traveling at 3500 feet per second (fps) actually has a slight edge over a .243 moving a 100 grain nullet. At 300 yards, the .243 strikes one inch lower than the .30-06 bullet. Velocity increases are greater for the .30-06; consequently, trajectories are slightly flatter.

Lightweight bullets traveling at top velocities will produce flatter trajectories. This increases the likelihood of connecting on small targets at extended ranges. A simple example illustrates the significance of velocity to trajectory. Let's take a typical hunting bullet, such as a 180 grain spire point fired from a .300 Winchester Magnum traveling 3000 fps at the muzzle. Compare this with a 110 grain bullet speeding along at 3700 fps. Sighted in for a 100-yard zero, the heavier bullet is a foot low at 300 yards; but the 100 grain bullet strikes the target only eight inches low at 300 yards! In squeezing double duty from the .300 Winchester, therefore, the 100 grain bullet offers clear advantages in trajectory and velocity. Moreover, lightweight bullets will take varmints better at long range than will heavier deer hunting bullets. Deer bullets are designed to penetrate and then expand rapidly. They need the resistance of the tougher bone, hair, skin and musculature of the deer to open up properly. These same bullets will simply pass through thin-skinned varmints and small game. All the more reason, therefore, to choose the correct bullet.

When handloading your big game rifle for both big and small game, don't expect sub-minute-of-an-angle accuracy. To make consistent kills at long ranges, a rifle must group within one inch at 100

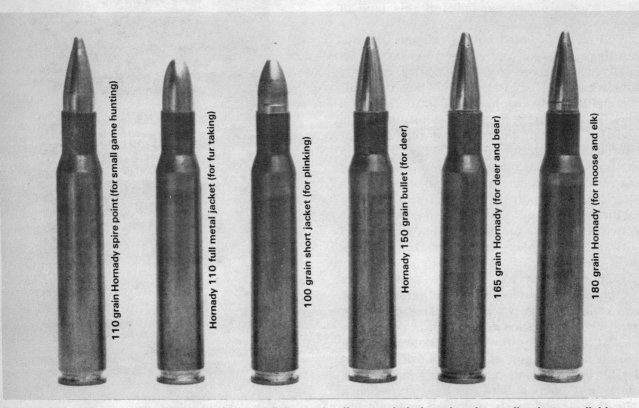

110 grain Hornady spire point (for small game hunting)

Hornady 110 full metal jacket (for fur taking)

100 grain short jacket (for plinking)

Hornady 150 grain bullet (for deer)

165 grain Hornady (for deer and bear)

180 grain Hornady (for moose and elk)

The .30-06 provides a good example of how judicious reloading can help broaden the applications available to the big game rifle hunter. The .30-06's shown here include various bullet weights as indicated.

Many big game cartridges can deliver long range accuracy for varmint and small game hunting. In doing so, the big game rifle should be used like a varmint gun (using a rest whenever possible).

yards. Varmint-weight rifles outfitted with heavy target-quality barrels will outshoot the average sporting rifle consistently with groups under three-quarters of an inch. Any hunter who thinks his sporting rifle will outdo a high-intensity varmint rig is only fooling himself.

Pleasant surprises do indeed await the shooter who has done things right. Many sporting weight rifles are capable of producing very tight groups, and superior handloading can tighten these groups even more. Applying varmint shooting techniques to sporting rifles can also improve results dramatically. Varminting is often done from the prone or sitting positions, frequently using a rest to support the forend. When these same tricks are applied to a plain deer-hunting rifle, above average results are likely.

One word of warning: shooting lightweight bullets is not a cure for an already poor shooting rifle. Improving the bedding, changing the pressure on the action screws, or free-floating the barrel are often necessary to improve grouping. But if your bolt or lever gun shoots a three-inch group at 100 yards, chances are new reloads will do the same.

The Importance of Testing and Experimenting

The real keys to squeezing greater versatility from your big bore rifle are *testing* and *experi-*

These Hornady bullets represent varying weights (left to right): 100 grain Hornady plinker; 110 grain full metal jacket; 110 grain spire point.

mentation. Reloading manuals and superior hand-loading computer programs can only provide starting points. It's up to the shooter to experiment with different bullet and powder combinations. This is a time-consuming process and it will take several weeks of shooting to come up with the perfect combination.

Powder selection is critical, of course. Traditionally, large caliber rifles have functioned best with the more coarse-grained, slow-burning powders. These include IMR 4064 (in the .30-06), H3031 (in the .308), IMR 4350 (in the .300 Winchester Magnum), and Win 748 (in the .30-30). These powders will also produce excellent accuracy with lightweight bullets. One load that has worked especially well is 57 grains of IMR 4064 behind the Sierra 100 grain hollow point bullet in the .30-06. Approach this full-power, high-end load with caution, however. All .30 caliber rifles shooting lightweight bullets generally fit the old rule that says any powder nearly filling the case will deliver the most accurate load.

Honest disagreements arise over which powders are best suited for developing loads pushing lightweight bullets. Such powders as W748, Reloader 7, H322, IMR 4895, IMR 3031, H4895 and H414 have all been recommended. Charges that favor the light end of the scale definitely produce better accuracy in .30 caliber lever and bolt guns than do top end weights. Compressed charges are not recommended. Also, powder weight must be consistent from load to load. During the reloading process, therefore, pay strict attention to quality control by checking the weight of every *fifth* powder charge. Whenever possible, weigh each charge,

especially if you're using extruded powders like IMR 4064. Other powders, including H322, which flow through the measure smoothly without bridging or binding, must also be checked. Even a slight overcharge can cause radical shifts in breech pressure.

When downloading, be sure you understand the special relationship between case capacity and the powder you've chosen. For example, the burning rate of powders like Winchester 748 is greatly affected by case capacity as well as bullet weight and rifle condition. Winchester 748 lacks enough bulk to give ideal loading density in large capacity cases; as a result, partially filled cases will yield erratic pressure curves. For this reason, W748 works fine in the .308 with lightweight bullets, but not so in the larger capacity .30-06. When moving from heavyweight bullets to lighter types, always check the primer carefully for signs of cratering. Avoid charges that produce these results, or switch to another powder.

When experimenting with lightweight bullets, never change more than one variable in a given test. When shooting for accuracy, stay with one bullet type until the various powders have all been tried. Then switch to another bullet weight or style and repeat the test using the same powders. In

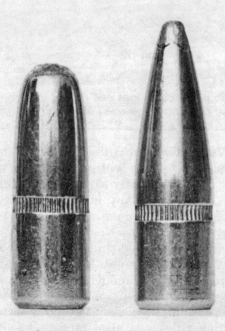

Bullet style is important. The bullets shown here—Hornady's 150 grain round nose and 150 grain spire point—are similar in weight but they behave quite differently.

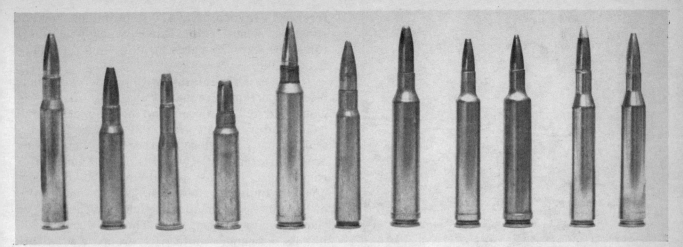

These popular big game cartridges can be reloaded for small game. L. to R.: .30-06, .308, .30-30, .300 Savage, .300 Win. Mag., 8 × 57 Mauser, 7mm Rem. Mag., 240 Wthby. Mag., 257 Wthby. Mag., .270, and .25-06.

this way, true comparisons can be reasonably made; otherwise, the results are questionable. Consistency is important, too. A load that performs the same way day after day under all kinds of field conditions is preferred over one that produces a variety of group sizes. Keep the same components throughout the testing procedure, and always shoot groups from the same position—preferably a solid bench. And always keep the things you might do differently from one time to the next under tight control. Maintaining accurate and up-to-date records is also important.

Setting Your Sights

As we've noted, different bullet weights produce vastly different points of impact. Scopes set to print 150 grain bullets at 100 yards will appear markedly off when a 110 grain bullet is driven from the barrel. Colonel Whelan agonized over this problem throughout his hunting career. The problem was particularly difficult to overcome in those days because scopes were crude and iron sights were still widely used. Whelan preferred graduated receiver sights, as did most serious riflemen of the day. He used these highly accurate sights to overcome the problem by marking the exact sight settings for each load. This enabled him to move confidently from one load to the next. Sometimes he slipped up and failed to match the setting to the correct load. At short ranges on big game, this was no problem—the bullet would simply strike a bit lower than desired. In this manner, the colonel was able to hunt in deep back country, switching

between loads designed for caribou and moose and a single light load he had made up for rabbits and grouse. For the conditions under which Whelan hunted, this simple dodge worked extremely well.

Today, of course, we enjoy the benefits derived from much improved equipment. American-made scopes and high-quality foreign products allow hunters to make their setting adjustments quickly and easily. Returning to a lower setting virtually ensures that the bullet will travel to the point of aim (all other factors being equal). Most good advice on scope settings states that once a scope has been correctly sighted in, it should be left alone. This advice was meant for a bygone era, one in which shooters were less sophisticated and the equipment was less reliable. Modern silhouette shooters are familiar with the need to move scope settings, and several scope models are now on the market with built-in bullet drop compensators. There's no reason why different loads can't be used in a good rifle outfitted with a quality scope.

A Final Briefing on Loads

How much practical difference is there between loads? Depending on what load is chosen, of course, the answer is, "Not really very much," especially under field conditions. A favorite .30-06 load with a 150 grain bullet sighted in at 200 yards, for example, will print six inches low at 300 yards. The 110 grain varmint hunting load for the same .30-06 leaves the muzzle at 3700 fps and, with no change in sighting, prints five inches low at the same distance. That's only a one-inch dif-

This prized rifle shoots to the same point of impact with different bullet weights.

ference in favor of the 110 grain bullet. For pot shooting, where edible game is taken at short range, perhaps 75 yards at most, this difference is negligible.

Wise experimentation with powder weights is most important. Frequently, backing off the big game load by half a grain and increasing the small game load by a half grain will produce two cartridges that print close together even though they are of different bullet weights. It's all a matter of compromise. It's easy to tell when you've discovered a winning combination. The characteristics of the successful small game load are the same as those for any hunting load. The small game load, like its big game counterpart, groups well within one minute of an angle (1½ inches) at 100 yards. It will usually (but not always) print higher than the big game load. Remember, *a winning load groups consistently when fired from the same rifle in the same manner.* Many hunters know that

Suggested Small Game Loads for Big Game Cartridges

Cartridge	Bullet		Powder		Case	Primer
	Maker	Grs	Type	Grs		
7-30 Waters	Hornady	139	IMR 4350	36	Win	CCI
7mm-08	Hornady	120	Hodgden	48	Rem	CCI
7 by 57	Hornady	100	IMR 4320	42	Fed	CCI
284 Win	Hornady	100	IMR 4320	46	Win	CCI
280 Rem	Hornady	100	IMR 4350	52	Rem	CCI
7mm Rem Mag	Hornady	100	IMR 4350	52	Rem	CCI
7mm Rem Mag	Hornady	120	IMR 4350	50	Rem	CCI
7mm Rem Mag	Sierra	120	IMR 4320	49	Rem	CCI
7mm Wea Mag	Speer	115	H4831	64	Weather	CCI
7mm Wea Mag	Hornady	120	H4831	62	Weather	CCI
30-30 Win	Speer	110	IMR 4064	33	Win	Win
30-30 Win	Sierra	125	IMR 4064	30	Win	Win
300 Sav	Hornady	110	H380	38	Win	CCI
307 Win	Sierra	125	IMR 4064	31	Win	Win
308 Win	Hornady	110	RL-7	40	Win	CCI
308 Win	Sierra	110	IMR 4064	44	Win	CCI
308 Win	Speer	110	W748	46	Win	Fed
308 Win	Sierra	125	W748	49	Win	Fed
308 Win	Speer	130	H380	48	Win	Fed
30-40 Kraig	Hornady	110	IMR 4350	45	Win	CCI

groups open up when one moves from bench shooting to kneeling to standing. The same applies to the small game load, but the pattern should parallel big game loads.

In practical terms, trajectories between the loads are not that much different. The truth is, field conditions—including wind, familiarity with the rifle, experience, and the like—have far more influence on where the bullet travels than all the fancy physics of trajectory. Under field conditions, the trajectory difference between many loads is not always significant. Woodchucks, for example, are large enough so that subtle differences in trajectory do not automatically translate into misses. There is, of course, the odd rifle (most frequently a .30-06) that prints bullets of all weights to the same point of impact without changes in scope settings. Any hunter lucky enough to find such a rifle should hold onto it like a prized treasure. Lighter calibers, such as the .243 and the .257 Roberts, rarely offer this ability. Under field conditions, it matters little that one bullet prints dead on, while another is an inch low (assuming all bullets are delivered accurately at working ranges).

The benefits of being able to swap one cartridge-bullet combo quickly for another more suited to a particular hunting situation cannot be overstated. And the advantages rest solely with the hunter. It's not much trouble, after all, to extract a loaded 150 grain cartridge, replace it with a 110, and take a shot at a distant coyote or a nearby rabbit. Small game animals are thus transformed into targets of opportunity. Be sure you take advantage of them.

Suggested Small Game Loads for Big Game Cartridges (cont.)

| Cartridge | Bullet | | Powder | | | |
	Maker	Grs	Type	Grs	Case	Primer
30-06	Hornady	110	IMR 4064	52	Win	Fed
30-06	Sierra	110	IMR 4320	50	Win	Fed
30-06	Speer	110	IMR 3031	49	Win	CCI
30-06	Sierra	125	IMR 3031	47	Win	CCI
30-06	Hornady	130	IMR 4350	55	Win	CCI
30-06	Speer	130	IMR 4320	49	Win	CCI
300 H and H	Sierra	110	IMR 4350	69	Rem	CCI
300 Win Mag	Hornady	110	IMR 4064	66	Win	Fed
300 Win Mag	Sierra	110	IMR 4350	73	Win	Fed
300 Win Mag	Hornady	130	H4831	77	Win	Fed
303 British	Hornady	150	IMR 4350	40	CIL	CIL
32 Win Spl	Hornady	170	IMR 4064	28	Win	CCI
8mm Mauser	Hornady	125	IMR 4064	47	Win	CCI
8mm Rem Mag	Hornady	125	IMR 4064	67	Rem	CCI
358 Win	Speer	180	IMR 4320	42	Win	Win
35 Whelan	Speer	180	IMR 4064	49	Custom	CCI
356 Win	Speer	180	IMR 4320	42	Win	CCI
375 Win	Hornady	220	IMR 4198	28	Win	Fed
44 Rem Mag	Hornady	200	2400	22	Rem	CCI
444 Marlin	Hornady	200	2400	27	Rem	CCI
45-70	Hornady	300	IMR 4198	42	Win	CCI

SHOOTER'S BIBLE CATALOG SECTION

Complete Illustrated Listing of Guns,
Specifications & Accessories

HANDGUNS

RIFLES

SHOTGUNS

BLACK POWDER

SCOPES & SIGHTS

AMMUNITION

BALLISTICS

RELOADING

Handguns

FOR ADDRESSES AND PHONE NUMBERS OF MANUFACTURERS AND DISTRIBUTORS INCLUDED IN THIS SECTION, SEE *DIRECTORY OF MANUFACTURERS AND SUPPLIERS*

ACTION ARMS PISTOLS

Crafted by the Swiss, this new double-action handgun is available in two sizes and calibers: 9mm and the new .41 Action Express. It can also be used cocked and locked.

AT-88S

SPECIFICATIONS
Operation: Locked breech, inertial firing pin
Ammunition: 9mm or .41 Action Express
Barrel length: 4.72″
Overall length: 8.1″
Weight: 35.3 oz. (empty)
Magazines: 9mm—15 rds.; 41 A.E.—10 rds.
Safety system: Thumb safety; cocked and locked or double action
Sights: Fixed blade front; drift adjustable rear
Stock: Checkered walnut
Finish: Blue or chrome
Price: $598.00

AT-88S

AT-88P

AT-88P

SPECIFICATIONS
Operation: Locked breech; inertial firing pin
Ammunition: 9mm or .41 Action Express
Barrel length: 3.66″
Overall length: 7.3″
Weight: 32.1 oz. (empty)
Magazines: 9mm—13 rds.; 41 A.E.—8 rds.
Safety system : Thumb safety; cocked & locked or double action
Sights: Fixed blade front; drift adjustable rear
Stock: Checkered walnut
Finish: Blue or chrome
Price: $598.00

Also available: **AT-88H**
Same specifications except:
Barrel length: 3.5″
Overall length: 6.9″
Weight: 30.5 oz. (empty)
Price: $598.00

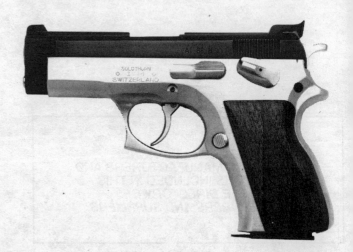

AMERICAN ARMS PISTOLS

MODEL PK-22 DA SEMIAUTO
$199.00

MODEL ZC-380 DA SEMIAUTO
$289.00

MODEL PX-22 DA SEMIAUTO
$189.00

MODEL TT9mm "TOKAREV"
SINGLE ACTION SEMIAUTO
$289.00

SPECIFICATIONS

MODEL	PK-22	PX-22	EP-380	ZC-380	TT-9mm
Caliber	22LR	22LR	380	380	9mm
Barrel Length	3⅓"	2¾"	3½"	3¾"	4½"
Overall Length	6⅓"	5⅓"	6½"	6½"	8"
Weight (empty)	22 oz.	15 oz.	25 oz.	26 oz.	31 oz.
Magazine	8 clip	7 clip	7 clip	8 clip	9 clip
Grip	Black Polymer	Black Polymer	Wood Checkered	Black Polymer	Black Polymer
Action	Straight Blowback Double Action	Straight Blowback Double Action	Delayed Blowback Locking Breech Double Action	Delayed Blowback Locking Breech Single Action	Delayed Blowback Locking Breech Single Action
Finish	Blued	Blued	Stainless	Blued	Blued
Safeties	Hammer & Firing Pin Block	Hammer & Firing Pin Block	Hammer & Firing Pin Block	Hammer Block	Hammer Block
Front Sights	Blade Fixed	Blade Fixed	Blade Fixed	Blade Fixed	Blade Fixed
Rear Sights	"V" Notch Fixed	"V" Notch Fixed	Square Notch Adjustable	Square Notch Adjustable	"V" Notch Fixed

AMERICAN DERRINGER PISTOLS

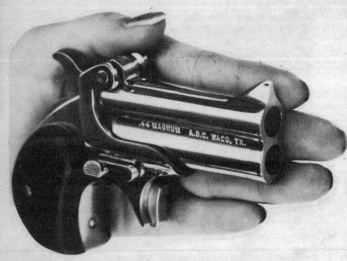

MODEL 1

SPECIFICATIONS
Calibers: 38 Super, 38 Special, 380 Auto, 9mm Luger, 32 Mag., 30-30 Win., 30 Luger, 223 Rem. Commercial Ammo, 22 LR, 22 Rimfire Mag., 22 Hornet, 45 Colt, 45 Auto, 45 Win. Mag., 45-70 (single shot), 44 Mag., 44-40 Win., 44 Special, 41 Mag., 410, 357 Maximum, 357 Magnum
Overall length: 4.82"
Barrel length: 3"
Weight: 15 oz. (in 45 Auto cal.)
Action: Single action w/automatic barrel selection
Number of shots: 2

Calibers	Prices
9mm Federal, 32 Magnum, 32 S&W Long, 32-20, 30 Luger, 38 Special	$187.50
22 LR, 22 Rimfire Magnum, 45 Auto, 45 Auto Shot Shell, 357 Magnum	218.00
30 Mauser (7.62 Tokarev)	200.00
38 Special Shot Shell, 38 Super	199.95
357 Maximum	250.00
380 Auto, 9mm Luger	179.95
41 Action Auto, 9mm x 21mm	225.00
45 Colt, 44-40, 44 Special	295.00
45 Colt (2½" .410), .410 x 2½" (45 Colt)	297.50
45 Win. Mag., 45-70 (single shot), 50 Saunders, 44 Magnum, 41 Magnum, 30-30 Winchester, 223 Rem. Comm. Ammo only, 22 Hornet	369.00

Also available: **Ultra Lightweight (7½ oz.) Model 7**

Calibers	Prices
22 LR	$187.50
32 Magnum, 32 S&W Long	137.50
38 S&W	157.50
38 Special	187.50
380 Auto	157.50
44 Special	500.00

Light Weight (11 oz.) Double Derringer Model 11
Available in 38 Special $157.50

Model 10 (10 oz.)
45 Colt $237.50
45 Auto 218.00

MODEL 3 (Stainless Steel Single Shot Derringer)
(not shown)

SPECIFICATIONS
Calibers: 32 Magnum, 38 Special
Barrel length: 2.5"
Overall length: 4.9"
Weight: 8.5 oz.
Safety: Manual "Hammer-Block"
Grips: Rosewood
Price: $95.00

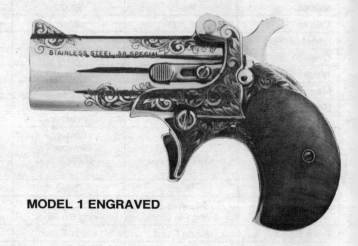

MODEL 1 ENGRAVED

AMERICAN DERRINGER PISTOLS

MODEL 4 (Stainless Steel Double Derringer)

SPECIFICATIONS
Calibers: 45-70 upper barrel, 45 Colt or 3″ .410 lower barrel
Barrel length: 4.1″
Overall length: 6″
Weight: 16.5 oz.
Number of shots: 2
Finish: Satin or high polish stainless steel
Price: $337.50

MODEL 6 (Stainless Steel Double Derringer)

SPECIFICATIONS
Calibers: 357 Magnum, 3″ .410, 45 Auto, 45 Colt
Barrel length: 6″
Overall length: 8.2″
Weight: 21 oz.
Number of shots: 2
Price: Grey matte finish $337.50
      Satin finish 357.00
      High polish finish 375.00

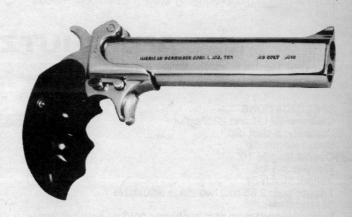

SEMMERLING LM-4 VEST-POCKET

SPECIFICATIONS
Caliber: 45 ACP or 9mm
Action: Double action
Capacity: 5 rounds
Overall length: 5″
Price: Blued finish (manual repeating) $1250.00
      Stainless steel 1500.00

AMT PISTOLS

22 AUTOMAG II RIMFIRE MAGNUM
$329.00

The only production semiautomatic handgun in this caliber, the Automag II is ideal for the small-game hunter or shooting enthusiast who wants more power and accuracy in a light, trim handgun. The pistol features a bold open slide design and employs a unique gas-channeling system for smooth, trouble-free action.

SPECIFICATIONS
Caliber: 22 Rimfire Magnum
Barrel lengths: 3³/₈", 4¹/₂", 6"
Magazine capacity: 9 shots
Weight: 32 oz.
Sights: Millett adjustable (white outline rear; red ramp)
Features: Squared trigger guard; grooved carbon fiber grips

ANSCHUTZ PISTOLS

EXEMPLAR
$395.00

SPECIFICATIONS
Calibers: 22 LR and 22 Magnum
Capacity: 5-shot clip
Barrel length: 10"
Overall length: 19"
Weight: 3¹/₃ lbs.
Action: Match 64
Trigger pull: 9.85 oz., two-stage adjustable
Safety: Slide
Sights: Hooded ramp post front; open notched rear; adjustable for windage and elevation
Stock: European walnut
Also available: **EXEMPLAR LEFT** featuring right-hand operating bolt. **Price: $419.50.**

EXEMPLAR

EXEMPLAR XIV
$405.00

SPECIFICATIONS
Calibers: 22 LR and 22 Magnum
Barrel length: 14"
Overall length: 23"
Weight: 4.15 lbs.
Action: Match 64
Trigger pull: 9.85 oz., two-stage
Safety: Slide
Also available: **EXEMPLAR HORNET.** A new centerfire version with Match 54 action. **Trigger pull:** 19.6 oz. **Barrel:** 10". **Overall length:** 20". **Weight:** 4.35 lbs. Tapped and grooved for scope mounting. Wing safety. **Price: $744.50.**

EXEMPLAR XIV

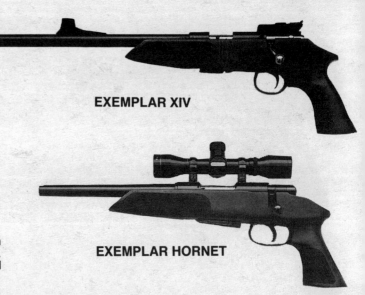

EXEMPLAR HORNET

ASTRA PISTOLS & REVOLVERS

BIG-BORE REVOLVERS

These large-frame, big-bore revolvers feature forged steel construction, large cylinders, magnum-sized bolts and recessed chambers (full 360 case-head support). A four-position adjustment for main spring tension tailors the trigger pull to the shooter's own specifications. **Calibers:** 357 Magnum, 44 Magnum, 45 ACP. **Capacity:** 6 rounds. **Barrel lengths:** 3″ in 357 Magnum; 6″ in 44 Mag. and 45 ACP. **Overall length:** 8½″ in 357 Magnum; 11½″ in 44 Mag. and 45 ACP. **Weight:** about 2½ lbs. **Finish: Blue or stainless steel.**

357 Magnum (Blue)	$395.00
44 Magnum	450.00
45 ACP	500.00

MODEL A-90

357 MAGNUM

ASTRA MODEL A-90

Double-action, semiautomatic pistol in 9mm Parabellum and 45 ACP.

Features include an advanced, smooth double-action mechanism, increased magazine capacity (15 rounds in 9mm, 9 rounds in 45 ACP), all-steel construction, compact size, loaded chamber indicator, combat-style trigger guard, optional right-side slide release. **Barrel length:** 3¾″. **Weight:** 36 oz. (37 oz. in 45 ACP). **Price:** $500.00
Also available: **Model A-80. Price:** 425.00

ASTRA CONSTABLE 22 L.R. & 380 ACP

The Astra Constable is a double-action, all-steel, small-frame auto, so you can safely carry it fully loaded with a round in the chamber and the safety off. A single pull of the trigger then cocks and fires the pistol without the necessity of cocking the hammer manually, as is necessary with most autos. The thumb safety completely blocks the hammer and actually locks the firing pin in place until released. The barrel is rigidly mounted in the frame for greater accuracy and the gun features quick, no-tool takedown, integral non-glare rib on the slide, push-button magazine release and a round, non-snagging hammer spur. **Barrel length:** 3½″. **Weight:** 37 oz. (380 ACP) and 28 oz. (22 LR). **Capacity:** 10 rds. (22 LR) and 7 rds. (380 ACP).

22 LR Blue	$365.00
22 LR Chrome	375.00
380 ACP Blue	350.00
380 ACP A-60 (13 rds.)	435.00

MODEL 44 (not shown)

Designed around the popular lines of its forerunner, the Astra 357, this revolver features wide-spur target hammers and a four-position main spring adjustment device that allows for custom tuning of trigger pull. Includes oversized, beefed-up frame and target-style grips to provide balanced weight distribution and minimize recoil.

The revolver, finished in deep astral blue, is available with 6-inch barrel that features integral sight ribs and shrouds for the ejector rods. Grooved trigger, ramp front sight and fully adjustable rear sight are standard. **Caliber:** 44 Magnum. **Price:** $450.00

CONSTABLE

BEEMAN PISTOLS AND REVOLVERS

BEEMAN/UNIQUE 2000-U 5-SHOT SEMIAUTOMATIC
$1198.00 (Right) $1260.00 (Left)

This improved version of the 823-U includes a reshaped grip, a redesigned firing mechanism, a faster falling hammer, and a dry firing mechanism that is easier to use. Trigger weight is only 3.5 oz. Features special light alloy frame and solid steel slide and shock absorber. Five vents reduce recoil; three removable vent screws adjust for jump control and velocity. Counter-weights available. **Caliber:** 22 Short. **Weight:** 2.7 lbs. Also available: **Beeman/Unique DES/32** (32 LG) $1235.00.

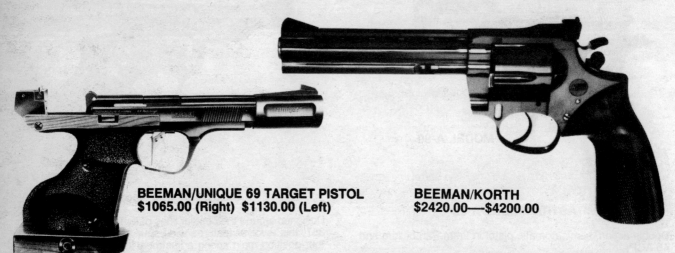

BEEMAN/UNIQUE 69 TARGET PISTOL
$1065.00 (Right) $1130.00 (Left)

BEEMAN/KORTH
$2420.00—$4200.00

SPECIFICATIONS
Caliber: 22 LR. **Capacity:** 5-shot magazine. **Sight radius:** 8.7″. **Weight:** 2.2 lbs. **Grips:** Adjustable, anatomically shaped. **Features:** Trigger adjusts for position and pull weight; several barrel counterweights available; dry firing device; meets all U.I.T. requirements.

The metal parts of these revolvers are hammer-forged steel super-hardened to high tensile strength. Cylinder gap of .002″ eliminates stretching of the frame while firing, reduces flash, and increases velocity. **Caliber:** 357 Mag. or 22 LR w/interchangeable combo cylinders of 357 Mag./9mm Para or 22 LR/22 WMR. **Grips:** Walnut. **Barrel lengths:** 3″; 4″; 6″ (Combat or Target).

MODEL MINI-P08
$389.50

SPECIFICATIONS
Caliber: 380 ACP. **Barrel length:** 3.5″. **Overall length:** 7.4″. **Weight:** I.4 lbs. **Grips:** Checkered hardwood.

MODEL PO8
$389.50

SPECIFICATIONS
Caliber: 22 LR. **Barrel length:** 3.8″. **Overall length:** 7.8″. **Weight:** 1.9 lbs. **Grips:** Checkered hardwood. Also features toggle-joint mechanism and magazine safety device.

BEEMAN/HÄMMERLI PISTOLS

MODEL 150 FREE PISTOL
$1980.00 ($2069.00 Left Hand)

SPECIFICATIONS
Caliber: 22 LR
Overall length: 17.2″
Weight: 45.6 oz.
Trigger action: Infinitely variable set trigger weight; cocking lever located on left of receiver; trigger length variable along weapon axis
Sights: Sight radius 14.8″; micrometer rear sight adj. for windage and elevation
Locking action: Martini-type locking action w/side-mounted locking lever
Barrel: Free floating, cold swaged precision barrel w/low axis relative to the hand

Ignition: Horizontal firing pin (hammerless) in line w/barrel axis; firing pin travel 0.15″
Grips: Selected walnut w/adj. hand rest for direct arm to barrel extension
MODEL 150L: Same as above but w/left-hand adjustable grips

MODEL 152 ELECTRONIC PISTOL
$2105.00 ($2195.00 Left Hand)

SPECIFICATIONS:
Same as **Model 150** except trigger action is electronic. Features short lock time (1.7 milliseconds between trigger actuation and firing pin impact), light trigger pull, and extended battery life.

BEEMAN/HÄMMERLI PISTOLS

MODEL 208 TARGET PISTOL
$1960.00

SPECIFICATIONS:
Caliber: 22LR
Barrel length: 6″
Overall length: 10.2″
Weight: 37.3 oz. (w/accessories)
Capacity: 8 rounds
Sight radius: 8.3″
Sights: Micrometer rear sight w/notch width; standard front blade
Left-hand version also available.

MODEL 215 TARGET PISTOL
$1560.00

SPECIFICATIONS
Same as **Model 208** except it has fewer "luxury" features. Also available: **MODEL 212 Hunter's Pistol** featuring safety catch, nonslip slide and optimal balance. **Price: $1550.00.**

MODEL 232 RAPID FIRE PISTOL
$1445.00

SPECIFICATIONS:
Caliber: 22 Short
Barrel length: 5.2″
Overall length: 10.5″
Weight: 44 oz.
Sight radius: 9.6″
Capacity: 5 rounds
Grips: Adjustable (add **$40** for wraparound grips)
Wraparound grips and left-hand version also available.

BERETTA PISTOLS

MODEL 21 DA SEMIAUTOMATIC
$205.00 ($227.00 Nickel)

A safe, dependable, accurate small-bore pistol in 22 LR or 25 Auto. Easy to load with its unique barrel tip-up system.

SPECIFICATIONS
Caliber: 22 LR or 25 Auto. **Magazine capacity:** 7 rounds (22 LR); 8 rounds (25 Auto). **Overall length:** 4.8″. **Barrel length:** 2.4″. **Weight:** 12 oz. **Sights:** Blade front, V-notch rear. **Safety:** Thumb operated. **Grips:** Walnut. **Frame:** Special alloy.
Also available:
Model 21 Engraved $237.00

MODEL 21

MODEL 950 BS-4″ (22 Short)

MODEL 950 BS
Single Action Semiautomatic

SPECIFICATIONS
Calibers: 25 ACP and 22 Short. **Barrel length:** 2¹/₂″. **Overall length:** 4¹/₂″. **Overall height:** 3.4″. **Safety:** External, thumb-operated. **Magazine:** 8 rounds (25 cal.); 6 rounds (22 Short). **Sights:** Blade front; V-notch rear. **Weight:** 10.2 oz. in 22 cal.; 9.9 oz. in 25 cal. **Frame:** Special alloy.

Model 950 BS $153.00
Model 950 BS Nickel 180.00
Model 950 EL Engraved 220.00

MODEL 92F (9mm)

This 9mm Parabellum semiautomatic pistol is specifically designed for use by law enforcement agencies. It has also been adopted as the official sidearm of the U.S. Armed Forces. Its 15-round firepower combines with flawless reliability and safety to make it the ideal police and military sidearm. Its firing mechanism will handle thousands of rounds without malfunction. And the ambidextrous triple-safety mechanism features a passive firing pin catch, a slide safety that acts as a decocking lever, plus a unique firing pin to insure that a falling hammer can never break safety and discharge accidentally.

SPECIFICATIONS
Caliber: 9mm Parabellum. **Overall length:** 8.54″. **Height:** 5.4″. **Barrel length:** 4.9″. **Weight** (empty): 34 oz. **Magazine:** 15 rounds, removable floorplate. **Sights:** Front, blade integral with slide; rear, square-notched bar, dovetailed to slide. **Slide stop:** Holds slide open after last round, manually operable.

Model 92F $600.00
(Wood grips $20.00 additional). Also available:
Model 92F Compact (13 round) 620.00
   Same as above with wood frame 647.00

MODEL 92F (9mm)

BERETTA PISTOLS

BERETTA MEDIUM FRAME PISTOLS
Calibers 22 LR and 380

MODEL 84

MODEL 85

This double action semiautomatic pistol features walnut grips, blued steel slide, ambidextrous safety, and anodized alloy frame with a single line 8-round magazine.

SPECIFICATIONS
Caliber: 380 Auto. **Barrel length:** 3.82″. **Weight** (empty): 21.8 oz. **Overall length:** 6.8″. **Overall height:** 4.8″. **Capacity:** 8 rounds. **Sights:** Blade integral with slide (front); square notched bar, dovetailed to slide (rear).

BERETTA MEDIUM FRAME PISTOLS

MODELS	PRICES
Model 84 Plastic (13 rounds)	$467.00
Model 84 Wood	493.00
Model 84 Nickel	533.00
Model 85 Plastic (8 rounds)	413.00
Model 85 Wood	440.00
Model 85 Nickel	480.00
Model 87 Wood (22 LR)	447.00
Model 87 (Long barrel, SA)	460.00
Model 87 Sport Wood (10 rds.)	620.00

MODEL 84

This pistol is pocket size with a large magazine capacity. The lockwork is of double-action type. The first shot (with hammer down, chamber loaded) can be fired by a double-action pull on the trigger without cocking the hammer manually.

The pistol also features a favorable grip angle for natural pointing, positive thumb safety (uniquely designed for both right- and left-handed operation), quick takedown (by means of special takedown button) and a conveniently located magazine release. Black plastic grips. Wood grips available at extra cost.

SPECIFICATIONS
Caliber: 380 Auto (9mm Short). **Weight:** 1 lb. 7 oz. (approx.). **Barrel length:** 3³/₄″. (approx.) **Overall length:** 6¹/₂″. (approx.) **Sights:** Fixed front and rear. **Magazine capacity:** 13 rounds. **Height overall:** 4¹/₄″ (approx.).

MODEL 85

MODEL 86

The Beretta Model 86 is a double-action 380 ACP medium-frame semiauto pistol with tip-up barrel that allows loading without actuating the slide. The slide is open in design to reduce the possibility of jamming. Also featured are a manual ambidextrous safety with firing-pin block and two types of grips: contoured cut-checkered walnut or standard black plastic.

SPECIFICATIONS
Caliber: 380 ACP
Capacity: 8 rounds
Barrel length: 4.33″
Weight: 23 oz.
Sights: Blade front; square notched rear
Sight radius: 5″
Price: On request

BERNARDELLI PISTOLS

P018 STANDARD
$499.00

MODEL P018

SPECIFICATIONS
Caliber: 9mm
Barrel length: 4.88"; 4.08" Compact Model
Overall length: 8.52"; 7.68" Compact Model
Weight: 35 oz. (empty); 33 oz. Compact Model
Frame: Steel
Sights: Welded blade front; notched bar rear, adjustable for
    windage
Finish: Blue
Grips: Plastic
Price: W/standard grips $499.00
    With walnut grips 539.00
    P018 COMPACT w/walnut grips 519.00

P018 COMPACT
$519.00

Also available:
**MODEL 69 COMPETITION/TARGET PISTOL (22
    LR)** $459.00
MODEL AMR (22 LR and 380) 309.00
MODEL USA (22 LR and 380) 289.00

P010 STANDARD
$519.00

MODEL P010 STANDARD

SPECIFICATIONS
Caliber: 22 LR
Barrel length: 5.9".
Weight: 40.5 oz.
Magazine capacity: 5 and 10 shot
Sight radius: 7.5".
Features: Matte black reflection-preventing finish; walnut grips
    for right- and left-hand shooters; interchangeable front and
    rear sights; external hammer with safety notch; pivoted
    trigger adjustable for pull weight and take-ups; external
    slide catch for hold-open device; manual safety; inertia safe
    firing pin.
Price: $519.00

BERSA AUTOMATIC PISTOLS

MODEL 380 DOUBLE ACTION
$280.00 ($349.95 in 13-Shot)

SPECIFICATIONS
Caliber: 380 Auto
Barrel length: 3½″
Action: Blow back
Sights: Front blade sight integral on slide; rear sight square notched adjustable for windage
Capacity: 7 + 1 in chamber or 13 + 1 in chamber
Grips: Custom wood
Also available in Nickel finish (13-shot): **$366.95**

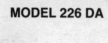

MODEL 226 DA

MODEL 22 DOUBLE ACTION
$280.00

SPECIFICATIONS
Caliber: 22 LR
Barrel length: 4″
Action: Blow back
Sights: Front blade sight on barrel; rear sight square notched adjustable for windage
Capacity: 10 + 1 in chamber
Grips: Custom wood
Finish: Blue
Also available: **MODEL 226 DA.** Same specifications as Model 22, but with 6″ barrel.

BRNO PISTOLS

MODEL CZ 75

MODEL CZ 75
$699.00

This 9mm double-action service pistol features an all-steel frame, 15-shot magazine, and two integral locking lugs on top of barrel that fit into matching recesses in the slide. When slide is pulled forward, the barrel is forced downward and unlocked from the slide stop pin (which fits through the slotted barrel tang.) A pivot-type extractor is pinned on the right side of the slide behind the ejection port. Trigger pull is 9 lbs.

SPECIFICATIONS
Caliber: 9mm Parabellum. **Barrel length:** 4.7″. **Overall length:** 8.1″. **Height:** 5.4″. **Weight:** 35 oz.

BROWNING AUTOMATIC PISTOLS

BUCK MARK .22 PISTOL
$182.95

Magazine capacity: 10 rounds. **Overall length:** 9¹/₂". **Barrel length:** 5¹/₂". **Height:** 5³/₈". **Weight:** 35 oz. **Grips:** Black molded. **Rear sights:** Screw adjusts for vertical correction; drift adjustable for windage.

Prices:
Standard **$207.95**
Plus (w/contoured, laminated wood grips) 252.95
Silhouette 352.95
Varmint 318.95

BUCK MARK SILHOUETTE

MODEL BDA-380.

MODEL BDA-380

A high-powered, double-action pistol with fixed sights in 380 caliber.
Nickel Finish **$477.95**
Standard Finish 452.75

SEMIAUTOMATIC PISTOL SPECIFICATIONS

	BUCK MARK VARMINT	BUCK MARK PLUS	BUCK MARK SILHOUETTE	BDA-380 (DOUBLE ACTION)
Capacity of Magazine	10	10	10	13
Overall length	14"	9¹/₂"	14"	6³/₄"
Barrel Length	9⁷/₈"	5¹/₂"	9⁷/₈"	3¹³/₁₆"
Height	5⁵/₁₆"	5³/₈"	5¹⁵/₁₆"	4³/₄"
Weight (Empty)	48 oz.	32 oz.	53 oz.	23 oz.
Sight radius	—	8"	13"	4¹⁵/₁₆"
Ammunition	22LR	22LR	22LR	380 Auto
Grips	Contoured Walnut	Black, Molded	Contoured Walnut	Walnut
Front Sights	None	¹/₈" wide	Interchangeable Post	Fixed blade
Rear Sights	None	Screw adjustable for windage and elevation.	Hooded Millett Gold cup	Square notch. Drift adjustable for windage.
Grades Available	standard	Standard	Standard	Polished Blue, Nickel

BROWNING AUTOMATIC PISTOLS

**9mm HI-POWER
SINGLE ACTION 9mm**

The Browning 9mm Parabellum, also known as the 9mm Browning Hi-Power, has a 14-cartridge capacity and weighs 2 pounds. The push-button magazine release permits swift, convenient withdrawal of the magazine.

The 9mm is available with either a fixed-blade front sight and a windage-adjustable rear sight or a non-glare rear sight, screw adjustable for both windage and elevation. The front sight is a 1/8-inch wide blade mounted on a ramp. The rear surface of the blade is serrated to prevent glare.

In addition to the manual safety, the firing mechanism includes an external hammer, making it easy to ascertain whether the pistol is cocked.

Prices:
Standard **$436.95**
Polished blue with adjustable sights **517.95**
Polished blue with fixed sights **473.95**

9MM SEMIAUTOMATIC PISTOL (SINGLE AND DOUBLE ACTION)

	SINGLE ACTION FIXED SIGHTS	SINGLE ACTION ADJUSTABLE SIGHTS
Finish	Polished Blue, Matte, or Nickel	Polished Blue
Capacity of Magazine	13	13
Overall Length	7³/₄″	7³/₄″
Barrel Length	4²¹/₃₂″	4²¹/₃₂″
Height	5″	5″
Weight (Empty)	32 oz.	32 oz.
Sight Radius	6⁵/₁₆″	6³/₈″
Ammunition	9mm Luger, (Parabellum)	9mm Luger, (Parabellum)
Grips	Checkered Walnut	Checkered Walnut
Front Sights	1/8″	1/8″ wide on ramp
Rear Sights	Drift adjustable for windage.	Screw adjustable for windage and elevation.

CHARTER ARMS REVOLVERS

357 MAGNUM REVOLVER BULLDOG "TRACKER"

SPECIFICATIONS
Caliber: 357 Magnum. **Type of action:** 5-shot. **Barrel length:** 2¹/₂″. **Overall length:** 7¹/₂″ (2¹/₂ bbl.). **Height:** 5¹/₈″. **Weight:** 21 oz. **Grips:** Hand-checkered walnut, square butt design. **Sights:** Ramp front sight; adjustable square-notched rear; elevation reference lines; definite click indicator. **Finish:** Service blue.

Price:
Blue finish and Neoprene or Bulldog grips **$250.35**

BULLDOG PUG 44 SPECIAL 5-SHOT

BULLDOG 44 SPECIAL

SPECIFICATIONS
Caliber: 44 Special. **Type of action:** 5-shot, single- and double-action. **Barrel length:** 3″. **Overall length:** 7³/₄″. **Height:** 5″. **Weight:** 19 oz. **Grips:** Neoprene or American walnut hand-checkered bulldog grips. **Sights:** Patridge-type, ⁹/₆₄″ wide front; square-notched rear. **Finish:** High-luster Service Blue or Stainless Steel.

  Also available: new **44SPL Bulldog Pug Model** with 2¹/₂″ barrel and ramp front sight. **Overall length:** 7¹/₄″.

Prices:
Blue finish (2¹/₂″ Bull or 3″)	**$232.35**
Blue finish (Pug)	250.35
Stainless Steel (2¹/₂″ Bull or 3″)	286.35
Stainless Steel (Pug)	325.00

POLICE BULLDOG

SPECIFICATIONS
Calibers: 32 Magnum, 38 Special, 357 Magnum. **Type of action:** 5-shot and 6-shot (38 Special only), single and double action. **Barrel lengths:** 2″ and 3¹/₂″ (32 Magnum only); 4″ (38 Special & 357 Mag. only). **Overall length:** 6¹/₂″ (32 Mag.), 8¹/₄″ (3¹/₂″ 32 Mag.) and 9″ (4″ barrel). **Weight:** 20 oz. (2″ 32 Mag.), 26 oz. (3¹/₂″ 32 Mag.) and 20-23¹/₂ oz. (38 Special & 357 Mag.).

Prices:
32 Mag. & 38 Special (w/3¹/₂″ shrouded barrel) . . .	**$250.35**
Same as above in stainless steel	292.89
32 Mag. & 38 Special (w/4″ tapered or bull barrel)	233.16
32 Mag. & 38 Special (w/4″ shrouded barrel stainless)	286.35
Same as above w/adjustable rear sight	325.00
357 Mag. (stainless steel only w/adj. rear sight) . . .	309.25

NEW POLICE BULLDOG (not shown) 44 SPECIAL

SPECIFICATIONS
Caliber: 44 Special. **Type of action:** 5-shot single and double action. **Barrel length:** 2¹/₂″ and 3¹/₂″. **Overall length:** 7″ (Bulldog grips); 7¹/₄″ (Neoprene grips); 8″ (3¹/₂″ barrel). **Height:** 5″. **Weight:** 19¹/₂ oz. (2¹/₂″ Bulldog); 21 oz. (2¹/₂″ Neoprene); 23 oz. (2¹/₂″ Stainless Steel); 23¹/₂ oz. (3¹/₂″). **Grips:** Bulldog and Neoprene. **Finish:** Stainless steel and service blue (2¹/₂″ barrel only).

Price:
44 Special	**$260.10**
In Stainless Steel	315.80

CHARTER ARMS REVOLVERS

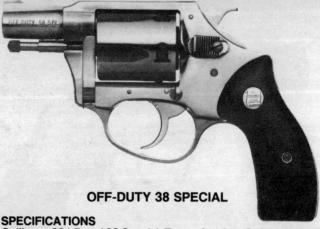

POLICE UNDERCOVER

SPECIFICATIONS
Caliber: 32 H&R Magnum and 38 Special. **Type of action:** 6-shot single and double action. **Barrel length:** 2″. **Height:** 4½″. **Weight:** 17½ oz. (2″ barrel) and 19 oz. (4″ barrel.) **Grips:** Checkered walnut panel. **Sights:** Patridge-type ramp front sight, square-notch rear sight. **Finish:** Blue.

Price **$250.35**
Stainless steel and checkered walnut panel 281.45

OFF-DUTY 38 SPECIAL

SPECIFICATIONS
Calibers: 22 LR and 38 Special. **Type of action:** 5-shot single- and double-action. **Barrel length:** 2″. **Overall length:** 6¼″. **Height:** 4¼″. **Weight:** 16 oz. (mat-black), 17 oz. (stainless steel). **Grips:** Select-a-grip (9 colors) or neoprene. **Sights:** Patridge-type ramp front sight (with new "red dot" feature); square notch rear sight on stainless.

Prices:
Matte black finish **$193.89**
Stainless steel 240.53

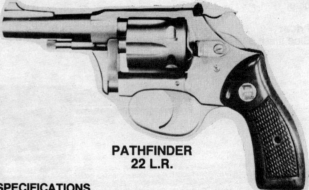

PATHFINDER 22 L.R.

SPECIFICATIONS
Caliber: 22 LR. **Type of action:** 6-shot, single and double action. **Barrel length:** 3″ or 6″. **Overall length:** 7¾″ (3″ bbl.); 10⅝″ (6″ bbl.). **Height:** 4¾″ (3″ bbl.); 5″ (6″ bbl.). **Weight:** 20 oz. (3″ bbl.); 22½ oz. (6″ bbl.). **Grips:** Hand-checkered square butt or checkered walnut panel. **Sights:** Patridge-type ramp front sight; fully adjustable notch rear sight. **Finish:** High luster service blue.

Prices:
With 3″ barrel **$229.89**
With 6″ barrel 233.16
With 3″ barrel in stainless steel 291.25

UNDERCOVER 38 SPECIAL

SPECIFICATIONS
Caliber: 38 Special (Mid-Range & Standard). **Type of Action:** 5 shots, single- and double-action. **Barrel length** (with shroud): 2″. **Overall length:** 6¼″. **Height:** 4¼″. **Weight:** 16 oz. **Grips:** American walnut hand-checkered. **Sights:** Patridge-type or standard ramp front, square-notched rear. **Finish:** High-luster Service Blue or Stainless Steel.

Prices:
Blued finish with checkered panel grips **$215.98**
Stainless steel with checkered panel grips 273.25

BONNIE AND CLYDE (not shown)

This matching pair of handguns in 32 Magnum and 38 Special are designed for couples who like to go to the shooting range together. Both guns come with their own "gun rug" identified by name. Each model also offers a scrolled name on the barrel and features Select-A-Grip color-coordinated grips. The fully shrouded barrels are 2½″ long with an attractive blue finish. Price on request.

COLT AUTOMATIC PISTOLS
MKIV SERIES

COMBAT COMMANDER

The semiautomatic Combat Commander, available in 45 ACP, 38 Super or 9mm Luger, boasts an all-steel frame that supplies the pistol with an extra measure of heft and stability. This outstanding Colt also offers fixed square-notch rear and fixed blade front, lanyard-style hammer and thumb and grip safety.

Caliber	Weight	Overall Length	Magazine Rounds	Finish	Price
45 ACP	36 oz.	7⁷/₈″	7	Blue	$593.50
38 Super	36¹/₂ oz.	7⁷/₈″	9	Blue	597.50
9mm Luger	36¹/₂ oz.	7⁷/₈″	9	Blue	597.50

COMBAT COMMANDER
4¹/₄″ barrel only

LIGHTWEIGHT COMMANDER

This lightweight, shorter version of the Government Model offers increased ease of carrying with the firepower of the 45 ACP. The Lightweight Commander features alloy frame, fixed-style sights, grooved trigger, lanyard-style hammer and walnut stocks; also thumb and grip safety, and firing pin safety.

SPECIFICATIONS
Weight: 27 oz.
Barrel length: 4¹/₄″
Overall length: 7⁷/₈″
Magazine rounds: 7
Finish: Blue
Price: $593.50

LIGHTWEIGHT COMMANDER
4¹/₄″ barrel only

GOLD CUP NATIONAL MATCH

SPECIFICATIONS
Caliber: 45 ACP
Capacity: 7 rounds
Barrel length: 5″
Weight: 38¹/₂ oz.
Overall length: 8³/₈″
Sights: Undercut front; adjustable rear
Hammer: Serrated target hammer
Stock: Checkered walnut
Finish: Colt blue or stainless
Price: $765.50 Blue
      821.95 Stainless steel
      876.50 Bright stainless
Also available:
COMBAT ELITE 45 ACP; features 3 dot front and rear combat sights, extended grip safety. **Price:** $723.50.

GOLD CUP NATIONAL MATCH

COLT AUTOMATIC PISTOLS
MKIV SERIES

GOVERNMENT MODEL

GOVERNMENT MODEL 380 AUTOMATIC

This scaled-down version of the 1911 A1 Colt Government Model does not include a grip safety. It incorporates the use of a firing pin safety to provide for a safe method to carry a round in the chamber in a "cocked and locked" mode. This provides for a consistent trigger pull rather than the double-action style of a heavy first pull. 380 ACP caliber. Now available in matte stainless steel finish with black composition stocks.

SPECIFICATIONS
Barrel length: 3.29″
Height: 4.4″
Weight (empty): 21.8 oz.
Overall length: 6″
Magazine capacity: 7 rounds
Sights: Fixed ramp blade in front; fixed square notch in rear
Grip: Composition stocks
Price: $383.95 Blue
    426.50 Satin Nickel
    405.95 Coltguard
    408.50 Stainless steel (NEW)

DELTA ELITE 10mm

The proven design and reliability of Colt's Government Model has been combined with the new powerful 10mm auto cartridge to produce a highly effective shooting system for hunting, law enforcement and personal protection. The velocity and energy of the 10mm cartridge make this pistol ideal for the serious handgun hunter and the law enforcement professional who insist on down-range stopping power. Now available in stainless steel and "Ultimate" stainless finish.

SPECIFICATIONS
Type: 0 Frame, semiautomatic pistol
Barrel length: 5″
Overall length: 8¹/₂″
Weight (empty): 38 oz.
Cylinder capacity: 8 rounds
Sights: 3-dot, high-profile front and rear combat sights
Sight radius: 6¹/₂″
Grip: Rubber combat stocks with Delta medallion
Safety: Trigger safety lock (thumb safety) is located on left-hand side of receiver; grip safety is located on backstrap
Rifling: 6 groove, left-hand twist, one turn in 16″
Price: $657.50 Blue
    699.95 Stainless steel
    762.95 "Ultimate" Bright Stainless (NEW)

GOVERNMENT MODEL

These full-size automatic pistols, available exclusively with 5-inch barrels, may be had in 45 ACP, 9mm Luger, 38 Super and 22 LR. The Government Model's special features include fixed military sights, grip and thumb safeties, grooved trigger, walnut stocks and Accurizor barrel and bushing.

SPECIFICATIONS
Overall length: 8³/₈″
Capacity: 9 rds.; 7 rds. (45 ACP)
Weight: 39 oz.; 38 oz. (45 ACP)
Price: $593.50 45 ACP blue
    628.95 45 ACP stainless
    691.95 45 ACP bright stainless
    597.50 Other calibers, blue

GOVERNMENT MODEL 380 AUTOMATIC

DELTA ELITE

Also available:
DELTA GOLD CUP. Same specifications as Delta Elite, except 39 oz. weight and 6³/₄″ sight radius. Price not set.
FIRST EDITION STAINLESS STEEL DELTA ELITE. Limited edition (1,000) from Colt's Custom Gun Shop. Complete with serial number and compact carrying case. **Price: $890.00.**

COLT PISTOLS
MKIV SERIES

COLT MUSTANG .380

This new backup automatic has four times the knockdown power of most 25 ACP automatics.

SPECIFICATIONS
Caliber: 380 ACP
Capacity: 5 rounds
Weight: 18.5 oz.
Overall length: 5.65"
Height: 3.9"
Price: $383.95
    426.50 in nickel
    405.95 in Coltguard
Also available:
MUSTANG POCKET LITE 380 with aluminum alloy receiver; 1/2" shorter than standard 380; weighs only 12.5 oz. **Price: $383.95.**
MUSTANG PLUS II features full grip length with shorter compact barrel and slide. **Price: $383.95.**

COLT MUSTANG .380

COLT OFFICER'S 45 ACP

SPECIFICATIONS
Caliber: 45 ACP
Barrel length: 3⁵/₈"
Overall length: 7¹/₄"
Weight: 34 oz.
Price: $576.50 matte finish
    628.95 stainless steel
    593.50 lightweight
    593.50 standard blue
    691.95 Ultimate stainless

MUSTANG POCKET LITE

COLT REVOLVERS

KING COBRA
357 MAGNUM

This "snake" revolver features a solid barrel rib, full-length ejector rod housing, red ramp front sight, white outline adjustable rear sight, and new "gripper" rubber combat grips. All stainless steel.

SPECIFICATIONS
Caliber: 357 Magnum
Barrel lengths: 2¹/₂", 4", 6"
Weight: 42 oz.
Price: $434.95
Also available: **"Ultimate"** bright stainless steel (4" and 6") **$471.95**
KING COBRA in blue finish with black neoprene finger-grooved, combat-style grips (4" and 6" barrels) **$408.95.**

KING COBRA

COLT REVOLVERS

PYTHON
357 MAGNUM (shown with 8″ barrel)

The Colt Python revolver, suitable for hunting, target shooting and police use, is chambered for the powerful 357 Magnum cartridge. Python features include ventilated rib, fast cocking, wide-spur hammer, trigger and grips, adjustable rear and ramp-type front sights, 1/8″ wide.

PYTHON

SPECIFICATIONS
Caliber: 357 Mag.
Barrel length: 2¹/₂″, 4″, 6″, 8″
Overall length: 11¹/₄″
Weight: 43¹/₂ oz.
Stock: Checkered walnut
Finish: Colt royal blue, stainless steel and "Ultimate" bright stainless steel

Finish	Price
Blued finish	$729.95
Stainless steel	835.95
"Ultimate" Bright Stainless Steel	859.95

COONAN ARMS

MODEL B 357 MAGNUM (Stainless Steel)
$680.00

Caliber: 357 Magnum
Magazine capacity: 7 rounds
Barrel length: 5″
Overall length: 8.3″
Weight (empty): 42 oz.
Height: 5.6″
Sights: Ramp interchangeable (front); fixed, adjustable for windage only (rear)
Grips: Smooth black walnut
Safety features: Hammer lock; half-notch lock; grip lock; inertia firing pin
Also available: w/6″ barrel $720.00

DAKOTA SINGLE ACTION REVOLVERS

MODEL 1873 (With Extra Cylinder)
$580.00

SPECIFICATIONS
Calibers: 22 LR, 22 Mag., 357 Mag., 45 Long Colt, 30 M1 Carbine, 38-40 cal., 32-20 cal., 44-40 cal. **Barrel lengths:** 3¹/₂″, 4³/₄″, 5¹/₂″, 7¹/₂″. **Finish:** Engraved models, blue or nickel. **Special feature:** Each gun is fitted with second caliber.

DAKOTA TARGET
$500.00

SPECIFICATIONS
Calibers: 45 Long Colt, 357 Magnum, 22 LR. **Barrel lengths:** 5¹/₂″ and 7¹/₂″. **Finish:** Polished blue. **Special features:** Case-hardened frame, one-piece walnut grips, brass back strap, ramp front blade target sight and adjustable rear sight.

MODEL 1875 "OUTLAW"
$485.00 ($520.00 Nickel)

SPECIFICATIONS
Calibers: 45 Long Colt, 357 Magnum, 44-40 cal. **Barrel length:** 7¹/₂″. **Finish:** Blue. **Special features:** Case-hardened frame, walnut grips; an exact replica of Remington #3 revolver produced from 1875 to 1889. Factory Engraved Model: $600.00

DAKOTA 1894 BISLEY
$540.00

SPECIFICATIONS
Calibers: 22, 44-40, 45 Long Colt, 357 Magnum. **Barrel lengths:** 4⁵/₈″, 5¹/₂″ and 7¹/₂″. Also available: **Dakota Bisley Engraved Model** with same barrel lengths and calibers. $700.00
Nickel finish 760.00

DAKOTA SINGLE ACTION REVOLVERS

1873 PREMIER SINGLE ACTION REVOLVER
$520.00

SPECIFICATIONS
Caliber: 45 Long Colt. **Barrel length:** 4⅝" or 5½". **Finish:** Blued, casehardened frame. **Grips:** One-piece walnut. **Features:** Set screw for cylinder pin release; parts are interchangeable with early Colts.

CUSTOM ENGRAVED SINGLE ACTION REVOLVER
$690.00

SPECIFICATIONS
Calibers: 45 Long Colt, 357 Magnum, 44-40. **Barrel lengths:** 5½" and 7½". **Finish:** Nickel. **Features:** Classic original-type scroll engraving.

DAVIS PISTOLS

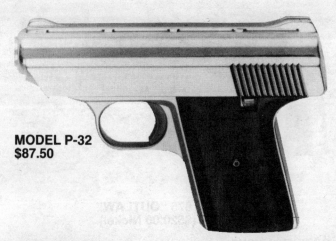

MODEL P-32
$87.50

MODEL D-22 DERRINGER
$87.50

SPECIFICATIONS
Calibers: 25 Auto, 22 LR, 32 Auto, 22 Mag.
Barrel length: 2.4"
Overall length: 4"
Height: 2.8"
Weight: 9.5 oz.
Capacity: 2 shot
Grips: Laminated wood
Finish: Black teflon or chrome (32 Auto in chrome only)

SPECIFICATIONS
Caliber: 32 Auto
Barrel length: 2.8"
Overall length: 5.4"
Height: 4"
Magazine capacity: 6 rounds
Weight (empty): 22 oz.
Grips: Laminated wood
Finish: Black teflon or chrome

DETONICS PISTOLS

COMBAT MASTER™ 45 ACP (Stainless Steel)

Calibers: 45 ACP, 6-shot clip; 38S and 9mm available on special order.
Barrel length: 3½″
Weight: 29 oz. (empty)
Overall length: 6¾″
Stock: Checkered walnut
Sights: Combat-type, fixed; adj. sights available
Features: Self-adjusting cone barrel centering system, beveled magazine inlet, "full clip" indicator in base of magazine; throated barrel and polished feed ramp.
Prices:
  MK I, matte stainless, fixed sights $725.00
  MK VI, polished stainless, adj. sights 795.95

**COMBAT MASTER
45 ACP**

SERIES II PISTOLS

Available in July 1989. Prices to be announced.

ERMA TARGET ARMS

MODEL 777 SPORTING REVOLVER

SPECIFICATIONS
Caliber: 357 Magnum
Capacity: 6 cartridges
Barrel length: 5½″ and 4″
Overall length: 11.3″ and 9.7″
Weight: 43.7 oz.; 39.2 oz. w/4″ barrel
Sight radius: 8″ and 6.4″
Grip: Checkered walnut
Price: $1093.00

Also available:
MODEL 773 MATCH (32 S&W Wadcutter). Same specifications as Model 777 (5½″ barrel only), but with adjustable match grip and 6″ barrel. **Weight:** 45.8 oz. **$1225.00**
MODEL 772 MATCH (22 LR). Same specifications as Model 773, except weight is 47¼ oz. **$1225.00**

MODEL 777

MODEL ESP 85A SPORTING PISTOL

SPECIFICATIONS
Caliber: 22 LR or 32 S&W Wadcutter
Action: Semiautomatic
Capacity: 5 cartridges (8 in 22 LR optional)
Barrel length: 6.″
Overall length: 10.2″
Weight: 40 oz.
Sight radius: 8″
Sights: Micrometer rear sight; fully adjustable interchangeable front and rear sight blade (3.5mm/4.0mm)
Grip: Checkered walnut grip with thumbrest
Price:
22 LR $1119.00
32 S&W 1169.00

MODEL ESP 85A

F.I.E. HANDGUNS

DERRINGER D-86 SINGLE SHOT
$92.95 ($99.95 Dyna-Chrome)

SPECIFICATIONS
Caliber: 38 Special
Barrel length: 3″
Weight: 12 oz.
Sights: Fixed
Safety: Transfer bar
Finish: Dyna-chrome hard matte or bright blue
Grips: Black nylon (Standard) and walnut (Deluxe)
Also available: $114.95 Dyna-Chrome Deluxe
            134.95 Misty Gold
            149.95 Misty Gold Deluxe

TITAN 25 SEMIAUTOMATIC
$72.95

SPECIFICATIONS
Caliber: 25 ACP
Barrel length: 2¹/₂″
Weight: 12 oz.
Sights: Ramp front, fixed rear
Hammer: Serrated external
Grips: European walnut
Trigger lock: Thumb operated
Also available: $ 74.95 Dyna-Chrome
            99.95 Gold Trim

TITAN TIGER DOUBLE ACTION REVOLVER
$174.95

SPECIFICATIONS
Caliber: 38 Special
Barrel length: 2″ or 4″
Sights: Ramp front, fixed rear
Grips: Composite, checkered
Features: Swing-out cylinder with thumb latch release

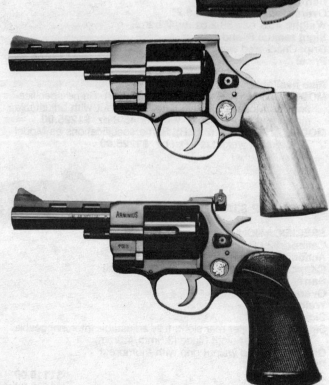

ARMINIUS DOUBLE ACTION REVOLVERS

SPECIFICATIONS
Calibers: 22S/L/LR, 22 WMR, 22 Combo w/interchangeable
   cylinders, 32 S&W Long, 38 Special, 357 Magnum
Barrel lengths: 2″, 3″, 4″ and 6″
Sights: Fixed or micro-adjustable
Weight: 26 oz. - 30 oz.
Capacity: 8 rds. (22), 7 rds. (32 S&W), 6 rds. (all others)
Prices: $184.95 (22 LR and 32 S&W snub nose)
   154.95 (22 LR 4″ and 6″)
   184.95 (38 Special 4″ and 6″)
   239.95 (357 Magnum 3″, 4″ and 6″)

F.I.E. PISTOLS

MODEL TZ75
$439.95

SPECIFICATIONS
Caliber: 9mm double action, 41 A.E.
Capacity: 15 + 1
Barrel length: 4½″
Overall length: 8¼″
Height: 5½″
Weight: 35 oz.
Sights: D/T ramp front (white insert); rear (white outline) adjustable for windage
Grips: European walnut, black rubber (optional)
Available in Satin Chrome: **$459.95**

COWBOY (not shown)
$79.95

SPECIFICATIONS
Calibers: 22 Short, Long, Long Rifle or 22 Magnum
Capacity: 6 rounds
Barrel length: 3¼″ or 6½″
Weight: 28 oz. (3¼″ bbl.); 32 oz. (6½″ bbl.)
Finish: Blue with ebony nylon grips
Sights: Blade front, fixed rear
Features: Floating firing pin, manual shell extraction
Also available: Convertible models supplied with 22 LR and 22 Magnum cylinders. **Price: $99.95.**

MODEL TITAN II

SPECIFICATIONS
Calibers: 22 LR, 380 ACP
Barrel length: 3¼″
Overall length: 6½″
Weight: 25½ oz.
Capacity: 10 + 1 (6 in 32 ACP and 380 ACP)
Finish: Blue
Grip: European walnut
Sights: Integral tapered post front sight; windage adjustable rear sight

SUPER TITAN II (not shown)
$259.95

SPECIFICATIONS
Calibers: 32 ACP, 380 ACP
Weight: 28 oz.
Barrel length: 3¼″
Finish: Blue

Models	Prices
22 LR Blue	$154.95
380 ACP Blue	219.95
380 ACP Chrome	229.95

FREEDOM ARMS

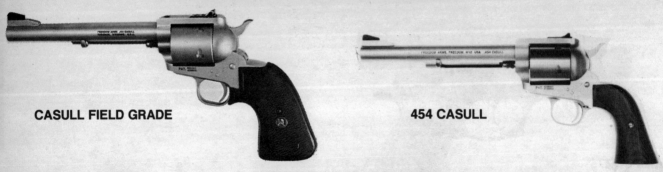

CASULL FIELD GRADE

454 CASULL

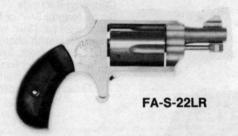

FA-S-22LR

Model	454 CASULL PREMIER GRADE	Prices
FA-454AS	Adjustable sight 454 Casull, 45 Colt and 44 Rem. Mag. with 4³/₄", 6", 7¹/₂" or 10" barrel, stainless steel, brush finish, impregnated hardwood grips.	$1149.75
FA-454FS	Same as above with fixed sight	1044.75
FA-454FGAS	Field Grade with stainless steel matte finish, adjustable sight, Pachmayr presentation grips	834.75

Model	22 LONG RIFLE REVOLVERS	Prices
FA-S-22LR	Stainless Steel Mini-Revolver with 1-inch contoured barrel, partial high-gloss finish. Caliber 22 Long Rifle.	$153.12
FA-S-22LR with FA/B	Same as above, with polished brass belt buckle. *Above prices include soft zipper pouch.*	192.62

NEW 22 PERCUSSION REVOLVERS

Model		Prices
FA-S-22P	Stainless Steel Percussion Mini-Revolver with 1-inch contoured barrel, partial high-gloss finish.	$203.02
FA-S-22P with FA/B	Same as above, with polished brass belt buckle. *All Percussion Revolver prices include the following: powder measure, bullet setting tool, twenty bullets and soft zipper pouch.*	242.56

22 WIN. MAGNUM REVOLVERS

Model		Prices
FA-S-22M	Stainless Steel Mini-Revolver with 1-inch contoured barrel, partial high-gloss finish.	$176.50
FA-S-22M with FA/BM	Same as above, with polished brass belt buckle.	216.00
FA-BG-22M	Stainless Steel Mini-Revolver with 3-inch tapered barrel, partial high-gloss finish and custom oversized grips. *Prices include soft zipper pouch.*	219.95

GLOCK PISTOLS

MODEL 17
$511.60

First launched in 1983, the Glock handgun represents a trend-setting development. The company's trial weapons have now passed 300,000 rounds of testfiring without visible wear and with continuing accuracy. The guns' main features include a limited number of components, a new ''safe-action'' system, low weight with soft recoil, 17-round capacity, and use of space-age polymers that can withstand extreme cold and heat (up to 200°C.) without structural damage.

SPECIFICATIONS
Caliber: 9mm Parabellum
Magazine capacity: 17 rounds
Barrel length: 4½″ (hexagonal profile with right-hand twist
Overall length: 7½″
Weight: 22 oz. (without magazine)
Sights: Fixed or adjustable rear sights

MODEL 17L COMPETITION
$773.53

SPECIFICATIONS
Caliber: 9mm Parabellum
Magazine capacity: 17 rounds
Barrel length: 6.02″
Overall length: 8.77″
Weight: 23.35 oz. (without magazine)
Sights: Fixed or adjustable rear sights

MODEL 19 COMPACT
$511.60

SPECIFICATIONS
Caliber: 9mm Parabellum
Magazine capacity: 17 rounds
Barrel length: 4.02″
Overall length: 6.74″
Weight: 21 oz. (without magazine)
Sights: Fixed or adjustable rear sights

HECKLER & KOCH PISTOLS

MODEL P7M8

MODEL P7M8 SELF-LOADING PISTOL

Features the Continuous Motion Principle in the form of a unique cocking lever. The gun can be drawn, cocked and fired with single-action accuracy in one continuous motion with either hand. Also featured are a low-profile slide, polygonal rifling and rugged forged, machined steel construction.

SPECIFICATIONS
Caliber: 9mm x 19 (Luger)
Capacity: 8 rounds
Barrel length: 4.13″
Overall length: 6.73″
Weight: 1.75 lbs. (empty)
Sight radius: 5.83″
Sights: Adjustable rear
Price: with 2 magazines . . . . $ 895.00

MODEL P7M13

Also available: **MODEL P7M13** with same barrel length, but slightly longer overall, heavier and 13-round capacity 1115.00

MODEL P7K3

Model P7K3 uses a unique oil-filled buffer to decrease recoil and increase control. An easy-to-install conversion kit in 22 LR is available as an accessory.

SPECIFICATIONS
Caliber: 380 (+22 LR Conversion Kit)
Capacity: 8 rounds
Barrel length: 3.8″
Overall length: 6.3″
Weight: 1.65 lbs. (empty)
Sight radius: 5.5″
Sights: Adjustable rear
MODEL P7K3 . . . . $895.00
    22 LR Conversion Kit 467.00

MODEL P7K3

IVER JOHNSON PISTOLS

POCKET PISTOL
TP22 (22LR) & TP25 (25ACP)
$191.65

These 22- and 25-caliber pocket pistols offer a maximum of convenience when carried. The 7-shot capacity, small size and light weight are enhanced by the hammer safety and fast-handling double-action design.
Barrel length: 3″. **Overall length:** 5.5″. **Weight:** 12 oz. (empty).
Grips: Black plastic. **Finish:** Blue

TP22 POCKET PISTOL

KASSNAR PISTOLS

MODEL PSP-25
$249.00

SPECIFICATIONS
Caliber: 25 ACP
Barrel length: 2¹/₈″
Overall length: 4¹/₈″
Weight: 9.5 oz. (empty)
Height: 2⁷/₈″
Features: Dual safety system; all-steel construction; honed, polished and blued.

MODEL PSP-25

MODEL 941 JERICHO (not shown)
$849.00

This multi-caliber semiautomatic pistol features interchangeable barrels and a conversion kit, plus all-steel construction, precision machined with a deep-blue satin matte finish.

SPECIFICATIONS
Calibers: 9mm/41 AE
Barrel length: 4.4″
Overall length: 7.9″
Height: 5.5″
Rifling: 1 turn in 10″ (9mm); 1 turn in 18.5″ (41 AE)
Weight: 2 lbs.
Features: 3-dot tritium sight system; custom loaded carrying case; custom RIG cleaning kit; 2 boxes of ammo; polygonal rifling; double action; easy-operating slide-mounted thumb safety; deep-groove serrated slide grip for positive operation; manual safety/decocking lever; non-slip modified combat hammer; impact-resistant Polymer grips.

L.A.R. GRIZZLY

MARK I
GRIZZLY WIN MAG
$725.00

This semiautomatic pistol is a direct descendant of the tried and trusted 1911-type .45 automatic, but with the added advantage of increased caliber capacity.

SPECIFICATIONS
Calibers: 45 Win. Mag., 45 ACP, 357 Mag.
Barrel length: 6½"
Overall length: 10½"
Weight (empty): 48 oz.
Height: 5¾"
Sights: Fixed, ramped blade (front); fully adjustable for elevation and windage (rear)

Magazine capacity: 7 rounds
Grips: Checkered rubber, nonslip, combat-type
Safeties: Grip depressor, manual thumb, slide-out-of-battery disconnect
Materials: Mil spec 4140 steel slide and receiver with non-corrosive, heat-treated, special alloy steels for other parts
Same model in 357 Magnum $750.00

Also available:
Win Mag Compensator 73.50

6½" BARREL

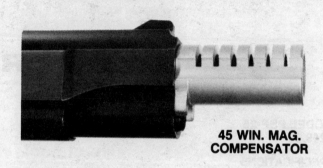

45 WIN. MAG. COMPENSATOR

Also available: Grizzly Win Mag with 8" and 10" Barrels in 45 Win Mag, 357 Magnum, 45 ACP and 357/45 Grizzly Win Mag.

Model G-WM8 (8" barrel in 45 Win Mag, 45 ACP, or 357/45 Grizzly Win Mag $1250.00
Model G357M8 (8" barrel in 357 Magnum) 1275.00
Model G-WM10 (10" barrel in 45 Win Mag, 45 ACP, or 357/45 Grizzly Win Mag 1313.00
Model G357M10 (10" barrel in 357 Magnum) 1337.50

8 " BARREL

10 " BARREL

LLAMA REVOLVERS

LLAMA COMANCHE

IN REVOLVERS TODAY, THERE'S A NEW NAME IN EXCELLENCE, IT'S THE LLAMA COMANCHE® SERIES. Designed for you and incorporating every feature worth having to make these Llamas the finest revolvers made today . . . at any price.

The sledgehammer 357 Magnum caliber utilizes massively forged solid-steel frames for tremendous strength and enduring reliability.

Up front, Llama added a precision-bored heavyweight barrel of target quality, complete with a solid shroud to protect the ejector rod, and a raised ventilated-rib that dissipates heat from the barrel to give you a clear, sharp sight image even when the action gets hot.

On the inside, everything is finely fitted and polished, for a double action that's slick and smooth, and a single-action trigger pull that's light, crisp and clean. Llama gave all Comanches a floating firing pin for greater safety and dependability.

COMANCHE III
357 Mag.
Satin Chrome
4″ and 6″ barrels

357 Mag. Standard Blue 4″, 6″ **$325.00**
357 Mag. Satin Chrome 4″, 6″ **380.00**

SPECIFICATIONS COMANCHE III

CALIBERS:	357 Magnum
BARREL LENGTH:	4 and 6-inch
NUMBER OF SHOTS:	6 shots
FRAME:	Forged high hensile strength steel. Serrated front and back strap.
ACTION:	Double-action.
TRIGGER:	Wide grooved target trigger
HAMMER:	Wide spur target hammer with serrated gripping surface.
SIGHTS:	Square notch rear sight with windage and elevation adjustments; serrated quick-draw front sight on ramp.
SIGHT RADIUS:	With 4-inch barrel—5³/₄″; with 6-inch barrel—7³/₄″.
GRIPS:	Oversized target, walnut. Checkered.
WEIGHT:	w/4″ bbl.—2 lbs., 4ozs. w/6″ bbl.—2 lbs., 7 ozs.
OVER-ALL LENGTH:	With 4-inch barrel—9¹/₄″; with 6-inch barrel—11″.
FINISH:	High-polished, deep blue. Deluxe models; satin chrome (.357 w/4″ & 6″ bbl.)
SAFETY FEATURE:	The hammer is mounted on an eccentric cam, the position of which is controlled by the trigger. Only when the latter is fully depressed can the firing pin contact the primer.

LLAMA REVOLVERS

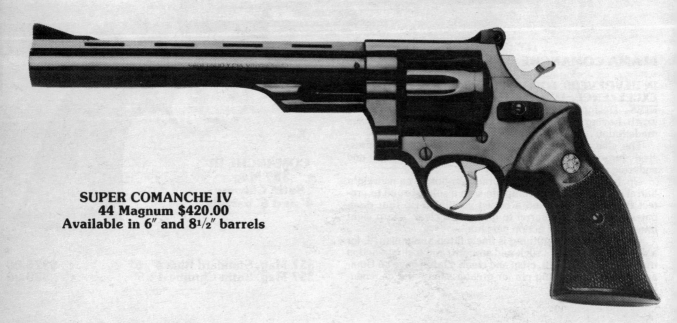

SUPER COMANCHE IV
44 Magnum $420.00
Available in 6″ and 8½″ barrels

LLAMA SUPER COMANCHE 44 MAGNUM

If ever a handgun was conceived, designed and built to fit the requirements of big bore handgunners, this one is it. The frame, for example, is massive. The weight and balance are such that the heavy recoil generated by the powerful .44 Magnum cartridge is easily and comfortably controlled.

Instead of a single cylinder latch, the Llama has two. In addition to the conventional center pin at the rear of the ratchet, there's a second latch up front that locks the crane to the frame, resulting in a safer, more secure lockup. The hammer is mounted on an eccentric cam, the position of which is controlled by the trigger. Only when the trigger is fully depressed can the firing pin contact the primer.

To minimize leading and to enhance accuracy, Llama has perfected a new honing process that imparts a mirror-smooth finish to the bore.

Additional features include a precision-lapped, heavyweight bull barrel with target accuracy. A matte finish, ventilated rib for more efficient heat dissipation, less glare and less target mirage. Oversized grips that soak up recoil for better control and a faster recovery for a second shot. A super-wide trigger for a more comfortable, controlled pull.

A three-point crane/cylinder provides support for a stronger, more rigid lockup.

The finish is highly polished and deeply blued with genuine walnut grips.

SPECIFICATIONS

	Super Comanche .44 Mag.	
Type:	Double action	
Calibers:	.44 Magnum	
Barrel Length:	6″	8½″
Number of Shots:	6	
Frame:	Forged high tensile strength steel.	
Trigger:	Smooth extra wide	
Hammer:	Wide spur, deep positive serrations.	
Sights:	Rear-click adjustable for windage and elevation, leaf serrated to cut down on glare. Front-ramped blade.	
Sight Radius:	8″	10³⁄₈″
Grips:	Oversized target, walnut. Checkered.	
Weight:	3 lbs., 2 ozs.	3 lbs., 8 ozs.
Over-all Length:	11³⁄₄″	14¹⁄₂″
Finish:	High polished, deep blue	

LLAMA AUTOMATIC PISTOLS

Llama's newest 9mm single action is a compact version of its 9mm semi-auto, a gun which over the years has earned the kind of trust that has made it the issued side arm of countless military and law enforcement agencies throughout the world

The small-frame Llama models, available in 22 LR, 32 and 380 Auto., are impressively compact handguns. All frames are precision machined of high strength steel, yet weigh a featherlight 23 ounces. A full complement of safeties . . . side lever, half-cock and grip . . . is incorporated.

Every small-frame Llama is complete with ventilated rib, wide-spur serrated target-type hammer and adjustable rear sight. NEW. Also available in 45 caliber automatic.

The large-frame Llama models, available in potent 45 ACP, are completely crafted of high strength steel.

NEW 9mm PARABELLUM STANDARD BLUE
$365.00

LLAMA COMPACT 45
$365.00

LLAMA SMALL-FRAME AUTOMATIC WITH DEEP BLUE FINISH
22, 32 and 380 Caliber
$315.00

LLAMA AUTOMATIC PISTOLS

LLAMA SMALL-FRAME AUTOMATIC PISTOL IN SATIN CHROME FINISH
22 and 380 Caliber
$390.00

LLAMA Automatic Pistol Specifications

	Small Frame Auto Pistols		Compact Frame Auto Pistols		Large Frame Auto Pistols
TYPE:	Small Frame Auto Pistols		Compact Frame Auto Pistols		Large Frame Auto Pistols
CALIBERS:	22 LR	380 Auto.	9mm Parabellum	45 Auto	45 Auto.
FRAME:	Precision machined form high strength steel. Serrated front strap, checkered (curved) backstrap.		Precision machined form high strength steel. Serrated front strap, checkered (curved) backstrap.		Precision machined from high strength steel. Plain front strap, checkered (curved) backstrap.
TRIGGER:	Serrated		Serrated		Serrated
HAMMER:	External. Wide spur, serrated.		External. Wide spur, serrated.		External. Wide spur, serrated.
OPERATION:	Straight blow-back.		Locked breech.		Locked breech.
LOADED CHAMBER INDICATOR:	No	Yes	No	No	Yes
SAFETIES:	Side lever thumb safety, grip safety.		Side lever thumb safety, grip safety.		Side lever thumb safety, grip safety.
GRIPS:	Modified thumbrest black plastic grips.		Genuine walnut on blue models. Genuine teakwood on satin chrome.		Genuine walnut on blue models. Genuine teakwood on satin chrome.
SIGHTS:	Square notch rear, and Patridge-type front, screw adjustable rear sight for windage		Square notch rear, and Patridge-type front, screw adjustable rear sight for windage.		Square notch rear, and Patridge-type front, screw adjustable rear sight for windage.
SIGHT RADIUS:	4¼"		6¼"		6¼"
MAGAZINE CAPACITY:	8-shot	7-shot	9-shot	7-shot	7-shot
WEIGHT:	23 ounces		34 ounces		36 ounces
BARREL LENGTH:	3¹¹/₁₆"		5"		5"
OVERALL LENGTH:	6½"		7⅞"		8½"
HEIGHT:	4⅜"		5⁷/₁₆"		5½"
FINISH:	Std. models; High-polished, deep blue. Deluxe models; satin chrome (22, 380, 45)		Std. models; High-polished, deep blue. Deluxe models; satin chrome (22, 380, 45)		Std. models; High-polished, deep blue. Deluxe models; satin chrome (22, 380, 45)

LLAMA AUTOMATIC PISTOLS

Machined and polished to perfection. These truly magnificent firearms come complete with ventilated rib for maximum heat dissipation, wide-spur checkered target-type hammer, adjustable rear sight and genuine walnut grips.

In addition to High Polished Deep Blue, the following superb handguns are available in handsome Satin Chrome 22 LR, 32, 380 Auto., 45 ACP.

**LLAMA LARGE-FRAME
AUTOMATIC PISTOL IN
SATIN CHROME FINISH**
45 Auto Caliber
$485.00

**LLAMA LARGE-FRAME
AUTOMATIC WITH
DEEP BLUE FINISH**
45 Auto Caliber
$365.00
38 SUPER $365.00

LLAMA PISTOLS

MODEL M-82 (9mm) DOUBLE ACTION
$975.00

SPECIFICATIONS

Caliber: 9mm Parabellum
Magazine: 15 cartridges (15 + 1 shot)
Barrel length: 4¼″
No. of barreling grooves: 6
Overall length: 8″
Height: 5⁵⁄₁₆″
Maximum width: 1³⁄₈″
Weight: 39 oz. (empty)
Sights: High visibility, 3-dot sights; rear sight drift adjustable
Sight radius: 6″
Grips: Matte black polymer
Stocks: Plastic
Finish: Blued satin

After nearly a decade of research, development and testing, the new Llama M-82 is being offered to the gun buying public. Representing the state-of-the-art in double action, semiauto pistol design, this handgun offers a unique blend of highly innovative technical features, combined with the kind of ergonomic design and practical performance that are so important in day-to-day use. It's the kind demanded by military and law enforcement personnel, as well as by competitive combat shooters and otherwise knowledgeable handgunners.

Whatever criteria are used in judging a DA semiauto—whether accuracy, reliability, simplicity of design, looks, compactness, quality of fit, or finish—all are effectively combined in the M-82. The following features indicate why pistol experts are already hailing this new Llama as the world's finest production handgun.

1. MINIMAL BARREL/SLIDE DISPLACEMENT: As the slide moves rearward during the firing cycle, the lineal displacement required to unlock the action is but a fraction of that in other double action designs. This translates into less wear and tear on the mechanism, as well as allowing tighter tolerances. That, in turn, means greater accuracy, greater durability.

2. POSITIVE SAFETY MECHANISM: Even when at rest and with the safety disengaged, the hammer does not contact the firing pin, making this gun one of the safest handguns available today.

3. TWIN LUG LOCK-UP: Unlike other DA's, which rely on a single locking lug engagement in the ceiling of the slide, the M-82 has two lugs in the "three and nine o'clock" position. This unique system provides greater strength, greater rigidity. . . . and greater accuracy.

4. FULL-LENGTH GUIDE RAILS: For more positive, accurate alignment of barrel, slide and frame, the Llama's slide is engaged by guide rails the entire length of its movement (some autos allow as much as two inches of unsupported slide movement).

5. MAXIMUM FIREPOWER: The M-82's staggered magazine holds 15 rounds, plus one in the chamber. This potent firepower is made possible by an overall grip dimension small enough to fit comfortably in the average hand.

6. RECESSED BREECH FACE: Unlike other guns featuring flat breech faces, the Llama's is recessed, much like most modern high-powered rifles. This additional support in the critical case head area means greater safety.

7. AMBIDEXTROUS SAFETY: Allows the M-82 to be used with equal speed and convenience by both right- and left-handed shooters.

8. CHANGEABLE MAGAZINE RELEASE: Normally positioned on the left side of the grip for right-handed shooters, the clip release button on the M-82 can be changed easily to the other side for southpaw use.

9. ARTICULATED FIRING PIN: Another excellent Llama feature is its virtually unbreakable firing pin. In fact, it's guaranteed not to break—for life.

10. COMPACT SIZE: Despite its 16-shot capability, the M-82 is neither heavy nor bulky. Its overall dimensions are short—8¼″ in length, 5⁵⁄₆″ in height, and 1³⁄₈″ in extreme width. Empty weight is 39 ounces.

11. ENLARGED EJECTION PORT: To preclude any sort of ejection problems brought about by variation in loads or in slide velocity, the ejection port is slightly oversize.

12. MODULAR GRIP DESIGN: The hammer strut and main spring are housed in a separate sub-assembly which easily detaches from the frame for routine cleaning and maintenance.

13. INSTANT DISASSEMBLY: The M-82 can be field stripped in less than five seconds—without tools.

LLAMA PISTOLS

LLAMA M-87 COMP PISTOL (9mm)
$1450.00

Llama, located in the heart of the Basque region of Spain, has been manufacturing high-grade quality handguns since 1903 and has recently made a substantial investment in high tech computer-controlled machining centers. This 21st-century hi-tech machinery has enabled the factory to produce the "match ready" LLAMA M-87 Comp pistol designed specifically for the professional shooter. All of the features demanded by the serious competitive shooter are already built into the M-87 so that it is virtually "out-of-the-box" ready for the range.

COMPENSATOR: Full profile • reduces muzzle lift • increased speed to get back "on target" • dual port internal expansion chamber • reduces recoil.

TRIGGER: Clean • crisp • smooth • positive • creep-free • concave, checkered and extended trigger guard.

SAFETIES: Manual thumb safety allows for quick release • oversized and extended lever for speed • conventional hammer block safety with ambidextrous (dual) levers.

MAGAZINE: 15 rounds • ambidextrous magazine release button is oversized and extended • tapered top allows for quick insertion • bumper pad ensures positive seating • pad also minimizes damage from dropping while rapid firing.

FRAME: Investment casting from Llama's state-of-the-art investment casting factory • beavertail extension for greater hand control and comfort • magazine well flared and beveled, providing for rapid magazine insertion.

SIGHTS: Low-profile combat sights • rapid target acquisition.

TILTING-BLOCK LOCK UP MECHANISM: Operates "in line" with the barrel • eliminates downward drop to unlock • no separate barrel bushing, which in turn provides a more solid and stable enclosure at the muzzle for greater accuracy.

SPECIFICATIONS

Caliber: 9mm double action
Capacity: 15 round magazine plus 1 in the chamber
Finish: Satin-nickel finish frame: matte black grip panels, operating levers, slide and compensator
Front sights: Low-profile combat; micrometer click; adjustable for windage
Grips: 2-piece polymer
Barrel length: $5\frac{1}{4}''$
Overall length: $9\frac{1}{2}''$
Weight: 40 oz.

MAGNUM RESEARCH
DESERT EAGLE PISTOL

SPECIFICATIONS	.357 MAGNUM	41/44 MAGNUM
Length, with 6 inch barrel	10.6 inches	10.6 inches
Height	5.6 inches	5.7 inches
Width	1.25 inches	1.25 inches
Trigger reach	2.75 inches	2.75 inches
Sight radius (with 6 inch barrel)	8.5 inches	8.5 inches
Additional available barrels	14 inch	14 inch & 10 inch
Weight	See below	See below
Bore rifling — Six rib	Polygonal: 1 turn in 14 inches	Polygonal: 1 turn in 18 inches
Method of operation	Gas operated	Gas operated
Method of locking	Rotating bolt	Rotating bolt
Magazine capacity	9 rounds (plus one in chamber)	8 rounds (plus one in chamber)

DESERT EAGLE — WEIGHT TABLES
357 Magnum

Frame	Without Magazine		With Empty Magazine	
	6" Barrel	14" Barrel	6" Barrel	14" Barrel
	ounces	ounces	ounces	ounces
Aluminum	47.8	55.0	51.9	59.1
Steel	58.3	65.5	62.4	96.6
Stainless	58.3	65.5	62.4	69.6

41/44 Magnum

Frame	Without Magazine		With Empty Magazine	
	6" Barrel	14" Barrel	6" Barrel	14" Barrel
	ounces	ounces	ounces	ounces
Aluminum	52.3	61.0	56.4	65.1
Steel	62.8	71.5	66.9	75.6
Stainless	62.8	71.5	66.9	75.6

**357 MAGNUM $629.00
(Alloy Frame Optional)
$629.00 w/Alloy Frame
$669.00 w/Stainless Steel
$799.00 w/14" barrel**

**DESERT EAGLE
44 MAGNUM SEMIAUTO PISTOL
(Standard Parkerized Finish)
$749.00 w/Alloy Frame
$789.00 w/Stainless Steel
$749.00 w/6" barrel
$889.00 w/10" barrel
$899.00 w/14" barrel
Note: Deduct $10.00 for
all 41 Magnum models**

**DESERT EAGLE
44 MAGNUM (14" Barrel)**

MITCHELL ARMS

SINGLE ACTION ARMY REVOLVERS

The Mitchell Arms Single Action Army Model Revolver is a modern version of the original "gun that won the West," adopted by the U.S. Army in 1873.½ Faithful to the original design, these revolvers are made of modern materials and use up-to-date technology; for example, a special safety device is built into the hammer assembly as a backstop to the traditional safety.

SPECIFICATIONS
Calibers: 22 LR, 357 Mag., 44 Mag., 45 Colt
Barrel lengths: 4³/₄", 5¹/₂", 6¹/₂", (7¹/₂" in 357 Mag., 44 Mag. and 45 Colt)
Frame: Forged steel, fully machined with traditional color casehardening. Two-piece style backstrap made of solid brass.
Action: Traditional single action with safety position and half-cock position for loading and unloading.
Sights: Rear sight is fully adjustable for windage and elevation. Front sight is two-step ramp style with non-glare serrations. Fixed sight models feature deep notch with fixed blade front sight.
Grip: One-piece solid walnut grip built in the style of the old black powder revolvers.
Accuracy: High-grade steel barrel honed for accuracy with smooth lands and grooves; precise alignment between cylinder and barrel. Fully qualified for big game hunting or silhouette shooting.

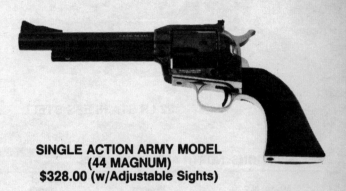

**SINGLE ACTION ARMY MODEL
(44 MAGNUM)
$328.00 (w/Adjustable Sights)**

Prices:
Fixed Sight Models $279.69-310.00
Target (Adjust.) Sight Models 310.00-359.00
Dual Cylinder Models (Target Sights) 345.00-359.95
Also available:
SPECIAL SILHOUETTE MODELS 44 Magnum/44-40 caliber; 10", 12" and 18" barrel lengths. **$395.95**

MOA MAXIMUM PISTOL

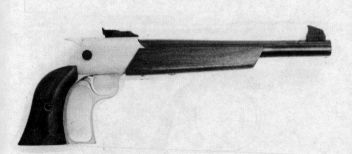

MAXIMUM

This single-shot pistol with its unique falling block action performs like a finely tuned rifle. The single piece receiver of chromoly steel is mated to a Douglas barrel for optimum accuracy and strength.

SPECIFICATIONS
Calibers: 22 Hornet to 358 Win.
Barrel lengths: 8³/₄", 10¹/₂" and 14"
Weight: 3 lbs. 8 oz. (8³/₄" bbl.); 3 lbs. 13 oz. (10¹/₂" bbl.); 4 lbs. 3 oz. (14" bbl.)
Price: $499.00

NORTH AMERICAN ARMS REVOLVERS

MINI-REVOLVERS

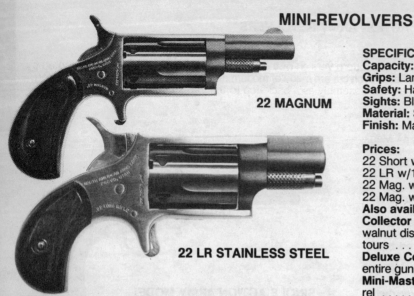

22 MAGNUM

22 LR STAINLESS STEEL

SPECIFICATIONS (Standard on all models)
Capacity: 5-shot cylinder
Grips: Laminated rosewood
Safety: Half-cock safety
Sights: Blade front (integral w/barrel); fixed, notched rear
Material: Stainless steel
Finish: Matte with brushed sides

Prices:
22 Short w/1⅛″ or 1⅝″ barrel	$138.00
22 LR w/1⅛″ or 1⅝″ barrel	139.00
22 Mag. w/1⅛″ or 1⅝″ barrel	158.00
22 Mag. w/2½″ barrel	174.00

Also available:
Collector Set—three-gun set with matching serial numbers, walnut display case, high polish finish w/matte contours . . . . **$630.00.**
Deluxe Collector 3-Gun Set includes high polish finish over entire gun . . . . **$681.00.**
Mini-Master 22 LR or Mag. w/4″ heavy vent barrel . . . . **$250.00.**

SPECIFICATIONS: NORTH AMERICAN ARMS

Model No.	Weight	Barrel Length	Overall Length	Overall Height	Overall Width
NAA-22S	4 oz.	1⅛″	4″	2⅜″	¾″
NAA-22SL	4.2 oz.	1⅝″	4⅜″	2⅜″	¾″
NAA-22SE	4.5 oz.	2½″	5⅜″	2⅜″	¾″
NAA-22LR	4.5 oz.	1⅛″	4¼″	2⅜″	¹³⁄₁₆″
NAA-22LLR	4.6 oz.	1⅝″	4¾″	2⅜″	¹³⁄₁₆″
NAA-22ELR	5.1 oz.	2½″	5¾″	2⅜″	¹³⁄₁₆″
*NAA-22MS	5.9 oz.	1⅛″	5″	2⅞″	⅞″
*NAA-22M	6.2 oz.	1⅝″	5⅜″	2⅞″	⅞″
*NAA-22ML	6.6 oz.	2½″	6⅜″	2⅞″	⅞″

* Available with Conversion Cylinder chambered for .22 long rifle.

RAVEN ARMS

MODEL P-25
$69.95

SPECIFICATIONS
Caliber: 25 Auto
Barrel length: 2⁷⁄₁₆″
Overall length: 4³⁄₄″
Height: 3⁷⁄₁₆″
Weight: (empty) 15 oz.
Capacity: 6 rounds
Features: Hand-polished surfaces; walnut grips; choice of finish (nickel, blue, chrome); all parts made in the U.S.

MODEL P-25

REMINGTON LONG-RANGE PISTOLS

**MODEL XP-100 BOLT
ACTION PISTOL**

"XP-100" LONG-RANGE CUSTOM PISTOLS

Remington's Model XP-100 Custom pistol is now chambered for two additional cartridges: the 6mm BR Rem. and the 250 Savage. Other cartridge options include the 223 Rem., 7mm BR Rem., 7mm-08 and 35 Rem. All XP-100 Custom pistols are hand-crafted from select English walnut in right- and left-hand versions. All chamberings except the 35 Rem. (standard barrel only) are offered in a choice of standard 14½" barrels with adj. rear leaf and front bead sights or 15½" barrels without sights. Receivers are drilled and tapped for scope mounts. Average weight is 4½ lbs. for standard models and 5½ lbs. for heavy barrel models. **Price: $907.00.**

MODEL XP-100 SILHOUETTE TARGET AND "VARMINT SPECIAL" PISTOLS

These unique single-shot centerfire, bolt-action pistols have become legends for their strength, precision, balance and accuracy. Now chambered for the 35 Rem. and 223 Rem. with a 14½" barrel, they are also available in 7mm BR, which many feel is the ideal factory-made metallic silhouette handgun for "unlimited" events. All XP-100 handguns have one-piece Du Pont "Zytel" nylon stocks with universal grips, two-position thumb safety switches, receivers drilled and tapped for scope mounts or receiver sights, and match-type grooved triggers.

Calibers: 35 Rem., 7mm BR Rem., 223 Rem. **Barrel length:** 14½". **Overall length:** 21¼". **Weight:** 4⅛ lbs. **Prices: $380.00** (7mm BR Rem.); **$393.00** (35. Rem.); **$373.00** (223 Rem.).

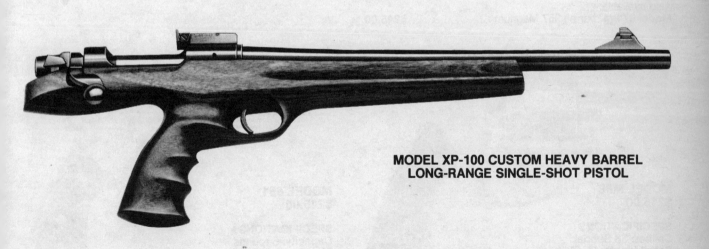

**MODEL XP-100 CUSTOM HEAVY BARREL
LONG-RANGE SINGLE-SHOT PISTOL**

ROSSI REVOLVERS

MODEL 68

SPECIFICATIONS
Caliber: 38 Special
Barrel length: 2″ and 3″
Overall length: 6½″ (2″ barrel); 7½″ (3″ barrel)
Weight: 21 oz. (2″ barrel); 23 oz. (3″ barrel)
Capacity: 5 rounds
Finish: Blue or nickel
Price: w/3″ barrel **$180.00**
       w/2″ barrel **185.00**
       w/3″ barrel (nickel) **195.00**

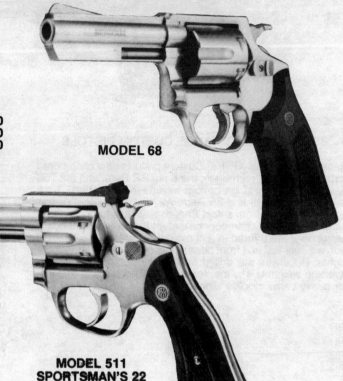

MODEL 68

MODEL 511 SPORTSMAN'S 22
$235.00

SPECIFICATIONS
Caliber: 22 LR
Barrel length: 4″
Overall length: 9″
Weight: 30 oz.
Capacity: 6 rounds
Finish: Stainless steel

**MODEL 511
SPORTSMAN'S 22**

MODEL M951 (not shown)
$225.00

SPECIFICATIONS
Caliber: 38 Special
Capacity: 6 rounds
Barrel length: 3″ and 4″
Overall length: 8″ and 9″
Weight: 27½ oz. and 30 oz.
Also available:
Model 971 (4″ barrel) 357 Magnum **$245.00**

MODEL M88
$215.00

SPECIFICATIONS
Caliber: 38 Special
Barrel length: 2″, 3″
Capacity: 5 rounds, swing-out cylinder
Weight: 21 oz.
Sights: Ramp front, square notch rear adjustable for windage
Finish: Stainless steel

MODEL 851
$245.00

SPECIFICATIONS
Capacity: 6 rounds
Barrel length: 3″ and 4″
Overall length: 8″ and 9″
Weight: 27½ oz. and 30 oz.
Frame: Medium

RUGER REVOLVERS

ALLOY STEEL REDHAWK

The popular Ruger Redhawk® double-action revolver is now available in an alloy steel model with blued finish in .41 Magnum and .44 Magnum calibers. The newest Redhawk, like the stainless steel model, is constructed of hardened chromemoly and other alloy steels. The revolver is satin polished to a high lustre and finished in a rich blue.

Catalog Number	Caliber	Barrel Length	Overall Length	Approx. Weight (Ounces)	Price
RUGER REDHAWK REVOLVER					
RH-415	41 Mag.	5¹/₂″	11″	52	$397.00
RH-41	41 Mag.	7¹/₂″	13″	52	397.00
RH-41R*	41 Mag.	7¹/₂″	13″	52	430.00
RH-445	44 Mag.	5¹/₂″	11″	52	397.00
RH-44	44 Mag.	7¹/₂″	13″	52	397.00
RH-44R*	44 Mag.	7¹/₂″	13″	52	430.00

*Scope model, with Integral Scope Mounts, 1″ Ruger Scope rings.

The **Super Redhawk** double-action revolver in stainless steel features a heavy extended frame with 7¹/₂″ and 9¹/₂″ barrels. Cushioned grip panels contain Goncalo Alves wood grip panel inserts to provide comfortable, nonslip hold.

REDHAWK DOUBLE-ACTION REVOLVER

There is no other revolver like the Ruger Redhawk. Knowledgeable sportsmen reaching for perfection in a big bore revolver will find that the Redhawk demonstrates its superiority at the target, whether silhouette shooting or hunting. Scope sight model shown above incorporates the patented Ruger integral Scope Mounting System with 1″ stainless steel Ruger scope rings.

Catalog Number	Caliber	Barrel Length	Overall Length	Approx. Weight (Ounces)	Price
RUGER REDHAWK REVOLVER					
KRH-415	41 Mag.	5¹/₂″	11″	52	$447.50
KRH-41	41 Mag.	7¹/₂″	13″	52	447.50
KRH-41R*	41 Mag.	7¹/₂″	13″	52	482.50
KRH-445	44 Mag.	5¹/₂″	11″	52	447.50
KRH-44	44 Mag.	7¹/₂″	13″	52	447.50
KRH-44R*	44 Mag.	7¹/₂″	13″	52	482.50

*Scope model, with Integral Scope Mounts, 1″ Stainless Steel Ruger Scope rings.

SUPER REDHAWK
DOUBLE ACTION REVOLVER

SPECIFICATIONS
Caliber: 44 Magnum
Barrel length: 7¹/₂″ and 9¹/₂″
Overall length: 13″ w/7¹/₂″ bbl.; 15″ w/9¹/₂″ bbl.
Weight (empty): 3 lbs. 5 oz. (7¹/₂″ bbl.); 3 lbs. 10 oz. (9¹/₂″ bbl.)
Sight radius: 9¹/₂″ (7¹/₂″ bbl.); 11¹/₄″ (9¹/₂″ bbl.)
Finish: Stainless steel; satin polished

KSRH-7 (7¹/₂″ barrel) $510.00
KSRH-9 (9¹/₂″ barrel) 510.00

RUGER REVOLVERS

BLACKHAWK SINGLE-ACTION REVOLVER

SPECIFICATIONS

Caliber: 357 Magnum (interchangeable with 38 Special); 41 Magnum
Barrel lengths: 4⁵/₈″ and 6¹/₂″
Frame: Chrome molybdenum steel with bridge reinforcement and rear-sight guard
Springs: Music wire springs throughout
Weight: 40 oz. with 4⁵/₈″ barrel and 42 oz. with 6¹/₂″ barrel (in 357 Mag.); 38 oz. with 4⁵/₈″ barrel and 40 oz. with 6¹/₂″ barrel (41 Mag.)
Sights: Patridge style, ramp front matted blade ¹/₈″ wide; rear sight click adjustable for windage and elevation
Grips: Genuine walnut
Finish: Polished and blued or stainless steel (357 Mag. only)

Catalog No./Specifications		Prices
BN-34	357 Mag.; 38 Special interchangeably; 4⁵/₈″ barrel	$297.50
KBN-34	Same as BN-34 in stainless steel	366.50
BN-36	357 Mag.; 38 Special interchangeably; 6¹/₂″ barrel	297.50
KBN-36	Same as BN-36 in stainless steel	366.50
BN-34X/36X	Same as BN-34/BN-36 fitted with 9mm Parabellum extra cylinder (not available in stainless steel)	311.25
BN-41	41 Magnum; 4⁵/₈″ barrel	297.50
BN-42	41 Magnum; 6¹/₂″ barrel	297.50
BN-44	45 Long Colt; 4⁵/₈″ barrel	297.50
BN-45	45 Long Colt; 7¹/₂″ barrel	297.50
S-45N	44 Magnum; 5¹/₂″ barrel	343.50

SUPER BLACKHAWK SINGLE-ACTION REVOLVER

SPECIFICATIONS

Caliber: 44 Magnum; interchangeable with 44 Special
Barrel: 7¹/₂″, 10¹/₂″
Frame: Chrome molybdenum steel with bridge reinforcement and rear sight guard
Springs: Music wire springs throughout
Weight: 48 oz. (7¹/₂″ bbl.) and 51 oz. (10¹/₂″ bbl.)
Sights: Patridge style, ramp front matted blade ¹/₈″ wide; rear sight click and adjustable for windage and elevation
Grip frame: Chrome molybdenum steel enlarged and contoured to minimize recoil effect

Trigger: Wide spur, low contour, sharply serrated for convenient cocking with minimum disturbance of grip
Overall length: 13³/₈″
Finish: Stainless steel

KS47N	7¹/₂″ barrel with steel grip frame	$375.25
KS411N	10¹/₂″ barrel with steel grip frame	375.25
S47N	7¹/₂″ barrel, with steel grip frame	343.50
S411N	10¹/₂″ barrel, with steel grip frame	343.50

RUGER REVOLVERS

NEW MODEL SUPER SINGLE-SIX REVOLVER

Caliber: 22 LR (fitted with WMR cylinder). **Barrel lengths:** 4⅝", 5½", 6½", 9½" (stainless steel model in 5½" and 6½" lengths only). **Weight** (approx.): 33 oz. (with 5½" barrel). **Sights:** Patridge-type ramp front sight; rear sight click adjustable for elevation and windage; protected by integral frame ribs. **Finish:** Blue or stainless steel. **Price: $255.00.** In stainless steel: **$321.00.**

NEW MODEL SINGLE-SIX SSM™ REVOLVER
$244.75

Caliber: 32 H&R Magnum; also handles 32 S&W and 32 S&W Long. **Barrel lengths:** 4⅝", 5½", 6½", 9½". **Weight** (approx.): 34 oz. with 6½" barrel.

NEW MODEL BISLEY REVOLVER
$354.50 (not shown)

Calibers: 357 Mag., 41 Mag., 44 Mag., 45 Long Colt. **Barrel length:** 7½". **Weight** (approx.): 48 oz. **Sights:** Adjustable rear sight, ramp-style front sight. **Special features:** Unfluted cylinder rollmarked with classic foliate engraving pattern (or fluted cylinder without engraving); hammer is low with smoothly curved, deeply checkered wide spur positioned for easy cocking.

Also available in 22LR and 32 Mag. **Weight:** 41 oz. **Barrel length:** 6½". **Sights:** Adjustable or fixed. **Price: $298.00.**

MODEL BN-31
BLACKHAWK SINGLE-ACTION REVOLVER
(In 30 Carbine Caliber) $286.00

Caliber: 30 Carbine. **Barrel length:** 7½"; 6-groove rifling; 20-inch twist. **Overall length:** 13⅛". **Weight:** 44 oz. **Springs:** Unbreakable music wire springs used throughout; no leaf springs. **Screws:** For security, Nylok® screws are used at all five locations that might be affected by recoil. **Sights:** Patridge-style, ramp front sight with ⅛" wide blade, matted to eliminate glare; rear sight adjustable for windage and elevation. **Ignition system:** Independent alloy steel firing pin, mounted in frame, transfer bar. **Frame:** Same cylinder frame as 44 Mag. Super Blackhawk. **Grips:** Genuine walnut. **Finish:** Polished, blued and anodized.

RUGER

MODEL P-85 AUTO PISTOL

MODEL P-85 AUTO PISTOL

SPECIFICATIONS
Caliber: 9mm. **Action:** Double action. **Capacity:** 15 rounds. **Weight:** 2.38 lbs. (loaded). **Barrel length:** 4½". **Overall length:** 7.84". **Sight radius:** 6.12". **Mechanism type:** Recoil-operated, semiautomatic. **Breech locking mode:** Tilting barrel, link actuated.

P-85 . . . . **$325.00**
P-85C w/plastic case and extra magazine **355.00**

MARK II GOVERNMENT TARGET MODEL (not shown)

SPECIFICATIONS
Caliber: 22 Rimfire. **Capacity:** 10-shot magazine. **Barrel length:** 6⅞" bull barrel. **Overall length:** 11⅛". **Weight:** 47½ oz. (loaded). **Sight radius:** 9¼"; laser sighting device.

MODEL MK678G **$300.25**

MODEL SP101

MODEL SP101 5-SHOT REVOLVER

SPECIFICATIONS
Calibers: 38 Special and 38 Special + P. **Barrel lengths:** 2¼" and 3". **Weight:** 1 lb. 9 oz. (2¼" barrel); 1 lb. 11 oz. (3" barrel). **Capacity:** 5 rounds. **Features:** One-piece Monsanto Santoprene grips and Xenoy resin inserts provide a secure hold and help reduce recoil. When cylinder is in firing position, it is securely locked to frame in two places, assuring proper cylinder/barrel alignment. Hammer locking mechanism is contained within trigger guard and inserted into frame as a single unit. Can be field-stripped in seconds without special tools.

KSP-182 (2¼" barrel) **$370.00**
KSP-183 (3" barrel) **370.00**

GP-100 357 MAGNUM

The GP-100 series is presented as a complete family of double-action models in three basic frame sizes handling all popular caliber handgun ammunition, from 22 rimfire to 44 Magnum. The GP-100 is designed for the unlimited use of 357 Magnum ammunition in all factory loadings; it combines strength and reliability with accuracy and shooting comfort.

Now available: **GP-100 COMPACT** with 3" barrel and fixed sight. **Price: $360.00.** In stainless steel: **$390.00.**

GP-100 357 MAGNUM

SPECIFICATIONS

BLUED FINISH GP-100 $375.00*		STAINLESS STEEL GP-100 $405.00*	
CAT. NO.	BARREL	CAT. NO.	BARREL
GP-141	4" Heavy	KGP-141	4" Heavy
GP-160	6"	KGP-160	6"
GP-161	6" Heavy	KGP-161	6" Heavy

* For fixed sights, deduct **$15.00**

RUGER 22 AUTOMATIC PISTOLS

**RUGER MARK II
STANDARD MODEL**

**RUGER MARK II
TARGET MODEL**

**RUGER MARK II
BULL BARREL MODEL**

SPECIFICATIONS
Caliber: 22 Long Rifle only, standard or high velocity. **Barrel:** 4³/₄″ or 6″ length; medium weight; 6-groove rifling; 14″ twist. **Weight:** 2¹/₄ lbs. with 4³/₄″ barrel. **Overall length:** 8⁵/₁₆″ with 4³/₄″ barrel; 10⁵/₁₆″ with 6″ barrel. **Sights:** Front sight is fixed, .093″ wide blade Patridge-type; square notch rear sight is dovetail mounted and can be adjusted for windage. **Sight radius:** 7¹/₂″ with 4³/₄″ barrel. Catalog No. MK-4 (4³/₄″ barrel) blued finish, MK-6 (6″ barrel) blued finish, KMK-4 (4³/₄″ barrel) Stainless Steel; KMK-6 (6″ barrel) Stainless Steel.

MK-4, MK-6	$208.00
KMK-4, KMK-6	277.00

SPECIFICATIONS
Same as for Mark II Model with the following exceptions. **Barrel:** 6⁷/₈″ tapered, button rifled. **Weight:** Approx. 2⁵/₈ lbs. **Overall length:** 11¹/₈″. **Sights:** Patridge-type front blade, .125″ wide, undercut to prevent glare; rear sight with click adjustments for windage and elevation. **Sight radius:** 9¹/₄″ for 6⁷/₈″ barrel.

MK-678 Blued	$259.75
KMK-678 Stainless steel	329.00
MK678G Bull barrel	300.25

The Mark II Bull barrel pistol is identical to the Mark II Target Model except that it is equipped with a heavier Bull barrel offered in two lengths, 5¹/₂ inches/10 inches. The Bull barrel configuration was developed to meet the needs of those shooters who prefer a greater concentration of weight at the muzzle. The longer barrel model meets all IHMSA regulations.

SPECIFICATIONS
Same as for Mark II model with the following exceptions: **Barrel:** 5¹/₂″ or 10″; button rifled; shorter barrel untapered, longer barrel has slight taper. **Weight:** Approx. 2⁵/₇ lbs. with 5¹/₂″ barrel; 3¹/₄ lbs. with 10″ barrel. **Sights:** Patridge-type front sight. Rear sight with click adjustments for windage and elevation. **Sight radius:** 7⁷/₈″ for 5¹/₂″ barrel, 12³/₈″ for 10″ barrel; blued finish. Catalog No. MK-512 5¹/₂″ barrel and MK-10 10″ barrel.

MK-512 and MK-10 Blued	$259.75
KMK-512 and KMK-10 Stainless steel	329.00

SIG SAUER DOUBLE ACTION PISTOLS

MODEL 220 "EUROPEAN"

MODEL 226

SPECIFICATIONS
Caliber: 9mm Parabellum
Capacity: 15 rounds
Barrel length: 4.4″
Overall length: 7³/₄″
Weight (empty): 26.5 oz.
Finish: Blue
Price: $780.00
        880.00 with "Siglite night sights
        815.00 with K-Kote

MODEL 220 "EUROPEAN"

SPECIFICATIONS
Caliber: 38 Super, 9mm Parabellum, 45 ACP
Capacity: 9 rounds; 7 rounds in 45 ACP
Barrel length: 4.4″
Overall length: 7.79″
Weight (empty): 26¹/₂ oz.; 25.7 oz. in 45 ACP
Finish: Blue
Prices:
In 9mm Para. & 38 Super $695.00
In 45 ACP 720.00
Electroless nickel w/"Siglite" night sights 890.00
"AMERICAN" Model in 45 ACP 720.00
    With "Siglite" night sights 820.00

MODEL 225 (not shown)

SPECIFICATIONS
Caliber: 9mm Parabellum
Capacity: 8 rounds
Barrel length: 3.85″
Overall length: 7″
Weight (empty): 26.1 oz.
Finish: Blue
Price: $750.00
        850.00 with "Siglite" night sights

MODEL 226

MODEL 230

MODEL 230

SPECIFICATIONS
Caliber: 380ACP
Capacity: 7 rounds
Barrel length: 3.6″
Overall length: 6.6″
Weight (empty): 16¹/₄ oz.; 20.8 oz. in stainless steel
Finish: Blue and stainless steel
Price: $495.00 in blue
        575.00 in stainless steel

SMITH & WESSON AUTO PISTOLS

MODEL 422
22 SINGLE ACTION
$199.80 (Fixed Sight)
$249.75 (Adjustable Sight)

Caliber: 22 LR
Capacity: 10 round (magazine furnished)
Barrel length: 4¹/₂″ and 6″
Overall length: 7¹/₂″ (4¹/₂″ barrel) and 9″ (6″ barrel)
Weight: 22 oz. (4¹/₂″ barrel) and 23 oz. (6″ barrel)
Stock: Plastic (field version) and checkered walnut w/S&W monogram (target version)
Front sight: Serrated ramp w/.125″ blade (field version); Patridge w/.125″ blade (target version)
Rear sight: Fixed sight w/.125″ blade (field version): adjustable sight w/.125″ blade (target version)
Hammer: .250″ internal
Trigger: .312″ serrated

22 CAL. AUTOMATIC PISTOL
MODEL NO. 41
$549.50 Blue Only

Caliber: 22 Long Rifle
Magazine capacity: 10 rounds
Barrel length: 5¹/₂″ and 7³/₈″
Overall length: 12″ with 7³/₈″ barrel
Sight radius: 9⁵/₁₆″ with 7³/₈″ barrel
Weight: 43¹/₂ oz. with 7³/₈″ barrel
Sights: Front, ¹/₈″ Patridge undercut; rear, S&W micrometer click sight adjustable for windage and elevation
Stocks: Checkered walnut with modified thumb rest, equally adaptable to right- or left-handed shooters
Finish: S&W Bright Blue
Trigger: ³/₈″ width, with S&W grooving and an adjustable trigger stop

38 MASTER MODEL NO. 52
$711.50 Bright Blue Only

Caliber: 38 S&W Special (for Mid-Range Wad Cutter only)
Magazine capacity: 5 rounds (2 five-round magazines furnished)
Barrel length: 5″
Overall length: 8⁵/₈″
Sight radius: 6¹⁵/₁₆″
Weight: 41 oz. with empty magazine
Sights: Front, ¹/₈″ Patridge on ramp base; rear, new S&W micrometer click sight with wide ⁷/₈″ sight slide
Stocks: Checkered walnut with S&W monograms
Finish: S&W Bright Blue with sandblast stippling around sighting area to break up light reflection
Trigger: ³/₈″ width with S&W grooving and an adjustable trigger stop

SMITH & WESSON PISTOLS

S&W THIRD GENERATION PISTOLS

Smith & Wesson's complete re-engineering of its double-action semiauto line has resulted in seven new custom-built pistols combining the following features: fixed barrel bushing for greater accuracy; smoother trigger pull plus a slimmer, con-toured grip and lateral relief cut where trigger guard meets frame; three-dot sights; wraparound grips; beveled magazine well for easier reloading; ambidextrous safety lever secured by spring-loaded plunger; low-glare bead-blasted finish.

MODEL 3900 SERIES
$495.50 (Model 3904)
$545.00 (Model 3906)

Caliber: 9mm Auto-Loading DA Luger (Parabellum)
Capacity: 8 rounds
Barrel length: 4"
Overall length: 7½"
Weight (empty): 25½ oz. (Model 3904); 34 oz. (Model 3906)
Sights: Post w/white dot front; fixed rear adj. for windage only w/2 white dots. Adjustable sight models include micrometer click, adj. for windage and elevation w/2 white dots. Add **$25** for adj. sights.
Finish: Blue (Model 3904); satin stainless (Model 3906)

**MODEL 3904
FIXED SIGHT**

**MODEL 3906
ADJUSTABLE SIGHT**

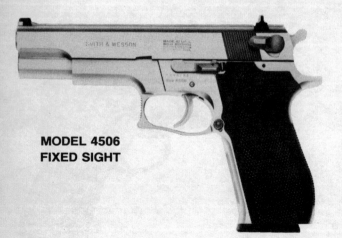

**MODEL 4506
FIXED SIGHT**

MODEL 4500 SERIES
$653.00 (Models 4506 and 4516)

Caliber: 45 ACP Auto-Loading DA
Capacity: 8 rounds (Model 4506); 7 rounds (Model 4516)
Barrel length: 5" (Model 4506); 3¾" (Model 4516)
Overall length: 8½"
Weight (empty): 36 oz. (Model 4506); 34 oz. (Model 4516)
Sights: Post w/white dot front; fixed rear, adj. for windage only. Adj. sight incl. micrometer click, adj. for windage and elevation w/2 white dots. Add **$33.00** for adj. sights.
Stocks: Delrin one-piece wraparound, arched backstrap, textured surface
Finish: Satin stainless

SMITH & WESSON PISTOLS

THIRD GENERATION PISTOLS

MODEL 5900 SERIES
$526.50 (Model 5904)
$579.00 (Model 5906)

Caliber: 9mm Auto-Loading DA Luger (Parabellum)
Capacity: 14 rounds
Barrel length: 4″
Overall length: 7$\frac{1}{2}$″
Weight (empty): 26 oz. (Model 5904); 34$\frac{1}{2}$ oz. (Model 5906)
Sights: Post w/white dot front; fixed rear, adj. for windage only w/2 white dots. Adjustable sight models include micrometer click, adj. for windage and elevation w/2 white dots. Add **$27** for adj. sights.
Finish: Blue (Model 5904); satin stainless (Model 5906)

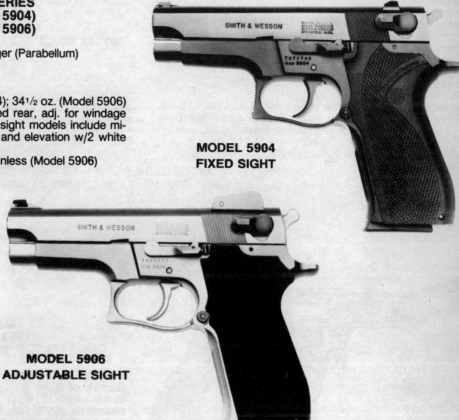

MODEL 5904
FIXED SIGHT

MODEL 5906
ADJUSTABLE SIGHT

MODEL 6904
FIXED SIGHT

MODEL 6900 SERIES
$502.50 (Model 6904)
$553.00 (Model 6906)

Caliber: 9mm Auto-Loading DA Luger (Parabellum)
Capacity: 12 rounds
Barrel length: 3$\frac{1}{2}$″
Overall length: 6$\frac{7}{8}$″
Weight (empty): 23$\frac{1}{2}$ oz.
Sights: Post w/white dot front; fixed rear, adj. for windage only w/2 white dots
Stocks: Delrin one-piece wraparound, arched backstrap, textured surface
Finish: Blue (Model 6904); clear anodized/satin stainless (Model 6906)

SMITH & WESSON REVOLVERS

LADY SMITH HANDGUNS
$368.00 (Model 36-LS)
$415.00 (Model 60-LS)

MODEL 36-LS

Caliber: 38
Capacity: 5 shots
Barrel length: 2″ or 3″
Sights: Serrated ramp front; fixed notch rear
Grips: Contoured rosewood (2″ barrel); Goncalo Alves finger-grooved stocks w/Carnauba wax finish (3″ barrel)
Finish: Glossy deep blue
Features: Model 36-LS is made of carbon steel
Also available:
Model 60-LS has the same specifications as Model 36-LS, but is made of stainless steel with a frosted finish. Both models come with carrying case and cleaning kit.

MODEL 60-LS

SMALL FRAME

MODEL NO. 34
1953 22/32 KIT GUN
$355.50 Blue

Caliber: 22 Long Rifle
Number of shots: 6
Barrel length: 2″, 4″
Overall length: 8″ with 4″ barrel and round butt
Weight: 22$\frac{1}{4}$ oz. with 4″ barrel and round butt
Sights: Front, $\frac{1}{10}$″ serrated ramp; rear, S&W micrometer click sight adjustable for windage and elevation
Stocks: Checked walnut Service with S&W monograms, round or square butt
Finish: S&W blue

MODEL NO. 63
1977 22/32 KIT GUN
$390.00

Caliber: 22 Long Rifle
Number of shots: 6
Barrel length: 4″
Weight: 24$\frac{1}{2}$ oz. (empty)
Sights: $\frac{1}{8}$″ red ramp front sight; rear sight is black stainless steel S&W micrometer click square-notch, adjustable for windage and elevation
Stocks: Square butt
Finish: Satin stainless

SMITH & WESSON REVOLVERS

SMALL FRAME

MODEL 649 BODYGUARD
$396.50

Caliber: 38 Special
Capacity: 5 shots
Barrel length: 2″
Overall length: 6¼″
Sights: Serrated ramp front, fixed square notch rear
Weight: 20 oz.
Grips: Round butt; checkered walnut service
Finish: Stainless steel

32 REGULATION POLICE
MODEL NO. 31
$354.00

Caliber: 32 S&W Long
Number of shots: 6
Barrel length: 2″, 3″
Overall length: 8½″ with 4″ barrel
Weight: 18¾ oz. with 4″ barrel
Sights: Front, fixed, 1/10″ serrated ramp; rear square notch
Stocks: Checked walnut Service with S&W monograms
Finish: S&W blue

38 CHIEFS SPECIAL MODEL 36
$328.00 Blue
$339.00 Nickel

Caliber: 38 S&W Special
Number of shots: 5
Barrel length: 2″ or 3″
Overall length: 6½″ with 2″ barrel and round butt
Weight: 19 oz. with 2″ barrel and round butt
Sights: Front, fixed, 1/10″ serrated ramp; rear square notch
Stocks: Checked walnut Service with S&W monograms, round or square butt
Finish: S&W blue or nickel
MODEL 37: Same as Model 36 except weight 14 oz. **$331.00;** with nickel finish **$344.00.**

SMITH & WESSON REVOLVERS

SMALL FRAME

38 CHIEFS SPECIAL STAINLESS
MODEL NO. 60
$375.00

Caliber: 38 S&W Special
Number of shots: 5
Barrel length: 2″
Overall length: 6 1/2″
Weight: 19 oz.
Sights: Front fixed, 1/10″ serrated ramp; rear square notch
Stocks: Checked walnut Service with S&W monograms
Finish: Satin

38 BODYGUARD "AIRWEIGHT"
MODEL NO. 38
$368.00 Blue
$381.00 Nickel

Caliber: 38 S&W Special
Number of shots: 5
Barrel length: 2″
Overall length: 6 3/8″
Weight: 14 1/2 oz.
Sights: Front, fixed 1/10″ serrated ramp; rear square notch
Stocks: Checked walnut Service with S&W monograms
Finish: S&W blue or nickel

38 BODYGUARD MODEL 49
$348.00

Caliber: 38 S&W Special
Capacity: 5-shot cylinder
Barrel length: 2″
Overall length: 6 1/4″
Weight (empty): 20 oz.
Sights: Serrated ramp (front); fixed square notch (rear)
Finish: S&W blue

SMITH & WESSON REVOLVERS

MEDIUM FRAME

K-22 MASTERPIECE
MODEL NO. 17
$368.00 (4" or 6" barrel)
$414.50 (8³/₈" barrel)

Caliber: 22 Long Rifle
Number of shots: 6
Barrel length: 4", 6", 8³/₈"
Overall length: 9⁵/₁₆" (4" barrel); 11¹/₈" (6" barrel); 13¹/₂" (8³/₈" barrel)
Weight loaded: 38¹/₂ oz. with 6" barrel; 42¹/₂ oz. with 8³/₈" barrel
Sights: Front, ¹/₈" plain Patridge; rear, S&W micrometer click sight adjustable for windage and elevation
Stocks: Checkered walnut Service with S&W monograms
Finish: S&W blue

38 MILITARY & POLICE
MODEL NO. 10
$323.00 Blue
$334.50 Nickel (4" barrel only)

Caliber: 38 S&W Special
Capacity: 6 shots
Barrel length: 2", (also 3" heavy barrel), 4" (also 4" heavy barrel)
Weight: 30¹/₂ oz. with 4" barrel
Sights: Front, fixed ¹/₈" serrated ramp; rear square notch
Stocks: Checkered walnut Service with S&W monograms, round or square butt
Finish: S&W blue or nickel

38 MILITARY & POLICE STAINLESS
MODEL NO. 64
$351.00

Caliber: 38 S&W Special
Capacity: 6 shots
Barrel length: 4" heavy barrel, square butt; 3" heavy barrel, round butt; 2" regular barrel, round butt
Overall length: 9¹/₄" w/4" barrel; 7⁷/₈" w/3" barrel; 6⁷/₈" w/2" barrel
Weight: With 4" barrel, 34 oz.; with 3" barrel, 30¹/₂ oz.; with 2" barrel, 28 oz.
Sights: Fixed, ¹/₈" serrated ramp front; square notch rear
Stocks: Checked walnut Service with S&W monograms
Finish: Satin
Ammunition: 38 S&W Special, 38 S&W Special Mid Range

SMITH & WESSON REVOLVERS

MEDIUM FRAME

38 COMBAT MASTERPIECE
MODEL NO. 15
$350.00

Caliber: 38 S&W Special
Number of shots: 6
Barrel lengths: 2″, 4″, 6″
Overall length: 7¼″ (2″ barrel); 9⁵/₁₆″ (4″ barrel); 11⅛″ (6″ barrel)
Weight (loaded): 34 oz. with 4″ barrel
Sights: Front, ⅛″ Baughman Quick Draw on plain ramp; rear, S&W micrometer click sight adjustable for windage and elevation
Stocks: Checkered walnut Service with S&W monograms
Finish: S&W blue or nickel

DISTINGUISHED COMBAT MAGNUM
MODEL 586
$381.50—$423.50 (Blue or Nickel)

Caliber: 357 Magnum
Capacity: 6 shots
Barrel length: 4″, 6″, 8⅜″
Overall length: 9¾″ with 4″ barrel; 11½″ with 6″ barrel; 13¹³/₁₆″ with 8⅜″ barrel
Weight: 42 oz. with 4″ barrel; 46 oz. with 6″ barrel; 53 oz. with 8⅜″ barrel
Sights: Front is S&W Red Ramp; rear is S&W Micrometer Click adjustable for windage and elevation; White outline notch. Option with 6″ barrel only—plain Patridge front with black outline notch
Stocks: Checkered Goncalo Alves with speedloader cutaway
Finish: S&W Blue or Nickel
Model 686: Same as Model 586 except finish is stainless steel, $394.00—$447.00.

357 COMBAT MAGNUM
MODEL NO. 66
$385.00—$437.00 Stainless Steel

Caliber: 357 Magnum (actual bullet dia. 38 S&W Spec.)
Number of shots: 6
Barrel length: 6″ or 4″ with square butt; 2½″ with round butt
Length overall: 9½″ with 4″ barrel; 7½″ with 2½″ barrel; 11⅜″ with 6″ barrel
Weight: 35 oz. with 4″ barrel; 30½ oz. with 2½″ barrel; 39 oz. with 6″ barrel
Sights: Front: ⅛″. Rear: S&W Red Ramp on ramp base, S&W Micrometer Click Sight, adjustable for windage and elevation
Stocks: Checked Goncalo Alves target with square butt with S&W monograms
Finish: Satin
Trigger: S&W grooving with an adjustable trigger stop
Ammunition: 357 S&W Magnum, 38 S&W Special Hi-Speed, 38 S&W Special, 38 S&W Special Mid Range

SMITH & WESSON REVOLVERS

MEDIUM FRAME

357 COMBAT MAGNUM
MODEL NO. 19
$338.50—$409.00 Bright Blue or Nickel

Caliber: 357 Magnum (actual bullet dia. 38 S&W Spec.)
Number of shots: 6
Barrel length: 2½", 4" and 6"
Overall length: 9½" with 4" barrel; 7½" with 2½" barrel; 11½" with 6" barrel
Weight: 35 oz. (2½" model weighs 31 oz.)
Sights: Front, ⅛" Baughman Quick Draw on 2½" or 4" barrel, ⅛" Patridge on 6" barrel; rear, S&W micrometer click sight adjustable for windage and elevation
Stocks: Checkered Goncalo Alves Target with S&W monograms
Finish: S&W bright blue or nickel

357 MILITARY & POLICE STAINLESS
HEAVY BARREL MODEL NO. 65
$357.00

Caliber: 357 Magnum and 38 S&W Special
Rounds: 6-shot cylinder capacity
Barrel length: 4" heavy barrel, square butt; 3" heavy barrel, round butt
Length overall: With 4" barrel, 9¼"; with 3" barrel, 7⁵/₁₆"
Weight: With 4" barrel, 34 oz.; with 3" barrel, 31 oz.
Sights: Fixed, ⅛" serrated ramp front; square notch rear
Stocks: Checked walnut Service with S&W monograms, square butt
Finish: Satin

357 MILITARY & POLICE (HEAVY BARREL)
MODEL NO. 13
$329.00

Caliber: 357 Magnum and 38 S&W Special
Rounds: 6-shot cylinder capacity
Barrel length: 3" and 4"
Overall length: 9¼"
Weight: 34 oz.
Sights: Front, ⅛" serrated ramp; rear square notch
Stocks: Checkered walnut Service with S&W monograms, square butt (3" barrel has round butt)
Finish: S&W blue

SMITH & WESSON REVOLVERS

LARGE FRAME

357 MAGNUM MODEL NO. 27
$451.00 (4″) $423.00 (6″)
$430.50 (8³/₈″)

Caliber: 357 Magnum (actual bullet dia. 38 S&W Spec.)
Number of shots: 6
Barrel length: 4″, 6″ and 8³/₈″
Weight: 44 oz. with 4″ barrel; 45¹/₂ oz.with 6″; 49 oz. with 8³/₈″
Sights: Front, S&W Red Ramp (4″ barrel) and Patridge (6″ and 8³/₈″ barrels); rear, S&W micrometer click sight adjustable for windage and elevation
Stocks: Checkered walnut Service with S&W monograms
Frame: Finely checked top strap and barrel rib
Finish: S&W bright blue or nickel

41 MAGNUM MODEL NO. 57
$427.00 (4″ and 6″)
$442.00 (8³/₈″)

Caliber: 41 Magnum
Number of shots: 6
Barrel length: 4″, 6″ and 8³/₈″
Overall length: 11³/₈″ with 6″ barrel
Weight: 48 oz. with 6″ barrel
Sights: Front, ¹/₈″ S&W Red Ramp; rear, S&W micrometer click sight adjustable for windage and elevation; white outline notch
Stocks: Special oversize Target type of checkered Goncalo Alves, with S&W monograms
Hammer: Checked target type
Trigger: Grooved target type
Finish: S&W bright blue

SMITH & WESSON REVOLVERS

LARGE FRAME

MODEL 657 STAINLESS $455.00 (6″)
$470.50 (8³/₈″)

Caliber: 41 Magnum
Magazine capacity: 6-shot cylinder
Barrel lengths: 6″, 8³/₈″
Overall length: 11³/₈″ (6″ barrel); 13¹⁵/₁₆″ (8³/₈″ barrel)
Weight (empty): 48 oz. (6″ barrel); 52¹/₂ oz. (8³/₈″ barrel)
Sights: Serrated black ramp on ramp base (front); Blue S&W micrometer click sight adj. for windage and elevation (rear)
Finish: Satin

44 MAGNUM MODEL NO. 29
$481.50 (4″ and 6″) $492.50 (8³/₈″)
$527.00 (8³/₈″, w/scope mount)
$535.00 (10⁵/₈″ Blue only)

Caliber: 44 Magnum
Number of shots: 6
Barrel lengths: 4″, 6″, 8³/₈″ and 10⁵/₈″ (blue only)
Overall length: 11⁷/₈″ with 6¹/₂″ barrel
Weight: 43 oz. with 4″ barrel; 47 oz. with 6″ barrel; 51¹/₂ oz. with 8³/₈″ barrel
Sights: Front, 1/8″ S&W Red Ramp; rear, S&W micrometer click sight adjustable for windage and elevation; white out-line notch
Stocks: Special oversize target type of checked Goncalo Alves; with S&W monograms
Hammer: Checkered target type
Trigger: Grooved target type
Finish: S&W bright blue or nickel
Also available in nickel: **$492.50** (4″ and 6″) and **$503.00** (8³/₈″).

MODEL 25
$429.00 (4″ and 6″)
$436.50 (8³/₈″)

Caliber: 45 Colt
Capacity: 6-shot cylinder
Barrel length: 4″, 6″, 8³/₈″
Overall length: 9⁹/₁₆″ (4″ barrel); 11³/₈″ (6″ barrel); 13⁷/₈″ (8³/₈″ barrel)
Weight (empty): 44 oz. (4″ barrel); 46 oz. (6″ barrel); 50 oz. (8³/₈″ barrel)
Sights: S&W red ramp on ramp base (front); S&W micrometer click sight w/white outline notch (rear), adj. for windage and elevation
Finish: S&W Bright blue or nickel

SPRINGFIELD ARMORY

**MODEL 1911-A1
STANDARD**

**MODEL 1911-A1
COMMANDER**

MODEL 1911-A1 STANDARD

An exact duplicate of the M1911-A1 pistol that served the U.S. Armed Forces for more than 70 years, this model has been precision manufactured from forged parts, including a forged frame, then hand-assembled.

SPECIFICATIONS
Calibers: 9mm Parabellum, 38 Super and 45 ACP
Capacity: 8 in mag. 1 in chamber (9mm); 7 in mag. 1 in chamber (45 ACP)
Barrel length: 5.04″
Overall length: 8.59″
Weight: 35.62 oz.
Trigger pull: 5 to 6.5 lbs.
Sight radius: 6.481″
Rifling: 1 turn in 16; left-hand, 4-groove (9mm); right-hand, 6-groove (45 ACP)
MODEL 1911-A1 (45 ACP or 9mm)
  Blued **$441.00**
  Same model with Parkerized finish **420.00**
1911-A1 DEFENDER w/fixed combat sights, bobbed
  hammer, walnut grips, beveled magazine well,
  extended thumb safety, in 45 ACP **535.00**
  Same as above w/blued finish **555.00**
1911-A1 COMMANDER with ½″ shortened
  slide and barrel, in 45 ACP **479.00**
  Same as above w/blued finish **499.00**
1911-A1 38 SUPER **420.00**
  Same as above w/blued finish **440.00**

MODEL 1911-A2 S.A.S.S.
(Springfield Armory Single Shot)

SPECIFICATIONS
Calibers: 22 LR, 44 Mag., 357 Mag., 7mm BR (10.7″ barrel); 358 Win., 7mm × 308, 223 and 308 (14.9″ barrel)
Barrel length: 10.7″ or 14.9″ (interchangeable)
Prices:
1911-A2 S.A.S.S. 14.9″ barrel **$519.00**
  10.7″ barrel **506.00**
Conversion Units 14.9″ barrel **259.00**
  10.7″ barrel **246.00**
Interchangeable Barrels 14.9″ barrel **128.70**
  10.7″ barrel **115.70**

**1911-A2 S.A.S.S.
SPRINGFIELD ARMORY SINGLE SHOT**

SPRINGFIELD ARMORY

OMEGA

Springfield's new Omega model is the first practical 10mm multi-caliber system available. Includes a ported slide with adjustable rear sight and interchangeable front sights; a hammer forged polygon barrel (with or without stabilizing ports); special lockup system for greater safety with high velocity loads; and a dual extractor system for fast barrel changes.

SPECIFICATIONS
Calibers: 10mm, 38 Super, 45 ACP (interchangeable)
Barrel length: 5″ or 6″
Overall length: 8.53″ (5″ barrel); 9.53″ (6″ barrel)
Weight: 42.88 oz. (5″ barrel); 45.36 oz. (6″ barrel)
Rifling: 6 grooves, right-hand; 1 turn in 14 (38 Spec.); 1 turn in 16 (10mm); 1 turn in 18 (45 ACP)
Grips: Rubberized wraparound
Finish: Blue
Price: $849.00
Note: in 6″ model, 38 Special is available unported only; 5″ available ported or unported in all 3 calibers.

OMEGA

MODEL P9 DOUBLE ACTION

MODEL P9 DOUBLE ACTION

SPECIFICATIONS
Caliber: 9mm Parabellum
Capacity: 16 rounds; 10 rounds Compact Model
Barrel length: 4.72″; 3.66″ Compact Model
Overall length: 8.1″; 7.24″ Compact Model
Weight: 35.3 oz.; 32.1 oz. Compact Model
Rifling: Right-hand; 1 turn in 10″, 4-groove
Features: Polished blue finish; checkered walnut grips; serrated front and rear frame straps; frame-mounted thumb safety, Commander-style hammer
Prices:
MODEL P9 STANDARD $454.00
COMPACT MODEL 467.00
IPSC MODEL 774.00

STAR AUTOMATIC PISTOLS

STAR BKM & BM
9mm PARABELLUM

The Model BM offers all-steel construction, and the BKM offers a high strength, weight-saving duraluminum frame. An improved thumb safety locks both the slide and hammer with hammer cocked or uncocked; further, an automatic magazine safety locks the sear when the magazine is removed.

Overall length: 7.17″. **Barrel length:** 3.9″. **Magazine capacity:** 8 rounds. **Weight:** 34.06 oz. (BM); 25.59 oz. (BKM)

Model BM Blue	$332.00
Model BM Chrome	395.00
Model BKM Blue	375.00

MODEL BM

STAR MODELS 30M & 30PK
9mm PARABELLUM

The Model 30 features a staggered 15-round button release magazine, square notch rear sight (click-adjustable for windage) and square front sight (notched to diffuse light). Removable backstrap houses complete firing mechanism. All-steel frame (Model 30/PK=alloy frame).

Overall length: 8.07″. **Height:** 5.32″. **Barrel length:** 4.33″ (Model 30PK=3.86″) **Weight:** 40.24 oz. (Model 30/Pk=30.36 oz.) **Price:** ....$535.00.

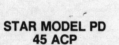

MODEL 30PK

STAR MODEL PD
45 ACP

Chambered for the sledgehammer 45 ACP, the PD is one of the smallest .45 caliber production pistols in the world.

Overall length: 7″. **Barrel length:** 4″. **Weight:** 25.5 oz. **Finish:** Blue. **Capacity:** 6 rounds. **Price:** ....$415.00.

MODEL PD

TANARMI

MODEL BTA90C
$430.00 Blue
$450.00 Chrome

SPECIFICATIONS
Caliber: 9mm Para
Barrel length: 4″
Weight: 30 oz
Capacity: 12 shots
Finish: Matte chrome
Frame: Steel
Grips: Neoprene

MODEL TA76M
"BUFFALO SCOUT" REVOLVER
$105.00

SPECIFICATIONS
Calibers: 22 LR and 22 WRM
Barrel length: 4³/₄″
Capacity: 6 shots
Finish: Satin blue
Frame: Alloy
Grips: Walnut

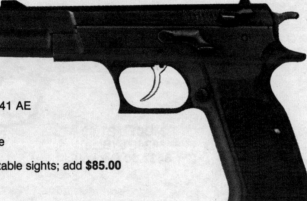

MODEL TA90B
$415.00 Blue
$430.00 Chrome

SPECIFICATIONS
Calibers: 9mm Parabellum, 41 AE
Barrel length: 4³/₄″
Capacity: 15 shots
Finish: Matte blue or chrome
Grips: Black Neoprene
Sights: Available with adjustable sights; add **$85.00**

TARGA SEMIAUTOMATIC PISTOLS

MODEL GT26S
$115.00

SPECIFICATIONS
Caliber: 25 ACP
Capacity: 6 shots
Barrel length: 2¹/₂″
Weight: 15 oz.
Frame: Steel
Finish: Satin blue
Grips: Walnut

MODEL GT22T
$200.00

SPECIFICATIONS
Caliber: 22 LR
Capacity: 12 shots
Barrel length: 6″
Weight: 28 oz.
Frame: Steel
Finish: Satin blue
Grips: Walnut

TARGA SEMIAUTOMATIC PISTOLS

MODEL GT380XE
$235.00

SPECIFICATIONS
Caliber: 380 ACP
Capacity: 11 shots
Barrel length: 3.88″
Weight: 26 oz.
Finish: Satin blue
Frame: Steel
Grips: Walnut

TAURUS PISTOLS

MODEL PT 92

Caliber: 9mm Parabellum
Action: Semiautomatic double action
Hammer: Exposed
Barrel length: 4.92″
Overall length: 8.54″
Height: 5.39″
Width: 1.45″
Weight: 34 oz. (empty)
Rifling: R.H., 6 grooves
Front sight: Blade integral with slide
Rear sight: Notched bar dovetailed to slide
Safeties: (a) Ambidextrous manual safety locking trigger mechanism and slide in locked position; (b) half-cock position; (c) inertia operated firing pin; (d) chamber loaded indicator
Magazine: Staggered 15-shot capacity
Slide: Hold open upon firing last cartridge
Finish: Blue or satin nickel
Grips: Smooth Brazilian walnut

MODEL PT 92
$424.75 (Blue)
$437.30 (Nickel)

MODEL PT 99

Caliber: 9mm Parabellum
Action: Semiautomatic double action
Hammer: Exposed
Barrel length: 4.92″
Overall length: 8.54″
Height: 5.39″
Width: 1.45″
Weight: 34 oz. (empty)
Rifling: R.H., 6 grooves
Front sight: Blade Integral with slide
Rear sight: Micrometer click adjustable for elevation and windage
Safeties: (a) Ambidextrous manual safety locking trigger mechanism and slide in locked position; (b) half-cock position; (c) inertia operated firing pin; (d) chamber loaded indicator. **Magazine:** Staggered, 15-shot capacity
Slide: Hold open upon firing last cartridge
Finish: Blue or satin nickel
Grips: Smooth Brazilian walnut

MODEL PT 99
$459.65 (Blue)
$474.50 (Nickel)

TAURUS PISTOLS

MODEL PT 58 (not shown)
$387.80 (Blue)
$394.50 (Nickel)

SPECIFICATIONS
Caliber: 380 ACP
Action: Semiautomatic double action
Capacity: Staggered 13 shot

Barrel length: 4″
Overall length: 7.1″
Weight: 30 oz.
Hammer: Exposed
Sights: Front, blade integral w/slide; rear, notched bar dove-tailed to slide
Finish: Blue or satin nickel
Grips: Smooth Brazilian walnut

TAURUS REVOLVERS

MODEL 73
$204.25 (Blue)
$222.35 (Nickel)

SPECIFICATIONS
Caliber: 32 Long
Capacity: 6 shot
Barrel length: 3″ heavy barrel
Weight: 20 oz.
Sights: Rear, square notch
Action: Double
Stock: Standard checkered
Finish: Blue or satin nickel

MODEL 83
$208.35 (Blue)
$219.25 (Nickel)

SPECIFICATIONS
Caliber: 38 Special
Action: Double
Number of shots: 6
Barrel length: 4″
Weight: 34 1/2 oz.
Sights: Ramp, front; rear micrometer click adjustable for windage and elevation
Finish: Blue or satin nickel
Stocks: Checkered walnut target

MODEL 86 TARGET MASTER
$276.50

SPECIFICATIONS
Caliber: 38 Special
Capacity: 6 shot
Barrel length: 6″
Weight: 34 oz.
Sights: Patridge-type front; micrometer click adjustable rear for windage and elevation
Action: Double
Stock: Checkered walnut target
Finish: Bright royal blue

Model 96 Target Scout: Same as Model 86 Target Master except 22 LR caliber. Blue.

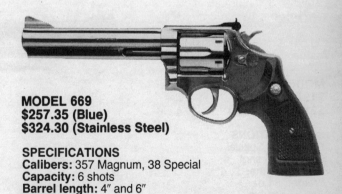

MODEL 669
$257.35 (Blue)
$324.30 (Stainless Steel)

SPECIFICATIONS
Calibers: 357 Magnum, 38 Special
Capacity: 6 shots
Barrel length: 4″ and 6″
Weight: 36 oz.
Action: Double
Sights: Serrated ramp front; rear micrometer click adjustable for windage and elevation
Finish: Royal blue or stainless
Stock: Checkered walnut target

TAURUS REVOLVERS

MODEL 94
$230.05

SPECIFICATIONS
Caliber: 22 LR
Barrel lengths: 3″ and 4″
Weight: 25 oz.
Number of shots: 9
Action: Double
Sights: Serrated ramp front; rear micrometer click adjustable
   for windage and elevation
Finish: Blue or satin nickel
Stock: Brazilian hardwood

MODEL 80
$197.90 (Blue)
$210.00 (Nickel)

SPECIFICATIONS
Caliber: 38 Special
Capacity: 6 shot
Barrel lengths: 3″, 4″
Weight: 33 oz.
Action: Double
Stock: Checkered walnut
Finish: Blue or satin nickel

MODEL 82
$197.90 (Blue)
$210.00 (Nickel)

SPECIFICATIONS
Caliber: 38 Special
Capacity: 6 shot
Barrel lengths: 3″, 4″
Weight: 34 oz.
Action: Double
Stock: Checkered walnut
Finish: Blue or satin nickel

TAURUS REVOLVERS

MODEL 65
$228.00 (Blue)
$239.70 (Nickel)

SPECIFICATIONS
Caliber: 357 Magnum
Capacity: 6 shot
Barrel length: 3″, 4″
Weight: 34 oz.
Sights: Rear square notch; front ramp
Action: Double
Stock: Checkered walnut target
Finish: Royal blue or satin nickel

MODEL 66
$248.35 (Blue) $259.45 (Nickel)
$315.35 (Stainless Steel)

SPECIFICATIONS
Caliber: 357 Magnum, 38 Special
Capacity: 6 shot
Barrel length: 3″, 4″, 6″
Weight: 35 oz.
Sights: Serrated ramp front; rear micrometer click adjustable
   for windage and elevation
Action: Double
Stock: Checkered walnut magna grips (3″); checkered walnut
   target grips (4″ & 6″)
Finish: Royal blue, satin nickel or stainless steel

MODEL 85
$216.90 (Blue) $232.70 (Nickel)
$274.60 (Stainless Steel)

SPECIFICATIONS
Caliber: 38 Special
Capacity: 5 shot
Barrel length: 2″ and 3″
Weight: 21 oz.
Sights: Notch rear sight, fixed sight
Action: Double
Stock: Brazilian checkered walnut
Finish: Blue, satin nickel or stainless steel

THOMPSON/CENTER

CONTENDER BULL BARREL

CONTENDER
OCTAGON BARREL MODELS

This standard barrel is interchangeable with any model listed here. Available in 10-inch length, it is supplied with iron sights. Octagon barrel is available in 22 LR. No external choke in this model **$335.00**

CONTENDER SUPER "14"

CONTENDER
SUPER "14" MODELS

Chambered in 11 calibers (22 LR, 222 Remington and 223 Remington, 7-30 Waters, 7mm T.C.U., 10mm Auto, 30/30 Winchester, 357 Rem. Max., 35 Remington and 44 Mag. and 445 Super Mag.), this gun is equipped with a 14-inch bull barrel, fully adjustable target rear sight and ramped front sight (Patridge-style). It offers a sight radius of 13½ inches. **Overall length: 18¼". Weight: 3½ lbs.** **$345.00**

CONTENDER
BULL BARREL MODELS

This pistol with 10-inch barrel features fully adjustable Patridge-style iron sights.

Standard and Custom calibers available:
22 Long Rifle, 22 Hornet, 22 Win. Mag., 7-30 Waters, 223 Rem., 32 H&R Mag., 32/20 Win., 7mm T.C.U., 30/30 Win., 357 Mag., 44 Mag., 357 Rem. Max., and 30 M1 Carbine.
Bull Barrel (less internal choke) **$335.00**
Standard calibers available w/internal choke:
45 Colt/.410 . . . . **340.00**

T/C ALLOY II CONTENDER

T/C Alloy II is a permanent, electroplated surface that will not separate from the base metal. It is harder than stainless steel and improves lubricity, causing actions to function smoother and enabling parts to move with less frictional drag. As a result, it provides 30% longer barrel life than stainless steel, reduces wear on moving parts, and shrugs off the effects of corrosion or erosion. It also reduces fouling to produce a more constant velocity shot after shot. All metal surfaces of this Contender Series, internal and external (excluding sights and springs) are finished in T/C Alloy II.

Calibers: 22 LR, 223 Rem., 357 Magnum, 357 Rem. Max., 44 Magnum, 7mm TCU, 30/30 Win. (10" Bull Barrel Model); 45 Colt/.410 (Vent rib/Internal Choke Model).
Prices:
Contender 10" Bull Barrel Model **$415.00**
Contender Vent Rib/Internal Choke Model **435.00**
Contender Super "14" Model (22LR, 223 Rem.,
   30/30 Win., 35 Rem., 7mm T.C.U., 7-30 Waters,
   44 Mag.) **425.00**

CONTENDER SUPER "16"
VENTILATED RIB/INTERNAL CHOKE MODELS
(not shown)

Featuring a raised ventilated (7/16-inch wide) rib, this Contender model is available in 45 Colt/.410 caliber. Its rear leaf sight folds down to provide an unobstructed sighting plane when the pistol is used with .410 ga. shot shells. A patented detachable choke (1⅞ inches long) screws into the muzzle internally. **Barrel length:** 10 inches **$375.00**

A. UBERTI REPLICAS

1871 ROLLING BLOCK TARGET PISTOL
$273.00

SPECIFICATIONS
Calibers: 22 LR, 22 Magnum, 357 Magnum
Capacity: Single shot
Barrel length: 9⅞″ (half octagonal, half round)
Overall length: 14″
Weight: 2.75 lbs.
Sights: Fully adjustable rear; ramp front
Grip and forend: Walnut
Trigger guard: Brass
Frame: Color casehardened steel

**1871 ROLLING BLOCK
TARGET PISTOL**

**1873 STALLION QUICK-
DRAW SINGLE-ACTION**

1873 STALLION QUICK DRAW SINGLE ACTION
$377.00

SPECIFICATIONS
Caliber: 22 LR, 22 Magnum (w/2 interchangeable cylinders)
Barrel length: 5½″ round (also avail. w/4 ¾″ or 6½″ barrel)
Overall length: 10¾″
Weight: 2.42 lbs.
Sights: Fully adjustable rear; ramp front
Capacity: 6 shots
Grip: One-piece walnut
Frame: Stainless steel + all metal parts

Also available:
Target Model Stainless **$399.00**
    Casehardened and blued steel 357.50

1873 CATTLEMAN QUICK DRAW
$309.00 (Brass)
$335.00 (Steel)

SPECIFICATIONS
Calibers: 22 LR, 22 Magnum, 357 Magnum, 38 Special, 38-40, 44 Special, 44-40, 45 L.C.
Barrel lengths: 4¾″, 5½″, 7½″; round tapered
Overall length: 10¾″ w/5½″ barrel
Weight: 2.42 lbs.
Capacity: 6 shots
Grip: One-piece walnut
Frame: Color casehardened steel

Also available:
Cattleman S.A. Target Brass **$332.00**
    Steel 357.50

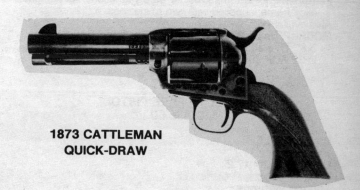

**1873 CATTLEMAN
QUICK-DRAW**

**1875 REMINGTON
ARMY S.A. "OUTLAW"**

1875 REMINGTON ARMY S.A. "OUTLAW"
$318.50

SPECIFICATIONS
Calibers: 357 Magnum, 45 Long Colt, 44-40
Barrel length: 7½″ round tapered
Overall length: 13¾″
Weight: 2.75 lbs.
Grips: Two-piece walnut
Frame: Color casehardened steel

Also available in nickel plate: **$350.00**

VICTORY ARMS

MODEL MC5

MODEL MC5
$499.00

SPECIFICATIONS
Calibers: 9mm Parabellum, 10mm, 38 Super, 41 Action Express, 45 ACP (interchangeable)
Capacity: 10 + 1 (45 ACP); 12 + 1 (41 AE); 17 + 1 (9mm Para, 38 Super)
Barrel lengths: 4³⁄₈″, 5⁷⁄₈″, 7¹⁄₂″
Overall length: 8¹⁄₂″
Weight: 45 oz. (empty)
Sight radius: 6¹⁄₂″ (w/standard 4³⁄₈″ barrel)
Automatic safeties: Firing pin lock; disconnector; hammer blocked unless slide is fully forward and locked
Finish: Service matte black; custom high-luster blue
Extra barrels $100.00
Magazines (each) 25.00

WALTHER PISTOLS

MODEL P-5 DA
$825.00

Caliber: 9mm Parabellum
Capacity: 8 rounds
Barrel length: 3¹⁄₂″
Overall length: 7″
Weight: 28 oz.
Finish: Blue
Features: Four automatic built-in safety functions; lightweight alloy frame; supplied with two magazines
Also available:
MODEL PP in 22, 32 ACP, or 380 ACP calibers. Barrel length: 3.8″. Overall length: 6.7″. Weight: 23.5 oz. Price: $875; in 32 ACP $850.00.

MODEL FP FREE PISTOL
$1850.00

Caliber: 22 LR
Barrel length: 11.7″
Overall length: 17.2″
Weight: 48 oz.
Trigger: Electronic

MODEL P-88 DA (not shown)
$1150.00

Caliber: 9mm Parabellum
Capacity: 15 rounds
Barrel length: 4″
Overall length: 7³⁄₈″
Weight: 31¹⁄₂ oz.
Finish: Blue
Sights: Rear adjustable for windage and elevation
Features: Internal safeties; ambidextrous de-cocking lever and magazine release button; lightweight alloy frame; loaded chamber indicator

MODEL FP

U.I.T.-BV UNIVERSAL
(not shown)

Caliber: 22 LR
Barrel length: 25¹⁄₂″
Overall length: 44³⁄₄″
Weight: 9 lbs.
Bolt action: Single shot; falling block
Prices:
U.I.T.-BV $1625.00
U.I.T. Match 1500.00

WALTHER TARGET PISTOLS

**WALTHER OSP
MATCH RAPID FIRE PISTOL
$1550.00
(22 Short only)**

WALTHER OSP

Walther match pistols are built to conform to ISU and NRA match target pistol regulations. The model GSP, caliber 22 LR is available with either 2.2 lb. (1000 gm) or 3.0 lbs. (1360 gm) trigger, and comes with 4½-inch barrel and special hand-fitting designed walnut stock. Sights consist of fixed front and adjustable rear sight. The GSP-C 32 S&W wadcutter center-fire pistol is factory tested with a 3.0 lb. trigger. The 22 LR conversion unit for the model GSP-C consists of an interchangeable barrel, a slide assembly and two magazines. **Weight:** 22-caliber model 44.8 oz.; 32 S&W 49.4 oz. **Overall length:** 11.8″. **Magazine capacity:** 5 shot.

Prices:
GSP—22 Long Rifle w/carrying case **$1400.00**
GSP-C—32 S&W wadcutter w/carrying case 1650.00
22 LR conversion unit for GSP-C 875.00
22 Short conversion unit for GSP-C 875.00
32 S&W wadcutter conversion unit for GSP-C 1050.00

**WALTHER GSP
MATCH PISTOL
22 LR & 32 S&W Wadcutter**

**GSP JR. SEMIAUTOMATIC (not shown)
$1400.00 (w/Carrying Case)**

Caliber: 22 LR
Capacity: 5 rounds
Barrel length: 4½″
Overall length: 11.8″
Weight: 40.1 oz.

WALTHER PISTOLS

DOUBLE-ACTION AUTOMATIC PISTOLS

The Walther double-action system combines the principles of the double-action revolver with the advantages of the modern pistol . . . without the disadvantages inherent in either design.

Models PP and PPK/S differ only in the overall length of the barrel and slide. Both models offer the same features, including compact form, light weight, easy handling and absolute safety. Both models can be carried with a loaded chamber and closed hammer, but ready to fire either single- or double-action. Both models in calibers 32 ACP and 380 ACP are provided with a live round indicator pin to signal a loaded chamber. An automatic internal safety blocks the hammer to prevent accidental striking of the firing pin, except with a deliberate pull of the trigger. Sights are provided with white markings for high visibility in poor light. Rich Walther blue/black finish is standard and each pistol is complete with extra magazine with finger rest extension. Available in calibers 22 LR, 32 ACP and 380 ACP.

The Walther P-38 is a double-action, locked breech, semi-automatic pistol with an external hammer. Its compact form, light weight and easy handling are combined with the superb performance of the 9mm Luger Parabellum cartridge. The P-38 is equipped with both a manual and automatic safety, which allows it to be carried safely while the chamber is loaded. Available in calibers 9mm Luger Parabellum, 30 Luger and 22 LR with either a rugged non-reflective black finish or a polished blue finish.

SPECIFICATIONS
Overall length: Model PP 6.7"; PPK/S 6.1"; P-38 8½"; P-38 IV 8"; TPH 5³/₈"

Height: Models PP, PPK/S 4.28"; P-38 5.39"; P-38 IV 5.39"; P-38K 5.39"

Weight: Model PP 23.5 oz; PPK/S 23 oz; P-38 28 oz.; P-38 IV (29 oz); TPH 14 oz.

MODEL PPK
6-SHOT AUTOMATIC

Caliber: 380 ACP
Barrel length: 3.2"
Finish: Walther blue or stainless steel
Price: (PPK & PPK/S) . . . . $ 529.00
Deluxe Engraved Blue 1550.00
   Chrome 1600.00

MODEL TPH DOUBLE ACTION

Considered by government agents and professional lawmen to be one of the top undercover/back-up guns available. A scaled-down version of Walther's PP-PPK series chambered for 22 LR.

Barrel length: 2¼". **Overall length:** 5³/₈". **Weight:** 14 oz. **Finish:** stainless steel. **Price:** $399.00

MODEL P-38 DOUBLE ACTION

Calibers: 22 LR, 9mm Parabellum
Barrel length: 5"
Weight: 28 oz. (alloy); 34 oz. (steel)
Finish: Blue
Prices: 22 Long Rifle $1050.00
9mm Parabellum 995.00
Deluxe Engraved (9mm Para. only) Blue 1750.00
   Silver 1950.00
   Chrome 1850.00
Now available: custom **all steel** classic (34 oz.) . . . 1400.00

DAN WESSON REVOLVERS

357 MAGNUM REVOLVERS

Introduced in 1935, the 357 Magnum is still the top selling handgun caliber. It makes an excellent hunting sidearm, and many law enforcement agencies have adopted it as a duty caliber. Take your pick of Dan Wesson 357s; then, add to its versatility with an additional barrel assembly option to alter it to your other needs.

SPECIFICATIONS
Action: Six-shot double and single action. **Ammunition:** 357 Magnum, 38 Special Hi-speed, 38 Special Mid-range. **Typical dimension:** 4″ barrel revolver, 9¼″×5¾″. **Trigger:** Smooth, wide tang (³/₈″) with overtravel adjustment. **Hammer:** Wide spur (³/₈″) with short double-action travel. **Sights: Models 14 and 714,** ¹/₈″ fixed serrated front; fixed rear integral with frame. **Models 15 and 715,** ¹/₈″ serrated interchangeable front blade; red insert standard, yellow and white available; rear notch (.125, .080, or white outline) adjustable for windage and elevation; graduated click. 10″, 12,″ 15″ barrel assemblies have special front sights and instructions. **Rifling:** Six lands and grooves, right-hand twist, 1 turn in 18.75 inches (2½″ thru 8″ lengths); six lands & grooves, right-hand twist, 1 turn in 14 inches (10″, 12″, 15″ lengths). **Note:** All 2½″ guns shipped with undercover grips. 4″ guns are shipped with service grips and the balance have oversized target grips.

38 SPECIAL REVOLVER

For decades a favorite of security and law enforcement agencies, the 38 special still maintains it's reputation as a fine caliber for sportsmen and target shooters. Dan Wesson offers a choice of many barrel lengths in either the service or target configuration.

SPECIFICATIONS
Action: Six-shot double and single action. **Ammunition:** 38 Special Hi-speed, 38 Special Mid-range. **Typical dimension:** 4″ barrel revolver, 9¼″×5¾″. **Trigger:** Smooth, wide tang (³/₈″) with overtravel adjustment. **Hammer:** Wide spur (³/₈″) with short double travel. **Sights: Models 8 and 708,** ¹/₈″ fixed serrated front; fixed rear integral with frame. Models 9 and 709, ¹/₈″ serrated interchangeable front blade; red insert standard, yellow and white available; rear, standard notch (.125, .080, or white outline) adjustable for windage and elevation; graduated click. **Rifling:** Six lands and grooves, right-hand twist, 1 turn in 18.75 inches. **Note:** All 2½″ guns shipped with undercover grips. 4″ guns are shipped with service grips and the balance have oversized target grips.

357 MAGNUM w/6″ Barrel

Price:
Pistol Pac Models 14-2S thru 715-VH . . . . \$455.80 to \$887.81

MODEL	CALIBER	TYPE	BARREL LENGTHS & WEIGHT IN OUNCES							FINISH
			2½″	4″	6″	8″	10″	12″	15″	
14-2	.357 Magnum	Service	30	34	38	NA	NA	NA	NA	Satin Blue
14-2B	.357 Magnum	Service	30	34	38	NA	NA	NA	NA	Brite Blue
15-2	.357 Magnum	Target	32	36	40	44	50	54	59	Brite Blue
15-2V	.357 Magnum	Target	32	35	39	43	49	54	59	Brite Blue
15-2VH	.357 Magnum	Target	32	37	42	47	55	61	70	Brite Blue
714	.357 Magnum	Service	30	34	40	NA	NA	NA	NA	Satin Stainless Steel
715	.357 Magnum	Target	32	36	40	45	50	54	59	Satin Stainless Steel
715-V	.357 Magnum	Target	32	35	40	43	49	54	59	Satin Stainless Steel
715-VH	.357 Magnum	Target	32	37	42	49	55	61	70	Satin Stainless Steel

Price:
38 Special Pistol Pacs . . . . \$455.80—804.85
Stainless Steel . . . . 516.68—887.81

MODEL	CALIBER	TYPE	BARREL LENGTHS & WEIGHT IN OUNCES				FINISH
			2½″	4″	6″	8″	
8-2	.38 Special	Service	30	34	38	N/A	Satin Blue
8-2B	.38 Special	Service	30	34	38	N/A	Brite Blue
9-2	.38 Special	Target	32	36	40	44	Brite Blue
9-2V	.39 Special	Target	32	35	39	43	Brite Blue
9-2VH	.38 Special	Target	32	37	42	47	Brite Blue
708	.38 Special	Service	30	34	38	N/A	Satin Stainless Steel
709	.38 Special	Target	32	36	40	44	Satin Stainless Steel
709-V	.38 Special	Target	32	35	39	43	Satin Stainless Steel
709-VH	.38 Special	Target	32	37	42	47	Satin Stainless Steel

DAN WESSON REVOLVERS

357 SUPER MAG

SPECIFICATIONS

Action: Six-shot double and single action. **Ammunition:** 357 Maximum. **Overall length:** 14.375″ with 8″ barrel. **Height:** 6.5″. **Trigger:** Clean let-off, wide tang with overtravel adjustment. **Hammer:** Wide spur with short double-action travel. **Sights:** 1/8″ serrated interchangeable front blade; red insert standard, yellow and white available; rear, new interchangeable blade (.125 or optional .080); screwdriver adjustable for windage and elevation. **Rifling:** Six lands and grooves, right-hand twist, 1 in 18 3/4 inches.

SPECIFICATIONS

Model	Caliber	Type	Barrel lengths & Weight (oz.)			Finish	Price*
			6″	8″	10″		
740-V	357 Max	Target	59.5	65	62	Stainless	
740-VH	357 Max	Target	62	72	76	Stainless	$568.97—641.89
740-V8S	357 Max	Target		64		Stainless	

*Model 40 (Blue): $508.32–574.50

32 MAGNUM SIX SHOT

This target and small-game gun offers a high muzzle velocity and a flat trajectory for better accuracy. Available in blue and stainless steel.

SPECIFICATIONS

Model	Caliber	Type	Barrel lengths & Weight in ounces				Finish	Pistol Pac
			2 1/2″	4″	6″	8″		
32	.32 Magnum	Target	35	39	43	48	Brite Blue	
32V	.32 Magnum	Target	35	39	43	48	Brite Blue	$614.73–$804.85
32VH	.32 Magnum	Target	35	40	46	53	Brite Blue	
732	.32 Magnum	Target	35	39	43	48	Satin Stainless Steel	
732V	.32 Magnum	Target	35	39	43	48	Satin Stainless Steel	$689.01–$887.81
732VH	.32 Magnum	Target	35	40	46	53	Satin Stainless Steel	

DAN WESSON REVOLVERS

41 AND 44 MAGNUM REVOLVERS

The Dan Wesson 41 and 44 Magnum revolvers are available with a patented "Power Control" to reduce muzzle flip. Both the 41 and the 44 have a one-piece frame and patented gain bolt for maximum strength.

SPECIFICATIONS
Action: Six-shot double- and single-action. **Ammunition:** Models 41 and 741, 41 Magnum; Models 44 and 744, 44 Magnum and 44 Special. **Typical dimension:** 6″ barrel revolver, 12″×6.″ **Trigger:** Smooth, wide tang ($^3/_8$″) with overtravel adjustment. **Hammer:** Wide checkered spur with short double-action travel. **Sights:** Front, $^1/_8$″ serrated interchangeable blade; red insert standard, yellow and white available; rear, standard notch (.125, .080, or white outline) adjustable for windage and elevation; click graduated. **Rifling:** Eight lands and grooves, right-hand twist, 1 turn in 18.75 inches. **Note:** 4″, 6″, and 8″ 44 Magnum guns will be shipped with unported and Power Control barrels. 10″ 44 Magnum guns available only without Power Control. Only jacketed bullets should be used with the 44 Mag. Power Control or excessive leading will result.

Price:
Pistol Pac Model 41 . . . . $623.60—672.27
  Stainless Steel . . . . 690.40—739.20
Pistol Pac Model 44 . . . . 707.52—757.80
  Stainless Steel . . . . 814.38—867.03

MODEL	CALIBER	TYPE	BARREL LENGTHS & WEIGHT IN OUNCES				FINISH
			4″	6″	8″	10″*	
41-V	.41 Magnum	Target	48	53	58	64	Brite Blue
41-VH	.41 Magnum	Target	49	56	64	69	Brite Blue
44-V	.44 Magnum	Target	48	53	58	64	Brite Blue
44-VH	.44 Magnum	Target	49	56	64	69	Brite Blue
741-V	.41 Magnum	Target	48	53	58	64	Satin Stainless Steel
741-VH	.41 Magnum	Target	49	56	64	69	Satin Stainless Steel
744-V	.44 Magnum	Target	48	53	58	64	Satin Stainless Steel
744-VH	.44 Magnum	Target	49	56	64	69	Satin Stainless Steel

22 RIMFIRE and 22 WIN. MAGNUM REVOLVERS

Built on the same frames as the Dan Wesson 357 Magnum, these 22 rimfires offer the heft and balance of fine target revolvers. Affordable fun for the beginner or the expert.

SPECIFICATIONS
Action: Six-shot double and single action. **Ammunition:** Models 22 & 722, 22 Long Rifle; Models 22M & 722M, 22 Win. Mag. **Typical dimension:** 4″ barrel revolver, $9^1/_4$″×$5^3/_4$″. **Trigger:** Smooth, wide tang ($^3/_8$″) with overtravel adjustment. **Hammer:** Wide spur ($^3/_8$″) with short double-action travel. **Sights:** Front, $^1/_8$″ serrated, interchangeable blade; red insert standard, yellow and white available; rear, standard wide notch (.125, .080, or white outline) adjustable for windage and elevation; graduated click. **Rifling:** Models 22 and 722, six lands and grooves, right-hand twist, 1 turn in 12 inches; Models 22M and 722M, six lands and grooves, right-hand twist, 1 turn in 16 inches. **Note:** All $2^1/_2$″ guns are shipped with undercover grips. 4″ guns are shipped with service grips and the balance have oversized target grips.

Price:
Pistol Pac Models 22 thru 722M . . . . . . $614.73—$922.52

MODEL	CALIBER	TYPE	BARREL LENGTHS & WEIGHT IN OUNCES				FINISH
			$2^1/_4$″	4″	6″	8″	
22	.22 L.R.	Target	36	40	44	49	Brite Blue
22-V	.22 L.R.	Target	36	40	44	49	Brite Blue
22-VH	.22 L.R.	Target	36	41	47	54	Brite Blue
22-M	.22 Win Mag	Target	36	40	44	49	Brite Blue
22M-V	.22 Win Mag	Target	36	40	44	49	Brite Blue
22M-VH	.22 Win Mag	Target	36	41	47	54	Brite Blue
722	.22 L.R.	Target	36	40	44	49	Satin Stainless Steel
722-V	.22 L.R.	Target	36	40	44	49	Satin Stainless Steel
722-VH	.22 L.R.	Target	36	41	47	54	Satin Stainless Steel
722M	.22 Win Mag	Target	36	40	44	49	Satin Stainless Steel
722M-V	.22 Win Mag	Target	36	40	44	49	Satin Stainless Steel
722M-VH	.22 Win Mag	Target	36	41	47	54	Satin Stainless Steel

HUNTER PACS

Offered in all magnum calibers with the following:
1. Complete gun in choice of caliber (22, 32, 357, 41, 44, 357 Supermag and 375 Supermag) with 8″ vent-heavy shroud.
2. 8″ vent shroud only, equipped with Burris scope mounts and scope ($1^1/_2$X-4X variable or fixed 2X).
3. Barrel changing tool and Dan Wesson emblem packed in attractive case.

Prices: $723.49 (32 Magnum w/2X) to **$1077.01** (357 Supermag Stainless w/$1^1/_2$X-4X)

WILDEY PISTOLS

These new gas-operated pistols are designed to meet the needs of hunters who want to use handguns for big game. The Wildey pistol includes such features as: • Ventilated rib • Reduced recoil • Double-action trigger mechanism • Patented hammer and trigger blocks and rebounding fire pin • Sights adjustable for windage and elevation • Stainless construction • Fixed barrel for increased accuracy • Increased action strength (with 3-lug and exposed face rotary bolt) • Selective single or autoloading capability • Ability to handle high-pressure loads.

SPECIFICATIONS
Calibers: 9mm Win. Mag., 45 Win. Mag., 475 Wildey Mag.
Capacity: 7 shots
Barrel lengths: 5″, 6″, 7″, 8″ and 10″
Overall length: 11″ w/7″ barrel
Weight: 64 oz. w/5″ barrel
Height: 6″
Prices: **$1079.95** (Serial #1001-2489) to **$2099.95** (Serial #001-200)
Also available:
Interchangeable barrel extension assemblies **$474.95** (5″) to **$499.95** (10″).
Presentation cases (incl. cleaning rod and accessories) **$149.95**

Rifles

FOR ADDRESSES AND PHONE
NUMBERS OF MANUFACTURERS AND
DISTRIBUTORS INCLUDED IN THIS
SECTION, SEE *DIRECTORY OF
MANUFACTURERS AND SUPPLIERS*

ANSCHUTZ SPORTER RIFLES
MATCH 54 SPORTER MODELS

MODEL 1700D CUSTOM
$999.50 (22 LR) $1029.00 (22 Magnum)
$1130.00 (22 Hornet & 222 Rem.)

BAVARIAN 1700
$999.50 (22 LR) $1029.00 (22 Magnum)
$1130.00 (22 Hornet & 222 Rem.)

MODEL 1700D CLASSIC
$988.50 (22 LR) $1015.00 (22 Magnum)
$1100.00 (22 Hornet & 222 Rem.)

SPECIFICATIONS

	Custom	Bavarian	Classic	1700 FWT
	22 Long Rifle, 22 Magnum, 22 Hornet, 222 Remington			22 LR
Length—Overall	43″	43″	43″	43″
Barrel	24″	24″	24″	24″
Pull	14″	14″	14″	14″
Drop at—Comb	1¼″	1¼″	1¼″	1¼″
Monte Carlo	1″	—	—	1″
Heel	1½″	1½″	1½″	1½″
Average Weight	7½ lbs.	7½ lbs.	6¾ lbs.	6¼ lbs.
Trigger—Single Stage 5095 (.222 Rem., 5096)	•	•	•	•
Rate of Twist	Right Hand—one turn in 16.5″ for .22 LR; 1–16″ for .22 Mag & .22 Hornet; 1–14″ for .222 Rem.			
Take Down Bolt Action With Removable Firing Pin	•	•	•	•
Swivel Studs	•	•	•	
Grooved for Scope	•	•	•	•
Tapped for Scope Blocks	•	•	•	•
Sights—Front-Hooded Ramp	•	•	•	
Rear-Folding Leaf	•	•	•	
Trigger Single Stage 5095 (.222 Rem. 5096)	5095 •	5095 •	5096 •	5095 •
*Adjustable for Creep, Pull, Overtravel	•	•		
Factory Set for 2.6 lbs.	•	•		
Adjustable for Overtravel	•	•		
Clip Magazine	•	•	•	•
Safety—Wing	•	•	•	•
Stock—Monte Carlo	•			•
Cheek Piece	•	•		•
Roll Over Cheek Piece	•			•

ANSCHUTZ SPORTER RIFLES
MATCH 64 SPORTER MODELS

MODEL 1416D CLASSIC

MODEL 1416D CUSTOM

MODEL 1416D CLASSIC/CUSTOM
$552.00 ($589.00 22 Magnum)
$630.00 (Left Hand)

1418D MANNLICHER
$830.00 ($847.00 22 Magnum)

MODEL 525 SPORTER
$435.00

RIFLES

SPECIFICATIONS

	Classic 1416D** 1516D	Custom 1416D 1516D	Mannlicher 1418D 1518D	Model 525 Sporter
Length—Overall	41″	41″	38″	43″
Barrel	22½″	22½″	19¾″	24″
Pull	14″	14″	14″	14″
Drop at—Comb	1¼″	1¼″	1¼″	1⅛″
Monte Carlo	1½″	1½″	1½″	1¾″
Heel	1½″	2½″	2½″	2⅝″
Average Weight	5½ lbs.	6 lbs.	5½ lbs.	6½ lbs.
Rate of Twist Right Hand—one turn in 16.5″ for .22 LR; 1–16″ for .22 Mag				
Take Down Bolt Action With Removable Firing Pin	•	•	•	
¾″ Swivel			•	
Swivel Studs	•	•		•

ANSCHUTZ MATCH RIFLES

MODEL 1403D

INTERMEDIATE MATCH RIFLES
$699.50 (1403D)
$806.00 (1803D)

THE ACHIEVER 22 LR
$319.50 (not shown)

SPECIFICATIONS
Capacity: 5 shot
Barrel length: 19½"
Overall length: 35½"-36⅔"
Weight: 5 lbs.
Action: Mark 2000 type repeating
Trigger: #5066-two stage 2.6 lbs.
Safety: Slide
Stock pull: 11⅞"-13"
Sights: Hooded ramp front; rear marble folding leaf; adj. for windage and elevation

SPECIFICATIONS

	1403D*	1803D*
Barrel Length	Precision rifled .22 long rifle only 25" medium heavy ¹¹⁄₁₆" dia.	25½"¾" dia.
Action	Match 64	Match 64
Trigger	1.1 lbs. Single stage, adjustable* for weight of pull, take-up over travel. #5093	#5091 2 stage adjustable* from 9.2 to 10.6 oz.
Safety	Slide safety locks sear and bolt.	Slide safety locks sear and bolt.
Stock	Walnut finished hardwood. Cheekpiece/Swivel Rail. Stippling.	Blonde finish, adjustable cheekpiece. Stippled pistol grip and fore stock. Swivel rail.
Sights	Takes Anschutz 6723 Sight Set (available separately.)	Takes Anschutz 6723 Sight Set (available separately.)
Overall Length	43¼"	43¼"
Weight (avg.)	8.6 lbs. with sights	8.6 lbs.
Left Hand		1803D Left

METALLIC SILHOUETTE RIFLES

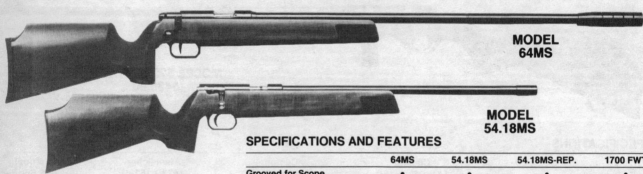

MODEL 64MS

MODEL 54.18MS

64MS	$ 717.00
1700 FWT	995.00
54.18MS	1212.00
Left Hand	1273.00
54.18MS-REP	1650.00

SPECIFICATIONS AND FEATURES

	64MS	54.18MS	54.18MS-REP.	1700 FWT
Grooved for Scope	•	•	•	•
Tapped for Scope Mount	•	•	•	•
Overall Length	39.5"	41"	41–49"	43"
Barrel Length	21½"	22"	22–30"	24"
Length of Pull	13½"	13¾"	13¾"	14"
High Cheekpiece with Monte Carlo Effect	•	•	•	
Drop at Comb	1½"	1½"	1½"	1¼"
Average Weight	8 lbs.	8 lbs. 6 oz.	7 lbs. 12 oz.	6¼ lbs.
Trigger:	#5091	#5018	#5018	#5096
Stage	Two	Two	Two	Single
Factory Adjusted Weight	5.3 oz.	3.9 oz.	3.9 oz.	2.6 lbs.
Adjustable Weight	4.9–7 oz.	2.1–8.6 oz.	2.1–8.6 oz.	2.6–4.4 lbs.
Safety	Slide	Slide	Slide	Wing
True Left-hand Model	•	•		

ANSCHUTZ INTERNATIONAL TARGET RIFLES

MODEL 1913
SUPER MATCH
$2255.00 ($2440.00 Left Hand)

MODEL 1910 (not shown)
SUPER MATCH II
$2013.00 ($2183.00 Left Hand)

MODEL 1911
PRONE MATCH
$1576.00 ($1714.00 Left Hand)

MODEL 1808ED (not shown)
SUPER RUNNING
$1290.00 ($1400.00 Left Hand)

MODEL 1907
ISU STANDARD
$1344.00 ($1462.00 Left Hand)

INTERNATIONAL MATCH RIFLES: SPECIFICATIONS AND FEATURES

	1913	1911	1910	1907	1808ED-Super
Barrel Length	27¼"	27¼"	27¼"	26"	32½"
O/D	1"	1"	1"	⅞"	⅞"
Stock	Int'l.-Thumb Hole Adj. Palm Rest Adj. Hand Rest	Prone	Int'l.-Thumb Hole	Standard	Thumb Hole
Cheek Piece	Adj.	Adj.	Adj.	Removable	Adj.
Butt Plate	Adj. Hook 10 Way Hook	Adj. 4 Way	Adj. Hook 10 Way Hook	Adj. 4 Way	Adj. 4 Way
Recommended Sights	6821, 6823 *6821 Left	6821, 6823 *6821 Left	6821, 6823 *6821 Left	6821, 6823 *6821 Left	Grooved for Scope Mounts
Overall Length	45"–46"	45"–46"	45"–46"	43¾"–44½"	50½"
Overall Length to Hook	49.6"–51.2"		49.6"–51.2"		
Weight (approx) without sights	15.4 lbs.	11.9 lbs.	13.9 lbs.	11 lbs.	9¼ lbs.
True Left-Hand Version	**1913 Left**	**1911 Left**	**1910 Left**	**1907 Left**	**1808 Left**
Trigger	#5018	#5018	#5018	#5018	5020D
Stage	Two	Two	Two	Two	Single
Factory Set Wt.	3.9 oz.	3.9 oz.	3.9 oz.	3.9 oz.	1.2 lbs.
Adjust. Wt.	2.1–8.6 oz.	2.1–8.6 oz.	2.1–8.6 oz.	2.1–8.6 oz.	14 oz.–2.4 lbs.

BEEMAN RIFLES

BEEMAN/WEIHRAUCH HW 60 SMALLBORE RIFLE
$698.00 (Right) $739.95 (Left)

Caliber: 22 LR, single shot. Improved bolt action. Adjustable match trigger with push button safety. Precision rifled barrel. Stippled forearm and pistol grip. Precision aperture sights, hooded front sight ramp. **Barrel length:** 26.8″. **Overall length:** 45.7″. **Weight:** 10.8 lbs.

BEEMAN/WEIHRAUCH HW 60J-ST
BOLT-ACTION RIFLE
$688.00 (60J) $488.00 (60J-ST)

Calibers: 222 Rem. (60J); 22 LR (60J-ST). Features include: walnut stock with cheekpiece; cut-checkered pistol grip and forend; polished blue finish; oil-finished wood. **Sights:** Hooded blade on ramp front; open rear adjustable. **Barrel length:** 22.8″. **Overall length:** 41.7″. **Weight:** 6½ lbs. Imported from West Germany by Beeman.

BEEMAN/WEIHRAUCH HW 660 MATCH RIFLE
$725.00 (Right Hand)

Caliber: 22 LR. Match-type walnut stock with adjustable cheekpiece and buttplate. Adjustable match trigger; stippled pistol grip and forend; forend accessory rail. **Sights:** Globe front; match aperture rear. **Barrel length:** 26″. **Overall length:** 45.3″. **Weight:** 10.7 lbs. Imported from West Germany by Beeman.

BEEMAN/FWB 2600
$1375.00 (Right) $1550.00 (Left)

Caliber: 22 LR. Designed as an identical small-bore companion to the Beeman/FWB 600 Match air rifle. Super rigid stock made of laminated hardwood. Bull barrel free floats. Stock is cut low to permit complete ventilation around barrel. Match trigger has fingertip weight adjustment dial. Adjustable comb; match sights; single shot.

BEEMAN/KRICO RIFLES

Beeman/Krico rifles bring West German tradition to the world of varmint and big game hunting and target shooting in North America. Noted worldwide for their superb balance and handling, these rifles feature hammer forged, precision rifled barrels, exceptionally fine triggers, smoothly operating bolt actions, and interchangeable trigger modules. All models have cheekpieces and fine handcut checkering on the grips and forearms (except target models, which are stippled). All Beeman/Krico rifles are proofed at the factory for accuracy (at 100 meters, hunting rifles must group shots under 1.2 inches; target rifles are under .75 inches).

MODEL 400
$1225.00

Classic German-style 22 Hornet varmint rifle. Beautifully designed for natural balance and easy handling. Detachable 5-shot magazine. Exceptional accuracy. Grooved for scopes. Smooth sliding bolt and crisp trigger action. **Overall length:** 43″. **Weight:** 6.8 lbs.

MODEL 720 BOLT ACTION
$899.00 (270 Win.) $799.00 (30-06)

Features full-length Mannlicher-style stock with metal schnabel forend tip; double-set trigger with optional match trigger available; receiver drilled and tapped for scope mounting. **Calibers:** 270 Win. and 30-06. **Barrel length:** 20³⁄₄″. **Weight:** 6.8 lbs.

MODEL 600/700 BIG GAME RIFLE
$1098.00 (Model 600) $999.00 (Model 700)

Features classic-style European walnut stock with Wundhammer palm swell, rosewood schnabel forend, checkering and rubber butt pad. Also a silent safety and barrel made of hammer-swaged chrome-moly steels, plus detachable 3-shot magazine. **Calibers:** 243 Win. (Model 600) and 30-06 (Model 700). **Barrel length:** 23¹⁄₂″. **Overall length:** 43¹⁄₂″. **Weight:** 7 lbs. **Sights:** Open rear adjustable for windage; hooded front ramp. Imported from West Germany by Beeman.

BLASER RIFLES

MODEL K 77A SINGLE SHOT

SPECIFICATIONS
Calibers: (interchangeable)
    Standard: 22-250, 243 Win., 6.5x55, 270 Win., 280 Rem., 7x57R, 7x65R, 30-06
    Magnum: 7mm Rem. Mag., 300 Win. Mag., 300 Weatherby Mag.
Barrel lengths: 23″ (Standard) and 24″ (Magnum)
Overall length: 39½″ (Standard); 40½″ (Magnum)
Weight: (w/scope mounts) 5½ lbs. (Standard) and 5¾ lbs. (Magnum)
Safety: Tang-mounted safety slide provides cocking and decocking of hammer spring

Stock: Two-piece Turkish walnut stock and forend; solid black recoil pad; handcut checkering (18 lines/inch, borderless)
Length of pull: 14″
Scope mounts: Low-profile Blaser one-piece steel (for 1″ dia. scopes)
Prices:
Standard calibers w/scope mounts. **$2280.00**
Magnum calibers w/scope mounts **2330.00**
Interchangeable barrels—Standard **730.00**
    Magnum. **778.00**

MODEL R 84 BOLT ACTION

SPECIFICATIONS
Calibers: (interchangeable)
    Standard: 22-250, 243 Win., 6mm Rem., 25-06, 270 Win., 280 Rem., 30-06
    Magnum: 257 Weatherby Mag., 264 Win. Mag., 7mm Rem. Mag., 300 Win. Mag., 300 Weatherby Mag., 338 Win. Mag., 375 H&H

Barrel lengths: 23″ (Standard) and 24″ (Magnum)
Overall length: 41″ (Standard) and 42″ (Magnum)
Weight: (w/scope mounts) 7 lbs. (Standard) and 7¼ lbs. (Magnum)
Safety: Locks firing pin and bolt handle
Stock: Two-piece Turkish walnut stock and forend; solid black recoil pad, handcut checkering (18 lines/inch, borderless)
Length of pull: 13¾″
Prices:
Standard calibers w/scope mounts **$1595.00**
Magnum calibers w/scope mounts **1595.00**
Left-Hand Standard w/scope mounts **1645.00**
Left-Hand Magnum w/scope mounts **1645.00**
Interchangeable barrels **545.00**

BRNO RIFLES

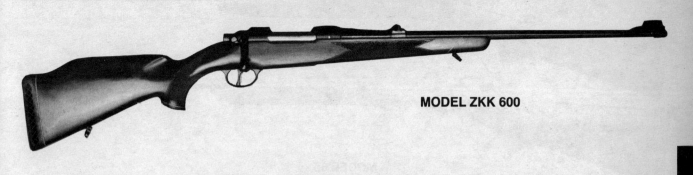

MODEL ZKK 600

MODEL ZKK 602

MODEL ZKK SPECIFICATIONS

Model	Action Type	Cal.	Barrel Specifications			Overall Length	Weight	Magazine Capacity	Sighted In
			Length	Rifling Twist	#Lands				
ZKK 600	bolt	270 Win	23.5 in	1 in 10″	4	44.0 in.	7 lbs. 2 oz.	5	110 yd.
		7×57		1 in 9″	4				
		7×64		1 in 9″	4				
		30.06 Spring			4				
ZKK 601	bolt	223 Rem	23.5 in.	1 in 12″	4	43.0 in.	6 lbs. 3 oz.	5	110 yd.
		243 Win		1 in 10″	4				
ZKK 602	bolt	300 Win mag	25.0 in.	1 in 10″	4	45.5 in.	9 lbs. 4 oz.	5	110 yd.
		8×68		1 in 11″	4				
		375 H&H		1 in 12″	4				

MODEL ZKK

Model	Prices
Model ZKK 600 Standard	$599.00
Model ZKK 601 Monte Carlo Stock	649.00
Model ZKK 602 Standard	689.00
Monte Carlo Stock	749.00

BROWNING LEVER ACTION RIFLES

MODEL 65
$550.00 (Grade I) $850.00 (High Grade)

This new lever-action centerfire rifle features an exposed, three-position hammer, full pistol grip with semi-beavertail forearm, select walnut with high-gloss finish (High Grade has cut-checkering on stock and forearm), and metal buttplate (straight style). **Caliber:** 218 Bee (round nose and hollow-point bullets only—no spitzer bullets). **Barrel length:** 24″. **Overall length:** 41³/₄″. **Weight:** 6 lbs. 12 oz. **Trigger:** Blued (High Grade is gold-plated). **Finish:** Deep blue on all metal surfaces (High Grade has grayed receiver with engraving and gold-plated animals). **Capacity:** 7 rounds. **Sights:** Open; hooded ramp-style front and buckhorn-style adjustable rear. **Sight radius:** 20¼″. **Length of pull:** 13¹/₂″. **Drop at comb:** 1³/₄″. **Drop at heel:** 2³/₈″.

MODEL 1885
$699.95

Calibers: 22-250; 223, 30-06, 270, 7mm Rem. Mag., 45-70 Govt. **Bolt system:** Falling block. **Barrel length:** 28″ (recessed muzzle). **Overall length:** 43¹/₂″. **Weight:** 8 lbs. 12 oz. **Action:** High wall type, single shot, lever action. **Sights:** Drilled and tapped for scope mounts; two-piece scope base available. **Hammer:** Exposed, serrated, three-position with inertia sear. **Stock and Forearm:** Select Walnut, straight grip stock and Schnabel forearm with cut checkering. Recoil pad standard.

MODEL 81 BLR SPECIFICATIONS

Calibers: 222 Rem., 223 Rem. 22-250 Rem., 243 Win., 257 Roberts, 7mm-08 Rem., 284 Win., 308 Win. and 358 Win. **Approximate Weight:** 6 lbs. 15 oz. **Overall length:** 39³/₄″. **Action:** Lever action with rotating head, multiple lug breech bolt with recessed bolt face. Side ejection. **Barrel length:** 20″. Individually machined from forged, heat treated chrome-moly steel; crowned muzzle. **Rifling:** 243 Win., one turn in 10″; 308 and 358 Win., one turn in 12″. **Magazine:** Detachable, 4-round capacity. **Trigger:** Wide, grooved finger piece. Short crisp pull of 4¹/₂ pounds. Travels with lever. **Receiver:** Non-glare top. Drilled and tapped to accept most top scope mounts. Forged and milled steel. All parts are machine-finished and hand-fitted.

Surface deeply polished. **Sights:** Low profile, square notch, screw adjustable rear sight. Gold bead on a hooded raised ramp front sight. Sight radius: 17³/₄″. **Safety:** Exposed, 3-position hammer. Trigger disconnect system. Inertia firing pin. **Stock and forearm:** Select walnut with tough oil finish and sure-grip checkering, contoured for use with either open sights or scope. Straight grip stock. Deluxe recoil pad installed.

Length of pull . . . . 13³/₄″
Drop at comb . . . . 1³/₄″
Drop at heel . . . . 2³/₈″
Price With sights **$472.50**
    Without sights **457.50**

BROWNING RIFLES

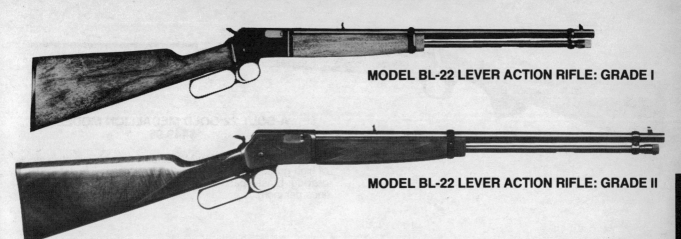

MODEL BL-22 LEVER ACTION RIFLE: GRADE I

MODEL BL-22 LEVER ACTION RIFLE: GRADE II

MODEL BL-22 SPECIFICATIONS

Action: Short throw lever action. Lever travels through an arc of only 33 degrees and carries the trigger with it, preventing finger pinch between lever and trigger on the upward swing. The lever cycle ejects the fired shell, cocks the hammer and feeds a fresh round into the chamber. **Magazine:** Rifle is designed to handle 22 caliber ammunition *in any combination* from tubular magazine. Magazine capacity is 15 Long Rifles, 17 Longs and 22 Shorts. The positive magazine latch opens and closes easily from any position. **Safety:** A unique disconnect system prevents firing until the lever and breech are fully closed and pressure is released from and reapplied to the trigger. An inertia firing pin and an exposed hammer with a half-cock position are other safety features. **Receiver:** Forged and milled steel. Grooved. All parts are machine-finished and hand-fitted. **Trigger:** Clean and crisp without creep. Average pull 5 pounds. Trigger gold-plated on Grade II model. **Stock and forearm:** Forearm and straight grip butt stock are shaped from select, polished walnut. Hand checkered on Grade II model. Stock dimensions:

Length of Pull . . . . 13 1/2"
Drop at Comb . . . . 1 5/8"
Drop at Heel . . . . 2 1/4"

Sights: Precision, adjustable folding leaf rear sight. Raised bead front sight. **Scopes:** Grooved receiver will accept the Browning 22 riflescope (Model 1217) and two-piece ring mount (Model 9417) as well as most other groove or tip-off type mounts or receiver sights. **Engraving:** Grade II receiver and trigger guard are engraved with tasteful scroll designs. **Barrel length:** 20"; recessed muzzle. **Overall length:** 36 3/4". **Weight:** 5 pounds.

Price: Grade I $286.95
Grade II 326.95

MODEL A-BOLT 22 BOLT ACTION
$339.95   ($349.95 w/Sights)

Caliber: 22 LR. **Barrel length:** 22". **Overall length:** 40 1/4". **Average weight:** 5 lbs. 9 oz. **Action:** Short throw bolt. Bolt cycles a round with 60° of bolt rotation. Firing pin acts as secondary extractor and ejector, snapping out fired rounds at prescribed speed. **Magazine:** Five and 15-shot magazine standard. Magazine/clip ejects with a push on magazine latch button. **Trigger:** Gold colored, screw adjustable. Pre-set at approx. 4 lbs. **Stock:** Laminated walnut, classic style with pistol grip. **Length of pull:** 13 3/4". **Drop at comb:** 3/4". **Drop at heel:** 1 1/2". **Sights:** Available with or without sights (add **$10** for sights). Ramp front and adjustable folding leaf rear on open sight model. **Scopes:** Grooved receiver for 22 mount. Drilled and tapped for full-size scope mounts.

NEW: Now available in 22 Magnum.
Price: (with open sights) . . . . **$399.95.**

SPECIFICATIONS RIMFIRE RIFLES

Model	Caliber	Barrel Length	Sight Radius	Overall Length	Average Weight
A-Bolt 22	22 Long Rifle	22"	17 5/8"	40 1/4"	5 lbs. 9 oz.
22 Semi-Auto	22 Long Rifle	19 1/4"	16 1/4"	37"	4 lbs. 4 oz.
BL-22	22 Long Rifle, Longs, Shorts	20"	15 3/8"	36 3/4"	5 lbs.

BROWNING RIFLES

A-BOLT 22 GOLD MEDALLION MODEL
$449.95

The A-Bolt Gold Medallion Model features a classic-style stock of high-grade select walnut with high-gloss finish; detailed engraving; brass spacers; and double-bordered checkering (22 lines per inch).

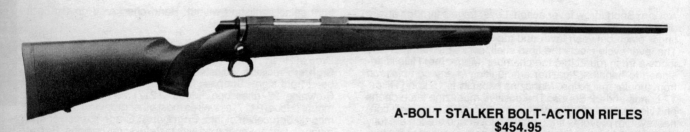

A-BOLT COMPOSITE STALKER

A-BOLT STALKER BOLT-ACTION RIFLES
$454.95

Browning's new graphite-fiberglass composite stock resists the nicks and scrapes of hard hunting and is resistant to weather and humidity. Its recoil-absorbing properties also make shooting a more pleasant experience. This series is available in three models: Stainless Stalker, Composite Stalker and Camo Stalker. The newest of these—the A-Bolt Composite Stalker—has the same features as Browning's A-Bolt Hunter plus the graphite-fiberglass composite stock, which helps ensure accuracy as well as durability. The stock is checkered for a good grip and has a nonglare textured finish. All exposed metal surfaces have a nonglare matte blued finish.

22 SEMIAUTOMATIC RIMFIRE RIFLES
GRADES I AND VI

SPECIFICATIONS
Caliber: 22 LR. **Overall length:** 37". **Barrel length:** 19¹/₄". **Weight:** 4 lbs. 4 oz. **Safety:** Cross-bolt type. **Capacity:** 11 cartridges in magazine, 1 in chamber. **Trigger:** Grade I is blued; Grade VI is gold colored. **Sights:** Gold bead front, adjustable folding leaf rear; drilled and tapped for Browning scope mounts. **Length of pull:** 13³/₄". **Drop at comb:** 1³/₁₆". **Drop at heel:** 2⁵/₈". **Stock & Forearm:** Grade I, select walnut with checkering (18 lines/inch); Grade VI, high-grade walnut with checkering (22 lines/inch).
Grade I $328.50
Grade VI 674.95

GRADE VI

BROWNING RIFLES

A-BOLT BOLT-ACTION RIFLES

Calibers: 25-06 Rem., 270 Win., 280 Rem., 30-06 Sprg., 375 H&H, 7mm Rem. Mag., 300 Win. Mag., 338 Win. Mag. **Action:** Short throw bolt of 60 degrees. Plunger-type ejector. **Magazine:** Detachable. Depress the magazine latch and the hinged floorplate swings down. The magazine can be removed from the floorplate for reloading or safety reasons. **Trigger:** Adjustable within the average range of 3 to 6 pounds. Also grooved to provide sure finger control. **Stock and forearm:** Stock is select grade American walnut cut to the lines of a classic sporter with a full pistol grip.

Scopes: Closed. Clean tapered barrel. Receiver is drilled and tapped for a scope mount; or select **Hunter** model w/open sights. **Barrel length:** 24″. Hammer forged rifling where a precision machined mandrel is inserted into the bore. The mandrel is a reproduction of the rifling in reverse. As hammer forces are applied to the exterior of the barrel, the barrel is actually molded around the mandrel to produce flawless rifling and to guarantee a straight bore. Free floated. **Overall length:** 44 1/4″. **Weight:** 7 lbs. 8 oz. in Magnum; 6 lbs. 8 oz. in Short Action; 7 lbs. in Standard (Long Action).

Hunter	$454.95
Hunter w/open sights	512.95
Medallion (no sights)	527.95
Left-Hand Model	550.95
Medallion 375 H&H (open sights)	617.95
Micro Medallion (no sights)	527.95
Gold Medallion	689.95
Stainless Stalker (no sights)	579.95
Camo Stalker (no sights)	482.95

Short Action A-Bolt available in 223 Rem., 22-250 Rem., 243 Win., 257 Roberts, 7mm-08 Rem., 308 Win.

A-BOLT HIGH-GRADE BOLT-ACTION RIFLE
BIG HORN SHEEP LIMITED EDITION
$1365.00

Calibers: 270. Win. **Barrel length:** 22″. **Overall length:** 42 3/4″. **Approx. weight:** 6 lbs. 11 oz. **Stock:** High grade walnut profiled in classic style, embellished with cut skipline checkering with pearl border design. Rosewood forearm and grip caps. Brass spacers between stock and forearm and grip caps; also between recoil pad and stock. **Engraving:** Deep relief engraving on receiver, barrel, floorplate and trigger guard as setting for game species displayed in 24K gold.

Pronghorn Antelope Issue (243 Win.): **$1240.00**

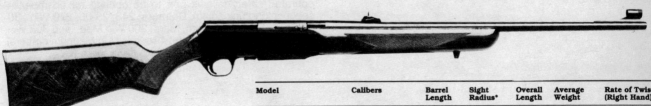

BAR SEMIAUTOMATIC RIFLES

Standard Calibers (Grade I)	$ 594.95
Magnum Calibers (Grade I)	644.95
North American Deer Issue	3550.00

Model	Calibers	Barrel Length	Sight Radius*	Overall Length	Average Weight	Rate of Twist (Right Hand)
Magnum	338 Win. Mag.	24″	19 1/2″	45″	8 lbs. 6 oz.	1 in 12″
Magnum	300 Win Mag.	24″	19 1/2″	45″	8 lbs. 6 oz.	1 in 10″
Magnum	7mm Rem Mag.	24″	19 1/2″	45″	8 lbs. 6 oz.	1 in 9 1/2″
Standard	30-06 Sprg.	22″	17 1/2″	43″	7 lbs. 6 oz.	1 in 10″
Standard	280 Rem.	22″	17 1/2″	43″	7 lbs. 9 oz.	1 in 10″
Standard	270 Win.	22″	17 1/2″	43″	7 lbs. 9 oz.	1 in 10″
Standard	308 Win.	22″	17 1/2″	43″	7 lbs. 9 oz.	1 in 12″
Standard	243 Win.	22″	17 1/2″	43″	7 lbs. 10 oz.	1 in 10″
Big Game Series Ltd. Edition	30-06 Sprg.	22″	—	43″	7 lbs. 6 oz.	1 in 10″

*All models (except Big Game Series) are available with or without open sights. All models drilled and tapped for scope mounts.

CHURCHILL RIFLES

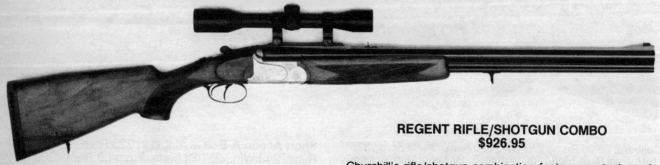

REGENT RIFLE/SHOTGUN COMBO
$926.95

Churchill's rifle/shotgun combination features a stock made of extra select European walnut with hand-checkering and natural oil finish. The integral dovetail mount, integral iron sights and engraved antique silver-finish receiver are standard features. The 12-gauge improved modified choke is available with the following calibers: 222 Rem., 223 Rem., 270 Win., 308 Win., 30-06 Springfield. **Barrel length:** 25″. **Chamber:** 3″. **Weight:** 8 lbs.

HIGHLANDER BOLT-ACTION RIFLE
$459.95

This repeating bolt-action rifle comes with an oil-finished walnut stock with classic design. Other features include twin locking lugs, gas relief port, swivel posts, positive non-slip thumb-operated safety (allows bolt to be opened for chamber inspection and unloading). **Calibers:** 243, 25-06, 270 Win., 30-06 Springfield, 7mm Rem. Mag., 300 Win Mag., and 308 Win. **Barrel length:** 22″. **Capacity:** 4 rounds (3 in Magnum calibers). **Weight:** 7½ to 8 lbs.

"ROTARY 22" RIFLE (not shown)
$129.95

This 22 LR model features a walnut-finished hardwood stock, bolt hold-open device, fixed front sight, adjustable rear sight, and a 10-shot rotary magazine. Drilled and tapped. **Barrel length:** 18″.

CLASSIC RIFLES

STANDARD GRADE
$1862.00

GRADE I (not shown)
$2564.00

GRADE II
$3517.00

CLASSIC RIFLES

Classic Rifles are presently offered in three grades: Standard, Grade I and Grade II. All stocks are made from French walnut and are fitted with forend tips (except Standard Grade), which are either ebony or striped ebony. Stocks are finished with a glass-type finish that is guaranteed for durability.

Standard Grade models feature A Grade French walnut stocks, Sako actions, Shilen Match Grade barrels, Pachmayr "Old English" recoil pads, Leonard Brownell steel grip caps, studs (for sling swivels), and checkering in a 3-point pattern with no wrap-around on the forend.

Grade I is the same as Standard except for the AAA Grade French walnut and checkering (a belted panel on the bottom of the forend).

Grade II features AAA Grade French walnut with fleurs-de-lis on each forend and checkering completely wrapped around. Two fleurs-de-lis appear on the pistol grip area and the floor plate is engraved with scrollwork (plus an animal of the owner's choice).

Specifications include the following: **Barrel lengths:** 22″ (medium calibers) and 24″ (long-action calibers and magnums). **Weight:** 6 lbs. (medium calibers) and 7¼ lbs. (long-action magnums). **Length of pull:** 13⅝″. Recoil pads are standard. Stocks can be made to order.

DAKOTA ARMS

CLASSIC GRADE

DAKOTA 76 RIFLES

Now available:

DAKOTA 76 Short Action, a scaled-down version of Dakota's standard length action designed specifically for shorter cartridges (standard chamberings include 22-250, 243, 6mm Rem., 250-3000, 7mm-08, 308 and 358). Available in right- and left-hand versions in two grades—Classic and Alpine. **Barrel length:** 21″. The Alpine Grade is a lighter weight rifle featuring a blind magazine, slimmer stock and barrel, with a 4-round capacity. **Weight:** approx. 6½ lbs. **Price:** $1850.00.

416 RIGBY African Grade Rifle is designed specifically for the 416 Rigby cartridge. Features include a special magazine (4-round capacity), select wood, cross bolts in the stock, and all other features found in Safari Grade rifles. **Price:** $3500.00.

SPECIFICATIONS
Calibers:
    Safari Grade: 338 Win. Mag., 300 Win. Mag., 375 H&H Mag., 458 Win. Mag.
    Classic Grade: 257 Roberts, 270 Win., 280 Rem., 30-06, 7mm Rem. Mag., 338 Win. Mag., 300 Win. Mag., 375 H&H Mag., 458 Win. Mag.

Barrel length: 23″
Weight: 7½ lbs. (Classic); 8½ lbs. (Safari)
Safety: Three-position striker-blocking safety allows bolt operation with safety on
Sights: Ramp front sight; standing leaf rear sight
Stock: Medium fancy walnut stock fitted with recoil pad (Classic); fancy walnut with ebony forend tip and recoil pad (Safari)
Prices:
Safari Grade	$2850.00
Classic Grade	1950.00
Barreled actions: Safari Grade	1800.00
Classic Grade	1450.00
Actions: Safari Grade	1400.00
Classic Grade	1200.00

Note: Numerous options are available, including choice of wood (English, Black/Claro, Bastogne), quarter rib, ebony forend tip, wraparound checkering, etc.

HECKLER & KOCH RIFLES

Based on the design of its dependable military firearms, which have been a standard of the industry for more than 25 years, Heckler & Koch has introduced three hunting rifles—Models 940, 770 and 630. Each one features a polygonal cold hammer-forged barrel that increases bullet velocities, prolongs barrel life and maintains accuracy. All three models feature a delayed roller-locked bolt system, providing soft recoil for big game rifles. They also include one-piece European walnut stocks and come designed for scope mounting.

MODEL HK 940
$961.00

SPECIFICATIONS
Caliber: 30-06
Capacity: 3 rounds
Barrel length: 21.6″
Rifling: Polygonal
Twist: 10.0″, right hand

Overall length: 47.2″
Weight: 8.62 lbs.
Sights: V-notch rear (adjustable for windage); post front (adjustable for elevation)
Stock: European walnut
Finish: Polished blue

MODEL HK 770
$887.00

SPECIFICATIONS
Caliber: 308
Capacity: 3 rounds
Barrel length: 19.7″
Rifling: Polygonal
Twist: 11″, right hand

Overall length: 44.4″
Weight: 7.92 lbs.
Sights: V-notch rear (adjustable for windage); post front (adjustable for elevation)
Stock: European walnut
Finish: Polished blue

MODEL HK 630
$813.00

SPECIFICATIONS
Caliber: 223
Capacity: 4 rounds
Barrel length: 17.7″
Rifling: Polygonal
Twist: 10.6″, right hand

Overall length: 42.1″
Weight: 7.04 lbs.
Sights: V-notch rear (adjustable for windage); post front (adjustable for elevation)
Stock: European walnut
Finish: Polished blue

HECKLER & KOCH RIFLES

RIFLES

MODEL HK PSG-1 HIGH PRECISION MARKSMAN'S RIFLE
$8728.00

SPECIFICATIONS
Caliber: 308
Capacity: 5 rounds and 20 rounds
Barrel length: 25.6″
Rifling: 4 groove, polygonal
Twist: 12″, right hand
Overall length: 47.5″
Weight: 17.8 lbs.
Sights: Hensoldt 6 × 42 telescopic
Stock: Matte black, high-impact plastic
Finish: Matte black, phosphated

SEMIAUTOMATIC VARMINT RIFLES
MODEL HK 300
$608.00

The Model HK 300 features a European walnut checkered stock. All metal parts are finished in a high-luster custom blue. The receiver is fitted with special bases for HK 05 quick snap-on clamp mount with 1-inch rings that will fit all standard scopes. The positive locking action of the HK 05 provides for instant scope mounting with no change in zero, even after hundreds of repetitions. The rifle has a V-notch rear sight, adjustable for windage, and a front sight adjustable for elevation. Scope mounts are available as an additional accessory.

SPECIFICATIONS
Caliber: 22 Winchester Magnum
Weight: 5.7 lbs.
Barrel length: 19.7″ (all-steel hammer forged, polygonal profile)
Overall length: 39.4″
Magazine: Box type; 5- and 15-round capacity
Sights: V-notch rear, adjustable for windage; post front, adjustable for elevation
Trigger: Single stage, 3½ lb. pull
Action: Straight blow-back inertia bolt
Stock: Top-grade European walnut, checkered pistol grip and forearm
Price: **$598.00**

HEYM RIFLES

SAFETY MODEL 22S SHOTGUN/RIFLE
$2400.00

The Model 22S offers a special break-open action in which the cocking is accomplished by manually pushing forward a cocking slide located on the tang. For ultimate safety, the gun will automatically uncock by means of a built-in rocker weight if it is dropped or jostled about.

The Model 22S comes with single-set trigger, left-side barrel selector, arabesque engraving, walnut stock and an integral dovetail base for scope mounting.

SPECIFICATIONS
Shotgun barrels: 12 ga., 2³/₄″; 16 ga., 2³/₄″; 20 ga., 2³/₄″ and 3″. **Rifle barrels:** 22 Mag., 22 Hornet; 222 Rem.; 222 Rem. Mag.; 5.6 × 50 R Mag.; 6.5 × 57 R; 7 × 57 R; 243 Win. **Barrel length:** 24″. **Length of pull:** 14¹/₂″. **Overall length:** 40″.
MODEL 22SZ:
Same as above, takedown model . . . . **add'l $370.00**

MAGNUM

STANDARD

MODEL SR20

Features two rugged Mauser-type locking lugs. A special guide rail allows the bolt to operate smoothly through the full length of travel. All parts are interchangeable. The magazine holds five regular or three Magnum cartridges. A hinged floorplate with convenient latch makes unloading easy.

SPECIFICATIONS
Calibers: (Standard) 243 Win., 270 Win., 308 Win., 30-06; (Magnum) 7mm Rem. Mag., 300 Win. Mag., 338 Win. Mag., 375 H&H Mag., plus metric calibers.
Barrel length: 22″ and 24″ (Standard); 23″ (Magnum)
Length of pull: 14″
Weight: 7 lb. 10 oz. (Standard); 8 lbs. (Magnum)
Stock: French walnut, hand checkering, Pachmayr Old English pad, oil finish, steel grip cap
Prices:
Model SR20 (Standard) **$1450.00**
Model SR20 (Magnum) 1500.00
Single set trigger for all models 125.00
Left-hand action and stock 350.00

MODEL SR20 CLASSIC
$1600.00

Features a hand-checkered, oil-finished stock, all-steel bottom metal with straddled floorplate and inside release, plus steel grip cap. Other specifications same as Model SR20.

HEYM RIFLES

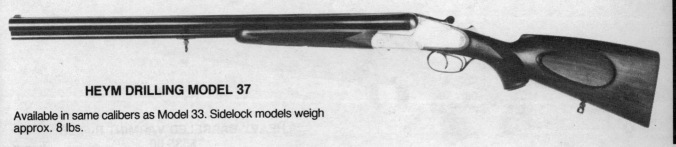

HEYM DRILLING MODEL 33

The Heym Drilling Model 33 is available in Standard or Deluxe boxlock versions in **calibers:** 222 Rem., 243 Win., 270 Win., 308 Win., and 30-06. **Weight:** approx. 6.8 lbs.

Prices:
Standard with arabesque engraving $6000.00
Deluxe with hunting scene engraving 6400.00

HEYM DRILLING MODEL 37

Available in same calibers as Model 33. Sidelock models weigh approx. 8 lbs.

Prices:
Standard with border engraving . . . . $ 9,400.00
Deluxe with hunting scene engraving 11,000.00

MODEL 88 SAFARI DOUBLE RIFLE

This German-built boxlock model has a modified Anson & Deeley action with standing sears, plus Purdey-type double underlocking lugs and Greener extension with crossbolt. Actions are furnished with sliding safeties and cocking indicators on the top tang, nonbreakable coil springs, front single set triggers and steel trigger guards.

SPECIFICATIONS
Calibers: 375 H&H, 458 Winchester, 470 & 500 Nitro Express
Barrel length: 25″
Overall length: 42″
Weight: 10 lbs. (approx.)
Sights: Three-leaf express sight with standing, shallow V-sight; large gold bead front sight

Prices:
Model 88 BW Safari in 375 H&H and 458 Win. . . . **$5600.00**

HOWA RIFLES

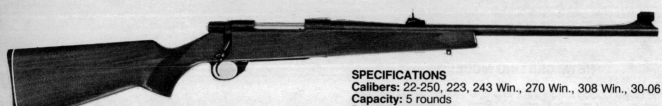

TROPHY SPORTING RIFLES
$495.00
($510.00 in 7mm Rem. Mag., 300 Win. Mag.)

SPECIFICATIONS
Calibers: 22-250, 223, 243 Win., 270 Win., 308 Win., 30-06
Capacity: 5 rounds
Barrel length: 22″
Overall length: 42¹/₂″
Weight: 7¹/₂ lbs.
Also available:
Model 1500 Trophy Grade $465.00
 In 7mm Rem. Mag and 300 Win. Mag.X **480.00**

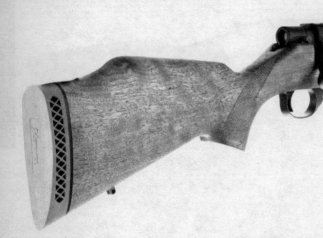

HEAVY-BARRELED VARMINT RIFLES
$535.00

SPECIFICATIONS
Calibers: 223 and 22-250
Barrel length: 24″
Overall length: 44¹/₂″
Weight: 9¹/₄ lbs.

HOWA LIGHTNING SPORTING RIFLES
$495.00
($510.00 in 7mm Rem. Mag.)

SPECIFICATIONS
Calibers: 270, 30-06, 7mm Rem. Mag.
Barrel length: 22″
Overall length: 42¹/₂″
Weight: 7 lbs.
Stock: Lightweight Carbolite

MODEL 1500 SERIES
BARRELED ACTIONS (not shown)
$275.00 (Standard Calibers)
$290.00 (300 Win. Mag. & 7mm Rem. Mag.)

SPECIFICATIONS
Calibers: 243 Win., 270 Win., 30-06, 308 Win. (standard); 223 Rem., 22-250 Rem. (heavy barreled varmint); 7mm Rem. Mag., 300 Win. Mag. (Magnum)
Capacity: 5 rounds (3 rounds in Magnum)
Barrel lengths: 22″ (standard); 24″ (heavy barreled varmint and Magnum)
Overall lengths: 27³/₄″ (standard); 29³/₄″ (heavy barreled and Magnum)
Weight: 5 lbs. 5 oz. (standard); 7 lbs. 1 oz. (heavy barreled varmint); 7 lbs. 9 oz. (Magnum)

IVER JOHNSON RIFLES

WAGONMASTER LEVER ACTION
$166.50 (22 S, L, LR)
$187.50 (22 Win. Mag.)

SPECIFICATIONS
Caliber: 22 Short, Long, Long Rifle (also available in 22 Win. Mag.)
Barrel length: 18½″
Weight: 5¾ lbs.
Overall length: 36½″

Sights: Hooded ramp front; adjustable rear
Capacity: 21 Short, 17 Long, or 15 Long Rifle; can be mixed and loaded simultaneously; Magnum has 12-shot capacity
Finish: Blue
Stock: Hardwood

TARGETMASTER
$166.50

SPECIFICATIONS
Caliber: 22 Short, Long, or Long Rifle
Magazine capacity: 19 Short, 15 Long, or 12 Long Rifle (can be mixed and loaded simultaneously
Barrel length: 18½″

Overall length: 36½″
Weight: 5¾ lbs.
Sights: Hooded ramp front; adjustable rear

L'IL CHAMP SINGLE SHOT BOLT .22
$89.00

SPECIFICATIONS
Caliber: 22 S, L & LR
Barrel length: 16¼″
Overall length: 32½″

Weight: 2 lbs. 11 oz.
Finish: Molded stock; nickel-plated bolt

K.D.F. RIFLES

MAUSER MODEL 225
$1400.00 ($1490.00 in Magnum)

SPECIFICATIONS

Calibers: 243, 25-06, 270, 7x57, 30-06, 308 Win., 308 Norma, 300 Win. Mag., 7mm Rem. Mag., 375 H&H Mag., 270 Weatherby Mag., 300 Weatherby Mag., 257 Weatherby Mag. Other calibers available on special request.
Magazine capacity: Standard, 4 cartridges; Magnum, 3 cartridges
Barrel length: Standard, 24"; Magnum, 26"
Overall length: Standard, 44⅞"; Magnum, 46⅞"
Weight: Approx. 8 lbs.
Trigger pull: 13⅞"
Shortest ignition time: Striker travels only 158-thousands of an inch. The extremely light striker is accelerated by a powerful striker spring . . . A patented two cocking cam design enables a very light and smooth cocking of the striker assembly . . . Two-piece firing pin.
Clip feature: Removable; can also be fed from top.
3 locking lugs: With large contact area . . . also Stellite locking insert.
60-Degree bolt lift only: For fast reloading.

Safety: Located on right-hand side . . . locking trigger and sear . . . Most convenient location.
Fine adjustable crisp trigger: 2½ lbs. to 7 lbs. . . . Two major moving parts only.
Stocks: American or European Walnut stocks with 1-inch recoil pad . . . Rosewood pistol grip cap . . . 20-line hand-checkering . . . Quick detachable swivels . . . Barrel is free floating . . . Oil finish . . . Available in right- or left-hand stocks . . . AAA grade stocks available. Monte Carlo style is standard. Classic, featherweight, thumbhole and competition-style stocks available.
Receiver: Drilled and tapped for scope mounts
Options: Iron sights . . . Set trigger . . . Recoil arrestor . . . KDF offers own bases to take 1" or 30mm rings.

Also available: .411 KDF Magnum Dangerous Game Rifle. Choice of iron sights or scope mounts and rings; also choice of finish. KDF recoil arrester included. Guaranteed to shoot 3 shots in ½" and 5 shots within 1" at 100 yards with proper loads. **Price: $1800.**

MAUSER MODEL 201 BOLT ACTION DELUXE
$650.00 (22 LR)
$715.00 (22 WMR)

SPECIFICATIONS

Caliber: 22 LR, 22 Mag.
Barrel length: 21.7"; chrome-moly steel, 4 grooves
Overall length: 40"
Weight: 6.6 lbs.

Action: Two locking lugs w/large contact area 60° bolt lift
Receiver: Two rails for scope mounting; scope mounts available from K.D.F.
Stock: European walnut, hand-checkered, rosewood forend, oil finish; sling swivels

KIMBER RIFLES

SPECIFICATIONS
Caliber: 22 LR
Capacity: 5 or 10-shot detachable magazine
Barrel length: 22" (6 grooves, 1 in 16" twist)
Overall length: 40½"
Weight: 6½lbs.
Stock: Deluxe grade is AA Claro walnut with ebony tip and Niedner-style checkered steel buttplate (no cheekpiece). Also includes hand-checkering and fully inletted swivel

MODEL 82 RIMFIRE SPORTING RIFLE

studs. **Super Grade** is AAA Claro walnut with ebony forend tip and beaded cheekpiece. Also hand-checkering, Niedner-style buttplate and fully inletted swivel studs. Both grades have round top receivers with screw-on two-piece scope mount bases.
Prices:
DELUXE GRADE (no sights, Sporterweight) . . . . . $ 995.00
SUPER GRADE (no sights, Sporterweight) 1095.00

SPECIFICATIONS
Caliber: 22 LR (rear-locking, bolt-action, single-shot target rifle)
Barrel length: 25" (6 grooves, 1 turn in 16")
Overall length: 43½
Weight: 10 to 10¾ lbs.
Stock: Claro walnut

MODEL 82 GOVERNMENT

Features: Single stage trigger fully adjustable for overtravel, sear engagement and pressure. Match-grade barrel is precision-rifled, step-crowned and air-gauge inspected. Grooved receiver accepts Kimber scope mounts. Barrel has 2 rear bases for barrel-mounted scopes.
Price:
MODEL 82 GOVERNMENT (without sights) **$575.00**

SPECIFICATIONS
Calibers: 17 Rem., 222 Rem., 223.
Magazine capacity: 5 shots
Barrel length: 24" varminter
Overall length: 40½" (Sporter); 42½" (Varminter)
Weight: 6½ lbs. (Sporter); 7¼ lbs. (Super Varminter)
Stocks: Deluxe Grade—AA Claro walnut w/ebony forend tip (no cheekpiece); hand-checkering; Niedner-style buttplate; fully inletted swivel studs and steel grip cap. **Super Grade**—AAA Claro walnut w/ebony forend tip; beaded cheekpiece; hand-checkering; Niedner-style buttplate; fully inletted swivel studs and steel grip cap. **Ultra Varminter** stock is made of laminated birch (no cheekpiece), plus curved rubber butt pad and conventional swivel studs. **Super Varminter**

MODEL 84 SPORTER

stock is AAA Claro walnut w/ebony forend tip, beaded cheekpiece, hand-checkering, curved rubber butt pad and fully inletted swivel studs.
Features: Mauser-type head locking repeater; steel trigger guard and hinged floorplate; fully adjustable trigger; positive rotating disc-type safety; round top receivers with two-piece screw-on scope mount bases.
Prices:
DELUXE GRADE (no sights, Sporterweight) **$1150.00**
SUPER GRADE (no sights; Sporterweight) 1250.00
ULTRA VARMINT (no sights; medium-heavy stainless barrel and laminated stock) 1165.00
SUPER VARMINT (no sights, medium-heavy barrel) 1265.00

KIMBER RIFLES

MODEL 89 BIG GAME RIFLE

SPECIFICATIONS
Calibers: 270, 280, 30-06, 7mm Rem. Mag., 300 Win. Mag., 338 Win. Mag., 375 H&H
Barrel length: 22" (24" for magnums)
Weight: 7 1/2 lbs. (8 1/2 lbs. in 300, 338 and 375 calibers)
Stocks: Deluxe Grades—AA Claro walnut w/ebony forend tip (270, 280, 30-06 calibers); "A" English walnut (magnum calibers). Plain buttstock (no cheekpiece). Rubber recoil pad and fully inletted swivel studs. **Super Grades**—AAA Claro walnut w/ebony forend tip (AA English walnut in magnum calibers). Beaded cheekpiece, rubber recoil pad and fully inletted swivel studs.

Features: Model 70-type override trigger design and Presentation Model 70-type ejector. Mauser-type head locking bolt action w/steel trigger guard and floorplate. Fully adjustable trigger; Mauser-type extractor. Chrome Moly barrel and 3-position Winchester-style safety.

Prices:
DELUXE GRADE (no sights, round top receiver)   **$1395.00**
  Same as above in 375 H&H 1495.00
SUPER GRADE (no sights, square bridge, dovetail receiver) 1495.00
  Same as above in 375 H&H 1595.00

MODEL 89 AFRICAN

Stock: AA grade English walnut w/ebony forend tip; beaded English-style cheekpiece
Features: Controlled feed head-locking Kimber magnum-sized action; Mauser-style extractor and bolt stop; express sights on contoured quarter rib; banded front sight. Also, barrel-mounted recoil lug and integral receiver lug, plus twin recoil cross pins in stock.
Price:
MODEL 89 AFRICAN **$3200.00**

SPECIFICATIONS
Calibers: 375 H&H, 404 Jeffrey, 416 Rigby, 460 Weatherby, 505 Gibbs
Barrel length: 24" (6 grooves, 1 turn in 10")
Overall length: 47"
Weight: 10 to 10 1/2 lbs.

KRIEGHOFF DOUBLE RIFLES

MODEL TECK O/U

MODEL TECK OVER/UNDER

SPECIFICATIONS
Calibers: 308, 30-06, 300 Win. Mag., 375 H&H, 458 Win.
Mag.
Barrel length: 25″
Action: Boxlock; double greener-type crossbolt and double
barrel lug locking, steel receiver
Weight: 7½ lbs.
Triggers: Double triggers; single trigger optional
Safety: Located on top tang
Sights: Open sight with right angle front sight
Stock: German-styled with pistol grip and cheekpiece; oil-fin-
ished
Length of stock: 14³/₈″
Finish: Nickel-plated steel receiver with satin grey finish
Prices:
Model Teck (Boxlock) $6990.00
In 375 H&H and 458 Win. Mag. 7850.00
Teck-Handspanner (16 ga. receiver only;
7x65R, 30-06, 308 Win.) 7990.00
Also available:
TRUMPF SBS (Side-by-side boxlock) 8400.00

MODEL ULM OVER/UNDER

SPECIFICATIONS
Calibers: 308 Win., 30-06, 300 Win. Mag., 375 H&H, 458 Win.
Mag.
Barrel length: 25″
Weight: 7.8 lbs.
Triggers: Double triggers (front trigger = bottom; rear trig-
ger = upper
Safety: Located on top tang
Sights: Open sight w/right angle front sight
Stock: German-styled with pistol grip and cheekpiece; oil-fin-
ished
Length of stock: 14³/₈″
Forearm: Semi-beavertail
Prices:
Model ULM (Sidelock) $11,500.00
Primus (Deluxe Sidelock) 14,500.00
Dekor (Light scroll engraving) 10,500.00
Also available:
NEPTUN SBS (Side-by-side sidelock) 13,500.00

MARK X RIFLES
ACTIONS & BARRELED ACTIONS

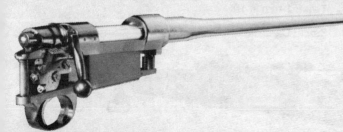

BARRELED ACTIONS
$275.00 (Standard Calibers)
$290.00 (7mm Rem. Mag., 300 Win. Mag.)
$355.00 (375 H&H, 458 Win. Mag.)

Hand-fitted with premium hammer-forged barrels created from
corrosion resistant chrome vanadium steel. Each barreled action is carefully proofed and marked under close government
control, ready to drop into the stock of your choice.

Calibers: 22-250, 243, 25-06, 270, 7 × 57, 7mm Rem. Mag.,
300 Win. Mag., 308, 30-06. **Barrel length:** 24″. **Weight:** 5½
lbs. (5¾ lbs. in 22-250, 243, and 25-06). **Rifling twist:** 10 (14
in 22-250 and 9.5 in 7 × 57).

Also available in 375 H&H Mag. and 458 Win. Mag. Same barrel length but different weights: 6 lbs. (375 H&H Mag.) and 5.75
lbs. (458 Win. Mag.). **Rifling twist:** 12 (375 H&H Mag.) and
14 (458 Win. Mag.). **Price: $340.00**

MAUSER SYSTEM ACTIONS
$185.00 (Single Shot)

Type A: 7×57mm to 30-06. Standard magazine
³/₈″) and bolt face (.470″) **$230.00**
Type B: 22-250 to 308. Short magazine (2⁷/₈″);
standard bolt face **230.00**
Type C: 7mm Rem. Mag. to 458 Win. Mag. Standard
magazine and Magnum bolt face (.532″) **235.00**

Also available:
Type D: 300 Win. Mag. to 375 H&H. Magnum
magazine (3¹¹/₁₆″) and Magnum bolt face **260.00**
Mini-Mark X (.17 to .223) **215.00**

MARK X RIFLES

MINI-MARK X
$385.00 (with sights)

SPECIFICATIONS
Caliber: 223
Capacity: 5 rounds
Barrel length: 20″
Twist: I turn in 10″
Overall length: 39³/₄″
Weight: 6.35 lbs.
Trigger: Adjustable

MARK X LTW SPORTER
$480.00 (270 and 30-06)
$495.00 (7mm Rem. Mag.)

SPECIFICATIONS
Calibers: 270, 30-06, 7mm Rem. Mag.
Capacity: 5 rounds; 3 in 7mm Rem. Mag.
Barrel length: 20″
Twist: 1 turn in 10″
Weight: 7 lbs.
Stock: Carbolite

AMERICAN FIELD MAUSER SYSTEM
SPORTING RIFLES $570.00
$585.00 (7mm Rem. Mag. and 300 Win. Mag.)

Features forged and machined Mauser System actions . . .
Hammer-forged, chrome, vanadium steel barrels . . . Drilled
and tapped for scope mounts and receiver sights . . . Hooded
ramp front and fully adjustable rear sight . . . All-steel button
release magazine floor plate . . . Detachable sling swivels . . .
Silent sliding thumb safety . . . Prime European walnut stocks
. . . Sculpted, low-profile cheekpiece . . . Rubber recoil butt
plate . . . Steel grip cap.

Calibers: 22-250, 243 Win., 25-06, 270 Win., 7 × 57, 308
Win., 30-06, 7mm Rem. Mag., 300 Win. Mag. **Barrel length:**
24″. **Overall length:** 44″. **Weight:** 7 lbs. **Capacity:** 5 rounds.

Also available: **VISCOUNT MAUSER SYSTEM SPORTING RI-
FLES.** Same as American Field, but without European walnut
stock: **$460.00.** In 7mm Rem. Mag. or 300 Win. Mag.: **$475.00.**

MARLIN RIFLES

MODEL 9 CAMP CARBINE
$311.95

SPECIFICATIONS
Caliber: 9mm
Capacity: 12-shot clip (20-shot magazine available)
Action: Semi-automatic. Manual bolt hold-open. Garand-type safety, magazine safety, loaded chamber indicator. Solid-top, machined steel receiver is sandblasted to prevent glare,

and is drilled and tapped for scope mounting.
Stock: Walnut finished hardwood with pistol grip; tough Mar-Shield™ finish; rubber rifle butt pad; swivel studs
Barrel length: 16½" with Micro-Groove® rifling

Sights: Adjustable rear, ramp front sight with brass bead; Wide-Scan™ hood. Receiver drilled and tapped for scope mount.
Overall length: 35½"
Weight: 6¼ lbs.

MODEL 45
$311.95

SPECIFICATIONS
Caliber: 45 Auto
Capacity: 7-shot clip
Barrel length: 16½"
Overall length: 35½"

Weight (approx.): 6.75 lbs.
Stock: Walnut finished hardwood with pistol grip; rubber rifle butt pad; swivel studs

Sights: Adjustable open rear; ramp front sight with brass bead; Wide-Scan hood

MARLIN 60
$123.95

SPECIFICATIONS
Caliber: 22 Long Rifle
Capacity: 17-shot tubular magazine with patented closure system
Barrel length: 22"
Weight: 5½ lbs.

Overall length: 40½"
Sights: Ramp front sight; adjustable open rear, receiver grooved for tip-off scope mount
Action: Semiautomatic; side ejection; manual and automatic "last-shot"

hold-open devices; receiver top has serrated, non-glare finish; cross-bolt safety
Stock: One-piece walnut-finished hardwood Monte Carlo stock with full pistol grip; Mar-Shield® finish

MARLIN RIFLES

MODEL 30AS
$286.95   ($334.95 w/scope)

SPECIFICATIONS

Caliber : 30/30
Capacity: 6-shot tubular magazine
Action: Lever action w/hammer block safety; solid top receiver w/side ejection; hammer block safety

Stock: Walnut-finish hardwood stock w/ pistol grip; Mar-Shield® finish
Sights: Tapped for scope mount and receiver sight; also available in combination w/4x, 32mm, 1″ scope

Barrel: 20″ Micro-Groove® barrel
Overall length: 38¹/₄″
Weight: Approx. 7 lbs.

MODEL 25MN
$150.95 with scope

SPECIFICATIONS

Caliber: 22 Win. Mag Rimfire (not interchangeable with any other 22 cartridge)

Capacity: 7-shot clip magazine
Stock: One-piece walnut-finished hardwood Monte Carlo with full pistol grip
Barrel length: 22″ with Micro-Groove® rifling

Overall length: 41″
Weight: 6 lbs.
Sights: Adjustable open rear, ramp front sight; receiver grooved for tip-off scope mount

MODEL 25N
$131.95

Same specifications as Model 25MN, except **caliber** 22 LR and **weight** 5¹/₂ lbs.

MARLIN RIFLES

MODEL 70HC
$138.95

SPECIFICATIONS
Caliber: 22 LR
Barrel length: 16¼"
Overall length: 35¼"
Weight: 3.75 lbs.

Capacity: 7-shot clip
Sights: Adjustable open rear; ramp front
Stock: Walnut-finished hardwood with full pistol grip

Action: Semiautomatic; side ejection; manual bolt hold-open; cross-bolt safety
Features: Zippered carrying case included

MODEL 70P "PAPOOSE"
$155.95 (without scope)

SPECIFICATIONS
Caliber: 22 LR
Capacity: 13-shot tubular magazine
Barrel length: 18"
Overall length: 36½"

Weight: 5½ lbs.
Stock: Monte Carlo walnut finish hardwood
Action: Semiautomatic; side ejection;

manual and "last-shot" automatic bolt hold-opens
Sights: Adjustable open rear; ramp front sight

MODEL 75C
$123.95

SPECIFICATIONS
Caliber: 22 LR
Capacity: 13-shot tubular magazine
Barrel length: 18"
Overall length: 36½"

Weight: 5½ lbs.
Stock: Monte Carlo walnut finish hardwood
Action: Semiautomatic; side ejection; manual and "last-shot" automatic

bolt hold-opens
Sights: Adjustable open rear; ramp front sight

MARLIN 22 RIFLES

MARLIN 995
$165.95

SPECIFICATIONS

Caliber: 22 Long Rifle
Action: Semiautomatic
Capacity: 7-shot clip magazine
Barrel: 18″ with Micro-Groove® rifling (16 grooves)

Stock: Monte Carlo genuine American black walnut with full pistol grip; checkering on pistol grip and forend
Sights: Adjustable folding semi-buckhorn rear; ramp front sight with brass bead, Wide-Scan™ hood

Overall length: 36³/₄″
Weight: About 5¹/₂ lbs.
Features: Receiver grooved for tip-off scope mount; bolt hold-open device; cross-bolt safety

MARLIN 15Y "LITTLE BUCKAROO™"
Single Shot 22 Beginner's Rifle
$120.95

SPECIFICATIONS

Caliber: 22 Short, Long or Long Rifle
Capacity: Single shot
Action: Bolt action; easy-load feed throat; thumb safety; red cocking indicator

Stock: One-piece walnut finish hardwood Monte Carlo with full pistol grip; tough Mar-Shield® finish
Barrel length: 16¹/₄″ (16 grooves)

Sights: Adjustable open rear; ramp front sight
Overall length: 33¹/₄″
Weight: 4¹/₄ lbs.

MARLIN BOLT ACTION RIFLES

MARLIN 880
$181.95

MARLIN 881
$188.95

SPECIFICATIONS (MODEL 880)
Caliber: 22 Long Rifle
Capacity: Clip magazine holds 7 cartridges
Action: Bolt action; serrated, anti-glare receiver top; positive thumb safety; red cocking indicator

Stock: Monte Carlo genuine American black walnut with full pistol grip; checkering on pistol grip and forend; tough Mar-Shield® finish; rubber butt pad; swivel studs
Barrel: 22" with Micro-Groove® rifling (16 grooves)
Sights: Adjustable folding semi-buckhorn rear; ramp front with Wide-Scan™ with hood; receiver grooved for tip-off scope mount
Overall length: 41"
Weight: About 5½ lbs.

MARLIN 881: Specifications same as Marlin 880, except with tubular magazine that holds 17 Long Rifle cartridges. **Weight:** About 6 lbs.

MARLIN 883 MAGNUM
$207.95

SPECIFICATIONS
Caliber: 22 Win. Magnum Rimfire (not interchangeable with any other 22 cartridge)
Capacity: 12-shot tubular magazine with patented closure system
Action: Bolt action; serrated, anti-glare receiver top; positive thumb safety; red cocking indicator

Stock: Monte Carlo genuine American black walnut with full pistol grip; checkering on pistol grip and underside of forend; rubber butt pad; swivel studs; tough Mar-Shield® finish
Barrel: 22" with Micro-Groove® rifling (20 grooves)
Sights: Adjustable folding semi-buckhorn rear; ramp front with Wide-Scan™ hood; receiver grooved for tip-off scope mount
Overall length: 41"
Weight: About 6 lbs.

MARLIN 882 MAGNUM: Specifications same as 883 Magnum, except with 7-shot clip magazine **$199.95**

MARLIN LEVER ACTION CARBINES

MARLIN 1895SS
$408.95

SPECIFICATIONS
Caliber: 45/70 Government
Capacity: 4-shot tubular magazine
Action: Lever action w/square finger lever; hammer block safety; receiver top sandblasted to prevent glare

Stock: American black walnut pistol grip stock w/rubber rifle butt pad and Mar-Shield® finish; white pistol grip and butt spacers
Barrel: 22″ Micro-Groove® barrel
Sights: Ramp front sight w/brass bead

and Wide-Scan™ hood; receiver tapped for scope mount or receiver sight
Overall length: 40¹/₂″
Weight: 7¹/₂ lbs.

MARLIN 1894S
$379.95

SPECIFICATIONS
Calibers: 41 Mag., 44 Rem. Mag./44 Special, 45 Colt
Capacity: 10-shot tubular magazine
Action: Lever action w/square finger lever; hammer block safety

Stock: American black walnut stock w/ Mar-Shield™ finish; blued steel forend cap
Barrel: 20″ Micro-Groove® barrel
Sights: Ramp front sight w/brass bead

and Wide-Scan™ hood; solid top receiver tapped for scope mount or receiver sight
Overall length: 37¹/₂″
Weight: 6 lbs.

MARLIN 1894CS 357 MAGNUM
$379.95

SPECIFICATIONS
Caliber: 357 Magnum, 38 Special
Capacity: 9-shot tubular magazine
Action: Lever action w/square finger lever; hammer block safety; side ejection; solid top receiver; deeply blued metal surfaces; receiver top sandblasted to prevent glare

Stock: Straight-grip two-piece genuine American black walnut with white butt plate spacer; tough Mar-Shield® finish.
Barrel: 18¹/₂″ long with modified Micro-Groove® rifling (12 grooves)
Sights: Adjustable semi-buckhorn folding rear, bead front; solid top receiver

tapped for scope mount or receiver sight; offset hammer spur for scope use—adjustable for right- or left-hand use
Overall length: 36″
Weight: 6 lbs.

MARLIN LEVER ACTION CARBINES

MODEL 1894 CLASSIC
$406.95

SPECIFICATIONS
Calibers: 25/20 Win. and 32/20 Win.
Capacity: 6-shot tubular magazine
Barrel length: 22″ (6-groove rifling)
Overall length: 38³/₄″
Weight: 6¹/₄ lbs.

Action: Lever action with squared finger lever; side ejection; solid receiver top sandblasted to prevent glare; hammer block safety
Sights: Adjustable semi-buckhorn folding rear, brass bead front; solid top receiver tapped for scope mount and receiver sight; offset hammer spur
Stock: Straight-grip American black walnut with Mar-Shield® finish; blued steel forearm cap

MARLIN 336CS
$337.95 (without scope)

SPECIFICATIONS
Caliber: 30/30 Win., 35 Rem., 375 Win.
Capacity: 6-shot tubular magazine
Action: Lever action w/hammer block safety; deeply blued metal surfaces; receiver top sandblasted to prevent glare

Stock: American black walnut pistol grip stock w/fluted comb and Mar-Shield® finish; deeply blued metal surfaces
Barrel: 20″ Micro-Groove® barrel
Sights: Adjustable folding semi-buckhorn rear; ramp front sight w/brass bead and removable Wide-Scan™ hood; tapped for receiver sight and scope mount; offset hammer spur for scope use (works right or left)
Overall length: 38¹/₂″
Weight: 7 lbs.

MODEL 336 LIGHTWEIGHT
$345.95

SPECIFICATIONS
Caliber: 30/30 Win.
Capacity: 5-shot tubular magazine
Barrel length: 16¹/₄″ with Micro-Groove® rifling (12 grooves)
Overall length: 34³/₈″

Weight: 6¹/₂ lbs.
Safety: Hammer block safety
Sights: Adjustable semi-buckhorn folding rear, brass bead front; offset hammer spur (right or left hand) for scope use

Stock: Straight-grip American black walnut with scaled-down forearm and rubber rifle butt pad
Action: Lever action; side ejection; solid top receiver; squared finger lever; deep blued metal surfaces

MARLIN LEVER ACTION CARBINES

MODEL 444SS
$408.95

Caliber: 444 Marlin
Capacity: 5-shot tubular magazine
Barrel: 22″ Micro-Groove®
Overall length: 40¹/₂″
Stock: American black walnut pistol grip stock with rubber rifle butt pad; swivel studs

Sights: Ramp front sight with brass bead and Wide-Scan® hood; receiver tipped for scope mount or receiver sight
Weight: 7¹/₂ lbs.

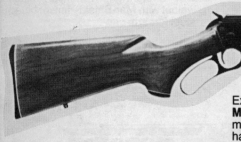

MARLIN GOLDEN 39AS
$338.95

The Marlin lever-action 22 is the oldest (since 1891) shoulder gun still being manufactured.
Solid Receiver Top. You can easily mount a scope on your Marlin 39 by screwing on the machined scope adapter base provided. The screw-on base is a neater, more versatile method of mounting a scope on a 22 sporting rifle. The solid top receiver and scope adapter base provide a maximum in eye relief adjustment. If you prefer iron sights, you'll find the 39 receiver clean, flat and sandblasted to prevent glare.

Exclusive brass magazine tube.
Micro-Groove® Barrel. Marlin's famous rifling system of multi-grooving has consistently produced fine accuracy because the system grips the bullet more securely, minimizes distortion, and provides a better gas seal.

And the Model 39 maximizes accuracy with the heaviest barrels available on any lever-action 22.

SPECIFICATIONS
Caliber: 22 Short, Long and Long Rifle
Capacity: Tubular magazine holds 26 Short, 21 Long and 19 Long Rifle Cartridges
Action: Lever action; solid top receiver; side ejection; one-step takedown; deeply blued metal surfaces; re-

ceiver top sandblasted to prevent glare; hammer block safety; rebounding hammer
Stock: Two-piece genuine American black walnut with fluted comb; full pistol grip and forend; blued-steel forend cap; swivel studs; grip cap; white butt plate and pistol-grip spacers; tough Mar-Shield® finish
Barrel: 24″ with Micro-Groove® rifling (16 grooves)
Sights: Adjustable folding semi-buckhorn rear, ramp front sight with new Wide-Scan™ hood; solid top receiver tapped for scope mount or receiver sight; scope adapter base; offset hammer spur for scope use—works right or left
Overall length: 40″
Weight: About 6¹/₂ lbs.

MODEL 39 TAKE-DOWN
$376.95 (incl. carrying case)

SPECIFICATIONS
Caliber: 22 Short, Long or Long Rifle
Capacity: Tubular magazine holds 16 Short, 12 Long, or 10 Long Rifle cartridges
Barrel length: 16¹/₂″ lightweight barrel (16 grooves)
Overall length: 32⁵/₈″

Weight: 5¹/₄ lbs.
Safety: Hammer block safety
Sights: Adjustable semi-buckhorn rear, ramp front with brass bead and Wide-Scan™ hood; top receiver tapped for scope mount and receiver sight; scope adapter base; offset hammer spur (right or left hand) for scope use

Stock: Two-piece straight-grip American black walnut with scaled-down forearm and blued steel forend cap; Mar-Shield® finish
Action: Lever action; solid top receiver; side ejection; rebounding hammer; one-step take-down; deep blued metal surfaces; gold-plated trigger

McMILLAN SIGNATURE RIFLES

CLASSIC SPORTER
$1750.00

SPECIFICATIONS
Calibers:
Model SA: 22-250, 243, 6mm Rem., 7mm-08, 284, 308
Model LA: 25-06, 270, 280 Rem., 30-06, 7mm Rem. Mag., 300 Win. Mag., 300 Weatherby
Model MA: 338 Win. Mag., 340 Weatherby, 375 H&H

Capacity: 4 rounds; 3 rounds in magnum calibers
Weight: 7 lbs; 7 lbs. 9 oz. in long action
Barrel lengths: 22″, 24″, 26″
Options: Fibergrain; wooden stock, optics, 30mm rings, muzzle brakes, steel floor plates, iron sights

ALASKAN
$2450.00

SPECIFICATIONS
Calibers:
Model LA: 270, 280, 30-06, 7mm Rem. Mag., 300 Win. Mag.
Model MA: 300 Weatherby, 358 Win., 340 Weatherby, 375 H&H

Other specifications same as the Classic Sporter, except McMillan action is fitted to a match-grade barrel, complete with single-leaf rear sight, barrel band front sight, 1″ detachable rings and mounts, steel floorplate, electroless nickel finish. Monte Carlo stock features cheekpiece, palm swell and special recoil pad.

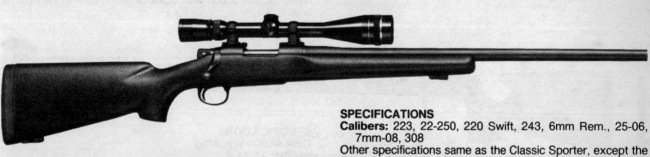

SUPER VARMINTER
$1850.00

SPECIFICATIONS
Calibers: 223, 22-250, 220 Swift, 243, 6mm Rem., 25-06, 7mm-08, 308
Other specifications same as the Classic Sporter, except the Super Varminter comes with heavy contoured barrel, adjustable trigger, field bipod and hand-bedded fiberglass stock.

TITANIUM MOUNTAIN RIFLE
(not shown) $2450.00

SPECIFICATIONS
Calibers:
Model LA: 270, 280 Rem., 30-06
Model MA: 7mm Rem. Mag., 300 Win. Mag.
Weight: 5½ lbs.
Other specifications same as the Classic Sporter, except barrel is made of chrome-moly (titanium alloy light contour match-grade barrel is available at additional cost of **$500.00**).

McMILLAN SIGNATURE RIFLES

SAFARI
$1450.00

SPECIFICATIONS
Calibers: 300 Win. Mag., 300 Weatherby, 338 Win. Mag., 340 Weatherby, 375 H&H, 378 Weatherby, 416 Taylor, 416 Rem., 416 Rigby, 458 Win.
Other specifications same as the Classic Sporter, except for match-grade barrel, positive extraction McMillan Safari action, quick detachable 1" scope mounts, positive locking steel floor-plate, multi-leaf express sights, barrel band ramp front sight, barrel band swivels, and McMillan's Safari stock.

NATIONAL MATCH RIFLE
$2000.00

SPECIFICATIONS
Caliber: 308
Mag. Capacity: 5 rounds
Weight: Approx. 11 lbs. (12½ lbs. with heavy contour barrel Available for right-hand shooters only. Features modified ISU fiberglass stock with adjustable butt plate, stainless steel match barrel with barrel band and Tompkins front sight; McMillan repeating bolt action with clip shot and Canjar trigger. Barrel twist is 1:12".

LONG RANGE RIFLE
$2000.00

SPECIFICATIONS
Caliber: 300 Win. Mag.
Weight: 14 lbs.
Barrel length: 26"
Available in right-hand only. Features a fiberglass stock with adjustable butt plate and cheekpiece. Stainless steel match barrel comes with barrel band and Tompkins front sight. McMillan solid bottom single-shot action and Canjar trigger. Barrel twist is 1:12".

McMILLAN BENCHREST RIFLE
(not shown) $2200.00

SPECIFICATIONS
Calibers: 6mm PPC, 243, 6mm BR, 6mm Rem., 308
Built to individual specifications to be competitive in hunter, light varmint and heavy varmint classes. Features solid bottom or repeating bolt action, Canjar trigger, fiberglass stock with recoil pad, stainless steel match-grade barrel and reloading dies. Right- or left-hand models.

PARKER-HALE RIFLES

MODEL M81 CLASSIC
$879.95

SPECIFICATIONS
Calibers: 22/250, 243 Win., 6mm Rem., 270 Win., 308 Win., 30-06, 300 Win. Mag., 7mm Rem. Mag.
Barrel length: 24″
Overall length: 44 1/2″
Capacity: 4 rounds
Weight: 7.75 lbs.
Length of pull: 13 1/2″

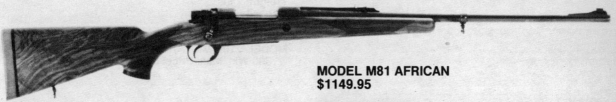

MODEL M81 AFRICAN
$1149.95

SPECIFICATIONS
Calibers: 375 H&H, 9.3 × 62mm
Barrel length: 24″
Overall length: 44 1/2″
Weight: 7.75 lbs.
Stock: Hand-checkered walnut
Features: All-steel trigger guard, adjustable trigger, barrel band front swivel, African express rear sight, hand-engraved receiver

MODEL 1100 LIGHTWEIGHT
$599.95

SPECIFICATIONS
Calibers: 22/250, 243 Win., 6mm Rem., 270 Win., 308 Win., 30-06
Barrel length: 22″
Overall length: 43″
Weight: 6 1/2 lbs.
Capacity: 4 rounds
Length of pull: 13 1/2″

MODEL 1100M AFRICAN MAGNUM (404 and 458 Win. Mag. only). **Barrel length:** 24″. **Overall length:** 46″. **Weight:** 9 1/2 lbs. **Price:** $999.95.

PARKER-HALE RIFLES

MODEL 2100 MIDLAND
$399.95

SPECIFICATIONS
Calibers: 22/250, 243 Win., 6mm Rem., 270 Win., 308 Win., 30-06
Barrel length: 22″ (24″ in cal. 22/250)
Overall length: 43″
Weight: 7 lbs.
Capacity: 4 rounds
Length of pull: 13½″
Also available:
MODEL 2100 MIDLAND MAGNUM in 7mm Rem. Mag. and 300 Win. Mag. **Price: $429.95.**

MODEL 1200 SUPER
$699.95

SPECIFICATIONS
Calibers: 22/250, 243 Win., 6mm Rem., 270 Win., 308 Win., 30-06
Barrel length: 24″
Overall length: 44½″
Weight: 7½ lbs.
Capacity: 4 rounds
Length of pull: 13½″
Also available:
MODEL 1200M SUPER MAGNUM (300 Win. Mag. and 7mm Rem. Mag. only): Same specifications as Model 1200 Super but capacity is 3 rounds. **Price: $699.95.**
MODEL 1200C SUPER CLIP (243 Win., 6mm Rem., 270 Win., 30-06 and 308 Win. only). Same specifications as Model 1200 Super but weighs 7¾ lbs. **Price: $699.95.** Also available in 300 Win. Mag. and 7mm Rem. Mag. (3 rounds only).

PARKER-HALE TARGET RIFLES

MODEL M87
$1299.95

This all-round high-precision long-range target rifle is available in several calibers suitable for silhouette or practical rifle competition and varmint shooting. The bolt is designed for smooth and rapid operation. The handle is tipped with a large diameter ball and allows ample clearance for aperture or telescopic sights. Integral dovetails on the action body provide positive scope mounting with Parker-Hale "Roll-Off" mounts.

SPECIFICATIONS
Calibers: 308 Win., 243 Win., 30-06 Springfield, 300 Win. Mag. (others on request). **Weight (empty):** 10 lbs. **Barrel length:** 26". **Overall length:** 45". **Sights:** none fitted; action body dovetailed for Parker-Hale "Roll-Off" Scope mounts.

MODEL M84 MK11 CANBERRA (not shown)
$1299.95 (7.62mm × 51 NATO)

Receiver is specifically designed for maximum rigidity with the framework of the rifle and a solid flat base with heavily reinforced flat top side. Action is securely fixed to the stock by two 1/4" socket head screws.

SPECIFICATIONS
Caliber: 7.62 × 51 NATO. **Barrrel length:** 27 1/2". **Overall length:** 48". **Weight:** 11 1/2 lbs. (w/sights & handstop). **Rifle twist:** 1 in 14" (1 in 10 and 1 in 12 made to order). **Capacity:** Single shot. **Trigger pull weight:** 3 1/2 lbs.

Also available:
MODEL M84 MK11 BISLEY. Same as "Canberra" but is produced in an alternative stock style (one for right-handed shooters and one for left-handers).

PRECISION SALES

INJEK NET PROJECTOR
$1950.00

This new product imported from Australia is designed exclusively for fast and simple capture of animals for purposes of relocation, tagging or veterinary treatment. The system includes a 10'×10' capture net that is shot from four barrels for a distance of 25 to 60 feet.

SPECIFICATIONS
Caliber: Special .308 Blank (with Injek power load)
Action: Mauser design with twin front locking lugs on bolt body; single loading
Barrel length: 11 1/2" (4 barrels chrome-plated, cold drawn steel)
Overall length: 37"
Weight : 12 lbs. (approx.)
Injek Capture Net: Made of 27-ply polypropylene, double-knotted (9cm square); four attached net-weights include anodized aluminum bodies with air-filled safety buffer tips
Manifold: Polished and blued, machined and hardened steel with 4 gas-metering jets

REMINGTON BOLT ACTION RIFLES

MODEL 700 LS

The Model 700 LS features a traditional wood stock made by laminating alternate strips of light and dark wood with waterproof adhesive and impregnating it with a phenolic resin for greater stability. Other features include low-gloss satin finish, cut checkering, sling swivel studs and open factory sights.

Calibers: 243 Win., 270 Win., 30-06 and 7mm Rem. Mag. **Capacity:** 5 (4 in 7mm Rem. Mag.). **Barrel length:** 22″ (24″ in 7mm Rem. Mag.). **Weight:** 7¼ lbs. **Stock dimensions:** drop at heel 1⁵⁄₁₆″; drop at comb ¹¹⁄₁₆″; length of pull 13³⁄₈″. **Price:** $440.00. In 7mm Rem. Mag.: $459.00.

MODEL 700 MOUNTAIN RIFLE
$469.00

A special lightweight version of the Remington Model 700 bolt action centerfire rifle. **Calibers:** 243 Win., 270 Win., 7mm-08 Rem., 280 Rem., 30-06 and 308 Win. **Weight:** 6¾ lbs. **Barrel length:** 22″. **Overall length:** 41⁵⁄₈″. **Stock:** Straight-line comb with cheekpiece; satin stock finish.

700 CUSTOM "KS" MOUNTAIN RIFLE
BOLT ACTION LIGHTWEIGHT SPORTER
Synthetic Stock w/Kevlar Aramid Fiber
$867.00

MODEL 700 CUSTOM GRADE RIFLES
(not shown)

GRADE I	$1263.00
GRADE II	2245.00
GRADE III	3508.00
GRADE IV	5473.00

REMINGTON BOLT ACTION RIFLES

MODEL 700 CLASSIC LIMITED EDITION
$485.00

Caliber: 300 Weatherby
Capacity: 3 shots (1 in chamber)
Barrel length: 24″
Overall length: 44 1/2″
Weight: 7 3/4 lbs.
Bolt: Jeweled with shrouded firing pin
Receiver: Drilled and tapped for scope mounts; fixed magazine with or without hinged floor plate
Stock: Cut-checkered select American walnut with quick detachable sling swivels installed; recoil pad standard equipment on Magnum rifles; installed at extra charge on others

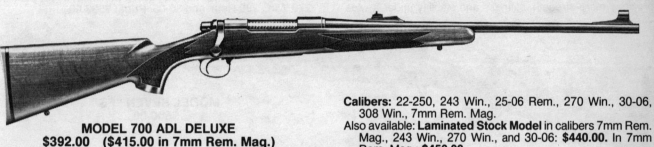

MODEL 700 ADL DELUXE
$392.00   ($415.00 in 7mm Rem. Mag.)

Calibers: 22-250, 243 Win., 25-06 Rem., 270 Win., 30-06, 308 Win., 7mm Rem. Mag.
Also available: Laminated Stock Model in calibers 7mm Rem. Mag., 243 Win., 270 Win., and 30-06: **$440.00.** In 7mm Rem. Mag.: **$459.00.**

MODEL 700 AS

Remington's new production-grade synthetic stock for the company's Model 700 bolt action rifle is called Model 700 AS. The rifle's stock is made of Arylon, a fiberglass-reinforced thermoplastic resin that matches other similar materials in strength and weight. Model 700 AS weighs only 6 1/2 lbs. All exposed metal surfaces of the action have a nonreflective, black matte finish, including the bolt body. Also nonreflective is the dull, flat finish of the stock, whose style includes a straight comb with cheekpiece, sling swivel studs and black recoil pad. The result is a lightweight, easy carrying, fast-handling rifle with the rigidity, barrel length and repetitive accuracy of a full-size Model 700. Specifications are listed in the table below. **Price: $479.00. In 7mm Rem. Mag.: $499.00.**

	Calibers	Mag. Capacity	Barrel Length	Overall Length	Twist R-H 1 turn in	Avg. Wt. (lbs.)
Model 700™ AS Arylon® Stock BDL (black)	22-250 Rem.	4	24″	43 5/8″	14″	6 1/2
	243 Win.	4	22″	41 5/8″	9 1/8″	6 1/2
	270 Win.	4	22″	42 1/2″	10″	6 1/2
	280 Rem.	4	22″	42 1/2″	9 1/4″	6 1/2
	30-06	4	22″	42 1/2″	10″	6 1/2
	308 Win.	4	22″	41 5/8″	10″	6 1/2
	7mm Rem. Mag.	3	24″	44 1/2″	9 1/4″	6 3/4

REMINGTON BOLT ACTION RIFLES

MODEL 700 "RS"
$547.00

MODEL 700 SYNTHETIC STOCKS

In answer to the demand for the lighter weight, strength and stability of synthetic stocks, Remington has introduced two new versions of its Model 700 centerfire rifle, as well as one version of its Model Seven. **Model 700 "RS"** introduces a new synthetic stock material called "Rynite", a DuPont thermoplastic resin with 35 percent glass reinforcement. This material provides more strength, stiffness and stability under a wide range of temperature and humidity conditions. This model includes the "Mountain Rifle" stock style featuring a straight comb and cheekpiece with Monte Carlo. A black, solid rubber recoil pad and pistol grip cap (with the "RA" logo) offer a smooth, uncluttered profile. Model 700 "RS" is available with a 22" barrel in right hand, long action with hinged floor plate in 270 Win., 280 Rem. and 30-06. **Price: $533.00**

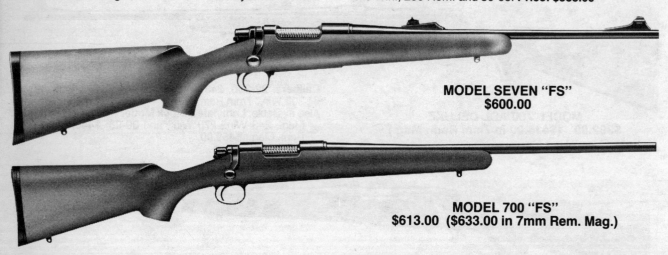

MODEL SEVEN "FS"
$600.00

MODEL 700 "FS"
$613.00 ($633.00 in 7mm Rem. Mag.)

Model 700 "FS" features a fiberglass stock reinforced with DuPont "Kevlar" aramid fiber for extra strength. The stock is shaped in the classic style with straight comb, no cheekpiece or Monte Carlo, and a black, Old English-style rubber recoil pad. The action has a blind magazine without floor plate. Model 700 "FS" is available in both long and short and right- and left-hand actions. Right-hand actions are chambered for 243 Win., 308 Win. and 7mm Rem. Mag. Left-hand actions are available in 270 Win., 30-06 and 7mm Rem. Mag.

MODEL SEVEN "FS" is available in 243 Win., 7mm-08 Rem. and 308 Win.

SYNTHETIC STOCK RIFLES

Calibers	Mag. capacity	Barrel length	Overall length	Avg. Wt.	Twist R-H 1 turn in
Model 700 RS Rynite Stock BDL					
270 Win.	4	22"	42 1/2	7 1/4	10"
280 Rem.	4	22"	42 1/2"	7 1/4	9 1/4"
30-06	4	22"	42 1/2"	7 1/4	10"
Model 700 FS Fiberglass Stock ADL					
243 Win.	4	22"	41 5/8"	6 1/4	9 1/8"
270 Win.	4	22"	42 1/2	6 1/4	10"
30-06	4	22"	42 1/2	6 1/4	10"
308 Win.	4	22"	41 5/8	6 1/4	10"
7mm Rem. Mag.	3	24"	44 1/2	6 3/4	10"
Model Seven FS Fiberglass Stock					
243 Win.	4	18 1/2"	37 1/2	5 1/4	9 1/8"
7mm-08 Rem.	4	18 1/2"	37 1/2	5 1/4	9 1/4"
308 Win.	4	18 1/2"	37 1/2	5 1/4	10"

REMINGTON BOLT ACTION RIFLES

The Model 700 BDL heavy barrel "Varmint Special" comes equipped with a 24-inch heavy target-type barrel. The "Varmint Special" is available in a wide range of popular high-velocity, varmint **calibers:** 222 Rem., 223 Rem., 22-250 Rem., 308 Win., 6mm Rem., 243 Win., 25-06 Rem., and 7mm-08 Rem. The "Varmint Special" was designed for maximum-range precision shooting, suitable for chucks, foxes and other varmints.

Features: hinged floor plate; quick release, swivels and strap; crisp trigger pull; American walnut stock, Monte Carlo style with cheekpiece; positive cut skip-line checkering on grip and all three sides of forend, grip cap with white line spacer and butt plate; DuPont developed RK-W wood finish. **Stock dimensions:** 13⅜-inch length of pull; 1⅜ inch drop at heel; ½-inch drop at comb (from open sight line). The safety is a thumb-lever type and is serrated. The bolt knob is oval shaped, serrated top and bottom. As in the Model 700 BDL, the cartridge head is completely encased by the bolt face and is supported by three rings of steel when the action is closed. The model is a very popular choice for metallic silhouette shooting.

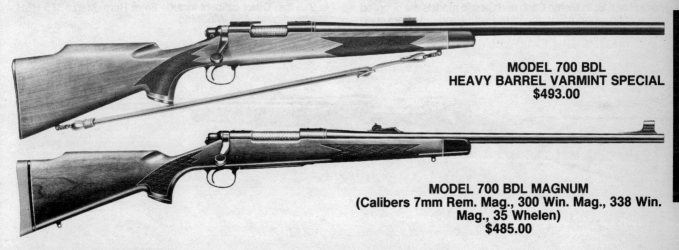

**MODEL 700 BDL
HEAVY BARREL VARMINT SPECIAL
$493.00**

**MODEL 700 BDL MAGNUM
(Calibers 7mm Rem. Mag., 300 Win. Mag., 338 Win. Mag., 35 Whelen)
$485.00**

MODEL 700 SPECIFICATIONS

Calibers	Mag. Cap	Barrel Length[1]	"Mountain Rifle"*	"Limited Classic"	Varmint Special	ADL, BDL & "Custom"	Twist R-H 1 turn in
			Overall Length/Avg. Wt. (lb.)				
17 Rem.	5	24"	—	—	—	43½"/7¼	9"
222 Rem.	5	24"	—	—	43½"/9	43½"/7¼	14"
22-250 Rem.	4	24"	—	—	43½"/9	43½"/7½	14"
223 Rem.	5	24"	—	—	43½"/9	43½"/7¼	12"
6mm Rem.*	4	22"	—	—	43½"/9	41½"/7¼	9⅛"
243 Win.	4	22"	—	—	43½"/9	41½"/7¼	9⅛"
25-06 Rem.	4	24"	—	—	—	41½"/7¼	10"
270 Win.	4	22"	42½"/6¾	—	—	41½"/7¼	10"
280 Rem.	4	22"	42½"/6¾	—	—	—	10"
7mm-08 Rem.	4	22"	—	—	43½"/9	41½"/7¼	9¼"
30-06	4	22"	42½"/6¾	—	—	41½"/7¼	10"
308 Win.	4	22"	—	—	43½"/9	41½"/7¼	10" / 12"
300 Wby. Mag.	3	24"	—	44½"/7¾	—	—	—
7mm Rem. Mag.[2]	3	24"	—	—	—	44½"/7¾	9¼"
300 Win. Mag.[2]	3	24"	—	—	—	44½"/7¾	10"
35 Whelen	4	22"	—	—	—	44½"/7¼	16"
338 Win. Mag.[2]	4	24"	—	44½"/7⁷/₄	—	—	10"
SAFARI GRADE (Custom Shop Only)							
8mm Rem. Mag.	3	24"	—	—	—	44½"/10	10"
375 H&H Mag.[2]	3	24"	—	—	—	44½"/9	12"
416 Rem. Mag.	—	24"	—	—	—	44½"	14"
458 Win. Mag.[2]	3	24"	—	—	—	44½"/9	14"

[1] "Varmint Special equipped only with a 24" barrel."   [2] Recoil pad included.

REMINGTON RIFLES
SAFARI GRADE BOLT ACTION RIFLES

Three versions of Model 700 Safari grade bolt action rifles are now chambered for the new .416 Remington Magnum cartridge, providing big-game hunters with a choice of three different stock styles and two stock materials. Model 700 Safari Monte Carlo (with Monte Carlo comb and cheekpiece) and Model 700 Safari Classic (with straight-line classic comb and no cheekpiece) are the wood-stocked models. Also available is Model 700 Safari KS with a synthetic stock of DuPont Kevlar aramid fiber. Both Monte Carlo and Classic models are supplied with a satin wood finish decorated with hand-cut checkering

18 lines to the inch and fitted with two reinforcing cross bolts covered with rosewood plugs. The Monte Carlo model also has a rosewood pistol grip cap and forend tip. Safari KS is completely impervious to temperature changes and moisture, making it ideal for hunting in the African jungle or the Alaskan peninsula. All three models are fitted with sling swivel studs. A barrel band replaces the front swivel on the Safari KS model. All three have 24" barrels with 1 in 14" twist. Average weight is 9½ lbs. Other calibers include 8mm Rem. Mag., 375 H&H Magnum, and .458 Win. Mag.

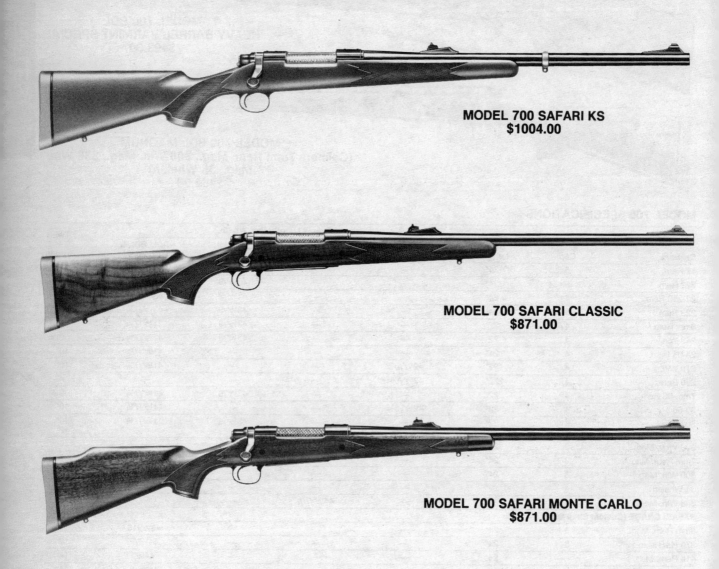

MODEL 700 SAFARI KS
$1004.00

MODEL 700 SAFARI CLASSIC
$871.00

MODEL 700 SAFARI MONTE CARLO
$871.00

REMINGTON BOLT ACTION RIFLES

Every Model Seven is built to the accuracy standards of our famous Model 700 and is individually test fired to prove it. Its 18½″ Remington special steel barrel is free-floating out to a single pressure point at the forend tip. And there is ordnance-quality steel in everything from its fully enclosed bolt and extractor system to its steel trigger guard and floor plate. Ramp front and fully adjustable rear sights, sling swivel studs are standard.

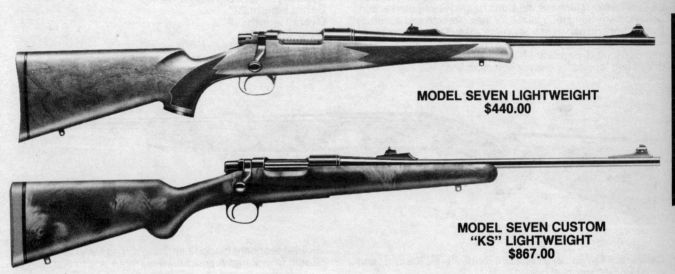

MODEL SEVEN LIGHTWEIGHT
$440.00

MODEL SEVEN CUSTOM "KS" LIGHTWEIGHT
$867.00

Models	Calibers	Clip Mag. Capacity	Barrel Length	Overall Length	Twist R-H 1 turn in	Avg. Wt. (lbs.)
MODEL SEVEN™	223 Rem.	5	18½″	37½″	12″	6¼
	243 Win.	4	18½″	37½″	9⅛″	6¼
	6mm Rem.	4	18½″	37½″	9⅛″	6¼
	7mm-08 Rem.	4	18½″	37½″	9¼″	6¼
	308 Win.	4	18½″	37½″	10″	6¼
SPORTSMAN® MODEL 78™ BOLT ACTION	223 Rem.	4	24″	43⅝″	12″	7
	243 Win.	4	22″	41⅝″	9⅛″	7
	270 Win.	4	22″	42½″	10″	7
	30-06*	4	22″	42½″	10″	7
	308 Win.*	4	22″	41⅝″	10″	7
MODEL 7400™ AND MODEL 7600™	243 Win.		22″	42″	9⅛″	7½
	270 Win.		22″	42″	10″	7½
	280 Rem.		22″	42″	9¼″	7½
	30-06 Carbine		18½″	38½″	10″	7¼
	30-06		22″	42″	10″	7½
	308 Win.		22″	42″	10″	7½
	35 Whelen		22″	42″	16″	8

STOCK DIMENSIONS: 13³/₁₆″ length of pull, ⁵/₁₆″ drop at heel, ⁹/₁₆″ drop at comb. Model 7600 also accepts 30-06 and 308 Accelerator® cartridges. Each has a positive cross-bolt safety switch.
* Also accepts Accelerator cartridge in same caliber.

REMINGTON RIFLES

BIG GAME REPEATING RIFLES "SPORTSMAN" 78 BOLT ACTION
$333.00

The popularly priced "Sportsman" 78 bolt-action centerfire rifle is chambered for the 243 Win., 308 Win., 270 Win. and 30-06 Springfield. It features the same rugged Remington action, bolt and barrel long recognized for their strength and accuracy by hunters and bench rest shooters alike. The straight comb, walnut-finished hardwood stock has classic lines and a rounded forend. Sights are fully adjustable and the receiver is drilled and tapped for easy scope mounting.

Calibers: 223 Rem., 243 Win., 270 Win., 30-06 Springfield and 308 Win.
Capacity: 4-shot clip magazine
Barrel length: 22″
Overall length: 42¹/₂″
Weight: 7 lbs.
Length of pull: 13³/₈″
Drop at heel: 1″ (from centerline of bore)
Drop at comb: ⁹/₁₆″ (from centerline of bore)

MODEL 7400
$459.00

Calibers: 243 Win., 270 Win., 280 Rem., 30-06, 308 Win., and 30-06 Carbine (see below)
Capacity: 5 centerfire cartridges (4 in the magazine, 1 in the chamber); extra 4-shot magazine available
Action: Gas-operated; receiver drilled and tapped for scope mounts
Barrel length: 22″
Weight: 7¹/₂ lbs.
Overall length: 42″

Sights: Standard blade ramp front; sliding ramp rear
Stock: Checkered American walnut stock and forend; curved pistol grip
Length of pull: 13³/₈″
Drop at heel: 2¹/₄″
Drop at comb: 1¹³/₁₆″

Also available:
MODEL 7400 CARBINE with 18¹/₂″ barrel; chambered for 30-06 cartridge

MODEL 7600
$439.00

Calibers: 243 Win., 270 Win., 280 Rem., 30-06, 308 Win., 35 Whelen, and 30-06 Carbine (see below)
Capacity: 5-shot capacity in all six calibers (4 in the removable magazine, 1 in the chamber)
Action: Pump action
Barrel length: 22″ (18¹/₂″ in 30-06 Carbine)
Weight: 8 lbs.
Overall length: 42″
Sights: Standard blade ramp front sight; sliding ramp rear, both removable

Stock: Checkered American walnut
Length of pull: 13³/₈″
Drop at heel: ¹⁵/₁₆″
Drop at comb: ⁹/₁₆″

Also available:
MODEL 7600 CARBINE with 18¹/₂″ barrel; chambered for 30-06 cartridge

REMINGTON RIMFIRE RIFLES

MODEL 541-T BOLT ACTION
$333.00

RIMFIRE RIFLE SPECIFICATIONS

Model	Action	Barrel Length	Overall Length	Average Wt. (lbs.)	Magazine Capacity
541-T	Bolt	24″	42½″	5⅞	5-Shot Clip
581-S	Bolt	24″	42½″	5⅞	5-Shot Clip
552 BDL Deluxe Speedmaster	Auto	21″	40″	5¾	15 Long Rifle
572 BDL Deluxe Fieldmaster	Pump	21″	40″	5½	15 Long Rifle

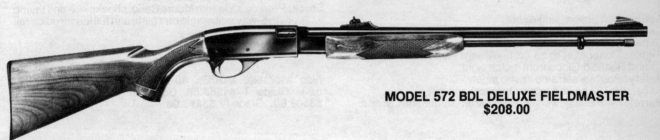

MODEL 572 BDL DELUXE FIELDMASTER
$208.00

MODEL 572 DELUXE

Features of this rifle with big-game feel and appearance are: DuPont's beautiful, tough RK-W finish; centerfire-rifle-type rear sight fully adjustable for both vertical and horizontal sight alignment; big-game style ramp front sight; handsome Remington impressed checkering on both stock and forend.

Action: Pump repeater
Caliber: 22 Short, Long and Long Rifle rimfire
Capacity: Tubular magazine holds 20 Short, 17 Long, 15 Long Rifle cartridges

Stock and forend: Model A, walnut finished hardwood; Model BDL, American walnut with tough DuPont RK-W lustrous finish and fine-line custom checkering
Sights: Model A, adjustable rear, bead front; Model BDL, fully adjustable rear, ramp front; screw removable
Safety: Positive cross bolt
Receiver: Grooved for "tip-off" scope mounts
Overall length: 40″
Barrel length: 21″
Average weight: 5½ lbs.

MODEL 552 BDL DELUXE SPEEDMASTER
$198.00

A deluxe model with all the tried and proven dependable mechanical features on the inside, plus special design and appearance extras on the outside. The 552 BDL sports tasteful Remington custom-impressed checkering on both stock and forend. Tough DuPont RK-W lifetime finish brings out the lustrous beauty of the walnut while protecting it. Sights are ramp-style in front and rugged big-game type fully adjustable in rear.

REMINGTON TARGET RIFLES

MODEL 40-XR
Rimfire Position Rifle
$983.00   ($1123.00 w/Kevlar Stock)

Stock designed with deep forend for more comfortable shooting in all positions. Butt plate vertically adjustable. Exclusive loading platform provides straight line feeding with no shaved bullets. Crisp, wide, adjustable match trigger. Meets all International Shooting Union standard rifle specifications.

Action: Bolt action, single shot
Caliber: 22 Long Rifle rimfire
Capacity: Single loading
Sights: Optional at extra cost. Williams Receiver No. FPTK and Redfield Globe front match sight
Safety: Positive serrated thumb safety
Receiver: Drilled and tapped for receiver sight
Barrel: 24″ medium weight target barrel countersunk at muzzle. Drilled and tapped for target scope blocks. Fitted with front sight base
Bolt: Artillery style with lock-up at rear. 6 locking lugs, double extractors
Trigger: Adjustable from 2 to 4 lbs.
Stock: Position style with Monte Carlo, cheekpiece and thumb groove; 5-way adjustable butt plate and full length guide rail
Overall length: 42¹/₂″
Average weight: 9¹/₄ lbs.

Also available: **MODEL 40-XR CUSTOM SPORTER** (22 cal.). Grade I **$1263.00.** Grade II **$2245.00.** Grade III **$3508.00.** Grade IV **$5473.00.**

MODEL 40-XC
National Match Course Rifle
$1052.00   ($1193.00 w/Kevlar Stock)

Chambered solely for the 7.62mm NATO cartridge, this match rifle was designed to meet the needs of competitive shooters firing the national match courses. Position-style stock, five-shot repeater with top-loading magazine, anti-bind bolt and receiver and in the bright stainless steel barrel. Meets all International Shooting Union Army Rifle specifications. Weighs about 11 lbs.

Action: Bolt action, single shot
Caliber: 22 Long Rifle rimfire
Capacity: Single loading
Sights: Optional at extra cost. Williams Receiver No. FPTK and Redfield Globe front match sight
Safety: Positive thumb safety
Length of pull: 13¹/₂″
Receiver: Drilled and tapped for receiver sight or target scope blocks
Barrel: 24″ heavy barrel
Bolt: Heavy, oversized locking lugs and double extractors
Trigger: Adjustable from 2 to 4 lbs.
Stock: Position style with front swivel block on forend guide rail
Overall length: 43¹/₂″
Average weight: 11 lbs.

REMINGTON TARGET RIFLES

MODEL 40-XB "RANGEMASTER"
Centerfire Rifle
$983.00

Barrels, in either standard or heavy weight, are unblued steel. Comb-grooved for easy bolt removal. Mershon White Line non-slip rubber butt plate supplied.

Action: Bolt—single shot in either standard or heavy barrel versions; repeater in heavy barrel only; receiver bedded to stock; barrel is free floating
Calibers: Single-shot, 222 Rem., 22-250 Rem., 6mm Rem., 243 Win., 7.62mm NATO (308 Win.), 30-06, 30-338 (30-7mm Mag.), 300 Win. Mag., 25-06 Rem., 7mm Rem. Mag.
Sights: No sights supplied; target scope blocks installed
Safety: Positive thumb operated
Receiver: Drilled and tapped for scope block and receiver sights

Barrel: Drilled and tapped for scope block and front target iron sight; muzzle diameter S2—approx. $^3/_4$", H2—approx. $^7/_8$"; unblued stainless steel only, 27$^1/_4$" long
Trigger: Adjustable from 2 to 4 lbs. pull; special 2-oz. trigger available at extra cost; single shot models only
Stock: American walnut; adjustable front swivel block on rail; rubber non-slip butt plate
Overall length: Approx. 45$^3/_4$"
Average weight: S2—9$^1/_4$ lbs.; H2—11$^1/_4$ lbs.

Also available: **MODEL 40-XB KEVLAR "Varmint Special."** Barrel length: 27$^1/_4$". Overall length: 45$^3/_4$". Weight: 9$^3/_4$ lbs. Price: $1123.00.

MODEL 40XB-BR
Bench Rest Centerfire Rifle
$1052.00

Built with all the features of the extremely accurate Model 40-XB-CF but modified to give the competitive bench rest shooter a standardized rifle that provides the inherent accuracy advantages of a short, heavy, extremely stiff barrel. Wider, squared off forend gives a more stable rest on sandbags or other supports and meets weight limitations for the sporter and light-varmint classes of National Bench Rest Shooters Association competition.

Action: Bolt, single shot only
Calibers: 222 Rem., 22 Bench Rest Rem., 7.62 NATO (308 Win.), 6mm Bench Rest Rem., 223 Rem., 6x47
Sights: Supplied with target scope blocks

Safety: Positive thumb operated
Receiver: Drilled and tapped for target scope blocks
Barrel: Unblued stainless steel only; 20" barrel for Light Varmint Class; 24" barrel for Heavy Varmint Class.
Trigger: Adjustable from 1$^1/_2$ to 3$^1/_2$ lbs.; special 2-oz. trigger available at extra cost
Stock: Selected American walnut; length of pull—12"
Overall length: 38" with 20" barrel; 44" with 24" barrel
Average weight: Light Varmint Class (20" barrel) 9$^1/_4$ lbs.; Heavy Varmint Class (24" barrel) 11 lbs.

Also available: **MODEL 40XB-BR KEVLAR. $1193.00**

ROSSI RIFLES

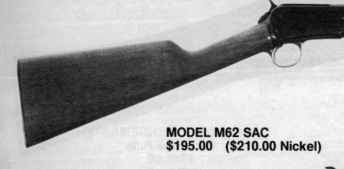

MODEL M62 SAC
$195.00   ($210.00 Nickel)

SPECIFICATIONS
Caliber: 22 LR
Capacity: 12 rds.
Barrel length: 16½"
Overall length: 32¾"
Weight: 4¼"
Finish: Blue

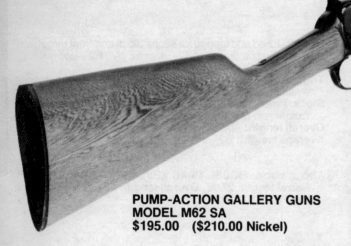

PUMP-ACTION GALLERY GUNS
MODEL M62 SA
$195.00   ($210.00 Nickel)

SPECIFICATIONS
Caliber: 22 LR
Capacity: 13 rds.
Barrel length: 23"
Overall length: 39¼"
Weight: 5½" lbs.
Finish: Blue
Model M62 SA w/Octagonal barrel $220.00
Model 59 22 Magnum 240.00

MODEL M92 SRC
$282.00 ($327.00 Engraved)

SPECIFICATIONS
Caliber: 38 Special or 357 Magnum
Capacity: 10 rounds
Barrel length: 20"
Overall length: 37"
Weight: 5¾"
Also available in 44 Magnum: $297.00

PUMA LEVER ACTION CARBINES
MODEL M92 SRS
$282.00 (not shown)

SPECIFICATIONS
Caliber: 38 Special or 357 Magnum
Capacity: 7 rounds
Barrel length: 16"
Overall length: 33"
Weight: 5 lbs.
Finish: Blue

RUGER CARBINES

RUGER MINI-14

Materials: Heat-treated chrome molybdenum and other alloy steels as well as music wire coil springs are used throughout the mechanism to ensure reliability under field-operating conditions. **Safety:** The safety blocks both the hammer and sear. The slide can be cycled when the safety is on. The safety is mounted in the front of the trigger guard so that it may be set to Fire position without removing finger from trigger guard. **Firing pin:** The firing pin is retracted mechanically during the first part of the unlocking of the bolt. The rifle can only be fired when the bolt is safely locked. **Stock:** One-piece American hardwood reinforced with steel liner at stressed areas. Handguard and forearm separated by air space from barrel to promote cooling under rapid-fire conditions. **Field stripping:** The Carbine can be field stripped to its eight (8) basic sub-assemblies in a matter of seconds and without use of special tools.

MINI-14 SPECIFICATIONS
Caliber: 223 (5.56mm). **Length:** 37¼″. **Weight:** 6 lbs. 4 oz. **Magazine:** 5-round, detachable box magazine. 20-shot and 30-shot magazines available. **Barrel length:** 18½″.

Mini-14/5 Blued	$421.75
Mini-14/5F Blued (folding stock)	503.00
K-Mini-14/5 Stainless Steel	465.00
K-MINI-14/5F (Stainless steel, folding stock)	535.00

Scopes not included

MINI-14 RANCH RIFLE

Caliber: 223 (5.56mm) or 7.62 × 39. **Length:** 37¼″. **Weight:** 6 lbs. 8 oz. **Magazine:** 10-shot and 20-shot magazines available. **Barrel length:** 18¼″.

Mini-14/5R Blued	$454.50
K-Mini-14/5R Stainless Steel	497.75
K-Mini-14/5RF Stainless Steel (folding stock)	562.75

RUGER CARBINES

STANDARD 10/22 CARBINE

DELUXE 10/22 SPORTER

MODEL 10/22 CARBINE
22 LONG RIFLE CALIBER

Identical in size, balance and style to the Ruger 44 Magnum Carbine and nearly the same in weight, the 10/22 is a companion to its high-power counterpart. Construction of the 10/22 Carbine is rugged and follows the Ruger design practice of building a firearm from integrated sub-assemblies. For example, the trigger housing assembly contains the entire ignition system, which employs a high-speed, swinging hammer to ensure the shortest possible lock time. The barrel is assembled to the receiver by a unique dual-screw dovetail system that provides unusual rigidity and strength—and accounts, in part, for the exceptional accuracy of the 10/22.

SPECIFICATIONS
Caliber: 22 Long Rifle, high-speed or standard-velocity loads. **Barrel:** 18 1/2" long; barrel is assembled to the receiver by unique dual-screw dovetail mounting for added strength and rigidity. **Weight:** 5 lbs. **Overall length:** 37". **Sights:** 1/16" gold bead front sight; single folding leaf rear sight, adjustable for elevation; receiver drilled and tapped for scope blocks or tip-off mount adapter. **Magazine:** 10-shot capacity, exclusive Ruger rotary design; fits flush into stock. **Trigger:** Curved finger surface, 3/8" wide. **Safety:** Sliding cross-button type; safety locks both sear and hammer and cannot be put in safe position unless gun is cocked. **Stocks:** 10/22 R Standard Carbine is walnut; 10/22 RB is birch; 10/22 SP Deluxe Sporter is American walnut. **Finish:** Polished all over and blued or anodized.

Model 10/22-R Standard (walnut stock) $203.85
Model 10/22-RB Standard (birch stock) 183.00
Model 10/22-DSP Deluxe 231.00

MINI THIRTY

This modified version of the Ruger Ranch rifle is chambered for the 7.62 × 39mm Russian service cartridge (used in the SKS carbine and AKM rifle). Designed for use with telescopic sights, it features a low, compact scope mounting for greater accuracy and carrying ease. **Barrel length:** 18 1/2". **Overall length:** 37 1/4". **Weight:** 7 lbs. 3 oz. (empty). **Magazine capacity:** 5 shots. **Rifling:** 6 grooves, right-hand twist, one turn in 10". **Finish:** polished and blued overall.

Price $454.50

RUGER SINGLE-SHOT RIFLES

The following illustrations show the variations currently offered in the Ruger No. 1 Single-Shot Rifle Series. Ruger No. 1 rifles come fitted with selected American walnut stocks. Pistol grip and forearm are hand-checkered to a borderless design. **Price for any listed model is $575.00** (except No. 1 International Model).

NO. 1A LIGHT SPORTER

Calibers: 243 Win.; 30/06; 270 Win., 7×57mm. **Barrel length:** 22″. **Sight:** Adjustable folding-leaf rear sight mounted on quarter rib with ramp front sight base and dovetail-type gold bead front sight; open. **Weight:** 7¼ lbs.

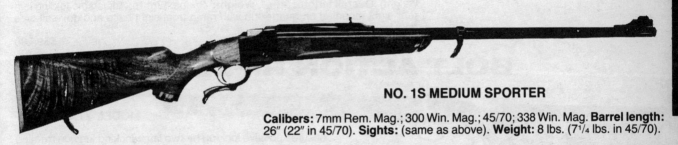

NO. 1S MEDIUM SPORTER

Calibers: 7mm Rem. Mag.; 300 Win. Mag.; 45/70; 338 Win. Mag. **Barrel length:** 26″ (22″ in 45/70). **Sights:** (same as above). **Weight:** 8 lbs. (7¼ lbs. in 45/70).

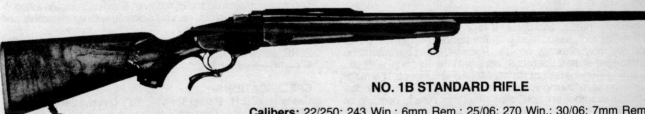

NO. 1B STANDARD RIFLE

Calibers: 22/250; 243 Win.; 6mm Rem.; 25/06; 270 Win.; 30/06; 7mm Rem. Mag.; 220 Swift; 338 Mag.; 280; 223; 257 Roberts, 270 Weatherby, 300 Mag., 300 Weatherby. **Barrel:** 26″. **Sights:** Ruger steel tip-off scope rings, 1″. **Weight:** 8 lbs.

NO. 1V SPECIAL VARMINTER

Calibers: 22/250; 25/06; 220 Swift; 223; 6mm. **Barrel length;** 24″. **Sights:** Ruger steel blocks and tip-off scope rings, 1″. **Weight:** 9 lbs.

RUGER RIFLES

NO. 1H TROPICAL RIFLE

Calibers: 375 H&H Mag.; 458 Win. Mag. **Barrel length:** 24″ (heavy). **Sights:** Adjustable folding-leaf rear sight mounted on quarter rib with ramp front sight base and dovetail-type gold bead front sight; open. **Weight:** 8¼ lbs. for 375; 9 lbs. for 458.
Price **$575.00**

NO. 1RSI INTERNATIONAL
With Mannlicher Style Forearm

SPECIFICATIONS
Caliber: 243 Win., 30-06, 270 Win., and 7×57mm. **Barrel length:** 20″ (lightweight). **Overall length:** 36½″. **Weight:** 7¼ lbs. **Sights:** Adjustable folding leaf rear sight mounted on quarter rib with ramp front sight base and dovetail-type gold bead front sight.
Price **$595.00**

BOLT ACTION RIFLES

MODEL 77/22 RS

MODEL 77/22 BOLT-ACTION RIMFIRE RIFLE

The Ruger 22-caliber rimfire 77/22 bolt-action rifle offers the sportsman quality and value. It represents a blend of characteristics long associated with the famous Ruger M-77 rifle and the internationally popular Ruger 10/22 semiautomatic rimfire rifle. It has been built especially to function with the patented Ruger 10-Shot Rotary Magazine concept. The magazine throat, retaining lips, and ramps that guide the cartridge into the chamber are solid alloy steel that resists bending or deforming.

The bolt assembly is built to military rifle standards of quality, but it has been modified to function with the 22 rimfire cartridge. Accordingly, the front part of the bolt is nonrotating and the locking lugs have been moved back to the middle of the action. The rear part of the bolt rotates and cams like that of the Ruger M-77 rifle, and it is connected to the nonrotating forward part of the bolt by a sturdy joint.

The 77/22 weighs just under six pounds and provides the smallbore shooter with a compact, featherweight arm that delivers performance and reliability. The heavy-duty receiver incorporates the integral scope bases of the patented Ruger Scope Mounting System, with 1-inch Ruger scope rings. A new 3-position safety offers a new dimension in security. With safety in its "lock" position, a dead bolt is cammed forward, locking the bolt handle down. In this position the action is locked closed and the handle cannot be raised.

A simplified bolt stop fits flush with the left side of the receiver and permits the bolt to be withdrawn from receiver merely by pressing down tightly. The new bolt locking system ensures positive lock-up by two large locking lugs on rotating part of bolt. A nonadjustable trigger mechanism is set for medium weight trigger pull. This mechanism includes a single strong coil spring for both sear recovery and trigger return. Lock time is 2.7 milliseconds.

All metal surfaces are finished in a deep, lustrous blue with nonglare surfaces on top of receiver. Stock is selected straight-grain American walnut, hand checkered with an attractive and durable polyurethane finish.

An all-new, All-Weather, all-stainless steel **MODEL K77/22RS** features a stock made of 6/6 glass-fiber reinforced nylon. **Weight:** approx. 6 lbs.

SPECIFICATIONS
Caliber: 22 LR. **Barrel length:** 20″. **Overall length:** 39¼″. **Weight:** 5¾ lbs. (w/o scope, magazine empty). **Feed:** Detachable 10-Shot Ruger Rotary Magazine.
Prices:
77/22R (plain barrel w/o sights, 1″ Ruger rings) . . . **$364.50**
77/22S (gold bead front sight, folding leaf rear sight) **364.50**
77/22RS (sights included, 1″ Ruger rings) **384.50**
77/22-RP (Synthetic stock), plain barrel with 1″ Ruger rings **300.00**
77/22-SP (Synthetic stock), gold bead front sight, folding-leaf rear sight **300.00**
77/22-RSP (Synthetic stock), gold bead front sight, folding-leaf rear sight and Ruger 1″ rings **320.00**
K77/22-RP (Synthetic stock), stainless steel, plain barrel with 1″ Ruger rings **360.00**
K77/22-SP (Synthetic stock), stainless steel, gold bead front sight, folding-leaf rear sight **360.00**
K77/22-RSP (Synthetic stock), stainless steel, gold bead front sight, folding-leaf rear sight, Ruger 1″ rings **380.00**

RUGER BOLT ACTION RIFLES

MODEL M-77RS

Integral Base Receiver, Ruger steel 1" rings, open sights. **Calibers:** (Magnum action) 270, 7 × 57mm, 30-06 (with 22" barrels), 25-06, 7mm Rem. Mag., 300 Win. Mag., 338 Win. Mag. (with 24" barrels); and (Short Stroke action) 243, 308 (with 22" barrels). **Weight:** Approx. 7 lbs.

Price $533.50
Also available in 458 Win. Mag. with steel trigger guard and floor
plate $618.00

MODEL M-77RL ULTRA LIGHT

New 6-pound big game rifle in both long- and short-action versions, with Integral Base Receiver and 1" Ruger scope rings. Luxury detailing throughout. **Calibers:** (Magnum action) 270, 30-06, 257 (all with 20" barrels); and (Short Stroke action) 22-250, 243, .250-3000, 308 (with 22" barrels). **Weight:** Approx. 6 lbs.

Price $513.00

MODEL M-77RLS ULTRA LIGHT

This big game bolt-action rifle encompasses the traditional features that have made the Ruger M-77 one of the most popular centerfire rifles in the world. It includes a sliding top tang safety, a one-piece bolt with Mauser-type extractor and diagonal front mounting system. American walnut stock is hand-checkered in a sharp diamond pattern. A rubber recoil pad, pistol grip cap and studs for mounting quick detachable sling swivels are standard. **Calibers:** 270, 30-06 (Magnum action); 243 and 308 (short stroke action). **Barrel length:** 18¹/₂". **Overall length:** 38⁷/₈". **Weight:** 6 lbs. (empty). **Sights:** Open.

Price $513.00

RUGER BOLT ACTION RIFLES

MODEL M-77RSI INTERNATIONAL

Mannlicher-type stock, Integral Base Receiver, open sights, Ruger 1" steel rings. **Calibers:** (Short Stroke action) 22-250, 250-3000, 243, 270, 30-06, and 308 (all with 18 1/2" barrels). **Weight:** Approx. 7 lbs.

Price **$539.75**

MODEL M-77V VARMINT

Integral Base Receiver, 1" scope rings. No sights. **Calibers:** 22-250, 6mm, 243, 25-06, 308 (with heavy 24" barrels); 220 Swift (with 26" barrel). **Weight:** Approx. 9 lbs.

Price **$496.50**

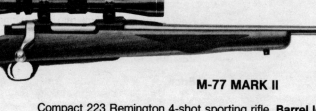

M-77 MARK II

Compact 223 Remington 4-shot sporting rifle. **Barrel lengths:** 20" (Ultra Light) and 22" (Standard). **Weight:** Approx. 6 1/2 lbs.

Price: **$483.00**

MODEL M-77R (not shown)

Integral Base Receiver, 1" scope rings. No sights. **Calibers:** (Magnum action) 270, 7×57mm, 257 Roberts, 280 Rem., 30-06 (all with 22" barrels); 25-06, 7mm Rem. Mag., 300 Win. Mag., 338 Win. Mag. (all with 24" barrels); and (Short Stroke action) 22-250, 6mm, 243, 308 (all with 22" barrels); 220 Swift (with 24" barrel). **Weight:** Approx. 7 lbs.

Price **$483.00**

MODEL M-77RS TROPICAL (not shown)

Integral Base Receiver (Magnum action only). Equipped with open sights and Ruger steel rings. **Caliber:** 458 Win. Mag. only. Steel trigger guard and floor plate. **Weight:** Approx. 8.75 lbs.

Price: **$618.00**

SAKO FIBERCLASS RIFLES

NEW ALL WEATHER FIBERGLASS-STOCKED CENTERFIRE RIFLE

FIBERCLASS

In answer to the increased demand for Sako quality and accuracy in a true "all-weather" rifle, this fiberglass-stock version of the renowned Sako barreled action has been created. Long since proven on the bench rest circuit to be the most stable material for cradling a rifle, fiberglass is extremely strong, light in weight, and unaffected by changes in weather. Because fiberglass is inert, it does not absorb or expel moisture, hence it cannot swell, shrink or warp. It is impervious to the high humidity of equatorial jungles, the searing heat of arid deserts, or the rain and snow of the high mountains. Not only is this new rifle lighter than its wood counterpart, it appeals to the performance-oriented hunter who seeks results over appearance.

Prices:
Short Action (AI): 223 Rem. $1175.00
Medium Action (AII): 22-250 Rem.,
   243 Rem., 308 Win. & 7mm-08 . . . . 1175.00
Long Action (AV):
25-06 Rem., 270 Win., 30-06 . . . . 1190.00
7mm Rem. Mag., 300 Win. Mag., 338
   Win. Mag., 375 H&H Mag. 1220.00

SAKO RIFLES

HUNTER RIFLE

HUNTER

Here's one case of less being more. Sako has taken its famed bolt-action, centerfire rifle, redesigned the stock and trimmed the barrel contour. In fact, in any of the short action (A1) calibers—.17 Rem., .222 or .223 Rem.—the Hunter weighs in at a mere 5³/₄ pounds, making it the lightest wood stock production rifle in the world.

The same cosmetic upgrading and weight reduction have been applied to the entire Hunter line in all calibers and action lengths, standard and magnum. All the precision, quality and accuracy for which this Finnish rifle has been so justly famous are still here. Now it just weighs less.

The Sako Trigger is a rifleman's delight—smooth, crisp and fully adjustable. If these were the only Sako features, it would still be the best rifle available. But the real quality that sets Sako apart from all others is its truly outstanding accuracy.

While many factors can affect a rifle's accuracy, 90 percent of any rifle's accuracy potential lies in its barrel. And the creation of superbly accurate barrels is where Sako excels.

The care that Sako takes in the cold-hammering processing of each barrel is unparalleled in the industry. As an example, after each barrel blank is drilled, it is diamond-lapped and then optically checked for microscopic flaws. This extra care affords the Sako owner lasting accuracy and a finish that will stay "new" season after season.

You can't buy an unfired Sako. Every gun is test fired using special overloaded proof cartridges. This ensures the Sako owner total safety and uncompromising accuracy. Every barrel must group within Sako specifications or it's scrapped. Not recycled. Not adjusted. Scrapped. Either a Sako barrel delivers Sako accuracy, or it never leaves the factory.

And hand-in-hand with Sako accuracy is Sako beauty. Genuine European walnut stocks, flawlessly finished and checkered by hand.

Prices (include lacquer finish without sights, or oil finish with sights)

Short Action (AI)

In 17 Rem.	$900.00
In 222 Rem. & 223 Rem.	860.00

Medium Action (AII)

In 22-250 Rem., 7mm-08, 243 Win. & 308 Win.	860.00

Long Action (AV)

In 25-06 Rem., 270 Win., and 30-06	890.00
In 7mm Rem. Mag., 300 Win. Mag., 338 Win. Mag.	900.00
In 375 H&H Mag.	920.00
In 300 Weatherby Mag.	935.00

SAKO CARBINES

SAKO CARBINE

Sako's Carbines combine the handiness and carrying qualities of the traditional, lever-action "deer rifle" with the power of modern, high-performance cartridges. An abbreviated 18½-inch barrel trims the overall weight of the Carbine to just over 40 inches in the long (or AV) action calibers, and 39½" in the medium (or AII) action calibers. Weight is a highly portable 7 and 6½ pounds, respectively (except in the 338 and 375 H&H calibers, which tip the scale at 7½ pounds).

As is appropriate for a rifle of this type, the Carbine is furnished with an excellent set of open sights; the rear is fully adjustable for windage and elevation, while the front is a nonglare serrated ramp with protective hood.

The Carbine is available in a choice of stocks: the traditional wood stock of European walnut done in a contemporary Monte Carlo style with a choice of hand-rubbed oil or gloss lacquer finish. Either way, hand-cut checkering is standard. The Mannlicher-style full stock Carbine wears Sako's exclusive two-piece forearm, which joins beneath the barrel band. This independent forward section of the forearm eliminates the bedding problems normally associated with the full forestock. A blued steel muzzle cap puts the finishing touches on this European-styled Carbine.

For the hunter whose primary concerns are ruggedness and practicality, there's the Fiberclass Carbine. Stocked in the same distinctive black fiberglass stock as Sako's famed Fiberclass Rifle model, the Carbine offers the same advantages but in a shorter, lighter configuration. The fiberglass Carbines in 338 and 375 H&H have become favorites withe Alaskan guides, bush pilots, and all those who work or travel regularly in big bear country.

Prices:

Sako Carbine

In 22-250 Rem. and 243 Rem. (Med. Action)	**$860.00**
In 270 Win. & 30-06 (Long Action)	890.00
In 7mm Rem. Mag. and 338 Win. Mag. (Long Action)	910.00

Sako Fiberclass Carbine

In 243 Win. (Medium Action)	**$1175.00**
In 25-06, 270 Win., & 30-06 (Long Action)	1190.00
In 7mm Rem. Mag., 300 Win. Mag. and 338 Win. Mag. (Long Action)	1220.00

Sako Mannlicher-Style Carbine

In 222 Rem. (Short Action)	**$ 945.00**
In 243 Win. & 308 Win. (Medium Action)	945.00
In 25-06, 270 Win., & 30-06 (Long Action)	960.00
In 7mm Rem. Mag., 300 Win. Mag. and 338 Win. Mag. (Long Action)	980.00
In 375 H&H Mag..........................	1020.00

SAKO MANNLICHER-STYLE CARBINE

SAKO RIFLES

LAMINATED STOCK MODELS

In response to the growing number of hunters and shooters who seek the strength and stability that a fiberglass stock provides, coupled with the warmth and feel of real wood, Sako introduces its Laminated Stock models.

Machined from blanks comprised of 36 individual layers of $1/16$-inch hardwood veneers that are resin-bonded under extreme pressure, these stocks are virtually inert. Each layer of hardwood has been vacuum-impregnated with a permanent brown dye. The bisecting of various layers of veneers in the shaping of the stock results in a contour-line appearance similar to a piece of slab-sawed walnut. Because all Sako Laminated Stocks are of real wood, each one is unique, with its own shading, color and grain.

These stocks satisfy those whose sensibilities demand a rifle of wood and steel, but who also want state-of-the-art performance and practicality. Sako's Laminated Stock provides both, further establishing it among the most progressive manufacturers of sporting rifles—and the *only* one to offer hunters and shooters their choice of walnut, fiberglass or laminated stocks in 18 calibers (10 in Left-Handed models), from .17 Remington to .375 H&H.

Prices:

Laminated Stock Models

In 223 Rem. (Short Action)	$ 965.00
In 22-250, 243 Rem., 308 Win. and 7mm-08 (Medium Action)	965.00
In 25-06 Rem., 270 Win. & 30-06 (Long Action)	980.00
In 7mm Rem. Mag., 300 Win. Mag. & 338 Win. Mag. (Long Action)	995.00
In 375 H&H Mag. (Long Action)	1020.00

Laminated Left-Handed Models:

In 25-06, 270 Win. & 30-06 (Long Action)	$1075.00
In 7mm Rem. Mag., 300 Win. Mag. & 338 Win. Mag. (Long Action)	1100.00
In 375 H&H Mag. (Long Action)	1115.00

SAKO CUSTOM RIFLES

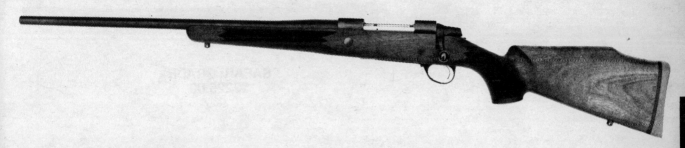

LEFT-HANDED MODELS

Sako's new Left-Handed models are based on mirror images of the right-handed models enjoyed by Sako owners for many years, with handle, extractor and ejection port all located on the port side. Naturally, the stock is also reversed, with the cheekpiece on the opposite side and the palm swell on the port side of the grip.

Otherwise these guns are identical to the right-hand models. That means hammer-forged barrels, one-piece bolts with integral locking lugs and handles, integral scope mount tails, three-way adjustable triggers, Mauser-type inertia ejections, and one-piece steel trigger guard/magazine frames.

Sako's Left-Handed rifles are available in all Long Action models. The Hunter Grade carries a durable, hand-rubbed oil finish with generous-size panels of hand-cut checkering, a presentation-style recoil pad, scope mounts, and sling swivel studs installed. The Deluxe model is distinguished by its rosewood forend tip and grip cap, its skip-line checkering and gloss lacquer finish atop a select-grade of highly figured European walnut. The metal work carries a deep, mirro-like blue that looks more like black chrome. Laminated and Fiberclass Long Action models are also available for lefthfanders.

Prices

Hunter Lightweight

In 25-06, 270 Win. & 30-06	$1010.00
In 7mm Rem. Mag., 300 Win. Mag. and 338 Win. Mag.	1025.00
In 375 H&H Mag.	1040.00

Deluxe (all Long Action)

In 25-06, 270 Win. Mag. & 30-06	$1250.00
In 7mm Rem. Mag, 300 Win. Mag. and 338 Win. Mag.	1265.00
In 375 H&H Mag.	1275.00

Fiberclass (all Long Action)

In 25-06, 270 Win. & 30-06	$1270.00
In 7mm Rem. Mag., 300 Win. Mag. and 338 Win. Mag.	1315.00
In 375 H&H Mag.	1330.00

Note: For **Laminated Left-Handed** models, see Laminated Stock Models.

SAKO RIFLES

**SAFARI GRADE
$2225.00**

Crafted in the tradition of the classic British express rifles, Safari Grade is truly a professional's rifle. Every feature has been carefully thought out and executed with one goal in mind: functionality. The magazine is extended, allowing four belted magnums to be stored inside (instead of the usual three). The steel floorplate straddles the front of the trigger guard bow for added strength and security.

An express-style quarter rib provides a rigid, non-glare base for the rear sight, which consists of a fixed blade and one auxiliary fold-down. The front swivel is carried by a contoured barrel band to keep the stud away from the off-hand under the recoil of big calibers. The front sight assembly is also a barrel-band type for maximum strength. The blade sits on a non-glare ramp and is protected by a steel hood.

The Safari's barreled action carries a subtle semi-matte blue, which lends an understated elegance to this eminently practical rifle. The functional, classic-style stock is of European walnut selected especially for its strength with respect to grain orientation as well as for color and figure. A rosewood forend tip, a steel grip cap, an elegant, beaded cheekpiece and presentation—style recoil pad complete the stock embellishments.

Calibers: 300 Win. Mag., 338 Win. Mag. & 375 H&H Mag. See also **Specifications Table.**

**VARMINT
$965.00**

The Sako Varmint is specifically designed with a prone-type stock for shooting from the ground or bench. The forend is extra wide to provide added steadiness when rested on sandbags or makeshift field rests.

Calibers: 17 Rem., 222 Rem. & 223 Rem. (Short Action); 22-250, 243 Rem., 7mm-08 & 308 Win. (Medium Action). Also available in 6mm PPC and 22 PPC (single shot only). **Price: $1085.00.**

SAKO RIFLES

Ever since Dr. Lou Palmisano and Farris Pindel introduced their custom-made PPC ammo in 1975, it has become widely recognized as the "world's most accurate cartridge," having broken well over 200 records since its debut. The impossible dream of making one-hole targets with five cartridges may never be realized, but PPC cartridges have come closer to that goal of perfection than anything in today's market.

Under an agreement with Dr. Palmisano, Sako has manufactured the PPC benchrest, single-shot rifle in both 6 PPC and 22 PPC since late 1987; in 1988 it introduced factory-made ammo and brass. Because of its outstanding success with the benchrest model, Sako has now made both calibers available in a repeater version of its new Hunter and Deluxe models. Each model features a soft, luxurious matte lacquer finish and is built to the demanding specifications and workmanship that have become synonymous with Finnish gunmakers.

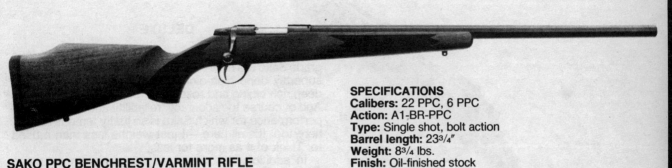

SAKO PPC BENCHREST/VARMINT RIFLE
$1085.00

SPECIFICATIONS
Calibers: 22 PPC, 6 PPC
Action: A1-BR-PPC
Type: Single shot, bolt action
Barrel length: 23³/₄"
Weight: 8³/₄ lbs.
Finish: Oil-finished stock

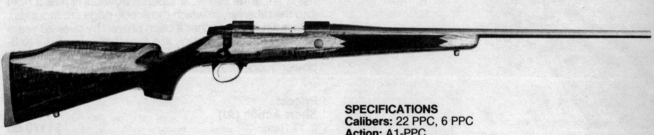

SAKO PPC HUNTER
$1085.00

SPECIFICATIONS
Calibers: 22 PPC, 6 PPC
Action: A1-PPC
Magazine capacity: 4
Barrel length: 21³/₄"
Weight: 6¹/₄ lbs.
Finish: Matte-lacquer stock

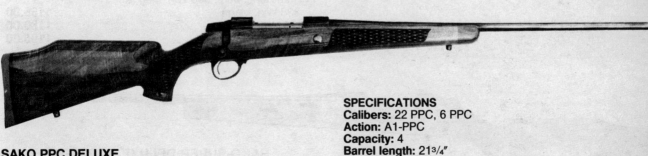

SAKO PPC DELUXE
$1360.00

SPECIFICATIONS
Calibers: 22 PPC, 6 PPC
Action: A1-PPC
Capacity: 4
Barrel length: 21³/₄"
Weight: 6¹/₄ lbs.
Finish: Matte-lacquer stock
Features: Deep-cut checkering; rosewood pistol-grip and forend caps; engraved floorplate; high-luster blue on barreled action

SAKO RIFLES

DELUXE SHORT ACTION

DELUXE

All the fine-touch features you expect of the deluxe grade Sako are here—beautifully grained French walnut, superbly done high-gloss finish, hand-cut checkering, deep rich bluing and rosewood forend tip and grip cap. And of course the accuracy, reliability and superior field performance for which Sako is so justly famous are still here too. It's all here—it just weighs less than it used to. Think of it as more for less.

In addition, the scope mounting system on these Sakos is among the strongest in the world. Instead of using separate bases, a tapered dovetail is milled right into the receiver, to which the scope rings are mounted. A beautiful system that's been proven by over 20 years of use. Sako scope rings are available in *low* (2½ to 3-power scopes), *medium* (4-power scopes) and *high* (6-power scopes). Available in one-inch only.

Prices:
Short Action (AI)
In 17 Rem. **$1170.00**
In 222 Rem. & 223 Rem. **1120.00**
Medium Action (AII)
In 22-250 Rem., 243 Rem., 7mm-08
    & 308 Win. **1120.00**
Long Action (AV)
In 25-06 Rem., 270 Win., 30-06 . . . . **1150.00**
In 7mm Rem. Mag., 300 Win. Mag. &
    338 Win. Mag. **1165.00**
In 375 H&H Mag. **1180.00**
In 300 Weatherby Mag. **1195.00**

SAKO SUPER DELUXE $2225.00

Sako offers the Super Deluxe to the most discriminating gun buyer. This one-of-a-kind beauty is available on special order.

SAKO RIFLES

	Model		Action*		Dimensions			Caliber/Rate of Twist																	Stock Finish			Sights			Mag.	Buttplate
			Action*	Left-handed	Total length (inches)	Barrel length (inches)	Weight (lbs)	17 Rem / 10″	222 Rem / 14″	223 Rem / 12″	22 PPC / 14″	6mm PPC / 14″	22-250 Rem / 14″	243 Win / 10″	7mm-08 / 9½″	308 Win / 12″	25-06 Rem / 10″	270 Win / 10″	30-06 / 10″	7mm / Rem Mag / 9½″	300 Win Mag / 10″	300 Wby Mag / 10″	338 Win Mag / 10″	375 H&H Mag / 12″	Lacquered	Matte Lacquered	Oiled	Without sights *	Open sights *	Base for telescopic sight mounts	Magazine capacity	Rubber
RIFLES	HUNTER		AI		41½	21¼	5¾	•	•	•		•													•		•	•		•	6	•
			AII		42½	21¾	6¾						•	•	•	•									•		•	•		•	5	•
			AV	•	44	22	7¼										•	•	•						•		•	•		•	5	•
			AV	•	44	24	7¼													•	•	•			•		•	•		•	3	•
			AV	•	46	24	7¾																•	•	•		•	•	•	•	3	•
	DELUXE		AI		41½	21¼	5¾	•	•	•															•			•		•	6	•
			AII		42½	21¾	6¾						•	•	•	•									•			•		•	5	•
			AV	•	44	22	7¼										•	•	•						•			•		•	5	•
			AV	•	44	24	7¼													•	•	•			•			•		•	3	•
			AV	•	46	24	7¾																•	•	•			•		•	3	•
	SUPERDELUXE		AI		41½	21¼	6¼	•	•	•															•		•	•		•	6	•
			AII		42½	21¾	7						•	•	•	•									•		•	•		•	5	•
			AV	•	43½	22	7½										•	•	•						•		•	•		•	5	•
			AV	•	43½	24	7½													•	•				•		•	•		•	3	•
			AV	•	45½	24	8																•	•	•		•	•		•	3	•
	FIBERCLASS		AI		41½	21¾	5¾			•																		•		•	6	•
			AII		42½	21¾	6¾						•	•	•	•												•		•	5	•
			AV	•	43½	22	7¼										•	•	•									•		•	5	•
			AV	•	43½	24	7¼													•	•							•		•	3	•
			AV	•	45½	24	7¾																•	•				•		•	3	•
	LAMINATED		AI		41½	21¾	5¾			•																•		•		•	6	•
			AII		42½	21¾	6¾						•	•		•										•		•		•	5	•
			AV	•	44	22	7¼										•	•	•							•		•		•	5	•
			AV	•	44	24	7¼													•	•					•		•		•	3	•
			AV	•	46	24	7¾																•	•		•		•		•	3	•
CARBINES	CARBINE MANNLICHER STYLE		AI		39½	18¼	6¾		•																		•		•	•	6	•
			AI		39½	18½	6¾						•	•	•	•											•		•	•	5	•
			AV		40½	18½	7¼										•	•	•								•		•	•	5	•
			AV		40½	18½	7¼													•	•						•		•	•	3	•
			AV		40½	18½	7¾																•	•			•		•	•	3	•
	CARBINE HANDY		AII		39½	18½	6½						•	•													•		•	•	5	•
			AV		40½	18½	7										•		•								•		•	•	5	•
			AV		40½	18½	7													•							•		•	•	3	•
			AV		40½	18½	7½																•	•			•		•	•	3	•
	CARBINE FIBERCLASS		AII		39½	18½	6½							•															•	•	5	•
			AV		40½	18½	7¼										•	•	•										•	•	5	•
			AV		40½	18½	7¼													•	•								•	•	3	•
			AV		40½	18½	7½																•	•					•	•	3	•
CUSTOM	SAFARI		AV		43	24	8½																•	•			•		•	•	4	•
	VARMINT		AI		43¾	23¾	8¾				•	•															•	•		•	0	•
			AI		42¾	22¾	8½	•	•	•																	•	•		•	6	•
			AII		43¼	22¾	8½						•	•	•	•											•	•		•	5	•
PPC	BENCHREST VARMINT		AI		43¾	23½	8¾				PPC	PPC																				
	HUNTER		AI		41½	21½	5¾				PPC	PPC																				
	DELUXE		AI		41½	21½	5¾				PPC	PPC																				

PPC: For varmint shooting, benchrest competition, target or hunting

STOEGER

BRASS AND AMMO ARE AVAILABLE FOR BOTH 6 PPC AND 22 PPC.

SAKO ACTIONS

Only by building a rifle around a Sako action do shooters enjoy the choice of three different lengths, each scaled to a specific family of cartridges. The A1 (Short) action is miniaturized in every respect to match the .222 family, which includes everything from .17 Remington to .222 Remington Magnum. The A11 (Medium) action is scaled down to the medium-length cartridges of standard (30-06) bolt face—.22-250, .243, .308 or similar length cartridges. The AV (Long) action is offered in either standard or Magnum bolt face and accommodates cartridges of up to 3.65 inches in overall length, including rounds like the .300 Weatherby and .375 H&H Magnum. **For left-handers, only the Long Action is offered in either standard or Magnum bolt face.** All actions are furnished in-the-white only.

AI-1 (SHORT ACTION)
CALIBERS:
17 Rem., 222 Rem.
222 Rem. Mag.
223 Rem.
$420.00

NEW:
AI PPC (Short Action) Hunter and Single Shot 22 PPC and 6 PPC
$460.00

AII-1 (MEDIUM ACTION)
CALIBERS:
22-250 Rem. (AII-3)
243 Win.
308 Win.
$420.00

AV-4 (LONG ACTION)
CALIBERS:
25-06 Rem. (AV-1)
270 Win. (AV-1)
7 × 64
30-06 (AV-1)
7mm Rem. Mag.
300 Win. Mag.
338 Win. Mag.
375 H&H Mag.
$420.00

Also available:
LEFT-HANDED ACTIONS
Long Action only: $445.00

 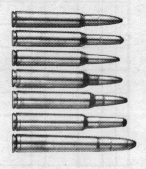

SAUER RIFLES

Maker of fine rifles and shotguns since 1751, the J.P. Sauer & Sohn Company of West Germany announces its Sauer 90 Bolt Action Rifle series in four configurations—Supreme, Lux, Stutzen and Safari. Each features a hammer-forged barrel and machined steel receiver; cam-activated lugs ensure positive lockup, while the 65° bolt facilitates rapid reloading.

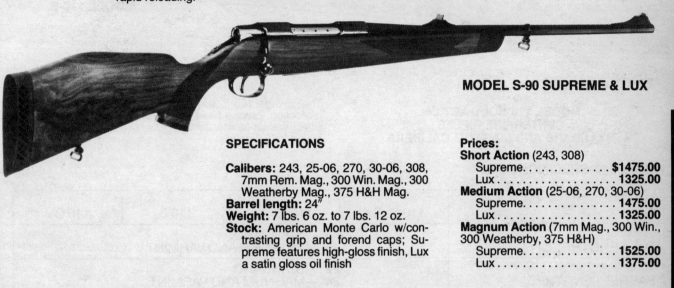

MODEL S-90 SUPREME & LUX

SPECIFICATIONS

Calibers: 243, 25-06, 270, 30-06, 308, 7mm Rem. Mag., 300 Win. Mag., 300 Weatherby Mag., 375 H&H Mag.
Barrel length: 24″
Weight: 7 lbs. 6 oz. to 7 lbs. 12 oz.
Stock: American Monte Carlo w/contrasting grip and forend caps; Supreme features high-gloss finish, Lux a satin gloss oil finish

Prices:
Short Action (243, 308)
  Supreme **$1475.00**
  Lux 1325.00
Medium Action (25-06, 270, 30-06)
  Supreme 1475.00
  Lux 1325.00
Magnum Action (7mm Mag., 300 Win., 300 Weatherby, 375 H&H)
  Supreme 1525.00
  Lux 1375.00

MODEL S-90 STUTZEN

SPECIFICATIONS
Calibers: 30-06, 270
Barrel length: 20″
Weight: 7½ lbs.
Stock: European Monte Carlo w/satin gloss oil finish
Price:
W/sights, no swivels **$1325.00**

MODEL S-90 SAFARI

SPECIFICATIONS
Caliber: 458 Win.
Barrel length: 24″
Weight: 10 lbs. 12 oz.
Stock: American Monte Carlo with matte oil finish
Price:
Incl. sights, swivels **$1675.00**

SAVAGE CENTERFIRE RIFLES

MODEL 110-E

MODEL 110 BOLT-ACTION
CENTERFIRE RIFLES
STANDARD AND MAGNUM CALIBERS

The Savage 100 Series features solid lockup, positive gas protection, precise head space, precision-rifled barrels, and select walnut Monte Carlo stocks. See specifications tables below for full details.

MODEL 110 SPECIFICATIONS

	110 G, GX	110 F, FX	110 B	110 GV
O.A. LENGTH	43"—STANDARD 45"— MAGNUM AND VARMINT			
BARREL LENGTH	22"—STANDARD 24"—MAGNUM AND VARMINT			
PULL	13¾"	13½"	13¾"	13¾"
COMB DROP	1⅝"			
MONTE CARLO DROP	1½"	N.A.	1½"	1½"
HEEL DROP	2¼"			
AVERAGE WEIGHT	6⅞–7¼	6¾	7–7¾	8¼
CAPACITY	5 RDS.—STANDARD 4 RDS.—MAGNUM			
FREE FLOATING BARREL	X	X	X	X
STOCK TYPE	WALNUT FINISH HARDWOOD	BLACK RYNITE®	BROWN LAMINATED	WALNUT FINISH HARDWOOD
RECOIL PAD	X	X	X	X
ADJUSTABLE SIGHTS	G ONLY	F ONLY	X	N.A.
RECEIVER DRILLED & TAPPED	G ONLY	F ONLY	X	X
INTEGRAL MOUNTS	GX ONLY	FX ONLY	N.A.	N.A.
CALIBERS AVAILABLE	.22/250, .223, .243, .308, .30/06, .270, 7mm REM MAG, 300 WIN MAG			.22/250 .223

SAVAGE CENTERFIRE RIFLES

MODEL 99-C LEVER ACTION
$441.00

Clip magazine allows for the chambering of pointed, high-velocity big-bore cartridges. **Calibers:** 243 Win., 308 Win. **Action:** Hammerless, lever action, cocking indicator, top tang safety. **Magazine:** Detachable clip; holds 4 rounds plus one in the chamber. **Stock:** Select walnut with high Monte Carlo and deep fluted comb. Cut checkered stock and forend with swivel studs. Recoil pad and pistol grip cap. **Sights:** Detachable hooded ramp front sight, bead front sight on removable ramp adjustable rear sight. Tapped for top mount scopes. **Barrel length:** 22″. **Overall length:** 41³/₄″. **Weight:** 8 lbs.

SAVAGE RIFLE/SHOTGUNS

SAVAGE MODEL 24F-20

SAVAGE MODEL 24-F COMBINATION RIFLE/SHOTGUN

Available in 222/20, 223/20, and 30-30/20. Match a 20-gauge shotgun with any of five popular centerfire calibers. Frame is color casehardened and barrel is a deep, lustrous blue and tapped, ready for scope mounting. Two-way top opening lever.

The original, all-purpose combination gun, **Savage Model 24** gives the shooter a choice of three different rifle calibers over a 12- or 20-gauge shotgun. All models are stocked with tough Du Pont Rynite™, plus hammerblock safeties that limit hammer travel in the safe position. Other features include interchangeable chokes (extra full tube supplied), and factory swivel studs.

Model 389 has a select hand-checkered walnut stock, folding rear sight, twin trigger for instant barrel selection, and interchangeable choke tubes. Price for either models on request. Additional specifications are listed in the accompanying table.

SPECIFICATIONS	24F-20	24F-12	24F-12T (TURKEY)	389
O.A. LENGTH	40″	40″	40″	43″
BARREL LENGTH	24″	24″	24″	25³/₄″
3″ CHAMBERS	X	X	X	X
GAUGE/CHOKE	20/MOD.	12/TUBES	12/TUBES	12/TUBES
RIFLE CALIBERS AVAILABLE	.222/.223/.30-30		.222/.223	.222/.308
STOCK TYPE	BLACK RYNITE®		CAMO RYNITE®	WALNUT CHECKERED
APPROX. WEIGHT	7¹/₂		7¹/₂	7

STEYR-MANNLICHER RIFLES

MODEL SSG MARKSMAN
(Shown with synthetic stock and optional Kahles ZF69 scope)

SPECIFICATIONS
Calibers: 243 Win., 308 Win. (7.62mm NATO)
Barrel length: 26″
Weight: 8.6 lbs. (9.9 lbs. with Kahles scope)
Overall length: 44.5″
Stock: Choice of synthetic half stock of ABS "Cycolac" or walnut; removable spacers in butt section adjusts length of pull from 12³/₄″ to 14″
Sights: Hooded blade front; folding rear leaf sight

Features: Parkerized finish; choice of interchangeable single- or double-set triggers; detachable 5-shot rotary straight-line feed magazine of "Makrolon"; 10-shot magazine optional; heavy-duty receiver drilled and tapped for scope mounting.

Prices:
Cycolac half stock	$1598.00
Walnut half stock	1995.00
SSG Scope Mount	194.00
Model SSG P-11 Sniper (308 Win.)	1682.00

Features 26″ heavy barrel, 10-shot box magazine, match bolt, Walther target peep sights, mirage cover, and adjustable rail in forend to adjust sling travel. **Weight:** 11 lbs. **Caliber:** 308 Win.

MODEL SSG MATCH UIT

Price:
With walnut half stock	$2350.00

Also available:
SSG MATCH RIFLE w/26″ heavy barrel, 308 caliber, synthetic stock. **Price: $1875.00.** With walnut stock: **$2125.00.**

LUXUS MODELS L, M & S
(L=Light M=Medium S=Magnum)

Barrel lengths: 20″ (full stock); 23.6″ (half stock); 26″ (Model S)
Weight: 6.8 lbs. (full stock); 6.9 lbs. (half stock)
Overall length: 39″ (full stock); 43″ (half stock)
Stock: Hand-checkered walnut with Monte Carlo cheekpiece; either full Mannlicher or half stock; European hand-rubbed oil finish or high-gloss lacquer finish
Sights: Ramp front adjustable for elevation; open U-notch rear adjustable for windage
Features: Single combination trigger (becomes hair trigger when moved forward before firing); detachable 3-shot steel straight-line feed magazine (6-shot optional). 6 rear locking lugs; drilled and tapped for scope mounts

SPECIFICATIONS
Calibers:
Model L (standard calibers) 22-250 Rem., 6mm Rem., 243 Win., 308 Win.
Model L (optional metric calibers) 5.6×57
Model M (standard calibers) 25-06 Rem., 270 Win., 7×57, 7×64, 30-06
Model M (optional metric calibers) 6.5×55, 6.5×57, 7.5 Swiss, 9.3×62
Model S 300 Win. Mag., 7mm Rem. Mag., 6.5×68, 8×68S

Prices:
Full stock (in **Model L & M** calibers)	$2495.00
Half stock (in **Model L & M** calibers)	2364.00
Half stock (in **Model S** calibers)	2567.00

STEYR-MANNLICHER RIFLES

MODEL L (LIGHT)
shown with full stock
and double triggers

MODEL M (MEDIUM)
shown with half stock
and single trigger

MODEL M PROFESSIONAL
with synthetic stock
& parkerized finish

SPECIFICATIONS
Calibers:
  Model SL (Super Light, standard calibers only) 222 Rem.,
   222 Rem. Mag., 223 Rem.
  Model L (standard calibers) 22-250 Rem., 6mm Rem., 243
   Win., 308 Win.
  Model L (optional metric caliber) 5.6×57
  Model M (standard calibers) 25-06 Rem., 270 Win., 7×57,
   7×64, 30-06 Spr.
  Model M (optional metric calibers) 6.5×57, 7.5 Swiss,
   8×57JS, 9.3×62
Barrel length: 20″ (full stock); 23.6″ (half stock)
Weight: 6.8 lbs. (full stock); 6.9 lbs. (half stock); 7.5 lbs.
 (Professional)
Overall length: 39″ (full stock); 43″ (half stock)
Stock: Full Mannlicher or standard half stock with Monte Carlo

cheekpiece and rubber recoil pad; hand-checkered walnut
in skip-line pattern; Model M with half stock is available in
a "Professional" version with a parkerized finish and synthetic stock made of ABS "Cycolac" (made with right-
handed action only); left-handed action available in full
stock and half stock.
Features: Choice of fine-crafted single- or double-set triggers.
 Detachable 5-shot rotary magazine of "Makrolon"; 6 rear
 locking lugs; drilled and tapped for scope mounting.
Prices:

Models SL, L, M Full stock	$1939.00
Models SL, L, M Half stock	1812.00
Full stock, with left-handed action	2212.00
Half stock, with left-handed action	2083.00
Professional, with iron sights	1532.00
Model SL, L Varmint (270 Win., 30-06)	1939.00

MODEL S AND S/T MAGNUM

SPECIFICATIONS
Calibers:
  Model S 257 Weatherby Mag., 264 Win. Mag., 300 Win.
   Mag., 7mm Rem. Mag., 300 H&H Mag., 375 H&H Mag.
  Model S (Optional calibers) 6.5×68
  Model S/T (Heavy barrel) 375 H&H Mag., 458 Win. Mag.
  Model S/T (Optional caliber) 9.3×64
Barrel length: 26″ Model S/T (with 26″ heavy barrel)
Weight: 8.4 lbs. (Model S); 9.02 lbs. (Model S/T); add .66 lbs.
 for butt mag. opt.

Overall length: 45″
Stock: Half stock with Monte Carlo cheekpiece and rubber recoil pad; hand-checkered walnut in skip-line pattern; available with optional spare magazine inletted in butt stock.
Features: Choice of fine-crafted single- or double-set triggers;
 detachable 4-shot rotary magazine of "Makrolon"; 6 rear
 locking lugs; drilled and tapped for scope mounting.
Prices:

Model S	$1952.00
Model S/T with opt. butt magazine	2176.00

THOMPSON/CENTER RIFLES

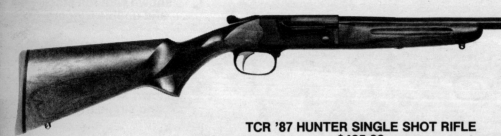

TCR '87 HUNTER SINGLE SHOT RIFLE
$425.00
Calibers: 22 Hornet, 222 Rem., 223 Rem., 22/250 Rem., 243 Win., 270 Win., 7mm-08, 308 Win., 32-40 Win. or 30-06

Barrels quickly interchange from one caliber to the next

Chambered for 10 popular hunting cartridges, this superbly accurate sports rifle offers the simplicity and strength of a break-open design coupled with the unique feature of interchangeable barrels. Triggers function double set or single stage. A positive lock cross-bolt safety offers maximum security. Wood is hand-selected American black walnut from the Thompson/Center mill. All barrels are equipped with iron sights, removable for scope mounting.

SPECIFICATIONS
Barrel lengths: 23″ (Light Sporter) and 25⅞″ (Medium Sporter)
Overall length: 39½″ (Light Sporter) and 43⅜″ (Medium Sporter)
Weight: 6 lbs. 14 oz. (Light Sporter) and 7 lbs. 8 oz. (Medium Sporter)

THE CONTENDER CARBINE
$375.00

Available in nine **calibers:** 22 LR, 22 Hornet, 223 Rem., 7mm T.C.U., 7×30 Waters, 30/30 Win., 35 Rem., 44 Mag. and 357 Rem. Max. Barrels are 21 inches long and are interchangeable, with adjustable iron sights and tapped and drilled for scope mounts.
Also available:
Contender Vent Rib Carbine
  With 21″ .410 barrel **$395.00**
Contender Youth Model Carbine w/16½″ bbl. **345.00**
  With 16½″ 45 Colt/.410 barrel **370.00**

TIKKA RIFLES

NEW GENERATION RIFLES

With the consolidation of three renowned Finnish fire-arms manufacturers—Tikka, Sako and Valmet—a "new generation" of Tikka rifles becomes a reality. These new rifles feature a "smooth as silk" bolt action made possible by a sleeve constructed of a space-age synthetic Polyarylamide material reinforced with fiberglass. The overall look of the rifle is enhanced by a walnut stock with matte lacquer finish and diamond point checkering. The short bolt throw allows for rapid firing. A free-floating barrel increases accuracy, and barrel quality itself is ensured by means of Tikka's cold-hammered forging process. The trigger guard is made of synthetic materials for added strength and is oversized for ease of shooting while wearing gloves. The magazine release is located conveniently for quick release and is recessed to avoid accidental release. The wood-to-metal fit reflects the high standards of Finnish craftsmanship throughout. The "New Generation" rifles are available in **calibers:** 223 Rem., 243 Win., 270 Win., 30-06, 7mm Rem. Mag. and 338 Win. Mag. **Barrel length:** 22". **Weight:** 7$1/8$ lbs.

Prices:
Calibers 223 Rem., 243 Win., 270 Win.
   and 30-06 . . . . **$720.00**
Calibers 7mm Rem. Mag. & 338 Win. Mag. **740.00**
Magazines (3 rounds) **46.00**

A. UBERTI REPLICA
RIFLES & CARBINES

SPECIFICATIONS
Calibers: 22 LR, 22 Magnum, 38 Special, 44-40
Barrel length: 24¼", octagonal, tapered
Overall length: 43¼"
Weight: 8.16 lbs.
Frame: Elevator and buttplate in brass
Stock: Walnut
Sights: Vertically adjustable rear; horizontally adjustable front

MODEL 1866 SPORTING RIFLE
$590.00

MODEL 1866 INDIAN CARBINE
$624.00

SPECIFICATIONS: Same as Model 1866, except **barrel length** is 19", **overall length** is 38¼" and **weight** is 7.38 lbs.

SPECIFICATIONS
Calibers: 22 LR, 22 Magnum, 357 Magnum
Barrel length: 22"
Overall length: 35½"
Weight: 4.85 lbs.
Stock & forend: Walnut
Trigger guard: Brass
Sights: Fully adjustable rear; ramp front
Frame: Color casehardened steel

MODEL 1871 ROLLING BLOCK
BABY CARBINE
$325.00

MODEL 1873 SPORTING RIFLE
$702.00

SPECIFICATIONS
Calibers: 22 LR, 22 Magnum, 357 Magnum, 38 Special and 44-40. Other specifications same as Model 1866.

A. UBERTI REPLICA RIFLES & CARBINES

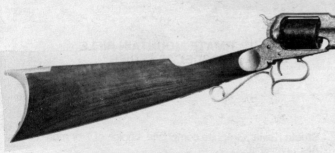

MODEL 1875 ARMY S.A. TARGET REVOLVING CARBINE
$477.00

SPECIFICATIONS
Calibers: 357 Magnum, 45 Long Colt, 44-40
Barrel length: 18″
Overall length: 37″
Weight: 4.96 lbs.
Stock: Walnut
Trigger guard & buttplate: Brass
Sights: Vertically adjustable rear; ramp front
Also available with nickel plate: $582.00

SPECIFICATIONS
Calibers: 22 LR, 22 Magnum, 38 Special, 44-40, 45 LC
Barrel length: 19″ round, tapered
Overall length: 38¼″
Weight: 7.38 lbs.
Sights: Fixed front; vertically adjustable rear
Also available:
1873 RIFLE w/24¼″ barrel (43¼″ overall) $700.00.

1873 CARBINE
$670.00 ($760.00 Nickel)

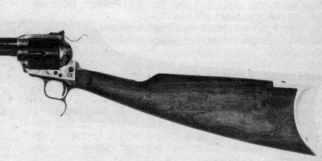

SPECIFICATIONS
Caliber: 44 Magnum (44-40 convert.)
Barrel length: 18″ round
Overall length: 34″
Weight: 4.41 lbs.
Stock: Walnut with brass buttplate
Also available:
BUCKHORN S.A. BUNTLINE w/23″ overall length $442.00.

BUCKHORN REVOLVING CARBINE
$427.75

ULTRA LIGHT ARMS

ULTIMATE MOUNTAIN RIFLE
MODEL 20 SERIES
$2000.00 ($2100.00 Left Hand)

SPECIFICATIONS

Calibers: 17 Rem., 222 Rem., 223 Rem., 22-250 Rem., 243 Win., 6mm Rem., 250-3000 Savage, 257 Roberts, 257 Ack., 7mm Mauser, 7mm Ack., 7mm-08 Rem., 284 Win., 300 Savage, 308 Win., 358 Win.
Barrel length: 22″
Weight: 4.75 lbs.
Safety: Two-position safety allows bolt to open or lock with sear blocked

Stock: Kevlar/Graphite composite; choice of 7 or more colors
Also available:
MODEL 24 SERIES (Long Action) in 270 Win.,
  30-06, 25-06, 7mm Express **$2100.00**
  Same as above in Left-Hand Model **2200.00**
MODEL 28 SERIES (Magnum Action) in 264 Win.,
  7mm Rem., 300 Win., 338 . . . . **2500.00**
  Same as above in Left-Hand Model **2600.00**

VALMET RIFLES

VALMET HUNTER RIFLE
$795.00

The most reliable semiautomatic sporting rifle available, the Hunter incorporates the durability and reliability of Valmet's military weapons manufactured for the Finnish Defense Forces. Its main features are as follows:

Durability: Precision-machined steel receiver.
Reliability: Simple but rugged design with few moving parts. Dependable gas piston mechanism. Proven to function in arctic sub-zero extremes as well as hot, muggy conditions.
Minimal recoil: Barrel is positioned centerline from barrel tip through the stock, minimizing barrel lift. Gas piston mechanism reduces recoil.
Accuracy: Heavy barrel with precision rifling. Less recoil and reduced barrel lift add to accuracy of following shots. Gas-operated rotating bolt ensures a secure lockup. Locked-down dust cover provides secure surface accommodating quick detachable scope mount with 1″ rings.
Caliber versatility: Available in 223, 243, 308 and 30-06.
Fast sighting: Flush-folding rear sight with luminous dots. Luminous vertical bar front sight assures fast, accurate sight picture.

Speed: Fast sighting, minimal recoil and barrel lift, plus large magazine capacity, enable shooter to stay "on target" with fast, accurate firepower.
American walnut stock: Deep-cut checkering and palm swell for added control. Length and angle (pitch) adjustable with factory spacers. Quick, detachable sling swivel.
Ejection buffer: Optional buffer protects brass for reloading.

SPECIFICATIONS

Type: Gas-operated semiautomatic
Calibers: 223, 243, 308, 30-06
Capacity:
  223 cal., 15 rounds (30 rds. optional)
  243 cal., 9 rounds (5 rds. optional)
  308 cal., 5 rounds (9 and 20 rds. optional)
  30-06 cal., 5 rounds (9 rds. optional)
Barrel length: 20½″
Overall length: 42″
Weight: 8 lbs.

VALMET RIFLES

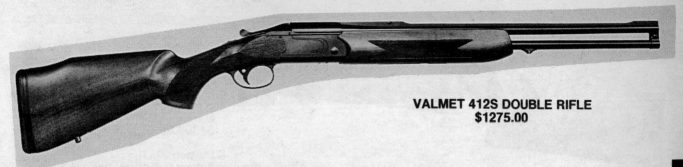

VALMET 412S DOUBLE RIFLE
$1275.00

Valmet's double rifle offers features and qualities no other action can match: rapid handling and pointing qualities and the silent, immediate availability of a second shot. As such, this model overcomes the two major drawbacks usually associated with this type of firearm: price and accuracy. Other features include:

Barrel regulation: Regulate windage through adjustment at the muzzle. Elevation is regulated by the sliding wedge between the barrels. Shooters can use their favorite loads and are not limited to the specific load used by the factory. Point-of-impact can be changed for any desired distance.

Accuracy: Compares favorably with most lever actions, pumps and autoloaders.

Speed: Faster initial shot due to excellent handling qualities inherent to a double rifle. Second shot is as fast as you can pull the trigger. No noise or distraction from a lever, moving bolt or pumping action.

Excellent handling qualities: Bulk of the weight is between the hands, enabling the gun to come up fast and swing smoothly.

American walnut stock: Available either cast-on or cast-off for right- or left-handed shooters. Deep-cut checkering for secure grip with palm swell for greater control and comfort.

Length and angle adjustable with factory spacer. Quick, detachable sling swivel. Semi-Monte Carlo design.

Interchangeability: Receiver will accept Valmet over/under shotgun barrels in both 12 and 20 gauge, plus shotgun/rifle barrels, with minor initial fitting.

Optional triggers: Equipped with single selective trigger. Double triggers also available.

Mechanical triggers: Operate mechanically and do not depend on inertia from recoil to activate trigger for second shot.

Automatic safety: Automatically goes to safe position when gun is opened. Optional safety locks safety out and in fire position.

Other features: Strong steel receiver, superior sliding locking mechanism, cocking indicators, and two-piece firing pin.

SPECIFICATIONS
Calibers: 30-06, 9.3 × 74R
Barrel length: 24″
Overall length: 40″
Weight: 8½ lbs.
Stock: American walnut
Other: Extractors, automatic ejectors

VARNER SPORTING ARMS

FAVORITE HUNTER MODEL
(Single Shot) $369.00

SPECIFICATIONS (FIELD GRADE)
Caliber: 22 LR
Barrel length: 21½″; 12-groove, match grade; half-round, half-octagonal
Weight: 5 lbs.
Sights: Peep and open rear sights adjustable for windage and elevation
Stock: Straight-grain American walnut
Finish: Blued steel

Also available:
HUNTER DELUXE (Hand-checkered AAA Fancy Walnut) **$499.00.**
PRESENTATION GRADE (w/AAA Fancy American walnut stock; color-hardened frame and lever; hand-checkered grip and forearm) **$569.00.**

WALTHER TARGET RIFLES

U.I.T. MATCH
$1300.00

Caliber: 22 LR
Action: Bolt action, single shot
Barrel length: 25½"
Overall length: 44¾"
Weight: 13 lbs.
Also available:
U.I.T. BV UNIVERSAL: $1700.00

MODEL GX-1
$2200.00

Caliber: 22 LR
Action: Bolt action, single shot
Barrel length: 25½"
Overall length: 46"
Weight: 16½"

KK/MS SILHOUETTE
$1100.00

Caliber: 22 LR
Action: Bolt action, single shot
Barrel length: 25½"
Overall length: 44¾"
Weight: 8¾ lbs

RUNNING BOAR (not shown)
$1300.00

Caliber: 22 LR
Action: Bolt action, single shot
Barrel length: 23½"
Overall length: 42"
Weight: 10¼ lbs.

WEATHERBY RIFLES

MARK V FIBERMARK

The Fibermark's hand-molded fiberglass stock is impervious to climatic changes. It shoots with constant accuracy no matter what the weather—from desert heat to mountain snow. The stock is finished with a non-glare black wrinkle finish for a positive grip, even in wet, humid weather. Available in right-hand only, 24″ or 26″ barrels. **Weight:** 7¼ lbs. (24″) and 8 lbs. (26″).

Additional specifications are listed on the following page.

Calibers	Prices
240, 257, 270, 7mm & 300 Wby.Mag. and 30-06	$1123.00
(24″ barrel; add $20 for 26″ barrel)	
340 Win. Mag. (26″ barrel)	1143.00

MARK V EUROMARK

The principal features of this Mark V model include a hand-rubbed, satin oil finish Claro walnut stock and non-glare special process blue matte barreled action. Specifications are listed on the following page. All calibers are available in right- or left-hand models, unless stated otherwise.

Calibers	Prices
240, 257, 270, 7mm, 30-06	
24″ barrel	$1040.00
26″ barrel	1060.00
300 Wby. Mag., L.H., 26″ bbl. only	1060.00
340 Wby. Mag., 26″ barrel	1060.00
378 Wby. Mag., 26″ barrel	1214.00
416 Weatherby Mag.	
24″ barrel	1320.00
26″ barrel	1340.00
460 Weatherby Mag.	
24″ barrel	1385.00
26″ barrel	1405.00

MARK V ULTRAMARK

Features a hand-honed action with a damascened bolt and follower, checkered bolt knob and floorplate. Also, an extra-fancy American Claro Walnut stock with hand-checkering. **Calibers:** 240, 257, 270, 7mm, 300 Wby. Mag., 30-06, and 416 Wby. Mag. **Price: $1575.00.** With 26″ barrel: **$1595.00.**

WEATHERBY RIFLES

MARK V DELUXE RIFLE

300 Wby. Mag., L.H., 26″ bbl. only 1011.00
340 Weatherby Mag., 26″ barrel 1011.00
378 Weatherby Mag., 26″ barrel 1165.00
416 Weatherby Mag.
  24″ barrel 1270.00
  26″ barrel 1290.00
460 Weatherby Mag.
  24″ barrel 1330.00
  26″ barrel 1350.00

All calibers are available in right- or left-hand models, unless stated otherwise.

Calibers   **Prices**

224 Weatherby Mag. or 22/250 Varmintmaster
  Right-hand only, 24″ barrel . . . . $ 971.00
  Right-hand only, 26″ barrel 987.00

240, 257, 270, 7mm, 30-06
  24″ barrel 991.00
  26″ barrel 1011.00

MARK V SPECIFICATIONS

CALIBER	.224 WBY MAG	.22/250	.240 WBY MAG	.257 WBY MAG	.270 WBY MAG	7mm WBY MAG	.30-06	.300 WBY MAG	.340 WBY MAG	.378 WBY MAG	.460 WBY MAG
Model	Right hand 24″ or 26″ bbl. Left hand model not available		Right or left hand 24″ bbl. Right hand 26″ bbl. Left hand 26″ bbl. **available in .300 cal. only**						Right or left hand 26″ bbl. only.	Right or left hand 26″ bbl. only.	Right or left hand 24″ or 26″ bbl.*
**Weight w/o sights	6½ lbs.		7¼ lbs.						8½ lbs.		10½ lbs.
Overall length	43⅜″ or 45⅜″ dependent on barrel length		44⅝″ or 46⅝″ dependent on barrel length						46⅝″		44¾″ or 46¾″
Magazine Capacity	4, +1 in chamber	3, +1 in chamber	4, +1 in chamber		3, +1 in chamber			4, +1 in chamber	3, +1 in chamber		2, +1 in chamber
Barrel	24″ standard or 26″ semi-target		24″ standard or 26″ #2 contour						26″ #2 contour	26″ #3 contour	24″ or 26″ #4 contour*
Rifling	1-14″ twist		1-10″ twist							1-12″ twist	1-16″ twist
Sights	Scopes or iron sights extra										
Stocks:	Drop dimensions from bore centerline: **Mark V—** Comb: ¾″ Monte Carlo: ½″ Heel: 1½″ **Varmintmaster—** Comb: ⁹⁄₁₆″ Monte Carlo: ¼″ Heel: 1⅛″										
Ultramark	Not available		Full fancy American walnut, individually hand-bedded to assure precision accuracy. High lustre, durable stock finish, quick detachable sling swivels, basket weave checkering with extension of checkering on pistol grip. Customized action.								Not available
Deluxe	American walnut, individually hand-bedded to assure precision accuracy. High lustre, durable stock finish. Quick detachable sling swivels. Basket weave checkering. Monte Carlo style with cheek piece, especially designed for both scope and iron sighted rifles. Length of pull 13⅝″.										European Walnut Pull: 14″
Euromark	American walnut, individually hand-bedded to assure precision accuracy. Satin finish. Ebony pistol grip cap and fore end tip. Custom fine line checkering with extension on pistol grip. Solid black recoil pad. Quick detachable sling swivels. Monte Carlo style with cheek piece, especially designed for both scope and iron sighted rifles. Length of pull 13⅝″.										European Walnut Pull: 14″
Lazermark	American walnut, individually hand-bedded to assure precision accuracy. High lustre, durable stock finish. Quick detachable sling swivels. Laser carving on forearm, pistol grip and under cheek piece. Monte Carlo style with cheek piece, especially designed for both scope and iron sighted rifles. Length of pull 13⅝″.										European Walnut Pull: 14″
Fibermark	Not available		Molded fiberglass, individually hand-bedded to assure precision accuracy. Non-glare, black, wrinkle finish. Quick detachable sling swivels. Monte Carlo style with cheek piece, especially designed for both scope and iron sighted rifles. Length of pull 13⅝″.							Not available	
Safari Grade Custom	Not available								European walnut with satin oil finish. Ebony tip and cap. Black presentation recoil pad. Fine line checkering with Fleur de Lis. Matte finish bluing with customized action. Floorplate is engraved ''Weatherby Safari Grade.'' Standard rear stock swivel and barrel band front swivel. Sight is ¼ rib rear with stationary leaf and one folding shallow. ''V'' leaf hooded ramp front with brass bead. Available left or right hand. 13⅞″ pull.			
Crown Custom	Not available		Fully checkered bolt knob. Damascened bolt and follower. Hand-honed action. ''Weatherby Custom.'' Super fancy walnut stock with pattern #7 butt stock and forearm inlays and pattern #16 stock carving. Gold monogram with name or initials. 13⅝″ pull. Avail. in right hand only.							Not available	
Action	A scaled-down version of the popular Mark V action, with 6 precision locking lugs in place of 9.		Featuring the Mark V, world's strongest and safest action. The nine locking lugs have almost double the shear area of the lugs found on conventional bolt rifles. The cartridge case head is completely enclosed in the bolt and barrel. .460: action includes hand honing, bolt knob fully checkered, bolt and follower damascened, custom engraved floor plate.								
Safety	Forward moving release, accessible and positive.										

BARRELED ACTION SPECIFICATIONS

CALIBER	.224 WBY MAG	.22/250	.240 WBY MAG	.257 WBY MAG	.270 WBY MAG	7mm WBY MAG	.30-06	.300 WBY MAG	.340 WBY MAG	.378 WBY MAG	.460 WBY MAG
Model	Right hand 24″ or 26″ bbl. Left hand model not available		Right or left hand 24″ bbl. Right hand 26″ bbl. Left hand 26″ bbl. **available in .300 cal. only**						Right or left hand 26″ bbl. only.	Right or left hand 26″ bbl. only.	Right or left hand 24″ or 26″ bbl. only.

*Available only with Pendleton Dekicker, KDF or Mag-Na-Port muzzle brake.   **Weight varies due to wood density.

WEATHERBY RIFLES

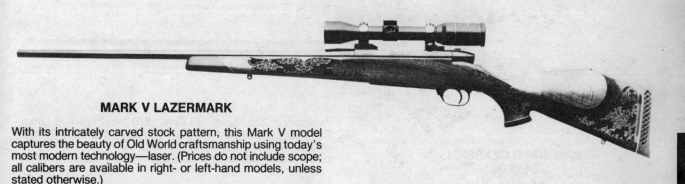

MARK V LAZERMARK

With its intricately carved stock pattern, this Mark V model captures the beauty of Old World craftsmanship using today's most modern technology—laser. (Prices do not include scope; all calibers are available in right- or left-hand models, unless stated otherwise.)

Calibers	Prices
224 Weatherby Mag. or 22/250 Varminter	
Right-hand only, 24″ barrel	$1085.00
Right-hand only, 26″ barrel	1100.00
240, 257, 270, 7mm, 300 Wby. Mag. & 30-06	
24″ barrel	1105.00
26″ barrel	1125.00
340 Wby. Mag., 26″ barrel	1127.00

Calibers	Prices
378 Wby. Mag., 26″ barrel	1281.00
416 Weatherby Mag.	
24″ barrel	1390.00
26″ barrel	1410.00
460 Weatherby Mag.	
24″ barrel	1450.00
26″ barrel	1470.00

MARK XXII SEMIAUTOMATIC

Although lighter and handier than Weatherby's big game rifle, this .22 semiautomatic boasts the same pointing characteristics and basic stock design. It is also the only .22 which allows hunters to choose single shot or semiautomatic fire. The Mark XXII is available in both clip and tubular models. The tubular model has a 15 shot capacity; the clip model comes with a 10 shot magazine. Folding leaf rear iron sights adjustable for windage and elevation and ramp front sights are standard. The receiver is precision-grooved for dovetailed scope mounts. Other features include non-skid rubber butt pad, Monte Carlo stock, and rosewood forend tip.

Price (clip or tube) **$454.00**

MARK XXII .22 AUTOMATIC SPECIFICATIONS

Action	Semi-automatic with single shot selector
Caliber	.22 long rifle cartridges only
Barrel	24″, special steel, contoured barrel
Overall length	42¼″
Magazine	Clip model—comes with 10-shot magazine. Extra 5 or 10-shot magazines available. Tubular model—15-shot capacity.
Stock	Select walnut, hand-checkered, Monte Carlo stock with cheek piece, Rosewood fore-end tip and pistol grip cap with diamond inlay. Non-skid rubber butt pad. Length of pull 13½″.
Sights	Adjustable folding rear sight; ramp front sight.
Safety	Shotgun type tang safety.
Weight	Approx. 6 lbs. without scope.
Trigger	Crip, clean precision trigger pull.
Mounts	Receiver is precision-grooved for dovetail scope mounts.

WEATHERBY RIFLES

VANGUARD CLASSIC I
$465.00

Available in 223 Rem., 243 Rem., 270 Win., 7mm-08, 7mm Rem. Mag., 30-06 and 308 Win. Features include black recoil pad (on magnum calibers) and solid black butt pad on regular calibers. See table for additional information and specifications.

VANGUARD CLASSIC II
$600.00

Utilizing the classic styling of an American walnut stock with oil finish, the Classic II stock design features a 90-degree black forend tip (rather than Weatherby's original 45-degree models). The black pistol grip cap with a walnut diamond inlay and a solid black recoil pad make this a distinctive stock. All **barrels** are 24″ with matte finish bluing. Available in **calibers:** 22/250, 243 Win., 270 Win., 7mm Rem. Mag., 30-06, 270 Wby. Mag., 300 Win. Mag., 300 Wby. Mag., and 338 Win. Mag. For additional information and specifications, see the Vanguard table.

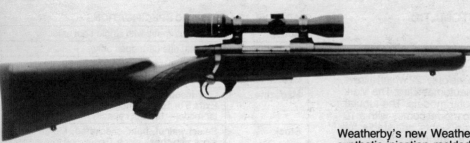

VANGUARD WEATHERGUARD
$399.00

Weatherby's new Weatherguard features a 24″ barrel and a synthetic injection molded stock designed to resist weather and humidity. Normal scratches from wear and tear are not visible because the black finish penetrates the entire stock. Stock comes complete with basket-weave checkering, solid black recoil pad, and front and rear swivel studs. **Calibers:** 223 Rem., 243 Rem., 270 Win., 7mm-08, 7mm Rem. Mag., 30-06 and 308 Win. For additional information and specifications, see the Vanguard table.

WEATHERBY RIFLES

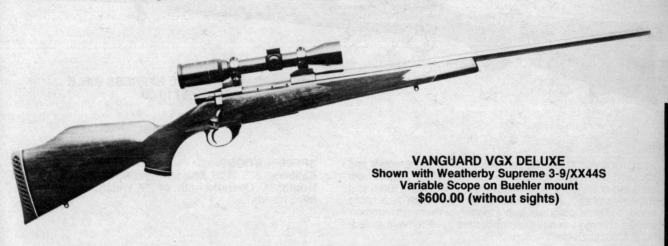

VANGUARD VGX DELUXE
Shown with Weatherby Supreme 3-9/XX44S
Variable Scope on Buehler mount
$600.00 (without sights)

VANGUARD SPECIFICATIONS

VGX DELUXE AND CLASSIC II									
CALIBER	.22/250 Rem.	.243 Rem.	.270 WBY. MAG.	.270 Win.	7mm Rem. Mag.	.30-06	.300 Win. Mag.	.300 WBY. MAG.	.338 Win. Mag.
Barrel Length	24"	24"	24"	24"	24"	24"	24"	24"	24"
Barrel Contour	No. 3	No. 2	No. 2	No. 2	No. 2	No. 2	No. 2	No. 2	No. 2
**Approx. Weight	8 lb. 8 oz.	7 lb. 12 oz.	7 lb. 14 oz.	7 lb. 14 oz.	7 lb. 14 oz.	7 lb. 14 oz.	7 lb. 14 oz.	7 lb. 14 oz.	7 lb. 14 oz.
Overall Length	*44"	*44"	44½"	44½"	44½"	44½"	44½"	44½"	44½"
Magazine Capacity	5 rnds.	5 rnds.	3 rnds.	5 rnds.	3 rnds.	5 rnds.	3 rnds.	3 rnds.	3 rnds.
Rifling	1-14"	1-10"	1-10"	1-10"	1-10"	1-10"	1-10"	1-10"	1-10"

CLASSIC I AND WEATHERGUARD							
CALIBER	.223 Rem.	.243 Win.	.270 Win.	7mm/08 Rem.	7mm Rem. Mag.	.30-06	.308 Win.
Barrel Length	24"	24"	24"	24"	24"	24"	24"
Barrel Contour	No. 1	No. 1	No. 1	No. 1	No. 1	No. 1	No. 1
**Weight—Classic I	7 lb. 5 oz.	7 lb. 5 oz.	7 lb. 7 oz.	7 lb. 5 oz.	7 lb. 7 oz.	7 lb. 7 oz.	7 lb. 5 oz.
Weight—Weatherguard	7 lb. 14 oz.	7 lb. 14 oz.	8 lbs.	7 lb. 14 oz.	8 lbs.	8 lbs.	7 lb. 14 oz.
Overall Length	*44"	*44"	44½"	*44"	44½"	44½"	*44"
Magazine Capacity	5 rnds.	5 rnds.	5 rnds.	5 rnds.	3 rnds.	5 rnds.	5 rnds.
Rifling	1-12"	1-10"	1-10"	1-9.5"	1-10"	1-10"	1-10"

ALL MODELS	
Sights	Scope or iron sights available at extra cost.
Stocks: Classic II	American walnut, 13⅝" pull, custom hand checkered, satin finish, 90 degree black tip and pistol grip cap, solid black recoil pad.
VGX Deluxe	American walnut, 13⅝" pull, custom checkering, recoil pad, high lustre finish; 45 degree rosewood fore end tip and pistol grip cap.
Classic I	American walnut, 13⅝" pull, hand checkered, satin finish, black butt pad. (Recoil pad on 7mm Rem. Mag.)
Weatherguard	Synthetic checkered stock, wrinkle finish, 13⅞" pull, black butt pad. (Recoil pad on 7mm Rem. Mag.)
Action	Vanguard action of the improved Mauser type. *Action is ½" shorter than the standard action.
Safety	Side operated, forward moving release, accessible and positive.
Mounts	Vanguard action accepts same bases as Mark V action.

**Weight Approximate—varies due to stock density.

WHITWORTH SPORTING RIFLES

SAFARI GRADE EXPRESS RIFLE
$710.00

Features three safety-lug bolt design for added strength and security . . . Hand-rubbed European walnut stocks with sculpted continental-style cheekpiece . . . Custom three-leaf Express sight . . . Ramp mounted front sight with detachable hood . . . Three-point adjustable trigger . . . Premium hammer-forged chrome-vanadium steel barrels . . . Premium milled-steel Mauser System Action.

SPECIFICATIONS
Calibers: 375 H&H Magnum and 458 Win. Mag. **Barrel length:** 24″. **Overall length:** 44.75″. **Weight:** 7½ lbs. **Capacity:** 3 rounds.

WINCHESTER BOLT ACTION RIFLES

MODEL 70 FEATHERWEIGHT
$472.00

Model 70 Featherweight hunting rifles minimize weight for easy handling and carrying. Barrel and receiver have integral recoil lug machined from chrome molybdenum steel. Bolt body and locking lugs are machined from a single steel bar. Thermoplastic bedding mates the receiver recoil lug and the stock for maximum strength and accuracy. Bolt features a jeweled finish and knurled bolt handle. Three-position safety. Receivers drilled and tapped for scope mounting. One-piece walnut stocks are hand-worked and finished with genuine cut checkering.

SPECIFICATIONS: MODEL 70 FEATHERWEIGHT (WALNUT)

Caliber	Magazine Capacity (A)	Barrel Length	Overall Length	Nominal Length Of Pull	Nominal Drop At			Nominal Weight (Lbs.)	Rate of Twist 1 Turn In	Bases & Rings or Sights
					Comb	Heel	MC			
22-250 Rem.	5	22″	42″	13½″	⁹⁄₁₆″	⁷⁄₈″	—	6½	14″	B + R
223 Rem.	6	22	42	13½	⁹⁄₁₆	⁷⁄₈	—	6½	12	B + R
243 Win.	5	22	42	13½	⁹⁄₁₆	⁷⁄₈	—	6½	10	B + R
270 Win.	5	22	42½	13½	⁹⁄₁₆	⁷⁄₈	—	6¾	10	B + R
280 Rem.	4	22	42½	13½	⁹⁄₁₆	⁷⁄₈	—	6¾	10	B + R
30-06 Spgfld.	5	22	42½	13½	⁹⁄₁₆	⁷⁄₈	—	6¾	10	B + R
308 Win.	5	22	42	13½	⁹⁄₁₆	⁷⁄₈	—	6½	12	B + R

(A) For additional capacity, add one round in chamber when ready to fire. Drops are measured from center line of bore. B + R—Bases and Rings included. Rate of twist is right-hand.

WINCHESTER BOLT ACTION RIFLES

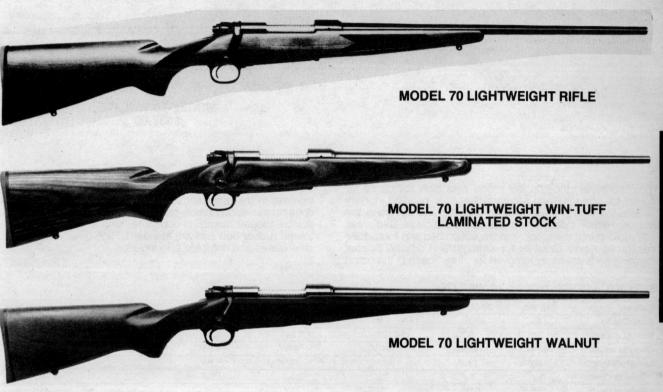

MODEL 70 LIGHTWEIGHT RIFLE

MODEL 70 LIGHTWEIGHT WIN-TUFF LAMINATED STOCK

MODEL 70 LIGHTWEIGHT WALNUT

MODEL 70 LIGHTWEIGHT RIFLE

Model 70 Lightweight Walnut	$430.00
Model 70 Win-Tuff Lightweight	442.00
Model 70 Win-Cam Lightweight	442.00

SPECIFICATIONS: MODEL 70 LIGHTWEIGHT

Model		Caliber	Magazine Capacity (A)	Barrel Length	Overall Length	Nominal Length Of Pull	Nominal Drop At Comb	Nominal Drop At Heel	Nominal Drop At MC	Nominal Weight (Lbs.)	Rate of Twist 1 Turn In	Sights
70 WALNUT Checkered, No Sights		22-250 Rem.	5	22"	42"	13½"	$^9/_{16}$"	⅞"	—	6¼	14"	—
		223 Rem.	6	22	42	13½	$^9/_{16}$	⅞	—	6¼	12	—
		243 Win.	5	22	42	13½	$^9/_{16}$	⅞	—	6¼	10	—
		270 Win.	5	22	42½	13½	$^9/_{16}$	⅞	—	6½	10	—
		280 Rem.	4	22	42½	13½	$^9/_{16}$	⅞	—	6½	10	—
		30-06 Spgfld.	5	22	42½	13½	$^9/_{16}$	⅞	—	6½	10	—
		308 Win.	5	22	42	13½	$^9/_{16}$	⅞	—	6¼	12	—
70 WIN-TUFF Warm Brown Laminate, Checkered, No Sights	New	223 Rem.	4	22	42	13½	$^9/_{16}$	⅞	—	6¾	12	—
		243 Win.	5	22	42	13½	$^9/_{16}$	⅞	—	6¾	10	—
		270 Win.	5	22	42½	13½	$^9/_{16}$	⅞	—	7	10	—
		30-06 Spgfld.	5	22	42½	13½	$^9/_{16}$	⅞	—	7	10	—
	New	308 Win.	5	22	42	13½	$^9/_{16}$	⅞	—	6¾	12	—
70 WIN-CAM Camo Green Laminate	New	270 Win.	5	22	42½	13½	$^9/_{16}$·	⅞	—	7	10	—
	New	30-06 Spgfld.	5	22	42½	13½	$^9/_{16}$	⅞	—	7	10	—

(A) For additional capacity, add one round in chamber when ready to fire. Drops are measured from center line of bore. Rate of twist is right-hand.

WINCHESTER BOLT ACTION RIFLES

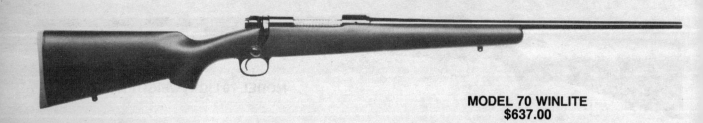

MODEL 70 WINLITE
$637.00

The fiberglass stock on this model sets high standards for lightness, strength, and accuracy. Receiver bedding stability is assured with the use of thermoplastic and by fitting the barreled action individually to the stock. Critical inletted areas are molded into the stock, and the action bed and forend are reinforced Kevlar/Graphite for strength and rigidity. Special bedding pads are easily removed for "free-floating" the barrel if desired. Despite a dramatic weight reduction, there is no increase in the recoil sensation since the fiberglass material compresses during recoil, becoming a total recoil absorption device. Hinged magazine floorplate, sling swivel studs, contoured rubber butt pad are standard. High-quality adjustable steel bases and rings are also included.

SPECIFICATIONS: MODEL 70 WINLITE

Caliber	270 Win.	30-06 Spfd.	7mm Rem. Mag.	338 Win. Mag.	280 Rem.	300 Win. Mag.	300 Weath. Mag.
Mag. Cap.*	5	5	3	3	4	3	3
Barrel Length:	22″	22″	24″	24″	22″	24″	24″
Overall Length:	42½″	42½″	44½″	44½″	42½″	44½″	44½″
Length of Pull:	13½″	13½″	13½″	13½″	13½″	13½″	13½″
****Drop at Comb:**	$^9/_{16}$″	$^9/_{16}$″	$^9/_{16}$″	$^9/_{16}$″	$^9/_{16}$″	$^9/_{16}$″	$^9/_{16}$″
****Drop at Heel:**	½″	½″	½″	½″	½″	½″	½″
Weight (lbs.)	6¼″	6¼″	6½″	6½″	6¼	6½	6½
Rate of Twist:	10″	10″	9½″	10″	10″	10″	10″

* For additional capacity, add one round in chamber when ready to fire.
** Drops are measured from centerline of bore.

WINCHESTER BOLT ACTION RIFLES

MODEL 70 SPORTER & SUPER EXPRESS RIFLES
$472.00

Featuring five standard calibers and eight magnum calibers (see table below), Winchester's Sporter and Super Express rifles feature one-piece Monte Carlo stocks with sculptured undercut cheekpieces, satin finish, deep-cut wraparound checkering, tapered forends and contoured rubber butt pads. Each rifle has a 24″ cold-formed chrome molybdenum steel barrel, a field-strippable jeweled bolt, and 3-position safety.

**MODEL 70 SUPER EXPRESS™
WALNUT MAGNUM
(375 H&H Magnum/458 Win. Mag.)
$792.00**

This big game pair of rifles boasts all the Sporter Magnum features in 375 H&H and 458 Winchester Magnum calibers. The Sporter stock design has the same innovative cheekpiece, but is reinforced with two steel crossbolts for added strength. The forward sling swivel is mounted directly on the rifle barrel for improved carrying balance and strength. Magazine capacity is three Magnum cartridges. The Monte Carlo stock with sculpted cheekpiece on Model 70 XTR Sporter Magnum and Super Express Magnum rifles is shown in the photo above.

SPECIFICATIONS: MODEL 70 SPORTER & SUPER EXPRESS

Model		Caliber	Magazine Capacity (A)	Barrel Length	Overall Length	Nominal Length Of Pull	Nominal Drop At Comb	Heel	MC	Nominal Weight (Lbs.)	Rate of Twist 1 Turn In	Bases & Rings or Sights
70 SPORTER WALNUT	*New*	22-250 Rem.	5	24″	44″	13½″	$^9/_{16}$″	$1^5/_{16}$″	¾″	7¾″	14″	Sights
		22-250 Rem.	5	24	44	13½	$^9/_{16}$	$1^5/_{16}$	¾	7¾	14	B + R
	New	223 Rem.	6	24	44	13½	$^9/_{16}$	$1^5/_{16}$	¾	7¾	12	Sights
	New	223 Rem.	6	24	44	13½	$^9/_{16}$	$1^5/_{16}$	¾	7¾	12	B + R
	New	243 Win.	5	24	44	13½	$^9/_{16}$	$1^5/_{16}$	¾	7¾	10	Sights
		243 Win.	5	24	44	13½	$^9/_{16}$	$1^5/_{16}$	¾	7¾	10	B + R
	New	264 Win. Mag.	3	24	44½	13½	$^9/_{16}$	$1^5/_{16}$	¾	7¾	9	Sight
		264 Win. Mag.	3	24	44½	13½	$^9/_{16}$	$1^5/_{16}$	¾	7¾	9	B + R
		270 Win.	5	24	44½	13½	$^9/_{16}$	$1^5/_{16}$	¾	7¾	10	Sights
		270 Win.	5	24	44½	13½	$^9/_{16}$	$1^5/_{16}$	¾	7¾	10	B + R
	New	270 Weath. Mag.	5	24	44½	13½	$^9/_{16}$	$1^5/_{16}$	¾	7¾	10	Sights
		270 Weath. Mag.	5	24	44½	13½	$^9/_{16}$	$1^5/_{16}$	¾	7¾	10	B + R
		7mm Rem. Mag.	3	24	44½	13½	$^9/_{16}$	$1^5/_{16}$	¾	7¾	9½	Sights
		7mm Rem. Mag.	3	24	44½	13½	$^9/_{16}$	$1^5/_{16}$	¾	7¾	9½	B + R
		30-06 Spgfld.	5	24	44½	13½	$^9/_{16}$	$1^5/_{16}$	¾	7¾	10	Sights
		30-06 Spgfld.	5	24	44½	13½	$^9/_{16}$	$1^5/_{16}$	¾	7¾	10	B + R
	New	300 H&H Mag.	3	24	44½	13½	$^9/_{16}$	$1^5/_{16}$	¾	7¾	10	Sights
	New	300 H&H Mag.	3	24	44½	13½	$^9/_{16}$	$1^5/_{16}$	¾	7¾	10	B + R
		300 Win. Mag.	3	24	44½	13½	$^9/_{16}$	$1^5/_{16}$	¾	7¾	10	Sights
		300 Win. Mag.	3	24	44½	13½	$^9/_{16}$	$1^5/_{16}$	¾	7¾	10	B + R
	New	300 Weath. Mag.	3	24	44½	13½	$^9/_{16}$	$1^5/_{16}$	¾	7¾	10	Sights
		300 Weath. Mag.	3	24	44½	13½	$^9/_{16}$	$1^5/_{16}$	¾	7¾	10	B + R
		338 Win. Mag.	3	24	44½	13½	$^9/_{16}$	$1^5/_{16}$	¾	7¾	10	Sights
		338 Win. Mag.	3	24	44½	13½	$^9/_{16}$	$1^5/_{16}$	¾	7¾	10	B + R
70 SUPER EXPRESS		375 H&H Mag.	3	24	44½	13½	$^9/_{16}$	$1^5/_{16}$	¾	8½	12	Sights
WALNUT MAGNUM		458 Win. Mag.	3	22	42½	13½	$^9/_{16}$	$1^5/_{16}$	¾	8½	14	Sights

(A) For additional capacity, add one round in chamber when ready to fire. Drops are measured from center line of bore. B + R—Bases and Rings included. Rate of twist is right-hand.

WINCHESTER BOLT ACTION RIFLES

MODEL 70 HEAVY BARREL VARMINT RIFLE
$482.00

Winchester's Varmint Rifle features a Sporter stock with undercut cheekpiece and 26" counter-bored barrel. Rubber butt pad, swivel studs and receiver drilled and tapped for scope are standard, as is Winchester's 3-position safety.

MODEL 70 HEAVY BARREL VARMINT RIFLE SPECIFICATIONS

Model		Caliber	Magazine Capacity (A)	Barrel Length	Overall Length	Nominal Length Of Pull	Nominal Drop At			Nominal Weight (Lbs.)	Rate of Twist 1 Turn In	Sights
							Comb	Heel	MC			
70 VARMINT	*New*	22-250 Rem.	5	26"	46"	13½"	9/16"	1 5/16"	¾"	8⅞	14"	—
	New	223 Rem.	6	26	46	13½	9/16	1 5/16	¾	8⅞	12	—
	New	243 Win.	5	26	46	13½	9/16	1 5/16	¾	8⅞	10	—

(A) For additional capacity, add one round in chamber when ready to fire. Drops are measured from center line of bore. Rate of twist is right-hand.

WINCHESTER RANGER®
BOLT ACTION CENTERFIRE RIFLE
$387.00

The Ranger Bolt Action Rifle comes with an American hardwood stock, a wear-resistant satin walnut finish, ramp bead-post front sight, steel barrel, three-position safety and engine-turned, anti-bind bolt. The receiver is drilled and tapped for scope mounting; accuracy is enhanced by thermoplastic bedding of the receiver. Barrel and receiver are brushed and blued.

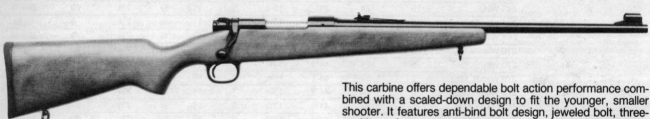

WINCHESTER RANGER®
YOUTH BOLT ACTION CARBINE
$396.00

This carbine offers dependable bolt action performance combined with a scaled-down design to fit the younger, smaller shooter. It features anti-bind bolt design, jeweled bolt, three-position safety, contoured recoil pad, ramped bead front sight, semi-buckhorn folding leaf rear sight, and sling swivels. Receiver is drilled and tapped for scope mounting. Stock is of American hardwood with protective satin walnut finish. Pistol grip, length of pull, overall length, and comb are all tailored to youth dimensions (see table).

RANGER & YOUTH RIFLE SPECIFICATIONS

Model	Caliber	Magazine Capacity (A)	Barrel Length	Overall Length	Nominal Length Of Pull	Nominal Drop At			Nominal Weight (Lbs.)	Rate of Twist 1 Turn In	Bases & Rings Sights
						Comb	Heel	MC			
RANGER BOLT ACTION	270 Win.	5	22"	42¾"	13½"	9/16"	7/8"	—	6	10"	Sights
	30-06 Spgfld.	5	22	42¾	13½	9/16	7/8	—	6	10	Sights
RANGER YOUTH/LADIES BOLT ACTION	243 Win.	5	22"	41¼	12½"	¾"	1"	—	5¾	10"	Sights

(A) For additional capacity, add one round in chamber when ready to fire. Drops are measured from center line of bore. Rate of twist is right-hand.

WINCHESTER LEVER ACTION CARBINES & RIFLES

Model 94™ Side Eject® Lever Action Centerfire carbines have been developed and refined through almost a century of sporting use and technological advancement. The new angled ejection system throws the spent cartridge away from the shooter's line of vision and does not interfere with top-mounted scopes. It features an improved, stabilized trigger mechanism with controlled pre-travel and short, crisp let-off.

Receivers are of forged steel. Chromium molybdenum barrels assure long-lasting strength. Chamber and rifling are cold-forged in a single operation for precise alignment and accuracy. The receiver is ported for angled ejection and scopes can be top-mounted.

Model 94 Standard Walnut Rifle is top choice for lever-action styling and craftsmanship. Metal surfaces are highly polished and blued. American walnut stock and forearm have a protective stain finish with precise-cut wraparound checkering. It has a 20-inch barrel with hooded blade front sight and semi-buckhorn rear sight. **Calibers:** 30-30 Win., 307 Win., 356 Win. and 7-30 Waters. **Prices:**

30-30 Win., checkered, 307 Win., 356 Win.	**$299.00**
30-30 Win., 7-30 Waters	283.00
30-30 Win. with scope	342.00

Model 94 Walnut Trapper Carbine is a 16-inch short-barrel lever action with straight forward styling. Compact and fast-handling in dense cover, it has a magazine capacity of five shots (9 in 45 Colt or 44 Rem. Mag./44 S&W Special). **Calibers:** 30-30 Winchester, 45 Colt, and 44 Rem. Mag./44 S&W Special. **Prices:**

30-30 Winchester	**$283.00**
45 Colt, 44 Rem. Mag./44 S&W Special	299.00

MODEL 94 SPECIFICATIONS

Model	Caliber	Magazine Capacity (A)	Barrel Length	Overall Length	Nominal Length Of Pull	Nominal Drop At Comb	Nominal Drop At Heel	Nominal Weight (Lbs.)	Rate of Twist 1 Turn In	Rings Sights
94 CHECKERED WALNUT	30-30 Win.	6	20″	37¾″	13″	1⅛″	1⅞″	6½	12″	Rifle
With 1.5-4.5 scope	30-30 Win.	6	20	37¾	13	1⅛	1⅞	6⅞	12	R/S
94 STANDARD WALNUT	30-30 Win.	6	20	37¾	13	1⅛	1⅞	6½	12	Rifle
	7-30 Waters	6	20	37¾	13	1⅛	1⅞	6½	9.9	Rifle
94 TRAPPER CARBINE WALNUT	30-30 Win.	5	16	33¾	13	1⅛	1⅞	6⅛	12	Rifle
	44 Rem. Mag. 44 S&W Spec.	9	16	33¾	13	1⅛	1⅞	6	38	Rifle
	45 Colt	9	16	33¾	13	1⅛	1⅞	6	38	Rifle

(A) For additional capacity, add one round in chamber when ready to fire. Drops are measured from center line of bore. Rate of twist is right-hand.

WINCHESTER LEVER ACTION RIFLES

MODEL 94 RANGER
$251.00 ($287.00 with Scope)

Model 94 Ranger is an economical version of the Model 94. Lever action is smooth and reliable. In 30-30 Winchester, the rapid-firing six-shot magazine capacity provides two more shots than most centerfire hunting rifles.

MODEL 94 BIG BORE WALNUT
$299.00

Winchester's powerful .307 and .356 hunting calibers combined with maximum lever-action power and angled ejection provide hunters with improved performance and economy.

MODEL 94 WIN-TUFF RIFLE
$299.00 (20" Barrel)

Includes all features and specifications of standard Model 94 plus tough laminated hardwood styled for the brush-gunning hunter who wants good concealment and a carbine that can stand up to all kinds of weather.

MODEL 94 SPECIFICATIONS

Model	Caliber	Magazine Capacity (A)	Barrel Length	Overall Length	Nominal Length Of Pull	Nominal Drop At Comb	Nominal Drop At Heel	Nominal Weight (Lbs.)	Rate of Twist 1 Turn In	Sights
94 WIN-TUFF	30-30 Win.	6	20"	37¾"	13"	1⅛"	1⅞"	6½	12"	Rifle
94 BIG BORE WALNUT	307 Win.	6	20	37¾	13	1⅛	1⅞	6½	12	Rifle
	356 Win.	6	20	37¾	13	1⅛	1⅞	6½	12	Rifle
RANGER	30-30 Win.	6	20	37¾	13	1⅛	1⅞	6½	12	Rifle
Scope 4 × 32 see-through mounts	30-30 Win.	6	20	37¾	13	1⅛	1⅞	6⅞	12	R/S

(A) For additional capacity, add one round in chamber when ready to fire. Drops are measured from center line of bore. R/S-Rifle sights and Bushnell® Sportview™ scope with mounts. Rate of twist is right-hand.

WINCHESTER LEVER ACTION RIFLES

MODEL 9422 LEVER-ACTION RIMFIRE RIFLES

These Model 9422 rimfire rifles combine classic 94 styling and handling in ultra-modern lever action 22s of superb craftsmanship. Handling and shooting characteristics are superior because of their carbine-like size.

Positive lever action and bolt design ensure feeding and chambering from any shooting position. The bolt face is T-slotted to guide the cartridge with complete control from magazine to chamber. A color-coded magazine follower shows when the brass magazine tube is empty. Receivers are grooved for scope mounting. Other functional features include exposed hammer with half-cock safety, hooded bead front sight, semi-buckhorn rear sight and side ejection of spent cartridges.

Stock and forearm are American walnut with checkering, high-luster finish, and straight-grip design. Internal parts are carefully finished for smoothness of action.

Model 9422 Walnut is considered one of the world's finest production sporting arms. It holds 21 Short, 17 Long or 15 Long Rifle cartridges.

Model 9422 Walnut Magnum gives exceptional accuracy at longer ranges than conventional 22 rifles. It is designed specifically for the 22 Winchester Magnum Rimfire cartridge and holds 11 cartridges.

Also available: **Model 9422 Win-Cam Magnum** featuring laminated non-glare, green-shaded stock and forearm. American hardwood stock is bonded to withstand all weather and climates. **Model 9422 Win-Tuff** is also available to ensure resistance to changes in weather conditions, or exposure to water and hard knocks.

RIFLES

SPECIFICATIONS

Model	Caliber	Magazine Capacity	Barrel Length	Overall Length	Nominal Length Of Pull	Nominal Drop At Comb	Nominal Drop At Heel	Nominal Weight (Lbs.)	Rate of Twist 1 Turn In	Sights	Prices
9422 WALNUT	22	21S,17L,15LR	20½"	37⅛"	13½"	1⅛"	1⅞"	6¼	16"	Rifle	$323.00
	22WMR	11	20½	37⅛	13½	1⅛	1⅞	6¼	16	Rifle	331.00
9422 WIN-TUFF	22	21S,17L,15LR	20½"	37⅛"	13½"	1⅛"	1⅞"	6¼	16"	Rifle	335.00
	22WMR	11	20½	37⅛	13½	1⅛	1⅞	6¼	16	Rifle	342.00
9422 WIN-CAM	22WMR	11	20½"	37⅛"	13½"	1⅛"	1⅞"	6¼	16"	Rifle	342.00

WMR-Winchester Magnum Rimfire. S-Short, L-Long, LR-Long Rifle. Drops are measured from center line of bore.   * Indicates NEW.

WINSLOW RIFLES

SPECIFICATIONS

Stock: Choice of two stock models. **The Plainsmaster** offers pinpoint accuracy in open country with full curl pistol grip and flat forearm. **The Bushmaster** offers lighter weight for bush country; slender pistol with palm swell; beavertail forend for light hand comfort. Both styles are of hand-rubbed black walnut. Length of pull—13½ inches; plainsmaster ⅜ inch castoff; Bushmaster ³/₁₆ inch castoff; all rifles are drilled and tapped to incorporate the use of telescopic sights; rifles with receiver or open sights are available on special order; all rifles are equipped with quick detachable sling swivel studs and whiteline recoil pad. All Winslow stocks incorporate a slight castoff to deflect recoil, minimizing flinch and muzzle jump. **Magazine:** Staggered box type, four shot. (Blind in the stock has no floorplate). **Action:** Mauser Mark X Action. **Overall length:** 43″ (Standard Model); 45″ (Magnum); all Winslow rifles have company name and serial number and grade engraved on the action

and caliber engraved on barrel. **Barrel:** Douglas barrel premium grade, chrome moly-type steel; all barrels, 20 caliber through 35 caliber, have six lands and grooves; barrels larger than 35 caliber have eight lands and grooves. All barrels are finished to (.2 to .4) micro inches inside the lands and grooves. **Total weight** (without scope): 7 to 7½ lbs. with 24″ barrel in standard calibers 243, 308, 270, etc; 8 to 9 lbs. with 26″ barrel in Magnum calibers 264 Win., 300 Wby., 458 Win., etc. Winslow rifles are made in the following calibers:

Standard cartridges: 22-250, 243 Win., 244 Rem., 257 Roberts, 308 Win., 30-06, 280 Rem., 270 Win., 25-06, 284 Win., 358 Win., and 7mm (7×57).

Magnum cartridges: 300 Weatherby, 300 Win., 338 Win., 358 Norma, 375 H.H., 458 Win., 257 Weatherby, 264 Win., 270 Weatherby, 7mm Weatherby, 7mm Rem., 300 H.H., 308 Norma.

Left-handed models available in most calibers.

WINSLOW BASIC RIFLE

The Basic Rifle, available in the Bushmaster stock, features one ivory diamond inlay in a rose-wood grip cap and ivory trademark in bottom of forearm. Grade 'A' walnut jeweled bolt and follower. **Price: $1475.00.** With **Plainsmaster stock: $100.00** extra. **Left-hand model: $1575.00.**

WINSLOW VARMINT

This 17-caliber rifle is available with Bushmaster stock or Plainsmaster stock, which is a miniature of the original with high roll-over cheekpiece and a round leading edge on the forearm, modified spoon billed pistol grip. Available in 17/222, 17/222 Mag. 17/233, 222 Rem. and 223. Regent grade shown. With **Bushmaster stock: $1475.00.** With **Plainsmaster stock: $100.00** extra. **Left-hand model: $1575.00.**

Shotguns

FOR ADDRESSES AND PHONE
NUMBERS OF MANUFACTURERS AND
DISTRIBUTORS INCLUDED IN THIS
SECTION, SEE *DIRECTORY OF
MANUFACTURERS AND SUPPLIERS*

AMERICAN ARMS

WATERFOWL SPECIAL SIDE-BY-SIDE
$609.00

WATERFOWL SPECIAL O/U 10 GAUGE

SPECIFICATIONS
Gauge: 10
Chambers: 3½″
Barrel length: 32″ with F/F (steel full)
Weight: 10 lbs. 13 oz.
Triggers: Double
Stock: Dull finish walnut, pistol-grip stock and beavertail forend with hand-checkering
Length of pull: 14⁵/₁₆″
Drop at comb: 1³/₈″
Drop at heel: 2³/₈″
Features: Flat rib; fitted rubber recoil pad; precision-made boxlocks; one-piece, steel-forged receiver; manual thumb safety; sling swivels and camouflaged sling

Also available:
WATERFOWL SPECIAL OVER/UNDER 10 GAUGE. Same specifications as side-by-side model, except for the following. **Weight:** 9 lbs. 15 oz. **Length of pull:** 14½″. Also includes ¼″ vent rib and single selective trigger. **Price:** $829.00
WATERFOWL SPECIAL OVER/UNDER 12 GAUGE. Same specifications as 10 gauge model, except for the following. **Chambers:** 3″. **Barrel length:** 28″. **Trigger:** Single selective. **Weight:** 6 lbs. 15 oz. Also has automatic selective ejectors and 3½″ chamber choke tubes. **Price:** $609.00

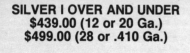

SILVER I OVER AND UNDER
$439.00 (12 or 20 Ga.)
$499.00 (28 or .410 Ga.)

SILVER II
(W/Choke Tubes & Automatic Selective Ejectors)
$579.00

SPECIFICATIONS
Gauges: 12, 20, 28 or .410
Chambers: 3″ (2³/₄″ in 28 ga.)
Barrel lengths: 26″, choked IC/M (all gauges); 28″, choked M/F (12 and 20 ga.)
Trigger: Single selective
Weight: 6 lbs. 15 oz. (12 ga.); 6 lbs. 10 oz. (20 ga.); 5 lbs. 14 oz. (28 ga.); 6 lbs. 6 oz. (.410 ga.)

Stock: Hand-checkered, walnut, pistol-grip stock and forend
Length of pull: 14¹/₈″
Drop at comb: 1³/₈″
Drop at heel: 2³/₈″
Features: Fitted recoil pad; ¼″ vent rib; manual thumb safety; scroll-engraved, precision-made boxlocks; one-piece, steel-forged receiver; locking cross bolt; monobloc chrome-lined barrels; extractors

AMERICAN ARMS

SPECIFICATIONS
Gauges: 12, 20 and .410
Chamber: 3"
Barrel length: 28", choked M/F (12 and 20 ga.); 26", choked F (.410 ga. only)
Features: Manual thumb safety; chrome-lined barrels; checkered stock and forearm with walnut-style finish; non-folding

AASB SINGLE BARREL SHOTGUN
$99.00

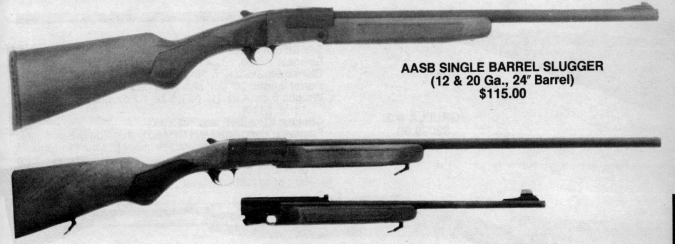

AASB SINGLE BARREL SLUGGER
(12 & 20 Ga., 24" Barrel)
$115.00

AASB COMBO
(22 H/12 Ga. or 22 LR/20 Ga.)
$235.00

AASB SINGLE BARREL 10 GAUGE (Not shown)
$149.00

SPECIFICATIONS
Gauge: 10
Chamber: 3½"
Barrel length: 30" choked Full
Finish: Same as above with non-reflective finish

Also available:
AASB SINGLE BARREL TURKEY SPECIAL. Same specifications as above, except for the following. **Barrel length:** 26" with choke tube. **Price: $179.00**

AASB CAMPER SPECIAL
$108.00

Same specifications as the single barrel model, except for the following. **Barrel length:** 21", choked Modified only. **Overall length:** 27".

AMERICAN ARMS

BRITTANY
$649.00

SPECIFICATIONS
Gauges: 12, 20
Chamber: 3″
Barrel lengths: 25″ and 27″
Weight: 6 lbs. 7 ozs. (25″); 6 lbs. 15 oz. (27″)
Chokes: Tubes IC/M/F
Features: Engraved case-colored frame; single selective trigger with top tang selector; automatic selective ejectors; manual safety; hard chrome-lined barrels; walnut English-style straight stock and semi-beavertail forearm w/cut checkering and oil-rubbed finish; ventilated rubber recoil pad; and choke tubes with key

GRULLA #2
$2099.00

SPECIFICATIONS
Gauges: 12, 20, 28, .410
Chambers: 2³/₄″ (12 & 28 ga.); 3″ (20 & .410 ga.)
Barrel length: 26″ (28″ also in 12 ga.)
Weight: 6 lbs. 4 oz. (12 ga.); 5 lbs. 11 oz. (20 & 28 ga.); 5 lbs. 13 oz. (.410)
Chokes: IC/M (M/F also in 12 ga.)
Features: Hand-fitted and finished high-grade classic double; double triggers; automatic selective ejectors; fixed chokes; concave rib; case-colored sidelock action w/engraving; English-style straight stock; splinter forearm and checkered butt of oil rubbed walnut

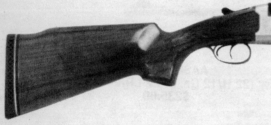

MODEL RS/COMBO (O/U RIFLE/SHOTGUN)
$749.00

SPECIFICATIONS
Caliber/Gauge: 308/12 or 222/12
Chamber: 3″
Weight: 7 lbs. 14 oz.
Features: Fitted w/vent rib; open rifle sights; grooved for scope mounting; fully adj. for windage & elevation w/barrel connectors; walnut pistol-grip stock w/Monte Carlo rollover cheekpiece and cut checkering; positive shell extraction; top tang safety; engraved frame w/antique silver finish.

STERLING OVER AND UNDER
$825.00

SPECIFICATIONS
Gauge: 12 or 20
Chambers: 3″
Barrel length: 26″ (28″ barrel avail. with 12 ga.)
Trigger: Single selective with gold color
Weight: 7 lbs. 1 oz. (12 ga.); 6 lbs. 12 oz. (20 ga.)
Frame: Old silver finish
Stock: Oil-finished walnut stock and forend with hand-checkering; pistol grip

Length of pull: 14¹/₈″
Drop at comb: 1³/₈″
Drop at heel: 2³/₈″
Features: Precision-made boxlocks with hand-engraved scrollwork on false side plates; one-piece, steel-forged receiver; monbloc chrome-lined barrels; locking cross bolt; manual thumb safety; fitted recoil pad; automatic selective ejector; ¹/₄″ vent rib with matte finish; choke tubes

AMERICAN ARMS

GENTRY SIDE-BY-SIDE
$469.00 (12, 16 or 20 Ga.)
$499.00 (28 or .410 Ga.)

Features boxlocks with engraved English-style scrollwork on side plates; one-piece, steel-forged receiver; chrome barrels; manual thumb safety; independent floating firing pin.

SPECIFICATIONS
Gauges: 12, 16, 20, 28, .410
Chambers: 3″ (except 28 gauge, 2³⁄₄″)
Barrel lengths: 26″, choked IC/M (all gauges); 28″, choked M/F (12, 16 and 20 gauges)

Weight: 6 lbs. 14 oz. (12 and .410 ga.); 6 lbs. 4 oz. (20 and 28 ga.)
Drop at comb: 1³⁄₈″
Drop at heel: 2³⁄₈″
Other features: Fitted recoil pad; flat matted rib; walnut pistol-grip stock and beavertail forend with hand-checkering; gold front sight bead

DERBY SIDE-BY-SIDE
Single or Double Trigger

Features functioning side locks with English-style hand-engraving on side plates; one-piece, steel-forged receiver; chrome barrels; automatic safety

SPECIFICATIONS
Gauges: 12, 20, 28, .410 (20/28 gauge in two-barrel set)
Chambers: 3″
Barrel lengths: 26″, choked IC/M (all gauges); 28″, choked M/F (12 and 20 gauges)
Weight: 7 lbs. 1 oz. (12 ga.); 6¹⁄₄ lbs. (20, 28 and .410 ga.)
Sights: Gold bead front sight
Stock: Walnut and splinter forend with hand-checkering

Length of pull 14¹⁄₈″
Drop at comb: 1³⁄₈″
Drop at heel: 2³⁄₈″
Finish: Hand-rubbed oil finish wood
Prices:

12 or 20 ga. double trigger	$ 789.00
12 or 20 ga. single trigger	825.00
28 or .410 ga. double trigger	825.00
28 or .410 ga. single trigger	859.00
20/28 ga. double trigger set	1029.00
20/28 ga. single trigger set	1069.00

TURKEY SPECIAL SIDE-BY-SIDE
$655.00

Features: Fitted recoil pad; flat rib; precision-made boxlocks with one-piece, steel-forged receiver; non-reflective, chrome-lined barrels; manual thumb safety; sling swivels and camouflaged sling
Also available:
TURKEY SPECIAL SIDE-BY-SIDE 12 GAUGE. Same specifications as 10 gauge model, except for the following. **Chambers:** 3″. **Weight:** 6 lbs. 14 oz. **Length of pull:** 14¹⁄₈″. **Price:** $559.00
TURKEY SPECIAL OVER/UNDER. Same specifications as side-by-side model, except for the following. **Length of pull:** 14¹⁄₂″. Also includes ¹⁄₄″ vent rib, choke tubes and extractors. **Price:** $875.00

SPECIFICATIONS
Gauge: 10
Chambers: 3¹⁄₂″
Barrel length: 26″ with choke tubes
Weight: 9 lbs. 15 oz.
Stock: Dull finish walnut stock and beavertail forend with hand-checkering; pistol grip
Length of pull: 14⁵⁄₁₆″
Drop at comb: 1³⁄₈″
Drop at heel: 2³⁄₈″

ARMSPORT SHOTGUNS

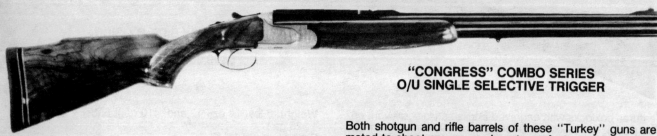

"CONGRESS" COMBO SERIES
O/U SINGLE SELECTIVE TRIGGER

Both shotgun and rifle barrels of these "Turkey" guns are mated to shoot groups as close to perfect as possible. The fine-grained palm swell full pistol grip rollover cheekpiece, walnut stock and forend are all hand-checkered. Both 12 and 20 gauge top shotgun barrels are chambered to accept 3" magnum shells. The Deluxe Single Selective Trigger models are available in both 12 and 20 gauge over either .222, .243 or .270.

Models	Prices
Model 2783 Deluxe 12 gauge/222 w/lateral rib	**$1495.00**
Model 2784 Deluxe 12 gauge/243 w/lateral rib	**1495.00**
Model 2785 Deluxe 12 gauge/270 w/lateral rib	**1495.00**

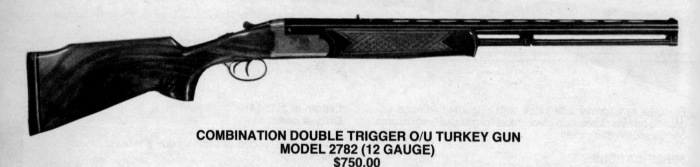

COMBINATION DOUBLE TRIGGER O/U TURKEY GUN
MODEL 2782 (12 GAUGE)
$750.00

Armsport's over/under shotgun/rifle combination turkey gun is manufactured by one of Italy's finest gun factories. This 12 gauge, 3" mag. shotgun with .222 caliber rifle features chrome-lined barrels with an extra wide upper vent rib. The frame is built from a special solid steel block and has tempered antique silver finish or basic blue, both beautifully engraved. Its high luster walnut palm swell pistol grip and stock are gracefully made with schnabel forend, both checkered for sure grip. Fitted with rubber recoil pad.

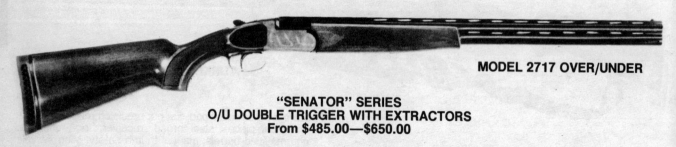

MODEL 2717 OVER/UNDER

"SENATOR" SERIES
O/U DOUBLE TRIGGER WITH EXTRACTORS
From $485.00—$650.00

The Armsport over/unders with double triggers are lightweight, well balanced and are chambered for 3" Mag. shells. The special grade steel barrels are chrome-lined, with both an upper vent rib and lateral vent rib. The fine grain walnut stock has a palm swell pistol grip and both the stock and schnabel-type forend have a deep, sure-grip checkering. The beautifully engraved antique silver receiver is engineered from the finest gun steel. The double trigger instantly allows the shooter his barrel choice.

Available in:
Model 2701 12 Ga. 28" O/U 3" Mag. 2 Trig. Ext. Mod. & Full
Model 2703 20 Ga. 26" O/U 3" Mag. 2 Trig. Ext. Imp. & Mod.
Model 2705 .410 Ga. 26" O/U 3" Mag. 2 Trig. Ext. Imp. & Mod.
Model 2708-3 12 Ga. 20" O/U BBL Slug Gun
Also available:
SINGLE TRIGGER Models 2711, 2713, 2720
SINGLE TRIGGER Models 2727-3 & 2729-3 w/auto ejectors

ARMSPORT SHOTGUNS

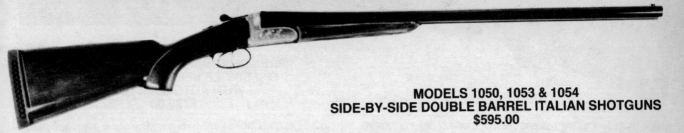

MODELS 1050, 1053 & 1054
SIDE-BY-SIDE DOUBLE BARREL ITALIAN SHOTGUNS
$595.00

Chambered for 3″ magnum with hard chrome-lined barrels, these shotguns feature center ribs, fluorescent front sights, Italian box lock actions and gloss finish stocks and forends. Also antique silver finish receivers engraved with bird scenes.

Model 1050 is 12 gauge with 28″ barrel with Modified & Full choke. Model 1053 is 20 gauge with 26″ barrel with Imp. & Modified choke. Model 1054 is .410 gauge with 26″ barrel with Imp. & Modified choke.

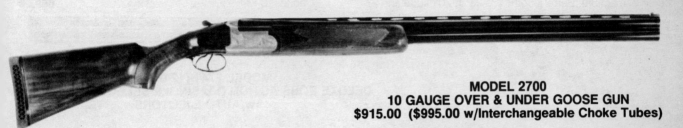

MODEL 2700
10 GAUGE OVER & UNDER GOOSE GUN
$915.00 ($995.00 w/Interchangeable Choke Tubes)

This 10 gauge 3½″ "Fowler" Magnum Boss-type action O/U Goose gun has two bottom locking lugs on its OM8 steel barrels attached to an antiqued silver finished action. Three Canada geese scenes are engraved on the two sides and bottom of the receiver. The hard chrome-lined barrels have an extra wide 12mm top vent rib with a fluorescent front sight and a brass mid-bead sight. Both the 32″ barrels choked full and the 28″ barrels choked Imp. and Mod. will shoot steel BB's effectively. The walnut stock with rubber recoil pad and matching forend are hand-checkered.

MODEL 2900
ITALIAN TRI-BARREL SHOTGUN
$1495.00

The only three-barrel shotgun being manufactured, Model 2900 features 28″ barrels (12 gauge) lined and chambered for 3″ magnum shells choked improved, modified and full. The front trigger fires the top two barrels and the rear trigger fires the bottom barrel. Made on a boss type action from special steel, the shotgun frame has two bottom locking lugs. The select grain walnut palm swell pistol grip stock and forend has a rubber recoil pad, high gloss finish and checkering.

ARMSPORT SHOTGUNS

MODELS 2730 & 2731
"PRESIDENT SUPERIMPOSED SERIES"
O/U SINGLE SELECTIVE TRIGGER
WITH AUTO EJECTORS
$730.00

Milled from special high-strength steel, these shotguns feature engraved antique silver finished boss-type receiver fitted to special steel barrels with jeweled engine turned barrel lugs and hand-checkered walnut stock with rubber recoil pad, palm swell full pistol grip and matching checkered semi-schnabel forend. Also, extra-wide 12mm top vent rib with front fluorescent sight and brass mid-bead sight, plus lateral vent rib. All President models have single selective triggers and are chambered 3" magnum. Barrel lengths are 26" in 20 gauge and 27"

in 12 gauge. Chokes are Skeet and Skeet 6 Interchangeable Deluxe.
Also available:
Model 2741 12 Ga. 26" O/U Mod. & Full $620.00
Model 2743 20 Ga. 26" O/U Imp. & Mod. 620.00
Model 2742 12 Ga. 28"/3 Interchangeable
    Chokes IC-M-F 660.00
Model 2744 20 Ga. 26"/3 Interchangeable
    Chokes IC-M-F 660.00

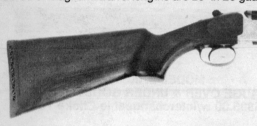

MODEL 2741 (12 GAUGE)
DELUXE BOSS ACTION O/U SINGLE SELECTIVE TRIGGER
w/AUTO EJECTORS

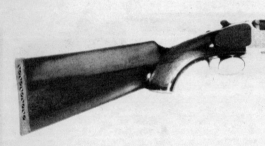

MODEL 2733 (12 GAUGE)
DELUXE BOSS ACTION SINGLE SELECTIVE TRIGGER
$575.00

This is a superbly designed, handsomely engraved over-and-under shotgun with ventilated rib. The single selective trigger allows you to fire either barrel at will. It has exceptionally fine hand-picked walnut stock and forend, hand-crafted and fitted for generations of fine shooting. Gloss or oil finish. 12 gauge. 28-inch barrels choked Mod. and Full (Extractors). 3-inch Mag. shells.

Also available:
Model 2735 20 Ga. 26" O/U 3" Mag. Imp. & Mod.
    Deluxe Boss Action $575.00

MODELS 1125, 1126, 1127 & 1128
TAKEDOWN SINGLE BARREL SHOTGUNS
$110.00

Machined from solid block of gun steel drop forging. Features a bottom lever takedown opening action and a complete iron cross removable forend. Barrels are chambered for 3" magnum shells with hard chrome-lined barrels and bores for steel shot use. High-gloss walnut finish stock and forend are checkered. **Models 1125 and 1126** are 12 gauge with 28" barrels (Model 1125 has Modified choke; Model 1126 has Full). **Model 1127** is 20 gauge with 26" barrel, Modified choke. **Model 1128** is .410 gauge with full choke.

BENELLI SHOTGUN

MODEL M1 SUPER 90 DEFENSE
$644.00 (w/Pistol Grip)

MODEL M1 SUPER 90 SLUG
$606.00

MODEL M1 SUPER 90 FIELD
$648.00

This 12 gauge autoloader functions on a rotating bolt system that minimizes recoil and maximizes accuracy. It features an adjustable rear sight as standard equipment, a one-piece alloy receiver for lighter weight and quick maneuverability, and a stock and forend made of a rugged fiberglass reinforced polymer. The Super 90 has a free carrier and an external shell release for lightning-like ammo changes or speedy reloads. A pistol grip stock is available as an accessory and the grip is enclosed in molded rubber to insulate the hand from recoil.

SPECIFICATIONS
Gauge: 12
Chamber: 3″
Mag. capacity: 7
Chokes: Cylinder (screw-in: Full, Imp. & Mod. with Field Model)
Barrel length: 19³/₄″ (26″ Field Model)
Overall length: 39³/₄″ (45¹/₂″ Field Model)
Weight: 7 lbs. 4 oz.; 7 lbs. 8 oz. Field Model; 7 lbs. 10 oz. Defense Model
Finish: Matte black
Stock: High impact polymer
Sights: Rifle; bead in Field Model

BENELLI SHOTGUNS

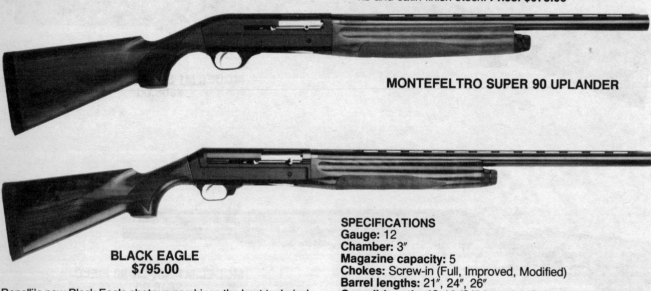

MONTEFELTRO SUPER 90
$675.00 ($734.00 Left Hand)

The Montefeltro Super 90 combines the fast firing character-istics of the M1 Super 90 with the look of a classic sporting shotgun. The heart of this Benelli remains the Montefeltro ro-tating bolt system, a rugged and simple inertia recoil design that functions with all types of 3″ and 2¾″ loads. A drop ad-justment kit allows the stock to be custom-fitted to any shooter.

SPECIFICATIONS (Standard Hunter)
Gauge: 12
Capacity: 5 rounds
Chamber: 3″

SUPER 90 LEFT HAND

Chokes: Screw-in, Full, Improved & Modified
Barrel lengths: 26″ and 28″
Overall length: 45″ with 26″ barrel
Weight: 7 lbs. 2 oz. with 26″ barrel; 7 lbs. 5 oz. w/28″ bbl.
Stock: High-gloss walnut with drop adjustment kit
Finish: Matte black
Also available:
MONTEFELTRO SUPER 90 TURKEY GUN w/24″ vent. rib and satin finish stock. **Price: $675.00**
MONTEFELTRO SUPER 90 UPLANDER GUN with 21″ vent. rib and satin finish stock. **Price: $675.00**

MONTEFELTRO SUPER 90 UPLANDER

BLACK EAGLE
$795.00

Benelli's new Black Eagle shotgun combines the best technical features of the Montefeltro Super 90 and the classic design of the old SL 80 Series. It comes standard with a specially designed two-piece receiver of steel and aluminum, adding to its reliability and resistance to wear. A premium high-gloss walnut stock and gold-plated trigger are included, along with a Montefeltro rotating bolt. The Black Eagle has no complex cylinders and pistons to maintain.

SPECIFICATIONS
Gauge: 12
Chamber: 3″
Magazine capacity: 5
Chokes: Screw-in (Full, Improved, Modified)
Barrel lengths: 21″, 24″, 26″
Overall length: 42½″ (21″ barrel); 45½″ (24″ barrel); 47½″ (26″ barrel)
Weight: 7 lbs. 1 oz. (21″ barrel); 7 lbs. 4 oz. (24″ barrel); 7 lbs. 6 oz. (26″ barrel)
Operation system: Inertia recoil; Montefeltro rotating bolt
Sights: Bead
Finish: Black lower receiver; deep blued upper receiver and barrel

BENELLI M3 SUPER 90
COMBINATION PUMP/AUTO
$801.00

BERETTA SHOTGUNS

SERIES 682 COMPETITION TRAP O/U

Available in Competition Mono, Over/Under or Mono Trap-O/U Combo Set, the 12-gauge 682 trap guns boast premium-grade hand-checkered walnut stock and forend with International or Monte Carlo left- or right-hand stock and choice of 3 stock dimensions.

Features: Adjustable gold-plated, single selective sliding trigger for precise length of pull fit; fluorescent competition front sight; step-up top rib; Bruniton non-reflective black matte finish; low profile improved boxlock action; manual safety with barrel selector; 2³/₄" chambers; auto ejector; competition recoil pad butt plate; light hand-engraving; stock with silver oval for initials; silver inscription inlaid on trigger guard; handsome fitted case. **Weight:** Approx. 8 lbs.

Barrel length/Choke	Prices
30" Imp. Mod./Full (Silver)	$2053.00
30" or 32" Mobilchoke (Black or Silver)	2120.00
Top Single 32" or 34" Mobilchoke	2187.00
Combo.: 30" or 32" Mobilchoke (Top)	2827.00
30" or 32" IM/F (Top or Mono)	2773.00
30" or 34" Mobilchoke (Mono)	2827.00
32" or 34" Mobilchoke (Top)	2827.00

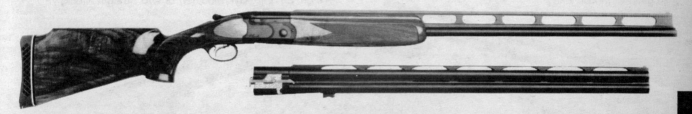

682 COMPETITION W/MONO AND COMBO O/U BARRELS

682 COMPETITION SKEET O/U
26" or 28" SK/SK $2073.00
4-Barrel Set (28") $4913.00
12, 20, 28, .410 Gauge

This skeet gun sports hand-checkered premium walnut stock, forged and hardened receiver, manual safety with trigger selector, auto ejector, stock with silver oval for initials, silver inlaid on trigger guard. Price includes fitted case.
Action: Low profile hard chrome-plated boxlock
Trigger: Single adjustable sliding trigger
Barrels: 26" or 28" rust blued barrels with 2³/₄" chambers
Stock dimensions: Length of pull 14³/₈"; drop at comb 1¹/₂"; drop at heel 2¹/₃"
Sights: Fluorescent front and metal middle bead
Weight: Approx. 8 lbs.

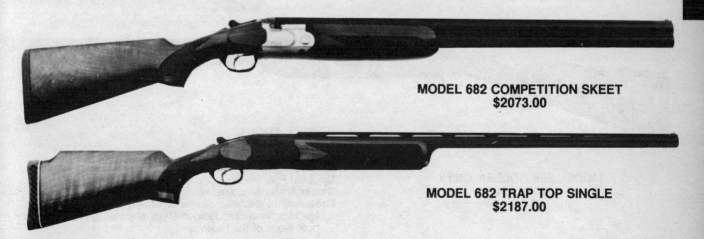

MODEL 682 COMPETITION SKEET
$2073.00

MODEL 682 TRAP TOP SINGLE
$2187.00

BERETTA SHOTGUNS

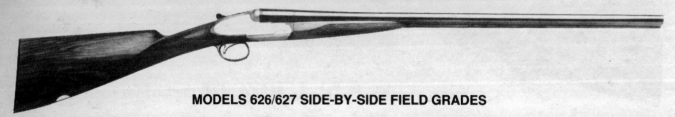

MODELS 626/627 SIDE-BY-SIDE FIELD GRADES

These good-looking field models feature low profile solid box-lock design, hand-fitted stocks and forends of handsome European walnut with deep diamond hand-checkering, tang-mounted safety/barrel selectors, single-selective trigger, metal bead sight and knurled rib. 12 gauge barrels are chambered 2³/₄"; 20 gauge barrels, 3" Mag. **Model 626** has bright chrome finish, full hand-engraving. **Model 627** boasts hand-engraved side plates.

MODEL 626 ONYX SERIES

The **Model 626 Onyx** has a full-figured American walnut stock, lustrous black semi-matte finish on the barrels and receiver, and front and center sighting beads on a vent rib.

Model 626 Onyx $1533.00
12 ga., 26" Mobilchoke
20 ga., 26" Mobilchoke

Model 627EL Field $2600.00
12 ga., 26" Imp. Cyl./Mod.
12 ga., 28" Mod./Full

Model 627EELL $4453.00
12 ga. 28" Mod./Full (w/ or w/o Straight Stock)
12 ga. 26" Imp. Cyl./Mod. (w/ or w/o Straight Stock)

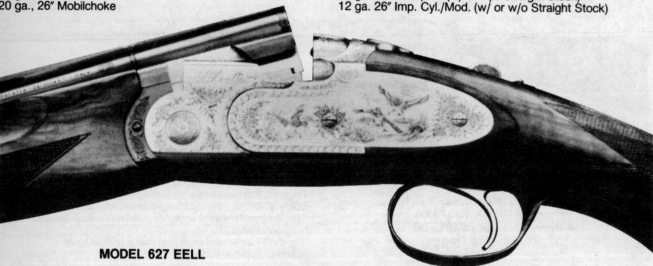

MODEL 627 EELL

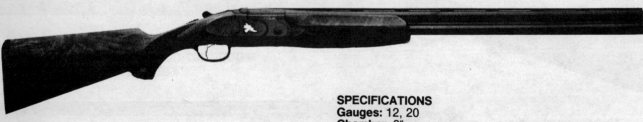

**MODEL 686 GOLDEN ONYX
$1167.00**

SPECIFICATIONS
Gauges: 12, 20
Chamber: 3"
Barrel lengths: 26" and 28"
Chokes: Full, Modified and Improved Cylinder
Stock: American walnut with recoil pad
Features: Mobilchoke Screw-in Choke System; automatic ejectors; vent ribs; Golden Onyx features game birds on both sides of the receiver

BERETTA SHOTGUNS
SPORTING CLAY SHOTGUNS 12 GAUGE

MODEL 682 SPORTING

MODEL 682 SPORTING
$2153.00

This competition-style 12-gauge shotgun for sporting clays features 28″ or 30″ barrels with four flush-mounted screw-in choke tubes (Full, Modified, Improved Cylinder and Skeet), plus hand-checkered stock and forend of fine walnut, 2³/₄″ chambers and adjustable trigger.

Also available:
MODEL 303 Sporting	$ 733.00
MODEL 686 Sporting	1653.00
MODEL 687 Sporting (12 or 20 Ga.)	2173.00
SUPER SPORT (12 Ga., 28″ or 30″ bbl.)	2287.00

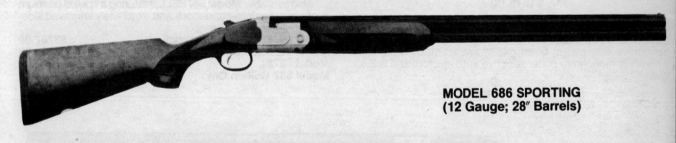

MODEL 686 SPORTING
(12 Gauge; 28″ Barrels)

MODEL 687 SPORTING
(12 and 20 Gauge, 28″ Barrels w/Mobilchoke)

SHOTGUNS

BERETTA SHOTGUNS

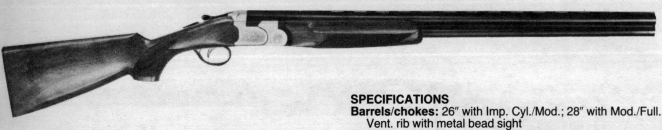

MODEL 686 FIELD OVER/UNDER
$1147.00 (28 Gauge)

SPECIFICATIONS
Barrels/chokes: 26″ with Imp. Cyl./Mod.; 28″ with Mod./Full. Vent. rib with metal bead sight
Action: Low profile, improved boxlock
Trigger: Selective single trigger, auto safety
Extractors: Auto ejectors
Stock: Choice walnut, hand-checkered and hand-finished with a tough gloss finish
Weight: Less than 7 lbs.

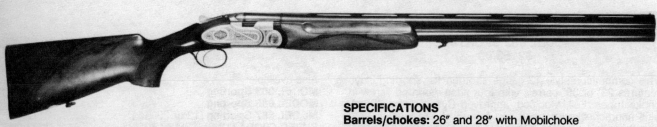

MODEL 687L FIELD GRADE O/U
12 & 20 Gauge (Mobilchoke)
$1573.00

The **687L** features Mobilchoke in 12 and 20 gauge; strong boxlock action handsomely tooled with floral hand-engraved decorative side plates, finest quality walnut stock accented with silver monogram plate, selective auto ejectors and fitted case.

SPECIFICATIONS
Barrels/chokes: 26″ and 28″ with Mobilchoke
Action: Low-profile improved boxlock
Trigger: Single selective with manual safety
Extractors: Auto ejectors
Weight: 7 lbs. 2 oz.
    Also available: **Model 687EELL,** featuring a special premium walnut, custom-fitted stock and exquisitely engraved side-plate, game-scene motifs.

Model 687EELL with fixed choke $3767.00
Model 687EELL with Mobilchoke 3820.00
Model 687EL 2607.00
Model 687 Golden Onyx 1800.00

MODEL 1200F
$580.00

This All-Weather 12 gauge semiautomatic shotgun features space-age technopolymer stock and forend. Lightweight (only 7+ pounds), it has a 28″ barrel chamber for 2³/₄″ shells and sports a unique weather-resistant matte black finish to reduce glare, resist corrosion and aid in heat dispersion.

SPECIFICATIONS
Gauge: 12
Chamber: 2³/₄″ or 3″
Barrel length: 28″
Choke: Modified
Weight: 7.3 lbs.
Length of pull: 14³/₈″
Mag. Capacity: 6

Also available: **MODEL 1200 RIOT** (Law Enforcement) with 20″ barrel (2³/₄″ or 3″ shells) and Improved Cylinder choke (7-round capacity). **Price: $560.00**

BERETTA SHOTGUNS

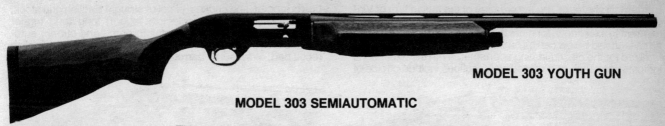

MODEL 303 YOUTH GUN

MODEL 303 SEMIAUTOMATIC

This unique autoloader features flush-mounted, screw-in choke tubes, and a magazine cut off that allows shooters to hand-feed a lighter or heavier load into the breech without emptying the magazine. Disassembly takes one minute.

SPECIFICATIONS
Gauge: 12 (3″ Magnum chamber)
Barrel lengths: 26″, 28″, 30″
Chokes: F, MC (24″, 30″ and 32″ barrels)
    IC, F, MC (26″ barrel)
    M, IM, F, MC (28″ barrel)

Gauge: 12 (2³/₄″ chamber)
Barrel lengths: 24″, 26″, 28″, 30″
Chokes: IC, C (24″ barrel); IM, M, IC, MC (26″ barrel)
    M, IM, F, MC (28″ barrel); F (30″ barrel)

Gauge: 20 (2³/₄″ or 3″ Magnum)
Barrel lengths: 26″ and 28″
Chokes: IC, M, MC (26″ barrel)
    M, IM, F, MC (28″ barrels)

---

303 YOUTH
Gauge: 20 (3″ chamber)
Barrel length: 24″
Chokes: F, M, IC
Length of pull: 13¹/₂″

303 SLUG
Gauges: 12, 20 (2³/₄″ and 3″ chambers)
Barrel lengths: 22″
Choke: Slug (C)
Weight: 7 lbs.

GENERAL 303 SPECIFICATIONS

Weight: 7 lbs. (12 gauge) and 6 lbs. (20 gauge)
Safety: Cross bolt
Action: Locked breech, gas operated
Sight: Vent. rib with front metal bead
Stock length: 14⁷/₈″ length of pull
Capacity: Plugged to 2 rounds

Prices:
303 Field w/Mobilchoke, 12 & 20 ga., 2³/₄″ or 3″ Magnums	$653.00
303 Slug	680.00
303 Youth	733.00
303 Skeet 12 & 20 ga., 2³/₄″, 26″ Skeet	673.00
303 Trap 12 ga., 2³/₄″, 30″ Full	673.00
303 Trap w/Monte Carlo 12 ga., 2³/₄″, 30″ and 32″ Mobilchoke	727.00
303 Upland 12 ga., 2³/₄″, 24″ Mobilchoke	680.00

MODEL 303 COMPETITION TRAP
(not shown)

The Beretta A303 Trap is the competition version of the proven A303 semiautomatic. Its gas-operated system lessens recoil; other features include wide floating vent rib with flourescent front and mid-rib bead sights, plus Monte Carlo stock fitted with American trap pad. The A303 also comes with hand-checkered stock and forend of select European walnut, plus gold-plated trigger.

SPECIFICATIONS
Gauge: 12
Barrel lengths: 30″ and 32″ (Full or Mobilchoke)

Sight: Ventilated rib with fluorescent front bead, metal middle bead
Action: Semiautomatic, locked breech, gas operated
Safety: Cross bolt
Ejector: Auto
Trigger: Gold plated
Stock: Select walnut
Weight: 8 lbs.
Butt plate: Special trap recoil pad
Chamber: 2³/₄″

BERNARDELLI SHOTGUNS

Bernardelli shotguns are the creation of the Italian firm of Vincenzo Bernardelli, known for its fine quality firearms and commitment to excellence for more than a century. Most of the long arms featured below can be built with a variety of options, customized for the discriminating sportsman. With the exceptions indicated for each gun respectively, options include choice of barrel lengths and chokes; pistol or straight English grip stock; single selective or non-selective trigger; long tang trigger guard; checkered butt; beavertail forend; hand-cut rib; automatic safety; custom stock dimensions; standard or English recoil pad; extra set of barrels; choice of luggage gun case.

ELIO SIDE-BY-SIDE

BRESCIA SIDE-BY-SIDE

ELIO SIDE-BY-SIDE

For gunners who prefer a lightweight 12 gauge double, the Elio weighs about 6¼ pounds and is designed around the Anson-Deeley action with Purdey locks. Intricate English rosette and scroll engraving and a coin finished receiver, fine hand-checkered European walnut stock, hinged front trigger on double trigger models. Prices on request.

BRESCIA SIDE-BY-SIDE

Available in 12, 16, or 20 gauge, the Brescia side-by-side features Greener or Purdey locks, small engravings, hardened marbled mounting, chrome-lined barrels, finely grained stock.

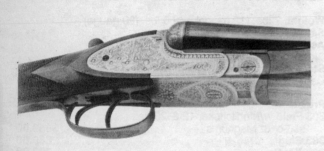

SLUG SIDE-BY-SIDE & SLUG LUSSO DELUXE

Especially designed to pattern well with slugs and buckshot, this 12 gauge side-by-side has Anson & Deeley action, Purdey-type locks, reinforced breech, richly engraved hunting scene on white-finish receiver, automatic ejectors, rear adjustable sight with overturning leafs, cheekpiece, double triggers. Deluxe model has fully engraved sideplates. Prices on request.

MODEL 120 O/U SHOTGUN/RIFLE COMBINATION

The Model 120 combination rifle/shotgun offers auto ejectors that can be changed into normal extractors by a patented device; set trigger, strong hinge pin, cross-bolt on the lumps, cheekpiece with walnut stock. Shotgun barrel in 12 gauge. Rifle barrel available in calibers 5.6×50R Mag., 5.6×57R, 6.5×55, 6.5×57R, 7×57R, 7×65R, 8×57JRS, 9.3×74R, 222 Rem., 243 Win., 308 Win., 30-06. Supplied on request with scope and interchangeable 12-gauge shotgun barrels. Prices on request.

An elegant and light 12 gauge side-by-side suitable for upland bird hunting, the Hemingway features 23½-inch barrels without monobloc, right bore open and left one slightly Improved Cylinder, automatic ejectors, special rib with white bead front sight, hinged front trigger, woodcock hunting scenes engraved, long-type trigger guard and forend, hand-checkered walnut woods, metal shield for intials. Special steel frame and barrels. **Weight:** 6¼ lbs. Also available:
HEMINGWAY DELUXE $1856.00

HEMINGWAY SIDE-BY-SIDE
$1542.00
W/Single Non-selective Trigger $1608.00

BERNARDELLI SHOTGUNS

HOLLAND LUSSO

HOLLAND V.B.

HOLLAND LUSSO
HOLLAND V.B.
HOLLAND LISCIO (not shown)

These 12 gauge Holland & Holland style sidelock side-by-sides feature sidelocks with double safety levers, reinforced breech, three round Purdey locks, automatic ejectors, right trigger folding, striker retaining plates, best-quality walnut stock and finely chiselled high-grade engravings. The three shotguns differ only in the amount and intricacy of engravings. Prices on request.

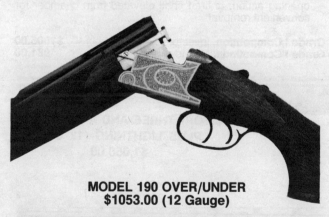

MODEL 190 OVER/UNDER
$1053.00 (12 Gauge)

High-quality hunting over/under shotgun with special steel integral frame, strong cross hinge pin and locks on the lumps, automatic ejectors, ventilated rib, special steel barrels with chrome-plated bores, richly engraved frame, hand-checkered selected walnut stock and forend. Available with double trigger or single selective trigger. **Gauge:** 12; 2³/₄″ or 3″ chambers. **Weight:** 6³/₄ pounds.

S. UBERTO F.S. WITH EJECTORS

S. UBERTO F.S.
$1580.00
S. UBERTO F.S. WITH EJECTORS
$1375.00

The S. Uberto F.S. side-by-side offers shotgunners Anson & Deeley hammerless action, Purdey-style locks, reinforced breech, fine relief engravings with hunting scenes, finest walnut checkered stock and forend, right trigger folding. Available in 12 and 20 gauge.

S. Uberto 1 with modest engraving, marbled
   mounting $1173.00
S. Uberto 1E w/ejectors 1279.00
S. Uberto 1E w/ejectors and single trigger 1346.00
S. Uberto 2 E w/ejectors 1343.00

ROMA 6

ROMA 6
$1726.00
ROMA 6E WITH EJECTORS
$1833.00

Available in 12, 16, 20 and 28 gauge, the Roma 6 is Bernardelli's premier boxlock and a most popular model. This side-by-side shotgun features Anson & Deeley action with Purdey-style locks, sideplated and coin-finished receiver with elaborate scroll engraving covering 100% of the action, precision-bored barrels made of superior chromium steel, double triggers with front hinged trigger, hand-selected European walnut stock and forend with fine, hand-cut checkering.

BROWNING AUTOMATIC SHOTGUNS

"SWEET SIXTEEN" AUTO-5

AUTO-5

The Browning Auto-5 Shotgun is offered in an unusually wide variety of models and specifications. The Browning 12-gauge 3-inch Magnum accepts up to and including the 3-inch, 1⁷/₈ ounce, 12-gauge Magnum load, which contains only ⅛ ounce of shot less than the maximum 3¹/₂-inch 10-gauge load. The 2³/₄-inch Magnums and 2³/₄-inch high velocity shells may be used with equal pattern efficiency. Standard features include a special shock absorber and a hunting-style recoil pad. The Auto-5 is also available with the Invector screw-in choke system.

Browning also offers the 20 gauge in a 3-inch Magnum model. This powerful, light heavyweight offers maximum versatility to 20-gauge advocates. It handles the 20-gauge, 2³/₄-inch high velocity and Magnums, but it literally thrives on the 3-inch, 1¹/₄-ounce load which delivers real 12-gauge performance in a 20-gauge package.

The 12-gauge Auto-5, chambered for regular 2³/₄-inch shells, handles all 12-gauge, 2³/₄-inch shells, from the very lightest 1 ounce field load to the heavy 1¹/₂-ounce Magnums. The Browning 20-gauge Auto-5 is lightweight and a top performer for the upland hunter. Yet, with 2³/₄-inch high velocity or 2³/₄-inch Magnums, it does a fine job in the duck blind.

24-inch barrels are available as an accessory.

Hunting Models	Prices
Light 12, Sweet 16 and Light 20 gauge, Invector	$ 684.95
3″ Magnum 12 and Magnum 20 gauge, Invector	706.95
Gold Classic edition, 500 issued	6500.00

BT-99 SINGLE SHOT TRAP SPECIAL

SPECIFICATIONS
Receiver: Machined steel, tastefully hand-engraved and richly blued
Barrel: Choice of 32″ or 34″ lengths; choke choice of Full, Improved Modified or Modified; chambered for 12 gauge, 2³/₄″ shells only
Trigger: Gold-plated, crisp, positive, pull approximately 3¹/₂ lbs.
Stock and forearm: Select French walnut, hand-rubbed finish, sharp 20-line hand-checkering; Monte Carlo or conventional stock available; full pistol grip; length of pull 14³/₈″; drop at comb 1³/₈″; drop at heel 2″; full beavertail forearm

Safety: No manual safety, a feature preferred by trap shooters
Sights: Ivory front and center sight beads
Rib: High post, ventilated, full floating, matted, ¹¹/₃₂″ wide
Recoil pad: Deluxe, contoured trap style
Weight: 8 lbs. with 32″ barrel; 8 lbs. 3 oz. with 34″ barrel
Automatic ejection: Fired shell ejected automatically on opening action, unfired shell elevated from chamber for convenient removal

Grade I Competition, Invector (32″ or 34″ bbl.)	$1005.00
Grade I Competition, Non-Invector	981.00

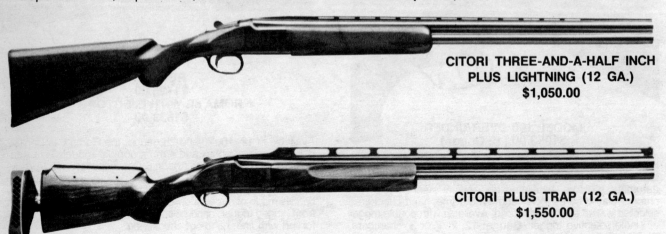

CITORI THREE-AND-A-HALF INCH PLUS LIGHTNING (12 GA.)
$1,050.00

CITORI PLUS TRAP (12 GA.)
$1,550.00

BROWNING SHOTGUNS

CITORI STANDARD

FIELD GRADE
Gauge: 12, 16, 20, 28 and .410 gauge
Barrels: 24″, 26″, 28″, or 30″ in 12 gauge; 28″ in 16 gauge; 24″, 26″, or 28″ in 20 gauge; ventilated rib with matted sighting plane; medium raised German nickel-silver sight bead; 26″ or 28″ in 28 gauge; 26″ or 28″ in .410 gauge
Overall length: All gauges 41″ with 24″ barrels; 43″ with 26″ barrels; 45″ with 28″ barrels; 47″ with 30″ barrels
Chokes: Mod.-Full, Invector in 30″ barrels; choice of Invector, Mod.-Full or Imp. Cyl.-Mod. in 28″ and 26″ barrels
Trigger: Single selective; gold-plated, fast and crisp
Chamber: All 20-gauge Field models and all 12-gauge Field models accept all 3″ Magnum loads as well as 2³/₄″ loads; 16 and 28-gauge accepts 2³/₄″ loads; .410-gauge accepts 2¹/₂″, 3″, or 3″ Mag. loads
Safety: Manual thumb safety; combined with barrel selector mechanism

Automatic ejectors: Fired shells thrown out of gun; unfired shells are elevated for easy removal

Approximate Weight:

	12 gauge	16 gauge	20 gauge
24″ barrels	.6 lbs. 9 oz.		5 lbs. 12 oz.
26″ barrels	.7 lbs. 9 oz.		6 lbs. 11 oz.
28″ barrels	.7 lbs. 11 oz.	7 lbs	6 lbs. 13 oz.
30″ barrels	.7 lbs. 13 oz		

Stock and forearm: Dense walnut; skillfully checkered; full pistol grip; hunting Beavertail forearm; field-type recoil pad installed on 12 gauge models.

	12 gauge	20 gauge
Length of pull	14¹/₄″	14¹/₄″
Drop at comb	1⁵/₈″	1¹/₂″
Drop at heel	2¹/₂″	2³/₈″

CITORI HUNTING, LIGHTNING, SUPERLIGHT & UPLAND SPECIAL MODELS*

HUNTING & LIGHTNING 28 GA., .410 BORE	PRICES
Grade I Hunting	$ 975.00
Grade I Lightning	985.00
Grade III Hunting	1525.00
Grade III Lightning	1535.00
Grade VI Hunting	2125.00
Grade VI Lightning	2150.00
SUPERLIGHT 12 & 20 GA. (UPLAND SPECIAL)	
Grade I Invector	1005.00
Grade III Invector	1410.00
Grade VI Invector	2035.00
HUNTING & LIGHTNING 12 & 20 GA.	
Grade I Invector	985.00
Grade I Lightning Invector	995.00
Grade III Invector	1385.00
Grade III Lightning Invector	1400.00
Grade VI Invector	1995.00
Grade VI Lightning Invector	2025.00

*NOTE: All Invector model Citori's are available in the High Grades, except Upland Special (Grade I only).

SUPERLIGHT 28 GAUGE & .410 BORE	
Grade I	$ 975.00
Grade III	1525.00
Grade VI	2125.00
TRAP MODELS (High Post Target Rib)	
Standard 12 Gauge	
Grade I Invector	$1105.00
Grade III	1525.00
Grade VI Invector	2125.00
SKEET MODELS (High Post Target Rib)	
Standard 12 and 20 Gauge	
Grade I Invector	1090.00
Grade I	1055.00
Grade III Invector	1525.00
Grade VI Invector	2125.00
Standard 28 Gauge and .410 Bore	
Grade I	1100.00
Grade III	1525.00
Grade VI	2125.00

4-BARREL SKEET SET
12 Gauge with one removable forearm and four sets of barrels, 12, 20, 28 and .410 gauges, high post target rib.
(Furnished with fitted luggage case for gun and extra barrels)

Grade 1	$3530.00
Grade III	4025.00
Grade VI	4515.00

BROWNING SHOTGUNS

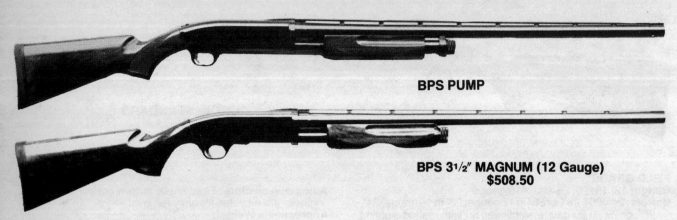

BPS PUMP

BPS 3½" MAGNUM (12 Gauge)
$508.50

BPS PUMP SHOTGUN

Gauge: 10, 12 and 20
Barrels: Choice of 22", 26", 28", 30" or 32" lengths with high-post ventilated rib; Hunting model has German nickel sight bead
Action: Pump action with double-action bars; bottom loading and ejection; serrated slide release located at rear of trigger guard
Choke: Invector only
Trigger: Crisp and positive; let-off at 4½ lbs.
Chamber: 3" chamber in Hunting models accepts all 2¾", 2¾" Magnum and 3" Magnum shells; target models 2¾" shells only
Safety: Convenient knurled-thumb, top-receiver safety; slide forward to shoot
Approximate weight: 7 lbs. 12 oz. with 28" barrel

Overall length: 42¾" with 22" barrel; 46¾" with 26" barrel; 48¾" with 28" barrel; 50¾" with 30" barrel
Stock and forearm: Select walnut, weather-resistant finish, sharp 18-line checkering; full pistol grip; semi-beavertail forearm with finger grooves; length of pull 14¼"; drop at comb 1½"; drop at heel 2½"
Prices:
Invector Hunting, 12 and 20 ga., V.R. $433.50
Invector Hunting, 10 ga. 508.50
Invector PLUS Hunting & Stalker 508.50
Upland Special, 22" barrel with Invector,
  12 and 20 ga., V.R. 433.50
Invector Stalker, 12 ga. only 433.50
Buck Special, 12 ga. only 439.50

BPS YOUTH & LADIES MODEL

SPECIFICATIONS
Chamber: 20 gauge only
Barrels: 22" invector w/ventilated rib; interchangeable within gauge
Overall length: 41¾"
Weight (approx.): 6 lbs. 11 oz.
Stock and forearm: Straight grip stock of select walnut in durable gloss finish

Length of pull: 13¼"
Drop at comb: 1½"
Drop at heel: 2½"

BPS Youth & Ladies Model $433.50

BROWNING SHOTGUNS

MODEL A-500 12 GAUGE SEMIAUTOMATIC

Designed and built in Belgium, the A-500 employs a short recoil system with a strong four-lug bolt design. There is no gas system to collect powder residues or grime, and no pistons, ports or cylinders to clean. Only one extractor is needed to pull the shell from the chamber. The stock has no drilled holes to accommodate action springs, making it that much stronger (especially where it bolts against the receiver).

SPECIFICATIONS
Barrel lengths: 26″, 28″ and 30″
Overall lengths: 45½″, 47½″ and 49½″
Weight: 7 lbs. 3 oz. (26″ barrel); 7 lbs. 5 oz. (28″ barrel) and 7 lbs. 7 oz. (30″ barrel)
Chamber: 3″
Choke: Invector
Stock dimensions: length of pull 14¼″; drop at comb 1½″; drop at heel 2½″
Safety: cross bolt, right or left hand
Action: short recoil operated with four lug rotary bolt
Barrel/receiver finish: deep high polish blued finish; receiver lightly engraved with scroll pattern
MODEL A-500 . . . . **$559.95**
   Extra barrels **199.95**

BT-99 PLUS
SINGLE BARREL TRAP SPECIAL

SPECIFICATIONS
Gauge: 12 (2¾″ shells only)
Barrel length: 34″ (.745 over bore; barrel porting optional)
Weight: 8 lbs. 12 oz.
Choke: Invector Plus system (Invector Plus Full, Imp. Mod., and Modified tubes and wrench included)
Rib: High post, ventilated, tapered, target rib; matted sight plane

Stock & Forearm: Select walnut with high-gloss finish and cut checkering; Monte Carlo stock; modified beavertail forearm; stock fully adjustable for length of pull (14-14½″), drop at comb (2½-2″) and drop at Monte Carlo (2⅜-1⅛″)
Prices:
MODEL BT-99 PLUS **$1570.00**
   Without ported barrels **1520.00**

BROWNING SHOTGUNS

MODEL 12 PUMP SHOTGUN

After more than 75 years, the ageless Winchester Model 12, one of the most popular shotguns ever produced (over 2 million), is offered as part of Browning's Limited Edition Model 12 Program. The first Model 12 is available in 20 gauge, with 28 gauge and .410 bore (Model 42) to follow. A total of 12,500 20 gauge Model 12's will be produced, including 8,500 Grade I models and 4,000 Grade V's.

SPECIFICATIONS
Gauge: 20
Barrel length: 26″
Overall length: 45″
Chamber: 2³/₄″
Choke: Modified
Weight: 7 lbs. 1 oz.

Length of pull: 14″
Drop at heel: 2¹/₂″
Drop at comb: 1¹/₂″
Trigger: Approx. 4¹/₂ lbs. trigger pull
Capacity: 5 loads in magazine (w/plug removed), one in chamber; 2 loads in magazine (w/plug installed), one in chamber
Receiver: Grade I: deeply blued. Grade V: engraved with gold game scenes
Stock and forearm: Grade I: select walnut w/semi-gloss finish and cut checkering. Grade V: select high grade walnut with high gloss finish (both grades include steel grip cap)
Prices:
GRADE I . . . . $ 734.95
GRADE V 1187.00

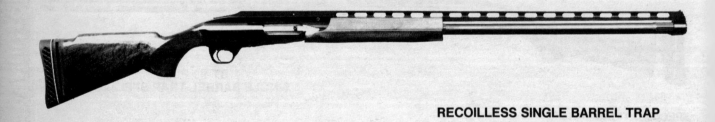

RECOILLESS SINGLE BARREL TRAP

SPECIFICATIONS
Gauge: 12 (2³/₄″ shells only; .745 back-bored)
Barrel length: 30″ (regular model); 27″ (short model)
Action: Special action, single shot design
Sights: Front and center ivory sight beads
Rib: High post, ventilated with three-position adjustment for point of impact

Stock & Forearm: Select walnut with high-gloss finish and cut checkering
Choke: Invector Plus system (Full, Imp. Mod., and Modified tubes and wrench)
Receiver: Black anodized
Price: To be announced

BROWNING SHOTGUNS

SPORTING CLAYS MODELS

Browning introduces its new line of Sporting Clays shotguns, including GTI, Special Sporting (with high post vent ribs), and Lightning Sporting models. All GTI models feature semi-pistol grips with slightly grooved semi-beavertail forearms and satin finish. The Special Sporting guns have full pistol grip stocks with palm swells, classic forearms, and high-gloss wood finish. All Lightning Sporting models feature rounded pistol grips with classic forearms and high-gloss wood finish.

Gauge: 12
Barrel lengths: 28″ & 30″ (GTI); 28″, 30″ & 32″ (Special Sporting); 30″ (Lightning)

Overall lengths: 45″ & 47″ (GTI); 45″, 47″ & 49″ (Special Sporting); 47″ (Lightning Sporting)
Weight: 8 lbs. & 8 lbs. 2 oz. (GTI); 8 lbs. 1 oz., 8 lbs. 3 oz. & 8 lbs. 5 oz. (Special Sporting); 8 lbs. 10 oz. (Lightning Sporting)
Chokes: Invector (GTI); IC/M (Special Sporting and Lightning Sporting)
Prices:
GTI $1125.00
SPECIAL SPORTING 1100.00
LIGHTNING SPORTING 1100.00

GTI SPORTING CLAY
$1125.00

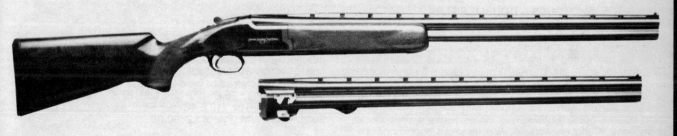

SPECIAL SPORTING CLAY
$1100.00

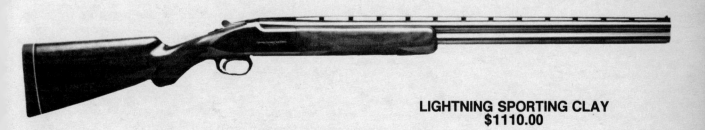

LIGHTNING SPORTING CLAY
$1110.00

CHAPUIS SHOTGUNS & DOUBLE RIFLES

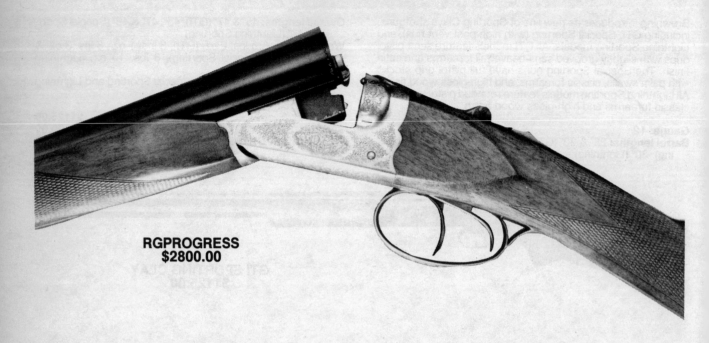

RGPROGRESS
$2800.00

SHOTGUNS & DOUBLE RIFLES

Manufactured in France, Chapuis side-by-side double rifles (RGEXpress Model 89) and side-by-side shotguns (RGProgress) are distributed in the U.S. by Armes de Chasse (see Directory for address). The **RGEXpress Model 89** is available in 375 H&H (plus 3 metric calibers) and features a notched action zone, long trigger guard, coin metal finish, automatic ejectors, barrels with double hook, Blitz system center side lock, quarter rib, adjustable rear sight, deluxe walnut stock with Monte Carlo cheekpiece, fine hand-cut checkering, oil finish, and grip cap with reservoir for extra front sight. **Barrel length:** 23.6″. **Overall length:** 40.35″. **Weight:** 7 lbs. 6. oz. **Price: $6500.00.**

The RGProgress side-by-side shotguns are available in 12, 16, and 20 gauges (plus rifled slug). This field gun features notched (and patented) ejector boxlock action with coin metal finish, French walnut stock (pistol or English grip), varnish (or oil) finish, checkered or hard butt plate. **Chamber:** 2³/₄″ & 3″. **Barrel lengths:** 26.8″ (20 ga.) and 27.6″ (12 and 16 ga.). **Weight:** 6 lbs. 6 oz. (12 & 16 ga.); 5 lbs. 8 oz. (20 ga.). **Chokes:** Full/M and IM/M. **Price: $2800.00.**

CHURCHILL SHOTGUNS

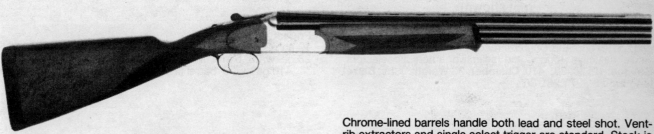

WINDSOR III OVER/UNDER SHOTGUNS
$624.95

Chrome-lined barrels handle both lead and steel shot. Vent-rib extractors and single select trigger are standard. Stock is checkered European walnut with schnabel forend and pistol grip. **Gauges:** 12 and 20. **Chamber:** 3″. **Barrel lengths:** 27″ and 30″ (ICT). **Weight:** 7 lbs. 3 oz.

COMPETITION SHOTGUNS
$962.95
$999.95 (w/Recoil Pad)

Available in trap or skeet, both guns feature select European walnut stocks with oil finish, 28-line checkering and sculpted schnabel forend. Receiver is engraved. Other features include selective automatic ejectors, single selective triggers, top tang safety, wide vent ribs. **Gauges:** 12 and 20. **Chamber:** 2³/₄″. **Barrel lengths:** 26″ and 30″. **Weight:** 8 lbs. **Chokes:** Skeet/Skeet (26″ barrel w/o recoil pad) and IM/Full (30″ barrel, 12 ga.).

REGENT VII OVER/UNDER SHOTGUNS (not shown)
$1099.95

Extra select European walnut stock has an oil-rubbed finish with 22-line checkering on forend and pistol grip. Features an 11mm-wide vent rib, single selective trigger, selective automatic ejectors, automatic top tang safety, interchangeable choke tubes. Barrels are chrome-lined. **Gauges:** 12 and 20. **Barrel length:** 27″. **Chamber:** 3″. **Weight:** 7 lbs. 5. oz. **Choke:** ICT.

MONARCH OVER/UNDER SHOTGUNS (not shown)

Blued steel receiver features scroll engraving. Stock is checkered, European walnut with hard matte finish. Other features: selective trigger, extractors and vent rib. **Gauges:** 12, 20, 28, .410. **Chamber:** 3″. **Barrel lengths:** 25″, 26″, 28″. **Weight:** 7 lbs.
Prices:
12 and 20 ga. w/26″ and 28″ barrels
  (IC-Modified & Modified/Full) **$528.95**
.410 ga. w/26″ barrel (Modified/Full) **596.95**
28 ga. w/25″ barrel (IC/Modified or
  w/28″ barrel (Modified/Full) **495.95**

CHURCHILL SHOTGUNS

WINDSOR IV OVER/UNDER SHOTGUNS
(not shown)

Features checkered European walnut stock with schnabel for-end, pistol grip and Churchill recoil pad. Also, ventilated rib, single selective trigger and selective automatic ejectors. **Gauges:** 12, 20, 28, .410. **Chamber:** 3″. **Weight:** 7 lbs. **Barrel lengths:** 26″, 27″, 28″, 30″.

Prices:

12 and 20 ga. w/27″ or 30″ barrel (ICT)	**$851.95**
28 ga. w/28″ barrel (Modified/Full) and	
.410 ga. w/26″ barrel (IC/Modified)	**799.95**

Chromed barrel with concave rib, double-hinged triggers, extractors, casehardened receiver and English-style walnut stock (checkered with splinter forend) are all included in this hunting gun. **Gauges:** 10, 12, 20, 28, .410. **Barrel lengths:** 25″, 26″, 28″, 30″. **Chamber** 3″. **Weight:** 6 lbs. 4 oz.

ROYAL SIDE X SIDE SHOTGUNS

Prices:

10 ga. w/30″ barrel, Full/Full	**$814.95**
12 and 20 ga. w/26″ or 28″ barrels,	
Modified/Full or IC/Modified	**539.95**
28. ga. w/25″ barrel, Modified/Full	**570.95**
.410 ga. w/26″ barrel, Full/Full	**613.95**

This handsome side-by-side offers hand-checkered European walnut stock with Churchill recoil pad and scroll-engraved antique silver receiver. Also double triggers, automatic top tang, safety and extractors. **Gauges:** 10, 12, 16, 20, 28, .410. **Barrel lengths:** 25″, 26″, 28″, 32″. **Chamber:** 3″ (16 ga. has 2¼″). **Weight:** 8 lbs.

WINDSOR I SIDE X SIDE SHOTGUN

Prices:

12, 16 and 20 ga. w/26″ and 28″ barrels,	
Modified/Full or IC/Modified	**$652.95**
28 ga. w/25″ barrel (Skeet/Skeet) and	
410 ga. w/26″ barrel (Mod./Full)	**707.95**
10 ga. w/32″ barrel (Full/Full)	**802.95**

CLASSIC DOUBLES

MODEL 101 OVER/UNDER

Formerly distributed by Olin/Winchester, Model 101 has been acquired by Classic Doubles International. These guns will continue to be produced in Japan by OK Firearms. All models feature chrome molybdenum steel barrels with chrome-lined chambers and bores suitable for steel shot, plus forged steel frames and trigger guards, single selective triggers, and top-grade semi-fancy American walnut.

Included in the new Classic Doubles line is Olin/Winchester's former Model 23 side-by-side, which is now Model 201. Prices and specifications for all models are listed below.

Prices:

MODEL 101 FIELD GRADE I	$2335.00
Waterfowler	1865.00
MODEL 101 FIELD GRADE II	2685.00
Field Set	4190.00
MODEL 101 SPORTERS	2425.00
Combo (28″ and 30″ Barrels)	3610.00
MODEL 101 TRAP SINGLE BARREL	2535.00
Over/Under	2335.00
Combo (Over/Under Single)	3460.00
MODEL 101 SKEET	2335.00
Four-Barrel Set (12, 20, 28, .410)	5840.00
MODEL 201 SIDE/SIDE GRADE I (12 Ga.)	2335.00
20 Ga. Skeet/Skeet Choke	2830.00
Set (28 & .410 Ga.)	4500.00

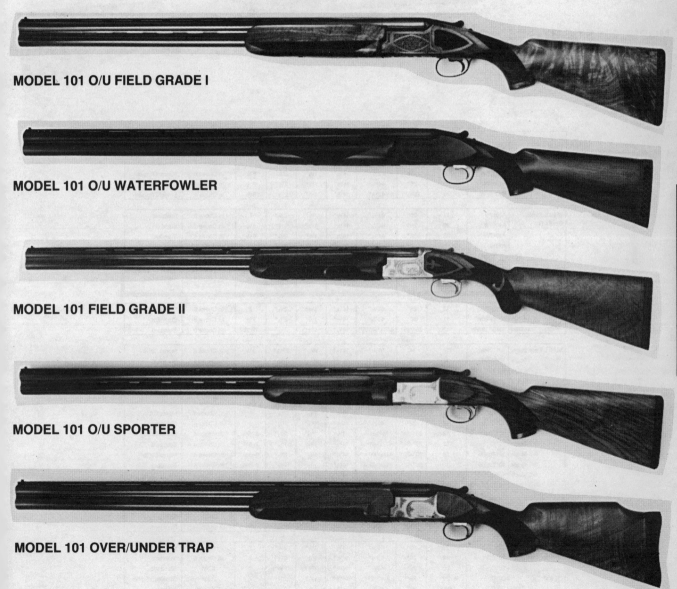

MODEL 101 O/U FIELD GRADE I

MODEL 101 O/U WATERFOWLER

MODEL 101 FIELD GRADE II

MODEL 101 O/U SPORTER

MODEL 101 OVER/UNDER TRAP

CLASSIC DOUBLES

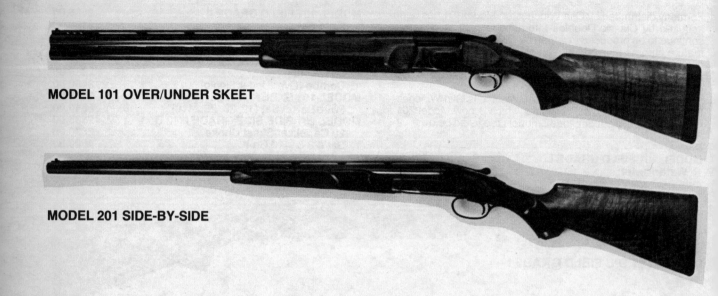

MODEL 101 OVER/UNDER SKEET

MODEL 201 SIDE-BY-SIDE

Model	Symbol	Gauge	BBL Lgth.	O/A Lgth.	Lgth. of Pull	Drop at Comb	Drop at Heel	Nominal Weight	Choke	Stock
M101 Field-Grade I	B1012W	12	28"	44⁷/₈"	14½"	1½"	2¼"	7	In Choke 6	Standard
	B1012EW	12	25½"	42¼"	14½"	1½"	2½"	6¾	In Choke 6	Straight English
	B1015W	20	28"	44⁷/₈"	14½"	1½"	2¼"	6½	In Choke 4	Standard
	B1015EW	20	25½"	42¼"	14½"	1½"	2½"	6¼	In Choke 4	Straight English
M101 Field-Grade II	A1012W	12	28"	44⁷/₈"	14½"	1½"	2¼"	7	In Choke 6	Standard
	A1015W	20	28"	44⁷/₈"	14½"	1½"	2¼"	6½	In Choke 4	Standard
	A1017W	28	28"	44⁷/₈"	14½"	1½"	2¼"	6½	In Choke 4	Standard
	A1019	410	28"	44⁷/₈"	14½"	1½"	2¼"	6¼	M/F	Standard
SET	A10128W2	12/20	28"/26"	44⁷/₈"/42⁷/₈"	14½"	1½"	2¼"	7/6½	In Choke 6/4	Standard
M101 Waterfowler	101CWF	12	30"	46⁷/₈"	14½"	1½"	2¼"	7½	In Choke 4	Standard
M101 Sporter	101SP28W	12	28"	44⁷/₈"	14½"	1½"	2¹/₈"	7	In Choke 6	Standard
New Model	101SP20W	12	30"	46⁷/₈"	14½"	1½"	2¹/₈"	7¼	In Choke 6	Standard
COMBO	101SP28W2	12	28"/30"	44⁷/₈"/46⁷/₈"	14½"	1½"	2¹/₈"	7/7¼	In Choke 6	Standard
M101 Trap Single	101T014M	12	34"	51¼"	14½"	1⁷/₁₆"	2³/₁₆"	8½	In Choke 4	Monte Carlo
Single	101T014S	12	34"	51¼"	14½"	1⁷/₁₆"	1⁷/₁₆"	8½	In Choke 4	Standard
Single	101T0112M	12	32"	49¼"	14½"	1⁷/₁₆"	2³/₁₆"	8½	In Choke 4	Monte Carlo
Single	101T012S	12	32"	49¼"	14½"	1⁷/₁₆"	1⁷/₁₆"	8½	In Choke 4	Standard
O/U	101T20M	12	30"	47¼"	14½"	1³/₈"	2¹/₈"	8¾	In Choke 4	Monte Carlo
O/U	101T20S	12	30"	47¼"	14½"	1³/₈"	1³/₈"	8¾	In Choke 4	Standard
O/U	101T22M	12	32"	49¼"	14½"	1³/₈"	2¹/₈"	9	In Choke 4	Monte Carlo
O/U	101T22S	12	32"	49¼"	14½"	1³/₈"	1³/₈"	9	In Choke 4	Standard
COMBO; O/U-Single	101T30M	12	30"-34"	47¼–51¼"	14½"	1³/₈"	2¹/₈"	9–8¾	In Choke 4	Monte Carlo
O/U-Single	101T30S	12	30"-34"	47¼–51¼"	14½"	1³/₈"	1³/₈"	9–8¾	In Choke 4	Standard
O/U-Single	101T302M	12	30"-32"	47¼–49¼"	14½"	1³/₈"	2¹/₈"	9–8¾	In Choke 4	Monte Carlo
O/U-Single	101T302S	12	30"-32"	47¼–49¼"	14½"	1³/₈"	1³/₈"	9–8¾	In Choke 4	Standard
O/U-Single	101T32M	12	32"-34"	49¼–51¼"	14½"	1³/₈"	2¹/₈"	9–8¾	In Choke 4	Monte Carlo
O/U-Single	101T32S	12	32"-34"	49¼–51¼"	14½"	1³/₈"	1³/₈"	9–8¾	In Choke 4	Standard
M101 Skeet	101527W	12	27½"	44⁵/₈"	14¼"	1³/₈"	2¹/₈"	7¼	In Choke 4	Standard
	101557	20	27½"	44⁵/₈"	14¼"	1³/₈"	2¹/₈"	6½	SK/SK	Standard
	10154	12,20,28,410	27½"	44⁵/₈"	14¼"	1½"	2¹/₈"	7½	SK/SK	Standard
M201 Side-by-Side	201C2	12	26"	43¼"	14½"	1½"	2¼"	7	IC/M	Standard
	201C2W	12	26"	43¼"	14½"	1½"	2¼"	7	In Choke 6	Standard
New Model	201C5	20	26"	43¼"	14½"	1½"	2¼"	7	IC/M	Standard
	201C5E	20	26"	43¼"	14½"	1½"	2¼"	7	IC/M	Straight English
SET	201C79	28/410	28"	45¼"	14½"	1½"	2¼"	6½/5⁷/₈	IC/M, M/F	Standard

CHARLES DALY SHOTGUNS

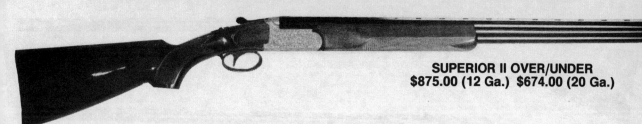

SUPERIOR II OVER/UNDER
$875.00 (12 Ga.) $674.00 (20 Ga.)

The Superior II Over/Under is a rugged shotgun that boasts a beautifully engraved silver receiver, single selective trigger, checkered pistol grip stock and forearm with recoil pad, ventilated rib, high-gloss wood finish with blued barrels. Selective, auto ejectors.

SPECIFICATIONS

Gauge	Barrel Length	Chokes
20	28″	Mod./Full
20	26″	Imp. Cyl./Mod.
12, 20	26″	Skeet

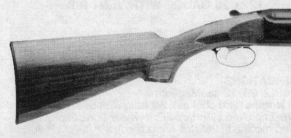

FIELD III OVER/UNDER
$425.00

This field grade over/under offers the same fine features as the other Charles Daly shotguns: excellent construction with a sound marriage of metal to wood. Checkered pistol grip and forearm, straight stock with high-gloss finish, 26- or 28-inch barrels with ventilated rib and single selective trigger. Nonselective extractors.

SPECIFICATIONS

Gauge	Barrel Length	Chokes
12 or 20	28″	Mod./Full
12 or 20	26″	Imp. Cyl./Mod.

FERLIB SHOTGUNS

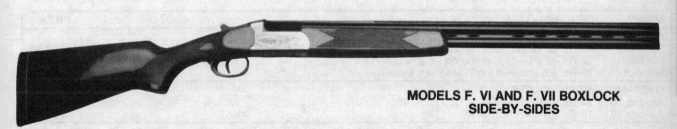

MODELS F. VI AND F. VII BOXLOCK
SIDE-BY-SIDES

Hand-crafted by the small European artisan firm of the same name, Ferlib shotguns are high-quality, hand-fitted side-by-sides. With Anson & Deeley boxlock design, all Ferlib doubles are available in 12, 16, 20 and 28 gauge and .410 bore, with automatic ejectors, double triggers with front trigger hinged (non-selective single trigger is optional), hand-rubbed oil-finished straight grip stock with classic forearm (beavertail optional). Dovetail lump barrels have soft-luster blued finish; top rib is concave with file-cut matting. **Barrel length:** 25″-28″. **Stock dimensions:** Length of pull, 14 1/2″; drop at comb, 1 1/2″; drop at heel, 2 1/4. **Weight:** 12 ga., 6 lbs. 8 oz.—6 lbs. 14 oz.; 16 ga., 6 lbs. 4 oz.—6 lbs. 10 oz.; 20 ga., 5 lbs. 14 oz.—6 lbs. 4 oz.; 28 ga. and .410, 5 lbs. 6 oz.—5 lbs. 11 oz.

Model F. VI w/scalloped frame, border-line engraving, casehardened colors, select walnut stock **$4200.00**
Model F. VII w/scalloped frame, full-coverage English scroll engraving, coin finish, select walnut stock **4900.00**
Model F. VII/SC w/scalloped frame, game scene with either bulino engraved or gold inlayed birds and scroll accents with coin finish, special walnut stock with extra figure and color **6200.00**
Model F. VII/Sideplate w/game scene engraving, gold inlayed birds and coin finish, special walnut stock, extra figure and color **8700.00**

FRANCHI AUTOLOADING SHOTGUNS

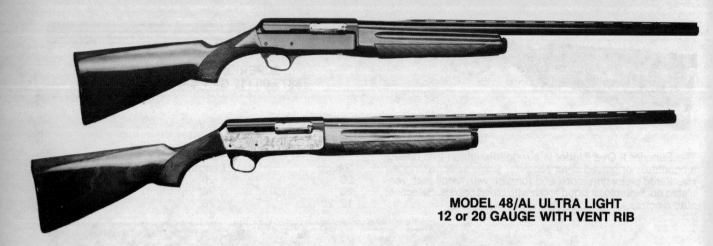

**MODEL 48/AL ULTRA LIGHT
12 or 20 GAUGE WITH VENT RIB**

Model 48/AL Ultra Lights feature specially selected European stock, forend; fully engraved light weight receiver covered by a lifetime guarantee; the automatic safety, which securely locks the hammer, is silent and positive; hand safety can be reversed for left-handed shooters; chrome-lined barrel for light weight and maximum strength; checkered pistol grip; reliable recoil action requiring no maintenance and no cleaning. Chambered for 2¾ shells.

SPECIFICATIONS
Gauge: 12, 20, 12 ga. Magnum
Barrel lengths (and chokes): 24″ (slug w/rifled sights; cylinder bore; improved cylinder); 26″ (cylinder bore; improved cylinder; modified); 28″ (full & modified); 30″ (full); 32″ (full)
Mechanism: Recoil
Chamber: 2¾″ (3″ in 12 ga. Magnum)
Overall length: 47⅞″ (w/28″ barrel)
Weight: 6 lbs. 4 oz. (12 ga); 5 lbs. 2 oz. (20 ga)
Capacity: 5 shots
Safety: Lateral push button safety
Stock: Stock and forearm have machine cut diamond checkering (Magnum models equipped with recoil pads)

MODEL 48 ULTRA-LIGHT AUTOLOADERS

MODEL	DESCRIPTION	PRICE
AUTOLOADING SHOTGUNS		
Standard	12 Ga. or 20 Ga. (chambered for 2¾″ shells)	$524.95
Hunter	12 Ga. or 20 Ga. (chambered for 2¾″ shells)	559.95
Magnum	12 Ga. (chambered for 3″ Magnum shells)	559.95
OVER-AND-UNDER MODELS		
Alcione 28	12 Ga. (28-inch M/F)	$799.95
Alcione 26	12 Ga. (26-inch I.C./M)	799.95

BARREL LENGTH AND CHOKE SELECTION		24″ Slug. R/S	24″ Cyl. V/R	24″ IC V/R	26″ Cyl. V/R	26″ Skeet V/R	26″ IC V/R	26″ Mod. V/R	28″ Mod. V/R	28″ Full V/R	30″ Full V/R	32″ Full V/R
	12 Gauge	X	X	X	X	X	X	X	X	X	X	X
	20 Gauge	X	X	X	X	X	X	X	X	X		

R/S = Rifle sights   V/R = Vent. rib
Note: 12 ga. Magnum in 32 Full only

FRANCHI AUTOLOADING SHOTGUNS

GAS-OPERATED SEMIAUTOMATICS
PRESTIGE & ELITE MODELS

ELITE

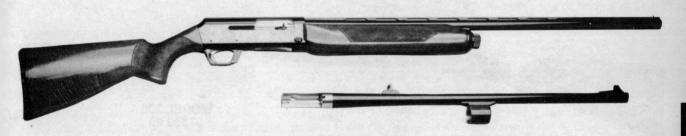

PRESTIGE

SPECIFICATIONS
Gauge: 12 (2³/₄″ chamber)
Mechanism: Gas operated semiautomatic
Magazine capacity: 5
Barrel lengths (and chokes): 24″ (slug barrel w/rifles sights); 26″ (Modified, Improved cylinder); 28″ (Full/Modified); 30″ (Full)
Overall length: 50″
Weight: 7 lbs. 6 oz.
Features: Double cocking slide (dual rails); chrome plated sleeve; stainless steel piston; patented magazine disconnect system; gold plated trigger

Finish: Hand rubbed satin finish; grip holding checkering
Note: Elite Model features hand filed ventilated rib (7mm wide to reduce glare); red phosphorescent front sight; European walnut stock and forend; oil finish w/hand patterned checkering on forend and pistol grip stock; engraved receiver illustrates shooting scenes
Prices: $759.95 (Prestige)
  784.95 (Elite) $739.95 w/o Franchoke
Also available: **TURKEY MODEL** in matte black finish w/Franchoke. $759.95

GARBI SIDELOCK SHOTGUNS

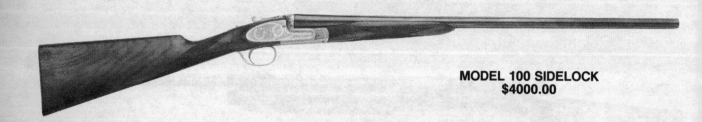

MODEL 100 SIDELOCK
$4000.00

Like this Model 100 shotgun, all Spanish-made Garbi models featured here are Holland & Holland pattern sidelock ejector guns with chopper lump (demibloc) barrels. They are built to English gun standards with regard to design, weight, balance and proportions, and all have the characteristic "feel" associated with the best London guns. All of the models offer fine 24-line hand-checkering, with outstanding quality wood-to-metal and metal-to-metal fit. The Model 100 is available in 12, 16, 20 and 28 gauge and sports Purdey-style fine scroll and rosette engraving, partly done by machine.

MODEL 200
$7300.00

MODELS 101, 103A and 120 (not shown)

Available in 12, 16, 20, and 28 gauge, the sidelocks are hand-crafted with hand-engraved receiver and select walnut straight grip stock.

SPECIFICATIONS
Barrels: 25″ to 30″ in 12 ga.; 25″ to 28″ in 16, 20 and 28 ga.; high-luster blued finish; smooth concave rib (optional Churchill or level, file-cut rib)
Action: Holland & Holland pattern sidelock; automatic ejectors; double triggers with front trigger hinged; case-hardened
Stock/forend: Straight grip stock with checkered butt (optional pistol grip); hand-rubbed oil finish; classic (splinter) forend (optional beavertail)

Weight: 12 ga. game, 6 lbs. 8 oz. to 6 lbs. 12 oz.; 12 ga. pigeon or wildfowl, 7 lbs.—7lbs. 8 oz.; 16 ga., 6 lbs. 4 oz. to 6 lbs. 10 oz.; 20 ga., 5 lbs. 15 oz.—6 lbs. 4 oz.; 28 ga., 5 lbs. 6 oz.—5 lbs. 10 oz.
Prices:
Model 101 . . . . $4100.00
Model 103A 5500.00
Model 120 . . . . 7000.00
Also available:
MODEL 200 in 12, 16, 20 or 28 gauge; features Holland pattern stock ejector double, heavy-duty locks, Continental-style floral and scroll engraving, walnut stock.

ITHACA SHOTGUNS

MODEL 87 FIELD GRADES

Made in much the same manner as 50 years ago, Ithaca's Model 37 pump (now designated as Model 87) features Roto-forged barrels hammered from 11″ round billets of steel, then triple-reamed, lapped and polished. The receivers are milled from a solid block of ordnance grade steel, and all internal parts—hammer, extractors, slides and carriers—are milled and individually fitted to each gun.

Prices:
MODEL 87 w/Supreme Vent Rib	$819.00
MODEL 87 w/Deluxe Vent Rib and choke tubes	495.00
MODEL 87 ULTRA DELUXE w/Choke Tubes	514.00
MODEL 87 Deluxe Combo	582.00
MODEL 87 FIELD	458.00
MODEL 87 ULTRAFIELD	481.00

MODEL 87 DEERSLAYER

The first shotgun developed to handle rifled slugs successfully, Ithaca's Deerslayer shotgun remains first choice for many big-game hunters around the world. The Deerlayer's design results in an "undersized" cylinder bore—from the forcing cone all the way to the muzzle. This enables the slug to travel smoothly down the barrel with no gas leakage or slug rattle. The new Deerslayer II features the world's first production rifled barrel for shotguns; moreover, the Deerslayer's barrel is permanently screwed into the receiver for solid frame construction, which insures better accuracy to about 85 yards.

Prices:
MODEL 87 DEERSLAYER	$391.00
MODEL 87 DEERSLAYER ULTRA	444.00
MODEL 87 MONTE CARLO DEERSLAYER II w/Rifled Barrel	525.00
MODEL 87 DELUXE DEERSLAYER	462.00
MODEL 87 FIELD DEERSLAYER	407.00

MODEL 87 TURKEY GUN
(Camo-seal Finish)

See Specifications for Ithaca 87 Models on following page.

ITHACA SHOTGUNS

SPECIFICATIONS: ITHACA MODEL 87 SHOTGUNS

Model	Grade	Gauge	Barrel Length	Choke*	Chamber	Weight (lbs.)
87	Supreme	12	30″	3 Tubes	3″	7
87	Supreme	12	28″	3 Tubes	3″	7
87	Supreme	12	26″	3 Tubes	3″	7
87	Supreme	20	26″	3 Tubes	3″	6¾
87	Deluxe	12	30″	3 Tubes	3″	7
87	Deluxe	12	28″	3 Tubes	3″	7
87	Deluxe	12	26″	3 Tubes	3″	7
87	Deluxe	20	26″	3 Tubes	3″	6¾
87	Field	12	30″	3 Tubes	3″	7
87	Field	12	28″	3 Tubes	3″	7
87	Field	12	26″	3 Tubes	3″	7
87	Field	20	26″	3 Tubes	3″	6¾
87	Ultra Deluxe	12	26″	3 Tubes	3″	6
87	Ultra Deluxe	20	26″	3 Tubes	3″	5
87	Ultra Deluxe	20	24″	3 Tubes	3″	5
87	Ultra Field	12	26″	3 Tubes	3″	6
87	Ultra Field	20	26″	3 Tubes	3″	5
87	Ultra Field	20	24″	3 Tubes	3″	5
87	Camo Field	12	28″	3 Tubes	3″	7
87	Deluxe Deerslayer	12	20″	DS	3″	7
87	Deluxe Deerslayer	12	25″	DS	3″	7
87	Deluxe Deerslayer	20	20″	DS	3″	6¾
87	Deluxe Deerslayer	20	25″	DS	3″	6¾
87	Ultra Deerslayer	20	20″	DS	3″	5
87	Deluxe Deerslayer	12	20″	DSR	3″	7
87	Deluxe Deerslayer	12	25″	DSR	3″	7
87	Deluxe Deerslayer	20	20″	DSR	3″	6¾
87	Deluxe Deerslayer	20	25″	DSR	3″	6¾
87	Field Deerslayer	12	20″	DS	3″	7
87	Field Deerslayer	12	25″	DS	3″	7
87	Field Deerslayer	20	20″	DS	3″	6¾
87	Field Deerslayer	20	25″	DS	3″	6¾
87	Basic Field Deerslayer	12	20″	DS	3″	7
87	Basic Field Deerslayer	12	25″	DS	3″	7
87	Monte Carlo Deerslayer II	12	25″	DS II	3″	7

Model	Grade	Gauge	Barrel Length	Choke*	Chamber	Weight (lbs.)
87	Deluxe Combo	20	28″ & 20″	3 Tubes/DS	3″	6¾
87	Deluxe Combo	12	28″ & 20″	3 Tubes/DS	3″	7
87	Deluxe Combo	12	28″ & 20″	3 Tubes/DSR	3″	7
87	Deluxe Combo	12	28″ & 25″	3 Tubes/DSR	3″	7
87	Deluxe Combo	20	28″ & 20″	3 Tubes/DSR	3″	6¾
87	Deluxe Combo	20	28″ & 25″	3 Tubes/DSR	3″	6¾
87	Basic Field/C	12	28″ & 20″	Mod Tube/DS	3″	7
87	Basic Field/C	12	28″ & 25″	Mod Tube/DS	3″	7
87	Basic Field/C	20	28″ & 20″	Mod Tube/DS	3″	6¾
87	Basic Field/C	12	28″ & 20″	Mod Tube/DSR	3″	7
87	Basic Field/C	12	28″ & 25″	Mod Tube/DSR	3″	7
87	Basic Field/C	20	28″ & 20″	Mod Tube/DSR	3″	6¾
87	Basic Field/C	20	28″ & 25″	Mod Tube/DSR	3″	6¾
87	Turkey Gun Matte Blue	12	24″	Full Tube	3″	7
87	Turkey Gun Matte Blue	12	24″	Full Choke	3″	7
87	Turkey Gun Camo	12	24″	Full Tube	3″	7
87	Turkey Gun Camo	12	24″	Full Choke	3″	7
87	Hand Grip	12	18½″	Cylinder	3″	5¼
87	Hand Grip	20	18½″	Cylinder	3″	4½
87	Hand Grip	20	18½″	Cylinder	3″	4½
87	M&P	12	20″	Cylinder	3″	7
87	M&P	12	18½″	Cylinder	3″	7
87	DSPS	12	20″	DS	3″	7
87	M&P 8 Shot	12	20″	Cylinder	3″	7
87	DSPS 8 Shot	12	20″	DS	3″	7
Custom Trap	M5E Custom	12	32″	Full	2¾″	8½
Custom Trap	M5E Custom	12	34″	Full	2¾″	8½
Custom Trap	Dollar Grade	12	32″	Full	2¾″	8½
Custom Trap	Dollar Grade	12	34″	Full	2¾″	8½

Model	Grade	Caliber	Barrel Length	Choke*	Chamber	Weight (lbs.)
Pistol	Pistol	.22	10″	N/A	N/A	3½
Pistol	Pistol	.44	10″	N/A	N/A	3½
Pistol	Pistol	.44	15″	N/A	N/A	3½
Pistol	Pistol Combo	.22/.44	10″ & 15″	N/A	N/A	3½
Pistol	Pistol Combo	.22/.44	10″ & 10″	N/A	N/A	3½

*3 tubes furnished are Improved Cylinder, Modified, and Full.
DS = Deer, Special Bore   DSR = Deer, Rifled Bore   DS II = Deer, Rifled Barrel

CUSTOM TRAP

SINGLE BARREL CUSTOM TRAP

SPECIFICATIONS

Model	Gauge	Chamber	Barrel Length	Choke	Weight (Lbs.)
Custom	12	2¾″	32″	Full	8½
	12	2¾″	34″	Full	8½
Trap	12	2¾″	32″	Full	8½
	12	2¾″	34″	Full	8½

Standard dimensions are: Length of pull is 14⅜″ with 1¾″ drop at both comb and heel. Custom stock fitting at no extra charge.

Prices:
CUSTOM TRAP 32″ and 34″ Barrel . . . . $ 7,500.00
DOLLAR TRAP w/Grade AA Fancy American
walnut stock & forend 10,000.00

KRIEGHOFF SHOTGUNS

· **K-80 LIVE PIGEON**

MODEL K-80 TRAP, SKEET, SPORTING CLAY AND LIVE PIGEON

Barrels: Made of Boehler steel; free-floating bottom barrel with adjustable point of impact; standard Trap and Live Pigeon ribs are tapered step; standard Skeet, Sporting Clay and International ribs are tapered or parallel flat.
Receivers: Hard satin-nickel finish; casehardened; blued finish available as special order
Triggers: Wide profile, single selective, position adjustable
Weight: 8½ lbs. (Trap); 8 lbs. (Skeet)

Ejectors: Selective automatic
Sights: White pearl front bead and metal center bead
Stocks: Hand-checkered and epoxy-finished Select European walnut stock and forearm; silver soldered metal-to-metal assemblies; quick-detachable palm swell stocks available in five different styles and dimensions
Safety: Push button safety located on top tang.

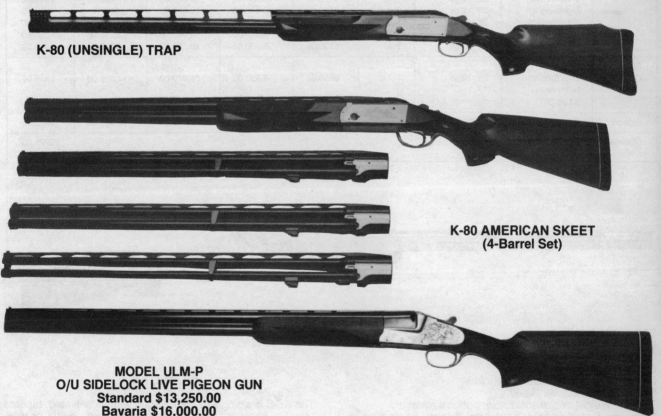

K-80 (UNSINGLE) TRAP

**K-80 AMERICAN SKEET
(4-Barrel Set)**

MODEL ULM-P
O/U SIDELOCK LIVE PIGEON GUN
Standard $13,250.00
Bavaria $16,000.00

SPECIFICATIONS
Gauge: 12
Chamber: 2¾″
Barrel: 28″ or 30″ long; tapered, ventilated rib
Choke: Top, Full; bottom, Imp. Mod.
Trigger action: Single trigger, non-selective bottom-top; hand-detachable sidelocks with coil springs; optional release trigger

Stock: Selected fancy English walnut, oil finish; length, 14⅜″; drop at comb, 1⅜″; optional custom-made stock
Forearm: Semi-beavertail
Engraving: Light scrollwork; optional engravings available
Weight: Approx. 8 lbs.
Also available in Skeet (28″) and Trap (30″) models (same prices as above)

KRIEGHOFF SHOTGUNS

SPECIFICATIONS AND PRICES

Model	Description	Bbl Length	Choke	Standard	Bavaria	Danube	Gold Target	Extra Barrels
Trap	Over & Under	30″/32″	IM/F	$4850.00	$8,475.00	$10,490.00	$13,875.00	$1895.00
	Unsingle	32″/34″	Full	5675.00	9,170.00	11,290.00	14,575.00	2550.00
	Top Single	34″ only	Full	4995.00	8,550.00	10,650.00	13,940.00	1895.00
		30″ + 32″						
	Combo	30″ + 34″	IM/F	7295.00	10,975.00	13,150.00	16,380.00	
		32″ + 34″	+F	6650.00	10,330.00	12,395.00	15,750.00	

Optional Features:
Screw-in chokes (O/U, Top or Unsingle) $325
Single factory release   285
Double factory release   480

Model	Description	Bbl Length	Choke	Standard	Bavaria	Danube	Gold Target	Extra Barrels
Skeet		28″/12 ga.	Tula	9650.00	13,750.00	15,800.00	20,500.00	2100.00
		28″/20 ga.	Skeet					1995.00
	4-Barrel Set	28″/28 ga.	Skeet					1995.00
		28″/.410 ga.	Skeet					1995.00
	2-Barrel Set	28″/12 ga.	Tula	8475.00	12,195.00	14,300.00	17,750.00	3345.00
	Lightweight	28″/12 ga.	Skeet	4750.00	8,375.00	10,390.00	N/A	1895.00
	Standardweight	28″/12 ga.	Tula	4950.00	8,575.00	10,590.00	13,975.00	2100.00
		28″/12 ga.	Skeet	4750.00	8,375.00	10,390.00	13,775.00	1895.00
	International	28″/12 ga.	Tula	5100.00	8,700.00	10,700.00	14,100.00	2100.00
Sporting Clays	Over/Under w/screw-in tubes (5)	28″/12 ga.	Tubes	5350.00	8,950.00	10,970.00	14,350.00	2380.00
Pigeon	Pigeon	28″/29″/30″	IM/SF	4850.00	8,475.00	10,490.00	13,875.00	1895.00

Optional engravings: Super Standard . . . .$$275.00
                              Super Scroll 600.00

SPECIFICATIONS
Gauge: 12
Chamber: 2³/₄″
Barrel length: 32″ or 34″
Choke: Full; optional screw-in chokes
Rib: Tapered step; ventilated
Trigger: Weight of pull adjustable; optional release
Receiver: Casehardened; satin grey finished in electroless nickel; now available in blue
Grade: Standard; engraved models on special order
Weight: Approximately 8.6-8.8 lbs.
Case: Aluminum
Price: With full choke and case $2670.00
With screw-in choke and case 2995.00
Screw-in choke barrels 1725.00
Regular barrels 1400.00
Engraved models (start at) 3495.00

MODEL KS-5

The KS-5 is a single barrel trap gun with a ventilated, tapered step rib, casehardened receiver in satin grey matte or blue, finished in electroless nickel. It features an adjustable point of impact by means of different optional fronthangers. Screw-in chokes and factory adj. stock are optional. Trigger is adjustable externally for poundage.

LAURONA SHOTGUNS

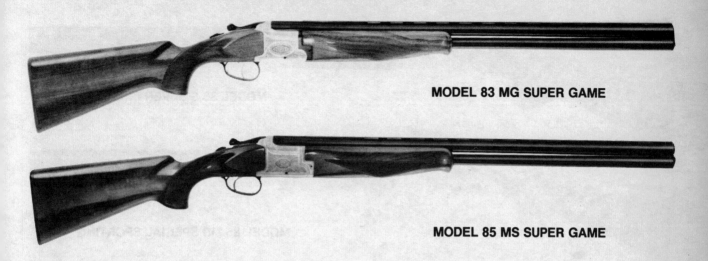

MODEL 83 MG SUPER GAME

MODEL 85 MS SUPER GAME

MODEL 83 MG SUPER GAME
$995.00

SPECIFICATIONS
Gauges: 12 and 20
Chamber: 2¾" or 3"
Barrel lengths: 26" (20 ga.) and 28" (12 ga.)
Chokes: Multichokes (or screw-in)
Rib: 5/16"

Frame finish: Old Silver
Weight: 6 lbs. 10 oz. (20 ga.); 7 lbs. (12 ga.)
Also available: **Model 85 MS** (12 and 20 Gauge).
Specifications same as Model 83, but with selective single trigger. **Price: $995.00.**

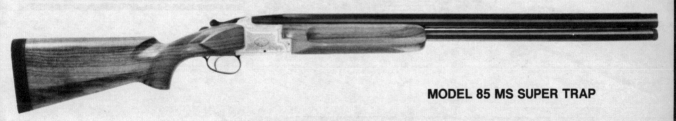

MODEL 85 MS SUPER TRAP

MODEL 85 MS SUPER TRAP
$1135.00

SPECIFICATIONS
Gauge: 12
Chamber: 2¾"
Barrel length: 29"
Choke: Multichoke/Full
Rib: 1/2"

Frame finish: Old silver
Weight: 7 lbs. 12 oz.
Also available: **MODEL 85 MS SUPER PIGEON** (12 ga.). Same specifications as Super Trap model except **Barrel length:** 28" and **Weight:** 7 lbs. 4 oz. **Price: $1117.00.**

SHOTGUNS

LAURONA SHOTGUNS

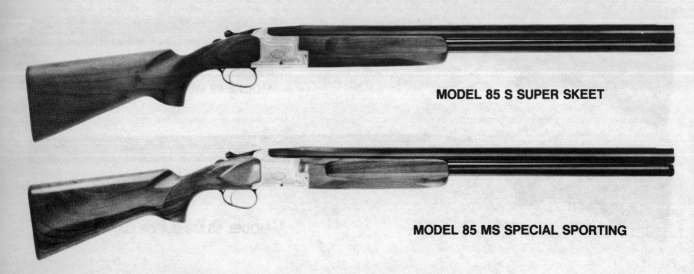

MODEL 85 S SUPER SKEET

MODEL 85 MS SPECIAL SPORTING

MODEL 85 S SUPER SKEET
$1061.00

SPECIFICATIONS
Gauge: 12
Chamber: 2³/₄″
Barrel length: 28″
Choke: Skeet/Skeet
Rib: ¹/₂″

Frame finish: Old silver
Weight: 7 lbs. 1 oz.
Also available: MODEL 85 MS SPECIAL SPORTING (12 ga.). Same specifications as Super Skeet model but without choke. **Weight:** 7 lbs. 4 oz. **Price: $1085.00**

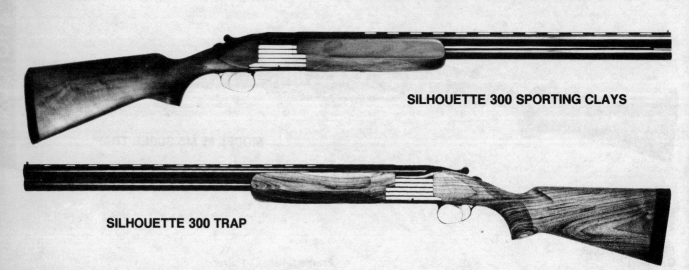

SILHOUETTE 300 SPORTING CLAYS

SILHOUETTE 300 TRAP

SILHOUETTE 300 SPORTING CLAYS
$1019.00

SPECIFICATIONS (Game, Trap & Sporting Clay Models)
Gauge: 12
Chamber: 2³/₄″ (3″ in Game model only)
Barrel length: 28″ (29″ in Trap & Sporting Clay models)
Choke: Multichoke

Rib: ⁵/₁₆″ (⁷/₁₆″ in Trap & Sporting Clay models)
Ejectors: Automatic selective ejectors
Stock: Full pistol grip
Weight: 7 lbs. (7 lbs. 15 oz. in Trap; 7 lbs. 4 oz. in Sporting Clays)

MARLIN SHOTGUNS

**MARLIN MODEL 55
GOOSE GUN
$228.95**

High-flying ducks and geese are the Goose Gun's specialty. The Marlin Goose Gun has an extra-long 36-inch full-choked barrel and Magnum capability, making it the perfect choice for tough shots at wary waterfowl. It also features a quick-loading 2-shot clip magazine, a convenient leather carrying strap and a quality ventilated recoil pad.

SPECIFICATIONS
Gauge: 12; 2³/₄″ Magnum, 3″ Magnum or 2³/₄″ regular shells

Choke: Full
Capacity: 2-shot clip magazine
Action: Bolt action; positive thumb safety; red cocking indicator
Stock: Walnut-finish hardwood with pistol grip and ventilated recoil pad; swivel studs; tough Mar-Shield® finish
Barrel length: 36″
Sights: Bead front sight and U-groove rear sight
Overall length: 56³/₄″
Weight: About 8 lbs.

Information on the new Maverick pump shotguns was received too late for inclusion in this edition.

MERKEL OVER & UNDER SHOTGUNS

Merkel over-and-unders are the first hunting guns with barrels arranged one above the other, and they have since proved to be able competitors of the side-by-side gun. Merkel superiority lies in the following details:

- Available in 12, 16, 20 and .410 gauges
- Lightweight (5³/₄ to 6³/₄ lbs.)
- The high, narrow forend protects the shooter's hand from the barrel in hot or cold climates.
- The forend is narrow and therefore lies snugly in the hand

to permit easy and positive swinging.
- The slim barrel line provides an unobstructed field of view and thus permits rapid aiming and shooting.
- The over-and-under barrel arrangement reduces recoil error; the recoil merely pushes the muzzle up vertically.

Additional specifications on the following page. For details and prices on Merkel options, contact Armes de Chasse (see Directory of Manufacturers & Suppliers).

**MODEL 200E SIDELOCK
$2835.00**

**MODEL 201E SIDELOCK
$3675.00**

MERKEL OVER/UNDER SHOTGUNS

MERKEL OVER/UNDER SHOTGUN SPECIFICATIONS

Gauges: 12, 16, 20, 28, .410
Barrel lengths: 26″, 26¾″, 28″
Weight: 6 to 7 lbs.
Stock: English or pistol grip in European walnut
Features: Models 200E and 201E are boxlocks; Models 203E and 303E are sidelocks. All models include three-piece forearm, automatic ejectors, articulated front triggers. Automatic safety, selective and nonselective triggers are optional, as are upgraded wood, recoil pad and special engraving. All Merkel shotguns are made by VEB Fahrzeug and Jagdwaffenwerk Ernst Thalman, West Germany, and are distributed in the U.S. by Armes de Chasse.

MODEL 203E SIDELOCK
$8020.00

MODEL 303E SIDELOCK
$9060.00

MERKEL SIDE-BY-SIDE SHOTGUNS

MERKEL SIDE-BY-SIDE SHOTGUN SPECIFICATIONS

Gauges: 12, 16, 20
Barrel lengths: 26″, 26¾″, 28″
Weight: 6 to 7 lbs.
Stock: English or pistol grip in European walnut

Features: Models 47E and 147E are boxlocks; Models 47S, 147S, 247S, 347S, and 447S are sidelocks. All guns have cold hammer-forged barrels, double triggers, double lugs and Greener crossbolt locking systems and automatic ejectors. Choking and patterning for steel shot (using U.S. Steel shotshells), upgraded wood, automatic safety, recoil pad and special engraving are available as options.

MODEL 347S SIDELOCK
$4715.00

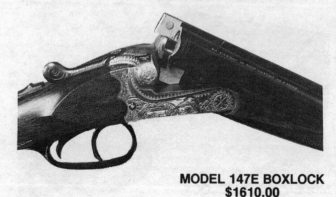

MODEL 147E BOXLOCK
$1610.00

MERKEL SIDE-BY-SIDE SHOTGUNS

MODEL 47S SIDE-BY-SIDE
$3275.00

MODEL 147S & 247S
$4030.00

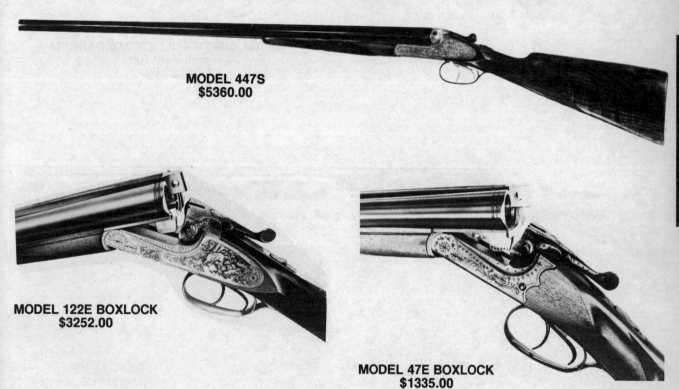

MODEL 447S
$5360.00

MODEL 122E BOXLOCK
$3252.00

MODEL 47E BOXLOCK
$1335.00

MOSSBERG PUMP SHOTGUNS

These slide-action Model 500's offer lightweight action and high tensile-strength alloys. They also feature the famous Mossberg "Safety on Top" and a full range of interchangeable barrels. Stocks are walnut-finished birch with rubber recoil pads with combs checkered pistol grip and forend.

MODEL 500 SPECIFICATIONS

Action: Positive slide-action

Barrel: 12 or 20 gauge and .410 bore with free-floating vent. rib; ACCU-CHOKE II interchangeable choke tubes; chambered for 2³/₄" standard and Magnum and 3" Magnum shells

Receiver: Aluminum alloy, deep blue/black finish; ordnance steel bolt locks in barrel extension for solid "steel-to-steel" lockup

Capacity: 6-shot (one less when using 3" Magnum shells); plug for 3-shot capacity included

Safety: Top tang, thumb-operated; disconnecting trigger

Stock/forend: Walnut-finished American hardwood with checkering; rubber recoil pad

Standard stock dimensions: 14" length of pull; 2¹/₂" drop at heel; 1¹/₂" drop at comb

Sights: Metal bead front

Overall length: 48" with 28" barrel

Weight: 12 ga. 7¹/₂ lbs.; 20 ga. 6³/₄ lbs.; .410 bore 6¹/₂ lbs.; Slugster 6³/₄ lbs.; Magnums 8¹/₂ lbs. (weight varies slightly due to wood density)

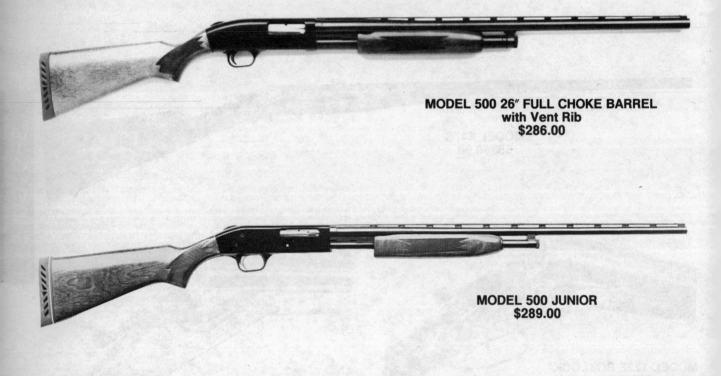

MODEL 500 26" FULL CHOKE BARREL
with Vent Rib
$286.00

MODEL 500 JUNIOR
$289.00

MOSSBERG SHOTGUNS

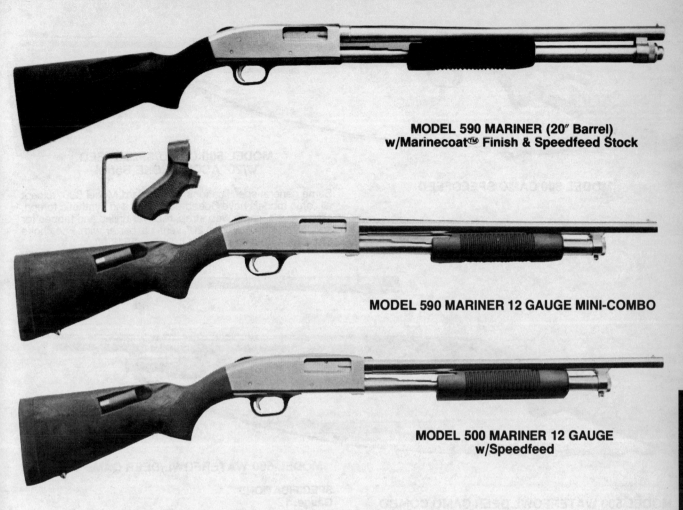

MODEL 590 MARINER (20″ Barrel)
w/Marinecoat™ Finish & Speedfeed Stock

MODEL 590 MARINER 12 GAUGE MINI-COMBO

MODEL 500 MARINER 12 GAUGE
w/Speedfeed

MODEL 500 & 590 MARINER

All carbon steel parts of these 12 gauge shotguns are treated with MARINECOAT® protective finish, a unique Teflon and metal coating. This finish makes each Mariner 500 shotgun resistant to salt spray and water damage by actually penetrating into the steel pores. All stock and forearms are made of a high-strength synthetic material rather than wood to provide extra durability with minimum maintenance. Mossberg's Speedfeed stock allows shooters to carry up to four extra 2³/₄″ rounds in the buttstock—two on each side. Mariners are available in a variety of 6- or 9-shot versions. The Mini-Combo offers a full-length buttstock and extra pistol grip. Pistol grip models include heat shields.

SPECIFICATIONS
Gauge: 12
Chambers: 2³/₄″ and 3″
Capacity: 6-shot model—5-shot (3″ chamber) and 6-shot (2³/₄″ chamber)
8-shot model—7-shot (3″ chamber) and 8-shot (2³/₄″ chamber)

Barrel lengths: 18¹/₂″ and 20″
Overall length: 40″ w/20″ barrel; 38¹/₂″ w/18¹/₂″ barrel
Weight: 6¹/₂ lbs. w/18¹/₂″ barrel
Stock dimensions: 14″ pull; 1¹/₂″ drop at comb; 2¹/₂″ drop at heel
Features: Double slide bars; twin extractors; dual shell latches; ambidextrous safety

Prices:
MODEL 500 MARINER 6-SHOT
Pistol Grip & Synthetic Field Models **$358.00**
MODEL 590 MARINER 9-SHOT
Pistol Grip & Synthetic Field Models 428.00
Speedfeed Model 443.00
MODEL 500 MARINER 6-SHOT MINI-COMBO
Synthetic Field 367.00
Speedfeed Model 383.00
MODEL 590 MARINER 9-SHOT MINI-COMBO
Synthetic Field Model 436.00
Speedfeed Model 452.00

MOSSBERG PUMP SHOTGUNS

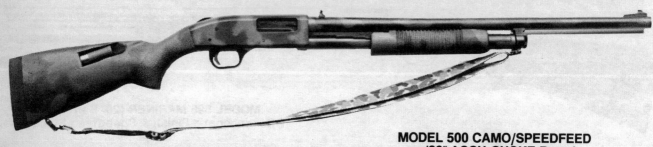

MODEL 500 CAMO/SPEEDFEED

MODEL 500 CAMO/SPEEDFEED w/20" ACCU-CHOKE Barrel

Same general specifications as standard Model 500, except all camo models have Speedfeed stock and synthetic forend, sling swivels, camo web strap, receiver drilled and tapped for scope mounting. **Price:** 20" vent rib barrel with Full choke **$334.00**; 24" vent rib ACCU II Turkey **$317.00**.

MODEL 500 WATERFOWL/DEER CAMO COMBO

MODEL 500 WATERFOWL/DEER CAMO COMBO

SPECIFICATIONS
Gauge: 12
Barrel length: 28" (Accu-Choke w/one Accu-Steel choke tube and 20" Slugster barrel
Features: Synthetic forearm and Speedback buttstock; receiver drilled and tapped for scope mounting; quick disconnect posts and swivels, plus camo web sling, are supplied
Price: $358.00

MODEL 500 CAMPER

MODEL 500 CAMPER

SPECIFICATIONS
Gauges: 12, 20 & .410
Chambers: 2¹/₂" and 3" Magnum
Barrel length: 18¹/₂"
Weight: 4¹/₂ lbs. (.410 ga.); 5 lbs. (20 ga.); 5¹/₂ lbs. (12 ga.)
Features: Synthetic pistol grip; camo carrying case
Price: $292.00; in .410 gauge **$298.00**

MOSSBERG PUMP SHOTGUNS

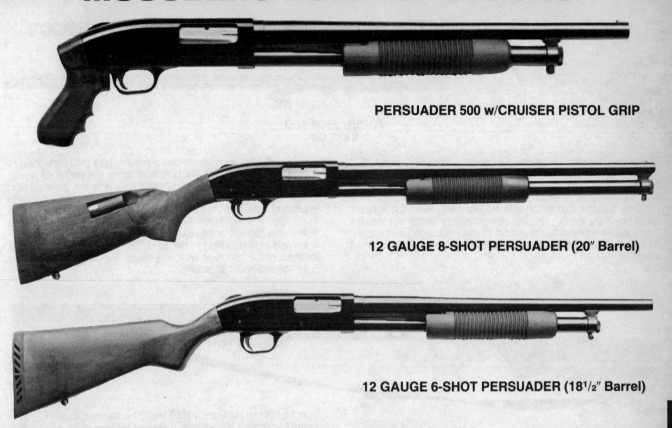

PERSUADER 500 w/CRUISER PISTOL GRIP

12 GAUGE 8-SHOT PERSUADER (20″ Barrel)

12 GAUGE 6-SHOT PERSUADER (18¹/₂″ Barrel)

MODEL 500 SLIDE-ACTION LAW ENFORCEMENT "PERSUADER"

These slide-action shotguns are available in 6- or 8-shot versions, chambered for both 2³/₄-inch and 3-inch shells.

Six-shot models have 18¹/₂-inch barrel, overall length of 37³/₄ inches and a weight of 6¹/₄ pounds with full buttstock. Also available in 20 gauge and .410 bore.

Eight-shot models have 20-inch barrels, overall length of 39³/₄ inches and weigh 6³/₄ pounds with full buttstock.

Both 6- and 8-shot models are available in choice of blued, parkerized or nickel metal finish; satin or oiled walnut wood finish. Lightweight aluminum alloy receiver with steel locking bolt into barrel extension affords solid "steel-to-steel" lockup. Heavy-duty rubber recoil pads come on all full stock models; sling swivels on all models. Optional pistol grip and other accessories.

PERSUADER 8-SHOT
Synthetic Field Model	$276.00
With rifle sight	296.00
Speedfeed Model	276.00

PERSUADER 8-SHOT MINI-COMBO Blued 284.00

PERSUADER 6-SHOT—Blued
With wood stock, bead sights	$259.00
Synthetic Field stock, blued, bead sight	259.00
Both models w/rifle sights	278.00
Cruiser Model, blued	259.00
Speedfeed stock, blued (12, 20 ga.)	276.00

PERSUADER 6-SHOT MINI-COMBO
Blued, 12 and 20 gauge	268.00
Synthetic Field Model	268.00

PERSUADER 6-SHOT MAXI-COMBO—Blued 294.00
Wood stock model	289.95
With ACCU-II Choke	317.00
Wood stock Model 20 gauge	294.00
With ventilated rib	305.00

MOSSBERG AUTOLOADING SHOTGUNS

MODEL 5500 MKII
$433.00

Mossberg's new semiauto 12-gauge "Shooting System," Model 5500 MKII, is equipped with two barrels—one for non-magnum 2³/₄" 12-gauge loads only, and the other for magnum 2³/₄" or 3" loads. A larger gas port in the non-magnum barrel ensures reliable extraction and ejection with even the lightest target or field loads. The 26" non-magnum barrel is ideal for close cover upland hunting and comes equipped with three ACCU-II choke tubes (Imp. Cyl., Modified, and Full) for lead shot.

The 28" magnum barrel has a smaller gas port designed to regulate the speed of the bolt and tame the recoil of heavy hunting loads. The magnum barrel provides the balance and longer sighting plane preferred by waterfowl hunters. It comes equipped with two ACCU-STEEL choke tubes (Modified and Full). Model 5500 MKII Auto has a full 5-shot capacity and features a high-strength aluminum alloy receiver for good balance and fast handling in the field. The positive tang safety is located in the top rear of the receiver for easy operation by right- or left-hand shooters.

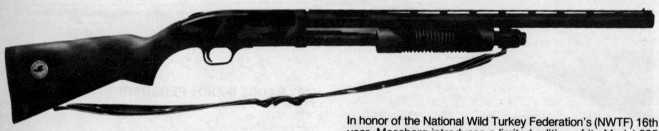

MODEL 835 "NWTF" ULTI-MAG
$477.00

In honor of the National Wild Turkey Federation's (NWTF) 16th year, Mossberg introduces a limited edition of its Model 835 Ulti-Mag 12-gauge 3¹/₂" chambered pump-action shotgun. Each gun features CAMO finish and a 24" vent ribbed barrel with ACCU-MAG chokes. A special Wild Turkey Federation medallion is inlaid in the stock (*see* photo). A 10-pack of Federal Cartridge's 3¹/₂" 12-gauge copper-plated #6 lead shot turkey load is included.

MODEL 835 ULTI-MAG
$416.00 (Blued) $443.00 (Camo)

The world's first shotgun chambered specifically for Federal Cartridge's new 3¹/₂" 12 gauge Magnum shotshell, the **Ulti-Mag** fires all standard 12 gauge 2³/₄" and 3" field and target loads as well. Designed for waterfowlers who need a shotshell capable of delivering larger payloads of steel shot, the high-velocity (1300+ fps) load provides a 23 percent or more increase in steel shot capacity compared to conventional 12 gauge 3" Magnums.

The **Ulti-Mag** also features a "backbored" barrel, thus increasing diameter bore, reducing recoil, and improving patterns. With the ACCU-MAG choke tube system, stainless steel tubes fit flush with the muzzle to handle high-velocity steel shot loads with efficiency. Capacity is five shots with 3" or 3¹/₂" shells, and six shots with 2³/₄" shells. Other features include an ambidextrous safety, solid "steel-to-steel" lockup, and high-strength aluminum alloy receivers with anodized finish.

NAVY ARMS SHOTGUNS

**MODEL 96
$575.00**

Five fully interchangeable chokes make the Model 96 Over/ Under a versatile shotgun, useful for all types of upland and waterfowl hunting as well as target shooting. Italian made, this 12-gauge gun features 28-inch chrome-lined barrels with 3- inch chambers, ejectors, double ventilated rib construction, an engraved hard chrome reciver, European walnut stock with checkered wrist and forend and gold-plated single trigger. Chokes: Full; Imp. Cyl./ Mod.; Mod.; Imp. Cyl./Skeet; Cyl.

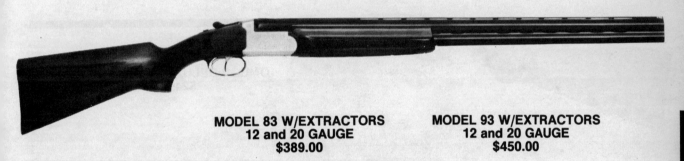

**MODEL 83 W/EXTRACTORS
12 and 20 GAUGE
$389.00**

**MODEL 93 W/EXTRACTORS
12 and 20 GAUGE
$450.00**

The Model 83/93 Bird Hunter is a quality field grade over/under available in 12 or 20 gauge. Manufactured in Italy, it features 28-inch chrome-lined barrels with 3-inch chambers; double vent rib construction, European walnut stock, hand-checkered wrist and forend, chrome engraved receiver and gold-plated triggers. Both gauges available in Mod./Full or Imp. Cyl./ Mod. chokes.

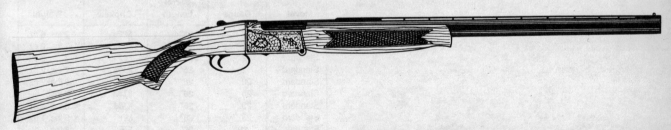

**MODEL 100 SHOTGUN
$299.00**

The Model 100 Italian-made over/under shotgun features European walnut stock checkered at the wrist and forend, 26- inch chrome-lined barrels with 3-inch chambers, ventilated rib barrel and an engraved, hard chrome receiver. **Chokes:** Full/ Full (.410), Mod./Full (28 ga.), Imp. Cyl./Mod. (20 ga.), and Imp. Cyl./Mod. or Mod./Full (12 ga.). **Weight:** 6¼ lbs.

SHOTGUNS

OMEGA SHOTGUNS

Omega side-by-side shotguns are available in two models, both with double triggers and non-automatic safety. The Standard model has a checkered beechwood stock and semi-pistol grip. The Deluxe model has a checkered European walnut stock and low barrel rib. Both models come in .410 gauge with 26-inch barrels and Full/Full chokes. **Overall length:** 40½". **Weight:** 5½ lbs.

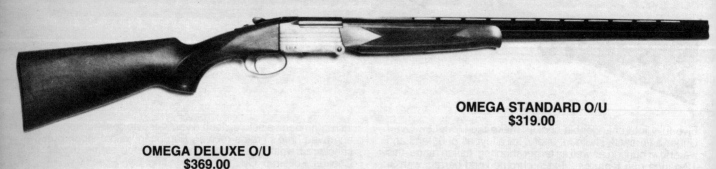

OMEGA STANDARD O/U
$319.00

OMEGA DELUXE O/U
$369.00

The Omega over/under is truly a premium shotgun featuring single trigger, automatic safety, ventilated rib and checkered European walnut stock.

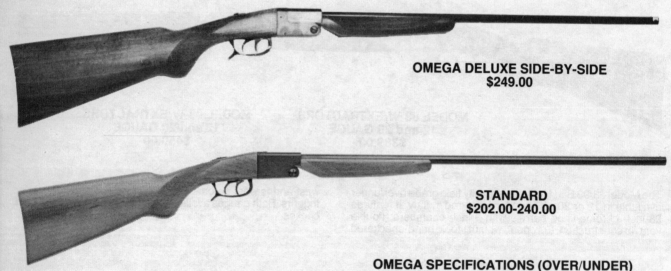

OMEGA DELUXE SIDE-BY-SIDE
$249.00

STANDARD
$202.00-240.00

OMEGA SPECIFICATIONS (OVER/UNDER)

Movel	Gauge	Barrel Length	Chokes	Weight
Deluxe	12	28"	M/F	7 lbs. 6 oz.
Deluxe	12	26"	IC/M	7 lbs. 2 oz.
Standard	12	28"	M/F	7 lbs. 6 oz.
Standard	12	26"	IC/M	7 lbs. 2 oz.
Standard	20	28"	M/F	6 lbs. 2 oz.
Standard	20	26"	IC/M	6 lbs.
Standard	28	26"	IC/M	6 lbs. 1 oz.
Standard	28	26"	M/F	6 lbs. 1 oz.
Standard	.410	26"	F/F	6 lbs.

OMEGA SPECIFICATIONS (SIDE-BY-SIDE)

Deluxe	.410	26"	F/F	5 lbs. 7 oz.
Standard	20	26"	IC/M	5 lbs. 7 oz.
Standard	28	26"	M/F	5 lbs. 7 oz.
Standard	.410	26"	F/F	5 lbs. 7 oz.

PARKER-HALE SHOTGUNS

Now available in the U.S., Parker-Hale side-by-side shotguns have long been favorites in Great Britain. Superbly crafted by the Spanish gunmaking firm of Ignacio Ugartechea, the "600" Series doubles are available in field grade boxlock models and "best" grade sidelock versions. Field grade models are offered in either extractor or ejector configurations. All models boast stocks of hand-checkered walnut finished with hand-rubbed oil, actions and parts machined from ordnance steel, standard auto safety, forged barrels, deep lustrous bluing and English scroll design engraving. **American** (A) models: Single non-selective trigger, pistol grip, beavertail forend, butt plate, raised matted rib. **English** (E) models: Double triggers, straight grip, splinter forend, checkered butt, concave rib; XXV models have Churchill-type rib. **Chokes:** Imp. Cyl./Mod.; Mod./Full. **Weight:** 12 ga., 6³/₄-7 lbs.; 20 ga. 5³/₄ lbs.-6 lbs.; 28 and .410 ga., 5¹/₄-5¹/₂ lbs. 3″ chambers on 20 and .410 ga.; 2³/₄ chambers on others. Bi-Gauge models have two sets of barrels, one set in each gauge.

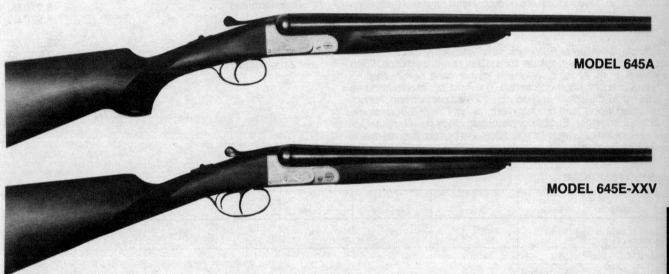

MODEL 645A

MODEL 645E-XXV

PARKER-HALE SIDE-BY-SIDE SHOTGUNS "600" SERIES

Model	Gauges	Action	Barrel Length	Price
640E (English)	12, 16, 20	Boxlock Ex.	26″, 28″	$ 564.95
640E (English)	28, .410	Boxlock Ex.	27″	634.95
640A (American)	12, 16, 20, 28, .410	Boxlock Ex.	26″, 28″	664.95
640A (American)	28, .410	Boxlock Ex.	27″	734.95
640M "Big Ten"	10 Magnum	Boxlock Ex.	30″ F/F	674.95
645E (Bi-Gauge)	20/28 or 28/410	Boxlock Ej.	26″	1299.95
645E (English)	12, 16, 20	Boxlock Ej.	26″, 28″	714.95
645E (English)	28, .410	Boxlock Ej.	27″	784.95
645A (American)	12, 16, 20	Boxlock Ej.	26″, 28″	814.95
645A (American)	28, .410	Boxlock Ej.	27″	884.95
645A (Bi-Gauge)	20/28 or 28/410	Boxlock Ej.	27″	1399.95
645E-XXV (English)	12, 16, 20	Boxlock Ej.	25″	744.95
645E-XXV (English)	28, .410	Boxlock Ej.	25″	814.95
670E (English)	12, 16, 20	Sidelock Ej.	26″, 28″	3100.00
670E (English)	28, .410	Sidelock Ej.	27″	3300.00
680E-XXV (English)	12, 16, 20	Sidelock Ej.	25″	2900.00
680E-XXV (English)	28, .410	Sidelock Ej.	25″	3100.00

* Ex.=Extractor; Ej.=Ejector

PARKER REPRODUCTIONS

PARKER A-1 SPECIAL

Recognized by the shooting fraternity as the finest American shotgun ever produced, the Parker A-1 Special is again available. Exquisite engraving and rare presentation grade French walnut distinguish the A-1 Special from any other shotguns in the world. Currently offered in 12, 20 and 28 gauge (.410 is pending). Each gun is custom-fitted in its own oak and leather trunk case. Two models are offered: Hand Engraved and Custom Engraved. Also available in B and D Grades. For specifications, see the table below.

Standard features: Automatic safety, selective ejectors, skeleton steel butt plate, splinter forend, engraved snap caps, fitted leather trunk case, canvas and leather case cover, chrome barrel interiors, hand-checkering. The A-1 Special also features a 24k gold initial plate or pistol cap, 32 lines per inch checkering, selected wood, and fine hand-engraving. Choose from single or double trigger, English or pistol grip stock (all models). Options include beavertail forend, additional barrels, internal screw chokes, vent rib.

Prices:
A-1 SPECIAL
 One barrel set . . . . $ 8,740.00
 Two barrel set 9,740.00
A-1 SPECIAL CUSTOM ENGRAVED . . . . From 10,500.00
B-GRADE BANK NOTE LTD. EDITION
 One barrel set 3,970.00
 Two sets of barrels 4,970.00
D-GRADE
 One barrel set $2,970.00
 Two sets of barrels 3,600.00
 12 ga. w/internal screw chokes 3,120.00

SPECIFICATIONS

Gauge	Barrel Length	Chokes	Chambers	Drop At Comb	Drop At Heel	Length of Pull	Nominal Weight	Overall Length
12	26	Skeet I & II or IC/M	2³/₄	1³/₈	2³/₁₆	14¹/₂	6³/₄	42⁵/₈
12	28	IC/M or M/F	2³/₄	1³/₈	2³/₁₆	14¹/₈	6³/₄	44⁵/₈
12+	28	Internal Screw Choke	3	1³/₈	2³/₁₆	14¹/₈	7+	44⁵/₈
12+	28	IC/M	3	1³/₈	2³/₁₆	14¹/₈	7+	44⁵/₈
20	26	Skeet I & II or IC/M	2³/₄	1³/₈	2³/₁₆	14³/₈	6¹/₂	42³/₈
20	28	M/F	3	1³/₈	2³/₁₆	14³/₈	6¹/₂	44⁵/₈
28	26	Skeet I & II or IC/M	2³/₄	1³/₈	2³/₁₆	14³/₈	5¹/₂	42⁵/₈
28	28	M/F	2³/₄	1³/₈	2³/₁₆	14¹/₈	5¹/₃	44⁵/₈
+28/.410	26	IC/M	3	1³/₈	2³/₁₆	14³/₈	5¹/₂	42⁵/₈
+28/.410	26	Skeet I & II	3	1³/₈	2³/₁₆	14³/₈	5¹/₂	42⁵/₈
*.410	26	IC/M	3	1³/₈	2³/₁₆	14³/₈	under 5	42⁵/₈
*.410	26	Skeet I & II	3	1³/₈	2³/₁₆	14³/₈	under 5	42⁵/₈

Note: *Dimensions may vary slightly as each stock is hand-carved.*
 + Steel Shot Special, 3-inch chambers, IC/M chokes—note weight
 ★ Sporting Clays Classic, six choke tubes: Skeet I, Skeet II, IC, M, IM, F

† .410 Bore barrels on 28 gauge, 00 frame
★ .410 Bore on 0000 frame, projected weight

PERAZZI SHOTGUNS

For the past 20 years or so, Perazzi has concentrated solely on manufacturing competition shotguns for the world market. Today the name has become synonymous with excellence in competitive shooting. The heart of the Perazzi line is the classic over/under, whose barrels are soldered into a monobloc that holds the shell extractors. At the sides are the two locking lugs that link the barrels to the action, which is machined from a solid block of forged steel. Barrels come with flat, step or raised ventilated rib. The walnut forend, finely checkered, is available with schnabel, beavertail or English styling, and the walnut stock can be of standard, Monte Carlo, Skeet or English design. Double or single non-selective or selective triggers. Sideplates and receiver are masterfully engraved and transform these guns into veritable works of art.

MODEL DB81 SPECIAL

AMERICAN TRAP STANDARD COMBO SET MODELS MX8 SPECIAL COMBO, MX3 SPECIAL COMBO, GRAND AMERICAN 88 SPECIAL COMBO & DB81 SPECIAL COMBO

SPECIFICATIONS
Gauge: 12
Chamber: 2¾"
Barrel lengths: 29½" and 31½" (O/U); 32" and 34" (single barrel)
Chokes: Mod./Full (O/U); Full (single barrel)
Trigger group: Detachable and interchangeable with flat "V" springs
Stock: Interchangeable and custom made

Forend: Beavertail
Weight: 8 lbs. 6 oz.
Prices:

Standard Grade	$ 6,650.00-11,550.00
SC3 Grade	10,950.00-11,550.00
SCO Grade	16,700.00-18,750.00
Gold Grade	18,550.00-20,650.00
Grand American 88 Special	7,650.00-20,150.00
DB81 Special	8,100.00-20,650.00

HUNTING MODEL MX20C

HUNTING MODELS MX12, MX12C, MX20, & MX20C

SPECIFICATIONS
Gauges: 12 (MX12 & MX12C); 20 (MX20 & MX20C); 28 & .410 (MX20)
Chambers: 2¾" (MX20 & MX20C also avail. in 3")
Barrel lengths: 26" (except MX12C) and 27" (MX12 & MX12C only)
Chokes: Mod./Full (MX12 & MX20); Chokes (MX12C & MX20C)
Trigger group: Non-detachable with coil springs and selective trigger

Stock: Interchangeable and custom made
Forend: Schnabel
Weight: 7 lbs. 4 oz. (MX12 & MX12C); 6 lbs. 6 oz. (MX20 & MX20C)
Prices:

Standard Grade	$ 5,200.00-	6,000.00
With gold outline	7,450.00-	8,550.00
SC3 Grade	9,000.00-	9,500.00
SCO Grade	15,200.00-	15,750.00

PERAZZI SHOTGUNS

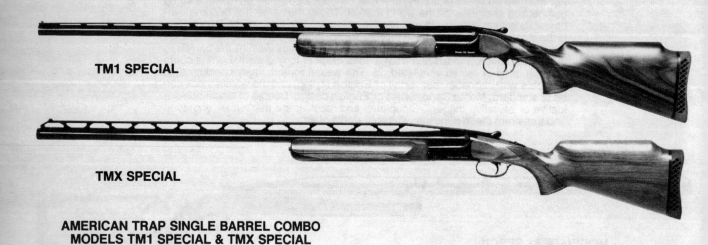

TM1 SPECIAL

TMX SPECIAL

AMERICAN TRAP SINGLE BARREL COMBO
MODELS TM1 SPECIAL & TMX SPECIAL
$4250.00

SPECIFICATIONS
Gauge: 12
Chamber: 2³/₄″
Barrel lengths: 32″ and 34″
Choke: Full

Trigger group: Detachable and interchangeable with coil springs
Stock: Interchangeable and custom made
Forend: Beavertail
Weight: 8 lbs. 6 oz.

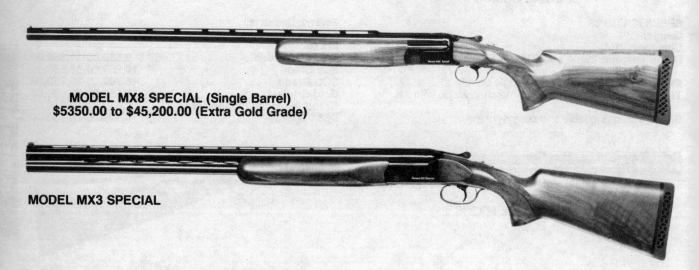

MODEL MX8 SPECIAL (Single Barrel)
$5350.00 to $45,200.00 (Extra Gold Grade)

MODEL MX3 SPECIAL

AMERICAN TRAP SINGLE BARREL MODELS
MX8 SPECIAL, MX3 SPECIAL & GRAND AMERICAN
88 SPECIAL

SPECIFICATIONS
Gauge: 12
Chamber: 2³/₄″
Barrel lengths: 32″ and 34″
Choke: Full
Trigger group: Detachable and interchangeable with flat "V" springs
Stock: Interchangeable and custom made
Forend: Beavertail
Weight: 8 lbs. 6 oz.

Prices:
Standard Grade . . . . $ 4,250.00- 7,950.00
SC3 Grade 8,000.00- 9,350.00
SCO Grade 12,350.00-15,550.00
Gold Grade 13,750.00-17,250.00
Also available:
SCO & Gold Grade Sideplates $22,800.00-26,450.00
Extra & Extra Gold Grades 41,850.00-45,700.00

PERAZZI SHOTGUNS

MX3 SPECIAL SPORTING

OLYMPIC TRAP OVER/UNDER MODELS
MX8-MX8 SPECIAL, MX3 SPECIAL & GRAND
AMERICAN 88 SPECIAL

SPECIFICATIONS
Gauge: 12
Chamber: 2³/₄″
Barrel lengths: 29¹/₂″ and 31¹/₂″ (Grand American 29¹/₂″ only)
Chokes: Imp./Mod. and X Full
Trigger group: Detachable & interchangeable with flat "V" springs
Stock: Interchangeable and custom made
Forend: Beavertail
Weight: 8 lbs. 4¹/₂ oz. (MX8); 8 lbs. 6 oz. (MX3 & Grand American)

Prices:
Model MX8 . . . . $5,350.00-15,400.00
Model MX8 Special 5,600.00-15,600.00
Model MX3 Special 5,330.00-14,750.00
Grand American 88 Special 5,600.00-15,400.00
Note: Gold Grade, SCO Grade or Gold Sideplates, Extra and Extra Gold Grade and O/U Sidelock Medals are also available at prices ranging from **$17,000.00 to $46,000.00.**

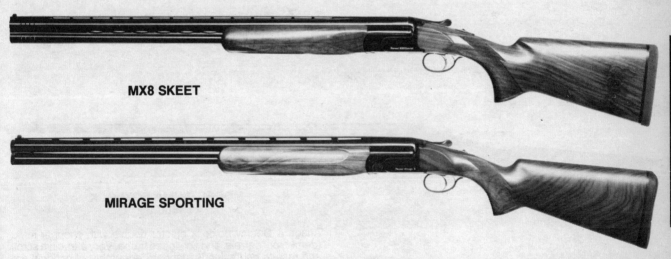

MX8 SKEET

MIRAGE SPORTING

AMERICAN SKEET MODELS MX8
& MIRAGE SPECIAL

SPECIFICATIONS
Gauge: 12
Chamber: 2³/₄″
Barrel length: 27⁵/₈″
Choke: Skeet/Skeet
Trigger group: Detachable and interchangeable with flat "V" springs
Stock: Interchangeable and custom made

Forend: Beavertail
Weight: 7 lbs. 15 oz.
Prices:
Standard Grade . . . . $ 5,030.00-18,650.00
SC3 Grade 8,250.00-18,350.00
SCO Grade 14,450.00-25,650.00
Gold Grade 16,200.00-27,700.00

PIOTTI SHOTGUNS

One of Italy's top gunmakers, Piotti limits its production to a small number of hand-crafted, best-quality double-barreled shotguns whose shaping, checkering, stock, action and barrel work meets or exceeds the standards achieved in London prior to WWII. The Italian engravings are the finest ever and are becoming recognized as an art form in themselves.

All of the sidelock models exhibit the same overall design, materials and standards of workmanship; they differ only in the quality of the wood, shaping and sculpturing of the action, type of engraving and gold inlay work and other details. The Model Piuma differs from the other shotguns only in its Anson & Deeley boxlock design.

SPECIFICATIONS
Gauges: 10, 12, 16, 20, 28, .410
Chokes: As ordered
Barrels: 12 ga., 25″ to 30″; other gauges, 25″ to 28″; chopper lump (demi-bloc) barrels with soft-luster blued finish; level, file-cut rib or optional concave or ventilated rib
Action: Boxlock, Anson & Deeley; Sidelock, Holland & Holland pattern; both have automatic ejectors, double triggers with front trigger hinged (non-selective single trigger optional), coin finish or optional color case-hardening
Stock: Hand-rubbed oil finish (or optional satin luster) on straight grip stock with checkered butt (pistol grip optional)
Forend: Classic (splinter); optional beavertail
Weight: Ranges from 4 lbs. 15 oz. (.410 ga.) to 8 lbs. (12 ga.)

MODEL MONTE CARLO SIDELOCK
$10,400.00

Best-quality Holland & Holland pattern sidelock ejector double with chopper lump barrels. Choice of Purdey-style scroll and rosette or Holland & Holland-style large scroll engraving.

MODEL PIUMA BOXLOCK
$6600.00

Anson & Deeley boxlock ejector double with chopper lump (demi-bloc) barrels, and scalloped frame. Very attractive scroll and rosette engraving is standard. A number of optional engraving patterns including game scene and gold inlays are available at additional cost.

PIOTTI SHOTGUNS

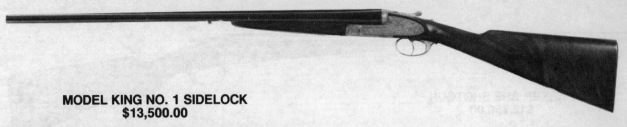

MODEL KING NO. 1 SIDELOCK
$13,500.00

Best-quality Holland & Holland pattern sidelock ejector double with chopper lump barrels, level file-cut rib, very fine, full coverage scroll engraving with small floral bouquets, gold crown in top lever, name in gold, and gold crest in forearm, finely figured wood.

MODEL LUNIK SIDELOCK
$14,400.00

Best-quality Holland & Holland pattern sidelock ejector double with chopper lump (demi-bloc) barrels, level, filecut rib, Renaissance-style, large scroll engraving in relief, gold crown in top lever, gold name, and gold crest in forearm, finely figured wood.

MODEL KING EXTRA (With Gold)
$20,000.00

Best-quality Holland & Holland pattern sidelock ejector double with chopper lump barrels, level filecut rib, choice of either bulino game scene engraving or game scene engraving with gold inlays, engraved and signed by a master engraver, exhibition grade wood.

REMINGTON SHOTGUNS

PARKER AHE SHOTGUN
$12,750.00

Produced by the Parker Gun Works (a division of Remington Arms Company at Ilion, N.Y.), this new version of a time-honored American firearms tradition is available in 20 gauge AHE Grade. It will be handcrafted in limited quantities on special order from the Remington Custom Shop. The Parker model features a new single selective trigger mechanism, the first new side-by-side trigger design in over 60 years. Automatic ejectors have a more simplified and reliable design, as do the updated automatic safeties. Stocks are produced from highly select Circassian or American walnut, and custom checkering

(28 lines/inch) adorns both forend and butt stock, with AHE-grade side panels on each side of the tang. Fine-scroll engraving and game scenes decorate the casehardened receivers.

Additional specifications include **Barrel length:** 28″. **Chambers:** 2³/₄″. **Weight:** 6¹/₂ lbs. Raised ventilated ribs are standard, with front and mid-barrel ivory beads. Customers may specify stock dimensions and any combination of chokes, including Skeet, Improved Cylinder, Modified and Full.

MODEL 870 EXPRESS MAGNUM

MODEL 870 EXPRESS (12 GAUGE)
$326.00

Model 870 Express features the same action as the Wingmaster and is available with 3″ chamber and 28″ vent-rib barrel only. It has a hardwood stock with low-luster finish and solid butt pad. Choke is Modified REM Choke tube and wrench. **Overall length:** 48¹/₂″. **Weight:** 7¹/₄ lbs.

MODEL 870 EXPRESS COMBO (not shown)
$349.00

Model 870 Express offers all the features of the standard Model 870, including twin-action bars, quick-changing barrels, REM Choke plus low-luster, checkered hardwood stock and no-shine finish on barrel and receiver. The Model 870 Combo is packaged with an extra 20″ deer barrel, fitted with rifle sights and fixed, Improved Cylinder choke (additional REM chokes can be added for special applications). The 3-inch chamber handles all 12 gauge ammo without adjustment.

REMINGTON PUMP SHOTGUNS

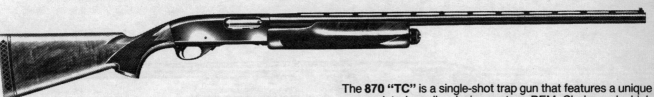

MODEL 870 "TC" TRAP (12 GAUGE ONLY)
$572.00   ($585.00 w/Monte Carlo Stock)

The **870 "TC"** is a single-shot trap gun that features a unique gas-assisted recoil-reducing system, REM, Choke and a high step-up ventilated rib. REM chokes include regular full, extra full and super full. **Stock:** Redesigned stock and forend of select American walnut with cut-checkering and satin finish; length of pull 14³/₈"; drop at heel 1⁷/₈"; drop at comb 1³/₈". **Weight:** 8¹/₂ lbs. **Barrel length:** 30".

Also available in **Fixed Full Choke: $559.00**; with Monte Carlo stock: **$572.00.**

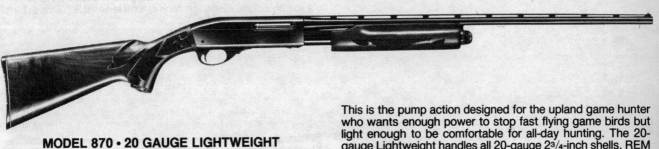

MODEL 870 • 20 GAUGE LIGHTWEIGHT
$439.00

This is the pump action designed for the upland game hunter who wants enough power to stop fast flying game birds but light enough to be comfortable for all-day hunting. The 20-gauge Lightweight handles all 20-gauge 2³/₄-inch shells. REM choke and ventilated rib. **Stock:** American walnut stock and forend. **Barrel lengths:** 26" and 28". **Average weight:** 6 lbs.

MODEL 870 "YOUTH" GUN
20 Gauge Lightweight
$423.00

The Model 870 "Youth" Gun brings Remington's pump action perfection to a whole new range of shooters. The Model 870 shotgun has been specially designed for youths and smaller-sized adults. It's a 20-gauge lightweight with a 1-inch shorter stock and 5-inch shorter barrel. Yet it is still all 870, complete with REM Choke and ventilated rib barrel. **Barrel length:** 21". **Stock Dimensions:** Length of pull 12¹/₂" (including recoil pad); drop at heel; 2¹/₂" drop at comb 1⁵/₈". **Overall length:** 40". **Average Weight:** 6 lbs. **Choke:** Mod. and Imp. Cyl.

REMINGTON PUMP SHOTGUNS

MODEL 870 WINGMASTER 12 GAUGE
$439.00 ($495.00 Left Hand)

This new restyled 870 "Wingmaster" pump has cut checkering on its satin finished American walnut stock and forend for confident handling, even in wet weather. An ivory bead "Bradley" type front sight is included. Rifle is available with 26", 28" and 30" barrel with REM Choke and handles 3" and 2¾" shells interchangeably. **Overall length:** 46½ (26" barrel), 48½" (28" barrel), 50½ (30" barrel). **Weight:** 7¼ lbs.

Also available: **WINGMASTER DEER GUN** with Imp. Cyl. and rifle sights, 12 gauge only. **Barrel length:** 20". **Price:** Left-hand model: **$454.00**

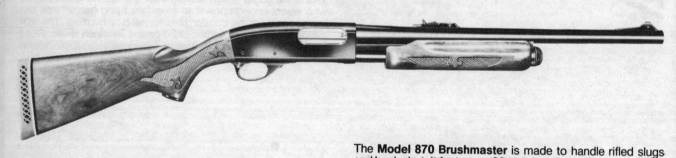

MODEL 870 DEER GUN
$414.00 ($386.00 in Lightweight 20 Ga.)

The **Model 870 Brushmaster** is made to handle rifled slugs and buck shot. It features a 20-inch barrel with 3-inch chamber and fully adjustable rifle-type sights. Stock fitted with rubber recoil pad and white-line spacer. Also available in standard model, but with lacquer finish, no checkering, recoil pad, grip cap; special handy short forend. **Choke:** Imp. Cyl. **Weight:** 6¼ lbs.

TURKEY EXTRA FULL "REM" CHOKE TUBE

STANDARD "REM" CHOKE TUBE

REMINGTON PUMP SHOTGUNS

MODEL 870 SPECIAL FIELD
$439.00

The **Model 870 "Special Field"** shotgun combines the traditional, straight-stock styling of years past with features never before available on a Remington pump. Its 21-inch vent rib barrel, slimmed and shortened forend, straight, cut-checkered stock offers upland hunters a quick, fast-pointing shotgun. The

"Special Field" is chambered for 3-inch shells and will also handle all 2¾-inch shells interchangeably. Barrels will not interchange with standard 870 barrels. **Overall length:** 41½". **Weight:** 7 lbs. (12 ga.); 6 lbs. (20 ga.).

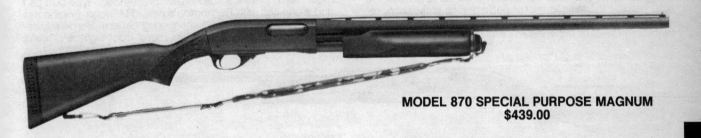

MODEL 870 SPECIAL PURPOSE MAGNUM
$439.00

Available in 12 gauge Magnum with 3-inch Mag. chamber, the **Model 870 SP (Special Purpose) Magnum** pump gun has been designed with waterfowlers and turkey hunters in mind. For concealment, all metal surfaces have been finished in non-glare, non-reflective Parkerized black. And all wood surfaces have been given a dull, non-reflective oil finish with a slightly rough feel for firmer grip. For ease of carrying, the SP Mag. Pump comes factory-equipped with a camo-patterned padded

sling, attached at both ends by quick-detachable sling swivels. More than 2 inches wide at the shoulder, the sling is made of durable Du Pont nylon "Cordura." **Barrel:** 26" or 30" chrome-lined barrel bore; ventilated rib. **Choke:** Full. **Stock:** Supplied with dark-colored recoil pad and black line spacers. **Overall length:** 46½" with 26" barrel; 50½" with 30" barrel. **Weight:** Approx. 7¼ lbs.

MODEL 870 SPECIAL PURPOSE DEER GUN
$414.00

Gauge: 12. **Choke:** Imp. Cyl. Equipped with rifle sights, recoil pad. **Barrel length:** 20". **Overall length:** 40½." **Average weight:** 7 lbs. **Price:** With cantilever barrel for scope mounting and Extra Full Turkey choke $476.00.

REMINGTON SHOTGUNS
MODEL 11-87 PREMIER

MODEL 11-87 "PREMIER" AUTOLOADER
(3" Chamber)
$559.00 ($612.00 Left Hand)

Model 11-87 "Premier" with REM Choke offers the dependability of a pump along with the easy shootability of an autoloader, the magnum power of a waterfowl gun, and the light handling of an upland gun. This new shotgun's standout attraction to the practical shooter is its ability to handle a broad variety of 12-gauge ammunition interchangeably. Switching from light, 2¾" field loads to heavy 3" magnums is simply a matter of inserting different shotgun shells. A new, patented pressure compensating gas system accomplishes this without the need for adjustments. An additional bonus to shooters is a 50 percent increase in overall performance endurance, revealed by extensive testing. Among the factors contributing to this high level of dependability and durability are:

- Extractor 30 percent thicker
- A redesigned, more durable firing pin retractor spring
- Heat treated pistol and piston seal
- Corrosion and rust resistant stainless steel magazine tube

The standard version of the 11-87 "Premier" shotgun is available in three ventilated rib barrel lengths: 26", 28" and 30"—all with REM Choke. A left-hand mirror image version is available in 28" only. The stock is satin finished with new cut-checkering (20 lines per inch), featuring a "floating diamond" motif. Also, there's a solid brown presentation-type butt pad and a grip cap with Remington's new "RA" logo. Forend has the same satin finish and checkering pattern. Barrel and receiver have Bradley-type white-faced front sight and metal bead on barrel.

MODEL 11-87 PREMIER TRAP 12 GAUGE
$618.00
$633.00 (w/Monte Carlo Stock)

A 30" trap barrel offers trap shooters a REM Choke system with three interchangeable choke constrictions: trap full, trap extra full, and trap super full.

Also available in **Fixed Full Trap Choke: $605.00**; with Monte Carlo stock: **$618.00**

MODEL 11-87 PREMIER SHOTGUNS

Gauge	Barrel Length & Choke	Overall length	Avg. Wt. (lbs.)
	30" REM Choke	50½	8⅜
12	28" REM Choke	48¼	8¼
	28" REM Choke	48¼	8¼
	26" REM Choke	46	8⅛

EXTRA BARRELS. 11-87 barrels are not interchangeable with the Remington Model 1100. Also, target barrels are designed for optimal performance with target loads and therefore are not pressure compensated. These guns will, however, be pressure compensating and shoot all 12-gauge loads when equipped with an 11-87 Premier field barrel.

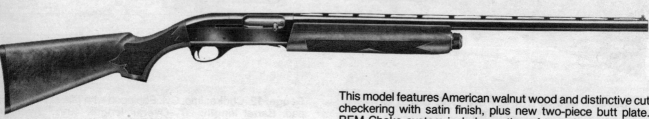

MODEL 11-87 PREMIER SKEET 12 GAUGE
$612.00

This model features American walnut wood and distinctive cut checkering with satin finish, plus new two-piece butt plate. REM Choke system includes option of two skeet chokes—skeet and improved skeet. Trap and skeet guns are designed for 12-gauge target loads and are set to handle 2¾" shells only.

Also available in **Fixed Skeet Choke: $597.00**.

REMINGTON SHOTGUNS

MODEL 11-87 SPECIAL PURPOSE MAGNUM
$559.00

Features non-reflective wood and metal finish for all types of hunting where concealment is critical. Exposed metal surfaces of both barrel and receiver are Parkerized; bolt and carrier have non-glare blackened coloring. **Barrel lengths:** 26″ and 30″. **Chamber:** 3″. **Choke:** REM Choke.

MODEL 11-87 SPECIAL PURPOSE DEER GUN
3″ MAGNUM
$543.00

Features same finish as other SP models plus a padded, camostyle carrying sling of Cordura nylon with Q.D. sling swivels. Barrel is 21″ with rifle sights and slug choke (handles all 2³/₄″ and 3″ rifled slug and buckshot loads as well as high-velocity field and magnum loads; does not function with light 2³/₄″ field loads).

Also available with cantilever barrel and rings for scope mount. Includes interchangeable rifled and IC "REM" chokes. **Price: $596.00.**

SP-10 MAGNUM SHOTGUN
$1265.00

Remington's new SP-10 Magnum is the only gas-operated semiautomatic 10 gauge shotgun made today. Engineered to shoot steel shot, the SP-10 delivers up to 34 percent more pellets to the target than standard 12 gauge shotgun and steel shot combinations. This autoloader features a non-corrosive, stainless steel gas system, in which the cylinder moves—not the piston. This reduces felt recoil energy by spreading the recoil over a longer period of time. The SP-10 has a ³/₈″ vent rib with middle and front sights for a better sight plane. It is also designed to appear virtually invisible to the sharp eyes of waterfowl. The American walnut stock and forend have a protective, low-gloss satin finish that reduces glare, and positive deep-cut checkering for a sure grip. The receiver and barrel have a matte finish, and the stainless steel breech bolt features a non-reflective finish. Remington's new autoloader also has a brown vented recoil pad and a padded camo sling of Cordura nylon for easy carrying. The receiver is machined from a solid billet of ordnance steel for total integral strength. The SP-10 vented gas system reduces powder residue buildup and makes cleaning easier.

Gauge: 10. **Barrel lengths & choke:** 26″ REM Choke and 30″ REM Choke. **Overall length:** 51¹/₂″ (30″ barrel) and 47¹/₂″ (26″ barrel). **Weight:** 11¹/₄ lbs. (30″ barrel) and 11 lbs. (26″ barrel).

REMINGTON AUTOLOADING SHOTGUNS

MODEL 1100 AUTOLOADING SHOTGUNS

The Remington Model 1100 is a 5-shot gas-operated auto-loading shotgun with a gas metering system designed to reduce recoil effect. This design enables the shooter to use all 2¾-inch standard velocity "Express" and 2¾-inch Magnum loads without any gun adjustments. Barrels, within gauge and versions, are interchangeable. The 1100 is made in gauges of 12, 20, Lightweight 20, 28 and .410. All 12 and 20 gauge versions include REM Choke; interchangeable choke tubes in 26″, 28″ and 30″ (12 gauge only) barrels. The solid-steel receiver features decorative scroll work. Stocks come with fine-line checkering in a fleur-de-lis design combined with American walnut and a scratch-resistant finish. Features include white-diamond inlay in pistol-grip cap, white-line spacers, full bea-vertail forend, fluted-comb cuts, chrome-plated bolt and metal bead front sight. Made in U.S.A.

MODEL 1100 SPECIAL FIELD (12 GAUGE)
$545.00

The **Model 1100 "Special Field"** shotgun combines traditional, straight-stock styling with its 21-inch vent-rib barrel and slimmed and shortened forend, which offer upland hunters a quick, fast-pointing shotgun. Non-engraved receiver; non-Magnum extra barrels are interchangeable with standard Model 1100 barrels. **Overall length:** 41″. **Stock dimensions:** Length of pull 14⅛″; drop at comb 1½″; drop at heel 2½″. **Choke:** REM Choke system. **Weight:** 7¼ lbs. (12 ga.); 6½ lbs. (20 ga.).

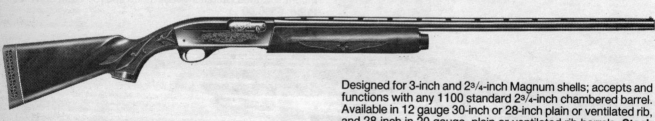

MODEL 1100 3″ MAGNUM
20 & Lightweight 20 Gauges
$545.00

Designed for 3-inch and 2¾-inch Magnum shells; accepts and functions with any 1100 standard 2¾-inch chambered barrel. Available in 12 gauge 30-inch or 28-inch plain or ventilated rib, and 28-inch in 20 gauge, plain or ventilated rib barrels. **Stock dimensions:** 14″ long including pad; 1½″ drop at comb; furnished with recoil pad. **Weight:** About 8 lbs., 12 ga.; 6¾ lbs., 20 ga.

MODEL 1100 DEER GUN
Lightweight 20 Gauges
$492.00

Features 20-inch (LT-20 gauge) barrels, Improved Cylinder choke. Rifle sights adjustable for windage and elevation. Recoil pad. Choked for both rifled slugs and buck shot. **Weight:** 6½ lbs. **Overall length:** 40″.

REMINGTON AUTOLOADING SHOTGUNS

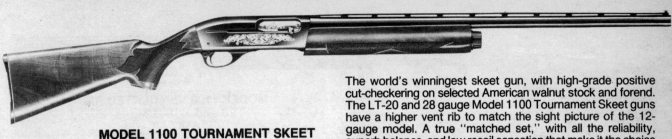

MODEL 1100 TOURNAMENT SKEET
$618.00

The world's winningest skeet gun, with high-grade positive cut-checkering on selected American walnut stock and forend. The LT-20 and 28 gauge Model 1100 Tournament Skeet guns have a higher vent rib to match the sight picture of the 12-gauge model. A true "matched set," with all the reliability, superb balance, and low recoil sensation that make it the choice of over 50% of the entrants in the world skeet shooting championships. Available in LT-20 and 28 gauges. **Barrel length:** 26" 5. **Choke:** REM Choke. **Weight:** 6¾ lbs. (20 ga.), 6½ lbs. (28 ga.).

MODEL 1100 TOURNAMENT SKEET
Small Gauge
$618.00

Quality and economy, American walnut stock and forend, and receiver engraving identical to that of the higher grade models distinguish this SA Grade Model 1100 auto Skeet gun. Available in 28 ga., and .410 bore. **Stock dimensions:** Length of pull 14"; drop at heel 2½"; drop at comb 1½". **Barrel length:** 25". **Choke:** Skeet.

MODEL 1100 LT-20 YOUTH GUN • LIGHTWEIGHT
20 Gauge Only
$532.00

The Model 1100 LT-20 Youth Gun autoloading shotgun features a shorter barrel (21") and stock. **Overall length:** 39½". **Weight:** 6½ lbs.

REMINGTON SHOTGUNS

MODEL 1100 VENTILATED RIB
28 and .410 Gauges
$587.00

The Remington Model 1100 Autoloading shotguns in 28 and .410 gauges are scaled-down models of the 12-gauge version. Built on their own receivers and frames, these small gauge shotguns are available in full (.410 only) and modified chokes with either plain or ventilated rib barrels.

SPECIFICATIONS. Type: Gas-operated. **Capacity:** 5-shot with 28 ga. shells; 4-shot with 3" .410 ga. shells; 3-shot plug furnished. **Barrel:** 25" of special Remington ordnance steel; extra barrels interchangeable within gauge. **Chamber:** 3" in .410, 2³/₄" in 28 ga. **Overall length:** 45". **Safety:** Convenient cross-bolt type. **Receiver:** Made from solid steel, top matted, scroll work on bolt and both sides of receiver. **Stock dimensions:** Walnut; 14" long; 2¹/₂" drop at heel; 1¹/₂" drop at comb. **Average weight:** 6¹/₂ lbs. (28 ga.); 7 lbs. (.410).

ROSSI SHOTGUNS

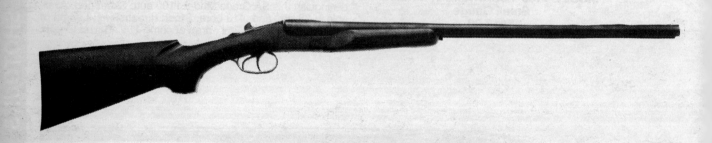

THE SQUIRE

SQUIRE DOUBLE. Available in .410 bore or 12 or 20 gauge, the Squire has 3-inch chambers to handle the full range of shotgun loads. Features double triggers, raised matted rib, beavertail forend and pistol grip. Twin underlugs mesh with synchronized sliding bolts for double-safe solid lockup.

Gauge	Barrel Length	Choke	Price
12	20"	IC&M	$340.00
12	28"	M&F	340.00
20	26"	IC&M	340.00
.410 bore	26"	F&F	345.00

RUGER SHOTGUNS

No Slots

3 Slots

2 Slots

1 Slot

RUGER RED LABEL OVER/UNDER 20 GAUGE
$920.00

Hardened chrome molybdenum, other alloy steels and music wire coil springs are used throughout. Features single-selective trigger, automatic top safety, standard gold bead front sight. Stock and semi-beavertail forearm are shaped from American walnut with hand-cut checkering (20 lines per inch). Pistol grip cap and rubber recoil pad are standard, and all wood surfaces are polished and beautifully finished. Stainless steel receiver available on 12 gauge version; 20 gauge is satin polished and blued. Also available in 12 gauge with **stainless receiver: $920.00**

RUGER SCREW-IN CHOKE INSERTS

Designed especially for the popular 12 gauge "Red Label" over/under shotgun. Easily installed with a key wrench packaged with each shotgun. Choke fits flush with the muzzle. Every shotgun is equipped with a Full, Modified, Improved Cylinder and two Skeet screw-in chokes. The muzzle edge of the chokes has been slotted for quick identification in or out of the barrels. Full choke has 3 slots; Modified has 2 slots, and Improved Cylinder has 1 slot (Skeet has no slots).

Models with Screw-in Chokes $1050.00

SPECIFICATIONS
RUGER OVER & UNDER SHOTGUN SPECIFICATIONS

Catalog Number	Gauge	Chamber	Choke	Barrel Length	Overall Length	Length of Pull	Drop at Comb	Drop at Heel	Sights	Weight
RL 2008	20	3″	F&M	28″	45″	14″	1 1/2″	2 1/2″	GBF	7 lbs.
RL-2016	20	3″	IC&M	26″	43″	14″	1 1/2″	2 1/2″	GBF	7 lbs.
RL-2018	20	3″	IC&M	28″	45″	14″	1 1/2″	2 1/2″	GBF	7 lbs.
RL-2026	20	3″	S/S	26″	43″	14″	1 1/2″	2 1/2″	GBF	7 lbs.
RL-2028	20	3″	S/S	28″	45″	14″	1 1/2″	2 1/2″	GBF	7 lbs.
Stainless Steel										
KRL-1232	12	3″	F&M	26″	42 7/8″	14″	1 1/2″	2 1/2″	GBF	7 1/2 lbs.
KRL-1235	12	3″	F&M	28″	44 7/8″	14″	1 1/2″	2 1/2″	GBF	7 1/2 lbs.
KRL-1230	12	3″	IC&M	26″	42 7/8″	14″	1 1/2″	2 1/2″	GBF	7 1/2 lbs.
KRL-1233	12	3″	IC&M	28″	44 7/8″	14″	1 1/2″	2 1/2″	GBF	7 1/2 lbs.
KRL-1231	12	3″	S/S	26″	42 7/8″	14″	1 1/2″	2 1/2″	GBF	7 1/2 lbs.
KRL-1234	12	3″	S/S	28″	44 7/8″	14″	1 1/2″	2 1/2″	GBF	7 1/2 lbs.
Screw-in Chokes										
KRL-1226	12	3″	F,M,IC,S	26″	42 7/8″	14″	1 1/2″	2 1/2″	GBF	7 1/2 lbs.
KRL-1227	12	3″	F,M,IC,S	28″	42 7/8″	14″	1 1/2″	2 1/2″	GBF	7 1/2 lbs.

F-Full, M-Modified, IC-Improved Cylinder, S-Skeet, GBF-Gold Bead Front Sight

SILMA OVER/UNDER SHOTGUNS

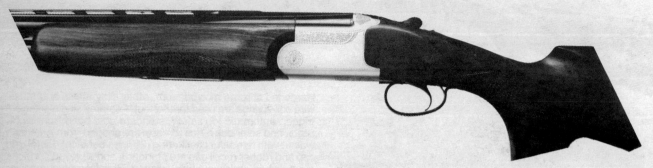

MODEL 70

SPECIFICATIONS
Gauges: 12, 20, .410
Barrel length: 27⁵/₈″
Chambers: 2³/₄″ and 3″
Chokes: Mod./IM and IM/Full
Weight: 7 lbs. (approx.)
Trigger: Single/double selective single trigger
Stock: Full pistol grip or straight hand

Prices:
MODEL 70—12 ga., std., extractor, double
trigger **$363.00**
With side plates **414.00**
With automatic ejectors **429.00**
Same as above with side plates **480.00**
MODEL 70—20 ga., std. extractor, double
trigger **416.00**
With automatic ejectors **494.00**
MODEL 70—.410 ga., std. extractor, double
trigger **457.00**
With automatic ejectors **544.00**
MODEL T.J. 70—competition trap/skeet **715.00**

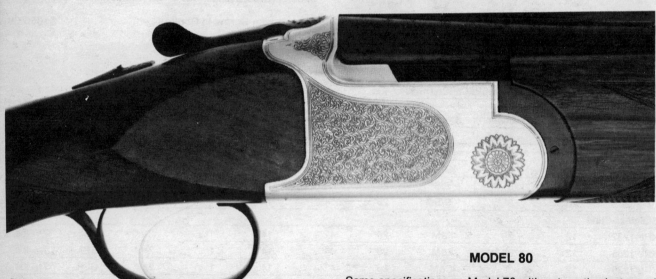

MODEL 80

Same specifications as Model 70 with automatic ejector and double triggers, but features English-style engraved body action, side plates and longer hinge pins (to increase wear resistance). Also features hand-checkered stock and forend, gold-plated trigger and ventilated ribs.

Price:
MODEL 80—12 Gauge **$504.00**
MODEL 80—20 Gauge **579.00**

SKB SHOTGUNS

GAS-OPERATED AUTOMATICS FOR FIELD & TRAP

MODEL 1900

Same specifications as Model 1300, but includes Field Outdoor Scene engraved on receiver with gold trigger and Interchoke.
Price: $550.00
Also available: **DELUXE AUTO TRAP** (12 ga. only with 2³/₄″ chamber).

MODEL 3000 (not shown)

Same specifications as Models 1300 and 1900, but with Field Presentation features.
Also available: **PRESENTATION AUTO TRAP** (12 ga. only with 2³/₄″ chamber).

MODEL 1300 (not shown)

SPECIFICATIONS
Gauges: 12 and 20
Chambers: 3″
Choke: Interchoke
Barrel lengths: 26″ and 28″ (Field); 30″ (Trap)
Overall length: 48¼″ (Field); 50¹¹/₁₆″ (Trap)
Weight: 6 lbs. 6 oz. (20 ga.); 7 lbs. 4 oz. (12 ga.)
Also available: **SLUG GUN** with sights (22″ barrel), 12 ga. only.

Also available: **SLUG GUN** with sights (22″ barrel), 12 ga. only:
    $499.00

OVER & UNDER TRAP GUNS

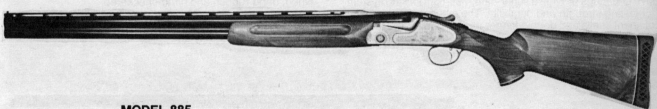

MODEL 885

SPECIFICATIONS
Gauge: 12
Chambers: 2³/₄″
Choke: Interchoke
Barrel lengths: 30″, 32″, 34″
Overall length: 47³/₈″
Weight: 8 lbs. 2 oz.
Stock: Standard or Monte Carlo
Finish: Silver engraved receiver

Also available: **MODEL 605**—Same specifications as Model 885, but without engraving on side plate. **MODEL 505**—Same specifications as Models 885 and 605, but with blued receiver.

STOEGER SHOTGUNS

CONDOR I OVER/UNDER SINGLE TRIGGER
Available in 12 and 20 Gauge
$450.00

The **STOEGER OVER/UNDER SINGLE TRIGGER** is a workhorse of a shotgun, designed for maximum dependability in heavy field use. The super-safe lock-up system makes use of a sliding underlug, the best system for over/under shotguns. A massive monobloc joins the barrel in a solid one-piece assembly at the breech end. Reliability is assured, thanks to the mechanical extraction system. Upon opening the breech, the spent shells are partially lifted from the chamber, allowing easy removal by hand. Stoeger barrels are of chrome-moly steel with micro-polished bores to give tight, consistent patterns.

They are specifically formulated for use with steel shot where Federal migratory bird regulations require. Atop the barrel is a sighting rib with an anti-glare surface. The buttstock and forend are of durable hardwood, hand-checkered and finished with an oil-based formula that takes dents and scratches in stride.

The Stoeger over/under shotgun is available in 12 or 20 gauge with 26-inch barrels choked Imp. Cyl./Mod. with 3-inch chambers; 12 or 20 gauge with 28-inch barrels choked Mod./Full, 3-inch chambers.

COACH GUN
Available in 12, 20 and .410 Gauge
$285.00

The **STOEGER CLASSIC SIDE-BY-SIDE COACH GUN** sports a 20-inch barrel. Lightning fast, it is the perfect shotgun for hunting upland game in dense brush or close quarters. This endurance-tested workhorse of a gun is designed from the ground up to give you years of trouble-free service. Two massive underlugs provide a super-safe, vise-tight locking system for lasting strength and durability. The mechanical extraction of spent shells and double-trigger mechanism assure reliability. The automatic safety is actuated whenever the action is opened, whether or not the gun has been fired. The polish and blue is deep and rich, and the solid sighting rib is matte-finished for glare-free sighting. Chrome-moly steel barrels with micro-polished bores give dense, consistent patterns. The classic stock and forend are of durable hardwood . . . oil finished, hand-rubbed and hand-checkered.

Improved Cylinder/Modified choking and its short barrel make the Stoeger coach gun the ideal choice for hunting in close quarters, security and police work. 3-inch chambers.

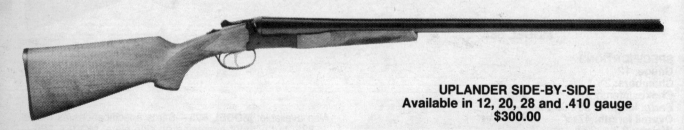

UPLANDER SIDE-BY-SIDE
Available in 12, 20, 28 and .410 gauge
$300.00

The **STOEGER SIDE-BY-SIDE** is a rugged shotgun, endurance-tested and designed to give years of trouble-free service. A vise-tight, super-safe locking system is provided by two massive underlugs for lasting strength and durability. Two design features which make the Stoeger a standout for reliability are its positive mechanical extraction of spent shells and its traditional double-trigger mechanism. The safety is automatic in that every time the action is opened, whether the gun has been fired or not, the safety is actuated. The polish and blue is deep and rich. The solid sighting rib carries a machined-in matte finish for glare-free sighting. Barrels are of chrome-moly steel with micro-polished bores to give dense, consistent patterns. The stock and forend are of classic design in durable hardwood . . . oil finished, hand-rubbed and hand-checkered.

STOEGER SHOTGUNS

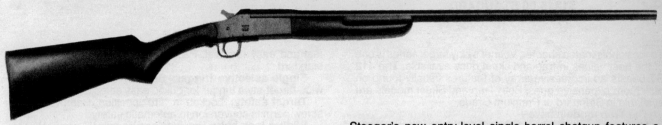

SINGLE BARREL
$110.00

Stoeger's new entry-level single barrel shotgun features a unique locking system. By pulling rearward on the trigger guard, the underlug engagement is released, thus opening the action. Single mechanical extraction makes for convenient removal of spent shells. For ease of operation and maximum safety, this single barrel shotgun is equipped with an exposed hammer, which must be cocked manually. A half-cocked setting on the hammer provides the safety mode.

The buttstock and semi-beavertail forearm are of durable Brazilian hardwood. Stoeger's new single barrel shotgun is available in 12, 20 gauge, and .410 bore.

STOEGER SHOTGUN SPECIFICATIONS

Model	Gauge	Chokes	Chamber	Barrel Length	Length of Pull	Drop at Comb	Drop at Heel	Approx. Average Weight	Safety	Extractors
Single Barrel	12	M, F, IC	2³/₄″	28″/26″	14¹/₂″	1¹/₂″	2¹/₂″	5¹/₈ lbs.	Manual	Yes
	20	M, F, IC	3″	28″/26″	14¹/₂″	1¹/₂″	2¹/₂″	5¹/₈ lbs.	Manual	Yes
	.410	M, F, IC	3″	28″	14¹/₂″	1¹/₂″	2¹/₂″	5¹/₈ lbs.	Manual	Yes
Side-by-Side	12	M/F IC&M	3″	28″/26″	14¹/₂″	1¹/₂″	2¹/₂″	7 lbs.	Automatic	Yes
	20	M/F IC&M	3″	28″/26″	14¹/₂″	1¹/₂″	2¹/₂″	6³/₄ lbs.	Automatic	Yes
	28	IC/M	2³/₄″	26″	14¹/₂″	1¹/₂″	2¹/₂″	7 lbs.	Automatic	Yes
	.410	F/F, IC/M	3″	26″	14¹/₂″	1¹/₂″	2¹/₂″	7 lbs.	Automatic	Yes
Over/Under	12	M/F IC&M	3″	28″/26″	14¹/₂″	1¹/₂″	2¹/₂″	7 lbs.	Manual	Yes
	20	M/F IC/M	3″	28″/26″	14¹/₂″	1¹/₂″	2¹/₂″	7 lbs.	Automatic	Yes
Coach Gun	12	M/F IC/M	3″	20″	14¹/₂″	1¹/₂″	2¹/₂″	6³/₄ lbs.	Automatic	Yes
Coach Gun	12	IC&M	3″	20″	14¹/₂″	1¹/₂″	2¹/₂″	6¹/₂ lbs.	Automatic	Yes
	20	IC&M	3″	20″	14¹/₂″	1¹/₂″	2¹/₂″	6¹/₂ lbs.	Automatic	Yes
	20	M/F IC/M	3″	20″	14¹/₂″	1¹/₂″	2¹/₂″	6³/₄ lbs.	Automatic	Yes

SHOTGUNS

VALMET SHOTGUNS

VALMET 412 ST TRAP & SKEET
$1215.00 STANDARD
$1550.00 PREMIUM

To the sophisticated shooter, Valmet's clay target series is one of the best values in trap and skeet guns available. The 412 ST boasts an impressive array of features usually found on only more expensive guns. Both Trap and Skeet models are available in Standard or Premium Grade.

The **Trap models** have—

High stepped, tapered vent rib: Gets the shooter "on target" quickly. Cross-file pattern reduces glare and improves heat dissipation. Fluorescent front and metal middle beads are standard.

Perfectly balanced: Lines up easily, swings smoothly and provides a superior sighting plane.

Reliable and durable 412 action: Designed to withstand large centerfire rifle calibers. Incorporates precision honing to ensure satisfaction from demanding competitive shooters.

Mechanical triggers: Not dependent upon the inertia from recoil to reset the trigger. Provides a faster and more reliable second shot.

Elongated forcing cones: Greatly reduce recoil.

Stainless steel screw-in choke tubes: Add versatility; corrosion-resistant stainless steel gives added strength over common carbon or alloy steel.

American walnut stock: Double palm swells for both right- and left-handed shooters with Monte Carlo and full comb stock in trap models. Quick-change stock bolt and key permit fast and easy removal. Pachmayr competition recoil pad is standard.

Single selective trigger: Selector button is located on wide target-style trigger for quick, easy selection.

Target safety: Locked in "fire" position. Removal of set screw permits conversion to automatic safety.

Sliding lock bolt: Provides secure barrel lockup. Wears in, not loose.

Steel receiver: Forged and machined for durability.

Automatic ejectors: Eject fired rounds.

Two-piece firing pin: For better durability.

Trap combo sets: Lets the shooter add barrels; precision tolerances require only minor initial fitting.

Skeet 12 and 20 gauge: Start with the gauge of your choice and add the other barrel/gauge at your convenience.

Premium Grade Models: Offer additional features such as Select, semi-fancy American walnut stock and forearm.

Matte nickel receiver: More resistant to wear and corrosion.

Matte blued locking bolt and lever: With non-reflective finish.

Pre-drilled stock: 1-inch diameter hole is provided for insertion of recoil reducer.

Gold trigger: For a subtle touch of class.

Stock wrist checkering: For improved grip.

MODEL 412 ST PREMIUM GRADE SKEET

SPECIFICATIONS MODEL 412 ST PREMIUM & STANDARD GRADE SKEET

Gauges: 12 and 20
Chambers: 2³/₄"
Barrel length: 28"
Chokes: Stainless steel, screw-in Skeet/Skeet
Weight: 8 lbs.
Stock: Premium Grade, Select semi-fancy American walnut; Standard Garde, American walnut

Length of pull: 14¹/₈"
Drop at comb: 1¹/₂"
Drop at heel: 2¹/₈"
Trigger: Single selective mechanical

VALMET SHOTGUNS

MODEL 412 ST STANDARD MONO TRAP

SPECIFICATIONS MODEL 412 ST PREMIUM GRADE TRAP

Gauge: 12
Chambers: 2³/₄″
Barrel lengths: 30″ and 32″
Chokes: Stainless steel, screw-in M, IM, F
Weight: 9 lbs.
Stock: Select semi-fancy American walnut
Length of pull: 14⁵/₈″

Drop at comb: 1¹/₂″
Drop at heel: 1¹/₂″
Trigger: Single selective mechanical
Combo sets: 30″ o/u bbl. w/32″ or 34″ single bbl.
32″ o/u bbl. w/32″ or 34″ single bbl.
Optional hard case available

SPECIFICATIONS MODEL 412 ST STANDARD GRADE TRAP

Gauge: 12
Chambers: 2³/₄″
Barrel lengths: 30″ and 32″
Chokes: Stainless steel, screw-in M, IM, F
Weight: 9 lbs.
Stock: American walnut
Length of pull: 14⁵/₈″

Drop at comb: 1¹/₂″
Drop at heel: 1¹/₂″
Trigger: Single selective mechanical
Combo sets: 30″ o/u bbl. w/32″ or 34″ single bbl.
32″ o/u bbl. w/32″ or 34″ single bbl.
Optional hard case available

VALMET 412S SHOTGUN/RIFLE
$1165.00

Valmet's unique 412S Shotgun/Rifle combination continues to be the most popular gun of its type in the U.S. Its features are identical to the 412S Field Grade over/under shotguns, including strong steel receiver, superior sliding locking mechanism with automatic safety, cocking indicators, mechanical triggers and two-piece firing pin. In addition, note the other features of this model—

Barrel regulation: Adjusts for windage simply by turning the screw on the muzzle. Elevation is adjustable by regulating the sliding wedge located between the barrels.

Compact: 24-inch barrels mounted on the low-profile receiver limit the overall length to 40 inches (about 5″ less than most bolt-action rifles with similar 24-inch barrels).

Single selective trigger: A barrel selector is located on the trigger for quick, easy selection. Double triggers are also available.

Wide choice of calibers: Choose from 222, 30-06, 308

or the new 9.3×74R. All are under the 12 gauge, 3″ chamber with Improved Modified choke.

Sighting options: The vent rib is cross-filed to reduce glare. The rear sight is flush-folding and permits rapid alignment with the large blade front sight. The rib is milled to accommodate Valmet's one-piece scope mount with 1″ rings. Scope mount is of "quick release" design and can be removed without altering zero.

American walnut stock: Stocks are available either cast-on or cast-off for either right- or left-handed shooters, with palm swell for greater control and comfort. Quick detachable sling swivel. Length or pitch adjustable with factory spacers. Semi-Monte Carlo design.

Interchangeability: Receiver will accommodate Valmet's 12 and 20 gauge over/under shotgun barrels and double-rifle barrels with minor initial fitting.

SPECIFICATIONS MODEL 412S SHOTGUN/RIFLE

Gauge/Caliber: 12/.222, 12/30-06, 12/308 or 12/9.3×74R
Chamber: 3″ with Improved Modified choke
Barrel length: 24″

Overall length: 40″
Weight: 8 lbs.
Stock: American walnut with semi-Monte Carlo design

VALMET SHOTGUNS

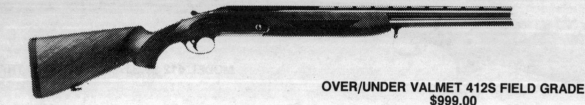

OVER/UNDER VALMET 412S FIELD GRADE
$999.00

Designed for the experienced hunter, Valmet's 412S represents the pride and skill of "Old World" European craftsmanship. The barrels are polished to a mirror finish and deeply blued. Select American walnut stock and forearm highlight fine, deep-cut checkering. Other features include:

Time-proven action: Designed to handle large centerfire calibers for more durability and reliability.

Mechanical trigger: Fires two shots as fast as you can pull the trigger. Does not rely on the inertia from the recoil of the first shot to set the trigger for the second. In the event of a faulty primer or light hit, inertia trigger shotguns cannot function on the second round.

Single selective trigger: Selector button is located on the trigger for fast, easy selection.

Large trigger guard opening: Designed for cold weather shooting; permits easy finger movement when wearing gloves.

American walnut stock and forearm: Add greatly to overall appearance.

Superior stock design: A straight stock that is not cast or "bent." Double palm swell for added comfort for both right- and left-handed shooters. Length and angle (pitch) can be altered for a perfect fit with addition of factory spacers. Fine, deep-cut checkering.

Palm-filling forearm: Rounded and tapered for comfort and smooth, true swing, plus fine, deep-cut checkering.

Automatic ejectors: Select and eject fired rounds. Raise unfired shells for safe removal.

Chrome-lined barrels: For more consistent patterns. Eliminates pitting and corrosion, extends barrel life even with steel shot.

Stainless steel choke tubes: Added strength over regular carbon and alloy materials. Easily handles steel shot. Recessed so as not to detract from appearance. Tight tolerances enable truer patterns and enhance choke versatility.

Sliding locking bolt: Secure lockup between receiver and barrels. Wears in, not loose.

Matte nickel receiver: Non-glare and more resistant to wear and corrosion.

Wide vent rib: Cross-file pattern reduces glare. Fluorescent front and middle beads.

Automatic safety: Goes to safe position automatically when gun is opened.

Cocking indicators: Allow shooter to determine (through sight or feel) which barrel has been fired.

Steel receiver: Forged and machined for durability.

Chamber: 3-inch on all models

Two-piece firing pin: For more durability

Versatility: Change from 12 to 20 gauge simply by adding a barrel. Change from over/under shotgun to shotgun/rifle, trap, skeet or double rifle. Precision tolerances require only minor initial fitting.

SPECIFICATIONS MODEL 412S FIELD GRADE OVER/UNDER

Gauge: 12
Chambers: 3"
Weight: 7¼ lbs. w/26" barrels; 7½ lbs. w/28" or 30" barrels

Barrel lengths/chokes:
26", IC, M, IM
28", M, IM, F
30" M, IM, F

WEATHERBY SHOTGUNS

ATHENA GRADE V

ATHENA GRADE IV OVER/UNDER

Receiver: The Athena receiver houses a strong, reliable box-lock action, yet it features side lock-type plates to carry through the fine floral engraving. The hinge pivots are made of a special high strength steel alloy. The locking system employs the time-tested Greener cross-bolt design. **Single selective trigger:** It is mechanically rather than recoil operated. This provides a fully automatic switchover, allowing the second barrel to be fired on a subsequent trigger pull, even in the event of a misfire. A flick of the trigger finger and the selector lever, located just in front of the trigger, is all the way to the left enabling you to fire the lower barrel first, or to the right for the upper barrel. The Athena trigger is selective as well. **Barrels:** The breech block is hand-fitted to the receiver, providing closest possible tolerances. Every Athena is equipped with a matted, ventilated rib and bead front sight. **Selective automatic ejectors:** The Athena contains ejectors that are fully automatic both in selection and action. **Slide safety:** The safety is the traditional slide type located conveniently on the upper tang on top of

the pistol grip. **Stock:** Each stock is carved from specially selected Claro walnut, with fine line hand-checkering and high luster finish. Trap model has Monte Carlo stock only. See Athena and Orion table for additional information and specifications.

GRADE IV PRICES:
Fixed Choke:
Field, 28 or .410 Ga. $1590.00
Skeet, 12 or 20 Ga. 1601.00
IMC Multi Choke:
Field, 12 or 20 Ga. 1590.00*
Trap, 12 Ga. 1611.00
Trap, single barrel, 12 Ga. 1611.00
Trap Combo, 12 Ga. 2100.00
Athena Master Skeet (tube set w/case) 3200.00
* Available in **GRADE V** with custom
metal engraving 2000.00

EIGHTY-TWO AUTOMATIC

MODEL 82 AUTOMATIC IMC (12 Ga.)
$500.00
BUCKMASTER AUTO SLUG $500.00

Gas-operated means no friction rings and collars to adjust for different loads. The barrel holds stationary instead of plunging backward with every shot. To these natural advantages, Weatherby has added revolutionary "Floating Piston" action. In the Weatherby Eighty-two, the piston "floats" freely on the magazine tube completely independent of every other part of the action. Nothing to get out of alignment. Nothing to cause drag or friction

MODEL EIGHTY-TWO AUTO SHOTGUN SPECIFICATIONS

All guns are 12 gauge and have ventilated rib barrels.
Magazine capacity is three shells (2¾″) with a removable plug limiting capacity to two shells in the magazine.

Model	Chamber	Bbl Length	Chokes	Overall Length	Length of Pull	Drop at: Comb	Drop at: Heel	Bead Sights	Approx. Weight
Choked Barrels									
Buckmaster	2¾″	22″	Skeet	46¼″	14¼″	1⅜″	2½″	Rifle	7½ lb.
IMC Barrels									
Field	2¾″	26″	M/IC/Sk	46½″	14¼″	1⅜″	2½″	Front bead	7½ lb.
Field	2¾″	28″	F/M/IC	48½″	14¼″	1⅜″	2½″	Front bead	7½ lb.
Field	2¾″	30″	F/M/IC	50½″	14¼″	1⅜″	2½″	Front bead	7½ lb.
Field	3″	28″	F/M/IC	48½″	14¼″	1⅜″	2½″	Front bead	7½ lb.
Field	3″	30″	F/M/IC	50½″	14¼″	1⅜″	2½″	Front bead	7½ lb.

SHOTGUNS

WEATHERBY SHOTGUNS

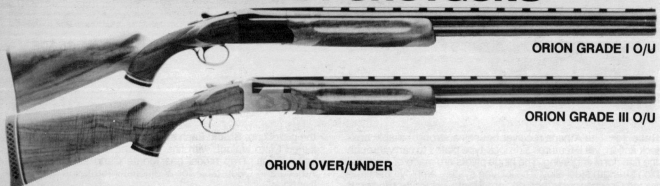

ORION GRADE I O/U

ORION GRADE III O/U

ORION OVER/UNDER

For greater versatility, the Orion incorporates the integral multi-choke (IMC) system. Available in Extra-full, Full, Modified, Improved Modified, Improved Cylinder and Skeet, the choke tubes fit flush with the muzzle without detracting from the beauty of the gun. Three tubes are furnished with each gun. The precision hand-fitted monobloc and receiver are machined from high-strength steel with a highly polished finish. The box-lock design uses the Greener cross-bolt locking system and special sears maintain hammer engagement. Pistol grip stock and forearm are carved of Claro walnut with hand-checkered diamond inlay pattern and high-gloss finish. Chrome moly steel barrels, and the receiver, are deeply blued. The Orion also features selective automatic ejectors, single selective trigger,

front bead sight and ventilated rib. The Trap model boasts a curved trap-style recoil pad and is available with Monte Carlo stock only. **Weight:** 12 ga. Field, 7½ lbs.; 20 ga. Field, 7½ lbs.; Trap, 8 lbs.

ORION PRICES:

Grade I
   IMC Multi-Choke, Field, 12 or 20 Ga. . . . . $ 850.00

Grade II
   Fixed Choke, Field, 28 or .410 Ga. 1000.00
   Fixed Choke, Skeet, 12 or 20 Ga. 1011.00
   IMC Multi Choke, Field, 12 or 20 Ga. 1000.00
   IMC Multi Choke, Trap, 12 Ga. 1051.00

Grade III
   IMC Multi-choke, Field, 12 or 20 Ga. 1100.00

Model	Chamber	Bbl Length	Chokes	Overall Length	Length Of Pull	Comb	Drop at Heel	**MC	Bead Sights	*Approx. Weight
IMC MULTI-CHOKE FIELD MODELS (12 GA., 20 GA.)										
Field	3"	26"	M/IC/Sk	43¼"	14¼"	1½"	2½"		Brilliant Front	6½ - 7½ lbs.
Field	3"	28"	F/M/IC	45¼"	14¼"	1½"	2½"		Brilliant Front	6½ - 7½ lbs.
Field (12 Ga. only)	3"	30"	F/M/F	47¼"	14¼"	1½"	2½"		Brilliant Front	7½ - 8 lbs.
FIXED CHOKE FIELD MODELS (28 GA., .410 GA.)										
28 Ga.	2¾"	26"	M/IC	43¼"	14¼"	1½"	2½"		Brilliant Front	6½ - 7½ lbs.
28 Ga.	2¾"	28"	F/M	45¼"	14¼"	1½"	2½"		Brilliant Front	6½ - 7½ lbs.
.410	3"	26"	M/IC	43¼"	14¼"	1½"	2½"		Brilliant Front	6½ - 7½ lbs.
.410	3"	28"	F/M	45¼"	14¼"	1½"	2½"		Brilliant Front	6½ - 7½ lbs.
IMC MULTI CHOKE TRAP MODELS (12 GA. only)**										
Trap	2¾"	30"	F/M/IM	47½"	14⅜"	1⅜"	2⅛"	1¾"	White Fr/Mid Br	8 - 8½ lbs.
Trap	2¾"	32"	F/M/IM	49½"	14⅜"	1⅜"	2⅛"	1¾"	White Fr/Mid Br	8 - 8½ lbs.
†Sgl Bbl Trap	2¾"	32"	F/M/IM	49½"	14⅜"	1⅜"	2⅛"	1¾"	White Fr/Mid Br	8 - 8½ lbs.
†Sgl Bbl Trap	2¾"	34"	F/M/IM	51½"	14⅜"	1⅜"	2⅛"	1¾"	White Fr/Mid Br	8½ - 9 lbs.
Single barrel trap available in combo set with 30" or 32" O/U barrels.										
FIXED CHOKE SKEET MODELS (12 GA., 20 GA., 28 GA., .410 GA.)										
12 Ga.	2¾"	26"	S/S	43¼"	14¼"	1½"	2½"		White Fr/Mid Br	6½ - 7½ lbs.
12 Ga.	2¾"	28"	S/S	45¼"	14¼"	1½"	2½"		White Fr/Mid Br	6½ - 7½ lbs.
20 Ga.	2¾"	26"	S/S	43¼"	14¼"	1½"	2½"		White Fr/Mid Br	6½ - 7½ lbs.
28 Ga.	2¾"	26"	S/S	43¼"	14¼"	1½"	2½"		White Fr/Mid Br	6½ - 7½ lbs.
.410	3"	26"	S/S	43¼"	14¼"	1½"	2½"		White Fr/Mid Br	6½ - 7½ lbs.
ATHENA MASTER SKEET TUBE SET (12 GA. Shotgun with 20 GA., 28 GA. and .410 GA. tubes)										
12 Ga.	2¾"***	28" & 26"	S/S	45¼"	14¼"	1½"	2½"		White Fr/Mid Br	7 - 8 lbs.
***.410 tube has 2½" chamber.										
Three choke tubes shown are furnished with IMC model. An Extra Full tube is also available as a separate item (12 ga. only).										
*Weight Varies due to wood density.										
**TRAP STOCKS AVAILABLE ONLY WITH MONTE CARLO.										
†Available in Athena model only.										

WINCHESTER SECURITY SHOTGUNS

This trio of tough 12-gauge shotguns provides backup strength for security and police work as well as all-around utility. The action is one of the fastest second-shot pumps made. It features a front-locking rotating bolt for strength and secure, single-unit lock-up into the barrel. Twin-action slide bars prevent binding.

All three guns are chambered for 3-inch shotshells. They handle 3-inch Magnum, 2³⁄₄-inch Magnum and standard 2³⁄₄-inch shotshells interchangeably. They have cross-bolt safety,

walnut-finished hardwood stock and forearm, black rubber butt pad and plain 18-inch barrel with Cylinder Bore choke. All are ultra-reliable and easy to handle.

Special chrome finishes on Police and Marine guns are actually triple-plated: first with copper for adherence, then with nickel for rust protection, and finally with chrome for a hard finish. This triple-plating assures durability and quality. Both guns have a forend cap with swivel to accommodate sling.

MODEL 1300 DEFENDER
$244.00

Security Defender™ is ideal for home security use. The compact 35⁵⁄₈-inch overall length handles and stores easily. The Defender has a deep blued finish on metal surfaces and features a traditional ribbed forearm for sure pumping grip. It has a metal bead front sight. The magazine holds eight 12-gauge 2³⁄₄-inch shells. Also available with a shotshell capacity of five 2³⁄₄″ shells with metal bead front sight or rifle type (front and rear): **$238.00.**

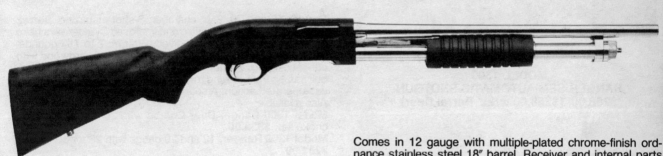

MODEL 1300 STAINLESS MARINE DEFENDER
$423.00

Comes in 12 gauge with multiple-plated chrome-finish ordnance stainless steel 18″ barrel. Receiver and internal parts are coated with Sandstrom 9A corrosion-inhibiting dry film lubricant. Stock and forend are made of corrosion and moisture-resistant material. **Capacity:** 7 shells (2³⁄₄″). **Sights:** Bead front (sling swivels incl.). Additional specifications same as Defender model described above.

SPECIFICATIONS: MODEL 1300 SECURITY

Model		Gauge	Chamber	Shotshell Capacity (A)	Choke	Barrel Length & Type	Overall Length	Nominal Length Of Pull	Nominal Drop At Comb	Nominal Drop At Heel	Nominal Weight (Lbs.)	Sights
Stainless Marine	*New*	12	3″Mag.	7¹	Cyl.	18″	38⁵⁄₈″	14″	1³⁄₈″	2³⁄₄″	7	MBF
Pistol Grip	*New*	12	3″Mag.	7¹	Cyl.	18	28½	14	—	—	—	MBF
Defender		12	3″Mag.	8¹	Cyl.	18	38⁵⁄₈	14	1³⁄₈	2³⁄₄	6¾	MBF
Pistol Grip		12	3″Mag.	8¹	Cyl.	18	28½	14	—	—	—	MBF
Defender		12	3″Mag.	5	Cyl.	18	38⁵⁄₈	14	1³⁄₈	2³⁄₄	6¼	MBF
Defender Combo		12	3″Mag.	5	Cyl.	18	38⁵⁄₈	14	1³⁄₈	2³⁄₄	6¼	MBF
Extra Barrel: Vent Rib		12	3″Mag.	5	W1M	28″VR	48⁵⁄₈	14	1³⁄₈	2³⁄₄	6½	MBF

(A) Includes one shotshell in chamber when ready to fire. VR—Ventilated rib. Cyl.—Cylinder Bore. W1M—Modified tube. MBF—Metal bead front. RT—Rifle type front and rear sights.

WINCHESTER SHOTGUNS

MODEL 1300
PISTOL GRIP SLIDE-ACTION DEFENDER
$244.00

Winchester Security shotguns are also available with high-strength pistol grip and forearm. The pistol grip features finger grooves and checkering for sure, fast handling. The shorter forearm is ribbed for positive grip and pumpability. Both pistol grip and forearm are high-impact-resistant ABS plastic with non-glare matte black finish. The Pistol Grip series is lighter in weight, compact, easily stored and fast handling.

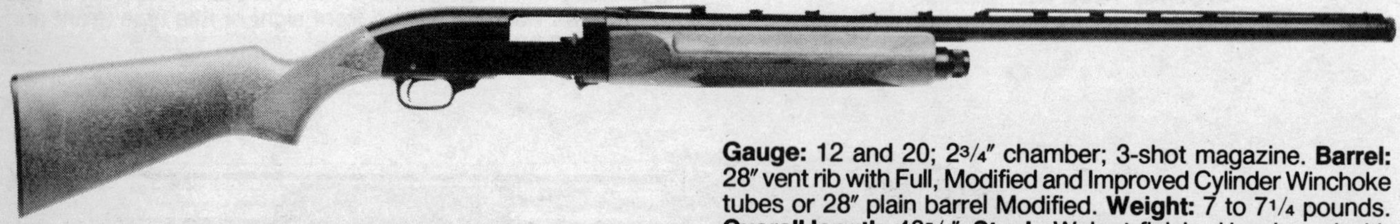

MODEL 1300
RANGER SEMIAUTOMATIC SHOTGUN
$268.00 ($258.00 w/22″ Barrel Deer)

Gauge: 12 and 20; 2³/₄″ chamber; 3-shot magazine. **Barrel:** 28″ vent rib with Full, Modified and Improved Cylinder Winchoke tubes or 28″ plain barrel Modified. **Weight:** 7 to 7¹/₄ pounds. **Overall length:** 48⁵/₈″. **Stock:** Walnut-finished hardwood with cut-checkering. **Sights:** Metal bead front. **Features:** Cross-bolt safety; front-locking rotating bolt; black serrated butt plate, gas-operated action. Also available in deer barrel.
Also available:
Model 1300 Ranger Deer Combo with 28″ barrel and Winchoke set: **$333.00**
Model 1300 Ranger, 12 and 20 gauge with 28″ or 30″ barrel: **$261.00**

SPECIFICATIONS: MODEL 1300 RANGER & YOUTH

Model	Gauge	Chamber	Shotshell Capacity (A)	Choke	Barrel Length & Type	Overall Length	Nominal Length Of Pull	Nominal Drop At Comb	Nominal Drop At Heel	Nominal Weight (Lbs.)	Sights
1300 Ranger	12	3″Mag.	5	W3	28″VR	48⁵/₈	14″	1½″	2½″	7¼	MBF
	20	3″Mag.	5	W3	28″VR	48⁵/₈	14	1½	2½	7¼	MBF
1300 Ranger Deer Combo	12	3″Mag.	5	Cyl.	22″VR	42⁵/₈	14	1½	2½	7¼	RT
12 ga. Extra Barrel	12	3″Mag.	5	W3	28″VR	48⁵/₈	14	1½	2½	7¼	MBF
1300 Ranger Deer Combo	20	3″Mag.	5	Cyl.	22″	42¾	14	1½	2½	6½	RT
20 ga. Extra Barrel	20	3″Mag.	5	W3	28″VR	48⁵/₈	14	1½	2½	7¼	MBF
1300 Ranger Deer Gun	12	3″Mag.	5	Cyl.	22″	42¾	14	1½	2½	6½	RT
	20	3″Mag.	5	Cyl.	22″	42¾	14	1½	2½	6½	RT
1300 Ranger	12	3″Mag.	5	W1M	28″VR	48⁵/₈	14	1½	2½	7¼	MBF
1300 Ranger	20	3″Mag.	5	W1M	28″VR	48⁵/₈	14	1½	2½	7¼	MBF
	12	3″Mag.	5	W1F	30″VR	50⁵/₈	14	1½	2½	7½	MBF
1300 Walnut Youth **New**	20	3″Mag.	5	W3	22″	41⁵/₈	13	1½	2½	6	MBF
1300 Youth	20	3″Mag.	5	W3	22″VR	41⁵/₈	13	1½	2½	6¼	MBF
	20	3″Mag.	5	W1M	22″	41⁵/₈	13	1½	2½	6	MBF

(A) Includes one shotshell in chamber when ready to fire. VR—Ventilated rib. Cyl.—Cylinder Bore. R—Rifled Barrel. MBF—Metal bead front. RT—Rifle type front and rear sights. Model 1300 and Ranger pump action shotguns have factory-installed plug which limits capacity to three shells. Ranger Youth has factory-installed plug which limits capacity to one, two or three shells as desired. Extra barrels for Model 1300 and Ranger shotguns are available in 12 gauge, plain or ventilated rib, in a variety of barrel lengths and chokes; interchangeable within gauge.

WINCHESTER SHOTGUNS

MODEL 1300 RANGER YOUTH PUMP-ACTION SHOTGUN
$257.00 ($286.00 w/vent. rib)

Gauge: 20 gauge only; 3" chamber; 5-shot magazine. **Barrel:** 22" plain barrel; Winchoke (Full, Modified, Improved Cylinder). **Weight:** 6½ lbs. **Length:** 41⅝". **Stock:** Walnut-finished hardwood with ribbed forend. **Sights:** Metal bead front. **Features:** Cross-bolt safety; black rubber butt pad; twin-action slide bars; front-locking rotating bolt; removable segmented magazine plug to limit shotshell capacity for training purposes; discount certificate for full-size adult stock. Also available in plain barrel w/Mod. choke.

MODEL 1300 PUMP-ACTION SHOTGUNS

The Model 1300 12- and 20-gauge pump guns are designed with shorter 22-inch barrels for upland shooting and small, quick game. At 6⅜ pounds, both are light-carrying, easy-swinging and lightning fast.

Their perfected slide action is one of the fastest, surest ever made. Twin-action slide bars prevent binding. The action permits ultra-fast follow-up shots. The front-locking rotating bolt locks the bolt into barrel with maximum strength and security. The ventilated rib barrel is chromium molybdenum steel, hot-formed for high strength.

Both 12- and 20-gauge versions handle 3-inch Magnum, 2¾-inch Magnum, and 2¾-inch standard shotshells interchangeably. Their 22-inch barrel is specially adapted for the Winchoke system, and each comes equipped with Full, Modified and Improved Cylinder Winchoke tubes and wrench. The Winchoke system and 3" Magnum capability give these new shotguns the versatility for most upland game—and great potential as utility guns.

Model 1300 Featherweight styling is clean-cut and handsome. Stock and forearm are American walnut with high-luster finish. Deep cut-checkering on pistol grip and traditional ribbing on the short, contoured forearm. Receivers are roll-engraved. Metal surfaces are highly polished and blued. Other features include cross-bolt safety with red indicator and metal front bead sight.

The 20-gauge Model 1300 Featherweight makes short work of upland birds. Equipped with serrated butt plate. The 12-gauge version delivers maximum versatility and performance for rabbits and small, fast game. The short barrel makes shotgun hunting for small game quick and responsive while the Winchoke system maximizes utility value. Equipped with rubber recoil pad. **Chamber:** 3". **Barrel length:** 22". **Overall length:** 42⅝". **Weight:** 6⅜ lbs.

WINCHESTER SHOTGUNS

MODEL 1300 MAGNUM WATERFOWL
$338.00 (12 GAUGE)

The Model 1300 Magnum Waterfowl pump is designed specifically for hunting ducks and geese. It features a 30-inch ventilated rib barrel with the Winchoke System of interchangeable choke tubes (Extra Full, Full and Modified). Stock and forearm are of American walnut with a low-luster protective finish. All exterior metal surfaces have a special non-glare matte finish to aid in hunter concealment. Other features include metal front bead sight, cross-bolt safety, rubber recoil pad and sling swivels. **Chamber:** 3" Mag. **Barrel length:** 30". **Overall length:** 50⅝". **Stock dimensions:** Length of pull, 14"; drop at comb, 1½"; drop at heel, 2½"; **Weight:** 7 lbs. Also available with WIN-TUFF brown laminated stock and forearm: **$349.00.**

MODEL 1300 TURKEY SHOTGUN
$368.00

Available in 12 gauge only, the Model 1300 Turkey gun comes equipped with a 22-inch ventilated rib barrel, which includes the Winchester Winchoke system with Extra Full, Full and Modified choke tubes and wrench. Its walnut stock and forearm have a special low-luster protective finish; the receiver, barrel and all exterior metal surfaces feature a non-glare matte finish. The receiver is roll engraved. The pistol grip has deep-cut checkering; the contoured forearm is ribbed for sure gripping and has been modified for positioning and comfort. Other features include cross-bolt safety with red indicator blocks and metal bead sights. The 1300 Turkey Gun handles 3" magnum, 2¾" Magnum and 2¾" standard shotshells interchangeably. See table below for complete specifications.

Also available:
Model 1300 Walnut Stock with satin finish, checkered, beavertail forend, and floating vent rib: **$338.00.**
Model 1300 Walnut Youth with scaled-down checkered stock with forend positioned rearward: **$344.00.**
Model 1300 Deer Gun with rifled matte-finish barrel: **$367.00.** With brown laminate: **$378.00.** With smoothbore barrel: **$328.00.**

SPECIFICATIONS: MODEL 1300 TURKEY

Model	Gauge	Chamber	Shotshell Capacity (A)	Choke	Barrel Length & Type	Overall Length	Nominal Length Of Pull	Nominal Drop At Comb	Nominal Drop At Heel	Nominal Weight (Lbs.)	Sights
1300 Special NWTF	12	3"Mag.	5	W3W	22"VR	42⅝	14	1½	2½	6⅜	MBF
1300 Turkey Gun Win-Cam	12	3"Mag.	5	W3W	22"VR	42⅝"	14"	1½"	2½"	6⅜	MBF
MODEL 1300 WATERFOWL & DEER											
1300 Waterfowl Walnut	12	3"Mag.	5	W3W	30"VR	50⅝"	14"	1½	2½	7	MBF
1300 Waterfowl Win-Tuff	12	3"Mag.	5	W3W	30"VR	50⅝	14	1½	2½	7	MBF
1300 Deer Gun Walnut	12	3"Mag.	5	Cyl/R	22"	42¾	14	1½	2½	6½	RT
1300 Deer Gun Win-Tuff	12	3"Mag.	5	Cyl/R	22"	42¾	14	1½	2½	6½	RT
1300 Deer Gun Walnut *New*	12	3"Mag.	5	Cyl.	22"	42¾	14	1½	2½	6½	RT

(A) Includes one shotshell in chamber when ready to fire. VR—Ventilated rib. Cyl.—Cylinder Bore. R—Rifled Barrel. MBF—Metal bead front. RT—Rifle type front and rear sights.

WINCHESTER SHOTGUNS
MODEL 1400 SEMIAUTO SHOTGUNS

The self-compensating gas-operated action in these shotguns enables the hunter to deliver follow-up shots as fast as the trigger can be pulled. A military-style lockup (Armor-Lock) assures high strength and low receiver weight. Front-locking rotary bolt is machined from solid chrome molybdenum steel and locks directly into a chrome molybdenum steel barrel extension by means of four locking bolts. The barrel is Winchester Proof steel; receiver is extruded from high strength, corrosion-resistant alloy; positive cross-bolt safety is located at the front of the trigger guard (blocking the trigger when "on," which in turn blocks the hammer). For other specifications, see the table below.

MODEL 1400 SEMIAUTO
(22″ Barrel, 12 Ga.)
$399.00

MODEL 1400 RANGER SEMIAUTO DEER GUN
$326.00
$333.00 (w/1 Mod. Winchoke Tube & Wrench)
$341.00 (w/Winchoke Set, Full Mod./Imp. Cyl. Tubes)
$406.00 DEER COMBO (12 Ga., 28″ Barrel, Winchoke Set)

SPECIFICATIONS: MODEL 1400 SEMI-AUTO

Model		Gauge	Chamber	Shotshell Capacity (A)	Choke	Barrel Length & Type	Overall Length	Nominal Length Of Pull	Nominal Drop At Comb	Nominal Drop At Heel	Nominal Weight (Lbs.)	Sights
1400 Walnut	New	12	2¾″	3	W3	22″VR	42¾″	14″	1½″	2½″	7	MBF
	New	20	2¾	3	W3	22″VR	42¾	14	1½	2½	7	MBF
	New	12	2¾	3	W3	28″VR	48⅝	14	1½	2½	7¾	MBF
1400 Ranger		12	2¾	3	W3	28″VR	48⅝	14	1½	2½	7¾	MBF
1400 Ranger	New	12	2¾	3	W1	28″VR	48⅝	14	1½	2½	7¾	MBF
1400 Ranger		20	2¾	3	W3	28″VR	48⅝	14	1½	2½	7¾	MBF
1400 Ranger	New	20	2¾	3	W1	28″VR	48⅝	14	1½	2½	7¾	MBF
1400 Ranger Deer Combo Extra Barrel		12	2¾	3		22″VR	42¾	14	1½	2½	7¼	RT
		12	2¾	3	W3	28″VR	48⅝	14	1½	2½	7¼	MBF
1400 Ranger Deer		12	2¾	3	Cyl.	22″	42¾	14	1½	2½	6½	RT

(A) Includes one shotshell in chamber when ready to fire. VR—Ventilated rib. Cyl.—Cylinder Bore. R—Rifled Barrel. MBF—Metal bead front. RT—Rifle type front and rear sights.

Black Powder Guns

FOR ADDRESSES AND PHONE NUMBERS OF MANUFACTURERS AND DISTRIBUTORS INCLUDED IN THIS SECTION, SEE *DIRECTORY OF MANUFACTURERS AND SUPPLIERS*

ARMSPORT
REPLICA REVOLVERS

MODEL 5133 COLT
1851 NAVY "REB"

A modern replica of a Confederate Percussion Revolver. It has a polished brass frame, a rifled blued barrel and polished walnut grips. **Price: $105.00.**

MODEL 5136 COLT
1851 NAVY STEEL

This authentic reproduction of the Colt Navy Revolver, which helped shape the history of America, features a rifled barrel, blued steel frame, engraved cylinder, polished brass trigger guard and walnut grips. **Price: $150.00.**

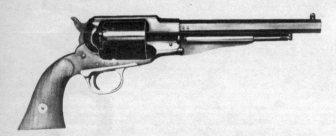

MODEL 5120 REMINGTON ARMY
44 CALIBER STEEL REVOLVER

One of the most accurate cap-and-ball revolvers of the 1880's. Its rugged steel frame and top strap made this the favorite of all percussion cap revolvers. **Price: $155.00.** With brass frame: **$110.00.**

MODEL 5138 REMINGTON ARMY
STAINLESS STEEL 44 CALIBER

This stainless-steel version of the 44-caliber Remington New Army Revolver is made for the shooter who seeks the best. Its stainless steel frame assures lasting good looks and durability. **Price: $250.00.**

MODEL 5139 COLT 1860 ARMY
44 CALIBER

This authentic reproduction offers the same balance and ease of handling for fast shooting as the original 1860 Army model. **Price: $160.00.**

MODEL 5140 COLT 1860 ARMY
(Not shown)

Same as the Model 5139 Colt Army replica, but with brightly polished brass frame. **Price: $115.00.**

Replica Revolvers Description	Model No. Finished	Barrel Length	Caliber	Recommended Ball Dia.
New Remington Army Stainless Steel	5138	8"	44	.451
New Remington Army	5120	8"	44	.451
1851 Navy Reb Brass	5133	7"	36	.376
1851 Navy Reb Brass	5134	7"	44	.451
1851 Navy Steel	5135	7"	36	.376
1851 Navy Steel	5136	7"	44	.451
1860 Colt Army	5139	8"	44	.451

ARMSPORT

MODEL 5145 COLT 1847 WALKER
$220.00

The largest of all Colt revolvers, this true copy of the original weighs 4½ lbs., making it also the most powerful revolver made at the time. **Caliber:** 44.

MODEL 5152 ENGRAVED REMINGTON OR COLT ARMY .44 CALIBER
$235.00

MODEL 5153 ENGRAVED COLT ARMY

MODEL 5154 ENGRAVED COLT NAVY
$235.00

Also available:
Model 5138 Remington Army SS $250.00
Model 5134 1851 Colt Navy Brass (36 & 44 Cal.) . . 105.00
   Kit 95.00
Model 5135 1851 Colt Navy Steel (36 & 44 Cal.) . . . 150.00
   Kit 140.00
Model 5150 1860 Colt Army SS 285.00

CVA REVOLVERS

1858 REMINGTON TARGET MODEL with adjustable target sights: **$229.95.**

Also available:
1858 REMINGTON ARMY REVOLVER with brass frame: **$159.95.** In Kit form: **$139.95.**

1858 REMINGTON ARMY STEEL FRAME REVOLVER $213.95

Caliber: 44
Cylinder: 6-shot
Barrel length: 8″ octagonal
Overall length: 13″
Weight: 38 oz.
Sights: Blade front; groove in frame (rear)
Grip: Two-piece walnut

COLT WALKER REVOLVER $261.95

Caliber: 44
Barrel: 9″ rounded with hinged-style loading lever
Cylinder: 6-shot engraved
Overall length: 15½″
Weight: 71 oz.
Grip: One-piece walnut
Front sight: Blade
Finish: Solid brass trigger guard

NEW MODEL POCKET REMINGTON
Finished $117.95
Kit $93.95

This single-action 31-caliber percussion revolver is a reproduction of a valued collector's item. Manufactured originally in the mid-1800s, the five-shot revolver was most effective at close ranges. Its brass frame and 4-inch blued barrel provide beauty as well as ruggedness.

Caliber: 31 percussion
Barrel length: 4″ octagonal
Cylinder: 5 shots
Overall length: 7½″
Sights: Post in front; groove in frame in rear
Weight: 15½ oz.
Finish: Solid brass frame

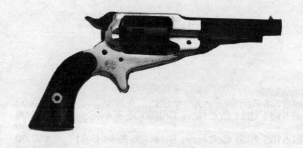

CVA REVOLVERS

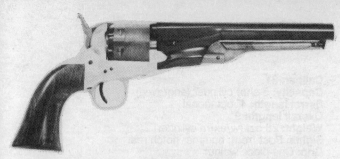

1861 COLT NAVY BRASS FRAMED REVOLVER
Finished $137.95
Kit $117.95

Caliber: 44
Barrel length: 7½″ rounded; creeping style
Weight: 44 oz.
Cylinder: 6-shot, engraved
Sights: Blade front; hammer notch rear
Finish: Solid brass frame, trigger guard and backstrap; blued barrel and cylinder
Grip: One-piece walnut

Also available in 36 caliber with steel frame: **$209.95**

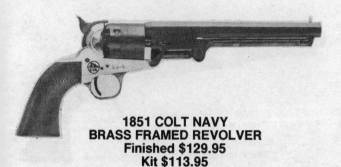

**1851 COLT NAVY
BRASS FRAMED REVOLVER**
Finished $129.95
Kit $113.95

Caliber: 36
Barrel length: 7½″ octagonal; hinged-style loading lever
Overall length: 13″
Weight: 44 oz.
Cylinder: 6-shot, engraved
Sights: Post front; hammer notch rear
Grip: One-piece walnut
Finish: Solid brass frame, trigger guard and backtrap; blued barrel and cylinder; color casehardened loading lever and hammer

Also available with steel frame: **$205.95**

COLT SHERIFF'S MODEL REVOLVER
Brass Frame $143.95
Kit $125.95

Caliber: 36
Barrel length: 5½″ (rounded w/creeping-style loading lever)
Overall length: 11½″
Weight: 40½ oz.
Cylinder: 6-shot semi-fluted
Grip: One-piece walnut
Sight: Hammer notch in rear
Finish: Solid brass frame, trigger guard and backstrap

Also available: **Engraved Nickel Plated Model** (with matching flask) **$221.95.** With steel frame: **$169.95.**

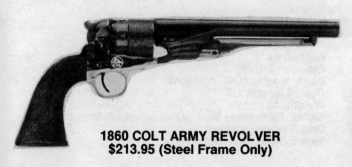

1860 COLT ARMY REVOLVER
$213.95 (Steel Frame Only)

Caliber: 44
Barrel length: 8″ rounded; creeping-style loading lever
Overall length: 13″
Weight: 44 oz.
Cylinder: 6-shot, engraved and rebated
Sights: Blade front; hammer notch rear
Grip: One-piece walnut
Finish: Solid brass trigger guard; blued barrel and cylinder with color casehardened loading lever, hammer and frame

CVA REVOLVERS

WELLS FARGO MODEL COLT
$117.95 Steel Frame $175.95
Kit $105.95

Caliber: 31
Capacity: 5-shot cylinder (engraved)
Barrel length: 4″ octagonal
Overall length: 9″
Weight: 28 oz. (w/extra cylinder)
Sights: Post front; hammer notch rear
Grip: One-piece walnut

COLT POCKET POLICE
$131.95 Steel Frame $179.95
Kit $109.95

Caliber: 36
Capacity: 5-shot cylinder
Barrel length: 5¹/₂″ (octagonal, with creeping-style loading lever
Overall length: 10¹/₂″
Weight: 26 oz.
Sights: Post front; hammer notch rear

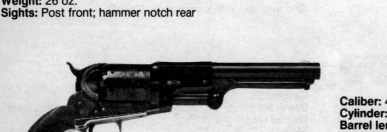

THIRD MODEL COLT DRAGOON
$225.95

Caliber: 44
Cylinder: 6-shot engraved
Barrel length: 7¹/₂″ rounded with hinged-style loading lever
Overall length: 14″
Weight: 75 oz.
Sights: Blade front; hammer notch rear
Grip: One-piece walnut

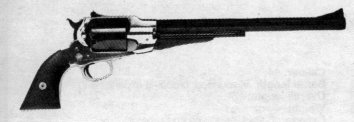

REMINGTON BISON
$247.95

Caliber: 44
Cylinder: 6-shot
Barrel length: 10¹/₄″ octagonal
Overall length: 18″
Weight: 48 oz.
Sights: Fixed blade front; screw adjustable target rear
Grip: Two-piece walnut
Finish: Solid brass frame

CVA PISTOLS

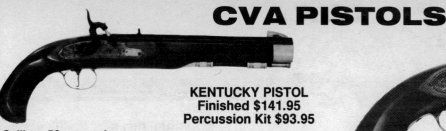

KENTUCKY PISTOL
Finished $141.95
Percussion Kit $93.95

Caliber: 50 percussion
Barrel: 10¼", rifled, octagonal
Overall length: 15½"
Weight: 40 oz.
Finish: Blued barrel, brass hardware
Sights: Brass blade front; fixed open rear
Stock: Select hardwood
Ignition: Engraved, color casehardened percussion lock, screw adjustable sear engagement
Accessories: Brass-tipped, hardwood ramrod; stainless steel nipple or flash hole liner

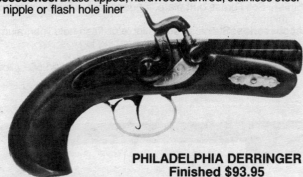

PHILADELPHIA DERRINGER
Finished $93.95
Kit $51.95

Caliber: 45 percussion
Barrel: 3¼" rifled
Overall length: 7⅛"
Weight: 16 oz.
Finish: Brass hardware; blued barrel
Stock: Select hardwood
Ignition: Color casehardened and engraved, coil-spring back-action lock
Accessories: Stainless steel nipple

VEST POCKET DERRINGER
Finished $57.95
Kit $49.95

Caliber: 31
Barrel length: 2½" (single shot)
Overall length: 5"
Weight: 16 oz.
Grip: Two-piece walnut
Frame: Brass

COLONIAL PISTOL
Finished $107.95
Percussion Kit $71.95

Caliber: 45 (451 bore) percussion
Barrel: 6¾", rifled, octagon
Overall length: 12¾"
Weight: 31 oz.
Finish: Casehardened lock; blued barrel; brass hardware
Sights: Dovetail rear; brass blade front
Stock: Select hardwood
Ignition: Engraved, color casehardened lock
Accessories: Steel ramrod, stainless steel nipple; kits available for percussion and flintlock

HAWKEN PISTOL
Finished $145.95
Kit $105.95

Caliber: 50
Barrel length: 9¾", octagonal
Overall length: 16½"
Weight: 50 oz.
Trigger: Early-style brass
Sights: Beaded steel blade front; fully adjustable rear (click adj. screw settings lock into position)
Stock: Select hardwood
Finish: Solid brass wedge plate, nose cap, ramrod thimbles, trigger guard and grip cap

SIBER PISTOL
$393.95

Caliber: 45
Barrel length: 10½", octagonal
Overall length: 16½"
Weight: 38 oz.
Sights: Blade front; rear adjustable for elevation
Stock: Fancy European walnut
Trigger: Adjustable single-set trigger with rear over-lateral limiting screw
Finish: Polished steel barrel, lock plate, hammer and trigger

CVA

SQUIRREL RIFLE
Percussion (Finished) $277.95
Percussion Kit $169.95

Ignition: Color case-hardened and engraved lockplate; bridle, fly, screw-adjustable sear engagement; authentic V-type mainspring
Caliber: 36 percussion or flintlock
Stock: Select hardwood
Barrel: 25″ octagonal; 11/16″ across flats; hooked breech for easy take down and cleaning; rifling, one turn in 48″; 8 lands, deep grooves; blued steel
Overall length: 40 3/4″
Weight: 5 lbs. 12 oz.

Trigger: Double set (will fire set or unset)
Front sight: Dovetail, beaded blade
Rear sight: Fully adjustable, open hunting-style dovetail
Finish: Solid brass butt plate, trigger guard, wedge plates and thimbles
Accessories: Stainless steel nipple or flash hole liner; aluminum ramrod with brass tips, cleaning jag
Also available:
SQUIRREL RIFLE HUNTING COMBO KIT (36 and 50 caliber percussion): **$229.95**

BLAZER RIFLE
Finished $149.95
Kit $121.95

Caliber: 50 percussion
Barrel length: 28″ octagonal (15/16″ across flats); in-line breech and nipple
Rifling: 1 turn in 66″ (8 lands and deep grooves)
Overall length: 43 1/2″

Weight: 7 lbs.
Sights: Brass blade front; fixed open rear
Stock: Select hardwood
Lock: Straight-through ignition (removable for cleaning and adjustment)

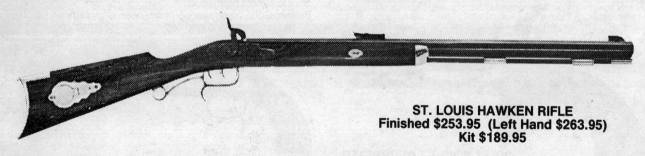

ST. LOUIS HAWKEN RIFLE
Finished $253.95 (Left Hand $263.95)
Kit $189.95

Calibers: 50 and 54
Barrel: 28″ octagonal 15/16″ across flats; hooked breech; rifling one turn in 66″, 8 lands and deep grooves
Overall length: 44″
Weight: 8 lbs.
Sights: Dovetail, beaded blade (front); adjustable open hunting-style dovetail (rear)
Stock: Select hardwood with beavertail cheekpiece
Triggers: Double set; fully adjustable trigger pull

Finish: Solid brass wedge plates, nose cap, ramrod thimbles, trigger guard and patch box
Also available:
50 Caliber Flintlock	**$263.95**
54 & 58 Caliber Percussion	253.95
Percussion Combos (50 and 54 calibers)	241.95
50 Cal./12 Ga. (full choke) Combo	343.95
Same as above, **in Kit**	269.95

CVA RIFLES

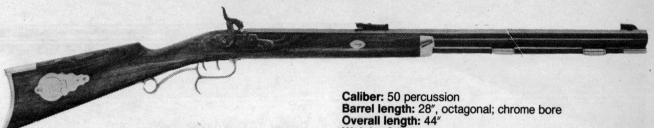

HAWKEN RIFLE
$389.95

Caliber: 50 percussion
Barrel length: 28″, octagonal; chrome bore
Overall length: 44″
Weight: 8 lbs.
Stock: Select walnut with fully formed beavertail cheekpiece
Sights: Beaded steel blade front; hunting-style rear, fully click adjustable for windage and elevation
Finish: Solid brass wedge plates, nose cap, ramrod thimbles, trigger guard, butt plate and patchbox

KENTUCKY RIFLE
$259.95
Kit $143.95

Caliber: 50 percussion
Barrel length: 33½″, octagonal
Overall length: 48″
Weight: 7½ lbs.
Sights: Brass blade front; fixed open rear
Stock: Select hardwood
Trigger: Early-style brass
Finish: Solid brass trigger guard, butt plate, toe plate, front sight, nose cap and thimble

HUNTER HAWKEN
$243.95
Kit $183.95

Calibers: 50 and 54
Barrel length: 28″, blued, octagonal
Overall length: 44″
Weight: 8 lbs.
Sights: Beaded steel blade front; hunting-style rear, fully click adjustable for windage and elevation
Stock: Select hardwood with non-glare finish; rubber recoil pad
Triggers: Double set with fully adjustable trigger pull
Finish: Black nose cap, trigger guard, thimbles and wedge plate
Also available: HUNTER HAWKEN CARBINE (24″ barrel; 40″ overall) **$243.95.**

BLACK POWDER

CVA

OVER/UNDER CARBINE
$579.95

Caliber: 50 Over/Under
Barrel length: 26″
Overall length: 41″
Twist: 1 in 66″; 8 lands and grooves
Features: Checkered English-style straight grip and beavertail forestock
Weight: 8 lbs. 8 oz.

TRAPPER COMBO
3 Interchangeable Chokes
Finished Combo $399.95
Single Barrel $283.95
Single Barrel Kit $237.95

Gauge: 12
Barrel length: 28″ round
Chokes: Interchangeable Improved, Modified and Full
Weight: 5½ lbs.
Stock: Select hardwood; English-style straight grip
Trigger: Early-style steel
Sights: Brass bead in front
Finish: Solid brass wedge plates; color-hardened lock plates, hammer, black trigger guard and tang
Features: Casehardened steel nipple, wooden ramrod w/brass tip

OZARK MOUNTAIN RIFLE
$397.95 (Chrome Bore)

Calibers: 50 and 54 percussion
Barrel length: 32″ octagonal (15/16″ across flats); with hooked breech for easy takedown and cleaning
Rifling: 1 turn in 66″ (8 lands and deep grooves)
Overall length: 48″
Weight: 9 lbs.
Sights: German silver blade front; screw adjustable ramp rear
Triggers: Double set, fully adjustable trigger pull
Stock: Select hardwood
Finish: Pewter nose cap, trigger guard and butt plate
Lock: Plate is color casehardened and engraved; internal features include bridle, fly, screw-adjustable sear engagement, V-type mainspring
Accessories: Stainless steel nipple, hardwood ramrod with aluminum tips
Also available: Same model with select finished hardwood stock w/low cheekpiece in 50 or 54 caliber **$289.95.**

CVA RIFLES

PENNSYLVANIA LONG RIFLE
Percussion (Finished) $475.95
Flintlock $485.95

Caliber: 50 percussion or flintlock
Stock: Select walnut
Barrel: 40″ octagonal, 7/8″ across flats; rifling 8 lands, deep grooves
Overall length: 55 3/4″
Weight: 8 lbs.
Trigger: Double set (will fire set or unset)
Rear sight: Fixed semi-buckhorn, dovetail
Finish: Brass butt plate, patchbox, trigger guard, thimbles and nose cap
Ignition: Color casehardened and engraved lockplate; bridle, fly, screw-adjustable sear engagement; authentic V-type mainspring
Accessories: Color casehardened nipple or flash hole liner; hardwood ramrod and brass tips

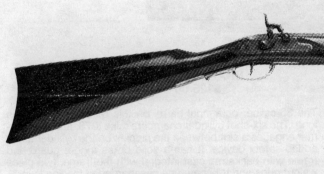

FRONTIER CARBINE
Finished $215.95
Kit $149.95

Caliber: 50 percussion
Barrel length: 24″ octagonal (15/16″ across flats)
Rifling: 1 turn in 48″ (8 lands and deep grooves)
Overall length: 40″
Weight: 6 1/2 lbs.
Sights: Brass blade front; fixed open rear
Trigger: Early-style brass with tension spring
Stock: Select hardwood
Finish: Solid brass butt plate, trigger guard wedge plate, nose cap and thimble
Accessories: Stainless steel nipple, hardwood ramrod with brass tips and cleaning jag

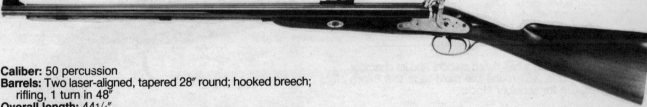

Caliber: 50 percussion
Barrels: Two laser-aligned, tapered 28″ round; hooked breech; rifling, 1 turn in 48″
Overall length: 44 1/4″
Weight: 9 lbs. 8 oz.
Locks: Plate is color hardened and engraved; includes bridle, fly, screw-adjustable sear engagement
Triggers: Double, color casehardened
Sights: Fully adjustable for windage and elevation, hunting style (rear); dovetail, beaded blade (front)
Stock: Select hardwood
Finish: Polished steel wedge plates; color casehardened locks, hammers, triggers and trigger guard; engraved locks, hammers and tang
Also available: Accessory barrel (12 Ga. Modified Choke) **$198.00.**

EXPRESS DOUBLE BARREL RIFLE
Finished $519.95
Kit $439.95

DIXIE

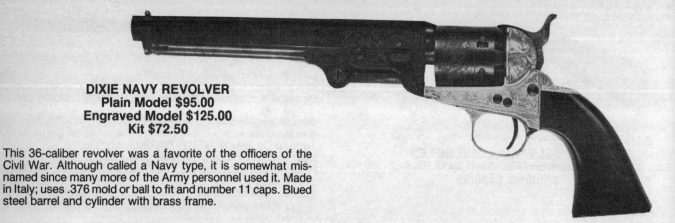

DIXIE NAVY REVOLVER
Plain Model $95.00
Engraved Model $125.00
Kit $72.50

This 36-caliber revolver was a favorite of the officers of the Civil War. Although called a Navy type, it is somewhat misnamed since many more of the Army personnel used it. Made in Italy; uses .376 mold or ball to fit and number 11 caps. Blued steel barrel and cylinder with brass frame.

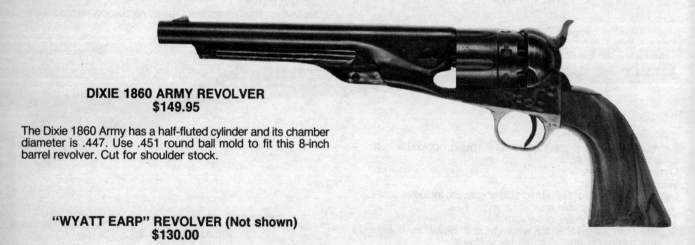

SPILLER & BURR 36 CALIBER BRASS FRAME REVOLVER
$125.00   Kit $65.00

The 36-caliber octagonal barrel on this revolver is 7 inches long. The six-shot cylinder chambers mike .378, and the hammer engages a slot between the nipples on the cylinder as an added safety device. It has a solid brass trigger guard and frame with backstrap cast integral with the frame, two-piece walnut grips and Whitney-type casehardened loading lever.

DIXIE 1860 ARMY REVOLVER
$149.95

The Dixie 1860 Army has a half-fluted cylinder and its chamber diameter is .447. Use .451 round ball mold to fit this 8-inch barrel revolver. Cut for shoulder stock.

"WYATT EARP" REVOLVER (Not shown)
$130.00

This 44-caliber revolver has a 12-inch octagon rifled barrel and rebated cylinder. Highly polished brass frame, backstrap and trigger guard. The barrel and cylinder have a deep blue luster finish. Hammer, trigger, and loading lever are case-hardened. Walnut grips. Recommended ball size is .451.

DIXIE

RHO200 WALKER REVOLVER
$185.00   Kit $164.00

This 4½-pound, 44-caliber pistol is the largest ever made. Steel backstrap; guard is brass with Walker-type rounded-to-frame walnut grips; all other parts are blued. Chambers measure .445 and take a .450 ball slightly smaller than the originals.

RHO301 THIRD MODEL DRAGOON
$192.00

This engraved-cylinder, 4½-pounder is a reproduction of the last model of Colt's 44 caliber "horse" revolvers. Barrel measures 7⅜ inches, ⅛ inch shorter than the original; color case-hardened steel frame, one-piece walnut grips. Recommended ball size: .454.

LINCOLN DERRINGER
$285.00   Kit $89.95

This 41-caliber, 2-inch browned barrel gun has 8 lands and 8 grooves and will shoot a .400 patch ball.

DSB-58 SCREW BARREL DERRINGER
(Not shown)
$89.00   Kit $53.00

Overall length: 6½″. Unique loading system; sheath trigger, color case-hardened frame, trigger and center-mounted hammer; European walnut, one-piece, "bag"-type grip. Uses #11 percussion caps.

DIXIE BRASS FRAMED "HIDEOUT" DERRINGER
(Not shown)
Plain $49.95   Engraved $85.95
Kit $42.50

Made with brass frame and walnut grips and fires a .395 round ball.

FHO201 FRENCH CHARLEVILLE FLINT PISTOL
(Not shown)
$145.00

Reproduction of the Model 1777 Cavalry, Revolutionary War-era pistol. Has reversed frizzen spring; forend and lock housing are all in one; casehardened, round-faced, double-throated hammer; walnut stock; casehardened frizzen and trigger; shoots .680 round ball loaded with about 40 grains FFg black powder.

ABILENE DERRINGER (Not shown)
$81.50   Kit $51.95

An all-steel version of Dixie's brass-framed derringers. The 2½-inch, 41-caliber barrel is finished in a deep blue black; frame and hammer are case-hardened. Bore is rifled with 6 lands and grooves. Uses a tightly patched .395 round ball and 15 or 20 grains of FFFg powder. Walnut grips. Comes with wood presentation case.

BLACK POWDER

DIXIE

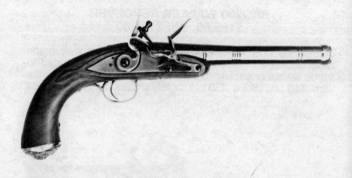

LePAGE PERCUSSION DUELING PISTOL
$225.00

This percussion pistol features a blued 10″ octagonal barrel with 12 lands and grooves. The 45-caliber sidearm has a brass-bladed front sight with open rear sight dovetailed into the barrel. Trigger guard and butt cap are polished silver plating. Right side of barrel is stamped "LePage á Paris." Double-set triggers are single screw adjustable. **Overall length:** 16″. **Weight:** 2½ lbs.

PEDERSOLI ENGLISH DUELING PISTOL
(Not shown)
$250.00

This reproduction of an English percussion dueling pistol, created by Charles Moore of London, features a European walnut halfstock with oil finish and checkered grip. The 45-caliber octagonal barrel is 11″ with 12 grooves and a twist of 1 in 15″. Nose cap and thimble are silver. Barrel is blued; lock and trigger guard are color casehardened.

PEDERSOLI MANG TARGET PISTOL (Not shown)
$595.00

Designed specifically for the precision target shooter, this 38-caliber pistol has a 10⁷/₁₆″ octagonal barrel with 7 lands and grooves. Twist is 1 in 15″. Blade front sight is dovetailed into the barrel, and rear sight is mounted on the breech-plug tang, adjustable for windage. **Overall length:** 17¼″. **Weight:** 2½ lbs.

QUEEN ANNE PISTOL
$131.50

Named for the Queen of England (1702-1714), this flintlock pistol has a 7½″ barrel that tapers from rear to front with a cannon-shaped muzzle. The brass trigger guard is fluted and the brass butt on the walnut stock features a grotesque mask worked into it. **Overall length:** 13″. **Weight:** 2¼ lbs.

DIXIE PENNSYLVANIA PISTOL (Not shown)
Percussion $105.00   Kit $72.50
Flintlock $119.95   Kit $88.75

Available in 44-caliber percussion or flintlock. Bright luster blued barrel measures 10 inches long; rifled, ⁷/₈-inch octagon, takes .430 ball; barrel held in place with a steel wedge and tang screw; brass front and rear sights. The brass trigger guard, thimbles, nose cap, wedge plates and side plates are highly polished. Locks are fine quality with early styling. Plates measure 4³/₄ inches × ⁷/₈ inch. Percussion hammer is engraved and both plates are left in the white. Flint is an excellent style lock with the gooseneck hammer having an early wide thumb piece. Stock is walnut stained and has a wide bird-head-type grip.

DIXIE

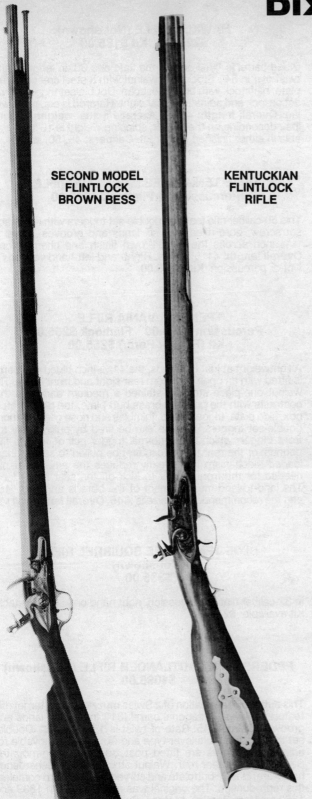

**SECOND MODEL
FLINTLOCK
BROWN BESS**

**KENTUCKIAN
FLINTLOCK
RIFLE**

SECOND MODEL BROWN BESS MUSKET
$450.00

This 75-caliber Brown Bess has a 41¾-inch smoothbore barrel that takes a .730 round ball. In keeping with the traditional musket, it has brass furniture on a walnut-stained stock. The lock is marked "Tower" and has the crown with the "GR" underneath. Barrel, lock and ramrod are left bright.
Kit: $375.00

THE KENTUCKIAN RIFLE
Flintlock $225.00
Percussion $210.00

This 45-caliber rifle, in flintlock or percussion, wears a 33½-inch blued octagonal barrel that is ¹³/₁₆ inch across the flats. The bore is rifled with 6 lands and grooves of equal width and about .006 inch deep. Land-to-land diameter is .453 with groove-to-groove diameter at. 465. Ball size ranges from .445 to .448. The rifle has a brass blade front sight and a steel open rear sight. The Kentuckian is furnished with brass butt plate, trigger guard, patch box, side plate, thimbles and nose cap plus case-hardened and engraved lock plate. Highly polished and finely finished stock in European walnut. **Overall length:** 48". **Weight:** Approx. 6¼ lbs.

DIXIE DOUBLE BARREL MAGNUM
MUZZLE LOADING SHOTGUN (Not shown)

A full 12-gauge, high-quality, double-barreled percussion shotgun with 30-inch browned barrels. Will take the plastic shot cups for better patterns. Bores are choked modified and full. Lock, barrel tang and trigger are case-hardened in a light gray color and are nicely engraved. In **12 Gauge: $325.00**. Also available: **10 Gauge Magnum** with double barrel (right-hand = cyl. bore; left-hand = Mod.), otherwise same specs as above: **$365.00**.

DIXIE

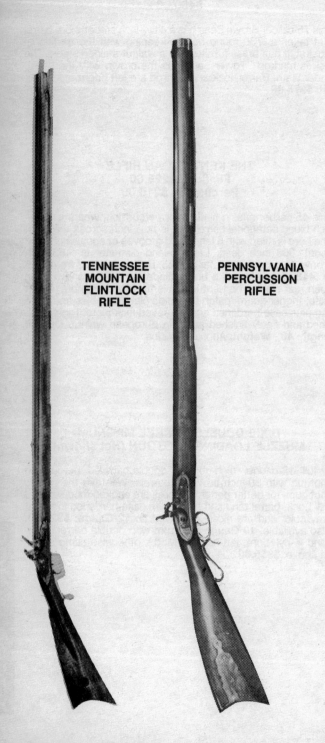

**TENNESSEE
MOUNTAIN
FLINTLOCK
RIFLE**

**PENNSYLVANIA
PERCUSSION
RIFLE**

HAWKEN RIFLE (Not shown)
$225.00   Kit $185.00

Blued barrel is ¹⁵/₁₆″ across the flats and 30″ in length with a twist of 1 in 64″. Stock is of walnut with a steel crescent buttplate, halfstock with brass nosecap. Double set triggers, front action lock and adjustable rear sight. Ramrod is equipped with jag. **Overall length:** 46½″. Average actual **weight:** about 8 lbs., depending on the caliber; shipping weight is 10 lbs. Available in either finished gun or kit. **Calibers:** 45, 50, and 54.

DIXIE TENNESSEE MOUNTAIN RIFLE
Percussion or Flintlock $335.00

This 50-caliber rifle features double-set triggers with adjustable set screw, bore rifled with six lands and grooves, barrel of ¹⁵/₁₆ inch across the flats, brown finish and cherry stock. **Overall length:** 41½ inches. Right- and left-hand versions in flint or percussion. **Kit: $275.00.**

PENNSYLVANIA RIFLE
Percussion $295.00   Flintlock $255.00
Kit (Flint or Perc.) $255.00

A lightweight at just 8 pounds, the 41½-inch blued rifle barrel is fitted with an open buckhorn rear sight and front blade. The walnut one-piece stock is stained a medium darkness that contrasts with the polished brass butt plate, toe plate, patchbox, side plate, trigger guard, thimbles and nose cap. Featuring double-set triggers, the rifle can be fired by pulling only the front trigger, which has a normal trigger pull of four to five pounds; or the rear trigger can first be pulled to set a spring-loaded mechanism that greatly reduces the amount of pull needed for the front trigger to kick off the sear in the lock. The land-to-land measurement of the bore is an exact .450 and the recommended ball size is .445. **Overall length:** 51½″.

DIXIE TENNESSEE SQUIRREL RIFLE
(Not shown)
$335.00

In 32-caliber flint or percussion, right hand only, cherry stock. Kit available: **$275.00**

PEDERSOLI WAADTLANDER RIFLE (Not shown)
$1095.00

This authentic re-creation of a Swiss muzzleloading target rifle features a heavy octagonal barrel (31″) that has 7 lands and grooves. **Caliber:** 45. Rate of twist is 1 turn in 48″. Double-set triggers are multi-lever type and are easily removable for adjustment. Sights are fitted post front and tang-mounted Swiss-type diopther rear. Walnut stock, color casehardened hardware, classic buttplate and curved trigger guard complete this reproduction. The original was made between 1839 and 1860 by Marc Bristlen, Morges, Switzerland.

DIXIE

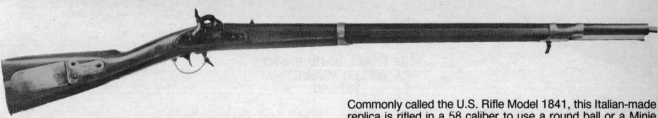

PRO401 MISSISSIPPI RIFLE
$430.00

Commonly called the U.S. Rifle Model 1841, this Italian-made replica is rifled in a 58 caliber to use a round ball or a Minie ball; 3 grooves and regulation sights; solid brass furniture; casehardened lock.

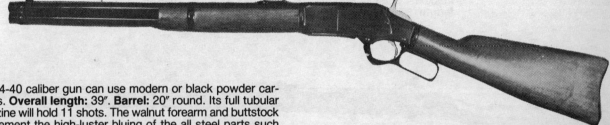

This 44-40 caliber gun can use modern or black powder cartridges. **Overall length:** 39″. **Barrel:** 20″ round. Its full tubular magazine will hold 11 shots. The walnut forearm and buttstock complement the high-luster bluing of the all steel parts such as the frame, barrel, magazine, loading lever and butt plate. Comes with the trap door in the butt for the cleaning rod; leaf rear sight and blade front sight. This carbine is marked "Model 1873" on the tang and caliber "44-40" on the brass carrier block.

WINCHESTER '73 CARBINE
$495.00
ENGRAVED WINCHESTER '73 RIFLE
$595.00

WESSON RIFLE
$395.00

The lock work for this rifle is housed in a steel frame or receiver. Barrel is a heavy $1\frac{1}{8}″ \times .50$ caliber measuring 28″ and fitted with a false muzzle. Two-piece European walnut stock is hand checkered at wrist and forearm. Barrel and underrib are finished in bright blue; receiver is case colored. Double set triggers and adjustable rear sight. **Overall length:** $43\frac{1}{2}″$. **Weight:** $10\frac{1}{4}$ lbs.

TRYON CREEDMOOR RIFLE (Not shown)
$495.00

This updated version of the Tryon rifle features a high-quality back-action lock, double-set triggers, steel buttplate, patchbox, toe plate and curved trigger guard. **Caliber:** 45. **Barrel:** $32\frac{3}{4}″$, octagonal, with 1 twist in 20.87″. **Sights:** Hooded post front fitted with replaceable inserts; rear is tang-mounted and adjustable for windage and elevation.

DIXIE

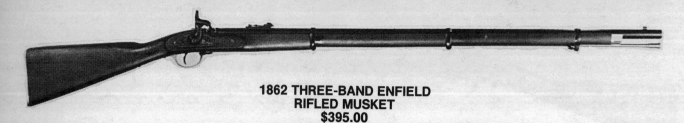

1862 THREE-BAND ENFIELD
RIFLED MUSKET
$395.00

One of the finest reproduction percussion guns available, the 1862 Enfield was widely used during the Civil War in its original version. This rifle follows the lines of the original almost exactly. The .58 caliber musket features a 39-inch barrel and walnut stock. Three steel barrel bands and the barrel itself are blued; the lock plate and hammer are case colored and the remainder of the furniture is highly polished brass. The lock is marked, "London Armory Co." **Weight:** 10½ lbs. **Overall length:** 55 inches.

1858 TWO-BAND ENFIELD RIFLE
$325.00

This 33-inch barrel version of the British Enfield is an exact copy of similar rifles used during the Civil War. The .58 caliber rifle sports a European walnut stock, deep blue-black finish on the barrel, bands, breech-plug tang and bayonet mount. The percussion lock is color casehardened and the rest of the furniture is brightly polished brass.

1863 SPRINGFIELD CIVIL WAR MUSKET
$475.00   Kit $330.00

An exact copy of the Model 1863 Springfield, which was the last of the regulation muzzleloading rifles. The barrel on this .58 caliber gun measures 40 inches. The action and all metal furniture is finished bright. The oil-finished walnut-stain stock is 53 inches long. **Overall length:** 56 inches. **Weight:** 9½ lbs.

EMF

SHERIFF'S MODEL 1851 REVOLVER
$114.00

SPECIFICATIONS
Caliber: 36 Percussion
Ball diameter: .376 round or conical, pure lead
Barrel length: 5″
Overall length: 10¹/₂″
Weight: 39 oz.
Sights: V-notch groove in hammer (rear); truncated cone in front
Percussion cap size: #11
Also available in complete **cased set** (36 caliber steel frame): **$160.00**

MODEL 1860 ARMY REVOLVER
$180.00

SPECIFICATIONS
Caliber: 44 Percussion
Barrel length: 8″
Overall length: 13⁵/₈″
Weight: 41 oz.
Frame: Casehardened
Finish: High-luster blue with walnut grips
Also available as a **cased set** with wood case, flask and mold: **$300.00**

MODEL 1851 STEEL NAVY REVOLVER
36 Caliber $170.00

SECOND MODEL 44 DRAGOON
$275.00

SPECIFICATIONS
Caliber: 44
Barrel length: 7¹/₂″ (round)
Overall length: 14″
Weight: 4 lbs.
Finish: Steel casehardened frame

MODEL 1862 POLICE REVOLVER
$225.00

SPECIFICATIONS
Caliber: 36 Percussion
Capacity: 5-shot
Barrel length: 6¹/₂″
Also available as a **cased set:** **$325.00**

EUROARMS OF AMERICA

SINGLE-BARRELED MAGNUM CAPE GUN
Model 2295: $400.00

Euroarms of America offers a beautiful reproduction of a classic English-styled single-barreled shotgun. The lock is left in the white and displays a scroll engraving, as does the bow of the trigger guard. Uses #11 percussion caps and recommended wads are felt overpowder and cardboard overshot.

Gauge: 12
Barrel: 32", open choke
Overall length: 47½"
Weight: 7½ lbs.
Stock: English style; European walnut with satin oil finish; moderate recoil, even with relatively heavy powder charges
Finish: Barrel, underrib, thimbles, nose cap, trigger guard and butt plate are deep, rich blue

COOK & BROTHER CONFEDERATE CARBINE
Model 2300: $367.00

Classic re-creation of the rare 1861, New Orleans-made Artillery Carbine. Lock plate is marked "Cook & Brother N.O. 1861" and is stamped with a Confederate flag at rear of hammer.

Caliber: 58
Barrel length: 24"
Overall length: 40⅓"
Weight: 7½ lbs.
Sights: Adjustable dovetailed front and rear sights
Ramrod: Steel
Finish: Barrel is antique brown; butt plate, trigger guard, barrel bands, sling swivels and nose cap are polished brass; stock is walnut
Recommended ball sizes: .575 r.b., .577 Minie and .580 maxi; uses musket caps

EUROARMS OF AMERICA

LONDON ARMORY COMPANY
2-BAND RIFLE MUSKET
Model 2270: $382.00

Caliber: 58
Barrel length: 33″, blued and rifled
Overall length: 49″
Weight: 8½–8¾ lbs., depending on wood density
Stock: One-piece walnut; polished "bright" brass butt plate, trigger guard and nose cap; blued barrel bands
Sights: Inverted 'V' front sight; Enfield folding ladder rear
Ramrod: Steel

LONDON ARMORY COMPANY
ENFIELD MUSKETOON
Model 2280: $350.00

Caliber: 58; Minie ball
Barrel length: 24″; round high-luster blued barrel
Overall length: 40½″
Weight: 7 to 7½ lbs., depending on density of wood
Stock: Seasoned walnut stock with sling swivels
Ramrod: Steel
Ignition: Heavy-duty percussion lock
Sights: Graduated military-leaf sight
Furniture: Brass trigger guard, nose cap and butt plate; blued barrel bands, lock plate, and swivels

LONDON ARMORY COMPANY
3-BAND ENFIELD RIFLED MUSKET
Model 2260: $427.00

Caliber: 58
Barrel length: 39″, blued and rifled
Overall length: 54″
Weight: 9½ — 9¾ lbs., depending on wood density
Stock: One-piece walnut; polished "bright" brass butt plate, trigger guard and nose cap; blued barrel bands
Ramrod: Steel; threaded end for accessories
Sights: Traditional Enfield folding ladder rear sight; inverted 'V' front sight

EUROARMS OF AMERICA

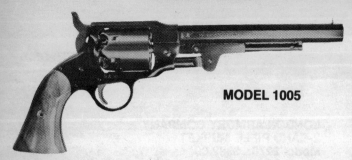

MODEL 1005

ROGERS & SPENCER REVOLVER
Model 1005
$192.00

Caliber: 44 Percussion; #11 percussion cap
Barrel length: 7½″
Sights: Integral rear sight notch groove in frame; brass truncated cone front sight
Overall length: 13¾″
Weight: 47 oz.
Finish: High-gloss blue; flared walnut grip; solid-frame design; precision-rifled barrel
Recommended ball diameter: .451 round or conical, pure lead

ROGERS & SPENCER ARMY REVOLVER
Model 1006 (Target)
$234.00

Caliber: 44; takes .451 round or conical lead balls; #11 percussion cap
Weight: 47 oz.
Barrel length: 7½″
Overall length: 13¾″
Finish: High-gloss blue; flared walnut grip; solid-frame design; precision-rifled barrel
Sights: Rear fully adjustable for windage and elevation; ramp front sight

MODEL 1006

ROGERS & SPENCER REVOLVER
Model 1007, London Gray
$234.00

Revolver is the same as Model 1005, except for London Gray finish, which is heat treated and buffed for rust resistance; same recommended ball size and percussion caps.

MODEL 1020

REMINGTON 1858
NEW MODEL ARMY REVOLVER
Model 1025: $164.00

This model is equipped with blued steel frame, brass trigger guard in 44 caliber.

Weight: 40 oz.
Barrel length: 8″
Overall length: 14¾″
Finish: Deep luster blue rifled barrel; polished walnut stock; brass trigger guard.
MODEL 1010: Same as Model 1025, except with 6½″ barrel and in 36 caliber: **$164.00**

REMINGTON 1858
NEW MODEL ARMY ENGRAVED
Model 1040: $275.00

Classical 19th-century style scroll engraving on this 1858 Remington New Model revolver.

Caliber: 44 Percussion; #11 cap
Barrel length: 8″
Overall length: 14¾″
Weight: 41 oz.
Sights: Integral rear sight notch groove in frame; blade front sight
Recommended ball diameter: .451 round or conical, pure lead

EUROARMS OF AMERICA

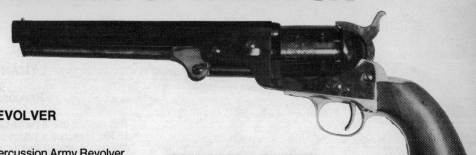

SCHNEIDER & GLASSICK
1851 NAVY CONFEDERATE REVOLVER
Model 1050 (36 Cal.): $104.00

A modern replica of a Confederate Percussion Army Revolver. Polished brass frame, rifled high-luster blued, octagonal barrel and polished walnut grips.

Weight: 40 oz.
Barrel length: 7$1/2$″
Overall length: 13″
Finish: Brass frame, backstrap and trigger guard; blued rifled barrel; casehardened hammer and loading lever; engraved cylinder with naval battle scene

SCHNEIDER & GLASSICK
1851 NAVY
CONFEDERATE REVOLVER

SCHNEIDER & GLASSICK
1851 NAVY (Not shown)
Model 1120: $137.00

Caliber: .36 percussion, #11 cap
Barrel length: 7$1/2$″, octagonal barrel, precision rifled
Overall length: 13″
Weight: 42 oz.
Finish: Blued barrel and frame; backstrap and trigger guard are polished brass; walnut grips.

GONIC ARMS

MODEL GA-87 RIFLE
$385.00 Standard
$410.50 Deluxe

SPECIFICATIONS
Caliber: 458 Express
Barrel lengths: 26″ (Rifle); 24″ (Carbine)
Overall length: 43″ (Rifle); 41″ (Carbine)
Weight: 6$1/2$ lbs. (Rifle); 6 lbs. (Carbine)
Sights: Bead front; open rear (adjustable for windage and elevation); drilled and tapped for scope bases

Stock: American walnut
Length of pull: 14″
Trigger: Single stage (4-lb. pull)
Mechanism type: Closed-breech muzzleloader
Features: Ambidextrous safety; non-glare satin finish; newly designed loading system; all-weather performance guaranteed; faster lock time

LYMAN

LYMAN PLAINS PISTOL
$174.95
Percussion Kit $144.95

This replica of the pistol carried by the Western pioneers of the 1830s features a pistol-sized Hawken lock with dependable coil spring and authentic rib and thimble styling. It has a richly stained walnut stock, blackened iron furniture and polished brass trigger guard and ramrod tips. Equipped with a spring-loaded trigger and a fast twist (1 in 30 inches both calibers) barrel for target accuracy. **Caliber:** 50 or 54 percussion.

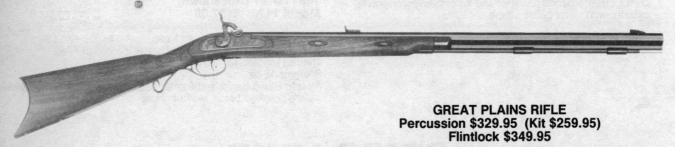

GREAT PLAINS RIFLE
Percussion $329.95 (Kit $259.95)
Flintlock $349.95

The Great Plains Rifle has a 32-inch deep-grooved barrel and 1 in 66-inch twist to shoot patched round balls. Blued steel furniture including the thick steel wedge plates and steel toe plate; correct lock and hammer styling with coil spring dependability; and a walnut stock without a patch box. A Hawken-style trigger guard protects double-set triggers. Steel front sight and authentic buckhorn styling in an adjustable rear sight. Fixed primitive rear sight also included. **Caliber:** 50 or 54.

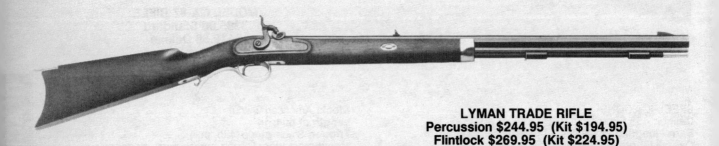

LYMAN TRADE RIFLE
Percussion $244.95 (Kit $194.95)
Flintlock $269.95 (Kit $224.95)

The Lyman Trade Rifle features a 28-inch octagonal barrel, rifled one turn at 48 inches, designed to fire both patched round balls and the popular maxistyle conical bullets. Polished brass furniture with blued finish on steel parts; walnut stock; hook breech; single spring-loaded trigger; coil-spring percussion lock; fixed steel sights; adjustable rear sight for elevation also included. Steel barrel rib and ramrod ferrule. **Caliber:** 50 or 54 percussion and flint. **Overall length:** 45".

MODERN MUZZLELOADING

KNIGHT MK-85 RIFLE

The Knight MK-85 muzzleloading rifle (designed by William A. "Tony" Knight of Schuyler County, Missouri) is a handcrafted, lightweight rifle capable of 1½-inch groups at 100 yards. It features a one-piece, in-line bolt assembly, patented double safety system, Timney featherweight deluxe trigger system, recoil pad, and Lothar Walther barrels (1 in 32″ twist in 50 and 54 caliber; 1 in 17″ twist in 45 caliber).

SPECIFICATIONS
Calibers: 45, 50 and 54
Barrel lengths: 20″, 22″ and 24″
Weight: 7 lbs.
Sights: Adjustable high-visibility open sights
Stock: Classic walnut, laminated, or composite
Features: Swivel studs installed; LS&B Perfect Memory nylon ramrod; combo tool; flush valve; hex keys, and more.
Prices:
KNIGHT MK-85 HUNTER (Walnut) $479.95
KNIGHT MK-85 STALKER (Laminated) 519.95
KNIGHT MK-85 PREDATOR (Stainless) 559.95

NAVY ARMS REVOLVERS

1862 POLICE MODEL

This is the last gun manufactured by the Colt Plant in the percussion era. It encompassed all the modifications of each gun starting from the early Paterson to the 1861 Navy. It was favored by the New York Police Dept. for many years. One-half fluted and rebated cylinder, 36 cal., 5 shot, .375 dia. ball, 18 grains of black powder, brass trigger guard and backstrap. Case-hardened frame, loading lever and hammer—balance blue. **Barrel length:** 5½″.

1862 Police $220.00
Law and Order Set 275.00

NAVY ARMS REVOLVERS

LE MAT REVOLVERS

Once the official sidearm of many Confederate cavalry officers, this 9 shot .44 caliber revolver with a central single shot barrel of approx. 65 caliber gave the cavalry man 10 shots to use against the enemy. **Barrel length:** 7⁵/₈″. **Overall length:** 14″. **Weight:** 3 lbs. 7 oz.

Cavalry Model	$550.00
Navy Model	550.00
Army Model	550.00

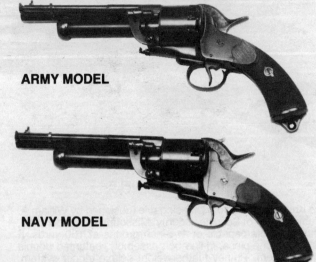

ARMY MODEL

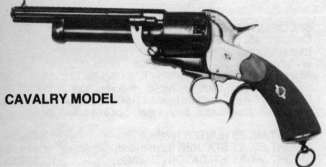

CAVALRY MODEL

NAVY MODEL

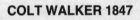

COLT WALKER 1847

The 1847 Walker replica comes in 44 caliber with a 9-inch barrel. **Weight:** 4 lbs. 8 oz. Well suited for the collector as well as the black powder shooter. Features include: rolled cylinder scene; blued and case-hardened finish; and brass guard. Proof tested.

Colt Walter 1847	$185.00
Single Cased Set	275.00

ROGERS & SPENCER NAVY REVOLVER

This revolver features a six-shot cylinder, octagonal barrel, hinged-type loading lever assembly, two-piece walnut grips, blued finish and case-hardened hammer and lever. **Caliber:** 44. **Barrel length:** 7¹/₂″. **Overall length:** 13³/₄″. **Weight:** 3 lbs.

Rogers & Spencer	$160.00
With satin finish	180.00

NAVY ARMS REVOLVERS

REB MODEL 1860

A modern replica of the confederate Griswold & Gunnison percussion Army revolver. Rendered with a polished brass frame and a rifled steel barrel finished in a high-luster blue with genuine walnut grips. All Army Model 60's are completely proof-tested by the Italian government to the most exacting standards. **Calibers:** 36 and 44. **Barrel length:** 7 1/4". **Overall length:** 13". **Weight:** 2 lbs. 10 oz.-11 oz. **Finish:** Brass frame, backstrap and trigger guard, round barrel hinged rammer on the 44 cal. rebated cylinder.

Reb Model 1860	$100.00
Single Cased Set	199.00
Double Cased Set	300.00
Kit	80.00

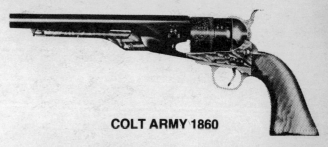

COLT ARMY 1860

These guns from the Colt line are 44 caliber and all six-shot. The cylinder was authentically roll engraved with a polished brass trigger guard and steel strap cut for shoulder stock. The frame, loading lever and hammer are finished in high-luster color case-hardening. Walnut grips. **Weight:** 2 lbs. 9 oz. **Barrel length:** 8". **Overall length:** 13 5/8". **Caliber:** 44. **Finish:** Brass trigger guard, steel back strap, round barrel creeping cylinder, rebated cylinder engraved. Navy scene. Frame cut for s/stock (4 screws). Also available with full fluted cylinder and in 5 1/2" barrel (Sheriff's model).

Army 1860	$150.00
Single Cased Set	225.00
Double Cased Set	350.00
Kit	120.00

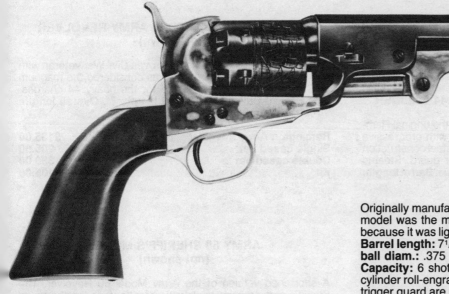

1851 NAVY "YANK"

Originally manufactured by Colt from 1850 through 1876, this model was the most popular of the Union revolvers, mostly because it was lighter and easier to handle than the Dragoon. **Barrel length:** 7 1/2". **Overall length:** 14". **Weight:** 2 lbs. **Rec. ball diam.:** .375 R.B. (.451 in 44 cal) **Calibers:** 36 and 44. **Capacity:** 6 shot. **Features:** Steel frame, octagonal barrel, cylinder roll-engraved with Naval battle scene, backstrap and trigger guard are polished brass.

1851 Navy "Yank"	$125.00
Kit	95.00
Single Cased Set	199.00
Double Cased Set	325.00

BLACK POWDER

NAVY ARMS REVOLVERS

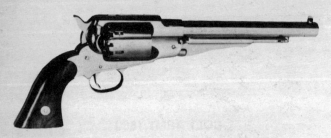

STAINLESS STEEL 1858 REMINGTON

Exactly like the standard 1858 Remington except that every part with the exception of the grips and trigger guard is manufactured from corrosion-resistant stainless steel. This gun has all the style and feel of its ancestor with all of the conveniences of stainless steel. **Caliber:** 44.

1858 Remington Stainless **$220.00**

TARGET MODEL REMINGTON REVOLVER

With its top strap and frame, the Remington Percussion Revolver is considered the magnum of Civil War revolvers and is ideally suited to the heavy 44-caliber charges. Based on the Army Model, the target gun has target sights for controlled accuracy. Ruggedly built from modern steel and proof tested.

Remington Percussion Revolver **$155.00**

DELUXE 1858 REMINGTON-STYLE 44 CALIBER

Built to the exact dimensions and weight of the original Remington 44, this model features an 8″ barrel with progressive rifling, adjustable front sight for windage, all-steel construction with walnut stocks and silver-plated trigger guard. Steel is highly polished and finished in rich charcoal blue. **Barrel length:** 8″. **Overall length:** 14¼″. **Weight:** 2 lbs. 14 oz.

Deluxe 1858 Remington-Style 44 Cal. **$300.00**

REMINGTON NEW MODEL ARMY REVOLVER
(not shown)

This rugged, dependable, battle-proven Civil War veteran with its top strap and rugged frame was considered the magnum of C.W. revolvers, ideally suited for the heavy 44 charges. Blued finish. **Caliber:** 44. **Barrel length:** 8″. **Overall length:** 14¼″. **Weight:** 2 lbs. 8 oz.

Remington Army Revolver **$135.00**
Single cased set **205.00**
Double cased set **330.00**
Kit **105.00**

ARMY 60 SHERIFF'S MODEL
(not shown)

A shortened version of the Army Model 60 Revolver. The Sheriff's model version became popular because the shortened barrel was fast out of the leather. This is actually the original snub nose, the predecessor of the detective specials or belly guns designed for quick-draw use. A piece of traditional Americana, the Sheriff's model was adopted by many local police departments. **Calibers:** 36 and 44.

Army 60 Sheriff's Model **$110.00**
Kit **80.00**

NAVY ARMS PISTOLS

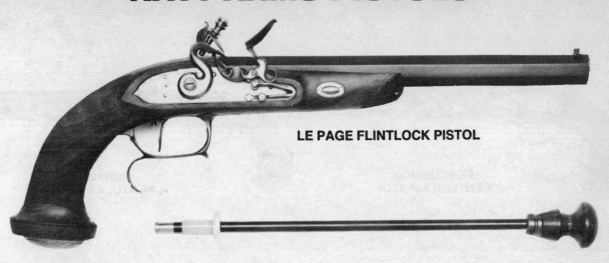

LE PAGE FLINTLOCK PISTOL

LE PAGE FLINTLOCK PISTOL
(45 Caliber)

The Le Page pistol is a beautifully hand-crafted reproduction featuring hand-checkered walnut stock with hinged buttcap and carved motif of a shell at the forward portion of the stock. Single-set trigger and highly polished steel lock and furniture together with a brown finished rifled barrel make this a highly desirable target pistol. **Barrel length:** 10½″. **Overall length:** 17″. **Weight:** 2 lbs. 2 oz.

Le Page Flintlock (rifled or smoothbore) $315.00
Single Cased Set 495.00

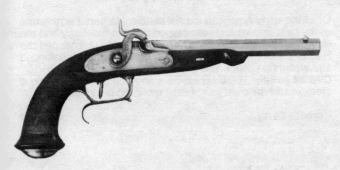

LE PAGE PERCUSSION PISTOL
(45 Caliber)

The tapered octagonal rifled barrel is in the traditional style with 7 lands and grooves. Fully adjustable single-set trigger. Engraved overall with traditional scrollwork. The European walnut stock is in the Boutet style. Spur-style trigger guard. Fully adjustable elevating rear sight. Dovetailed front sight adjustable for windage. **Barrel length:** 9″. **Overall length:** 15″. **Weight:** 2 lbs. 2 oz. **Rec. ball diameter:** 440 R.B.

Le Page Percussion $295.00

CASED LE PAGE PISTOL SETS
(45 Caliber)

The case is French-fitted and the accessories are the finest quality to match.

Double Cased Flintlock Set $850.00

Double Cased Set
French-fitted double-cased set comprising two Le Page pistols, turn screw, nipple key, oil bottle, cleaning brushes, leather covered flask and loading rod.

Double Cased Percussion Set $700.00

Single Cased Set
French-fitted single-cased set comprising one Le Page pistol, turn screw, nipple key, oil bottle, cleaning brushes, leather covered flask and loading rod.

Single Cased Percussion Set $420.00

NAVY ARMS PISTOLS

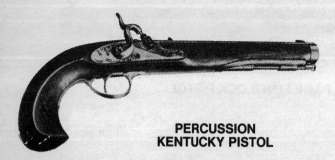

**PERCUSSION
KENTUCKY PISTOL**

**FLINTLOCK
KENTUCKY PISTOL**

KENTUCKY PISTOLS

The Kentucky Pistol is truly a historical American gun. It was carried during the Revolution by the Minutemen and was the sidearm of "Andy" Jackson in the Battle of New Orleans. Navy Arms Company has conducted extensive research to manufacture a pistol truly representative of its kind, with the balance and handle of the original for which it became famous.

Flintlock	$120.00
Single Cased Flintlock Set	195.00
Double Cased Flintlock Set	295.00
Percussion	100.00
Single Cased Percussion Set	175.00
Double Cased Percussion Set	270.00

HARPERS FERRY PISTOLS

Of all the early American martial pistols, Harpers Ferry is one of the best known and was carried by both the Army and the Navy. Navy Arms Company has authentically reproduced the Harper's Ferry to the finest detail, providing a well-balanced and well-made pistol. **Weight:** 2 lbs. 9 oz. **Barrel length:** 10". **Overall length:** 16". **Caliber:** 58 smoothbore. **Finish:** Walnut stock; casehardened lock; brass mounted browned barrel.

Harpers Ferry **$165.00**

ELGIN CUTLASS PISTOL

Part of Navy Arm's Classic Collection, this pistol represents the only combination gun (knife and pistol) ever issued by any U.S. military service. It was also the first percussion handgun officially used by the U.S. **Overall length:** 9" (12" blade). **Rec. ball diam.:** .440 R.B. **Weight:** 2 lbs.

Elgin Cutlass Pistol	$80.00
Kit	60.00

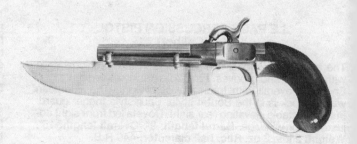

NAVY ARMS RIFLES

PARKER-HALE WHITWORTH MILITARY TARGET RIFLE

Recreation of Sir Joseph Whitworth's deadly and successful sniper and target weapon of the mid-1800s. Devised with a hexagonal bore with a pitch of 1 turn in 20 inches. Barrel is cold-forged from ordnance steel, reducing the build-up of black powder fouling. Globe front sight; open military target rifle rear sight has interchangeable blades of different heights. Walnut stock is hand-checkered. **Caliber:** 451. **Barrel length:** 36″. **Weight:** 9 1/2 lbs.

Parker-Hale Whitworth Military Target Rifle **$795.00**

PARKER-HALE 451 VOLUNTEER RIFLE

Originally designed by Irish gunmaker, William John Rigby, this relatively small-caliber rifle was issued to volunteer regiments during the 1860s. Today it is rifled by the cold-forged method, making one turn in 20 inches. Sights are adjustable: globe front and ladder-type rear with interchangeable leaves; hand-checkered walnut stock. **Weight:** 9 1/2 lbs.

Parker-Hale 451 Volunteer Rifle **$775.00**
    Same as above with 3-band barrel **795.00**

Other Parker-Hale muskets available:
2-BAND MUSKET MODEL 1858
    Barrel length: 33″. **Overall length:** 48 1/2″. **Weight:** 8 1/2 lbs. **500.00**
MUSKETOON MODEL 1861
    Barrel length: 24″. **Overall length:** 40 1/4″. **Weight:** 7 1/2 lbs. **400.00**
3-BAND MUSKET MODEL 1853
    Barrel length: 39″. **Overall length:** 55″. **Weight:** 9 lbs. **550.00**

ITHACA/NAVY HAWKEN RIFLE

Features a 31 1/2″ octagonal blued barrel crowned at the muzzle with buckhorn-style rear sight, blade front sight. Color case hardened percussion lock is fitted on walnut stock. Furniture is all steel and blued (except for nose cap and escutcheons). Available in 50 and 54 cal.

Ithaca/Navy Hawken Rifle **$225.00**
Kit **185.00**

NAVY ARMS RIFLES

#2 CREEDMOOR TARGET RIFLE

Features a color casehardened rolling block receiver, checkered walnut stock and forend, 30″ tapered barrel in 45/70 caliber with blued finish, hooded front sight and Creedmoor tang sight. **Barrel length: 30″. Overall length: 46″. Weight: 9 lbs.**

#2 Creedmoor Target Rifle	$640.00
Rolling Block Action	125.00

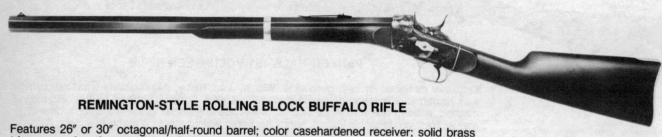

REMINGTON-STYLE ROLLING BLOCK BUFFALO RIFLE

Features 26″ or 30″ octagonal/half-round barrel; color casehardened receiver; solid brass trigger guard, walnut stock and forend. Available in 45/70 caliber only. Tang is drilled and tapped for Creedmoor sight.

Remington-Style Rolling Block Buffalo Rifle	$489.00

COUNTRY BOY RIFLE
(32, 36, 45, and 50 Caliber)

An authentic copy of one of the most effective percussion systems ever devised. The simple lock is trouble-free and with the nipple directly on the barrel gives fast, positive ignition. The quickest handling, fastest shooting rifle on the market today; ideal for the young beginner shooter. Features hooked breech and fully adjustable hunting sights. Simple, efficient and trustworthy. **Barrel length: 26″. Weight: 5½ lbs.**

Country Boy Rifle	$165.00
Rifle Kit	145.00

NAVY ARMS RIFLES

1853 ENFIELD RIFLE MUSKET

The Enfield Rifle Musket marked the zenith in design and manufacture of the military percussion rifle and this perfection has been reproduced by Navy Arms Company. This and other Enfield muzzleloaders were the most coveted rifles of the Civil War, treasured by Union and Confederate troops alike for their fine quality and deadly accuracy. **Caliber:** 557. **Barrel length:** 39″. **Weight:** 9 lbs. **Overall length:** 55″. **Sights:** Fixed front; graduated rear. **Rifling:** 3 groove, cold forged. **Stock:** Seasoned walnut with solid brass furniture.

1853 Enfield Rifle Musket **$400.00**

1858 ENFIELD RIFLE

In the late 1850s the British Admiralty, after extensive experiments, settled on a pattern rifle with a 5-groove barrel of heavy construction, sighted to 1100 yards, designated the Naval rifle, Pattern 1858. In the recreation of this famous rifle Navy Arms has referred to the original 1858 Enfield Rifle in the Tower of London and has closely followed the specifications even to the progressive depth rifling. **Caliber:** 557. **Barrel length:** 33″. **Weight:** 8 lbs. 8 oz. **Overall length:** 48.5″. **Sights:** Fixed front; graduated rear. **Rifling:** 5-groove; cold forged. **Stock:** Seasoned walnut with solid brass furniture.

1858 Enfield Rifle **$325.00**

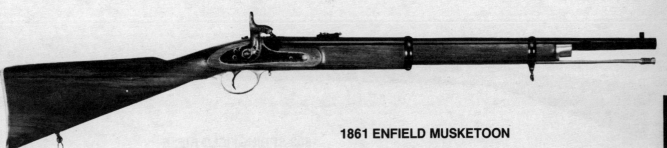

1861 ENFIELD MUSKETOON

The 1861 Enfield Musketoon is a Limited Collector's edition, individually serial numbered with certificate of authenticity. **Caliber:** 557. **Barrel length:** 24″. **Weight:** 7 lbs. 8 oz. **Overall length:** 40.25″. **Sights:** Fixed front; graduated rear. **Rifling:** 5-groove; cold forged. **Stock:** Seasoned walnut with solid brass furniture.

1861 Enfield Musketoon **$295.00**
Kit **250.00**

BLACK POWDER

NAVY ARMS RIFLES

MISSISSIPPI RIFLE MODEL 1841

The historic percussion lock weapon that gained its name as a result of its performance in the hands of Jefferson Davis' Mississippi Regiment during the heroic stand at the Battle of Buena Vista. Also known as the "Yager" (a misspelling of the German Jaeger), this was the first rifle adopted by Army Ordnance to fire the traditional round ball. In 58 caliber, the Mississippi is handsomely furnished in brass, including patch box for tools and spare parts. **Weight:** 9½ lbs. **Barrel length:** 32½". **Overall length:** 48½". **Caliber:** 58. **Finish:** Walnut finish stock, brass mounted.

Mississippi Rifle Model 1841 . . . . **$400.00**

RIGBY-STYLE TARGET RIFLE

This affordable reproduction of the famed Rigby Target Rifle of the 1880s features a 32-inch blued barrel, target front sight with micrometer adjustment, fully adjustable vernier rear sight (adjustable up to 1000 yards), hand-checkered walnut stock color casehardened breech plug, hammer lock plate, and escutcheons. This .451 caliber gun is cased with loading accessories, including bullet starter and sizer and special ramrod.

Rigby-Style Target Rifle **$500.00**

1863 SPRINGFIELD RIFLE

An authentically reproduced replica of one of America's most historical firearms, the 1863 Springfield rifle features a full-size, three-band musket and precision-rifled barrel. **Caliber:** 58. **Barrel length:** 40". **Overall length:** 56". **Weight:** 9½ lbs. **Finish:** Walnut stock with polished metal lock and stock fittings.

1863 Springfield Rifle **$475.00**
Springfield Kit **400.00**

NAVY ARMS RIFLES

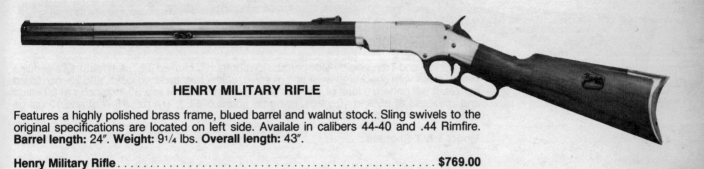

HENRY MILITARY RIFLE

Features a highly polished brass frame, blued barrel and walnut stock. Sling swivels to the original specifications are located on left side. Availale in calibers 44-40 and .44 Rimfire. **Barrel length:** 24″. **Weight:** 9¼ lbs. **Overall length:** 43″.

Henry Military Rifle **$769.00**

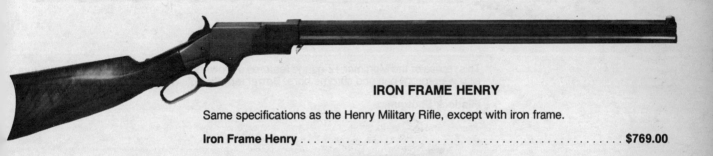

IRON FRAME HENRY

Same specifications as the Henry Military Rifle, except with iron frame.

Iron Frame Henry **$769.00**

HENRY TRAPPER MODEL

This short, lightweight 44/40 is ideal for the hunter. **Barrel length:** 16½″. **Overall length:** 34½″. **Weight:** 7¼ lbs.

Henry Trapper Model **$769.00**

HENRY CARBINE

The arm first utilized by the Kentucky Cavalry. Available in either original 44 rimfire caliber or in 44/40 caliber. Oil-stained American walnut stock, blued finish with brass frame. **Barrel length:** 23⅝″. **Overall length:** 45″.

Henry Carbine **$769.00**

NAVY ARMS SHOTGUNS

MODEL T & T SHOTGUN (12 GAUGE PERCUSSION)

This Turkey and Trap side-by-side percussion shotgun is choked full/full. It features a genuine walnut stock with checkered wrist and oil finish, color casehardened locks, and 28-inch blued barrels. It will pattern a load of #6 shot size in excess of 85% in a 30-inch circle at 30 yards and in excess of 65% at 40 yards, using 96 grains of FFg, 1¼ oz. #6 shot and 13 gauge overshot, over powder and cushion wads.

Model T & T Shotgun **$325.00**

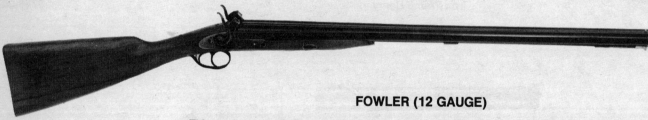

FLINTLOCK SHOTGUN

This replica of the Mortimer 12-gauge features a browned barrel and casehardened furniture, also waterproof pan and chrome bore. **Barrel length:** 36″. **Weight:** 7½ lbs. **Stock:** Walnut.

Flintlock Shotgun **$595.00**

FOWLER (12 GAUGE)

This traditional side-by-side percussion field gun features blued barrels and English-style straight stock design. It also sports a hooked breech, engraved and color casehardened percussion locks, double triggers and checkered walnut stained stock. **Gauge:** 12. **Chokes:** Cylinder/Cylinder. **Barrel length:** 28″. **Overall length:** 44½″. **Weight:** 7½ lbs.

Fowler (12 Gauge) **$350.00**

STEEL SHOT FOWLER (10 GAUGE)

Same general specifications as 12-Gauge Fowler (above), but with heavier barrels and designed for steel shot.

Steel Shot Fowler **$350.00**
Extra 10-Gauge Barrels **130.00**

SHILOH SHARPS

MODEL 1874 BUSINESS RIFLE
$725.00

Calibers: 45-70, 45-90, 45-120, 50-70, 50-90 and 50-140. **Barrel:** 28-inch heavy-tapered round; dark blue. Double-set triggers adjustable set. **Sights:** Blade front, and sporting rear with leaf. Buttstock is straight grip rifle butt plate, forend sporting schnabel style. Receiver group and butt plate case-colored; wood is American walnut oil-finished. **Weight:** 9 lbs. 8 oz.

MODEL 1874 MILITARY RIFLE
$845.00

Calibers: 45-70 and 50-70. **Barrel:** 30-inch round; dark blue. Blade front and Lawrence-style sights. Military-style forend with 3 barrel bands and 1¼-inch swivels. Receiver group, butt plate and barrel bands case-colored. Wood is oil finished. **Weight:** 8 lbs. 2 oz.
Also available: **1874 MILITARY CARBINE** with 22″ round barrel. **Weight:** 7 lbs. 8 oz. **Price: $765.00.**

MODEL 1874 CARBINE
$725.00

Calibers: 45-70 and 45-90. **Barrel:** 24-inch round; dark blue. Single trigger, blade front and sporting rear sight, buttstock straight grip, steel rifle butt plate, forend sporting schnabel style. Case-colored receiver group and butt plate; wood has oil finish. **Weight:** 8 lbs. 4 oz.

SHARPS MODEL 1874 RIFLE and CARTRIDGE AVAILABILITY TABLE

MODEL	CALIBERS									
	40-50 1¹¹/₁₆″BN	40-70 2¼″BN	40-90 2⁵/₈″BN	45-70 2¹/₁₀″ST	45-90 2⁴/₁₀″ST	45-100 2⁶/₁₀″ST	45-110 2⁷/₈″ST	45-120 3¼″ST	50-70 1³/₄″ST	50-100 2½″ST
Long Range Express	•	•	•	•	•	•	•	•		•
No. 1 Sporting Rifle	•	•	•	•	•	•	•	•		•
No. 3 Sporting Rifle	•	•	•	•			•	•		•
Saddle Rifle	•	•	•	•	•					
Business Rifle	•	•	•	•	•	•		•	•	•
Carbine	•	•	•	•	•	•	•			
1874 Military Rifle	•	•	•	•					•	

• Standard
BN = Bottleneck, ST = Straight

SHILOH SHARPS

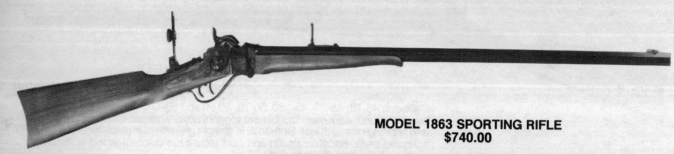

MODEL 1863 SPORTING RIFLE
$740.00

Caliber: 54. **Barrel:** 30″ tapered octagonal. Blade front sight, sporting rear with elevation leaf; double-set triggers with adjustable set; curved trigger plate, pistol grip buttstock with steel butt plate, forend schnable style; optional Tang sight. **Weight:** 9 lbs.
Also available:
MODEL 1863 PERCUSSION MILITARY RIFLE $850.00
MODEL 1863 PERCUSSION CARBINE 740.00

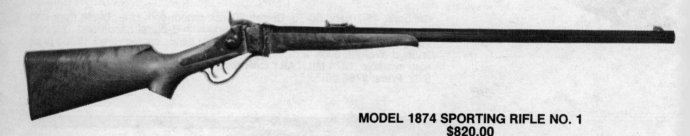

MODEL 1874 SPORTING RIFLE NO. 1
$820.00

Calibers: 45-70, 45-90, 45-120, 50-70, 50-90 and 50-140. Features 28-inch or 30-inch tapered octagon barrel. Double-set triggers with adjustable set, blade front sight, sporting rear with elevation leaf and sporting tang sight adjustable for elevation and windage. Buttstock is pistol grip, shotgun butt, sporting forend style. Receiver group and butt plate case colored. Barrel is high finish blue-black; wood is American walnut oil finish. **Weight:** 10 lbs.

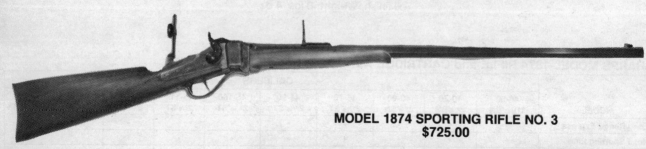

MODEL 1874 SPORTING RIFLE NO. 3
$725.00

Calibers: 45-70, 45-90, 45-120, 50-70, 50-90 and 50-140. **Barrel:** 30-inch tapered octagonal; with high finish blue-black. Double-set triggers with adjustable set, blade front sight, sporting rear with elevation leaf and sporting tang sight adjustable for elevation and windage. Buttstock is straight grip with rifle butt plate; trigger plate is curved and checkered to match pistol grip. Forend is sporting schnabel style. Receiver group and butt plate is case colored. Wood is American walnut oil-finished. **Weight:** 9 lbs. 8 oz.

THOMPSON/CENTER

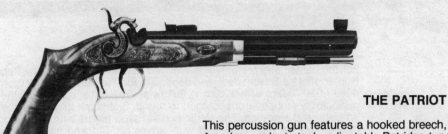

THE PATRIOT

This percussion gun features a hooked breech, double-set triggers, first-grade American walnut stock, adjustable Patridge-type target sights, solid brass trim, beautifully decorated and color casehardened lock with a small dolphin-shaped hammer. **Weight:** Approx. 36 oz. Inspired by traditional gallery and dueling-type pistols, its carefully selected features retain the full flavor of antiquity, yet modern metals and manufacturing methods have been used to ensure its shooting qualities.

Patriot Pistol 45 caliber **$235.00**
Kit **165.00**

THE NEW ENGLANDER RIFLE

This percussion rifle features 26″ round, 50 or 54 caliber rifled barrel (1 in 48″ twist). **Weight:** 7 lbs. 15 oz.
New Englander Rifle **$220.00**
Left-Hand Model **235.00**

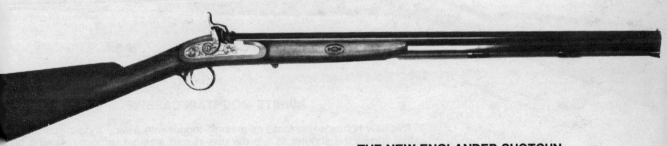

THE NEW ENGLANDER SHOTGUN

This new 12-gauge muzzleloading percussion shotgun weighs only 5 lbs. 2 oz. It features a 28-inch (improved cylinder) round barrel and is stocked with selected American black walnut.
New Englander Shotgun **$220.00**
Left-Hand Model **235.00**

THOMPSON/CENTER

PENNSYLVANIA HUNTER

For the hunter who prefers (or is required to use) a round ball, the Pennsylvania Hunter offers a firearm designed especially for that purpose. Its 31″ barrel is cut rifled (.010″ deep) with 1 turn in 66″ twist. The outer contour of the barrel is distinctively stepped from octagon to round. Sights are fully adjustable for both windage and elevation. The single hunting style trigger with large trigger guard bow allows the rifle to be fired with gloves on. Stocked with select American black walnut; metal hardware is all blued steel. Features a hooked breech system and coil spring lock. **Caliber:** Caplock and flintlock models are available in .50 caliber only. **Overall length:** 48″. **Weight:** Approx. 7.6 lbs.

Pennsylvania Hunter Caplock .50 caliber $265.00
Pennsylvania Hunter Flintlock .50 caliber 280.00

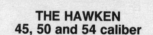

THE HAWKEN
45, 50 and 54 caliber

Similar to the famous Rocky Mountain rifles made during the early 1800's, the Hawken is intended for serious shooting. Button-rifled for ultimate precision, the Hawken is available in 45, 50 or 54 caliber, flint or percussion. Featuring a hooked breech, double-set triggers, first-grade American walnut, adjustable hunting sights, solid brass trim, beautifully decorated and color casehardened lock.

Hawken Caplock 45, 50 or 54 caliber $325.00
Hawken Flintlock 50 caliber 340.00
Kit: Percussion 230.00
Flintlock 245.00

WHITE MOUNTAIN CARBINE

This new hunter's rifle features a single trigger with a wide trigger guard bow that allows the shooter to fire the rifle in cold weather without removing his gloves. Its stock is of select American black walnut finished off with a rifle-type rubber recoil pad, and equipped with swivel studs and quick detachable sling swivels. A soft leather hunting-style sling is included. The barrel's outer surface is stepped from octagonal to round. **Caliber:** 50 (Hawken or Renegade loads). **Barrel length:** 21″. **Overall length:** 38″. **Weight:** 6½ lbs. **Sights:** Open hunting (Patridge) style, fully adjustable. **Lock:** Heavy-duty coil springs; decorated with floral design and color-cased. **Breech:** Hooked breech system.

White Mountain Carbine (right-hand only) $275.00

THOMPSON/CENTER

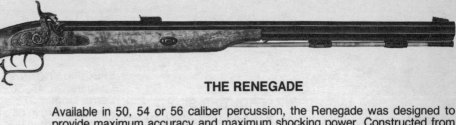

THE RENEGADE

Available in 50, 54 or 56 caliber percussion, the Renegade was designed to provide maximum accuracy and maximum shocking power. Constructed from superior modern steel with investment cast parts fitted to an American walnut stock, the rifle features a precision-rifled (26-inch carbine-type) octagon barrel, hooked-breech system, coil spring lock, double-set triggers, adjustable hunting sights and steel trim. **Weight:** Approx. 8 lbs.

Renegade Caplock 50 and 54 caliber and 56 caliber smoothbore	$275.00
Renegade Caplock Left Hand	285.00
Renegade Caplock Kit (R.H. only)	200.00
Renegade Flintlock 50 caliber (R.H. only)	290.00
Renegade Flintlock Kit (R.H. only)	215.00

RENEGADE HUNTER
50 and 54 Caliber

This single trigger hunter model, fashioned after the double triggered Renegade introduced in 1974 with great success, features a large bow in the shotgun style trigger guard. This allows shooters to fire the rifle in cold weather without removing their gloves. The octagon barrel measures 26″ and the stock is made of select American walnut. **Weight:** About 8 pounds.

Renegade Hunter	$255.00

THE CHEROKEE

A light percussion sporting rifle with interchangeable barrels. **Caliber:** 32 or 45. **Barrel length:** 24″. **Weight:** About 6 lbs. Sights are open hunting style fully adjustable for windage and elevation. Stock is American walnut with contoured cheekpiece on left-hand side.

Cherokee Caplock	$265.00
Kit	210.00
Interchangeable barrels (w/ramrod) in 32 and 45 caliber	115.00
Kit barrels	80.00

BLACK POWDER

TRADITIONS

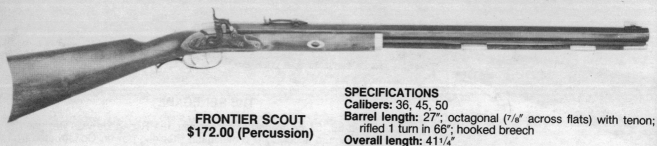

FRONTIER SCOUT
$172.00 (Percussion)

SPECIFICATIONS
Calibers: 36, 45, 50
Barrel length: 27"; octagonal (7/8" across flats) with tenon; rifled 1 turn in 66"; hooked breech
Overall length: 41 1/4"
Weight: 4.75 lbs.
Length of pull: 12 1/4"
Sights: Fully adjustable rear, brass blade front
Stock: Beech
Lock: Adjustable sear engagement with fly and bridle
Furniture: Solid brass, blued steel

HUNTER RIFLE
$321.00 (Percussion)

SPECIFICATIONS
Calibers: 50, 54
Barrel length: 29"; octagonal (1" across flats) with 2 tenons; hooked breech, rifled 1 turn in 66"
Overall length: 46"
Weight: 7 1/2 lbs.
Lock: Adjustable sear engagement with fly and bridle
Stock: Walnut with contoured beavertail cheekpiece
Sights: Fully screw adjustable for windage and elevation; beaded blade front with Patridge-style open rear; both dovetailed
Furniture: Black-chromed brass with German silver wedge plates and stock ornaments

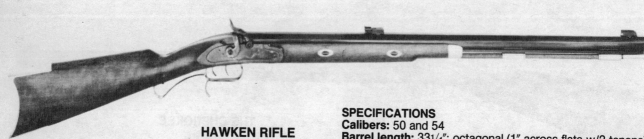

HAWKEN RIFLE
$316.00 (Percussion)
$213.00 (Kit)

SPECIFICATIONS
Calibers: 50 and 54
Barrel length: 33 1/4"; octagonal (1" across flats w/2 tenons)
Overall length: 50 3/8"
Weight: 9 lbs.
Lock: Adjustable sear engagement with fly and bridle
Stock: Walnut, beavertail cheekpiece
Triggers: Double set; will fire set and unset
Sights: Fully screw adjustable for windage and elevation; beaded front sight with Patridge-style open rear; both are dovetailed
Furniture: Solid brass, blued steel

TRADITIONS

HAWKEN WOODSMAN
$206.00 (Percussion)
$160.00 (Kit)

Overall length: 45³/₄″
Weight: 7 lbs.
Triggers: Double set; will fire set or unset
Lock: Adjustable sear engagement with fly and bridle
Stock: Beech
Sights: Fully screw adjustable for windage and elevation; beaded blade front with Patridge-style open rear
Furniture: Solid brass, blued steel

SPECIFICATIONS
Calibers: 50 and 54
Barrel length: 28″ (octagonal); hooked breech; rifled 1 turn in 66″

PENNSYLVANIA RIFLE
$369.00 (Flintlock)
$354.00 (Percussion)

Weight: 9 lbs.
Lock: Adjustable sear engagement with fly and bridle
Stock: Walnut, beavertail style
Triggers: Double set; will fire set and unset
Sights: Primitive-style adjustable rear; brass blade front
Furniture: Solid brass, blued steel

SPECIFICATIONS
Calibers: 45 and 50
Barrel length: 40¹/₄″; octagonal (⁷/₈″ across flats) with 3 tenons; rifled 1 turn in 66″
Overall length: 57¹/₂″

PIONEER RIFLE
$161.00

Weight: 7 lbs.
Trigger: Sear adjustable
Stock: Beech
Sights: Buckhorn rear with elevation ramp, ajustable for windage and elevation; German silver blade front
Lock: Adjustable sear engagement; V-type mainspring
Features: Blackened hardward; German silver furniture

SPECIFICATIONS
Calibers: 50 and 54 percussion
Barrel length: 27¹/₄″ octagonal w/tenon (rifled 1 turn in 66″ or 48″)
Overall length: 44″

TROPHY RIFLE
$321.00

Weight: 7 lbs.
Lock: Adjustable sear engagement with bridle, claw mainspring
Trigger: Sear adjustable
Stock: Walnut with cheekpiece
Sights: Hunting-style rear, click adjustable for windage and elevation; Patridge-style blade front
Features: Sling swivel, fiberglass ramrod, blackened furniture

SPECIFICATIONS
Calibers: 50 and 54
Barrel length: 27¹/₄″ octagonal-to-round with tenon (rifled 1 turn in 48″ or 66″)
Overall length: 44³/₄″

TRADITIONS

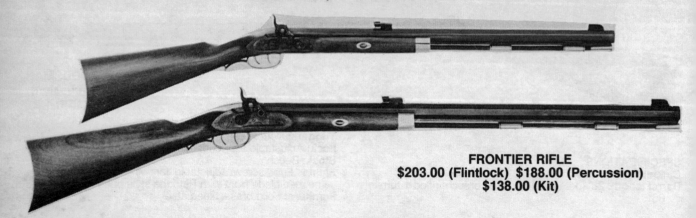

FRONTIER RIFLE
$203.00 (Flintlock) $188.00 (Percussion)
$138.00 (Kit)

SPECIFICATIONS
Calibers: 45 (percussion only) and 50
Barrel length: 28″ octagonal ($^{15}/_{16}$ across flats) with tenon; hooked breech, rifled 1 turn in 66″
Overall length: 44$^1/_4$″
Weight: 8 lbs.
Lock: Adjustable sear engagement with fly and bridle
Triggers: Double set; will fire set and unset

Stock: Beech
Sights: Fully screw adjustable for windage and elevation; beaded blade front with Patridge-style open rear (dovetailed)
Furniture: Solid brass, blued steel
Also available:
FRONTIER CARBINE with 24″ barrel, 40$^1/_2$″ overall length; weight 6$^1/_2$ lbs.; percussion only in 45 or 50 caliber. **Price: $188.00.** Kit $138.00.

TRAPPER RIFLE
$188.00 (Percussion)

SPECIFICATIONS
Calibers: 36, 45, and 50
Barrel length: 24″; 45 and 50 calibers rifled 1 turn in 66″; 36 caliber rifled 1 turn in 48″; hooked breech; octagonal ($^7/_8$ across flats)
Overall length: 40$^1/_2$″
Weight: 6 lbs.

Stock: Beech
Lock: Adjustable sear engagement with fly and bridle
Triggers: Double set, will fire set and unset
Sights: Fully screw adjustable for windage and elevation; beaded blade front with Patridge-style open rear
Furniture: Solid brass, blued steel

TRAPPER PISTOL
$128.00 (Percussion)
$98.00 (Kit)

SPECIFICATIONS
Calibers: 36, 45, 50
Barrel length: 9$^1/_4$″; octagonal ($^7/_8$″ across flats) with tenon
Overall length: 16″
Weight: 2$^3/_4$ lbs.
Stock: Beech
Lock: Adjustable sear engagement with fly and bridle
Triggers: Double set, will fire set and unset
Sights: Primitive-style adjustable rear; brass blade front
Furniture: Solid brass; blued steel on assembled pistol

A. UBERTI

SPECIFICATIONS
Caliber: 44
Capacity: 6 shots
Barrel length: 7½″ round forward of lug
Overall length: 13½″
Weight: 4 lbs.
Frame: Color casehardened steel
Grip: One-piece walnut
Features: Brass backstrap and trigger guard; engraved cylinder
Also available:
2nd Model Dragoon w/square cylinder bolt shot .. **$221.00**
3rd Model Dragoon w/loading lever latch, steel
  backstrap, cut for shoulder stock **247.00**
Texas Dragoon w/squareback trigger guard **227.50**

1st MODEL DRAGOON REVOLVER
$221.00

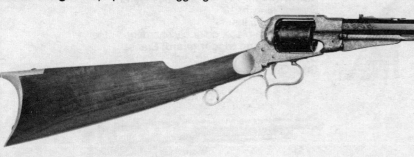

**1858 NEW ARMY TARGET
REVOLVING CARBINE
$362.70**

SPECIFICATIONS
Caliber: 44
Barrel length: 18″ octagonal, tapered
Overall length: 37″
Weight: 4.63 lbs.

Sights: Vertically adjustable rear; ramp front
Frame: Blued steel
Stock: Walnut
Features: Brass trigger guard and butt plate

1858 NEW ARMY 44 Revolver **$188.50**
  With Stainless Steel **253.50**
  Target Model, blued steel **227.50**

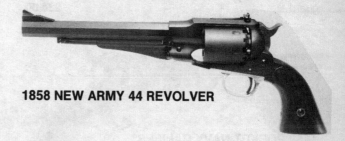

1858 NEW ARMY 44 REVOLVER

**SANTA FE HAWKEN RIFLE
$362.70**

SPECIFICATIONS
Caliber: 50 or 54
Barrel length: 32″ octagonal
Overall length: 50″
Weight: 9½ lbs.
Stock: Walnut with beavertail cheekpiece
Features: Brown finish; double trigger set; color casehardened
  lockplate; German silver wedge plates and stock turrule

A. UBERTI

SPECIFICATIONS
Caliber: 44
Barrel length: 9″ (round in front of lug)
Overall length: 15³/₄″
Weight: 4.41 lbs.
Frame: Color casehardened steel
Backstrap: Steel
Cylinder: 6 shots (engraved with "Fighting Dragoons" scene)
Grip: One-piece walnut

THE WALKER REVOLVER
$273.00

1851 NAVY REVOLVER
$214.50

SPECIFICATIONS
Caliber: 36
Barrel length: 7¹/₂″ (octagonal, tapered)
Overall length: 13″
Weight: 2.75 lbs.
Frame: One-piece, color casehardened steel
Backstrap and trigger guard: Brass
Cylinder: 6 shots (engraved)
Grip: One-piece walnut

SPECIFICATIONS
Caliber: 36
Capacity: 6 shots
Barrel length: 7¹/₂″
Overall length: 13″
Weight: 2.75 lbs.
Grip: One-piece walnut
Frame: Color casehardened steel
Also available:
Civil Type w/brass backstrap and trigger guard . . . **$214.50**
Western Type w/silver plated backstrap and trigger
   guard **234.00**
Fluted Cylinder Type w/steel backstrap and trigger
   guard **234.00**

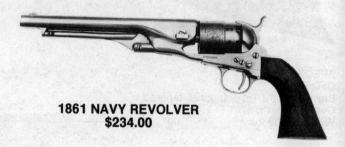

1861 NAVY REVOLVER
$234.00

1862 POCKET NAVY CALIBER
$195.00

SPECIFICATIONS
Caliber: 36
Barrel length: 6¹/₂″ (octagonal, tapered)
Overall length: 10¹/₂″
Weight: 1.68 lbs.
Frame: Color casehardened steel
Backstrap and trigger guard: Brass
Cylinder: 5 shots (engraved)
Grip: One-piece walnut
Also available: 4¹/₂″ and 5¹/₂″ barrels

SPECIFICATIONS
Caliber: 36
Barrel length: 5¹/₂″ (round, tapered)
Overall length: 10¹/₂″
Weight: 1.59 lbs.
Frame: Color case-hardened steel
Cylinder: 5 shots (fluted)
Grip: One-piece walnut
Backstrap & Trigger guard: Brass
Also available: 4¹/₂″ and 6¹/₂″ barrels

Sights, Scopes & Mounts

FOR ADDRESSES AND PHONE
NUMBERS OF MANUFACTURERS AND
DISTRIBUTORS INCLUDED IN THIS
SECTION, SEE *DIRECTORY OF
MANUFACTURERS AND SUPPLIERS*

ACTION ARMS SIGHTS

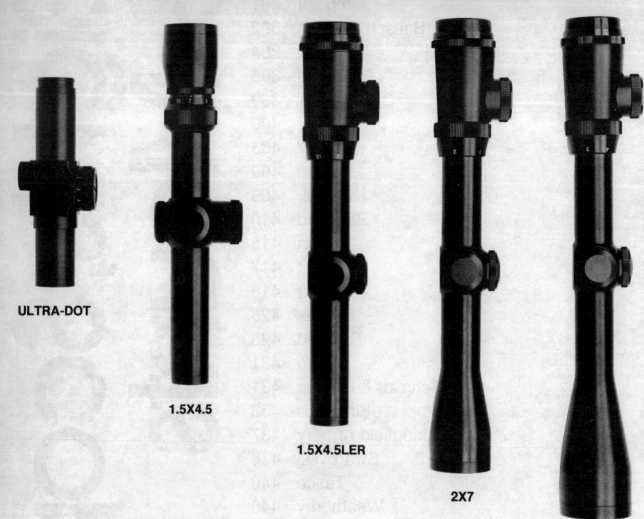

ULTRA-DOT

1.5X4.5

1.5X4.5LER

2X7

3X9

MICRO-DOT SIGHTS

Micro-Dot's red aiming point allows the hunter to aim with confidence even when he can no longer see the crosshairs. These 1″, waterproof sights feature an extended eye relief model, one-piece tube and coated optics. *See* table below for specifications.

Prices:

1½X4½ pistol sight	**$265.00**
1½X4½ rifle sight	270.00
2X7 rifle sight	290.00
3X9 rifle sight	295.00

ULTRA-DOT SIGHTS

The Ultra-Dot is lighter and more compact than the Micro-Dot sight. Its battery pack is built right into the small, click adjustable brightness control. Mounts easily with 1″ scope mounts on any firearm. *See* table below for specifications.

Price (Black or Silver) **$195.00**

MICRO-DOT SCOPES & ULTRA-DOT SIGHT SPECIFICATIONS

Model	Length	Tube Dia.	Weight	Objective Dia.	Eye Relief
3 × 9	12.2″	1″	13.3 oz.	40mm	3″
2 × 7	11.0″	1″	12.1 oz.	32mm	3″
1.5 × 4.5	9.8″	1″	10.5 oz.	20mm	3″
1.5 × 4.5 LER	8.8″	1″	9.5 oz.	20mm	12–24″
Ultra-Dot	5.1″	1″	4.0 oz.	1″	unlimited

AIMPOINT SIGHTS

SERIES 2000 ELECTRONIC SIGHTS

Aimpoint's Series 2000 Sights (Long only) is offered in two finishes—black and stainless. Primarily designed for handgun users, its versatility allows for multi-use. Shooters can easily move the sight from one firearm to another. Mounting requires standard one-inch rings and mounts. The Long 2000 is 7¹/₄ inches overall and weighs just over 6 ounces. It can be mounted on all firearms and will work well for hunters and marksmen who use rifles and require magnification.

SPECIFICATIONS
Length: 6⁷/₈″
Weight: 6³/₄ oz.
Diameter: 1″
Magnification: None
Scope Attachments: 3X
Material: Anodized Aluminum
Finish: Black or Stainless
Mounting: Standard 1″ rings
Positive sight adjustment: ¹/₂″ at 100 yards
Lens coating: Standard
Battery: One-piece lithium (DL ²/₃A) or two-piece mercury (PX1/RM1N)
Price: $229.95

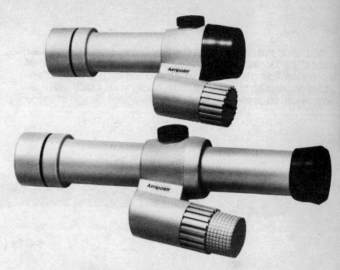

SERIES 2000 LONG STAINLESS

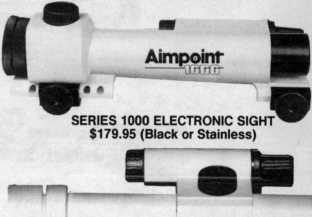

SERIES 1000 ELECTRONIC SIGHT
$179.95 (Black or Stainless)

SERIES 2000 LONG BLACK

Series 2000 Specifications	Long
Length	7¹/₄″
Weight	6 oz.
Diameter	1″
Magnification	None
Scope Attachments	3X
Material	Anodized Aluminum
Finish	Black or Stainless finish
Mounting	Standard 1″ rings
Positive sight adjustment	¹/₂″ at 100 yards
Lens coating	Standard
Battery types	Same
	Same
Price: 2000 Black or Stainless	**$229.95**

SERIES 3000

SERIES 3000 SIGHTS

This small, lightweight sight is easy to mount on all firearms, and features a sharp, adjustable red dot that covers only 2¹/₂″ of the target at 100 yards using a standard-type battery. Also includes a mil-spec on/off switch made to withstand the heaviest magnum recoil. Mounts easily on standard 1″ rings.

SPECIFICATIONS
System: Parallax free
Magnification: 1X
Optical: Anti-reflex coated lenses; polarizing filter
Batteries: Mercury, SP675 (or equivalent), or Lithium, DL ¹/₃N (or equivalent).
Length: 5¹/₂″
Width/Height: 1¹¹/₁₆″
Weight: 5.15 oz. (with batteries)
Diameter of Dot: 2³/₄″ at 110 yards
Price: $229.95

BAUSCH & LOMB

Since 1853 the name Bausch & Lomb has stood for superior optical performance. The repeatability—a critical factor—of Bausch & Lomb's variable and fixed power rifle-scopes enables sportsmen to enjoy optimum tracking accuracy with positive return to zero each time. The advanced design of these scopes eliminates point-of-impact shifts at high and low powers. To insure brightness, internal lens surfaces are multi-coated so light loss from reflection is minimized. Strong, durable one-piece body maintains optical alignment. All scopes are waterproof and fogproof.

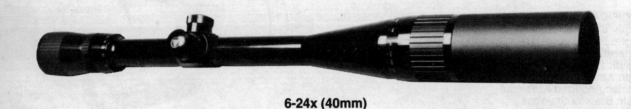

6-24x (40mm)

2.5-10 × (40mm)

3-9x (40mm)

1.5x-6 (20mm)

BALVAR RIFLESCOPES

Bausch & Lomb's variable 6-24x40, 3-9x40, and 1.5-6x21 riflescopes have been redesigned, reducing their weight by 15 percent each. When set at its lowest power, the variable 1.5-6x provides a full 60-foot field at 100 yards, making it an ideal optical sight for stalking in tall timber and dense brushy areas. For maximum visibility, this scope can also zoom up to a full 6x for long range shots at big game. It weighs only 13.9 ounces and measures 11 inches in length. For benchrest competitors, long-range varmint hunters and silhouette shooters, the 6x-24x scope is sufficiently short and light. Its 40mm focusing objective lens eliminates problems with parallax regardless of distance to target. Features positive click steel windage and elevation adjustments, plus precision internal adjustments for repeatability and return to zero.

Model 64 Balvar Riflescope

6-24x40mm	$600.95
3-9x40mm	500.95
1.5-6x32mm	533.95
2.5-10x40mm	556.95

BAUSCH & LOMB

TARGET RIFLESCOPES

Feature crisp, repeatable ¹/₈″ MOA click adjustments in two styles, plus hard surface, multi-coated optics, sunshades (3″ and 5″). Fogproof and waterproof.

36x(40mm) Dot Reticle	$733.95
36x(40mm) Fine Crosshair Reticle	722.95
24x(40mm) Dot Reticle	733.95
24x(40mm) Fine Crosshair Reticle	722.95
6x-24x(40mm) Fine Crosshair Reticle	733.95

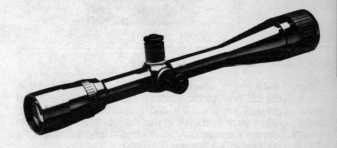

TARGET SCOPES

COMPACTS

Offer same features and performance as full-size Bausch & Lomb riflescopes in lightweight design. Include four times zoom ratio, resettable ¹/₄″ MOA click adjustments, hard surface multi-coated optics, one-piece body tube. Fogproof and waterproof.

2x-8x(32mm) Balvar Compact	$467.95
4x(32mm) Balfor Compact	356.95

COMPACTS

HANDGUN SCOPES

Feature one-piece body tube, resettable ¹/₄″ MOA click adjustments, wide margin of eye relief, hard surface, multi-coated optics. Fogproof and waterproof.

4x(28mm)	$333.95
2x(28mm)	322.95

Add **$22.00** for Matte Silver.

HANDGUN SCOPES

BEEMAN SCOPES

SS-3 SERIES

Offers 1.5-4x zoom power for greater flexibility. Glare-free black matte finish is anodized into metal for deep sheen and extra toughness. Instant action dial around front of scope dials away parallax error and dials in perfect focus from 10 feet to infinity. Scope measures only 5¾ inches in length and weighs only 8.5 ounces. **SS-3 Series: $250.00**

SS-1 AND SS-2 SERIES

Beeman SS-1 and SS-2 short scopes are extra compact and rugged, due largely to breakthroughs in optical engineering and computer programming of lens formulas. Less than 7 inches long, both scopes pack 11 lenses that actually gather light for bigger, brighter targets than "projected spot" targets. Scope body and built-in mounts are milled as a single unit from a solid block of hi-tensile aircraft aluminum.

SS-1 Series: $179.50
SS-2 Series: $225.00—$250.00

BEEMAN SS-2L "SKYLITE" RIFLESCOPE

Features a brightly illuminated reticle powered by daylight and even moonlight (no batteries necessary). In addition to standard black reticle, supplementary color filters are available for different lighting and shooting situations. Filter options include: white (for silhouette or target); red (for twilight and general purpose); yellow (for haze, fog and low light); green (for bright light and snow). A small electrical illuminator is also available for use in total darkness.

Beeman SS-2L w/color reticle, 3x **$275.00**
Beeman SS-2L w/color reticle, 4x 295.00
Lamp 29.95
Filter Kit (green or yellow) 18.95

BLUE RIBBON AND BLUE RING SCOPES

These versatile scopes have a Range Focus Ring by which parallax error can be dialed away and perfect focus dialed in from 13 feet to infinity. Model 66R also has Speed Dials—extra large windage and elevation knobs that are especially fast and easy to use. Beeman economy scopes (Models 30A, 35R and 45R) are notable for their high lens counts. **Prices:** range from **$36.95 - $379.95**

SCOPE SPECIFICATIONS

Model	Series	Power	Obj. Lens mm	Tube Dia. in. (mm)	Wgt. oz. (gm)	Length in. (mm)	Field of View 100 yds. (100m)	Eye Relief in. (mm)	Reticle
30A	Blue Ring	4	15	¾" (19)	4.5* (128)	10.2 (259)	21 (7m)	2 (50)	5 pt. TL
35R	Blue Ring	3	20	¾" (19)	5.2* (147)	11 (280)	25 (8.3m)	2.5 (64)	5 pt. TL
45R	Blue Ring	3-7	20	¾" (19)	6.3* (179)	10.8 (275)	26-12 (8.7-4m)	2.5 (64)	5 pt. TL
50R	Blue Ribbon	2.5	32	1" (25)	12.3 (350)	12 (305)	33 (11m)	3.5 (90)	5 pt. TL
54R	Blue Ribbon	4	32	1" (25)	12.3 (35)	12 (305)	29' (8.8m)	3.5 (90)	5 pt. TL
66R	Blue Ribbon	2.7	32	1" (25)	14.9 (422)	11.4 (290)	62-16 (18.9-5.3m)	3 (76)	5 pt. TL
66RL	Blue Ribbon	2-7	32	1" (25)	17 (482)	11.4 (290)	30.5'-11' (9.3-3.4m)	3 (76)	5 pt. TL
67R	Blue Ribbon	3-9	40	1" (25)	15.2 (431)	14.4 (366)	43.5-15' (13.3-4.6m)	3 (76)	5 pt. TL
68R	Blue Ribbon	4-12	40	1" (25)	15.2 (431)	14.4 (366)	30.5'-11' (9.3-3.4m)	3 (76)	5 pt. TL
MS-1	Blue Ribbon	4	18	1" (25)	8 (227)	7.5 (191)	23' (7m)	3.5	5 pt. TL
SS-1	Blue Ribbon	2.5	16	⅞" (22)	6.9* (195)	5.5 (137)	32.5 (10.8m)	3 (76)	5 pt. TL
SS-2	Blue Ribbon	3	21	1.38" (35)	13.6* (385)	6.8 (172)	34.5 (11.5m)	3.5 (90)	5 pt. TL
SS-2	Blue Ribbon	4	21	1.38" (35)	13.7 (388)	7 (182)	24.6 (8.2m)	3.5 (90)	5 pt. TL
SS-3	Blue Ribbon	1.5-4	16	⅞" (22)	8.6 (241)*	5.75 (146)	44.6'-24.6' (13.6-7.5m)	3 (76)	5 pt. TL

*Includes scope mount in price and weight. TL = Thin Line reticle.

BEEMAN MOUNTS

DOUBLE ADJUSTABLE SCOPE MOUNTS

Beeman Professional Pivot Mounts. The finest scope mounts in existence for big bore. These allow scopes to be quickly and easily detached for transporting, protecting from bad weather or repairing. No tools required. Just lift mount latch, pivot scope 90° and lift out. Scope returns to zero when reattached. Built-in windage adjustment allows full use of scope's windage adjustment. Also, bases sit so low mechanical sights may be used when scope is off. **No. 5099:$269.50**
Beeman Professional Dovetail Mounts. These are the finest scope mounts in existence for 22 caliber rifles. Same superb construction and built-in windage adjustment as the Pivot Mounts (above). A locking screw arrangement absolutely locks the mount into position with 11mm dovetails. **No. 5085** w/25-26mm (1") rings: **$98.95**
Double Adjustable Scope Mounts. The first mounts to have both clamp size and windage adjustment features. Using

DELUXE RING MOUNTS

spacer bars provided, clamp size adjusts to fit grooved receivers and scope bases on all known 22 rifles (1/4 to 5/8", 6mm to 15mm). Windage adjustment built into the mount center scope so that scope retains its full range of windage adjustments. These high-quality mounts are for 22 rimfire and airgun shooters who wish to mount high-performance 1" diameter scopes on their guns. **No. 5084: $29.98**
Beeman Deluxe Ring Mounts. Simpler version of 5084 without the double adjustable feature. Very sturdy and extremely solid. High tensile aviation aluminum with non-glare, honed blue-black finish. Blued steel clamping screws. **No. 5081: $28.98**
Beeman Sport Aperture Sights. Right side of mounting dovetail fits exactly by tightening hidden precision lock screws onto male receiver grooves. Made of rust-proof alloy with tensile strength of over 85,000 pounds. No machining required. **No. 5822 & 5823: $39.98** (with finger adjustable knobs).

MODEL 68R
$379.95

MODELS 67R & 68R

These two high power scopes—with 4-12 zoom power and 3-9 zoom power, respectively—are suitable for airguns, rimfire and centerfire rifles alike. Field shooters who must make precise head shots on small game will find the higher magnifications helpful. Both models incorporate the lens bracing required to protect them from the damaging two-way snap of spring piston airguns. Other features include a speed dial (for elevation) and range focus, plus a large 40mm objective lens that provides super-bright images. **Model 67R: $349.00**

MODEL M66R
$239.95

This scope, which was designed for centerfire, 22 caliber rimfire, and adult air rifles, can zoom instantly from 2 to 7x for long-range shots requiring pinpoint accuracy. It features speed dials with full saddle and range focus. There's also a special running target version—a delicate dot is set on each side of the horizontal member of a special, thin-line crosshair to provide proper leads for targets running right or left at 10 meters.

Also available: **Model 66RL** with color reticle (2x-7x): **$289.95.**

B-SQUARE SCOPE MOUNTS

44 MAGNUM RUGER BLACKHAWK MOUNTS
$49.95 (Stainless)
$39.95 (Blue)

M-94 ANGLE EJECT SCOPE MOUNT
For Winchester 94 Angle Eject
$49.95

1903 SPRINGFIELD SCOPE MOUNT
$59.95

ONE-PIECE BASES
$9.95

This new one-piece base fits both long and short actions. It provides better alignment than two-piece blocks for the straightest, strongest and best looking base available. It can be attached with socket screws and wrench provided. The Mauser 98 Large Ring and Small Ring bases have a notch that locates itself in the clip-lip, so there's no need to file for clip-lips or bolt handle clearance. Bases are available for Winchester 70, Savage 110, Browing A-Bolt, Remington 700, T/C Hawken, and many others.

MAUSER 98

OTHER POPULAR RIFLES

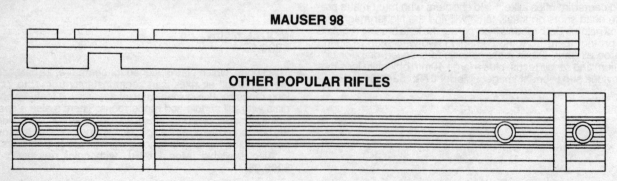

B-SQUARE SCOPE MOUNTS

RIFLE MOUNTS

RUGER MINI-14
$69.95 ($79.95 Stainless)

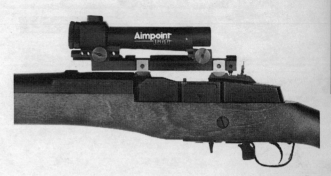

RUGER RANCH/MINI-THIRTY
$49.95

SHOTGUN MOUNTS

REMINGTON 870/1100
$39.95

MOSSBERG 500
$39.95

B-SQUARE SCOPE MOUNTS

RUGER MK I/II 22 AUTO (MONO-MOUNT)
$39.95 ($49.95 Stainless)

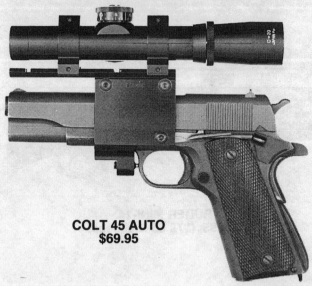

COLT 45 AUTO
$69.95

DAN WESSON/COLT PYTHON
$49.95 ($59.95 Stainless)

BROWNING BUCKMARK
$39.95

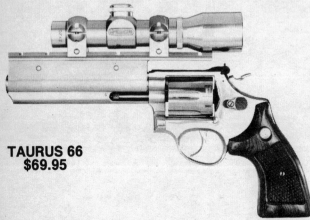

TAURUS 66
$69.95

RUGER BLACKHAWK
$59.95

BUEHLER SCOPE MOUNTS

BUEHLER TELESCOPIC SIGHT MOUNTS. By using one of the five basic styles of mount bases, you may position the scope of your choice in the best possible location—the one that positions the scope so that the shooter has a full field of view when his face is nestled in a comfortable, natural position against the stock. Scopes vary in eye relief from 3 to 5 inches. Sight adjustment turrets are in different locations. The amount of space available on the scope for the mount varies. Most important of all is the difference in shooters and in the way each one holds a rifle. One of the five styles of mounts will locate your scope in the best position for you. All Buehler mount rings fit and are interchangeable with all Buehler bases.

SHORT ONE-PIECE BASES

The short one-piece base locates the front ring over the top of the receiver ring about 1 inch aft of the long one-piece base. The rear ring is in about the same location. Thus, ring spacing averages 4 inches. The short base is recommended for shorter scopes, scopes with large and long objective bells, and scopes with turrets near the center of the tube. **Price: ea. $32.25.**

TWO-PIECE BASE

Two-piece bases locate the front ring over the receiver ring in the same place as the short one-piece base. The rear ring, however, is over the bridge on bolt-action rifles, not ahead of it as is the case with the one-piece bases. The ring spacing averages 4½ inches. Will accommodate scopes described under the *short* one-piece bases. The eye relief is shorter than either one-piece base but adequate for the average installation. **Two-Piece Scope Mount Base: $32.25.**

MICRO-DIAL UNIVERSAL MOUNT

Both windage and elevation features are built in. A twist of the fingers fixes the elevation desired on a dial clearly marked in minutes (one inch at 100 yards). Another twist on the lock wheel directly below the dial securely locks the setting. The windage screws are also calibrated in minutes on both sides. The Micro Dial is designed primarily for all scopes with internal adjustments, such as the Balvar 2½ to 8 (use Code 7 Rings for Balvar), but can be used to advantage with many other scopes. Dial also makes it possible to switch scopes between rifles. The ring spacing is 4 inches.

Prices:

Micro-Dial Base	$53.25
Mount Base, One or Two-piece	32.25
Mount Base, Sako, Mini-14	49.50
Mount Base, Pistol—Blue	32.25
Mount Base, Pistol—Stainless	40.50
Mount Base, Pistol M83, (Blue or Silver)	42.75

LOW SAFETY

For scoping bolt-action rifles. In the "ON" position, pressure of the striker spring holds both bolt and striker in closed position. Safety operates on right side of action, rotating through 70-degree arc with definite stops in "OFF" and "ON" positions. Can be used equally well with or without scope. Fits following models: Mauser M98 & F.N., Krag, Springfield, Winchester M54, 1891 Argentine Mauser, M93. **Price: $22.25.**

BUEHLER SCOPE MOUNTS

M83 BUEHLER PISTOL MOUNT
(shown on Ruger Blackhawk)

M83 PISTOL MOUNT

Installs without drilling or tapping (wrench included). Base is made of high tensile Aircraft Aluminum Alloy, anodized and dyed in black or silver to match blue or stainless steel pistols. Designed for calibers up through 357 Magnum. Use code 7 rings.

M83 (Base only). **$42.75**

BUEHLER RINGS FOR BOTH ONE AND TWO-PIECE MOUNTS

A double split-type ring with the added beauty of a smoothly rounded "ball turret top." The steel spacer at the top of each ring is made of 16 laminations .002" thick which may be peeled off one or more at a time, thus accurately fitting all scopes up to .01" smaller in size than the normal dimension of the ring.

MOUNT RINGS

Double split rings, codes 6, 7 & 8 (1") . . . . $ 42.25
Double split rings, codes 10, 11, 14, 15 (Special) . . . 54.00
Spec. 30mm, code 30 . . . . 65.00
Engraved split rings, codes 6, 8 . . . . 102.75

BURRIS SCOPES

3X-9X FULLFIELD (illustrated)

A versatile scope for big game and varmint hunting. The most popular variable power scope because it fulfills a variety of purposes from long-range varmint shooting to shorter ranges of heavy brush shooting. A rugged, factory-sealed hunting scope with a big 14-foot field of view at 9X and a 38-foot field at 3X.

3x-9x FULLFIELD

Plex $291.95
Plex w/satin finish 303.95
Plex Siver Safari 317.95
Post crosshair 303.95
3"–1" dot 304.95

2x-7x FULLFIELD (not illus.)
Field of view: at 7x, 18 ft.; at 2x, 47 ft.

Plex $276.95
Plex w/satin finish 289.95
Post crosshair 289.95
3"–1" dot 289.95

1³⁄₄x-5x FULLFIELD (not illus.)
Field of view: at 5x, 25 ft.; at 1³⁄₄x, 66 ft.

Plex $250.95
Post crosshair 260.95
3"–1" dot 261.95

BURRIS SCOPES

SIGNATURE SERIES 3X-12X PLEX
$491.95

This new Signature Series features a computer-designed optical system, using the most advanced optical glass available. All models have Hi-Lume (multi-coated) lenses for maximum light transmission. Also features full-field wide angle field-of-view sight picture.

Prices:

3x-12x	$491.95
3x-9x	392.95
3x-9x Safari	405.95
6X	339.95
6X Safari	352.95
4X	324.95
4X Safari	332.95

GUNSITE SCOUT SCOPE

Made for hunters who need a seven to 14-inch eye relief to mount just in front of the ejection port opening, allowing hunters to shoot with both eyes open. The 15-foot field of view and 2³/₄x magnification are ideal for brush guns and handgunners who use the "two-handed hold."

German 3 Post 1¹/₂X	$181.95
German 3 Post 2³/₄X	198.95
Gunsite Scout Scope 2³/₄x Plex XER	170.95
With satin finish	181.95
Gunsite Scout Scope 1¹/₂X Plex XER	163.95
With satin finish	174.95

GERMAN 3 POST
For close-in shooting
at fast-moving targets under
low light conditions

3x-9x FULLFIELD RAC SCOPE
with AUTOMATIC RANGEFINDER RETICLE

Once the crosshair has been zeroed in at 200 yards, it remains there regardless of the power setting. The range reticle automatically moves to a zero at ranges up to 500 yards as power is increased to fit the game between the stadia range wires. No need to adjust elevation knob. Bullet drop adjustment is automatic.

3x-9x Fullfield RAC Crosshair (Dot or Plex)	$312.95
3x-9x RAC CHP Safari Finish	321.95

BURRIS SCOPES

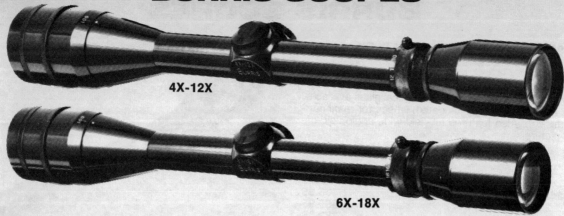

4X-12X

6X-18X

4X-12X FULLFIELD VARIABLE POWER

The ideal scope for long-range varmint hunting and testing hand loads. Can also be used for big-game hunting. Features crisp resolution, accurate parallax settings and a big field of view. Friction-type parallax settings from 50 yards to infinity with positive stop to prevent overturning. Fully sealed to withstand the worst field conditions and designed to deliver years of excellent service.

4x-12x FULLFIELD

Plex	$342.95
Fine Plex	342.95
2"-.7" Dot	356.95
ARC Crosshair Fine Plex	359.95

6X-18X FULLFIELD VARIABLE POWER

This versatile, high-magnification, variable scope can be used for hunting, testing hand loads or shooting bench rest. It features excellent optics, a precise parallax adjustment from 50 yards to infinity, accurate internal adjustments and a rugged, reliable mechanical design that will give years of dependable service. Fully sealed against moisture and dust.

6x-18x FULLFIELD

Plex	$355.95
Fine Plex	355.95
2"-.7" Dot	366.95
2"-.7" Dot Silhouette	386.95
Fine Plex Silhouette	374.95

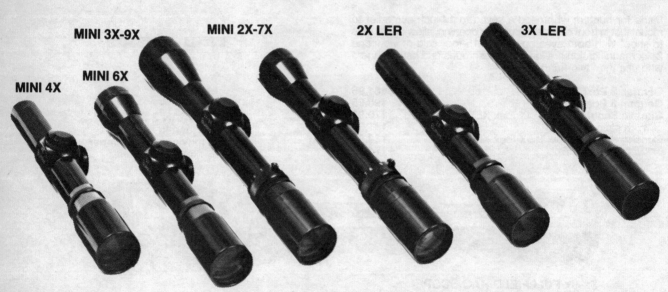

MINI 3X-9X   **MINI 2X-7X**   **2X LER**   **3X LER**

MINI 6X

MINI 4X

MINI SCOPES with PLEX RETICLE:

Mini 4x	$165.95
Mini 6x	181.95
Mini 6x 2" Dot P.A.	214.95
Mini 3x-9x	230.95
Mini 3x-9x Silver Safari	252.95
Mini 2x-7x	225.95
Mini 4x-12x	306.95

LONG EYE RELIEF SCOPE with PLEX RETICLE:

1x LER	$156.95
1½x-4x LER	266.95
2x LER	163.95
3x LER	176.95
4x LER	184.95
5x LER	198.95

INTERMEDIATE EYE RELIEF SCOPE with PLEX RETICLE:

7X IER	$213.95
10x IER	265.95

BURRIS SCOPES

1¹/₂X SHOTGUN

2¹/₂X SHOTGUN

10X, 12X & 6X-18X FULLFIELD SILHOUETTE SCOPES

These three scopes, with their precision click target-type knobs and Burris Hi-Lume lenses give silhouette shooters a real edge. All new design allows fast, precise reticle adjustments, free of backlash, on both windage and elevation. Graduated knobs are easy to read and can be reset to zero once initial sighting is made. Threaded dust covers included.

10x Fullfield Fine Plex Silhouette	$298.95
10x ¹/₂″ Dot Silhouette	308.95
12x Fullfield Fine Plex Silhouette	306.95
12x ¹/₂″ Dot Silhouette	317.95
6x-18x Fullfield Fine Plex Silhouette	374.95
6x-18x Fullfield 2″-.7″ Dot Silhouette	386.95

1¹/₂X & 2¹/₂X FULLFIELD SHOTGUN SCOPES

The huge field-of-view and recoil proof construction allows shotgun slug hunters to improve their accuracy. Running shots during low-light conditions are made possible with either scope.

1¹/₂X Fullfield Plex	$187.95
2¹/₂X Fullfield Plex	197.95

10X SILHOUETTE SCOPE

12X SILHOUETTE SCOPE

6X–18X SILHOUETTE SCOPE

MOUNT BASE (For Ruger Mark I & II)

Installs in seconds without drilling or tapping. Accepts one-inch .22 rings and Burris long eye relief handgun scopes.

Price:	$35.95
With Silver Safari Finish	40.95

BURRIS RINGS, BASES AND MOUNTS

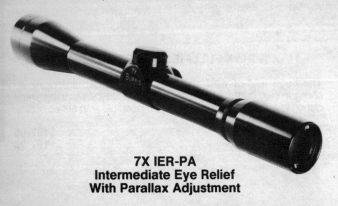

7X IER-PA
Intermediate Eye Relief
With Parallax Adjustment

This popular handgun scope has parallax settings from 25 meters to infinity. Target knobs with precision click adjustments are standard.

7x IER Plex	$213.95
7x IER 2″ Dot	227.95
7x IER 2″ Dot P.A.	257.95
7x IER Plex P.A.	245.95
With Silver Safari	265.95

UNIVERSAL BASE (LU) LONG EYE RELIEF

Tough all steel bases feature a recoil stop-screw that lets the rear ring absord the recoil generated by larger caliber handguns. They provide versatility of a universal dovetail base and magnum proof performance.

Universal Base Long Eye Relief $27.95

SUPREME BASE,
UNIVERSAL DOVETAIL
$24.95

MEDIUM EXTENSION FRONT RING,
STANDARD REAR RING,
UNIVERSAL DOVETAIL
$43.95

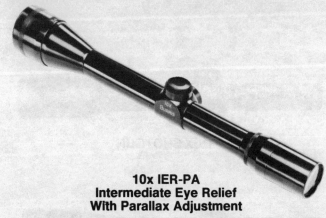

10x IER-PA
Intermediate Eye Relief
With Parallax Adjustment

Designed for precision shooting handguns with barrels that are a minimum of 14 inches in length. Eye relief is 9 inches minimum and 14 inches maximum.

10x IER Plex	$265.95
10x IER ½″ Dot	279.95
10x IER Plex P.A.	287.95

SILVER SAFARI BASE FOR HANDGUNS

A special nickel-chrome finish gives these bases a tough but beautiful stainless look. Features a recoil stop-screw that lets the rear ring absorb the recoil genrated by large caliber handguns.

Silver Safari Base $40.95

TRUMOUNT BASE,
UNIVERSAL DOVETAIL
$22.95

BUSHNELL RIFLESCOPES

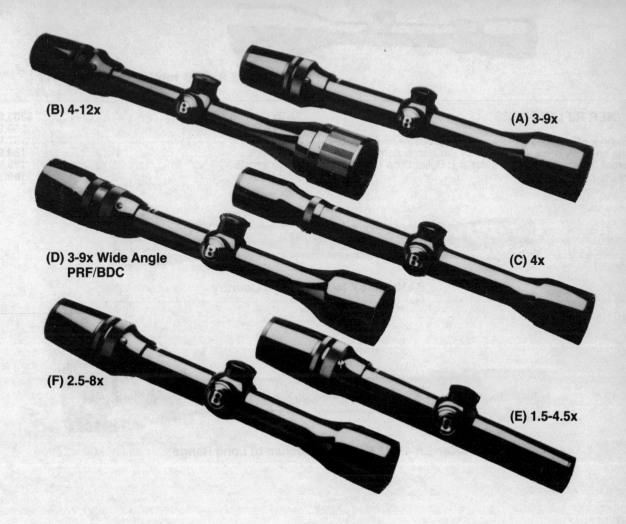

(B) 4-12x

(A) 3-9x

(D) 3-9x Wide Angle PRF/BDC

(C) 4x

(F) 2.5-8x

(E) 1.5-4.5x

SCOPECHIEF RIFLESCOPES

To maximize light transmission and image brightness, the precision ground polished lenses in the Scope Chief riflescope line are now multi-coated on all air-to-glass surfaces. Precision 1/4 M.O.A. click adjustments are standard, as is durable one-piece body tube. Scopes are hermetically sealed for full waterproof and fogproof integrity. Bullet Drop Compensator and Prismatic Range Finder included on 4-12x and 3-9x models.

3-9x40mm	$296.95
4-12x40mm PRF/BDC	367.95
3-9x40mm Wide Angle PRF/BDC	369.95
1.5-4.5x20mm	258.95
2.5-8x32mm	262.95
4x32mm	189.95

SCOPECHIEF SPECIFICATION CHART

	Variable Powers			Fixed Power
Magnification	3x-9x	2.5x-8x	1.5x-4.5x	4x
Objective Lens Aperture (mm)	40	32	20	32
Field of View at 100 yards (ft)	3x-34 9x-13	2.5x-45 8x-14	1.5x-73.7 4.5x-24.5	28
Weight (oz)	13.6	11.6	9.5	9.3
Length (in)	12.1	11.2	9.6	12
Eye Relief (in)	3x-3.5 9x-3.3	2.5x-3.7 8x-3.3	1.5x-3.5 4.5x-3.5	3.5
Exit Pupil (mm)	3x-13.3 9x-4.4	2.5x-12.8 8x-4	15x-13.3 4.5x-4.4	8
Relative Light Efficiency	3x-267 9x-30	2.5x-247 8x-96	1.5x-267 4.5x-30	96
MX Center CH Width at 100 yards	3x-.67 9x-.22	2.5x-.8 8x-.25	1.5x-1.3 4.5x-44	.5
Mix Distance Post Tip to Post Tip (in) at 100 yards	3x-24 9x-8	2.5x-28.8 8x-9	1.5x-48 4.5x-16	18
100 yards (in)	.5			

BUSHNELL RIFLESCOPES

BANNER 3-9x (56 mm) EXTRA BRIGHT

BANNER RIFLESCOPES

All Banner riflescopes feature precise resettable click adjustments and fully coated optics. They are also waterproof and fogproof. Prismatic Range Finder and Bullet Drop Compensator are optional.

3x-9x (56mm)	$302.95
4x-12x (40mm) BDC	269.95
3x-9x (40mm)	167.95
6x (40mm)	189.95
4x (32mm) BDC	136.95
2.5x (20mm)	100.95

BANNER 6X (40mm) Open Country

BANNER 4X-12X (40mm) Medium to Long Range

BANNER 4X (32mm) General-purpose w/BDC

BANNER 2.5X (20mm) Short Range

BUSHNELL RIFLESCOPES

BANNER COMPACT RIFLESCOPES

Light in weight (11 ounces for the 2-8x and 8 ounces for the 4x), these scopes complement the popular lightweight rifles. They feature large 28mm objective lens for bright, sharp images, precise internal click adjustments, and a Multi-X reticle for a clearly visible aiming point.

2-8x (28mm) Banner Compact Riflescope **$233.95**
4x (28mm) Banner Compact Riflescope **156.95**

(A) 2-8X (28mm) BANNER COMPACT RIFLESCOPE

(B) 4x (28mm) BANNER COMPACT RIFLESCOPE

BANNER RIFLESCOPE SPECIFICATION CHART

VARIABLE POWER

Magnification	Bullet Drop Compensator	Field of view at 100 yds. (ft.)	Weight (oz.)	Length (inches)	Eye distance (inches)	Entrance pupil (mm)	Exit pupil (mm)	Relative Light Efficiency	MX center CH width at 100 yds. (inches)	MX distance post tip to post tip (inches)	Graduation at 100 yds. (inches)
4x-12x 40mm	BDC	29 at 4x 10 at 12x	15.5	13.5	3.2	40	10 at 4x 3.3 at 12x	150 17	0.5 .17	18 6	.75
3x-9x 40mm		35 at 3x 12.6 at 9x	13	13	3.5	40	13.3 at 3x 4.4 at 9x	267 30	.66 .22	24 8	.75
3x-9x 38mm	BDC	43 at 3x WIDE ANGLE 14.6 at 9x	14	12.1	3	38	12.7 at 3x 4.2 at 9x	241 26.5	.66 .22	24 8	1.0
3x-9x 32mm	BDC	39 at 3x 13 at 9x	11	11.5	3.5	32	10.7 at 3x 3.6 at 9x	171 19	.66 .22	24 8	1.0
1.75x-4.5x 21mm	BDC	71 at 1.75x WIDE ANGLE 27 at 4.5x	11.5	10.2	2.9	21	12 at 1.75x 4.7 at 4.5x	216 33	1.18 .44	45.7 17.8	1.5
1.5x-4x 21mm	BDC	63 at 1.5x 28 at 4x	10.3	10.5	3.5	21	14 at 1.5x 5 at 4x	294 41	1.3 0.5	48 18	1.5

FIXED POWER

Magnification	Bullet Drop Compensator	Field of view at 100 yds. (ft.)	Weight (oz.)	Length (inches)	Eye distance (inches)	Entrance pupil (mm)	Exit pupil (mm)	Relative Light Efficiency	MX center CH width at 100 yds. (inches)	MX distance post tip to post tip (inches)	Graduation at 100 yds. (inches)
10x 40mm	BDC	12	14.0	14.5	3	40	4	24	0.2	7.2	.66
6x 40mm		19.5	11.5	13.5	3	40	6.7	67	0.3	12	.75
4x 40mm	BDC	37.3 WIDE ANGLE	12	12.3	3	40	10	150	0.6	21	1.0
4x 32mm	BDC	29	10	12.0	3.5	32	8	96	0.5	18	1.0
2.5x 20mm		45	8	10.9	3.5	20	8	96	0.8	28.8	1.5

BUSHNELL RIFLESCOPES

ARMOR-SIGHT RIFLESCOPE

Bushnell's Armorlite riflescope offers a proven optical system in Graphlon-VI, a graphite composite material that is stronger than steel, lighter than aluminum, and impervious to any field hazard the hunter might encounter. The scope is available in 3 to 9 power variable and features multicoated optics. It is nitrogen-purged for waterproof and fogproof integrity. One-quarter-minute adjustments provide precise targeting, and the one-piece body tube ensures positive optical alignment.

MODEL 65-3940 . . . . **$444.95**

SPORT VIEW TRUSCOPE

Lets the hunter confirm that the rifle is shooting where he is aiming in the field (where firing a shot would spook the game).

Truscope w/22 & 30 caliber arbor **$73.95**

HOLDEN IRONSIGHTER MOUNTS

BLACK POWDER BASES
$24.95

Available in one-piece and adjustable models. Shown on a T/C Hawken Rifle. These new bases are precision-machined from an extra strong aluminum alloy for maximum scope rigidity.

MODEL 732
$24.95
($54.95 Stainless Steel)

Wide Ironsighter "SEE-THRU" mounts for Ruger 22 caliber rifles are investment-cast from alloy steel. Side clamps assure maximum rigidity. Also fit Ruger 77/22S, 77/22R, #1, and Ranch Rifle (plus RH 41R and 44R revolvers).

KIMBER SCOPES

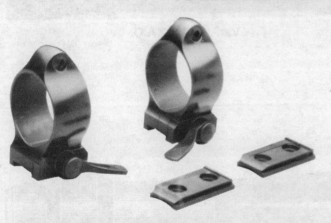

DOUBLE-LEVER QUICK-DETACHABLE MOUNTS
$89.00

Kimber mounts feature all-steel construction and are polished by hand. They are easily detached by turning two thumb levers and will return precisely to the same zero each time they are replaced. The levers synchronize in the closed position and the rings clamp to a dovetail on steel screw-on bases. A positive recoil retention shoulder is located on both front and rear bases. The double-lever mounts accept 1" scopes and have been tested on rifles from .22 rimfires to .458 Magnums. Available in one height only.

DELUXE MOUNTS
$59.95

This non-detachable version of Kimber's double-lever mount is also made of solid steel and has the same size dovetail as the double-lever mounts. Utilizing the same bases, the Deluxe mount is clamped to the dovetail by tightening an Allen head screw. These 1" diameter mounts are available in two heights.

LEUPOLD RIFLE SCOPES

VARIABLE POWER SCOPES

VARI-X II 2x7

A compact scope, no larger than the Leupold M8-4X, offering a wide range of power. It can be set at 2X for close ranges in heavy cover or zoomed to maximum power for shooting or identifying game at longer ranges. **$317.15.** With Dot or CPC reticle: **$338.15**

Vari-X II 2x7

Vari-X II 3x9

VARI-X II 3x9

A wide selection of powers lets you choose the right combination of field of view and magnification to fit the particular conditions you are hunting at the time. Many hunters use the 3X or 4X setting most of the time, cranking up to 9X for positive identification of game or for extremely long shots. The adjustable objective eliminates parallax and permits precise focusing on any object from less than 50 yards to infinity for extra-sharp definition. **$340.70.** With Dot or CPC reticle: **$361.70.** Also available with adjustable objective: **$378.20**

Vari-X II 4x12 A.O.

VARI-X II 4x12 (Adj. Objective)

The ideal answer for big game and varmint hunters alike. At 12.25 inches, the 4x12 is virtually the same length as Vari-X II 3x9. **$410.55**

SPOTTING SCOPES

Leupold's Golden Ring 30x60mm Spotting Scope features extraordinary eye relief and crisp, bright roof prism optics housed in a lightweight, sealed, waterproof body. The 12.9-inch, 19.5-ounce Spotting Scope comes complete with a self-storing screw-on sunshade, lens caps, and a green canvas case. **$513.60**

Now available: Leupold's new 20x50mm and 25x50mm compact Waterproof Spotting Scopes with nearly 1″ of eye relief for comfortable viewing with or without glasses.

20x50mm Compact	**$459.00**
20x50mm Compact Armored	486.35
25x50mm Compact	486.35
25x50mm Compact Armored	573.60
With reticle	540.95

LEUPOLD SCOPES
THE COMPACT SCOPE LINE

The introduction of the Leupold Compacts has coincided with the increasing popularity of the new featherweight rifles. Leupold Compact scopes give a more balanced appearance atop these new scaled-down rifles and offer generous eye relief, magnification and field of view, yet are smaller inside and out. Fog-free.

2.5X COMPACT

2.5X COMPACT
The 2.5X Compact is only 8½ inches long and weighs just 7.4 ounces. **$218.00**

4X COMPACT
& 4X RF Special

4X COMPACT
The 4X Compact is over an inch shorter than the standard 4X. The 4X RF Special is focused to 75 yards and has a Duplex reticle with finer crosshairs. **$244.20**

6X COMPACT

6X COMPACT
To make the 6X Compact, Leupold's shaved an ounce and a half and .7 inch off the standard scope of the same magnification. **$260.70**

6X COMPACT
(with adjustable objective)

6X COMPACT (Adj. Objective)
The popularity of this magnification seems to be growing at the same rate as the availability of lighter or so-called "mountain" rifles. Now available with adjustable objective lens. **$298.20**

2X7 COMPACT

2X7 COMPACT
Two ounces lighter and a whole inch shorter than its full-size counterpart, this 2x7 is one of the world's most compact variable power scopes. It's the perfect hunting scope for today's trend toward smaller and lighter rifles. **$308.00**

3x9 COMPACT

3X9 COMPACT
The 3x9 Compact is a full-blown variable that's 3½ ounces lighter and 1.3 inches shorter than a standard 3x9. Also available in new flat black, matte finish. **$332.05**

3x9 COMPACT
(with adjustable objective)

3X9 COMPACT (Adj. Objective)
Big scope performance in a package compatible with the growing list of scaled down and featherweight rifles. Now available with adjustable objective lens. **$369.55**

LEUPOLD RIFLE SCOPES
VARIABLE POWER SCOPES
VARI-X III LINE

The Vari-X III scopes feature a power-changing system that is similar to the sophisticated lens systems in today's finest cameras. Some of the improvements include an extremely accurate internal control system and a sharp, superb-contrast sight picture. Reticles are the same apparent size throughout power range, stay centered during elevation/windage adjustments. Eyepieces are adjustable and fog-free.

VARI-X III 1.5x5
Here's a fine selection of hunting powers for ranges varying from very short to those at which big game is normally taken. The exceptional field at 1.5X lets you get on a fast-moving animal quickly. With the generous magnification at 5X, you can hunt medium and big game around the world at all but the longest ranges. **$368.70.** Also available in black matte finish: **$386.50**

Vari-X III 1.5 × 5

VARI-X III 2.5x8
This is an excellent range of powers for almost any kind of game, inlcuding varmints. In fact, it possibly is the best all-around variable going today. The top magnification provides plenty of resolution for practically any situation. **$415.85.** In matte finish: **$433.65**

Vari-X III 2.5 × 8

Vari-X III 3.5 × 10

VARI-X III 3.5x10
The extra power range makes these scopes the optimum choice for year-around big game and varmint hunting. The adjustable objective model, with its precise focusing at any range beyond 50 yards, also is an excellent choice for some forms of target shooting. **$435.05.** With adjustable objective: **$472.50**

**Vari-X III 6.5 × 20
(with adjustable objective)**

VARI-X III 6.5x20
This scope has the widest range of power settings in our variable line, with magnifications that are especially useful to hunters of all types of varmints. In addition, it can be used for any kind of big game hunting where higher magnifications are an aid. **$515.25**

LEUPOLD SCOPES

THE TARGET SCOPE LINE

Shooters using Leupold target scopes are dominating both local and national bench rest and silhouette matches. Fog-free. Adjustable objective.

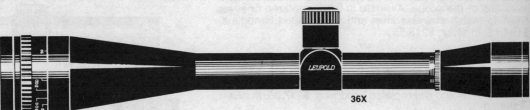

36X

36X TARGET SCOPE
A full 36 power magnification with clear, sharp resolution is possible with Leupold's 36X target scope, all in a package that is only 13.9 inches long and weighs just 15½ ounces. Adjustable objective. **$623.20.** With Target Dot: **$644.20**

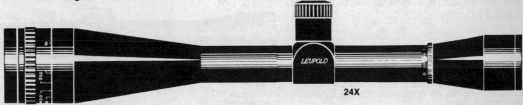

24X

24X TARGET SCOPE
The 24X is just 13.6 inches long and weighs only 14½ ounces. It is compact enough to be receiver mounted and light enough to permit transfer of significant weight from scope to rifle. Adjustable objective. **$623.20.** With ⅛ min. or ½ min. Target Dot: **$644.20**

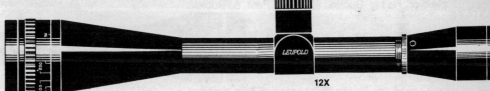

12X

12X TARGET SCOPE
The 12X target scope has the magnification and clear, sharp-contrast sight picture that target shooters need. Two types of redesigned windage/elevation adjustment knobs are included. Adjustable objective. **$437.95.** With CPC reticle or Dot: **$458.95**

VARI-X III 6.5x20

VARI-X III 6.5x20 TARGET SCOPE
The 6.5x20 target allows a shooter to not only change magnifications quickly to match target range, but also rapidly select the windage and elevation needed for each shot, knowing he can unerringly return to a previous setting with ease. Adjustable objective. **$581.60.** With CPC reticle or Dot: **$602.60**

LEUPOLD SCOPES

EXTENDED EYE RELIEF HANDGUN SCOPE LINE

2X EER
With an optimum eye relief of 12-24 inches, the 2X EER is an excellent choice for most handguns. It is equally favorable for carbines and other rifles with top ejection that calls for forward mounting of the scope. Available in black anodized or silver finish to match stainless steel and nickel-plated handguns. **$194.15.** In silver: **$215.55**

4X EER
Only 8.4 inches long and 7.6 ounces. Optimum eye relief 12-24 inches. Available in black anodized or silver finish to match stainless steel and nickel-plated handguns. **$237.05.** In silver: **$258.50**

FIXED-POWER SCOPE LINE

4X
The all-time favorite is the 4X, which delivers a widely used magnification and a generous field of view. Also available in new flat black, matte finish. **$244.20.** With CPC reticle or Dot: **$265.20**

6X
Gaining popularity fast among fixed power scopes is the 6X, which can extend the range for big game hunting and double, in some cases, as a varmint scope. **$260.70.** CPC reticle or Dot: **$281.90**

6X42mm
Large 42mm objective lens features increased light gathering capability and a 7mm exit pupil. Great for varmint shooting at night. Duplex or Heavy Duplex: **$298.90.** Post & Duplex: **$319.90**

8X
A true varmint scope, the 8X has the sharp resolution, contrast and accuracy that also make it effective for some types of target shooting. Adjustable objective permits precise, parallax-free focusing. **$347.90.** CPC reticle or Dot: **$368.60**

 Also available: **8x36mm.** Features a target-style dot and thinner Duplex reticle for long-range use (focused at 300 yds. instead of 150). **$347.60.** With target-style dot: **$406.50.** With adj. objective: **$368.40**

12X
Superlative optical qualities, outstanding resolution and magnification make the 12X a natural for the varmint shooter. Adjustable objective is standard for parallax-free focusing. **$359.15.** CPC reticle or Dot: **$380.15**

2X EER

4X EER

4X

6X

8X

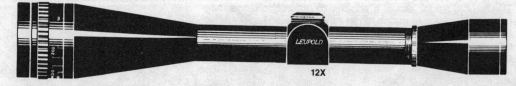

12X

LYMAN RECEIVER SIGHTS

LYMAN 57 and 66 UNIVERSAL RECEIVER SIGHTS

An unobtrusive micrometer receiver sight for hunting or target shooting with sporter, target or military rifle. This sight is equipped with a push-button quick release slide that makes it ideal for alternating use on a scope-equipped rifle.

Fully adjustable with audible 1/4-minute clicks for windage and elevation. Coin-slotted stayset knobs for hunting.

Slide adjustments are equipped with precision scales to aid in pre-setting sights for specific ranges or wind conditions. Slide furnished with elevation stop screw that facilitates return to "zero" if removed and reattached. Slide operates in dovetail channel.

No. 57 and 66 Receiver Sights, complete **$58.95**

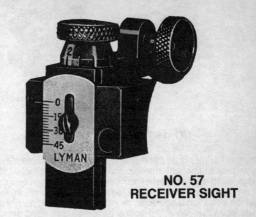

NO. 57 RECEIVER SIGHT

NO. 66 RECEIVER SIGHT

SERIES 17A TARGET FRONT SIGHTS

Teamed with a Lyman receiver sight, these low silhouette front sights provide precise, X-ring accuracy on the range. Designed for use with dovetail slot mounting, they are supplied with seven interchangeable inserts (see descriptions below) that are locked into place with a threaded cap.

Series 17A Target Front Sight w/inserts **$24.95**

LYMAN HUNTING FRONT SIGHTS

Despite the exceptionally sharp definition provided by a fine aperture receiver sight, an equally fine front sight is necessary for consistently accurate shooting, particularly in extreme glare and overcast in the field. Lyman ivory bead front sights are the ideal field front sights. They present a flat optical surface that's equally illuminated by bright or dull light, and they keep their "color" under all light conditions. The Lyman ivory bead front sight is the perfect teammate for your favorite Lyman receiver sight, and will give you a reliable, sharply defined, glareless aiming surface, even under the worst conditions. You can fit a ready adaptable Lyman bead front sight to your rifle in minutes.

NO. 31 FRONT SIGHT
1/16-inch BEAD

This sight is designed to be used on ramps. Standard 3/8-inch dovetail. Ivory bead. See Sight Selection Chart.

No. 31 Front Sight **$7.95**
Also available: **No. 28** 3/32" **Bead** 7.95

NO. 18 SCREW-ON TYPE RAMP

The screw-on ramp is designed to be secured with a heavy 8-40 screw (it may be brazed on if desired). Screw-on ramps are ruggedly built and extremely versatile. They use A width front sights, and are available in the following heights:

18A—Low Ramp: .100-inch from top of barrel to bottom of dovetail.
18C—Medium Ramp: .250-inch from top of barrel to bottom of dovetail.
18E—High Ramp: .350-inch from top of barrel to bottom of dovetail.

No. 18 Screw-On Ramp less sight **$14.95**

LYMAN SIGHTS

BASES
NO. 25 BASES

Permit the installation of dovetail rear sights (such as Lyman 16 leaf sight) on rifles that do not have dovetail rear sights cut in barrel. They also supply a higher line of sight when needed. The No. 25 Base is mounted by drilling and tapping the barrel for two 6-48 screws. Screws are supplied with base.

No. 25 Base **$7.95**

STANDARD BASES	HEIGHT FROM TOP OF BARREL TO BOTTOM OF DOVETAIL	BARREL RADIUS
25A Base (Low)	.025″	.875 or larger
25C Base (High)	.125″	.875 or larger
SPECIAL BASES		
25B Base	.125″	.875 or larger
Fits factory screw holes on Remington 740, 742, 760, 725 & replaces factory rear		

LEAF SIGHTS
NO. 16 FOLDING LEAF SIGHT

Designed primarily as open rear sights with adjustable elevation, leaf sights make excellent auxiliary sights for scope-mounted rifles. They fold close to the barrel when not in use, and they can be installed and left on the rifle without interfering with scope or mount. Two lock screws hold the elevation blade adjustments firmly in place. A sight of this type could save the day if the scope becomes damaged through rough handling. Leaf sights are available in the following heights:

16A—.400″ high; elevates to .500″.
16B—.345″ high; elevates to .445″.
16C—.500″ high; elevates to .600″.

For installation on rifles without a dovetail slot, use Lyman No. 25 Base.

No. 16 Folding Leaf Sight **$11.50**

NO. 12 SLOT BLANKS

These blanks fill the standard 3/8-inch rear barrel dovetail when a receiver sight is installed. They are also available for front sight dovetails and ramps when a scope is being used. **Price: $3.50**

No. 12S (³/₈″ × ⁵/₈″ long) for standard rear barrel slots.

SHOTGUN SIGHTS

Lyman shotgun sights are available for all shotguns. Equipped with oversized ivory beads that give perfect definition on either bright or dull days, they are easy to see under any light conditions. They quickly catch your eye on fast upland targets, and point out the lead on long passing shots. Lyman shotgun sights are available with white bead, and can be fitted to your gun in minutes.

No. 10 Front Sight (press fit) for use on double barrel, or ribbed single
-barrel guns **$3.95**
No. 10D Front Sight (screw fit) for use on non-ribbed single-barrel guns;
supplied with a wrench **4.95**
No. 11 Middle Sight (press fit). This small middle sight is intended for use on
double-barrel and ribbed single-barrel guns **3.95**

When you replace an open rear sight with a receiver sight, it is usually necessary to install a higher front sight to compensate for the higher plane of the new receiver sight. The table below shows the increase in front sight height that's required to compensate for a given error at 100 yards.

AMOUNT OF ADJUSTMENT NECESSARY TO CORRECT FRONT SIGHT ERROR																					
DISTANCE BETWEEN FRONT AND REAR SIGHTS	14″	15″	16″	17″	18″	19″	20″	21″	22″	23″	24″	25″	26″	27″	28″	29″	30″	31″	32″	33″	34″
1	.0038	.0041	.0044	.0047	.0050	.0053	.0055	.0058	.0061	.0064	.0066	.0069	.0072	.0074	.0077	.0080	.0082	.0085	.0088	.0091	.0093
Amount of **2**	.0078	.0083	.0089	.0094	.0100	.0105	.0111	.0116	.0122	.0127	.0133	.0138	.0144	.0149	.0155	.0160	.0156	.0171	.0177	.0182	.0188
Error **3**	.0117	.0125	.0133	.0142	.0150	.0159	.0167	.0175	.0184	.0192	.0201	.0209	.0217	.0226	.0234	.0243	.0251	.0259	.0268	.0276	.0285
100 Yards **4**	.0155	.0167	.0178	.0189	.0200	.0211	.0222	.0234	.0244	.0255	.0266	.0278	.0289	.0300	.0311	.0322	.0333	.0344	.0355	.0366	.0377
Given in **5**	.0194	.0208	.0222	.0236	.0250	.0264	.0278	.0292	.0306	.0319	.0333	.0347	.0361	.0375	.0389	.0403	.0417	.0431	.0445	.0458	.0472
Inches **6**	.0233	.0250	.0267	.0283	.0300	.0317	.0333	.0350	.0367	.0384	.0400	.0417	.0434	.0450	.0467	.0484	.0500	.0517	.0534	.0551	.0567

EXAMPLE: Suppose your rifle has a 27-inch sight radius, and shoots 4 inches high at 100 yards, with the receiver sight adjusted as low as possible. The 27-inch column shows that the correction for a 4-inch error is .0300 inch. This correction is added to the overall height of the front sight (including dovetail). Use a micrometer or similar accurate device to measure sight height. Thus, if your original sight measured .360 inch, it should be replaced with a sight .390 inch high, such as a J height sight.

MERIT SHOOTING AIDS

SCOPES

IRIS SHUTTER DELUX MASTER TARGET DISC WITH FLEXIBLE NEOPRENE LIGHT SHIELD

May be cut to size. Particularly adapted for use with extension, telescope height and tang sights. The 1½-inch diameter flexible neoprene light shield is permanently attached to the eye cup, which is replaceable by removing three screws. The shield is concentrically ribbed on its concave face for cutting to suitable size. It is more advantageous than a large metal disc since it protects the sighting equipment in case the disc is accidentally bumped.

The Master Target Disc may be used on all sights having clearance for a disc 7/16-inch thick and 3/4-inch or larger in diameter.

Merit Delux Master Disc $60.00
Replacement Shield 8.95
Delux Replacement Shield and Steel Cup 10.00

MERIT DELUX NO. 3 SERIES DISC

Side View	Front Views
	(minimum and maximum opening)

Other size apertures are obtained by simply turning the knurled eyepiece right or left respectively to decrease or increase the opening.

Merit Delux No. 3LS **$50.00**
Outside diameter of disc 11/16". Shank 11/32" long.
Merit Delux No. 3A 50.00
Outside diameter of disc 11/16". Shank 15/32" long. Disc thickness 7/32".

Merit No. 4SS—Outside diameter of disc 1/2". Shank 5/16" long. Disc thickness 1/4". **$40.00**
Merit No. 4LS—Outside diameter of disc 1/2". Shank 11/32" long. Disc thickness 1/4". 40.00
Merit No. 4ELS—Outside diameter of disc 1/2". Shank 1/2" long. Disc thickness 1/4". 40.00

MERIT OPTICAL ATTACHMENT

Provides an instantly adjustable aperture to accommodate changing light conditions. Weighs less than 1/5 ounce. Stores in a compact box (1"×1"×1").

Optical attachment **$60.00**
Replacement suction cup 8.00

SIGHT CHART

Popular Peep Sights and the proper Merit Discs to fit them. The Merit Master Target Disc may be had with any of the No. 3 series shanks. All of the sights marked ★ will take the Master Disc depending on the front sight used. See chart below:

Sight Model No.	Merit Discs Target	Hunting	Sight Model No.	Merit Discs Target	Hunting
LYMAN 48WH, 48WJ, 48WJS, 48W, 45, 35, *30½, *2, *2A, *103	Deluxe 3LS	4SS	**REDFIELD** All of Series 70-*75-80-90 and 100; *Olympic (See Adaptor Page); *International (See Adaptor Page)	3SS or 3LS	Deluxe 4LS
All Other 48 Sights	Deluxe 3LS		All of Series 102		
*All 52, 54, *524, *525, *Tube Sight		4LS	All Williams FP		4SS
All 57, 34, All 38, All 41, 45, All 42, All 55, All 56, All 66		4SS	**PACIFIC** K1, S1, W1, SA1, S1R, L1, LB1, EN1, EN3, EN5		4SS
*58E	3A	4ELS	K2, S2, W2, SA2, S2R, LB2, EN2, EN4	Deluxe 3LS	4LS
40					

WITTEK-VAVER					
*All Wittek-Vaver Sights Most of these sights will take the Master Disc with 3A shank	Deluxe 3A	4ELS
*Savage 15, 3S, 4S, 5S, 6S, 7S	3LS / 3S	4LS
*Remington Model 37 Std. Peep Sight	3SL or Master Disc 3SL	
Remington 41P, 341P, 510P, 511P, 512P, Springfield 084, 085, 086, 087	Deluxe 3S	

WINCHESTER Rifle Model	Sight Model	Target	Hunting
74	88A		474
71, 64, 65	Win Special		4SS
*75	84A	3A	4ELS
72	80A	3S72	4SP72
69A	80A		

	Target	Hunting
*All of Marble-Goss Receiver, Tang and Extension Sights	3LS	4LS
Ranger and Stevens Standard Peep Sights	3LS	4LS
Marlin Standard Peep Sights		4-S
Marble Flexible Rear Sights		4-S
King 210 Rear Sights		4-K

MILLET SCOPE MOUNTS

SCOPE-SITE™ FOR RIFLES & SHOTGUNS

Scope-Site solves two major problems that arise in effective use of telescopic sights. First, scopes are not useable for low-light, close-in shots in densely wooded areas. Second, scopes on high magnification take too much time to align on distant shots for fast, elusive game.

Scope-Site provides open patridge-style high visibility sights above the telescopic sight. The rear sights are either click-adjustable or fixed. Both types come with white outline apertures. Front post sights are blaze orange.

Scope-Site is far superior to see-through type mounts, because the telescopic sight remains close to the bore for proper cheeking on the stock comb. Scope-Site requires the rifleman to move his head only one inch to see through his open sights.

Adjustable Rear

Fixed Rear

Front Sight

Scope-Site Ring Set Adjustable	$77.95
Scope-Site Ring Set Fixed	44.95
Convertible Top Cap Set Adjustable	62.95
Scope-Site Ruger M77-Fixed	44.95
Scope-Site Ruger M77-Adjustable	77.95
Scope-Site Remington 870 & 1100 Shotguns	43.95
Same as above w/Adjustable	76.95

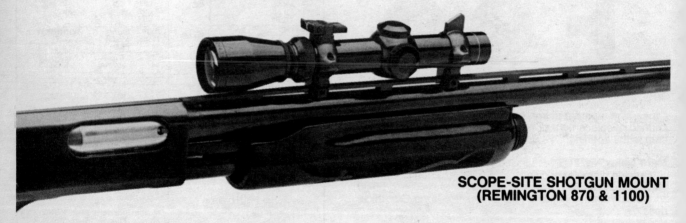

SCOPE-SITE SHOTGUN MOUNT (REMINGTON 870 & 1100)

ANGLE-LOC™ SCOPE RINGS (not shown) (for Weaver-Type Bases and Ruger Rings)

Millett's 1″ Angle-Loc™ scope rings (for use with Weaver-type bases) feature positive clamping mounts for solid alignment of the base to the ring, and windage adjustment integral to the rings enabling shooters to fine-tune the scope rings to their firearms. Available in three heights. Choice of smooth, engraved or Scope-Site.

Angle-Loc Engraved Rings (low, medium, high)	$44.95
Angle-Loc Smooth Rings (low, medium, high)	30.65
Ruger M77 or Super Redhawk Engraved Rings (front & rear, set), medium only	44.95
Same as above w/smooth rings, medium only	30.65

UNIVERSAL CUSTOM SCULPTURED BASES (not shown)

Millett's 2-piece scope bases have outstanding features. Custom crafted style on the outside with all of the excess mass remove from the underside, makes these bases the lightest, heat treated, nickel steel bases on the market, 40% lighter.

700 Series (Two piece set)	SB70001	$23.95
FN Series (Two piece set)	FN00002	23.95
70 Series (Two Piece Set)	WB70003	23.95
Browning Bar, Blr (2 piece set)	BB00004	23.95
Browning A-Bolt (2 piece set)	BB00005	23.95
Rem 7400/7600/4/6 (2 piece set)	RB00006	23.95
Marlin 336 & Similar (2 piece set)	MB00007	23.95
Winchester 94, Angle Eject (2-pc set)	WB00008	23.95
Savage 110, All Models (2-pc set)	SB00009	23.95

MILLETT SIGHTS

RIFLE SIGHTS

COLT AR-15 (and similar models)

Riflemen will appreciate this new peep sight system for AR-15's. Fully adjustable for windage and elevation at the rear sight. No more difficult front sight adjustment. The Millett front sight is a serrated post design that provides a sharp, crisp sight picture under all lighting conditions. A real improvement over the round factory front sight. The rear peep sight blade has a large eye piece that blocks out the surrounding light and allows a sharp, crisp image to show through the cone-shaped aperture. Easy to install requiring no special tools.

Combo Peep Sight (Peep Sight Rear/Serrated Ramp Front)	$62.65
Rear Only Peep Sight (.080 Dia. Aperture)	51.45
Front Only Serrated Ramp	12.25
Rear Peep Blade (.050 Dia. Aperture)	18.95

RUGER MINI-14

Mini-14 owners will be elated with this new Series 100 adjustable sight system. Precision click adjustments for windage and elevation with easy return to zero. The large eye piece on the peep sight blade blocks out surrounding light to provide a sharp sight picture which greatly improves shooting accuracy. The cone-shaped aperture totally eliminates sighting error caused by reflected light. Easy to install with no special tools or gunsmithing required.

Mini-14 Rear Peep Sight (.080 Dia. Aperture)	$51.45
Mini-14 Front Sight	17.85
Mini-14 Combo (Rear peep/post front)	68.25
Rear Peep Blade only; .050 diam. aperture	18.95

OPEN RIFLE SIGHTS
Dovetail Rear Mount

The Series 100 Adjustable Sight System for Dovetail rear mount rifles provide a highly visible sight picture and fast, accurate sightings every time. Precision click adjustments for windage and elevation insure fine sighting. Made of heat treated steel and easy to install. Especially recommended for Marlin 336 owners. Front sights feature blaze orange and white bar enhance contrast, especially in dim light. Rear sight blade provides a sharp horizontal sighting plane with deep notch for fast sighting (choice of white outline or target rear blades). **Rear Sight: $52.95. Front Sight: $11.75.**

FRONT SIGHT CHART

HEIGHT	MAKE & MODEL
.540	Ruger 44 Carbine, #3, 375
.540	Marlin 336, 375
.540	Winchester 94 Trapper
.540	Browning, BLR 22
.500	Winchester 77, 94 Carbine
.500	Remington 740-760, 700 Old Model with Dovetail
.500	Ruger 10/22
.460	Marlin 44, 88-89, 39 A-M
.460	Remington 121, 241, 510-513T
.460	Savage 110, 170, 99T-E-C
.430	Savage 340 Old Model, 99 Old Model
.400	Winchester 88, 70 pre 1964, 94 pre 1964, 71 pre 1964
.400	Marlin 780 22 LR, 1894-1895
.400	Browning Bar 22
.400	Savage 340
.343	Winchester 9422
.343	Use with Interchangeable Base to make .500 height

MILLET SIGHTS

FLUSH-MOUNT SLING SWIVELS

Millett's flush-mount redesigned Pachmayr sling swivels are quick detachable and beautifully styled in heat treated nickel steel. The sling swivel loop has been redesigned to guide the sling into the loop, eliminating twisitng and fraying on edges of sling. Millett flush-mount bases are much easier to install than the old Pachmayr design, with no threading and an easy to use step drill.

Flush-Mount Swivels (pair)	SS00001	$15.65
Loops Only	SS00002	8.70
Installation Drill	SS00003	16.75

FLUSH-MOUNT HARRIS BIPOD ADAPTER (not shown)

Millett's flush-mount sling swivels have a simple-to-use adapter for the Harris bipod, that detaches quickly so the loop can then be installed in the bipod loop receptacle. Will also fit Pachmayr flush-mount bases.

Harris Bipod Adapter	SS00004	$8.70

DUAL-CRIMP INSTALLATION TOOL KIT

The Dual-Crimp System is a new revolutionary way of installing front sights on autos. Now it is not necessary to heliarc or silver solder to get a good secure job. Dual-Crimp has a two-post, hollow rivet design that works very much like an aircraft rivet and withstands the heavy abuse of hardball ammo. Your choice of four styles and nine heights. Dual-Crimp is the quick and easy system for professionals. Requires a drill press.

Dual-Crimp Tool Set, Complete	$142.95
Application Tool	76.95
Reverse counterbore (solid carbide)	36.85
3/16" Drill (solid carbide)	17.05
Drill Jig	21.95
Complete Tool Kit (Stake-On)	87.95

SHURSHOT RIBBED SHOTGUN SIGHTS

The greatest deterrent to shotgun accuracy is raising your head from the stock when shooting. With the Millett ShurShot, accuracy is improved by giving the shooter a reference point to align his head position on the stock. The blaze orange inserts are highly visible in low light and aids the eye in picking up the target. Late in the day deer hunters or early morning duck hunters can get on the game quickly and accurately. ShurShot works great with slugs or shot. Shooting is quick and natural. Eye instinct will automatically align and center the rib and sight bar.

ShurShot Shotgun Sight Combo (Orange) Fits Rem. 1100 & 870	SG00001	$20.95
ShurShot Shotgun Sight (Rear Only Orange) Fits Rem. 1100 & 870	SG00002	12.50
ShurShot Shotgun Sight (Front Only Orange)	SG00003	8.70
ShurShot Shotgun Combo (Orange)	SG00004	27.40
Other Models ShurShot Shotgun Sight (Rear Only Orange)	SG00005	12.50
Other Models ShurShot Adj. Shotgun Sight Combo (Orange)	SG00006	20.95

GLOCK 17 REPLACEMENT SIGHT

The Innovative Glock 17 pistol, the first production pistol to use plastic for the major part of its construction, leaves many shooters looking for better, fully adjustable sights. The Millet sight, in either white outline or target black blade) retrofits the factory dovetail. The plastic factory front sight must be replaced with a Millett Dual-Crimp front (.340 height) and is available in white, orange or black serrated ramp. Rear sight is fully adjustable with positive clicks for windage and elevation. All-steel construction.

GLOCK 17 Sight

Rear Sight (white outline)	52.95
Rear Sight (target)	52.95

MILLET SIGHTS ™

REVOLVER SIGHTS

COLT REVOLVER

The Series 100 Adjustable Sight System offers today's discriminating Colt owner the finest quality replacement sight available. 12 crisp click stops for each turn of adjustment, delivers ⅝″ of adjustment per click at 100 yards with a 6″ barrel. Easy to install, using factory front sight. Guaranteed to give your Colt that custom look.

For Colt Python, Trooper, Diamond Back, and new Frontier single action army.

Rear Only (White Outline)	CR00001	**$46.95**
Rear Only (Target Blade)	CR00002	46.95
Rear Only (Silhouette)	CR00003	46.95

Colt owners will really appreciate the high visibility feature of Colt front sights. Easy to install—just drill 2 holes in the new sight and pin on. All steel. Your choice of blaze orange or white bar. Fits 4″, 6″ & 8″ barrels only.

Colt Python (White or Orange Bar)	FB00007-8	**$12.95**
Trooper, Diamond Back, King Cobra, Peace-maker	FB00015-16	12.95

SMITH & WESSON

The Series 100 Adjustable Sight System for Smith & Wesson revolvers provides the sight picture and crisp click adjustments desired by the discriminating shooter. ½″ of adjustment per click, at 100 yards on elevation, and ⅝″ on windage, with a 6″ barrel. Can be installed in a few minutes, using factory front sight.

K&N frames manufactured prior to 1974 did not standardize on front screw hole location, so the front hole must be drilled and counterbored on these sights.

Smith & Wesson **N** Frame
N.312—Model 25-5, all bbl., 27-3½″ & 5″, 28-4″ & 6″
N.360—Model 25, 27, 29, 57, & 629-4, 6 & 6½″ bbl.
N.410—Model 27, 29, 57, 629 with 8⅜″ bbl.

Smith & Wesson **K&L** Frame
K.312—Models 14, 15, 18, 48-4″, & 53
K&L360—Models 16, 17, 19, 48-6″, 8⅜″, 66, 686, 586

Smith & Wesson K&L-Frame		
Rear Only .312 (White Outline)	SK00001	**$46.95**
Rear Only .312 (Target Blade)	SK00002	46.95
Rear Only .360 (White Outline)	SK00003	46.95
Rear Only .360 (Target Blade)	SK00004	46.95
Rear Only .410 (White Outline)	SK00005	46.95
Rear Only .410 (Target Blade)	SK00006	46.95
Smith & Wesson K&N Old Style		
Rear Only .312 (White Outline)	KN00001	**$46.95**
Rear Only .312 (Target Blade)	KN00002	46.95
Rear Only .360 (White Outline)	KN00003	46.95
Rear Only .360 (Target Blade)	KN00004	46.95
Rear Only .410 (White Outline)	KN00005	46.95
Rear Only .410 (Target Blade)	KN00006	46.95
Smith & Wesson N-Frame		
Rear Only .312 (White Outline)	SN00001	**$46.95**
Rear Only .312 (Target Blade)	SN00002	46.95
Rear Only .360 (White Outline)	SN00003	46.95
Rear Only .360 (Target Blade)	SN00001	46.95
Rear Only .410 (White Outline)	SN00005	46.95
Rear Only .410 (Target Blade)	KN00006	46.95

RUGER

The high visibility white outline sight picture and precision click adjustments of the Series 100 Adjustable Sight System will greatly improve the accuracy and fast sighting capability of your Ruger. ¾″ per click at 100 yard for elevation, ⅝″ per click for windage, with 6″ barrel. Can be easily installed, using factory front sight or all-steel replacement front sight which is a major improvement over the factory front. Visibility is greatly increased for fast sighting. Easy to install by drilling one hole in the new front sight.

The Red Hawk all-steel replacement front sight is highly visible and easy to pickup under all lighting conditions. Very easy to install. Fits the factory replacement system.

SERIES 100 Ruger Double Action Revolver Sights	
Rear Sight (fits all adjustable models)	**$46.95**
Front Sight (Security Six, Police Six, Speed Six)	12.95
Front Sight (Redhawk and GP-100)	15.25

SERIES 100 Ruger Single Action Revolver Sights	
Rear Sight (Black Hawk Standard & Super; Bisley Large Frame, Single-Six	**$46.95**
Front Sight (Millet Replacement sights not available for Ruger single action revolvers).	

DAN WESSON

This sight is exactly what every Dan Wesson owner has been looking for. The Series 100 Adjustable Sight System provides 12 crisp click stops for each turn of adjustment, with ⅝″ per click for windage, with a 6″ barrel. Can be easily installed, using the factory front or new Millett high visibility front sights.

Choice of white outline or target blade.

Rear Only (White Outline)	DW00001	**$46.95**
Rear Only (Target Blade)	DW00002	46.95
Rear Only (White Outline) 44 Mag.	DW00003	46.95
Rear Only (Target Blade) 44 Mag.	DW00004	46.95

If you want super-fast sighting capability for your Dan Wesson, the new Millett blaze orange or white bar front is the answer. Easy to install. Fits factory quick-change system. All steel, no plastic. Available in both heights.

Dan Wesson .44 Mag & 15-2 (White Bar) (high)	FB00009	**$12.95**
Dan Wesson .44 Mag & 15-2 (Orange Bar) (high)	FB00010	12.95
Dan Wesson 22 Caliber (White Bar) (low)	FB00011	12.95
Dan Wesson 22 Caliber (Orange Bar) (low)	FB00012	12.95

MILLET SIGHTS ™

PISTOL SIGHTS FOR RUGER P85

Combo (White rear/White front) $66.95
Combo (White rear/Orange front) 66.95
Rear only (White outline) 52.95
Front only (White ramp) 15.25
Front only (Orange ramp) 15.25
Front only (Serrated ramp) 15.25

SCOPE-SITE FOR HANDGUNS

Colt Python/Trooper/Diamondback/
  Peacekeeper (fully adjustable) $80.25
Dan Wesson (calibers thru 357; fully
  adjustable; 2 rings) 80.25
Ruger Redhawk Engraved (also Ranch Rifle, #1,
  #3; adj. for windage, medium) 44.95
Ruger Super Redhawk Engraved
  (also M77; adj. for windage) 44.95

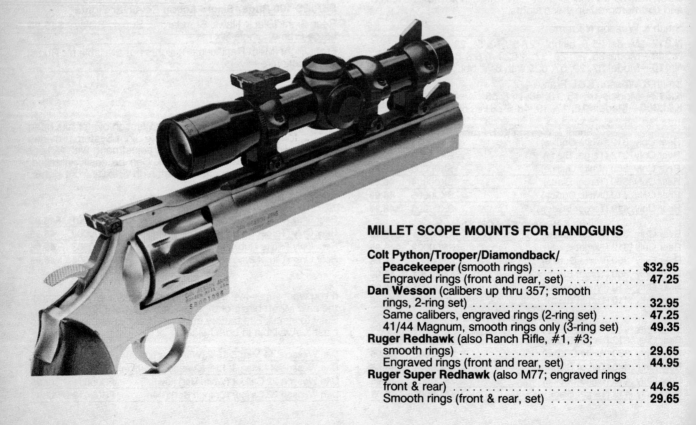

MILLET SCOPE MOUNTS FOR HANDGUNS

Colt Python/Trooper/Diamondback/
  Peacekeeper (smooth rings) $32.95
  Engraved rings (front and rear, set) 47.25
Dan Wesson (calibers up thru 357; smooth
  rings, 2-ring set) 32.95
  Same calibers, engraved rings (2-ring set) 47.25
  41/44 Magnum, smooth rings only (3-ring set) . . . 49.35
Ruger Redhawk (also Ranch Rifle, #1, #3;
  smooth rings) 29.65
  Engraved rings (front and rear, set) 44.95
Ruger Super Redhawk (also M77; engraved rings
  front & rear) 44.95
  Smooth rings (front & rear, set) 29.65

MILLETT SIGHTS™

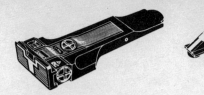

SMITH & WESSON 39/59

This sight system provides fast and accurate sighting capability even under low light conditions. The unique white outline rear blade teamed up with the blaze orange or white bar front sight creates a highly visible sight picture, ideal for match or duty use.

Combo (White rear/Dual-Crimp White Front)	SW39591	$70.50
Combo (White rear/Dual-Crimp Orange Front	SW39592	70.50
Rear Only (White outline)	SW39595	56.45
Rear Only (Target Blade)	SW39596	56.45

Requires .340 Dual-Crimp Front

SMITH & WESSON 469, 669, 659, 459, 645 AUTOPISTOL SIGHTS

Rear Sight (white outline)	$54.10
Front Sight DC 312 white or orange	15.25
Rear/Front Combination	66.95

SMITH & WESSON 400/500/600 SERIES AUTOPISTOL SIGHTS

Rear Sight (white outline)	$52.95
Front Sight DC 312 white or orange	15.25
Rear/Front Combination	68.95

COLT 45

This Series 100 High Profile Adjustable Sight is rugged, all steel, precision sight which fits the standard factory dovetail with no machine modifications required. This sight provides a highly visible sight picture even under low light conditions. Blaze orange or white bar front sight, precision click adjustments for windage and elevation makes the Colt .45 Auto Combo the handgunner's choice.

Combo (White rear/Stake-On White Front)	CA00001	$66.95
Combo (White rear/Stake-On Orange Front)	CA00002	66.95
Combo (White rear/Dual-Crimp White Front)	CA00003	66.95
Combo (White rear/Dual-Crimp Orange Front)	CA00004	66.95
Rear Only (White Outline)	CA00009	52.95
Rear Only (Target Blade)	CA00010	52.95

Colt Gov. and Com. Require .312 High Front Sight.

BROWNING HI-POWER

The Series 100 Adjustable Sight System for Browning Hi-Power will provide accurate high visibility sighting for both fixed and adjustable slides with no machine modifications required to the dovetail. Most adjustable slide model Hi-Powers can use the factory front sight as shown in the photo. The fixed slide model requires a new front sight installation. We highly recommend the Dual-Crimp front sight installation on this gun.

Browning Hi-Power (Adjustable Slide Model)		
Combo (White rear/Stake-On White Front)	BA00001	$66.95
Combo (White rear/Stake-On Orange Front)	BA00002	66.95
Combo (White rear/Dual-Crimp White Front)	BA00003	66.95
Combo (White rear/Dual-Crimp Orange Front)	BA00004	66.95
Rear Only (White Outline)	BA00009	52.95
Rear Only (Target Blade)	BA00010	52.95

High-Power Requires .340 High Front Sight.

Browning Hi-Power (Fixed Slide Model)		
Combo (White rear/Stake-On White Front)	BF00001	$66.95
Combo (White rear/Stake-On Orange Front)	BF00002	66.95
Combo (White rear/Dual-Crimp White Front)	BF00003	66.95
Combo (White rear/Dual-Crimp Orange Front)	BF00004	66.95
Rear Only (White Outline)	BF00009	52.95
Rear Only (Target Blade)	BF00010	52.95

High-Power Requires .340 High Front Sight.

MODELS CZ75/TZ75/TA90 AUTOPISTOL SIGHTS	
Rear Sight (white and Target) only	$52.95

BERETTA ACCURIZER COMBO

This amazing new sight system not only provides a highly visible sight picture but also tunes the barrel lockup to improve your accuracy and reduce your group size by as much as 50%. The Beretta Accurizer sight system fits the 92S, 92SB, 84 and 85 models. Easy to install. Requires the drilling of one hole for installation. Your choice of rear blade styles. Front sight comes in white bar, serrated ramp or blaze orange.

Combo (White Rear/White Bar Front)	BE00001	$75.35
Combo (White Rear/Orange Bar Front)	BE00002	75.35
Rear Only (White Outline)	BE00005	53.70
Rear Only (Target Blade)	BE00006	53.70
Front Only (White Bar)	BE00007	23.95
Front Only (Orange Bar)	BE00008	23.95
Front Only (Serrated Ramp)	BE00009	23.95

Fits Models 92S, 92SB, 85, 84

MILLET AUTO PISTOL SIGHTS

RUGER STANDARD AUTO

The Ruger Standard Auto Combo provides a highly visible sight picture even under low light conditions. The blaze orange or white bar front sight allows the shooter to get on target fast. Great for target use or plinking. Uses Factory Front Sight on adjustable model guns when using Millett target rear only. All other installations use Millett Front Sight. Easy to install.

Combo (White rear/White front)	$66.95
Combo (White rear/Orange front)	66.95
Rear Only (White Outline)	52.95
Rear Only (Silhouette Target Blade)	52.95
Front Only (White)	15.25
Front Only (Orange)	15.25
Front Only (Serrated Ramp)	15.25
Front Only (Target-Adjustable Model/White Bar)	15.25
Front Only (Target-Adjustable Model/Orange Bar)	15.25
Front Only Bull Barrel (White or Orange Ramp)	16.75

INTERCHANGEABLE SIGHT BLADES (REAR ONLY)

The Millett Series 100 Adjustable Sight System is the first group of completely interchangeable component gun sights.

Rear Blades Only

.312 (White Outline)	$18.95
.312 (Target Blade)	18.95
.312 (Target Silhouette Blade)	18.95
.360 (White Outline)	18.95
.360 (Target Blade)	18.95
.360 (Target Silhouette Blade)	18.95
.360 Narrow Notch (White Outline)	18.95
.360 Narrow Notch (Target Blade)	18.95
.410 (White Outline)	18.95
.410 (Target Blade)	18.95

POCKET SIGHT ADJUSTMENT TOOL

This handy little tool prevents the bluing from being scratched and makes sight adjustment quick and easy.

Sight Adjusting Tool (Series 100 System)	SA00008	$3.40

COLT GOLD CUP

Colt Gold Cup Marksman Speed Rear Only (Target .410 Blade)	$46.95
Custom Combat Low Profile Marksman Speed Rear Only (Target .410 Blade)	52.95
Colt Government & Commander (High Profile) Marksman Speed Rear Only (Target .410 Blade) CA00018	52.95
Gold Cup & Low Profile Front .275	15.25
Colt High Profile Front .410	15.25

SIG/SAUER P-220, P-225, P-226

Now Sig Pistol owners can obtain a Series-100 adjustable sight system for their guns. Precision click adjustment for windage and elevation makes it easy to zero when using different loads. The high visibility features assures fast sight acquisition when under the poorest light conditions. Made of high quality heat treated nickel steel and built to last. Extremely easy to install on P-225 and P-226. The P-220 and Browning BDA 45 require the Dual-Crimp front sight installation.

Sig P220 Combo (White Rear/Dual-Crimp White Front)	SP22001	$66.95
Sig P220 Combo (White Rear/Dual-Crimp Orange Front)	SP22002	66.95
Sig P220-25-26 Rear Only (White)	SP22003	52.95
Sig P220-25-26 Rear Only (Target)	SP22004	52.95
Sig P225-6 Combo (White Rear/Dovetail White Front)	SP22561	66.95
Sig P225-6 Combo (White Rear/Dovetail Orange Front)	SP22562	66.95
Sig P225-6 (White) Dovetail Front	SP22565	15.25
Sig P225-6 (Orange) Dovetail Front	SP22566	15.25

The Sig P220 Uses .360 Dual-Crimp Front Sight. The Sig P225-6 Uses a Dovetail Mount Front Sight

PENTAX SCOPES

FIXED POWER

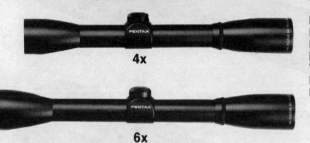

4x

6x

FIXED POWER RIFLESCOPES

Magnification: 4x
Field of view: 35′
Eye relief: 3.25″
Diameter: 1″
Weight: 12.2 oz.
Length: 11.6″
Prices: $260.00 (Glossy)
  280.00 (Pro finish)

Magnification: 6x
Field of view: 20′
Eye relief: 3.25″
Diameter: 1″
Weight: 13½ oz.
Length: 13.4″
Prices: $300.00 (Glossy)
  320.00 (Pro finish)

VARIABLE POWER

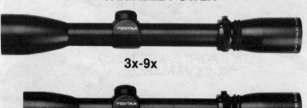

3x-9x

2x-7x

MINI 3x-9x

VARIABLE POWER RIFLESCOPES

Magnification: 1.5x-5x
Field of view: 66′-25′
Eye relief: 3″-3¼″
Diameter: 1″
Weight: 13 oz.
Length: 11″
Price: $300.00 (Matte only)

Magnification: 2x-7x
Field of view: 42.5′-17′
Eye relief: 3″-3¼″
Diameter: 1″
Weight: 14 oz.
Length: 12″
Prices: $355.00 (Glossy)
  375.00 (Pro finish)

Magnification: 3x-9x
Field of view: 33′-13½′
Eye relief: 3″-3¼″
Diameter: 1″
Weight: 15 oz.
Length: 13″
Prices: $375.00 (Glossy)
  390.00 (Pro finish)

Magnification: Mini 3x-9x
Field of view: 26½′-10½′
Eye relief: 3¼″
Diameter: 1″
Weight: 13 oz.
Length: 10.4″
Prices: $315.00 (Mini-glossy)
  335.00 (Mini-Pro finish)

PISTOL SCOPES

Magnification: 2x
Field of view: 21′
Eye relief: 10″-24″
Diameter: 1″
Weight: 6.8 oz.
Length: 8¼″
Prices: $220.00 (Glossy)
  240.00 (Chrome-matte)

Magnification: 1.5x-4x
Field of view: 16′-11′
Eye relief: 11″-25″/11″-18″
Diameter: 1″
Weight: 11 oz.
Length: 10″
Prices: $350.00 (Glossy)
  370.00 (Chrome-matte)

REDFIELD SCOPES

**LOW PROFILE WIDEFIELD
2X-7X VARIABLE**

**LOW PROFILE WIDEFIELD
3X-9X VARIABLE**

**3X-9X ACCU-TRAC
VARIABLE POWER**

LOW PROFILE WIDEFIELD

In heavy cover, game may jump out of the brush 10 feet away or appear in a clearing several hundred yards off, either standing or on the move.

The Widefield®, with 25% more field of view than conventional scopes, lets you spot game quicker, stay with it and see other animals that might be missed.

The patented Low Profile design means a low mounting on the receiver, allowing you to keep your cheek tight on the stock for a more natural and accurate shooting stance, especially when swinging on running game.

The one-piece, fog-proof tube is machined with high tensile strength aluminum alloy and is anodized to a lustrous finish that's rust-free and virtually scratch-proof. Available in 7 models.

WIDEFIELD LOW PROFILE SCOPES

1³/₄x-5x Low Profile Variable Power
113806 1³/₄x-5x 4 Plex **$305.95**
2x-7x Low Profile Variable Power
111806 2x-7x 4 Plex **314.95**
2x-7x Low Profile Accu-Trac Variable Power
111810 2x-7x 4 Plex AT **367.95**
3x-9x Low Profile Variable Power
112806 3x-9x 4 Plex **345.95**
3x-9x Low Profile Accu-Trac Variable Power
112810 3x-9x 4 Plex AT **398.95**
2³/₄x Low Profile Fixed Power
141807 2³/₄x 4 Plex **224.95**
4x Low Profile Fixed Power
143806 4x 4 Plex **249.95**
6x Low Profile Fixed Power
146806 6x 4 Plex **271.95**

REDFIELD SCOPES

GOLDEN FIVE STAR SCOPES

This series of seven scopes incorporates the latest variable and fixed power scope features, including multi-coated and magnum recoil-resistant optical system, plus maximum light-gathering ability. Positive quarter-minute click adjustments for ease of sighting and optimum accuracy. Anodized finish provides scratch-resistant surface.

Golden Five Star Scopes:

1x-4x Variable Power	$244.95
2x-7x Variable Power	254.95
3x-9x Variable Power	272.95
4x-12x Variable Power (adj. objective)	347.95
6x-18x Variable Power (adj. objective)	367.95
4x Fixed Power	197.95
6x Fixed Power	216.95

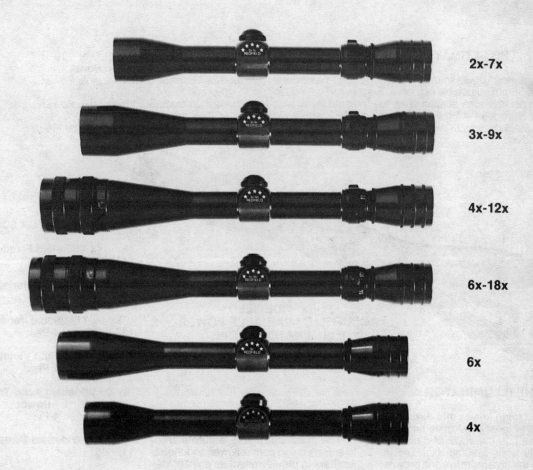

2x-7x

3x-9x

4x-12x

6x-18x

6x

4x

REDFIELD SCOPES

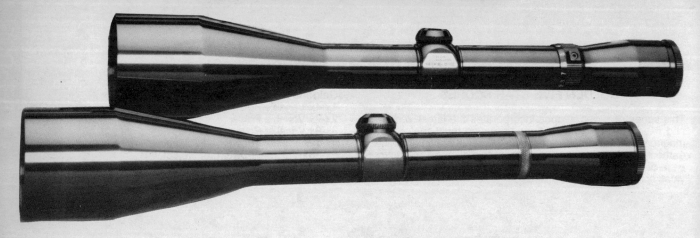

THE ULTIMATE ILLUMINATOR

The first American-made scopes with a 30mm one-piece outer tube and a 56mm adjustable objective. Engineered with quarter-minute positive click adjustments, the Ultimate Illuminator features a European #4 reticle. Comes complete with a set of 30mm steel rings with exclusive Rotary Dovetail System and lens covers.

4x Ultimate 30mm Fixed Power	**$535.95**
3x-9x Ultimate 30mm Var. Power	**625.95**
3x-12x Ultimate 30mm Variable Power (European #4 Adj. Obj.)	**714.95**
3x-12x Ultimate 30mm Variable Power (4 Plex Adj. Obj.)	**714.95**
3x-12x Ultimate 30mm Var. Matte Finish	**723.95**

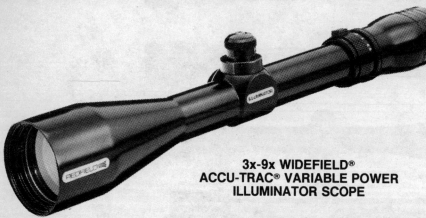

3x-9x WIDEFIELD®
ACCU-TRAC® VARIABLE POWER
ILLUMINATOR SCOPE

THE ILLUMINATOR

Every sportsman knows that dawn and dusk are the most productive times to hunt. Game use the cover of darkness for security while feeding, blending in easily with the greens, grays and browns of the outdoors during dim light conditions.

With this new Illuminator series, you can add precious minutes to morning and evening hunting. These scopes actually compensate for the low light, letting you "see" contrasts between field and game.

Optimum resolution, contrast, color correction, flatness of field, edge-to-edge sharpness and absolute fidelity are improved by the unique air-spaced, tri-

plet objective, and the advanced 5-element erector lens system.

The Illuminators also feature a zero tolerance nylon cam follower and thrust washers to provide absolute point of impact hold through all power ranges. The one-piece tube construction is virtually indestructible, tested at 1200g acceleration forces, and fog-free through the elimination of potential leak paths.

Offered in both the Traditional and Widefield® variable power configurations, the Illuminator is also available with the Accu-Trac® feature.

Also offered in a 30mm 3x-12x with a 56mm adjustable objective.

ILLUMINATOR SCOPES

4x Widefield Fixed Power
141807 4 Plex   **$375.95**

2x-7x Widefield Variable Power
112910 4 Plex   **$428.95**

3x-9x Traditional Variable Power
123886 3x-9x 4 Plex   **$435.95**

3x-9x Widefield Variable Power
112886 3x-9x 4 Plex   **$482.95**

3x-9x Widefield Accu-Trac Variable Power
112880 3x-9x 4 Plex   **$528.95**

3x9 Widefield Matte Finish
112888   **$491.95**

3x12 Ultimate Illuminator Variable Power
112902 3x12 30mm   **$714.95**

4x Ultimate 30mm Fixed Power
112926   **$535.95**

3x-9x Ultimate 30mm Var. Power
112920   **$625.95**

3x-12x Ultimate Var. Power Matte
112908   **$723.95**

REDFIELD SCOPES

THE TRACKER

The Tracker series brings you a superior combination of price and value. It provides the same superb quality, precision and strength of construction found in all Redfield scopes, but at an easily affordable price. Features include the tough, one-piece tube, machined and hand-fitted internal parts, excellent optical quality and traditional Redfield styling.

TRACKER SCOPES

2x-7x Tracker Variable Power
122300 2x-7x 4 Plex   **$182.95**

3x-9x Tracker Variable Power
123300 3x-9x 4 Plex   **$204.95**

4x Tracker Fixed Power
135300 4x 4 Plex   **$144.95**

Matte Finish
122308 2x-7x 4 Plex   **$190.95**
122308 3x-9x 4 Plex   **212.95**
122308 4x 4 Plex   **149.95**

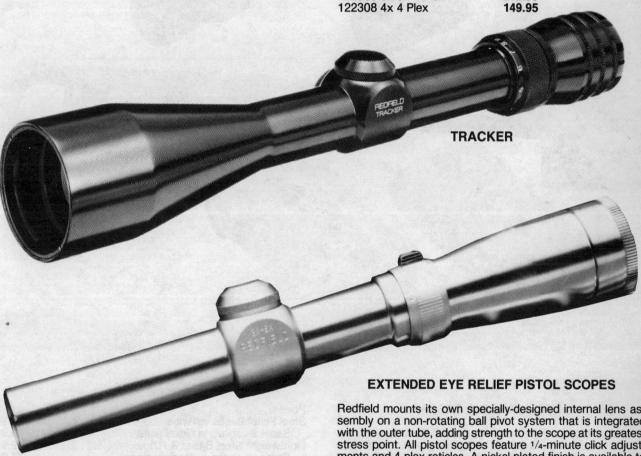

TRACKER

EXTENDED EYE RELIEF PISTOL SCOPES

Redfield mounts its own specially-designed internal lens assembly on a non-rotating ball pivot system that is integrated with the outer tube, adding strength to the scope at its greatest stress point. All pistol scopes feature ¼-minute click adjustments and 4-plex reticles. A nickel-plated finish is available to match stainless steel pistols and comes in three lengths.

Prices:

2½X Pistol Fixed Power **$204.95**
    Same as above in nickel plate 218.95
4X Pistol Fixed Power 215.95
    Same as above in nickel plate 229.95
2X-6X Pistol Variable Power 258.95
    Same as above in nickel plate 277.95

REDFIELD

STEEL RINGS & BASES

Redfield introduces new steel rings designed to fit Ruger rifles, a two-piece steel base that fits all Browning A-Bolt rifles, and a one-piece steel base for the Mini-Mark X rifle. All Redfield rings are precision-machined from solid steel and are available in sizes to mount both 1″ and 30mm tube scopes. Available in medium or high height variations.

Prices:

Steel Pistol Bases w/Rings	$58.95
Same as above in nickel plate	69.95
Lightweight Steel Bases & Rings	19.95
Same as above w/medium rings	27.95
Steel Rings for Ruger Rifles (1″)	32.95
Same as above in 30mm	43.95
Super Strength Steel Rings (1″)	$27.95 to 34.95

SAKO SCOPE MOUNTS

Weighing less than 3 ounces, these new Sako scope mounts are lighter, yet stronger than ever. Tempered steel allows the paring of every last gram of unnecessary weight without sacrificing strength. Like the original mount, these rings clamp directly to the tapered dovetails on Sako rifles, thus eliminating the need for separate bases and screws. Annular grooves inside the rings preclude scope slippage even under the recoil of the heaviest calibers. Nicely streamlined and finished in a rich blue-black to complement any Sako rifle.

Price: Low, medium, or high **$41.50**
Engraved (low, medium, high) **49.00**

SCHMIDT & BENDER RIFLE SCOPES

These fine Schmidt & Bender rifle scopes offer brightness and resolution, color fidelity, and excellent field-of-view. Each model comes with a 30-year guarantee and incorporates the essential ingredients every hunter looks for in rough hunting conditions: recoil-proof, centered reticles; dust and moisture-proof assembly (nitrogen-filled), and precise click adjustments. To guarantee that its scopes will stand up to the most severe hunting conditions, Schmidt & Bender subjects them to vibration tests exceeding the demands of the most powerful cartridges, environmental tests from −40° F to + 122° F, and heavy rain testing. All variable scopes have 30mm center tubes; all fixed power scopes have 1″ tubes.

VARIABLE POWER SCOPE 1¼-4x20
$625.00

VARIABLE POWER SCOPE 1½-6x42
$695.00

VARIABLE POWER SCOPE 2½-10x56
$825.00

SCHMIDT & BENDER

FIXED POWER SCOPE 1¹/₂x15
(steel tube w/o mounting rail)
$455.00

FIXED POWER SCOPE 4x36
(steel tube w/o mounting rail)
$490.00

FIXED POWER SCOPE 6x42
(steel tube w/o mounting rail)
$515.00

FIXED POWER SCOPE 12x42
(steel tube w/o mounting rail)
$565.00

FIXED POWER SCOPE 8x56
(steel tube w/o mounting rail)
$580.00

SIMMONS SCOPES

SILHOUETTE AND TARGET RIFLESCOPES

MODEL 1074
6.5-20x40mm

Field of view: 17.8'-6.2'
Eye relief: 3.5-3.3 Truplex
Weight: 16.2 oz.
Length: 15"
Price: $259.50

DOT RETICLE

MODEL 1075
6.5-20x40mm

Field of view: 17.8'-6.2'
Eye relief: 3.5-3.3 Dot
Weight: 16.2 oz.
Length: 15"
Price: $259.50

TRUPLEX RETICLE

MODEL 1076
15x40mm

Field of view: 11.5'
Eye relief: 3.4 Truplex
Weight: 15.6 oz.
Length: 15"
Price: $223.25

MODEL 1077
15x40mm

Field of view: 11.5'
Eye relief: 3.4 Dot
Weight: 15.6 oz.
Length: 15"
Price: $223.25

MODEL 1078
24x40mm

Field of view: 6.2'
Eye relief: 3.3 Truplex
Weight: 15.6 oz.
Length: 15"
Price: $223.25

MODEL 1079
24x40mm

Field of view: 6.2'
Eye relief: 3.3 Dot
Weight: 15.6 oz.
Length: 15"
Price: $223.25

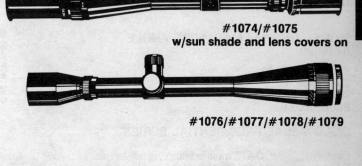

#1074/#1075

#1074/#1075
w/sun shade and lens covers on

#1076/#1077/#1078/#1079

WHITETAIL SERIES

MODEL WT01

Magnification: 4x32mm
Field of view: 36' at 100 yds.
Eye relief: 3.7'
Weight: 9.1 oz.
Length: 12"
Price: $80.25

MODEL WT02

Magnification: 3-9x32mm
Field of view: 37'-12.7' at 100 yds.
Eye relief: 3.1"-2.9"
Weight: 12.8 oz.
Length: 12.8"
Price: $100.50

MODEL WT03

Magnification: 3-9x40mm
Field of view: 37'-12.7' at 100 yds.
Eye relief: 3.1"-2.9"
Weight: 14.2 oz.
Length: 12.8"
Price: $117.75

MODEL WT03
3-9x40mm

SIMMONS SCOPES

**GOLD MEDAL SERIES
MODEL 1044**

GOLD MEDAL RIFLESCOPE SERIES

MODEL 1042 "44 MAG" WIDE ANGLE
6x44mm

Field of view: 22.5'
Eye relief: 3.0"
Weight: 14.5 oz.
Price: $202.00

GOLD MEDAL PRESIDENTIAL SERIES

Features "SIMCOAT" multi-coating on all lenses . . . 360°
Wide-angle . . . 44mm Objective lens . . . Anodized high gloss
finish . . . Speed focusing . . . 1/4-minute click adjustments

Also available:
Model 1066 (2-7x44mm) $308.25
Model 1067 (3-9x44mm) 330.00
Model 1068 (4-12x44mm) 337.50
Model 1069 (6.5-20x44mm) 360.00

#1065

#1066

MODEL 1043 "44 MAG" WIDE ANGLE
8x44mm

Field of view: 22.5'
Eye relief: 3.0"
Weight: 14.5 oz.
Price: $202.00

MODEL 1044 "44 MAG" WIDE ANGLE
3-10x44mm

Field of view: 36.2-10.5'
Eye relief: 3.4"-3.3"
Weight: 16.3 oz.
Price: $229.75

#1067

#1068

#1069

RIFLESCOPE RINGS

Low 1" Set **Model 1401** $10.00
High 1" Set **Model 1403** 10.00
1" See-Thru Set **Model 1405** 11.50
1" Rings for 22 Grooved Receiver **Model 1406** 10.00
1" Rings extention for Compact Scopes
    Model 1409 . . . . 18.00
22 Deluxe Rings for Grooved receivers
    Model 1408 . . . . 13.50

#1401   #1406

#1403

#1409

SIMMONS SCOPES

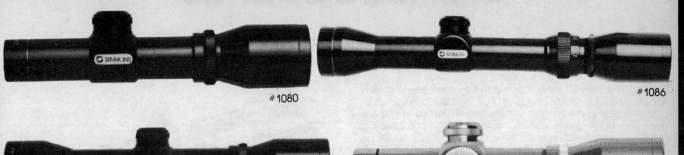

#1080

#1086

#1084

#1081

SILVER MEDAL PISTOLSCOPE SERIES

Fixed power, variable power and silhouette models are all available in this series in traditional blue or silver finish with multi-coated lenses and one-½ piece tubes (to withstand shock of magnum calibers).

Model 1080 2x20 . . . . **$124.00**
Model 1081 10x20 Polished Alum. **124.00**

Model 1082 1x20 . . . . **$146.50**
Model 1083 1x20 Polished Alum. **146.50**
Model 1084 4x32 . . . . **174.00**
Model 1086 1-3.5x32 . . . . **238.25**
Model 1087 2-6x32 w/Adj. Obj. **314.25**
Model 1088 4x32 Polished Alum. **174.50**
Model 1089 7x32 w/Adj. Obj. & Tar. Tur. **223.25**

#1013

#1015

#1017

#1018

SILVER MEDAL RIFLESCOPE SERIES
QUAD VARIABLES

Model 1013 1-4x20 Quad **$136.25**
Model 1015 3-12x40 Quad **130.75**
Model 1017 4-16x40 Quad **149.00**
Model 1018 6-24x40 Quad **174.50**
Model 1023 4x40 Wide Angle **138.50**
Model 1025 6x40 Wide Angle **140.25**

Model 1026 1.5-4.5x32 . . . . **$152.50**
Model 1027 2-7x32 . . . . **136.25**
Model 1029 3-9x40 Wide Angle **141.25**
Model 1030 3-9x32 Polished Alum. **142.50**
Model 1090 1.5x20 L.E.R. Matte **136.75**

SIMMONS SCOPES

RIMFIRE RIFLESCOPES

Features the new 22 MAG scope with fully coated lens system set precisely for rimfire shooting. Full big-bore configuration, plus windage and elevation capabilities. Trimmed in red and gold, this black scope comes complete with rings ready to mount to a grooved receiver. Also available: three additional 1" rimfire scopes (all with objective focus features) and two models with target turrets.

Model 100I (4x20mm Compact, ¾" diameter) .... $ 32.25
Model 1002 (4x15 22mm, ¾" diameter) 11.75
Model 1004 (3-7x20 22mm, ¾" diameter) 39.00
Model 1022 (4x32mm, 1" diameter) 83.00
Model 1073 (2-7x32mm, 1" diameter) 180.75
Model 1099 (4x32mm, 1" diameter) 109.50
Model 21007 (4x32mm, 1" diameter) 87.25

MODEL 1022

SPOTTING SCOPES

Features a finder scope whereby both eyes are used to locate the target with an electronically assisted seeker spot that is illuminated and controlled by a pulse switch. Also featured is a prismatic telescope that utilizes two separate prism systems. Complete with tripods, plus several options.

Model 1209 (25x50 camouflage compact) $161.00
Model 1210 (25x50mm) 225.50
Model 1212 (17-52x50mm zoom) 433.50
Model 1214 (50mm) 468.00
Model 1215 (25x50mm; camouflaged) 361.50
Model 1220 (25x60mm; deluxe tripod) 434.50
Model 1299 (15-60x60mm and 3x finder scope) ... 481.75

MODEL 1221 (20x56mm)

SPRINGFIELD ARMORY RIFLE SCOPES

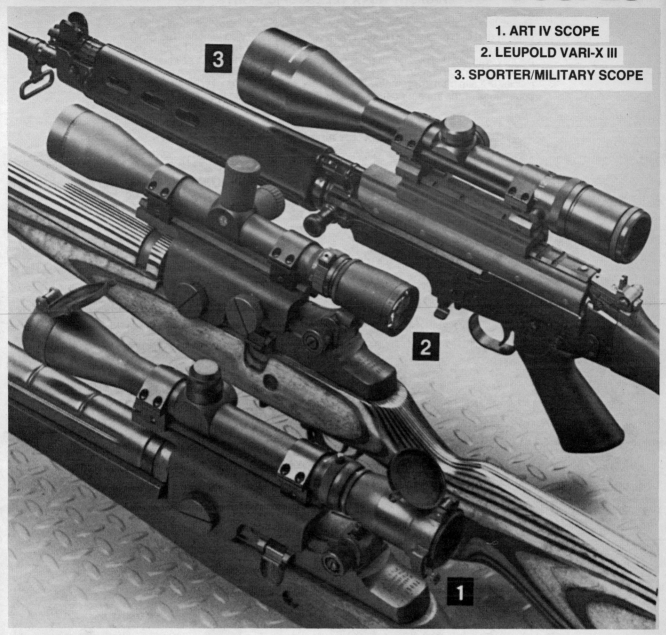

1. ART IV SCOPE
2. LEUPOLD VARI-X III
3. SPORTER/MILITARY SCOPE

SPORTER SCOPE $433.50
GOVERNMENT MODEL SCOPE $523.50

Available in 3x9x56 Sporter and 4x14x56 Government Model (30mm tube), these scopes provide range-finding capabilities out to 1,000 yards. They also enable shooters to use any power setting without changing the ranging effect, while leaving their hands in position. An internal level maintains vertical and horizontal alignment for maximum accuracy at extended ranges. The Sporter model comes with a one-inch tube.

Also available:
SPORTER MODEL (Non-range finding) **$208.50**
ART IV 3x9 Variable Power 387.00

LEUPOLD VARI-X III (3.5x10)
$487.50

This scope features infinitely variable power selector detents at regular intervals and a 15-minute dial with quarter-minute click adjustments for windage and elevation. It comes standard with a one-inch tube with matte black finish.

SWAROVSKI

HABICHT NOVA TELESCOPIC SIGHTS

These fine Austrian-made sights feature brilliant optics with high-quality lens coating and optimal sighting under poor light and weather conditions. The Nova ocular system with telescope recoil damping reduces the danger of injury, especially with shots aimed in an upward direction. The main tube is selectable in steel or light metal construction with a mounting rail. Because of Nova's centered reticle, the aiming mark remains in the center of the field of view regardless of corrections of the impact point. See **Specifications** table on the following page.

VARIABLE POWER
(Add $20.00 for aluminum tubes)

1.5-6x42
$665.00

2.2-9x42
$815.00

3-12x56
$910.00

FIXED POWER (STEEL TUBES ONLY)

1.5x20
$470.00

6x42
$540.00

8x56
$635.00

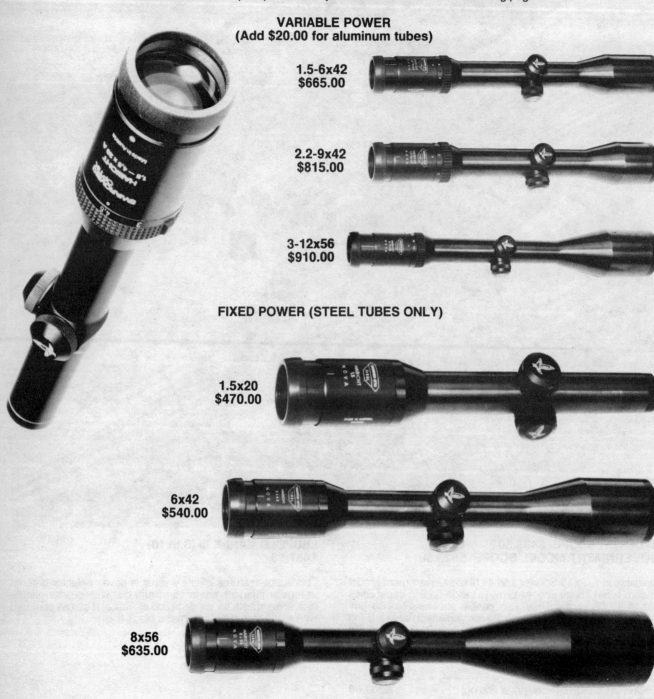

SWAROVSKI

SPECIFICATIONS

Telescopic Sights	1.5x20	4x32	6x42	8x56	1.5-6x42	2.2-9x42	3-12x56
Magnification	1.5x	4x	6x	8x	1.5-6x	2.2-9x	3-12x
Max. effective objective dia.	20mm	32mm	42mm	56mm	42mm	42mm	56mm
Exit pupil dia.	12.7mm	8mm	7mm	7mm	14.3-7mm	14.3-4.7mm	14.3-4.7mm
Field of view at 100m	18.5m	10m	7m	5.2m	18.5-6.5m	12-4.5m	9-3.3m
Twilight effective factor (DIN 58388)	4.2	11.3	15.9	21.1	4.2-15.9	6.2-19.4	8.5-25.9
Intermediary tube dia. Steel-Standard	26mm	26mm	26mm	26mm	30mm	30mm	30mm
Objective tube dia.	26mm	38mm	48mm	62mm	48mm	48mm	62mm
Ocular tube dia.	40mm	40mm	40mm	40mm	40mm	40mm	40mm
Scope length	247mm	290mm	322mm	370mm	322mm	342mm	391mm
Weight Steel	360g	430g	500g	660g	570g	580g	710g
(approx.) Light metal with rail		370g	400g	490g	480g	470g	540g
A change of the impact point per click in mm/100m	12	7	6	4	9	6	4

AMERICAN LIGHTWEIGHT RIFLESCOPE

This new model features precision ground, coated and aligned optics sealed in a special aluminum alloy tube to withstand heavy recoil. Eye relief is 85mm and the recoiling eyepiece protects the eye. Positive click adjustments for elevation and windage change the impact point (approx. 1/4") per click at 100 yards, with parallax also set at 100 yards. Weight is only 13 ounces.

Prices:
1.5-4.5x20 . . . . **$590.00**
4x32 with duplex reticle **450.00**
6x36 with duplex reticle **500.00**
3-9x36 with duplex reticle **655.00**

1.5-4.5x20
LOW MAGNIFICATION VARIABLE RIFLESCOPE

TASCO SCOPES

MODEL WA1.35×20

WORLD CLASS WIDE ANGLE® RIFLESCOPES

Features:
- 25% larger field of view
- Exceptional optics
- Fully coated for maximum light transmission
- Waterproof, shockproof, fog-proof
- Non-removable eye bell
- Free haze filter lens caps
- TASCO's unique World Class Lifetime Warranty

This member of Tasco's World Class Wide Angle line offers a wide field of view—115 feet at 1X and 31 feet at 3.5X—and quick sighting without depending on a critical view. The scope is ideal for hunting deer and dangerous game, especially in close quarters or in heavily wooded and poorly lit areas. Other features include 1/2-minute positive click stops, fully coated lenses (including Supercon process), nonremovable eyebell and windage/elevation screws. Length is 9³/₄″, with 1″ diameter tube. Weight is 10.5 ounces.

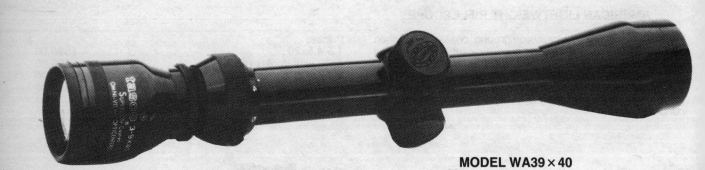

MODEL WA39 × 40

WIDE ANGLE VARIABLE ZOOM RIFLESCOPES (ALL WATERPROOF)

MODEL NO.	DESCRIPTION	RETICLE	PRICE
WA13.5×20	1X-3.5X Zoom (20mm)	Wide Angle 30/30	**239.95**
WA39X40TV	3X-9X (40mm)	Wide Angle 30/30	**209.95**
WA4×40	4X (40mm)	Wide Angle 30/30	**154.95**
WA6×40	6X (40mm)	Wide Angle 30/30	**159.95**
WA1.755×20	1.75X-5X Zoom (20mm)	Wide Angle 30/30	**239.95**
WA27×32	2X-7X Zoom (32mm)	Wide Angle 30/30	**209.95**
WA39×32	3X-9X Zoom (32mm)	Wide Angle 30/30	**199.95**
WA39×40	3X-9X Zoom (40mm)	Wide Angle 30/30	**209.95**
CW28×32	2X-8X (32mm)	Wide Angle 30/30	**229.95**
CW4×32	4X (32mm)	Wide Angle 30/30	**179.95**
ER39×40WA	3X-9X 200m Electric Reticle	Wide Angle 30/30 Electronic	**459.95**

TASCO SCOPES

**RIMFIRE RIFLESCOPE
FOR 22's WITH 22 RING MOUNTS**

MODEL RF4 × 15
$14.95

SPECIFICATIONS

Model	Power	Objective Diameter	Finish	Reticle	Field of View @ 100 yards	Eye Relief	Tube Diam.	Scope Length	Scope Weight	Price
RF4X15	4	15mm	Black	Cross Hair	21'	2½"	¾"	11"	4 oz.	$18.45
RF4X18	4	18mm	Black	30/30	20'	2½"	¾"	10½"	3.8 oz.	36.95
RF4X20DS	4	20mm	Dull Satin	Cross Hair	20'	2½"	¾"	10½"	3.8 oz.	27.95
RF37X20	3-7	20mm	Black	30/30	24'-11'	2½"	¾"	11½"	5.7 oz.	54.95
P1.5X15	1.5	15mm	Black	Cross Hair	22½'	9½"-20¾"	¾"	8¾"	3.25 oz.	36.95

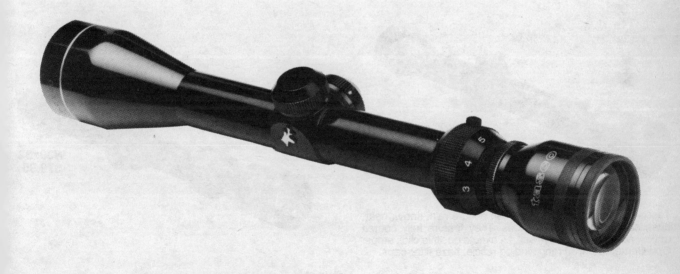

TRAJECTORY-RANGE FINDING RIFLESCOPE

All Tasco TR Scopes have fully coated optics, Opti-Centered® stadia reticle, ¼-minute positive click stops and haze filter caps. All are fog-proof, shockproof, waterproof and anodized.

MODEL NO.	DESCRIPTION	RETICLE	PRICE
TR39X40WA	3X-9X Zoom (40mm) Wide Angle	30/30 RF	$279.95
TR416X40	4X-16X Zoom (40mm)	30/30 RF	304.95
TR624X40	6X-24X Zoom (40mm)	30/30 RF	349.95

TASCO TS® SCOPES

For silhouette and target shooting, Tasco's TS® scopes adjust for varying long-range targets, with ⅛-minute Positrac® micrometer windage and elevation adjustments. All TS® scopes are waterproof, fog-proof, shockproof, fully Supercon-coated, and include screw-in metal lens protectors. All include two metal mirage deflection and sunshade hoods, five and eight inches in length, which can be used separately or together to eliminate image distortion resulting from excessive barrel temperatures or to shade the objective lens from direct sunlight. All include a focusing objective for precise parallax correction and extra-large 44mm objective lenses for extra brightness at high magnifications. Each scope is available in a choice of two reticle patterns: ¾-minute dot (A) and fine crosshair (B).

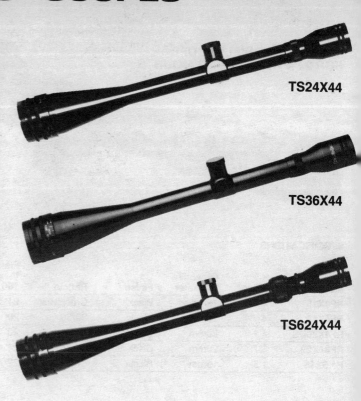

TS24X44

TS36X44

TS624X44

MODEL NO.	DESCRIPTION	PRICE
TS24X44B,A	24X (44mm)	$399.95
TS36X44B,A	36X (44mm)	439.95
TS624X44B,A	6X-24X Zoom (44mm)	489.95
TS832X44A	8X-32X (44 mm)	489.95
TS832X44B	8X-32X (44mm)	539.95

Standard features: Two mirage deflection and sunshine hoods (3″ and 5″)

W4x32
$59.95

W39x32
$79.95

TRADITIONAL RIFLESCOPES

Tasco's waterproof riflescopes can endure rain, snow, heat, dust, sand and altitude changes. They feature fully coated optics, non-removable eye bell, ¼ minute positive click stops, Opti-Centered 30/30 rangefinding reticle, haze filter caps.

Model	Power	Objective Diameter	Finish	Reticle	Field of View @ 100 yards	Eye Relief	Tube Diam.	Scope Length	Scope Weight	Prices
W4X32T	4	32mm	Black	30/30	27′	3⅛″	1″	11¾″	9 oz.	$89.95
W4X40	4	40mm	Black	30/30	32′	3⅛″	1″	12½″	11.2 oz.	114.95
W39X32V	3-9	32mm	Black	30/30	39′-13′	3″	1″	11.5″	11.5 oz.	109.95
W39X40V	3-9	40mm	Black	30/30	39′-13′	3⅛″	1″	12⅝″	12.3 oz.	134.95
W2.5X32	2.5	32mm	Black	30/30	42′	3¼	1″	12¼″	9.5 oz.	99.95
4X32V	4	32mm	Black	30/30	32′	3⅛″	1″	11¾	9 oz.	79.95
W6X40V	6	40mm	Black	30/30	20′	3″	1″	12½″	11.5 oz.	124.95

TASCO SCOPES

PRO-POINT MULTI-PURPOSE SCOPES

Tasco's ProPoint scopes are ideal for fast-action pistol competition and bull's-eye marksmanship, as well as rifle, shotgun, bow and blackpowder use. Available in matte black or matte aluminum. Features include: True 1X for unlimited eye relief. . . Electronic red dot reticle with manual rheostat control. . . 30mm tube with 30mm aluminum ringset included. . . Optically bright and wide field of view (54% over 1″ tubes). . . Windage and elevation controls. . . Positive click stops. . . waterproof, fogproof, shockproof. . . Lithium battery (mercury battery converter included). Also available: ProPoint II. Redesigned and streamlined with lithium battery pack housed inside the tube. Available with a T-3 reticle design and 3X power booster in black matte finish.

SPECIFICATIONS PROPOINT SCOPES

Model	Power	Objective Diameter	Finish	Reticle	Field of View @ 100 Yds.	Eye Relief	Tube Diam.	Scope Length	Scope Weight	Prices
PDP1L	1X	25mm	Matte Black	Illum. Red Dot	25′–12′	Unltd.	30mm	5″	5.5 oz.	349.95
PDP1LMA	1X	25mm	Matte Alum.	Illum. Red Dot	25′–12′	Unltd.	30mm	5″	5.5 oz.	349.95
PDP2	1X	25mm	Matte Black	Illum. Red Dot	25′–12′	Unltd.	30mm	5″	5.5 oz.	429.95
PDP2MA	1X	25mm	Matte Alum.	Illum. Red Dot	25′–12′	Unltd.	30mm	5″	5.5 oz.	429.95
PDP2T3	1X	25mm	Matte Black	Illum. T-3 Red Dot	25′–12′	Unltd.	30mm	5″	5.5 oz.	429.95
PB1	3X Power Booster	13mm	Matte Black	No reticle	For use with all models of ProPoint					199.95
PB2	3X Power Booster	13mm	Matte Black	Cross Hair	For use with PDP2 only			5.5″	6.1 oz.	189.95

TASCO PISTOL SCOPES

RUBBER ARMORED SCOPES

Extra padding helps these rugged scopes stand up to rough handling. Custom-fitting rings are included. Scopes feature:
- Fully coated optics
- Windage and elevation controls
- Waterproofing, fogproofing, shockproofing
- 1/4-minute positive click stops
- Opti-centered 30/30 rangefinding reticle
- Haze filter caps

Model	Power	Objective Diameter	Finish	Reticle	Field of View @ 100 Yards	Eye Relief	Tube Diam.	Scope Length	Scope Weight	Price
RC4X32A,B	4	32mm	Green Rubber	30/30	27'	3"	1"	11 3/4"	11.5 oz.	$134.95
RC4X40A,B	4	40mm	Green Rubber	30/30	27'	3 1/4"	1"	12 1/2"	14.2 oz.	159.95
RC39X40A,B	3-9	40mm	Green Rubber	30/30	35'-14'	3 1/4"	1"	12 5/8"	14.3 oz.	189.95

"A" fits standard dove tail base.
"B" fits 3/8" grooved receivers—most 22 cal. and airguns.

MAG IV RIFLESCOPES (not shown)

MAG IV scopes yield four times magnification range in a standard size riflescope and one-third more zooming range than most variable scopes. Features include: Fully coated optics and large objective lens to keep target in low light . . . Nonremovable eye bell. . . 1/4-minute positive click stops . . . Nonremovable windage and elevation screws. . . Opti-centered 30/30 rangefinding reticle . . . Waterproof, fogproof, shockproof.

SPECIFICATIONS

Model	Power	Objective Diameter	Finish	Reticle	Field of View @ 100 Yds.	Eye Relief	Tube Diam.	Scope Length	Scope Weight	Price
W312X40	3-12	40mm	Black	30/30	35'-9'	3 1/8"	1"	12 3/16"	12 oz.	159.95
W416X40†	4-16	40mm	Black	30/30	26'-6'	3 1/8"	1"	14 1/8"	15.6 oz.	209.95
W624X40†	6-24	40mm	Black	30/30	17'-4'	3"	1"	15 3/8"	16.75 oz.	279.95

† Indicates focusing objective.

TASCO PISTOL SCOPES

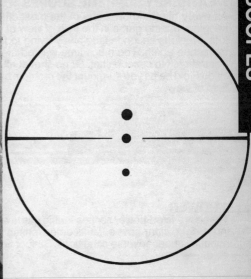

PRO-CLASS PISTOL SCOPES

OBJECTIVE DIAMETER: 22mm

POWER: 1 Model	Finish	Reticle	Field of View @ 100 yds	Eye Relief	Scope Length	Scope Weight	Price
P1X22	Dull Satin	GTD	65'-24'	8-28"	7³/₄"	8 oz.	$209.95
P1X22PA	Pol. Alum.	GTD	65'-24'	8-28"	7³/₄"	8 oz.	209.95
P1.254X22	Dull Satin	GTD	23'-18' (1.25X) 9'-7' (4X)	12"-28" (1.25X) 12"-20" (4X)	9¹/₄"	9.5 oz.	319.95
POWER: 2							
P2X22	Dull Satin	GTD	26'-18'	10-24"	7³/₄"	7.6 oz.	209.95
P2X22PA	Pol. Alum.	GTD	26'-18'	10-24"	7³/₄"	7.6 oz.	209.95
ER2X22P	Dull Satin	30/30 ER	25'-15'	8"-20"	8³/₄"	9.4 oz.	419.95
POWER: 3							
P3X22	Dull Satin	GTD	13'-6'	12-24"	8¹/₄"	8.5 oz.	239.95
P3X22PA	Pol. Alumin.	GTD	13'-6'	12-24"	8¹/₄"	8.5 oz.	239.95

OBJECTIVE DIAMETER: 30mm
POWER: 4

Model	Finish	Reticle	Field of View @ 100 yds	Eye Relief	Scope Length	Scope Weight	Price
P4X30	Dull Satin	GTD	7'-6'	12-24"	9³/₄"	12.1 oz.	279.95
P4X30PA	Pol. Alum.	GTD	7'-6'	12-24"	9³/₄"	12.1 oz.	279.95
ER4X30P	Dull Satin	30/30 ER	7'-6'	12"-24"	9³/₄"	12 oz.	459.95

OBJECTIVE DIAMETER: 40mm
POWER: 6

Model	Finish	Reticle	Field of View @ 100 yds	Eye Relief	Scope Length	Scope Weight	Price
P6X40	Dull Satin	GTD	5'2"-5'5"	12-23"	11"	14.2 oz.	379.95
P6X40PA	Pol. Alum.	GTD	5'2"-5'5"	12-23"	11"	14.2 oz.	379.95

OBJECTIVE DIAMETER: 22mm
POWER: 1

Model	Finish	Reticle	Field of View @ 100 yds	Eye Relief	Scope Length	Scope Weight	Price
P1X22S	Dull Satin	GTD	43'-22'	8-28"	6¹/₂"	7.7 oz.	249.95
POWER: 2							
A2X22S	Dull Satin	GTD	23'-18'	10-24"	6¹/₂"	7.7 oz.	249.95

WEATHERBY SUPREME SCOPES

WEATHERBY SUPREME SCOPES

As every hunter knows, one of the most difficult problems is keeping running game in the field of view of the scope. Once lost, precious seconds fade away trying to find the animal in the scope again. Too much time wasted means the ultimate frustration. No second shot. Or no shot at all. The Weatherby Wide Field helps you surmount the problem by increasing your field of view.

4 POWER

These are fixed-power scopes for big game and varmint hunting. Bright, clear image. Multicoated lenses for maximum luminosity under adverse conditions. 32-foot field of view at 100 yards.

Fixed Power:	PRICES
4 × 44	$270.00
Variable Power:	
1.75-5 × 20	260.00
2-7 × 34	270.00
3-9 × 44	320.00

FEATURES:

Optical excellence—now protected with multicoated anti-glare coating. • Fog-free and waterproof construction. • Constantly self-centered reticles. • Non-magnifying reticle. • ¼" adjustments. • Quick variable power change. • Unique luminous reticle. • Neoprene eyepiece. • Binocular-type speed focusing. • Rugged score tube construction. Autocom point-blank system.

3 TO 9 POWER

The most desirable variable for every kind of shooting from target to long-range big game. Outstanding light-gathering power. Fast, convenient focusing adjustment.

1³/₄ TO 5 POWER

A popular model for close-range hunting with large-bore rifles. Includes the Autocom system, which automatically compensates for trajectory and eliminates the need for range-finding without making elevation adjustments. Just aim and shoot!

SUPREME RIFLESCOPES SPECIFICATIONS

Item	1.75-5X20	4X34	2-7X34	4X44	3-9X44
Actual Magnification	1.7-5	4	2.1-6.83	3.9	3.15-8.98
Field of View @ 100 yards	66.6-21.4 ft.	32 ft.	59-16 ft.	32 ft.	36-13 ft.
Eye Relief (inches)	3.4	3.1	3.4	3.0	3.5
Exit Pupil dia. in mm	11.9-4	8	10-4.9	10	10-4.9
Clear Aperture of Objective	20mm	34mm	34mm	44mm	44mm
Twilight Factor	5.9-10	11.7	8.2-15.4	13.3	11.5-19.9
Tube Diameter	1"	1"	1"	1"	1"
O.D. of Objective	1"	1.610"	1.610"	2"	2"
O.D. of Ocular	1.635"	1.635"	1.635"	1.635"	1.635"
Overall Length	10.7"	11.125"	11.125"	12.5"	12.7"
Weight	11 oz.	9.6 oz.	10.4 oz.	11.6 oz.	11.6 oz.
Adjustment Graduations Major Divisions: Minor Divisions:	1 MOA 1/4 MOA	1 MOA 1/4 MOA	1 MOA 1/4 MOA	1 MOA 1/4 MOA	1 MOA 1/4 MOA
Maximum Adjustment (W&E)	60"	60"	60"	60"	60"
Reticles Available	LUMIPLEX	LUMIPLEX	LUMIPLEX	LUMIPLEX	LUMIPLEX

WEAVER SCOPES

MODEL V9
3x-9x38 Variable Hunting Scope
$159.29

MODEL K4
4x38 Fixed Power Hunting Scope
$122.10

MODEL V3
1x-3x20 Variable Hunting Scope
$147.63

MODEL K2.5
2.5x20 Fixed Power Hunting Scope
$112.55

MODEL K6
6x38 Fixed Power Hunting Scope
$132.98

MODEL RV7
2x-7x32 Rimfire Variable Scope
$125.54

MODEL V10
2x-10x38 Variable All-Purpose Scope
$169.16

Also available:
MODEL KT 15. 15x42 Target Silhouette Scope. **$266.40**

MODEL RK4
4x32 Rimfire Fixed Power Scope
$103.34

WEAVER RINGS AND BASES

1. **DETACHABLE TOP MOUNT RINGS.** Made with split rings in 7/8" and 1" diameters. The 1" blued rings are available in standard, medium, high and extension styles. New stainless steel rings in 1" medium also available. High Top Mount Rings and Medium Top Mount Rings (in 1" diameter only) provide adequate barrel and iron sight clearance for scopes with adjective diameters greater than 1 3/4". **$24.02 ($36.72 for 1" Medium Stainless Steel)**

2. **EXTENSION DETACHABLE MOUNT RINGS.** In 1" diameter only. Position scope 3/4" further forward, or backward, for improved eye relief. **$28.06**

3. **DETACHABLE SIDE MOUNTS.** Designed for Winchester 94 (except Angle Eject models) without drilling or tapping. Made with 1" diameter split-rings and brackets. Also offered in High style for greater clearance. **$25.40 (30.01 for 1" Long)**

4. **PIVOT MOUNT RINGS.** Change from scope to iron sights with a gentle push. Spring latch locks rings in place when scope is in sighting position. No drilling or tapping required. **$32.55**

5. **SEE-THRU MOUNT RINGS.** Attach to any bases which have square-cut cross bolt slots. Detach easily and offer built-in remounting precision. **$24.02 ($28.06 for 1" Extension; $17.32 for 7/8")**

6. **INTEGRAL 1" SEE-THROUGH RINGS.** No drilling or tapping, and no base needed. Large aperature offers wide field of view with iron sights. **$17.89**

7. **1" & 7/8" TIP-OFF MOUNTS, SPLIT RINGS.** For mounting 1" or 7/8" scopes on rimfire rifles with 3/8" dovetailed factory-grooved receiver. No bases required. **$23.55**

8. **BLUED MOUNT BASE SYSTEMS. $62.45**

9. **STAINLESS STEEL MOUNT BASE SYSTEMS.** Require no drilling or tapping. Simply remove rear sight and slip on barrel yoke. Base attaches easily with two screws. Includes two Detachable Mount Rings, Mount Base, barrel yoke, screws and Allen wrench. **$87.38**

10. **SCOPE MOUNT SYSTEMS.** For fast mounting on Mossberg 500, Remington 870 or 1100 shotguns with no drilling or tapping. System meshes with existing trigger plate pins. Remove pins, replace with bolts. **$62.45**

11. **MODEL 94 ANGLE EJECT BASES.** For scoping Angle Eject Winchester 94's. **$9.68**

12. **BASES. $2.42-$12.59** (top mount); **$5.77-$9.24** (pivot mount); **$10.39** (side mount)

WILLIAMS TWILIGHT SCOPES

1.5x-5x (and 2x-6x): $196.30

2¹/₂x: $138.95

4x: $145.25

3x-9x: $206.30

The "Twilight" series of scopes was introduced to accommodate those shooters who want a high-quality scope in the medium-priced field. The "Twilight" scopes are waterproof and shockproof, have coated lenses and are nitrogen-filled. Resolution is sharp and clear. All "Twilight" scopes have a highly polished, rich, black, hard anodized finish.

There are five models available: the 2¹/₂x, the 4x, the 1.5x-5x, the 2x-6x, and the 3x-9x. They are available in T-N-T reticle only (which stands for "thick and thin").

OPTICAL SPECIFICATIONS	2.5X	4X	2X-6X At 2X	2X-6X At 6X	3X-9X At 3X	3X-9X At 9X
Clear aperture of objective lens	20mm	32mm	32mm	Same	40mm	Same
Clear aperture of ocular lens	32mm	32mm	32mm	Same	32mm	Same
Exit Pupil	8mm	8mm	16mm	5.3mm	13.3mm	44.4mm
Relative Brightness	64	64	256	28	161.2	17.6
Field of view (degree of angle)	6°20'	5°30'	8°30'	3°10'	7°	2°20'
Field of view at 100 yards	32'	29'	45¹/₂'	16³/₄'	36¹/₂'	12³/₄'
Eye Relief	3.7"	3.6"	3"	3"	3.1"	2.9"
Parallax Correction (at)	50 yds.	100 yds.	100 yds.	Same	100 yds.	Same
Lens Construction	9	9	11	Same	11	Same
MECHANICAL SPECIFICATIONS						
Outside diameter of objective end	1.00"	1.525"	1.525"	Same	1.850"	1.850"
Outside diameter of ocular end	1.455"	1.455"	1.455"	Same	1.455"	Same
Ouside diameter of tube	1"	1"	1"	Same	1"	Same
Internal adjustment graduation	¼ min.	¼" min.	¼ min.	Same	¼" min.	Same
Minimum internal adjustment	75 min.	75 min.	75 min.	Same	60 min.	Same
Finish			Glossy Hard Black Anodized			
Length	10"	11³/₄"	11¹/₂"	11¹/₂"	12³/₄"	12³/₄"
Weight	8¹/₂ oz.	9¹/₂ oz.	11¹/₂ oz.	Same	13¹/₂ oz.	Same

WILLIAMS SIGHT-OVER-SCOPE

**S-O-S
(SIGHT-OVER-SCOPE)
MOUNTING SYSTEMS
Shown on a Marlin Model 336**

MODELS	S-O-S FRONT	S-O-S REAR
Remington Models 760-740-742, and Savage Model 170	1	2
Browning A-Bolt	3	3
Winchester Models 70 Standard, 670 & 770	4	3
*1917 Enfield and Sauer 200	4	4
Remington Models 700-721-722-725, L.H. and 40X; BSA; Weatherby MK-V and Vanguard; Ruger 77ST; and S&W 1500	4	5
Savage Models 110, 111 and 112V	4	16
Winchester Models 88 and 100	6	6
Browning BAR Auto and BLR Lever	7	7
Marlin Models 336, 1894 & 1894C	8	8
Remington Model 788	9	9
Thompson/Center 45 & 50 Cal. Hawken and 54 Cal. Renegade	10**	10**
Remington 541-S. Also, Remington Models 580-581-582 (require drilling & tapping)	11	11
Ruger Model 44	11	12
Ruger Model 10/22	13	12
Browning Safari Bolt and Mark X	14	15
Ithaca LSA-55 and LSA-65 Bolt	16	16
Rem. Models Four, Six, 7400 and 7600	17	18
Savage Model 99	19	20**
Winchester Model 94 Angle Eject	21	22**

*With the rear receiver radiused the same diameter as the front receiver ring.
**Requires sub-block

The S-O-S System (on a Ruger 10/22)

S-O-S Kit Complete for Williams Rings	$47.00
S-O-S Streamline Set (except w/sub-block)	54.15
S-O-S Streamline Set 10 & 10	61.75
S-O-S Streamline Set 19 & 20, 21 & 22	56.55

This concept in sighting known as the S-O-S (Sight-Over-Scope) allows the scope to be mounted low and permits instant use of open sight for quick, fast action shots at close range. The compact S-O-S has both elevation and windage in the rear sight, and the front sight has additional windage.

The "Guide-Line" S-O-S ring top kit will work with all Williams mounts having the two-piece 1-inch rings. The sights are made from an aluminum alloy. They are rustproof and attractively anodized.

The S-O-S front sight is furnished with a fluorescent orange ³/₃₂-inch bead (white or gold is optional.) The S-O-S rear sight is furnished with the WGRS-M/L Guide Receiver Sight with the regular ³/₈ × .125 Buckbuster long shank aperture. (Twilight or Regular apertures in the ³/₈ × .093 and ³/₈ × .050 are optional.) Specify the long shank aperture to fit the WGRS receiver sight.

WILLIAMS RECEIVER SIGHTS

TARGET FP RECEIVER SIGHT (HIGH)

TARGET FP RECEIVER SIGHT (LOW)

TARGET FP RECEIVER SIGHTS

Available in High or Low sight line models, Target FP receiver sights with proper attaching bases can be attached to most 22-caliber target rifles and many sporter-type rifles as well. In most cases, the High models are recommended on target-type rifles with globe front sights. The Low models are for sporter-type rifles and are compatible with standard sights or the lowest globe-type front sights. **Price: $64.85** (Base only: **$10.90**).

GUIDE RECEIVER SIGHTS

Features compact, low profile and positive windage and elevation locks. Lightweight, strong, and rustproof. These sights utilize dovetail or existing screws on top of receiver for installation. Made from an aluminum alloy that is stronger than many steels.

Prices:
GUIDE RECEIVER SIGHT	**$25.79**
With Twilight Aperture	27.26
With 1/4" "U" blade	23.69

FP RECEIVER SIGHTS

Internal micrometer adjustments have positive internal locks. The FP model is made of an alloy with a tensile strength of 85,000 lbs., yet it weighs only 1½ oz. Target knobs are available on all models if desired. FP sights fit more than 100 different guns.

Prices:
FP RECEIVER SIGHT	**$47.00**
With "Twilight" Aperture	49.37
With Target Knobs	56.90
With Target Knobs & "Twilight" Aperture	58.37

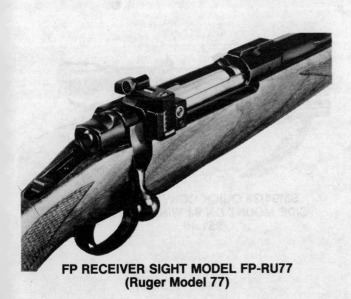

FP RECEIVER SIGHT MODEL FP-RU77
(Ruger Model 77)

WILLIAMS

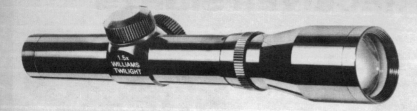

1.5X PISTOL & BOW SCOPE
$143.70

2X PISTOL & BOW SCOPE
$145.80

TWILIGHT SCOPES
FOR PISTOLS AND BOWS
WITH LONG EYE RELIEF

Built tough, compact and lightweight, the Twilight Scope was designed specifically for handgun hunters and precision target shooters. And for archers, these scopes offer the first practical scope-aiming device, including the new Wiliams bow scope mount, which opens up target and hunting possibilities never before available to the archer.

MECHANICAL SPECIFICATIONS	1.5X20	2.20
Outside Diameter of Objective End	1″	1″
Outside Diameter of Ocular End	36.5mm	36.5mm
Outside Diameter of Tube	1″	1″
Internal Adjustment Graduation	¼″	¼″
Minimum Internal Adjustment	170″	162″
Finish	Glossy Hard Black Anodized	
Length	209mm	216mm
Weight	6.4 oz.	6.6 oz.

OPTICAL SPECIFICATIONS	1.5X20	2X20
Clear Aperture of Objective Lens	20mm	20mm
Clear Aperture of Ocular Lens	30mm	30mm
Exit Pupil	13.3mm	10mm
Relative Brightness	177	100
Field of View (Degree of Angle)	3°4′	3°20′
Field of View at 100 Yards	19 ft.	17½ ft.
Eye Relief	18″-25″	18″-25″
Parallax Correciton (at)	50 yds.	50 yds.
Lens Construction	6	6

MOUNTING PLATES:

FOR 30-M1 CARBINE
(Attach with 8-40 fillister screws.) Use the Williams SM-740 side mount base with this mounting plate. Scope can be offset or high over bore. **Price: $12.10**

FOR SMLE NO. 1
(Attach with 8-40 fillister head mounting screws.) This mounting plate is supplied with long 8-40 fillister head screws to replace SM-70 short screws. Use the SM-70 base. Mount can be installed offset or central over bore. **Price: $7.80**

FOR M1 GARAND RIFLE
The mounting screws for this mounting plate are 8-40 × .475 fillister head. Use the Williams SM-740 (4 holes) side mount with this mounting plate. **Price: $12.10**

SM94/36 QUICK CONVERTIBLE
SIDE MOUNT ON 94 WINCHESTER
$51.40

WILLIAMS SCOPE MOUNTS

MODEL SW-N-44-S (on S&W Model 629)

MODEL BH-S-357 (on Ruger Blackhawk)

GUIDELINE HANDGUN SCOPE MOUNTS
FOR REVOLVERS
$63.95

- Lightweight
- Hard anodized finish
- Precision-machined
- No drilling and tapping required
- High strength, heat-treated aluminum alloy
- Fits Colt Python, King Cobra, Ruger Blackhawk, Redhawk, Super Blackhawk and Bisley revolvers

- Fits Smith & Wesson "N" frames (44 Magnum, 6" and 8³/₈" barrels) and Model 29

Also available:
GUIDELINE HANDGUN SCOPE MOUNTS Barrel Auto Pistols for Ruger Bull: **$52.60**

TWO-PIECE DOVETAIL SCOPE MOUNT
(on Winchester 9422)

STREAMLINE DOVETAIL SCOPE MOUNTS
(ONE- and TWO-PIECE)
$29.95

Williams' unique double dovetail clamp-on system allows for simple installation and superior strength. These mounts are made to fit most dovetails found on rimfire rifles and air guns. Mounts are made for 1" scopes and are constructed of precision-machined aluminum alloy.

ONE-PIECE DOVETAIL SCOPE MOUNT
(on Weatherby MKXXII)

WILLIAMS SCOPE MOUNTS

Shown on Model 70A Winchester

STREAMLINE TOP MOUNT

The Williams "Streamline" top mount is a revolutionary concept in two-piece mount design. Its solid ring-base construction allows the strongest possible installation of scope to rifle.

Because the bases are the rings, there can be no movement between the rings and bases as on other two-piece mounts. By design, the "Streamline" mount eliminates the need for extension rings as the mounts can be reversed allowing for installation of virtually all 1-inch scopes.

Features:
- Available for wide assortment of factory drilled rifles
- Precision-machined and lightweight
- Solid construction
- Eliminates need for extension rings—allows use of virtually all 1" scopes
- The bases are the rings
- Hard black anodized finish

Prices:

Williams "Streamline" Two-Piece Top Mount
Complete **$21.00**
Williams "Steamline" Front or Rear Base Only **10.50**
Williams "Streamline" Two-Piece Top Mount with
Sub-Blocks for Hawken M/L **28.65**

STREAMLINE TOP MOUNT MODELS	Front	Rear
Remington Models 760, 740, 742, and Savage Model 170	1	2
Browning A-Bolt	3	3
Winchester Models 70 Standard, 670 and 770	4	3
*1917 Enfield and Sauer 200	4	4
Remington Models 700, 721, 722, 725, Remington 700 L.H. and Remington 40X; BSA; Weatherby MK-V & Vanguard; Ruger 77ST; and S&W 1500	4	.5
Savage Models 110, 111 and 112V	4	16
Winchester Models 88 and 100	6	6
Browning BAR Auto and BLR Lever	7	7
Marlin Models 336, 1894 & 1894C	8	8
Remington Model 788	9	9
Thompson/Center 45 & 50 Cal. Hawken and 54 Cal. Renegade	10**	10**
Remington 541-S. Also, Remington Models 580, 581, 582 (require drilling & tapping)	11	11
Ruger Model 44	11	12
Ruger Model 10/22	13	12
Browning Safari Bolt and Mark X	14	15
Ithaca LSA-55 and LSA-65 Bolt	16	16
Rem. Models Four, Six, 7400 and 7600	17	18
Savage Model 99	19	20**
Winchester Model 94 Angle Eject	21	22

*With the rear receiver radiused the same diameter as the front receiver ring.

**Requires Sub-block

Shown on Thompson/Center Renegade w/Sub-blocks

WILLIAMS SIGHT CHART

AMOUNT OF ADJUSTMENT NECESSARY TO CORRECT FRONT SIGHT ERROR

DISTANCE BETWEEN FRONT AND REAR SIGHTS	14"	15"	16"	17"	18"	19"	20"	21"	22"	23"	24"	25"	26"	27"	28"	29"	30"	31"	32"	33"	34"
Amount of 1	.0038	.0041	.0044	.0047	.0050	.0053	.0055	.0058	.0061	.0064	.0066	.0069	.0072	.0074	.0077	.0080	.0082	.0085	.0088	.0091	.0093
Error 2	.0078	.0083	.0089	.0094	.0100	.0105	.0111	.0116	.0122	.0127	.0133	.0138	.0144	.0149	.0155	.0160	.0156	.0171	.0177	.0182	.0188
at 3	.0117	.0125	.0133	.0142	.0150	.0159	.0167	.0175	.0184	.0192	.0201	.0209	.0217	.0226	.0234	.0243	.0251	.0259	.0268	.0276	.0285
100 Yards 4	.0155	.0167	.0178	.0189	.0200	.0211	.0222	.0234	.0244	.0255	.0266	.0278	.0289	.0300	.0311	.0322	.0333	.0344	.0355	.0366	.0377
Given in 5	.0194	.0208	.0222	.0236	.0250	.0264	.0278	.0292	.0306	.0319	.0333	.0347	.0361	.0375	.0389	.0403	.0417	.0431	.0445	.0458	.0472
Inches 6	.0233	.0250	.0267	.0283	.0300	.0317	.0333	.0350	.0367	.0384	.0400	.0417	.0434	.0450	.0467	.0484	.0500	.0517	.0534	.0551	.0567

When you replace an open rear sight with a receiver sight, it is usually necessary to install a higher front sight, to compensate for the higher plane of the new receiver sight. The table above shows the increase in front sight height that's required to compensate for a given error at 100 yards. Suppose your rifle has a 19 inch sight radius, and shoots 6 inches high at 100 yards, with the receiver sight adjusted as low as possible. The

19 inch column shows that the correction for a 6 inch error is .0317 inch. This correction is added to the over-all height of the front sight (including dovetail). Use a micrometer or similar accurate device to measure sight height. Thus, if your original sight measured .250 inch, it should be replaced with a sight .290 inch high.

WILLIAMS SIGHT-THRU MOUNTS

SHOWN ON REMINGTON MODEL 742

SHOWN ON WINCHESTER MODEL 70

Features:
- One-piece construction
- Large field of view for Iron Sights right under the scope
- Available for a wide assortment of factory-drilled rifles
- All parts are precision-machined
- Lightweight
- Hard black anodized finish
- Fast, accurate sighting under all field conditions

The Williams Sight-Thru Mount provides instant use of scope above, or iron sights below. Easily installed. Uses existing holes on top of receiver. No drilling or tapping necessary. The Sight-Thru is compact and lightweight—will not alter balance of the rifle. The high tensile strength alloy will never rust. All parts are precision-machined. Completely rigid. Shockproof. The attractive streamlined appearance is further enhanced by a beautiful, hard black anodized finish. Rings are 1″ in size; ⁷/₈″ sleeves available.

Williams "Sight-Thru" Mount Complete.........$21.00

MODELS	FRONT	REAR
Winchester Models 88 and 100; Sako Finn-wolf; Ithaca 37†.	A	A
Remington Models 760, 740, 742 and Savage Model 170	A	B
Winchester Models 70 Standard, 670 and 770; Browning BBR.	D	C
Remington Models 700 R.H. and L.H., 721, 722, 725; Weatherby MK-V and Vanguard; BSA round top receivers; Ruger 77ST; Smith & Wesson Model 1500.	D	E
Savage Models 110, 111 and 112V	D	F
Browning BLR Lever Action	O	O
Browning BAR High Power Auto; Mossberg 800; Remington 541S †. Will also fit Ward's Western Field Model 72 and Mossberg Model 472 lever action.*.	G	G
Late models Marlin 336, 1894 and 1894C	H	H
FN Mauser; Browning Bolt Action; J. C. Higgins 50-51; Interarms Mark X Mauser	D	I
Savage 99 (New Style)	J	K**
Schultz & Larsen.	A	G
1917 Enfield	J	J
Ruger 10/22	L	M
Ruger 44	O	M
Ruger 77R and RS Series †	H	P
Remington Models 4, 7400, 6, and 7600 . .	R	S

*When ordering 'G' bases for Western Field Model 72 and Mossberg Model 472, please specify that 360 screws must be furnished.
**Requires Sub-block   †Drilling and Tapping Required

WILLIAMS FRONT SIGHT RISER BLOCK

This riser block adds .250 inch to the height of the dovetail. It is especially handy on such guns as the Ruger 10/22 and any other models that require a higher than normal front sight (when installing a receiver sight). This model is available in two widths—the .250 for Williams Streamlined ramps and other ramps having a ¹/₄-inch top width—and the .340 to work on all standard factory ramps (Winchester, Remington, Savage, etc.) having this base width. It incorporates the standard ³/₈-inch dovetail.

Price $4.60

ZEISS RIFLESCOPES

THE C-SERIES

The C-Series was designed by Zeiss specifically for the American hunter. It is based on space-age alloy tubes with integral objective and ocular bells, and an integral adjustment turret. This strong, rigid one-piece construction allows perfect lens alignment, micro-precise adjustments and structural integrity. Other features include quick focusing, a generous 3½" of eye relief, rubber armoring, T-Star multi-layer coating, and parallax setting (free at 100 yards).

DIATAL-C 10x36T*
$675.00

DIAVARI-C 3-9x36T*
$755.00

DIATAL-C 6x32T*
$565.00

DIATAL-C 4x32T*
$525.00

DIAVARI-C 1.5-4.5x18T*
$725.00

PRODUCT SPECIFICATIONS	4×32	6×32	10×36	3-9×36		C1.5-4.5×18	
Magnification	4X	6X	10X	3X	9X	1.5X	4.5X
Objective Diameter (mm)/(inch)	1.26"	1.26"	1.42"	1.42"		15.0/0.6	18.0/0.7
Exit Pupil	0.32"	0.21"	0.14"	0.39"	0.16"	10.0	4.0
Twilight Performance	11.3	13.9	19.0	8.5	18.0	4.2	9.0
Field of View at 100 yds.	30'	20'	12'	36'	13'	72'	27'
Eye Relief	3.5"	3.5"	3.5"	3.5"	3.5"	3.5"	
Maximum Interval Adjustment (elevation and windage (MOA)	80	80	50	50		10.5' @ 100 yds.	
Click-Stop Adjustment 1 click = 1 interval (MOA)	¼	¼	¼	¼		.36" @ 100 yds.	
Length	10.6"	10.6"	12.7"	11.2"		11.8"	
Weight approx. (ounces)	11.3	11.3	14.1	15.2		13.4	
Tube Diameter	1"	1"	1"	1"		1"	
Objective Tube Diameter	1.65"	1.65"	1.89"	1.73"		1"	
Eyepiece O.D.	1.67"	1.67"	1.67"	1.67"		1.8"	

ZEISS RIFLESCOPES
EUROPEAN ZA SERIES

These five new scopes include the following features: large objective diameter and good twilight performance; metric graduation of reticle adjustment (1 click = 1cm/100m); traditional reticle types; and constant relationship between reticle and target when changing power (enabling use of reticle also for range estimation).

DIATAL-ZA 4x32T*
$525.00

DIATAL-ZA 6x42T*
$620.00

DIATAL-ZA 8x56T*
$710.00

DIAVARI-ZA 1.5-6x42T*
$870.00

DIAVARI-ZA 2.5-10x52T*
$1030.00

CENTERFIRE PISTOL & REVOLVER AMMUNITION

CENTERFIRE RIFLE AMMUNITION

22 RIMFIRE AMMUNITION

SHOTSHELL AMMUNITION

Ammunition

FOR ADDRESSES AND PHONE
NUMBERS OF MANUFACTURERS AND
DISTRIBUTORS INCLUDED IN THIS
SECTION, SEE *DIRECTORY OF
MANUFACTURERS AND SUPPLIERS*

ACTIV AMMUNITION

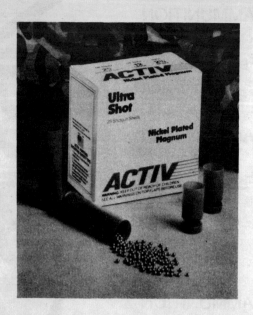

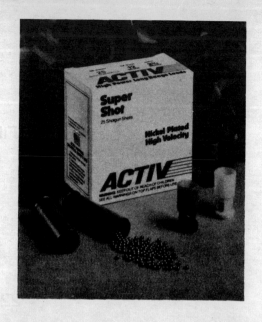

Ultrashot Nickel Magnum Loads Specifications

Model	Ga.	Length (in.)	Dram Equiv.	Ounces Shot	Standard Shot Sizes	Rnds. Per Box	Rnds. Per Case
N12B	12	3	4	1⅞	BB,2,4,6	25	250
N12C	12	3	4	1⅝	2,4,6	25	250
N12D	12	2¾	4½	1½	BB,2,4,6	25	250
N20F	20	3	3	1¼	2,4,6,7½	25	500
N20G	20	3	3¼	1⅛	4,6,7½	25	500
N20GL	20	2¾	2¾	1⅛	4,6,7½	25	500

Super Shot Nickel High Velocity Loads Specifications

Model	Ga.	Length (in.)	Dram Equiv.	Ounces Shot	Standard Shot Sizes	Rnds. Per Box	Rnds. Per Case
N12E	12	2¾	4	1⅜	4,6,7½	25	250
N12F	12	2¾	3¾	1¼	BB,2,4,5,6,7½,9	25	250
N16GL-X	16	2¾	3¼	1	4,6,7½	25	250
N20H	20	2¾	2¾	1	4,5,6,7½,9	25	500

Penetrator Series Nickel Turkey Load Specifications

Model	Ga.	Length (in.)	Dram Equiv.	Ounces Shot	Standard Shot Sizes	Rnds. Per Box	Rnds. Per Case
P123A	12	3	4	2	4,6	10	100
P12A	12	2¾	4	1¾	4,6,7½	10	100
P12D	12	2¾	4½	1½	4,6	10	100

All Purpose Field Loads Specifications

Model	Ga.	Length (in.)	Dram Equiv.	Ounces Shot	Standard Shot Sizes	Rnds. Per Box	Rnds. Per Case
G12F	12	2¾	3¼	1¼	6,7½,8,9	25	500
G12GL	12	2¾	3¼	1⅛	6,7½,8,9	25	500
G12H	12	2¾	3¼	1	6,7½,8,9	25	500
G16GL-X	16	2¾	2¾	1	6,7½,8,9	25	500
G16H	16	2¾	2½	1	6,7½,8,9	25	500
G20H	20	2¾	2½	1	6,7½,8,9	25	500
G20I	20	2¾	2½	⅞	6,7½,8,9	25	500

ACTIV AMMUNITION

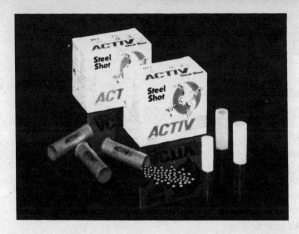

Buckshot Specifications

Model	Ga.	Length (in.)	# Of Pellets	Shot Size	Rnds. Per Box	Rnds. Per Case
*BK12Y	12	2¾	12	00	5	250
	12	2¾	20	1	5	250
	12	2¾	34	4	5	250
*BK12Z	12	2¾	9	00	5	250
	12	2¾	16	1	5	250
	12	2¾	27	4	5	250
BK12XL	12	3	15	00	5	250
	12	3	24	1	5	250
	12	3	41	4	5	250
BK12YL	12	2¾	12	00	5	250
	12	2¾	20	1	5	250
	12	2¾	34	4	5	250
BK12ZL	12	2¾	9	00	5	250
	12	2¾	16	1	5	250
	12	2¾	27	4	5	250

Steel Shot Specifications

Model	Ga.	Length (in.)	Dram Equiv.	Ounces Shot	Standard Shot Sizes	Rnds. Per Box	Rnds. Per Case
ST12E	12	3	Max	1⅜	BB, 1, 2, 4, 6	20	200
ST123F	12	3	Max	1¼	BB, 1, 2, 4	20	200
ST12F	12	2¾	Max	1¼	BB, 1, 2, 4, 6	20	200
ST12G	12	2¾	Max	1⅛	BB, 1, 2, 4	20	200
ST20J	20	2¾	Max	¾	4, 6	20	480

Steel Shot Information

Shot Sizes	Pellet Count Per Ounce	Average Pellet Count		
		1⅛	1¼	1⅜
BB	72	81	90	99
#1	103	116	129	142
#2	125	140	156	172
#4	192	216	240	264
#6	312	351	390	429

Target Load Specifications

Model	Ga.	Length (in.)	Dram Equiv.	Ounces Shot	Standard Shot Sizes	Rnds. Per Box	Rnds. Per Case
Tournament Grade: High Quality Target Loads. Trap and Skeet							
TG12G	12	2¾	3	1⅛	7½, 8, 8½, 9	25	500
TG12GL	12	2¾	2¾	1⅛	7½, 8, 8½, 9	25	500
TG12UL	12	Ultra Light		1⅛	7½, 8, 8½, 9	25	500
TG12H	12	2¾	2¾	1	7½, 8, 8½, 9	25	500
A20I	20	2¾	2½	⅞	7½, 8, 8½, 9	25	500
International Trap Loads. Nickel Plated Shot							
A12GH	12	2¾	3¼	1⅛	7½, 8, 9	25	500
Nickel Plated Pigeon Loads							
A12FH	12	2¾	3¼	1¼	6, 7½, 8, 9	25	500

Steel Shot Ballistics

ACTIV Loads	Average Pressure	Average Velocity	SAAMI Spec. Max. Dram
12 gauge – 1⅜ oz.	11.000	1280	1210
12 gauge – 1¼ oz.	10.800	1390	1375
12 gauge – 1⅛ oz.	11.000	1420	1365

Red Hornet Series Specifications

Model	Ga.	Length (in.)	Dram Equiv.	Ounces Shot	Standard Shot Sizes	Rnds. Per Box	Rnds. Per Case
Duck & Pheasant Promotional Loads							
H12F	12	2¾	3¾	1¼	4, 5, 6, 7½	25	500
H16G	16	2¾	3¼	1⅛	4, 5, 6, 7½	25	500
H20HH	20	2¾	2¾	1	4, 6, 7½	25	500
Small Game & Bird Promotional Loads							
H12FL	12	2¾	3¼	1¼	4, 6, 7½, 8	25	500
H12GL	12	2¾	3¼	1⅛	4, 6, 7½, 8	25	500
H16GL	16	2¾	2¾	1⅛	4, 6, 7½, 8	25	500
H20H	20	2¾	2½	1	4, 6, 7½, 8	25	500
Dove & Quail Promotional Loads							
H12HH	12	2¾	3¼	1	6, 7½, 8	25	500
H16H	16	2¾	2½	1	6, 7½, 8	25	500
H20I	20	2¾	2½	⅞	6, 7½, 8	25	500

Slugs Specifications

Model	Ga.	Length (in.)	Dram Equiv.	Weight	Rnds. Per Box	Rnds. Per Case
SL123F	12	3	Max	1¼ oz.	5	250
SL12F	12	2¾	Max	1¼ oz.	5	250
SL12H	12	2¾	Max	1 oz.	5	250
SL16H	16	2¾	Max	1 oz.	5	250
SL20I	20	2¾	Max	⅞ oz.	5	250

FEDERAL AMMUNITION

FEDERAL CENTERFIRE PISTOL CARTRIDGES

LOAD NO.	CARTRIDGES	BULLET TYPE	BULLET WEIGHT GRAINS

NYCLAD® PISTOL CARTRIDGES—50 rounds per box, 20 boxes per case. 1000 rounds per case.

LOAD NO.	CARTRIDGES	BULLET TYPE	BULLET WEIGHT GRAINS
N9BP	9mm Luger Auto Pistol	Hollow Point	124
N38A	38 Special	Wadcutter	148
N38B	38 Special	Round Nose	158
N38G	38 Special (High Vel + P)	SW Hollow Point	158
N38M	38 Special	Hollow Point	125
N38N	38 Special (High Vel + P)	Hollow Point	125
N357E	357 Magnum	SW Hollow Point	158

FEDERAL CENTERFIRE RIFLE CARTRIDGES

20 rounds per box, 25 boxes per case. 500 rounds per case.

	LOAD NO.	CARTRIDGES	BULLET TYPE	BULLET WEIGHT GRAINS
	222A	222 Remington	Soft Point	50
	222B	222 Remington	Metal Case Boat Tail	55
	22250A	22-250 Remington	Soft Point	55
	22250C	22-250 Remington	Varmint, Hollow Point	40
	223A	223 Remington (5.56 mm)	Soft Point	55
	223B	223 Remington (5.56 mm)	Metal Case Boat Tail	55
	223C	223 Remington (5.56 mm)	Hollow Point Boat Tail	55
	223D	223 Remington (5.56 mm)	Varmint, Hollow Point	40
NEW	223M	223 Remington (5.56 mm)	Boat Tail, Hollow Point Match	69
	6A	6mm Remington	Soft Point	80
	6B	6mm Remington	Hi-Shok Soft Point	100
	243A	243 Winchester	Soft Point	80
	243B	243 Winchester	Hi-Shok Soft Point	100
NEW	243V	243 Winchester	Varmint, Hollow Point	60
	257A	257 Roberts (High Vel + P)	Hi-Shok Soft Point	117
	2506A	25-06 Remington	Hollow Point	90
	2506B	25-06 Remington	Hi-Shok Soft Point	117
	270A	270 Winchester	Hi-Shok Soft Point	130
	270B	270 Winchester	Hi-Shok Soft Point	150
	7A	7mm Mauser	Hi-Shok Soft Point	175
	7B	7mm Mauser	Hi-Shok Soft Point	140
	7RA	7mm Remington Magnum	Hi-Shok Soft Point	150
	7RB	7mm Remington Magnum	Hi-Shok Soft Point	175
	30CA	30 Carbine	Soft Point	110
NEW	76239B	7.62x39 Soviet	Soft Point	123
	730A	7-30 Waters	Boat Tail Soft Point	120
	3030A	30-30 Winchester	Hi-Shok Soft Point	150
	3030B	30-30 Winchester	Hi-Shok Soft Point	170
	3030C	30-30 Winchester	Hollow Point	125

We accept orders for split cases of centerfire—5 boxes per individual load in increments of 5 boxes.

FEDERAL AMMUNITION

FEDERAL CENTERFIRE RIFLE CARTRIDGES

20 rounds per box, 25 boxes per case. 500 rounds per case.

	LOAD NO.	CARTRIDGES	BULLET TYPE	BULLET WEIGHT GRAINS
	3006A	30-06 Springfield	Hi-Shok Soft Point	150
	3006B	30-06 Springfield	Hi-Shok Soft Point	180
	3006C	30-06 Springfield	Soft Point	125
	3006D	30-06 Springfield	Boat Tail Soft Point	165
	3006H	30-06 Springfield	Hi-Shok Soft Point	220
	3006J	30-06 Springfield	Round Nose	180
	300A	300 Savage	Hi-Shok Soft Point	150
	300B	300 Savage	Hi-Shok Soft Point	180
	300WB	300 Winchester Magnum	Hi-Shok Soft Point	180
NEW	**303A**	303 British	Hi-Shok Soft Point	180
	308A	308 Winchester	Hi-Shok Soft Point	150
	308B	308 Winchester	Hi-Shok Soft Point	180
	308M	308 Winchester (Match)	Boat Tail Hollow Point Match	168
	8A	8mm Mauser	Hi-Shok Soft Point	170
	32A	32 Winchester Special	Hi-Shok Soft Point	170
NEW	**338C**	338 Winchester Mag.	Soft Point	225
	35A	35 Remington	Hi-Shok Soft Point	200
NEW	**375A**	375 H&H Magnum	Hi-Shok Soft Point	270
NEW	**375B**	375 H&H Magnum	Hi-Shok Soft Point	300
	†44A	44 Remington Magnum	Hollow Soft Point	240
	4570A	45-70 Government	Hollow Soft Point	300

† For Rifle or Pistol.

FEDERAL TARGET LOAD SHOTSHELLS

LOAD NO.	GAUGE	SHELL LENGTH (INCHES)	POWDER DRAMS EQUIV.	OUNCES SHOT	SHOT SIZES
TRAP LOADS–25 rounds per box, 20 boxes per case. 500 rounds per case.					
F105	12	2¾	2¾	1⅛	7½,8
F106	12	2¾	3	1⅛	7½,8
F114	12	2¾	**E.L.	1⅛	7½,8,8½
F115	12	2¾	2¾	1⅛	7½,8
F116	12	2¾	3	1⅛	7½,8
C117	12	2¾	2¾	1⅛	7½,8
C118	12	2¾	3	1⅛	7½,8
F113	12	2¾	2¾	1	8½
SKEET LOADS–25 rounds per box, 20 boxes per case. 500 rounds per case.					
F105	12	2¾	2¾	1⅛	9
F114	12	2¾	**E.L.	1⅛	9
F115	12	2¾	2¾	1⅛	9
F116	12	2¾	3	1⅛	9
C117	12	2¾	2¾	1⅛	9
C118	12	2¾	3	1⅛	9
F206	20	2¾	2½	⅞	8, 9
F280	28	2¾	2	¾	9
F412	410	2½	Max.	½	9
† SPORTING CLAYS LOAD–25 rounds per box, 20 boxes per case. 500 rounds per case.					
T122	12	2¾	3	1⅛	8, 9

C117, C118 and T122 have paper tubes, all others are plastic.
**EXTRA-LITE™
† Formerly "Special"

FEDERAL AMMUNITION

FEDERAL SHOTSHELLS

LOAD NO.	GAUGE	SHELL LENGTH (INCHES)	POWDER DRAMS EQUIV.	SHOT SIZES	
HI-POWER MAGNUM BUCKSHOT—5 rounds per box, 50 boxes per case. 250 rounds per case.					
F131	12	3	Mag.	000 Buck	10 Pellets
F131	12	3	Mag.	00 Buck	15 Pellets
F131	12	3	Mag.	1 Buck	24 Pellets
F131	12	3	Mag.	4 Buck	41 Pellets
F130	12	2¾	Mag.	00 Buck	12 Pellets
F130	12	2¾	Mag.	1 Buck	20 Pellets
F130	12	2¾	Mag.	4 Buck	34 Pellets
F207	20	3	Mag.	2 Buck	18 Pellets
HI-POWER BUCKSHOT—5 rounds per box, 50 boxes per case. 250 rounds per case.					
F127	12	2¾	Max.	000 Buck	8 Pellets
F127	12	2¾	Max.	00 Buck	9 Pellets
F127	12	2¾	Max.	0 Buck	12 Pellets
F127	12	2¾	Max.	1 Buck	16 Pellets
F127	12	2¾	Max.	4 Buck	27 Pellets
F164	16	2¾	Max.	1 Buck	12 Pellets
F203	20	2¾	Max.	3 Buck	20 Pellets

FEDERAL 22 RIMFIRE CARTRIDGES

LOAD NO.	CARTRIDGES	BULLET TYPE	BULLET WEIGHT GRAINS
HI-POWER® 22's—50 rounds per box, 100 boxes per case. 5000 rounds per case.			
701	22 Short	Copper Plated	29
706	22 Long	Copper Plated	29
700CB	22 Long	Copper Plated	29
710	22 Long Rifle	Copper Plated	40
712	22 Long Rifle	Copper Plated, Hollow Point	38
HI-POWER® 22's—100 PACK—50 boxes per case. 5000 rounds per case.			
810	22 Long Rifle	Copper Plated	40
812	22 Long Rifle	Copper Plated, Hollow Point	38
MAGNUM 22's—50 rounds per box, 50 boxes per case. 2500 rounds per case.			
737	22 Win. Mag.	Full Metal Jacket	40
747	22 Win. Mag.	Jacketed Hollow Point	40
757	22 Win. Mag.	Jacketed Hollow Point	50
22 SHOT—50 rounds per box, 50 boxes per case. 2500 rounds per case.			
716	22 Long Rifle	# 12 Shot	#12
SPITFIRE HYPER-VELOCITY 22's—6000 rounds per case; 50 rounds per Sport-Pak™, 20 packs per carton, 6 cartons per case.			
720	22 Long Rifle	Truncated Cone, Solid	36

FEDERAL AMMUNITION

FEDERAL SHOTSHELLS

LOAD NO.	GAUGE	SHELL LENGTH (INCHES)	POWDER DRAMS EQUIV.	OUNCES SHOT	SHOT SIZES
HI-POWER® POWER MAGNUM LOADS—25 rounds per box, 10 boxes per case, 250 rounds per case.					
F103	10	3½	4¼	2	BB, 2, 4
F131	12	3	4	1⅞	BB, 2, 4
F129	12	3	4	1⅝	2, 4, 6
F130	12	2¾	3¾	1½	BB, 2, 4,5,6
F165	16	2¾	3¼	1¼	4, 6
F207	20	3	3	1¼	2, 4, 6, 7½
F205	20	2¾	2¾	1⅛	4, 6, 7½
CLASSIC HI-BRASS—25 rounds per box, 10 boxes per case. 250 rounds per case.					
NEW H126	12	2¾	3¾	1¼	2, 4,5,6, 7½,8, 9
NEW H163	16	2¾	3¼	1⅛	4, 6, 7½
NEW H204	20	2¾	2¾	1	4,5,6, 7½,8
NEW H413	410	3	Max.	11/16	4,5,6, 7½,8
NEW H412	410	2½	Max.	½	6, 7½
STEEL SHOT HI-POWER MAGNUM LOADS—25 rounds per box, 10 boxes per case. 250 rounds per case.					
W104	10	3½	Max.	1⅝	F,T,**BBB**,BB, 2
NEW W135	12	3½	Max.	1 9/16	F,T, BB, 2
W149	12	3	Max.	1⅜	F,T,**BBB**,BB,1,2,**3**,4
W140	12	3	Max.	1¼	BB,1,2,**3**,4
W148	12	2¾	Max.	1¼	**T,BBB**,BB,1,2,**3**,4
W168	16	2¾	Max.	15/16	**2, 4**
W209	20	3	3¼	1	2,**3**,4, 6
STEEL SHOT HI-POWER® LOADS—25 rounds per box, 20 boxes per case. 500 rounds per case.					
W147	12	2¾	3¾	1⅛	BB, 2,**3**,4, 6
W208	20	2¾	3	¾	**3**,4, 6
STEEL SHOT TRI-POWER™—10 rounds per box, 25 boxes per case. 250 rounds per case.					
NEW W348	12	2¾	3½	1¼	BB-1-4
NEW W349	12	3	Max.	1⅜	T-BB-2
FIELD LOADS—25 rounds per box, 20 boxes per case. 500 rounds per case.					
*F125	12	2¾	3¼	1¼	7½,8
F124	12	2¾	3¼	1¼	7½,8, 9
25 rounds per box, 10 boxes per case. 250 rounds per case.					
H123	12	2¾	3¼	1⅛	4, 6, 7½,8, 9
H162	16	2¾	2¾	1⅛	6, 7½,8
H202	20	2¾	2½	1	6, 7½,8

*Flyer Load

LOAD NO.	GAUGE	SHELL LENGTH (INCHES)	POWDER DRAMS EQUIV.	OUNCES SHOT	SHOT SIZES
HI-SHOK® RIFLED SLUGS—5 rounds per box, 50 boxes per case. 250 rounds per case.					
F103	10	3½	Mag.	1¾	Rifled Slug
F131	12	3	Mag.	1¼	Rifled Slug
F130	12	2¾	Mag.	1¼	Rifled Slug
F127	12	2¾	Max.	1	Rifled Slug
F164	16	2¾	Max.	⅘	Rifled Slug
F203	20	2¾	Max.	¾	Rifled Slug
F412	410	2½	Max.	⅕	Rifled Slug

FEDERAL AMMUNITION

PREMIUM® SHOTSHELLS

LOAD NO.	GAUGE	SHELL LENGTH (INCHES)	POWDER DRAMS EQUIV.	OUNCES SHOT	SHOT SIZES
MAGNUM LOADS—25 rounds per box, 10 boxes per case. 250 rounds per case.					
P109	10	3½	4½	2¼	BB, 2, 4, 6
P159	12	3	4	2	BB, 2, 4, 6
P158	12	3	4	1⅞	BB, 2, 4, 6
P157	12	3	4	1⅝	4, 6
P156	12	2¾	4	1½	BB, 2, 4, 6
P258	20	3	3	1¼	4, 6
P256	20	2¾	2¾	1⅛	4, 6
HI-POWER LOADS—25 rounds per box, 20 boxes per case. 500 rounds per case.					
P154	12	2¾	3¾	1¼	4, 6, 7½
P254	20	2¾	2¾	1	6
P283	28	2¾	2¼	¾	6, 7½, 8
FIELD LOADS—25 rounds per box, 20 boxes per case. 500 rounds per case.					
P153	12	2¾	3¼	1¼	7½, 8
P152	12	2¾	3¼	1⅛	7½
P252	20	2¾	2½	1	7½, 8
BUCKSHOT—5 rounds per box, 50 boxes per case. 250 rounds per case.					
P108	10	3½	Magnum	00 Buck	18 Pellets
P108	10	3½	Magnum	4 Buck	54 Pellets
P158	12	3	Magnum	000 Buck	10 Pellets
P158	12	3	Magnum	00 Buck	15 Pellets
P158	12	3	Magnum	4 Buck	41 Pellets
P158	12	3	Magnum	1 Buck	24 Pellets
P156	12	2¾	Magnum	00 Buck	12 Pellets
P156	12	2¾	Magnum	4 Buck	34 Pellets
P154	12	2¾	Max	00 Buck	9 Pellets
P154	12	2¾	Max	4 Buck	27 Pellets

FEDERAL AMMUNITION

FEDERAL 22 RIMFIRE CARTRIDGES

LOAD NO.	CARTRIDGES	BULLET TYPE	BULLET WEIGHT GRAINS

CHAMPION™ STANDARD VELOCITY 22's–50 rounds per box, 100 boxes per case. 5000 rounds per case.

711	22 Long Rifle	Lead Lubricated	40

CHAMPION STANDARD VELOCITY 22's–100 PACK–50 boxes per case. 5000 rounds per case.

811	22 Long Rifle	Lead Lubricated	40

FEDERAL CENTERFIRE PISTOL CARTRIDGES
50 rounds per box, 20 boxes per case. 1000 rounds per case.

	Load No.	Cartridges	Bullet Type	Grains
	*25AP	25 Auto Pistol (6.35mm)	Metal Case	50
	32AP	32 Auto Pistol (7.65mm)	Metal Case	71
	32LA	32 S&W Long	Lead Wadcutter	98
	32LB	32 S&W Long	Lead Round Nose	98
	32HRA	32 H&R Magnum	Lead Semi-Wadcutter	95
	32HRB	32 H&R Magnum	Jacketed Hollow Point	85
	380AP	380 Auto Pistol	Metal Case	95
	380BP	380 Auto Pistol	Jacketed Hollow Point	90
	9AP	9mm Luger Auto Pistol	Metal Case	123
	9BP	9mm Luger Auto Pistol	Jacketed Hollow Point	115
	9CP	9mm Luger Auto Pistol	Jacketed Soft Point	95
	9MP	9mm Luger (Match)	Metal Case, S.W.C.	124
NEW	9FA	9mm Federal	Jacketed Hollow Point	115
	38A	38 Special (Match)	Lead Wadcutter	148
	38B	38 Special	Lead Round Nose	158
	38C	38 Special	Lead Semi-Wadcutter	158
	38E	38 Special (High Vel + P)	Jacketed Hollow Point	125
	38F	38 Special (High Vel + P)	Jacketed Hollow Point	110
	38G	38 Special (High Vel + P)	Lead SW Hollow Point	158
	38H	38 Special (High Vel + P)	Lead Semi-Wadcutter	158
	38J	38 Special (High Vel + P)	Jacketed Soft Point	125
	357A	357 Magnum	Jacketed Soft Point	158
	357B	357 Magnum	Jacketed Hollow Point	125
	357C	357 Magnum	Lead Semi-Wadcutter	158
	357D	357 Magnum	Jacketed Hollow Point	110
	357E	357 Magnum	Jacketed Hollow Point	158
	357G	357 Magnum	Jacketed Hollow Point	180
	41A	41 Remington Magnum	Jacketed Hollow Point	210
	***†44A	44 Remington Magnum	Hollow Soft Point	240
	44B	44 Remington Magnum	Jacketed Hollow Point	180
	**A44B20	44 Remington Magnum	Jacketed Hollow Point	180
	†44D	44 Remington Magnum	Metal Case Profile	250
	44SA	44 S&W Special	Lead SW Hollow Point	200
	45LCA	44 Colt	Lead SW Hollow Point	225
	45A	45 Automatic (Match)	Metal Case	230
	45B	45 Automatic (Match)	Metal Case, S.W.C.	185
	45C	45 Automatic	Jacketed Hollow Point	185

† For Rifle or Pistol.
  * 25AP packed 25 rounds per box. 40 boxes per case.
 ** A44B20 packed 20 rounds per box, 50 boxes per case.
*** 44A packed 20 rounds per box, 25 boxes per case. 500 rounds per case.

FEDERAL AMMUNITION

PREMIUM® HYDRA-SHOK™ PISTOL & REVOLVER CARTRIDGES

LOAD NO.	CARTRIDGES	BULLET TYPE	BULLET WEIGHT GRAINS

20 rounds per box, 25 boxes per case. 500 rounds per case.

	LOAD NO.	CARTRIDGES	BULLET TYPE	BULLET WEIGHT GRAINS
NEW	P38HS1	38 Special (+P)	Hydra-Shok	129
NEW	P357HS1	357 Magnum	Hydra-Shok	158
NEW	P9HS1	9mm Luger	Hydra-Shok	124
NEW	P9HS2	9mm Luger	Hydra-Shok	147
NEW	P45HS1	45 Automatic	Hydra-Shok	230

PREMIUM® CENTERFIRE RIFLE CARTRIDGES –20 rounds per box, 25 boxes per case, 500 rounds per case.

	LOAD NO.	CARTRIDGES	BULLET TYPE	BULLET WEIGHT GRAINS
NEW	P223E	223 Remington	Boat Tail Hollow Point	55
	P22250B	22-250 Remington	Boat Tail Hollow Point	55
	P2506C	25-06 Remington	Boat Tail Soft Point	117
	P6C	6mm Remington	Nosler Partition	100
	P243C	243 Winchester	Boat Tail Soft Point	100
	P243D	243 Winchester	Boat Tail Hollow Point	85
	P257B	257 Roberts (High Vel +P)	Nosler Partition	120
	P270C	270 Winchester	Boat Tail Soft Point	150
	P270D	270 Winchester	Boat Tail Soft Point	130
	P270E	270 Winchester	Nosler Partition	150
	P280A	280 Remington	Nosler Partition	150
	P7C	7mm Mauser	Nosler Partition	140
	P7RD	7mm Remington Magnum	Boat Tail Soft Point	150
	P7RE	7mm Remington Magnum	Boat Tail Soft Point	165
	P7RF	7mm Remington Magnum	Nosler Partition	160
	P7RG	7mm Remington Magnum	Nosler Partition	140
	P3030D	30-30 Winchester	Nosler Partition	170
	P3006D	30-06 Springfield	Boat Tail Soft Point	165
	P3006F	30-06 Springfield	Nosler Partition	180
	P3006G	30-06 Springfield	Boat Tail Soft Point	150
	P3006L	30-06 Springfield	Boat Tail Soft Point	180
	P300WC	300 Winchester Magnum	Boat Tail Soft Point	200
	P308C	308 Winchester	Boat Tail Soft Point	165

PREMIUM® SAFARI –20 rounds per box, 25 boxes per case, 500 rounds per case.

	LOAD NO.	CARTRIDGES	BULLET TYPE	BULLET WEIGHT GRAINS
NEW	P300WD2	300 Win. Magnum	Nosler Partition	180
NEW	P338A2	338 Win. Magnum	Nosler Partition	210
NEW	P338B2	338 Win. Magnum	Nosler Partition	250
NEW	P375C	375 H&H Magnum	Boat Tail Soft Point	250
NEW	P375D	375 H&H Magnum	Solid	300
NEW	P375E	375 H&H Magnum	Boat Tail Soft Point	300
NEW	P458A	458 Win. Magnum	Soft Point	350
NEW	P458B	458 Win. Magnum	Soft Point	510
NEW	P458C	458 Win. Magnum	Solid	500
NEW	P416A	416 Rigby	Soft Point	410
NEW	P416B	416 Rigby	Solid	410
NEW	P470A	470 Nitro Express	Soft Point	500
NEW	P470B	470 Nitro Express	Solid	500

FEDERAL/NORMA

LOAD NO.	CALIBER	BULLET TYPE	BULLET WEIGHT GRAMS	RETAIL BOX

NORMA CENTERFIRE RIFLE CARTRIDGES – Specialty Calibers
20 rounds per box, 10 boxes per case. 200 rounds per case.

LOAD NO.	CALIBER	BULLET TYPE	BULLET WEIGHT GRAMS	RETAIL BOX
15701	220 Swift	Soft Point	50	21.43
15604	22 Savage H.P.	Soft Point	71	22.71
16531	6.5x50 Japanese	Soft Point Boat Tail	139	22.71
16532	6.5x50 Japanese	Soft Point	156	22.71
16535	6.5x52 Carcano	Soft Point	156	22.71
New 16537	6.5x52 Carcano	Soft Point	139	22.71
16558	6.5x55 Swedish	Protected Power Cavity	139	22.71
16552	6.5x55 Swedish	Soft Point	156	22.71
17002	7x57 Mauser	Soft Point	150	21.01
17005	7x57 R	Soft Point	150	23.81
17013	7x64 Brenneke	Soft Point	150	23.81
17511	7.5x55 Swiss	Soft Point Boat Tail	180	23.81
17634	7.62x54R Russian	Soft Point Boat Tail	180	24.07
New 17637	7.62x54R Russian	Soft Point	150	24.07
17638	308 Norma Magnum	Dual Core	180	28.76
17701	7.65x53 Argentine	Soft Point	150	22.71
New 17702	7.65x53 Argentine	Soft Point	180	22.71
17712	.303 British	Soft Point	150	17.77
17721	7.7x58 Japanese	Soft Point	130	24.07
17722	7.7x58 Japanese	Soft Point Boat Tail	180	24.07
18017	8x57 JS Mauser	Protected Power Cavity	165	22.71
18003	8x57 JS Mauser	Soft Point	196	22.71
19303	9.3x57 Mauser	Soft Point	286	27.54
19315	9.3x62 Mauser	Soft Point	286	27.54

NORMA CENTERFIRE PISTOL CARTRIDGES
50 rounds per box, 20 boxes per case. 1000 rounds per case.

LOAD NO.	CALIBER	BULLET TYPE	BULLET WEIGHT GRAMS	RETAIL BOX
19022	9mm Luger	Full Metal Jacket	116	25.27
19119	38 Special (+P)	Jacketed Hollow Point	110	25.92
19114	38 Special (+P)	Full Metal Jacket	158	25.92
19106	357 Magnum	Full Metal Jacket	158	26.73

20 rounds per box, 25 boxes per case.

LOAD NO.	CALIBER	BULLET TYPE	BULLET WEIGHT GRAMS	RETAIL BOX
11002	10mm Auto	Jacketed Hollow Point	170	14.66
11001	10mm Auto	Full Metal Jacket	200	14.66
11103-5	44 Magnum	Jacketed Soft Point	240	18.14

HORNADY AMMUNITION

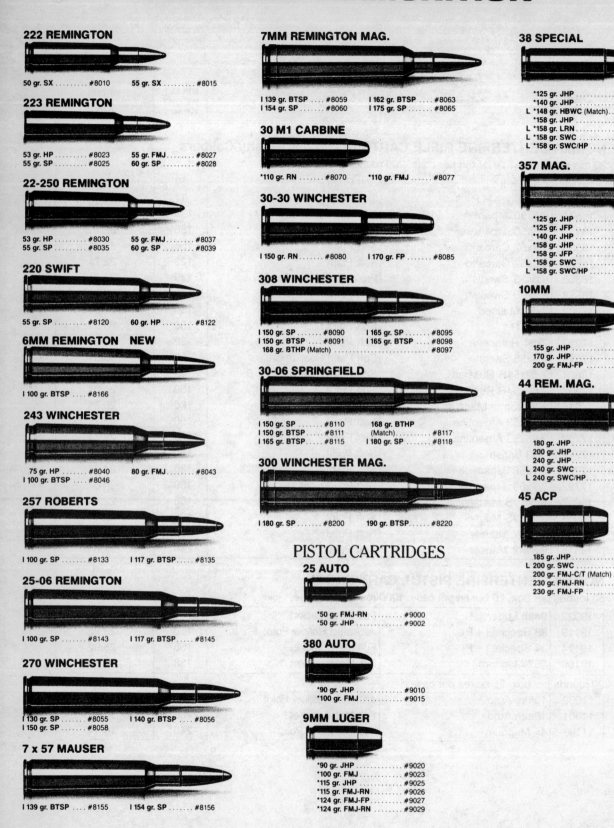

222 REMINGTON

50 gr. SX .... #8010   55 gr. SX .... #8015

223 REMINGTON

53 gr. HP .... #8023   55 gr. FMJ .... #8027
55 gr. SP .... #8025   60 gr. SP .... #8028

22-250 REMINGTON

53 gr. HP .... #8030   55 gr. FMJ .... #8037
55 gr. SP .... #8035   60 gr. SP .... #8039

220 SWIFT

55 gr. SP .... #8120   60 gr. HP .... #8122

6MM REMINGTON   NEW

I 100 gr. BTSP .... #8166

243 WINCHESTER

75 gr. HP .... #8040   80 gr. FMJ........ #8043
I 100 gr. BTSP ... #8046

257 ROBERTS

I 100 gr. SP ...... #8133   I 117 gr. BTSP..... #8135

25-06 REMINGTON

I 100 gr. SP ...... #8143   I 117 gr. BTSP..... #8145

270 WINCHESTER

I 130 gr. SP ...... #8055   I 140 gr. BTSP .... #8056
I 150 gr. SP ...... #8058

7 x 57 MAUSER

I 139 gr. BTSP .... #8155   I 154 gr. SP .... #8156

7MM REMINGTON MAG.

I 139 gr. BTSP .... #8059   I 162 gr. BTSP .... #8063
I 154 gr. SP ...... #8060   I 175 gr. SP ...... #8065

30 M1 CARBINE

*110 gr. RN ...... #8070   *110 gr. FMJ ...... #8077

30-30 WINCHESTER

I 150 gr. RN ...... #8080   I 170 gr. FP .... #8085

308 WINCHESTER

I 150 gr. SP .... #8090   I 165 gr. SP ..... #8095
I 150 gr. BTSP .... #8091   I 165 gr. BTSP .... #8098
168 gr. BTHP (Match) .... #8097

30-06 SPRINGFIELD

I 150 gr. SP .... #8110   168 gr. BTHP
I 150 gr. BTSP .... #8111   (Match).......... #8117
I 165 gr. BTSP .... #8115   I 180 gr. SP ..... #8118

300 WINCHESTER MAG.

I 180 gr. SP .... #8200   190 gr. BTSP..... #8220

PISTOL CARTRIDGES

25 AUTO

*50 gr. FMJ-RN .... #9000
*50 gr. JHP .... #9002

380 AUTO

*90 gr. JHP .... #9010
*100 gr. FMJ .... #9015

9MM LUGER

*90 gr. JHP .... #9020
*100 gr. FMJ .... #9023
*115 gr. JHP .... #9025
*115 gr. FMJ-RN .... #9026
*124 gr. FMJ-FP........ #9027
*124 gr. FMJ-RN .... #9029

38 SPECIAL

*125 gr. JHP .... #9032
*140 gr. JHP .... #9035
L *148 gr. HBWC (Match).. #9043
*158 gr. JHP .... #9036
L *158 gr. LRN .... #9045
L *158 gr. SWC .... #9046
L *158 gr. SWC/HP .... #9047

357 MAG.

*125 gr. JHP .... #9050
*125 gr. JFP .... #9053
*140 gr. JHP .... #9055
*158 gr. JHP .... #9056
*158 gr. JFP .... #9058
L *158 gr. SWC .... #9065
L *158 gr. SWC/HP .... #9066

10MM

155 gr. JHP .... #9122
170 gr. JHP .... #9125
200 gr. FMJ-FP .... #9128

44 REM. MAG.

180 gr. JHP .... #9081
200 gr. JHP .... #9080
240 gr. JHP .... #9085
L 240 gr. SWC .... #9087
L 240 gr. SWC/HP ...... #9086

45 ACP

185 gr. JHP .... #9090
L 200 gr. SWC .... #9110
200 gr. FMJ-C/T (Match) .. #9111
230 gr. FMJ-RN .... #9097
230 gr. FMJ-FP .... #9098

REMINGTON AMMUNITION

The centerfire cartridges pictured below and on the following page represent the most recent additions to Remington's ammunition lineup. They are being introduced in 1989 and will join the other cartridges pictured and described on the following pages.

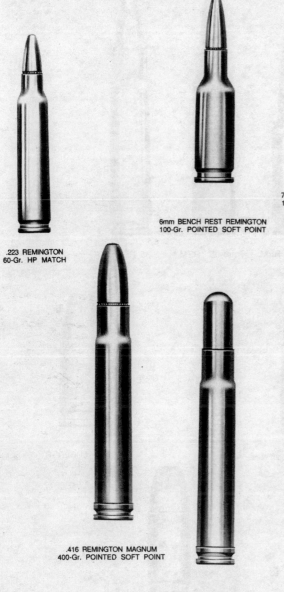

6mm BENCH REST REMINGTON
100-Gr. POINTED SOFT POINT

7mm BENCH REST REMINGTON
140-Gr. POINTED SOFT POINT

.223 REMINGTON
60-Gr. HP MATCH

.45 AUTO +P
185-Gr. JHP

.357 MAGNUM
125-Gr. SJHP
(Med. Velocity)

.416 REMINGTON MAGNUM
400-Gr. POINTED SOFT POINT

.416 REMINGTON MAGNUM
400-Gr. SOLID

.300 WEATHERBY MAGNUM
180-Gr. PSP "CORE-LOKT"
(Remington Version)

.300 WEATHERBY MAGNUM
220-Gr. SP "CORE-LOKT"
(Remington Version)

REMINGTON AMMUNITION

REMINGTON XP-100 CALIBERS
* Available in XP-100 Custom Only

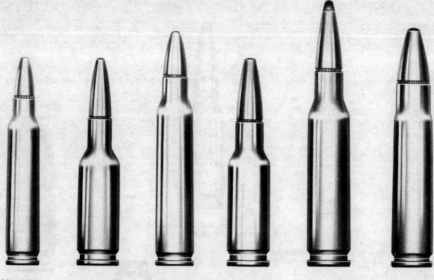

.223 REM. 6mm BR REM.* .250 SAVAGE* 7mm BR REM. 7mm-08 REM.* .35 REM.

10mm AUTO
170-Gr. HOLLOW POINT

10mm AUTO
200-Gr. METAL CASE

.30-06 SPRINGFIELD
168-Gr. Boattail HP Match

7.62 X 39mm
125-Gr. Pointed Soft Point

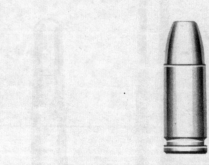

9mm LUGER +P
115-GR. JHP

9mm LUGER
140-Gr. SJHP
(Practice Round)

REMINGTON CENTERFIRE RIFLE CARTRIDGES

17 REMINGTON

No.	Bullet weight	Bullet style	Wt. case, lbs.
R17REM	25 gr.	Hollow Point Power-Lokt®	12

20 IN A BOX, 500 IN A CASE.

22 HORNET

No.	Bullet weight	Bullet style	Wt. case, lbs.
R22HN1	45 gr.	Pointed Soft Point	9
R22HN2	45 gr.	Hollow Point	9

20 IN A BOX, 500 IN A CASE.

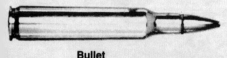

222 REMINGTON

No.	Bullet weight	Bullet style	Wt. case, lbs.
R222R1	50 gr.	Pointed Soft Point	14
R222R4	50 gr.	Hollow Point Power-Lokt®	14
R222R4	55 gr.	Metal Case	14

20 IN A BOX, 500 IN A CASE.

222 REMINGTON MAGNUM

No.	Bullet weight	Bullet style	Wt. case, lbs.
R222M1	55 gr.	Pointed Soft Point	15
R222M2	55 gr.	Hollow Point Power-Lokt®	15

20 IN A BOX, 500 IN A CASE.

22-250 REMINGTON

No.	Bullet weight	Bullet style	Wt. case, lbs.
R22501	55 gr.	Pointed Soft Point	21
R22502	55 gr.	Hollow Point Power-Lokt®	21

20 IN A BOX, 500 IN A CASE.

223 REMINGTON (5.56MM)

No.	Bullet weight	Bullet style	Wt. case, lbs.
R223R1	55 gr.	Pointed Soft Point	15
R223R2	55 gr.	Hollow Point Power-Lokt®	15
R223R3	55 gr.	Metal Case	15
R223R4†	60 gr.	Hollow Point	14

20 IN A BOX, 500 IN A CASE.

6MM REMINGTON

No.	Bullet weight	Bullet style	Wt. case, lbs.
R6MM1*	80 gr.	Pointed Soft Point	26
R6MM2*	80 gr.	Hollow Point Power-Lokt®	26
R6MM4	100 gr.	Pointed Soft Point Core-Lokt®	26

20 IN A BOX, 500 IN A CASE.

* May be used in rifles chambered for .244 Remington.

6MM BENCH REST REMINGTON

No.	Bullet weight	Bullet style	Wt. case, lbs.
R6MMBR†	100 gr.	Pointed Soft Point	21

20 IN A BOX, 500 IN A CASE.

243 WIN.

No.	Bullet weight	Bullet style	Wt. case, lbs.
R243W1	80 gr.	Pointed Soft Point	25
R243W2	80 gr.	Hollow Point Power-Lokt®	25
R243W3	100 gr.	Pointed Soft Point Core-Lokt®	25

20 IN A BOX, 500 IN A CASE.

25-06 REMINGTON

No.	Bullet weight	Bullet style	Wt. case, lbs.
R25061	87 gr.	Hollow Point Power-Lokt®	27
R25062	100 gr.	Pointed Soft Point Core-Lokt®	27
R25063	120 gr.	Pointed Soft Point Core-Lokt®	27

20 IN A BOX, 500 IN A CASE.

REMINGTON CENTERFIRE RIFLE CARTRIDGES

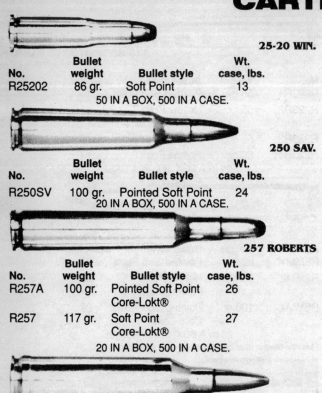

25-20 WIN.

No.	Bullet weight	Bullet style	Wt. case, lbs.
R25202	86 gr.	Soft Point	13

50 IN A BOX, 500 IN A CASE.

250 SAV.

No.	Bullet weight	Bullet style	Wt. case, lbs.
R250SV	100 gr.	Pointed Soft Point	24

20 IN A BOX, 500 IN A CASE.

257 ROBERTS

No.	Bullet weight	Bullet style	Wt. case, lbs.
R257A	100 gr.	Pointed Soft Point Core-Lokt®	26
R257	117 gr.	Soft Point Core-Lokt®	27

20 IN A BOX, 500 IN A CASE.

6.5MM REMINGTON MAGNUM

No.	Bullet weight	Bullet style	Wt. case, lbs.
R65MM2	120 gr.	Pointed Soft Point Core-Lokt®	31

20 IN A BOX, 500 IN A CASE.

(SUBJECT TO STOCK ON HAND)

264 WIN. MAG.

No.	Bullet weight	Bullet style	Wt. case, lbs.
R264W2	140 gr.	Pointed Soft Point Core-Lokt®	34

20 IN A BOX, 500 IN A CASE.

270 WIN.

No.	Bullet weight	Bullet style	Wt. case, lbs.
R270W1	100 gr.	Pointed Soft Point	32
R270W2	130 gr.	Pointed Soft Point Core-Lokt®	32
R270W3	130 gr.	Bronze Point™	32
R270W4	150 gr.	Soft Point Core-Lokt®	32

20 IN A BOX, 500 IN A CASE.

7MM-08 REMINGTON

No.	Bullet weight	Bullet style	Wt. case, lbs.
R7M082	120 gr.	Hollow Point	28
R7M081	140 gr.	Pointed Soft Point	30

20 IN A BOX, 500 IN A CASE.

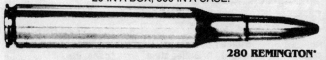

280 REMINGTON*

No.	Bullet weight	Bullet style	Wt. case, lbs.
R280R4	120 gr.	Hollow Point	32
R280R3	140 gr.	Pointed Soft Point	33
R280R1	150 gr.	Pointed Soft Point Core-Lokt®	33
R280R2	165 gr.	Soft Point Core-Lokt®	34

20 IN A BOX, 500 IN A CASE.

*Interchangeable with 7mm "Express" Rem.

7MM BENCH REST REMINGTON

No.	Bullet weight	Bullet style	Wt. case, lbs.
R7MMBR	140 gr.	Pointed Soft Point	28

20 IN A BOX, 500 IN A CASE.

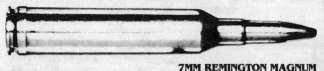

7MM REMINGTON MAGNUM

No.	Bullet weight	Bullet style	Wt. case, lbs.
R7MM4	140 gr.	Pointed Soft Point	36
R7MM2	150 gr.	Pointed Soft Point Core-Lokt®	37
R7MM3	175 gr.	Pointed Soft Point Core-Lokt®	37

20 IN A BOX, 500 IN A CASE.

7MM MAUSER (7X57)

No.	Bullet weight	Bullet style	Wt. case, lbs.
R7MSR1	140 gr.	Pointed Soft Point	32

20 IN A BOX, 500 IN A CASE.

REMINGTON CENTERFIRE RIFLE CARTRIDGES

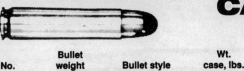

30 CARBINE

No.	Bullet weight	Bullet style	Wt. case, lbs.
R30CAR	110 gr.	Soft Point	15

50 IN A BOX, 500 IN A CASE.

30 REMINGTON

No.	Bullet weight	Bullet style	Wt. case, lbs.
R30REM	170 gr.	Soft Point Core-Lokt®	26

20 IN A BOX, 500 IN A CASE.

30-30 WIN.

No.	Bullet weight	Bullet style	Wt. case, lbs.
R30301	150 gr.	Soft Point,Core-Lokt®	27
R30302	170 gr.	Soft Point,Core-Lokt®	27
R30303	170 gr.	Hollow Point,Core-Lokt®	27

20 IN A BOX, 500 IN A CASE.

30-40 KRAG

No.	Bullet weight	Bullet style	Wt. case, lbs.
R30402	180 gr.	Pointed Soft Point Core-Lokt®	32

20 IN A BOX, 500 IN A CASE.

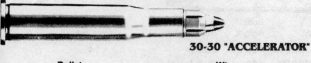

30-30 "ACCELERATOR"

No.	Bullet weight	Bullet style	Wt. case, lbs.
R3030A	180 gr.	Pointed Soft Point Core-Lokt®	32

20 IN A BOX, 500 IN A CASE.

30-06 "ACCELERATOR"

No.	Bullet weight	Bullet style	Wt. case, lbs.
R30069	55 gr.	Pointed Soft Point	26

20 IN A BOX, 500 IN A CASE.

30-06 SPFD.

No.	Bullet weight	Bullet style	Wt. case, lbs.
R30061	125 gr.	Pointed Soft Point	35
R30062	150 gr.	Pointed Soft Point Core-Lokt®	35
R30063	150 gr.	Bronze Point™	35
R3006B	165 gr.	Pointed Soft Point Core-Lokt®	35
R30064	180 gr.	Soft Point Core-Lokt®	35
R30065	180 gr.	Pointed Soft Point Core-Lokt®	35
R30066	180 gr.	Bronze Point™	35
R30067	220 gr.	Soft Point Core-Lokt®	35
R3006C†	168 gr.	Boat Tail Hollow Point (Match)	31

20 IN A BOX, 500 IN A CASE.

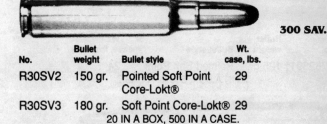

300 SAV.

No.	Bullet weight	Bullet style	Wt. case, lbs.
R30SV2	150 gr.	Pointed Soft Point Core-Lokt®	29
R30SV3	180 gr.	Soft Point Core-Lokt®	29

20 IN A BOX, 500 IN A CASE.

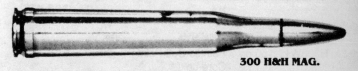

300 H&H MAG.

No.	Bullet weight	Bullet style	Wt. case, lbs.
R300HH	180 gr.	Pointed Soft Point Core-Lokt®	39

20 IN A BOX, 500 IN A CASE.

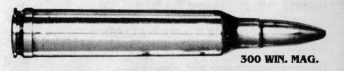

300 WIN. MAG.

No.	Bullet weight	Bullet style	Wt. case, lbs.
R300W1	150 gr.	Pointed Soft Point Core-Lokt®	39
R300W2	180 gr.	Pointed Soft Point Core-Lokt®	39

20 IN A BOX, 500 IN A CASE.

REMINGTON CENTERFIRE RIFLE CARTRIDGES

300 WEATHERBY MAG.

No.	Bullet weight	Bullet style	Wt. case, lbs.
R300WB1†	180 gr.	Pointed Soft Point Core-Lokt®	41
R300WB2†	220 gr.	Soft Point, Core-Lokt®	44

20 IN A BOX, 500 IN A CASE.

303 BRITISH

No.	Bullet weight	Bullet style	Wt. case, lbs.
R303B1	180 gr.	Soft Point, Core-Lokt®	67

20 IN A BOX, 500 IN A CASE.

7.62X39MM

No.	Bullet weight	Bullet style	Wt. case, lbs.
R762391†	125 gr.	Pointed Soft Point	24

20 IN A BOX, 500 IN A CASE.

308 WIN.

No.	Bullet weight	Bullet style	Wt. case, lbs.
R308W1	150 gr.	Pointed Soft Point Core-Lokt®	30
R308W6	165 gr.	Pointed Soft Point Core-Lokt®	30
R308W7	168 gr.	Boat Tail Hollow Point (Match)	30
R308W2	180 gr.	Soft Point Core-Lokt®	30
R308W3	180 gr.	Pointed Soft Point Core-Lokt®	30

20 IN A BOX, 500 IN A CASE.

308 WIN. "ACCELERATOR"

No.	Bullet weight	Bullet style	Wt. case, lbs.
R308W5	55 gr.	Pointed Soft Point	26

20 IN A BOX, 500 IN A CASE.

8MM (7.9MM) MAUSER

No.	Bullet weight	Bullet style	Wt. case, lbs.
R8MSR	170 gr.	Soft Point, Core-Lokt®	32

20 IN A BOX, 500 IN A CASE.

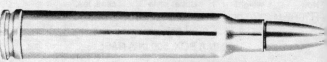

8MM REMINGTON MAGNUM

No.	Bullet weight	Bullet style	Wt. case, lbs.
R8MM1	185 gr.	Pointed Soft Point Core-Lokt®	40
R8MM2	220 gr.	Pointed Soft Point Core-Lokt®	42

20 IN A BOX, 500 IN A CASE.

32 WIN. SPECIAL

No.	Bullet weight	Bullet style	Wt. case, lbs.
R32WS2	170 gr.	Soft Point, Core-Lokt®	27

20 IN A BOX, 500 IN A CASE.

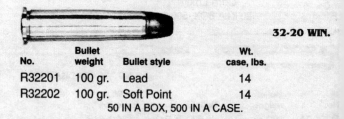

32-20 WIN.

No.	Bullet weight	Bullet style	Wt. case, lbs.
R32201	100 gr.	Lead	14
R32202	100 gr.	Soft Point	14

50 IN A BOX, 500 IN A CASE.

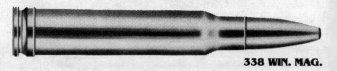

338 WIN. MAG.

No.	Bullet weight	Bullet style	Wt. case, lbs.
R338W1	225 gr.	Pointed Soft Point	42
R338W2	250 gr.	Pointed Soft Point	45

20 IN A BOX, 500 IN A CASE.

REMINGTON CENTERFIRE PISTOL AND REVOLVER CARTRIDGES

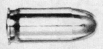

380 AUTO. PISTOL

No.	Bullet weight	Bullet style	Wt. case, lbs.
R380A1	88 gr.	Jacketed Hollow Point	12
R380AP	95 gr.	Metal Case	12

50 IN A BOX, 500 IN A CASE.

38 AUTO. COLT PISTOL

Adapted only for 38 Colt Sporting, Military and Pocket Model Automatic Pistols.

No.	Bullet weight	Bullet style	Wt. case, lbs.
R38ACP	130 gr.	Metal Case	16

50 IN A BOX, 500 IN A CASE.
(Subject to stock on hand)

38 SUPER AUTO. COLT PISTOL

Adapted only for 38 Colt Super and Colt Commander Automatic Pistols.

No.	Bullet weight	Bullet style	Wt. case, lbs.
R38SU1	115 gr.	Jacketed Hollow Point (+P)	14
R38SUP	130 gr.	Metal Case (+P)	16

50 IN A BOX, 500 IN A CASE.

38 S&W

No.	Bullet weight	Bullet style	Wt. case, lbs.
R38SW	146 gr.	Lead	16

50 IN A BOX, 500 IN A CASE.

38 SPECIAL

No.	Bullet weight	Bullet style	Wt. case, lbs.
R38S1	95 gr.	Semi-Jacketed Hollow Point (+P)	13
R38S10	110 gr.	Semi-Jacketed Hollow Point (+P)	13
R38S2	125 gr.	Semi-Jacketed Hollow Point (+P)	17
R38S13	125 gr.	Semi-Jacket Soft Point (+P)	17
R38S3	148 gr.	Targetmaster Lead Wadcutter, brass case	17
R38S4	158 gr.	Targetmaster Lead Round Nose	18
R38S5	158 gr.	Lead	18
R38S6	158 gr.	Lead Semi-Wadcutter	18
R38S14	158 gr.	Lead Semi-Wadcutter (+P)	18
R38S7	158 gr.	Metal Point	18
R38S8	158 gr.	Lead (+P)	18
R38S12	158 gr.	Lead Hollow Point (+P)	18
R38S9	200 gr.	Lead	21
R38SMB†	140 gr.	Multi-Ball	17

50 IN A BOX, 500 IN A CASE.

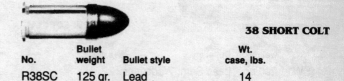

38 SHORT COLT

No.	Bullet weight	Bullet style	Wt. case, lbs.
R38SC	125 gr.	Lead	14

50 IN A BOX, 500 IN A CASE.

10MM AUTO.

No.	Bullet weight	Bullet style	Wt. case, lbs.
R10MM1†	170 gr.	Hollow Point	21
R10MM2†	200 gr.	Metal Case	24

50 IN A BOX, 500 IN A CASE.

> (+P) Ammunition with (+P) on the case headstamp is loaded to higher pressure. Use only in firearms designated for this cartridge and so recommended by the gun manufacturer.

REMINGTON CENTERFIRE PISTOL AND REVOLVER CARTRIDGES

41 REMINGTON MAGNUM

No.	Bullet weight	Bullet style	Wt. case, lbs.
R41MG3†	170 gr.	Semi-Jacketed Hollow Point	24
R41MG1	210 gr.	Soft Point	26
R41MG2	210 gr.	Lead	26

50 IN A BOX, 500 IN A CASE.

44 REMINGTON MAGNUM

No.	Bullet weight	Bullet style	Wt. case, lbs.
R44MG5	180 gr.	Semi-Jacketed Hollow Point	29
R44MG1	310 gr.	Semi-Jacketed Hollow Point	27
R44MG1	240 gr.	Lead, Gas-Check	29
R44MG4	240 gr.	Lead	29
R44MG2	240 gr.	Soft Point	29
R44MG3	240 gr.	Semi-Jacketed Hollow Point	29

20 IN A BOX, 500 IN A CASE.

44 S&W SPECIAL

No.	Bullet weight	Bullet style	Wt. case, lbs.
R44SW1	200 gr.	Lead Semi-Wadcutter	22
R44SW	246 gr.	Lead	25

50 IN A BOX, 500 IN A CASE.

45 COLT

No.	Bullet weight	Bullet style	Wt. case, lbs.
R45C1	225 gr.	Lead Semi-Wadcutter	24
R45C	250 gr.	Lead	26

50 IN A BOX, 500 IN A CASE.

45 AUTO.

No.	Bullet weight	Bullet style	Wt. case, lbs.
R45AP1	185 gr.	Targetmaster Metal Case Wadcutter	11
R45AP2	185 gr.	Jacketed Hollow Point	11
R45AP4	230 gr.	Metal Case	13
R45AP6†	185 gr.	Jacketed Hollow Point (+P)	21

50 IN A BOX, 500 IN A CASE.

.45 AUTO. SHOT CARTRIDGE

No.	Bullet style	Wt. case, lbs.
R45AP5	650 Pellets — No. 12 Shot	18

20 IN A BOX, 500 IN A CASE.

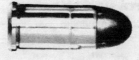

45 AUTO. RIM

No.	Bullet weight	Bullet style	Wt. case, lbs.
R45AR	230 gr.	Lead	27

50 IN A BOX, 500 IN A CASE.

REMINGTON CENTERFIRE BLANK

No.	Caliber	No. in case	Wt. case, lbs.
R32BLNK	32 S&W	500	4
R38SWBL	38 S&W	500	7
R38BLNK	38 Special	500	7

50 IN A BOX.

(+P) Ammunition with (+P) on the case headstamp is loaded to higher pressure. Use only in firearms designated for this cartridge and so recommended by the gun manufacturer.

REMINGTON RIMFIRE CARTRIDGES

"HIGH VELOCITY" CARTRIDGES WITH "GOLDEN" BULLETS

22 SHORT

No.	Bullet weight and style	Wt. case, lbs.
1022	29 gr., Lead	29
1122	27 gr., Lead, Hollow Point	28

50 IN A BOX, 5,000 IN A CASE.

22 LONG

No.	Bullet weight and style	Wt. case, lbs.
1322	29 gr., Lead	31

50 IN A BOX, 5,000 IN A CASE.

22 LONG RIFLE

No.	Bullet weight and style	Wt. case, lbs.
1522	40 gr., Lead	40
1622	36 gr., Lead, Hollow Point	38

50 IN A BOX, 5,000 IN A CASE.

100 PACK

No.	Bullet weight and style	Wt. case, lbs.
1500	40 gr., Lead	40
1600	36 gr., Lead, Hollow Point	38

100 IN A BOX, 5,000 IN A CASE.

"TARGET" STANDARD VELOCITY CARTRIDGES

22 SHORT

No.	Bullet weight and style	Wt. case, lbs.
5522	29 gr., Lead	29

50 IN A BOX, 5,000 IN A CASE.

22 LONG RIFLE

No.	Bullet weight and style	Wt. case, lbs.
6122	40 gr., Lead	40

50 IN A BOX, 5,000 IN A CASE.

.22 LONG RIFLE, TARGET 100 PACK

No.	Bullet weight and style	Wt. case, lbs.
6100	40 gr., Lead	40

100 IN A BOX, 5,000 IN A CASE.

CB22™ CARTRIDGES LOW NOISE LEVEL

Velocity of 720 f.p.s.; the quietness of an airgun, the impact of a .22 bullet.

22 SHORT

22 LONG

No.	Bullet weight and style	Wt. case, lbs.
CB-22S Short	30 gr., Lead	29
CB-22L Long	20 gr., Lead	30

50 IN A BOX, 5,000 IN A CASE.

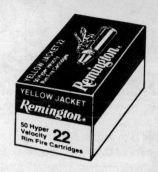

YELLOW JACKET® CARTRIDGES HYPER-VELOCITY

22 LONG RIFLE

No.	Bullet weight and style	Wt. case, lbs.
1722	33 gr., Truncated Cone, Hollow Point	36

50 IN A BOX, 5,000 IN A CASE.

"VIPER" CARTRIDGES HYPER-VELOCITY

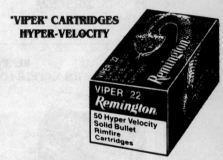

22 LONG RIFLE

No.	Bullet weight and style	Wt. case, lbs.
1922	36 gr., Truncated Cone, Solid Point, Copper Plated	38

50 IN A BOX, 5,000 IN A CASE.

"THUNDERBOLT" CARTRIDGES HI-SPEED

22 LONG RIFLE

No.	Bullet weight and style	Wt. case, lbs.
TB22A	36 gr., Truncated Cone, Solid Point	40

50 IN A BOX, 5,000 IN A CASE.

REMINGTON SHOTGUN SHELLS

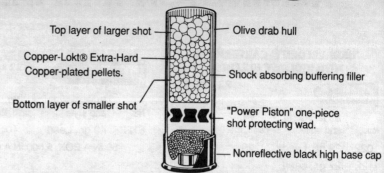

- Top layer of larger shot
- Olive drab hull
- Copper-Lokt® Extra-Hard Copper-plated pellets.
- Shock absorbing buffering filler
- Bottom layer of smaller shot
- "Power Piston" one-piece shot protecting wad.
- Nonreflective black high base cap

- Combined large and smaller shot sizes.
- Available in lead or steel shot magnum loads.

Patented Remington Duplex® Shotgun Shell

	No.	Gauge	Length shell, in.	Powder equiv. drams	Shot, oz.	Size shot	Wt. case, lbs.
MULTIRANGE	MRP12S	12	2 3/4	Max.	1 1/2	BBx4,2x4,,2x6, 4x6	35
DUPLEX®	MRP12H	12	3	Max.	1 7/8	BBx4, 2x4, 2x6, 4x6	41
MAGNUM							
COPPER PLATED							
LEAD SHOT							
MULTIRANGE	MRS10M	10	3 1/2	Max.	1 3/4	TxBB†,BBBx1†	48
DUPLEX®	MRS12	12	2 3/4	Max.	1 1/8	BBx1,BBx2,BBx4,2x6,1x3	29
MAGNUM	MRS12SM	12	2 3/4	Max.	1 1/4	BBx2†,1x3†	31
STEEL SHOT	MRS12H	12	3	Max.	1 1/4	BBx1, BBx2, BBx4, 2x6,1x3	29
	MRS12HM	12	3	Max.	1 3/8	BBBx1†, BBx2†, 1x3†	35

10 IN A BOX, 250 IN A CASE.

REMINGTON "PREMIER" HIGHEST GRADE SHOTSHELLS
WITH "COPPER-LOKT"EXTRA HARD PLATED SHOT AND "POWER-PISTON" WADS

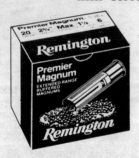

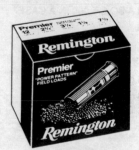

	No.	Gauge	Length shell, in.	Powder equiv. drams	Shot, oz.	Size shot	Wt. case, lbs.
PREMIER™	PR10H Mag.†	10	3 1/2	4 1/2	2 1/4	2, 4, 6	49
EXTENDED	PR12S Mag.	12	2 3/4	Max.	1 1/2	BB, 2,4, 6	34
RANGE	PR12 Mag.	12	3	4	1 5/8	4, 6	37
BUFFERD	PR12H Mag.	12	3	Max.	1 7/8	BB, 2, 4, 6†	41
MAGNUM	PR20S Mag.	20	2 3/4	Max.	1 1/8	4, 6	26
LOADS	PR20H Mag.	20	3	Max.	1 1/4	2, 4, 6	30
PREMIER™	PR12	12	2 3/4	2 3/4	1 1/4	2, 4, 6, 7 1/2	29
EXTRA LONG	PR20	20	2 3/4	2 3/4	1	4, 6	24
RANGE LOADS							
PREMIER™	PR12F	12	2 3/4	3 1/4	1 1/8	7 1/2, 8	29
"POWER-PATTERN"	PR12HF	12	2 3/4	3 1/4	1 1/4	7 1/2, 8	29
	PR20F	20	2 3/4	2 1/2	1	7 1/2, 8	23

25 IN A BOX, 250 IN A CASE.

REMINGTON SHOTGUN SHELLS

SHOTGUN SHELLS
REMINGTON PREMIER™ TARGET LOADS

	No.	Gauge	Length shell, in.	Powder equiv. drams	Size, oz.	Size shot	Wt. case, lbs.
PREMIER™ TARGET LOADS	RTL12L•	12	2 3/4	2 3/4	1 1/8	7 1/2, 8, 8 1/2, 9	27
	RTL12M•	12	2 3/4	3	1 1/8	7 1/2, 8, 9	27
	RTL20	20	2 3/4	2 1/2	7/8	9	41
"REMLITE" PREMIER™ TARGET LOAD	LRTL12†•	12	2 3/4	—	1 1/8	7 1/2, 8, 9	27
DUPLEX® PREMIER™ TARGET LOAD	MRTL12L†•	12	2 3/4	2 3/4	1 1/8	7 1/2X8	27
	MRTL12M†•			3	1 1/8	7 1/2X8	27
SKEET LOADS	SP28	28	2 3/4	2	3/4	9	37
	SP410	.410	2 1/2	Max.	1/2	9	22
PREMIER™ PIGEON LOADS	RTL12P•	12	2 3/4	3 1/4	1 1/4	7 1/2, 8	27
	RTL12PN•	12	2 3/4	3 1/4	1 1/4	7 1/2, 8 (nickel)	27
PREMIER™ INTERNATIONAL TARGET LOADS	IRT12•	12	2 3/4	3 1/4	1 1/8	7 1/2, 8	54
	NIRT12•	12	2 3/4	3 1/4	1 1/8	7 1/2, 8 (nickel)	54

25 IN A BOX, 500 IN A CASE • 25 IN A BOX, 250 IN A CASE

REMINGTON PROMOTIONAL SHOTSHELLS

	No.	Gauge	Length shell, in.	Powder equiv. drams	Size, oz.	Size shot	Wt. case, lbs.
DOVE/QUAIL FIELD LOADS	DQ12W•	12	2 3/4	3 1/4	1	7 1/2, 8	24
	DQ16W•	16	2 3/4	2 1/2	1	7 1/2, 8	24
	DQ20W•	20	2 3/4	2 1/2	7/8	7 1/2, 8	20
RABBIT/SQUIRREL FIELD LOADS	RS12W•	12	2 3/4	3 1/4	1	6	24
	RS16W•	16	2 3/4	2 1/2	1	6	24
	RS20W•	20	2 3/4	2 1/2	1	6	20
DUCK/PHEASANT FIELD LOADS	DP12	12	2 3/4	3 3/4	1 1/4	4, 5, 6, 7 1/2	58
	DP16	16	2 3/4	3 1/4	1 1/8	4, 6, 7 1/2	52
	SP20	20	2 3/4	2 2/3	1	4, 6, 7 1/2	46
SPORT LOADS	SL12•	12	2 3/4	3 1/4	1	8	24
	SL20•	20	2 3/4	2 1/2	7/8	8	20

25 IN A BOX, 500 IN A CASE • 25 IN A BOX, 250 PER CASE

REMINGTON SHOTGUN SHELLS

REMINGTON NITRO MAGNUM®, EXPRESS™, AND SHURSHOT® SHOTSHELLS

	No.	Gauge	Length shell, in.	Powder equiv. drams	Shot, oz.	Size shot	Wt. case, lbs.
NITRO	SP12SNM•	12	2 3/4	Max.	1 1/2	BB, 2, 4, 5, 6	34
MAGNUM™	SP12NM•	12	3	4	1 5/8	2, 4, 6	35
EXTENDED	SP12HNM•	12	3	Max.	1 7/8	BB, 2, 4	35
RANGE	SP20SNM•	20	2 3/4	Max.	1 1/8	4, 6, 7 1/2	26
BUFFERED	SP20HNM•	20	3	Max.	1 1/4	2, 4, 6, 7 1/2	30
MAGNUMS							
EXPRESS™	SP10MAG•	10	3 1/2	Max.	2	BB, 2, 4	45
LONG RANGE	SP12	12	2 3/4	3 3/4	1 1/4	BB, 2, 4, 5, 6, 7 1/2, 9	58
LOADS	SP16	16	2 3/4	3 1/4	1 1/8	4, 5, 6, 7 1/2, 9	52
	SP16CMAG	16	2 3/4	Max.	1 1/4	2, 4, 6	58
	SP20	20	2 3/4	2 3/4	1	4, 5, 6, 7 1/2, 9	47
	SP28	28	2 3/4	2 1/4	3/4	6, 7 1/2	36
	SP410	410	2 1/2	Max.	1/2	4, 6, 7 1/2	23
	SP4103	410	3	Max.	11/16	4, 5, 6, 7 1/2, 9	31
SHURSHOT®	R12H	12	2 3/4	3 1/4	1 1/8	4, 5, 6, 9	51
FIELD	R12H250CS•	12	2 3/4	3 1/4	1 1/8	7 1/2, 8	29
LOADS	RP12H250CS•	12	2 3/4	3 1/4	1 1/4	7 1/2, 8	30
	R16H	16	2 3/4	2 3/4	1 1/8	4, 6, 7 1/2, 8, 9	51
	R20M	20	2 3/4	2 1/2	1	4, 5, 6, 9	45
	R20M250CS•	20	2 3/4	2 1/2	1	7 1/2, 8	23

25 IN A BOX, 500 IN A CASE. • 25 IN A BOX, 250 PER CASE

REMINGTON STEEL SHOT WATERFOWL LOADS

	No.	Gauge	Length shell, in.	Powder equiv. drams	Shot, oz.	Size shot	Wt. case, lbs.
STEEL SHOT	STL10MAG	10	3 1/2	Max.	1 3/4	T†, BBB†, BB, 1, 2, 3	48
WATERFOWL	STL12	12	2 3/4	Max.	1 1/8	BB, 1, 2, 3, 4, 6	28
LOADS	STL12SMAG	12	2 3/4	Max.	1 1/4	1, 2, 3, 4	30
	STL12MAG	12	3	Max.	1 1/4	BB, 1, 2, 3, 4, 6	30
	STL12HMAG†	12	3	Max.	1 3/8	BB, 1, 2, 3, 4	32
	STL20HMAG	20	3	Max.	1	2, 3, 4, 6	23

25 IN A BOX, 250 PER CASE.

REMINGTON SHOTGUN SHELLS

REMINGTON PREMIER™ MAGNUM BUCKSHOT WITH EXTRA HARD NICKEL PLATED SHOT

Nickel plated extra-hard buckshot and granulated polyethylene filler for reduced deformation and improved pattern.

	No.	Gauge	Length shell, in.	Powder equiv. drams	Size Shot	Pellets	Wt. case, lbs.
PREMIER™	P12SN00	12	2 3/4	4	00	12	29
MAGNUM	P12SN4	12	2 3/4	4	4	34	31
EXTENDED	P12N000	12	3	4	000	10	40
RANGE	P12N00	12	3	4	00	15	40
BUCKSHOT	P12N1	12	3	Max.	1	24	40
WITH NICKEL	P12N4	12	3	4	4	41	42
PLATED SHOT							

10 IN A BOX, 250 RDS. PER CASE.

REMINGTON "EXPRESS" BUCKSHOT LOADS AND "SLUGGER" RIFLED SLUGS

	No.	Gauge	Length shell, in.	Powder equiv. drams	Size, oz.	Size shot	Wt. case, lbs.
"POWER PAKT"	SP12BK	12	2 3/4	3 3/4	—	000 Buck—8 Pellets	31
EXPRESS™	SP12BK	12	2 3/4	3 3/4	—	00 Buck—9 Pellets	29
BUCKSHOT	SP12BK	12	2 3/4	3 3/4	—	0 Buck—12 Pellets	32
LOADS	SP12BK	12	2 3/4	3 3/4	—	1 Buck—16 Pellets	32
	SP12BK	12	2 3/4	3 3/4	—	4 Buck—27 Pellets	31
	SP16BK	16	2 3/4	3	—	1 Buck—12 Pellets	26
	SP20BK	20	2 3/4	2 3/4	—	3 Buck—20 Pellets	24
"POWER PAKT"	SP12SMagBK	12	2 3/4	4	—	00 Buck—12 Pellets	34
EXPRESS™	SP12SMagBK	12	2 3/4	4	—	1 Buck—20 Pellets	34
MAGNUM	SP12HMagBK	12	3	4	—	000 Buck—10 Pellets	40
BUCKSHOT	SP12HMagBK	12	3	4	—	00 Buck—15 Pellets	40
LOADS	SP12HMagBK	12	3	4	—	1 Buck—24 Pellets	40
	SP12HMagBK	12	3	4	—	4 Buck—41 Pellets	42
SLUGGER®	SP12SMagRS†	12	2 3/4	Max.	1	Rifled Slug	26
MAGNUM	SP12MagRS†	12	3	Max.	1	Rifled Slug	26
RIFLED SLUG							
LOADS							
SLUGGER®	SP12RS	12	2 3/4	Max.	1	Rifled Slug H.P.	26
RIFLED SLUG	SP12SRS	12	2 3/4	Max.	1	Rifled Slug H.P.	26
LOADS	SP12MRS	12	3	Max.	1	Rifled Slug H.P.	26
	SP16RS	16	2 3/4	3	4/5	Rifled Slug H.P.	24
	SP20RS	20	2 3/4	2 3/4	5/8	Rifled Slug H.P.	19
	SP410RS	410	2 1/2	Max.	1/5	Rifled Slug	8

5 IN A BOX, 250 PER CASE

WINCHESTER AMMUNITION

Supreme™ Centerfire Rifle Cartridges
Packaged 20 per Box, 500 per Case.

WINCHESTER SYMBOL	CARTRIDGE	CASE CONTAINS M'S	BOXES PER CASE	APPROX. CASE WT. LBS.	SUGGESTED RETAIL PRICE PER M	PER CASE	PER BOX
	Supreme 22-250 Remington						
S22250R52	52 gr. Hollow Point Boattail	½	25	19	636.00	318.00	12.72
	Supreme 243 Winchester						
S243W100	100 gr. Soft Point Boattail	½	25	26	760.00	380.00	15.20
	Supreme 270 Winchester						
S270W140	140 gr. Silvertip Boattail	½	25	32	1048.00	524.00	20.96
	Supreme 30-30 Winchester						
S3030W150	150 gr. Silvertip	½	25	26	876.00	438.00	17.52
	Supreme 308 Winchester						
S308W180	180 gr. Silvertip Boattail	½	25	31	960.00	480.00	19.20
	Supreme 30-06 Springfield						
S3006S165	165 gr. Silvertip Boattail	½	25	34	960.00	480.00	19.20
	Supreme 30-06 Springfield						
S3006S180	180 gr. Silvertip Boattail	½	25	34	1048.00	524.00	20.96
	Supreme 300 Winchester Magnum						
S300WM190	190 gr. Silvertip Boattail	½	25	42	1308.00	654.00	26.16

Super-X Centerfire Pistol/Revolver Cartridges
Packaged 50 per Box unless noted—Smokeless Powder—Staynless Non-Corrosive Priming.

WINCHESTER SYMBOL	CARTRIDGE	CASE CONTAINS M'S	BOXES PER CASE	APPROX. CASE WT. LBS.	SUGGESTED RETAIL PRICE PER M	PER CASE	PER BOX
	25 Automatic (6.35mm)						
X25AXP	45 gr. Expanding Point**.................	2	40	23	299.52	599.04	14.98
X25AP	50 gr. Full Metal Case	2	40	24	276.48	552.96	13.82
	30 Luger (7.65mm)						
X30LP	93 gr. Full Metal Case	½	10	12	496.96	248.48	24.85
	30 Carbine						
X30M1	110 gr. Hollow Soft Point	1	20	29	456.00	456.00	22.80
X30M2	110 gr. Full Metal Case	1	20	29	456.00	456.00	22.80
	32 Smith & Wesson						
X32SWP	85 gr. Lead Round Nose	2	40	39	264.64	529.28	13.23
	32 Smith & Wesson Long (Colt New Police)						
X32SWLP	98 gr. Lead Round Nose	2	40	45	278.08	556.16	13.90
	32 Short Colt						
X32SCP	80 gr. Lead Round Nose	½	10	9	261.44	130.72	13.07
† X32LCP	**32 Long Colt** 82 gr. Lead Round Nose	½	10	10	273.60	136.80	13.68
	32 Automatic						
X32ASHP	60 gr. Silvertip Hollow Point	2	40	33	363.52	727.04	18.18
X32AP	71 gr. Full Metal Case	2	40	35	313.28	626.56	15.66
	38 Smith & Wesson						
X38SWP	145 gr. Lead Round Nose	2	40	66	293.44	586.88	14.67
	380 Automatic						
X380ASHP	85 gr. Silvertip Hollow Point	2	40	46	374.08	748.16	18.70
X380AP	95 gr. Full Metal Case	2	40	43	320.64	641.28	16.03
	38 Special						
X38S9HP	110 gr. Silvertip Hollow Point	2	40	57	432.96	865.92	21.65
X38S1P	158 gr. Lead Round Nose	2	40	71	294.72	589.44	14.74
X38WCPSV	158 gr. Lead Semi-Wad Cutter	2	40	72	306.88	613.76	15.34
† X38S2P	158 gr. Metal Point	2	40	71	375.36	750.72	18.77
	38 Special+P						
X38SSHP	95 gr. Silvertip Hollow Point +P	2	40	56	452.80	905.60	22.64
X38S6PH	110 gr. Jacketed Hollow Point +P	2	40	62	374.08	748.16	18.70
X38S7PH	125 gr. Jacketed Hollow Point +P	2	40	67	374.08	748.16	18.70
X38S8HP	125 gr. Silvertip Hollow Point +P	2	40	66	452.80	905.60	22.64
X38SPD	158 gr. Lead Hollow Point +P	2	40	74	320.64	641.28	16.03
X38WCP	158 gr. Lead Semi-Wad Cutter +P	2	40	74	325.76	651.52	16.29
	38 Special Match						
X38SMRP	148 gr. Lead Mid-Range (Clean Cutting) Match	2	40	65	306.88	613.76	15.34
	9mm Luger (Parabellum)						
X9LP	115 gr. Full Metal Case	2	40	57	389.12	778.24	19.46
X9MMSHP	115 gr. Silvertip Hollow Point	2	40	56	470.40	940.80	23.52

**Lubaloy coated   † Obsolete in 1989

+P = Ammunition with (+P) on the case head stamp is loaded to higher pressure. Use only in firearms designated for this cartridge and so recommended by the gun manufacturer.

WINCHESTER AMMUNITION

Shotshells—Staynless Non-Corrosive Priming.

WINCHESTER SYMBOL	GAUGE	LENGTH OF SHELL INCHES	POWDER DRAM EQUIV.	OZ. SHOT	SHOT SIZES	APPROX. CASE WT. LBS.	CASES PER PALLET	NET WEIGHT PER PALLET	SUGGESTED RETAIL PRICE PER M	PER CASE	PER BOX
Super-X Game Loads—Packed 25 per Box, 500 per Case											
X12	12	2¾	3¾	1¼	2,4,5,6,7½,9	56	60	3360	434.56	217.28	10.86
X16H	16	2¾	3¼	1⅛	4,6,7½	49	64	3136	419.84	209.92	10.50
X20	20	2¾	2¾	1	4,5,6,7½,9	44	80	3520	401.28	200.64	10.03
X28	28	2¾	2¼	¾	6,7½	34	90	3060	391.68	195.84	9.79
X28H **NEW**	28	2¾	MAX	1	6,7½,8	17	144	2448	391.68	195.84	9.79
X41	410	2½	Max.	½	4,6,7½	23	161	3703	300.80	150.40	7.52
X413	410	3	Max.	11/16	4,6,7½	29	108	3132	352.64	176.32	8.82
Double X Magnum Game Loads—Copperplated, Buffered Shot—Packed 25 per Box, 250 per Case unless noted											
X103XC	10	3½	4½	2¼	BB,2,4	47	60	2820	1082.24	270.56	27.06
X123XC	12	3	4	1⅞	BB,2,4,6	39	84	3276	680.96	170.24	17.02
†●X123XCT*	12	3	4	1⅞	4,6	40	84	3318	716.80	179.20	7.17
X12MXC	12	3	4	1⅝	2,4,5,6	39	84	3276	632.32	158.08	15.81
●X123MXCT	12	3	Max.	2	4,5,6	40	84	3360	747.20	186.80	7.47
X12XC	12	2¾	Max.	1½	BB,2,4,5,6	32	105	3360	592.64	148.16	14.82
●X12XCT	12	2¾	Max.	1½	4,6	33	84	2730	600.00	150.00	6.00
X16XC	16	2¾	3¼	1¼	4,6	27	112	3024	561.28	140.32	14.03
X203XC	20	3	3	1¼	2,4,6	26	84	2184	528.64	132.16	13.22
X20XC	20	2¾	2¾	1⅛	4,6,7½	26	112	2912	468.48	117.12	11.71
Xpert Field Loads—Packed 25 per Box, 500 per Case											
WW12SP	12	2¾	3¼	1¼	6,7½,8	56	60	3360	359.04	179.52	8.98
UWH12	12	2¾	3¼	1⅛	6,7½,8,9	50	60	3000	325.12	162.56	8.13
UWL12	12	2¾	3¼	1	6,7½,8	46	60	2760	292.48	146.24	7.31
UWH16#	16	2¾	2¾	1⅛	6,7½,8	50	64	3200	325.12	162.56	8.13
UWH20#	20	2¾	2½	1	6,7½,8,9	43	80	3440	304.00	152.00	7.60
UWL20	20	2¾	2½	⅞	6,7½,8	40	80	3200	292.48	146.24	7.31
Super-X Buckshot Loads with Buffered Shot—5 Round Pack—Packed 250 Rounds per Case unless noted											
X12000B5	12	2¾	8 Pellets		000 Buck	32	54	1728	608.00	152.00	3.04
X12RB▷	12	2¾	9 Pellets		00 Buck	52	60	3120	608.00	304.00	15.20
X12RB5	12	2¾	9 Pellets		00 Buck	27	54	1458	608.00	152.00	3.04
X120B5	12	2¾	12 Pellets		0 Buck	32	54	1728	608.00	152.00	3.04
X121B5	12	2¾	16 Pellets		1 Buck	33	54	1782	608.00	152.00	3.04
X124B5	12	2¾	27 Pellets		4 Buck	29	54	1566	608.00	152.00	3.04
X16B5	16	2¾	12 Pellets		1 Buck	26	91	2366	608.00	152.00	3.04
X20B5	20	2¾	20 Pellets		3 Buck	24	104	2496	608.00	152.00	3.04
Double X Magnum Buckshot Loads—Copperplated, Buffered Shot—5 Round Pack—Packed 250 Rounds per Case											
X10C4B	10	3½	54 Pellets		4 Buck	51	56	2856	1264.00	316.00	6.32
X123C000B	12	3	10 Pellets		000 Buck	35	54	1890	902.40	225.60	4.51
X12XC3B5	12	3	15 Pellets		00 Buck	39	54	2106	902.40	225.60	4.51
X12XC0B5	12	2¾	12 Pellets		00 Buck	33	54	1782	780.80	195.20	3.90
X12C1B	12	2¾	20 Pellets		1 Buck	38	54	2052	780.80	195.20	3.90
X12XCMB5	12	3	41 Pellets		4 Buck	38	54	2052	902.40	225.60	4.51
X12XC4B5	12	2¾	34 Pellets		4 Buck	33	54	1782	780.80	195.20	3.90
X1231B5	12	3	24 Pellets		1 Buck (Not Plated)	44	54	2376	902.40	225.60	4.51
Super-X Hollow Point Rifled Slug Loads—5 Round Pack—Packed 250 Rounds per Case											
X12RS15	12	2¾	Max.	1	Rifled Slug	26	63	1638	684.80	171.20	3.42
X16RS5	16	2¾	Max.	4/5	Rifled Slug	21	117	2457	684.80	171.20	3.42
X20RSM5	20	2¾	Max.	¾	Rifled Slug	19	117	2223	652.80	163.20	3.26
X41RS5	410	2½	Max.	1/5	Rifled Slug	8	198	1584	608.00	152.00	3.04
Super Steel Non-Toxic Game Loads—Packed 25 per Box, 500 per Case											
W12SD	12	2¾	Max.	1	2,4,6	46	60	2760	435.20	217.60	10.88
X12SSL	12	2¾	Max.	1⅛	1,2,3,4,5,6	52	60	3120	531.84	265.92	13.30
X20SSL	20	2¾	Max.	¾	4,6	36	80	2880	480.64	240.32	12.02
Super Steel Non-Toxic Magnum Loads—Packed 25 per Box, 250 per Case											
X10SSM	10	3½	Max.	1¾	BB,2	39	60	2340	899.84	224.96	22.50
X12SSM	12	3	Max.	1⅜	BB,1,2,3,4	33	84	2772	629.12	157.28	15.73
X123SSM	12	3	Max.	1¼	F,BB,1,2,3,4,5	32	84	2688	595.84	148.96	14.90
X12SSF▷	12	2¾	Max.	1¼	BB,1,2,3,4,5,6	56	60	3360	577.92	288.96	14.45
X20SSM	20	3	Max.	1	2,3,4,5,6	24	84	2016	504.96	126.24	12.62

#Loads with 7½ or 8 shot recommended for trap shooting
*Not Copperplated

●Packaged in 10 Round Trebark camouflage packaging, 250 Rounds per Case
▷Packed 25 Rounds per Box, 500 Rounds per Case
†Obsolete in 1989

Ballistics

FEDERAL BALLISTICS

Hi-Power Centerfire Rifle Ballistics (Approximate)

Usage Key: |1|=Varmints, predators, small game |2|=Medium game |3|=Large heavy game |4|=Dangerous game |5|=Target shooting, training, practice

Usage	Federal Load No.	Caliber	Grains	Grams	Bullet Style	Factory Primer No.	Muzzle	100 yds.	200 yds.	300 yds.	400 yds.	500 yds.	Muzzle	100 yds.	200 yds.	300 yds.	400 yds.	500 yds.
			Bullet Wgt. in				Velocity in Feet Per Second (To Nearest 10 Feet)						Energy in Foot/Pounds (To Nearest 5 Foot/Pounds)					
1	222A	222 Rem. (5.56x43mm)	50	3.24	Soft Point	205	3140	2600	2120	1700	1350	1110	1095	750	500	320	200	135
5	222B		55	3.56	FMJ Boat-tail	205	3020	2740	2480	2230	1990	1780	1115	915	750	610	485	385
1	22250A	22-250 Rem.	55	3.56	Soft Point	210	3680	3140	2660	2220	1830	1490	1655	1200	860	605	410	270
1	22250C		40	2.59	Hollow Point Varmint	210	4000	3320	2720	2200	1740	1360	1420	980	660	430	265	165
1	223A	223 Rem. (5.56x45mm)	55	3.56	Soft Point	205	3240	2750	2300	1910	1550	1270	1280	920	650	445	295	195
5	223B		55	3.56	FMJ Boat-tail	205	3240	2950	2670	2410	2170	1940	1280	1060	875	710	575	460
1	223C		55	3.56	Hollow Point Boat-tail	205	3240	2770	2340	1950	1610	1330	1280	935	670	465	315	215
1	223D		40	2.59	Hollow Point Varmint	205	3650	3010	2450	1950	1530	1210	1185	805	535	340	205	130
1	6A	6mm Rem.	80	5.18	Soft Point	210	3470	3060	2690	2350	2040	1750	2140	1665	1290	980	735	540
2	6B		100	6.48	Hi-Shok Soft Point	210	3100	2830	2570	2330	2100	1890	2135	1775	1470	1205	985	790
1	243A	243 Win. (6.16x51mm)	80	5.18	Soft Point	210	3350	2960	2590	2260	1950	1670	1995	1550	1195	905	675	495
2	243B		100	6.48	Hi-Shok Soft Point	210	2960	2700	2450	2220	1990	1790	1945	1615	1330	1090	880	710
1 NEW	243V		60	3.89	Hollow Point Varmint	210	3600	3110	2660	2260	1890	1560	1725	1285	945	680	475	325
2	257A	257 Roberts (H-Vel + P)	117	7.58	Hi-Shok Soft Point	210	2780	2560	2360	2160	1970	1790	2010	1710	1445	1210	1010	835
1	2506A	25-06 Rem.	90	5.83	Hollow Point Varmint	210	3440	3040	2680	2340	2030	1750	2365	1850	1435	1100	825	610
2	2506B		117	7.58	Hi-Shok Soft Point	210	2990	2730	2480	2250	2030	1830	2320	1985	1645	1350	1100	885
2	270A	270 Win.	130	8.42	Hi-Shok Soft Point	210	3060	2800	2560	2330	2110	1900	2700	2265	1890	1565	1285	1045
2	270B		150	9.72	Hi-Shok Soft Point RN	210	2850	2500	2180	1890	1620	1390	2705	2085	1585	1185	870	640
2	7A	7mm Mauser (7x57mm Mauser)	175	11.34	Hi-Shok Soft Point RN	210	2440	2140	1860	1600	1380	1200	2315	1775	1340	1000	740	565
2	7B		140	9.07	Hi-Shok Soft Point	210	2660	2450	2260	2070	1890	1730	2200	1865	1585	1330	1110	930
2	7RA	7mm Rem. Magnum	150	9.72	Hi-Shok Soft Point	215	3110	2830	2570	2320	2090	1870	3220	2670	2200	1790	1450	1160
3	7RB		175	11.34	Hi-Shok Soft Point	215	2860	2650	2440	2240	2060	1880	3180	2720	2310	1960	1640	1370
2	730A	7-30 Waters	120	7.77	Boat-tail Soft Point	210	2700	2300	1930	1600	1330	1140	1940	1405	990	685	470	345
1	30CA	30 Carbine	110	7.13	Hi-Shok Soft Point RN	205	1990	1570	1240	1040	920	840	965	600	375	260	210	175
2 NEW	76239B	7.62x39mm Soviet	123	7.97	Hi-Shok Soft Point	210	2300	2030	1780	1550	1350	1200	1445	1125	860	655	500	395
2	3030A	30-30 Win.	150	9.72	Hi-Shok Soft Point FN	210	2390	2020	1680	1400	1180	1040	1900	1355	945	650	460	355
2	3030B		170	11.01	Hi-Shok Soft Point FN	210	2200	1900	1620	1380	1190	1060	1830	1355	990	720	535	425
1	3030C		125	8.10	Hollow Point Varmint	210	2570	2090	1660	1320	1080	960	1830	1210	770	480	320	260
2	3006A	30-06 Springfield (7.62x63mm)	150	9.72	Hi-Shok Soft Point	210	2910	2620	2340	2080	1840	1620	2820	2280	1825	1445	1130	875
3	3006B		180	11.66	Hi-Shok Soft Point	210	2700	2470	2250	2040	1850	1660	2915	2435	2025	1665	1360	1105
1	3006C		125	8.10	Hi-Shok Soft Point	210	3140	2780	2450	2140	1850	1600	2735	2145	1660	1270	955	705
2	3006D		165	10.69	Boat-tail Soft Point	210	2800	2610	2420	2240	2070	1910	2870	2490	2150	1840	1580	1340
3	3006H		220	14.25	Hi-Shok Soft Point RN	210	2410	2130	1870	1630	1420	1250	2835	2215	1705	1300	985	760
3	3006J		180	11.66	Hi-Shok Soft Point RN	210	2700	2350	2020	1730	1470	1250	2915	2200	1630	1190	860	620
2	300A	300 Savage	150	9.72	Hi-Shok Soft Point	210	2630	2350	2100	1850	1630	1430	2305	1845	1460	1145	885	685
2	300B		180	11.66	Hi-Shok Soft Point	210	2350	2140	1940	1750	1570	1410	2205	1825	1495	1215	985	800
2	308A	308 Win (7.62x51mm)	150	9.72	Hi-Shok Soft Point	210	2820	2530	2260	2010	1770	1560	2650	2140	1705	1345	1050	810
2	308B		180	11.66	Hi-Shok Soft Point	210	2620	2390	2180	1970	1780	1600	2745	2290	1895	1555	1270	1030
3	300WB	300 Win. Magnum	180	11.66	Hi-Shok Soft Point	215	2960	2750	2540	2340	2160	1980	3500	3010	2580	2195	1860	1565
2 NEW	303A	303 British	180	11.66	Hi-Shok Soft Point	210	2460	2230	2020	1820	1630	1460	2420	1995	1625	1315	1060	850
2	*8A	8mm Mauser (8x57mm JS Mauser)	170	11.01	Hi-Shok Soft Point	210	2360	1970	1620	1330	1120	1000	2100	1465	995	670	475	375
2	32A	32 Win. Special	170	11.01	Hi-Shok Soft Point	210	2250	1920	1630	1370	1180	1040	1910	1395	1000	710	520	410
3 NEW	338C	338 Win. Magnum	225	14.58	Soft Point	215	2780	2570	2370	2180	2000	1830	3860	3305	2815	2380	2000	1670
2	35A	35 Rem.	200	12.96	Hi-Shok Soft Point	210	2080	1700	1380	1140	1000	910	1920	1280	840	575	445	370
2	357G	357 Magnum	180	11.66	Hollow Point	100	1550	1160	980	860	770	680	960	535	385	295	235	185
3 NEW	375A	375 H&H Magnum	270	17.50	Hi-Shok Soft Point	215	2690	2420	2170	1920	1700	1500	4340	3510	2810	2220	1740	1355
4 NEW	375B		300	19.44	Hi-Shok Soft Point	215	2530	2270	2020	1790	1580	1400	4265	3425	2720	2135	1665	1295
2	44A	44 Rem. Magnum	240	15.55	Hollow Point	150	1760	1380	1090	950	860	790	1650	1015	640	485	395	330
2	4570A	45-70 Government	300	19.44	Hollow Point	210	1880	1650	1430	1240	1110	1010	2355	1815	1355	1015	810	680

*Only for use in barrels intended for .323 inch diameter bullets. Do not use in 8x57mm J Commission Rifles (M1888) or in sporting or other military arms of .318 inch bore diameter.
These trajectory tables were calculated by computer using the best available data for each load. Trajectories are representative of the nominal behavior of each load at standard conditions (59°F temperature; barometric pressure of 29.53 inches; altitude at sea level). Shooters are cautioned that actual trajectories may differ due to variations in altitude, atmospheric conditions, guns, sights, and ammunition.
RN=Round Nose   FN=Flat Nose   FMJ=Full Metal Jacket   HP=Hollow Point

Match Rifle Ballistics (Approximate)   Usage Key: 5|=Target shooting, training, practice

Usage	Federal Load No.	Caliber	Grains	Grams	Bullet Style	Factory Primer No.	Muzzle	100 yds.	200 yds.	300 yds.	400 yds.	500 yds.	600 yds.	700 yds.	800 yds.	900 yds.	1000 yds.	Muzzle	100 yds.
			Bullet Wgt. in				Velocity in Feet Per Second (to Nearest 10 Feet)											Energy in Foot/Pounds	
5 NEW	223M	223 Rem. (5.56x45mm)	69	4.47	Boat-tail HP Match	205M	3000	2720	2460	2210	1980	1760	1560	1390	1240	1130	1060	1380	1135
5	308M	308 Win. (7.62x51mm)	168	10.88	Boat-tail HP Match	210M	2600	2420	2240	2070	1910	1760	1610	1480	1360	1260	1170	2520	2180

FEDERAL BALLISTICS

Wind Drift in Inches – 10 mph Crosswind					Height of Bullet Trajectory (Average Range)				Height of Bullet Trajectory (Long Range)						Test Barrel Length Inches	Federal Load No.
100 yds.	200 yds.	300 yds.	400 yds.	500 yds.	50 yds.	100 yds.	200 yds.	300 yds.	50 yds.	100 yds.	200 yds.	300 yds.	400 yds.	500 yds.		
1.7	7.3	18.3	36.4	63.1	−0.2	⊕	−3.7	−15.3	+0.7	+1.9	⊕	−9.7	−31.6	−71.3	24	222A
0.9	3.4	8.5	16.8	26.3	−0.2	⊕	−3.1	−12.0	+0.6	+1.6	⊕	−7.3	−21.5	−44.6	24	222B
1.2	5.2	12.5	24.4	42.0	−0.4	⊕	−2.1	−9.1	+0.1	+1.0	⊕	−6.0	−19.1	−42.6	24	22250A
1.3	5.7	14.0	27.9	49.2	−0.4	⊕	−1.7	−8.1	0	+0.8	⊕	−5.6	−18.4	−42.8	24	22250C
1.4	6.1	15.0	29.4	50.8	−0.3	⊕	−3.2	−12.9	+0.5	+1.6	⊕	−8.2	−26.1	−58.3	24	223A
0.8	3.3	7.8	14.5	24.0	−0.3	⊕	−2.5	−9.9	+0.3	+1.3	⊕	−6.1	−18.3	−37.8	24	223B
1.3	5.8	14.2	27.7	47.6	−0.3	⊕	−2.7	−10.8	+0.4	+1.4	⊕	−6.7	−20.5	−43.4	24	223C
1.5	6.5	16.1	32.3	56.9	−0.4	⊕	−2.4	−10.7	+0.2	+1.2	⊕	−7.1	−23.4	−54.2	24	223D
1.0	4.1	9.9	18.8	31.6	−0.3	⊕	−2.2	−9.3	+0.2	+1.1	⊕	−5.9	−18.2	−39.0	24	6A
0.8	3.3	7.9	14.7	24.1	−0.3	⊕	−2.9	−11.0	+0.5	+1.4	⊕	−6.7	−19.8	−40.6	24	6B
1.0	4.3	10.4	19.8	33.3	−0.3	⊕	−2.5	−10.2	+0.3	+1.3	⊕	−6.4	−19.7	−42.2	24	243A
0.9	3.6	8.4	15.7	25.8	−0.2	⊕	−3.3	−12.4	+0.6	+1.6	⊕	−7.5	−22.0	−45.4	24	243B
1.1	4.8	11.7	22.6	38.7	−0.4	⊕	−2.1	−9.2	+0.2	+1.1	⊕	−6.0	−18.9	−41.6	24	243V
0.8	3.3	7.7	14.3	23.4	−0.1	⊕	−3.8	−14.0	+0.8	+1.9	⊕	−8.2	−24.0	−48.9	24	257A
1.0	4.1	9.8	18.7	31.3	−0.3	⊕	−2.3	−9.4	+0.2	+1.1	⊕	−6.0	−18.3	−39.2	24	2506A
0.8	3.4	8.1	15.1	24.9	−0.2	⊕	−3.2	−12.0	+0.6	+1.6	⊕	−7.2	−21.4	−44.0	24	2506B
0.8	3.2	7.6	14.2	23.3	−0.2	⊕	−2.9	−11.2	+0.5	+1.5	⊕	−6.8	−20.0	−41.1	24	270A
1.2	5.3	12.8	24.5	41.3	−0.1	⊕	−4.1	−15.5	+0.9	+2.0	⊕	−9.4	−28.6	−61.0	24	270B
1.5	6.2	15.0	28.7	47.8	−0.1	⊕	−6.2	−22.6	+1.6	+3.1	⊕	−13.3	−40.1	−84.6	24	7A
1.3	3.2	8.2	15.4	23.4	−0.1	⊕	−4.3	−15.4	+1.0	+2.1	⊕	−9.0	−26.1	−52.9	24	7B
0.8	3.4	8.1	15.1	24.9	−0.3	⊕	−2.9	−11.0	+0.5	+1.4	⊕	−6.7	−19.9	−41.0	24	7RA
0.7	3.1	7.2	13.3	21.7	−0.2	⊕	−3.5	−12.6	+0.7	+1.7	⊕	−7.6	−22.1	−44.9	24	7RB
1.6	7.2	17.7	34.5	58.1	0	⊕	−5.2	−19.8	+1.2	+2.6	⊕	−12.0	−37.6	−81.7	24	730A
3.4	15.0	35.5	63.2	96.7	+0.6	⊕	−12.8	−46.9	+3.9	+6.4	⊕	−27.7	−81.8	−167.8	18	30CA
1.5	6.4	15.2	28.7	47.3	+0.2	⊕	−7.0	−25.1	+1.9	+3.5	⊕	−14.5	−43.4	−90.6	20	76239B
2.0	8.5	20.9	40.1	66.1	+0.2	⊕	−7.2	−26.7	+1.9	+3.6	⊕	−15.9	−49.1	−104.5	24	3030A
1.9	8.0	19.4	36.7	59.8	+0.3	⊕	−8.3	−29.8	+2.4	+4.1	⊕	−17.4	−52.4	−109.4	24	3030B
2.2	10.1	25.4	49.4	81.6	+0.1	⊕	−6.6	−26.0	+1.7	+3.3	⊕	−16.0	−50.9	−109.5	24	3030C
1.0	4.2	9.9	18.7	31.2	−0.2	⊕	−3.6	−13.6	+0.7	+1.8	⊕	−8.2	−24.4	−50.9	24	3006A
0.9	3.7	8.8	16.5	27.1	−0.1	⊕	−4.2	−15.3	+1.0	+2.1	⊕	−9.0	−26.4	−54.0	24	3006B
1.1	4.5	10.8	20.5	34.4	−0.3	⊕	−3.0	−11.9	+0.5	+1.5	⊕	−7.3	−22.3	−47.5	24	3006C
0.7	2.8	6.6	12.3	19.9	0.2	⊕	−3.6	−13.2	+0.8	+1.8	⊕	−7.8	−22.4	−45.2	24	3006D
1.4	6.0	14.3	27.2	45.0	−0.1	⊕	−6.2	−22.4	+1.7	+3.1	⊕	−13.1	−39.3	−82.2	24	3006H
1.5	6.4	15.7	30.4	51.2	−0.1	⊕	−4.9	−18.3	+1.1	+2.4	⊕	−11.0	−33.6	−71.9	24	3006J
1.1	4.8	11.6	21.9	36.3	0	⊕	−4.8	−17.6	+1.2	+2.4	⊕	−10.4	−30.9	−64.4	24	300A
1.1	4.6	10.9	20.3	33.3	+0.1	⊕	−6.1	−21.6	+1.7	+3.1	⊕	−12.4	−36.1	−73.8	24	300B
1.0	4.4	10.4	19.7	32.7	−0.1	⊕	−3.9	−14.7	+0.8	+2.0	⊕	−8.8	−26.3	−54.8	24	308A
0.9	3.9	9.2	17.2	28.3	−0.1	⊕	−4.6	−16.5	+1.1	+2.3	⊕	−9.7	−28.3	−57.8	24	308B
0.7	2.8	6.6	12.3	20.0	−0.2	⊕	−3.1	−11.7	+0.6	+1.6	⊕	−7.0	−20.3	−41.1	24	300WB
1.1	4.5	10.6	19.9	32.7	0	⊕	−5.5	−19.6	+1.4	+2.8	⊕	−11.3	−33.2	−68.1	24	303A
2.1	9.3	22.9	43.9	71.7	+0.2	⊕	−7.6	−28.5	+2.1	+3.8	⊕	−17.1	−52.9	−111.9	24	8A
1.9	8.4	20.3	38.6	63.0	+0.3	⊕	−8.0	−29.2	+2.3	+4.0	⊕	−17.2	−52.3	−109.8	24	32A
0.8	3.1	7.3	13.6	22.2	−0.1	⊕	−3.8	−13.7	+0.8	+1.9	⊕	−8.1	−23.5	−47.5	24	338C
2.7	12.0	29.0	53.3	83.3	+0.5	⊕	−10.7	−39.3	+3.2	+5.4	⊕	−23.3	−70.0	−144.0	24	35A
5.8	21.7	45.2	76.1	NA	⊕	−3.4	−29.7	−88.2	+1.7	⊕	−22.8	−77.9	−173.8	−321.4	18	357G
1.1	4.5	10.8	20.3	33.7	+0.4	⊕	−5.5	−18.4	+1.0	+2.2	⊕	−9.7	−28.8	−59.9	24	375A
1.2	5.0	11.9	22.4	37.1	+0.5	⊕	−6.3	−21.2	+1.3	+2.6	⊕	−11.2	−33.3	−69.1	24	375B
4.2	17.8	39.8	68.3	102.5	⊕	−2.2	−21.7	−67.2	+1.1	⊕	−17.4	−60.7	−136.0	−250.2	20	44A
1.7	7.6	18.6	35.7	NA	⊕	−1.3	−14.1	−43.7	+0.7	⊕	−11.5	−39.7	−89.1	−163.1	24	4570A

Energy in Foot/Pounds (to Nearest 5 Foot/Pounds)									Wind Drift in Inches – 10 mph Crosswind										Height of Bullet Trajectory (Sights 1.5 Inches Above Bore Line)									
200 yds.	300 yds.	400 yds.	500 yds.	600 yds.	700 yds.	800 yds.	900 yds.	1000 yds.	100 yds.	200 yds.	300 yds.	400 yds.	500 yds.	600 yds.	700 yds.	800 yds.	900 yds.	1000 yds.	100 yds.	200 yds.	300 yds.	400 yds.	500 yds.	600 yds.	700 yds.	800 yds.	900 yds.	1000 yds.
925	750	600	475	375	295	235	195	170	0.9	3.7	8.7	16.3	27.0	41.3	59.5	82.2	109.2	140.0	+1.6	⊕	−7.4	−21.9	−45.3	−79.8	−128.7	−194.1	−280.2	−388.7
1870	1600	1355	1150	970	815	690	590	510	0.8	3.1	7.4	13.6	22.2	33.3	47.1	64.1	84.2	107.5	+17.5	+30.5	+36.6	+34.5	+22.9	⊕	−36.1	−87.8	−157.5	−247.4

FEDERAL/NORMA BALLISTICS

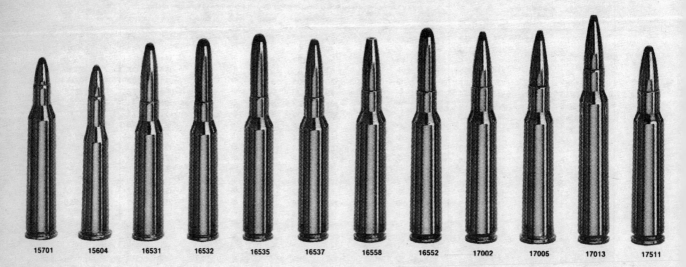

| 15701 | 15604 | 16531 | 16532 | 16535 | 16537 | 16558 | 16552 | 17002 | 17005 | 17013 | 17511 |

Norma Centerfire Rifle Ballistics (Approximate)   Usage Key: |1|=Varmints, predators, small game |2|=Medium game |3|=Large heavy game

Usage	Federal Load No.	Caliber	Bullet Wgt. in Grains	Grams	Bullet Style	Factory Primer	Velocity in Feet Per Second (to Nearest 10 Feet) Muzzle	100 yds.	200 yds.	300 yds.	400 yds.	500 yds.	Energy in Foot/Pounds (to Nearest 5 Foot/Pounds) Muzzle	100 yds.	200 yds.	300 yds.	400 yds.	500 yds.
|1|	15701	220 Swift	50	3.24	Soft Point	Large Rifle	4110	3570	3080	2640	2240	1870	1875	1415	1055	775	555	390
|1|	15604	22 Savage HiPwr (5.6x52Rmm)	71	4.60	Soft Point	Large Rifle	2790	2340	1930	1570	1280	1090	1225	860	585	390	260	190
|2|	16531	6.5x50mm Japanese	139	9.00	Boat-tail Soft Point	Large Rifle	2360	2160	1970	1790	1620	1470	1720	1440	1195	985	810	665
|2|	16532	6.5x50mm Japanese	156	10.10	Soft Point Alaska	Large Rifle	2070	1830	1610	1420	1260	1140	1475	1155	900	695	550	445
|2|	16535	6.5x52mm Carcano	156	10.10	Soft Point Alaska	Large Rifle	2430	2170	1930	1700	1500	1320	2045	1630	1285	1005	780	605
|2|	16537	6.5x52mm Carcano	139	9.00	Soft Point	Large Rifle	2580	2360	2160	1970	1790	1620	2045	1725	1440	1195	985	810
|2|	16558	6.5x55mm Swedish	139	9.00	Prot'd Power Cavity	Large Rifle	2850	2560	2290	2030	1790	1570	2515	2025	1615	1270	985	760
|2|	16552	6.5x55mm Swedish	156	10.10	Soft Point Alaska	Large Rifle	2650	2370	2110	1870	1650	1450	2425	1950	1550	1215	945	730
|2|	17002	7x57mm Mauser	154	9.97	Soft Point	Large Rifle	2690	2490	2300	2120	1940	1780	2475	2120	1810	1530	1285	1080
|2|	17005	7x57Rmm	154	9.97	Soft Point	Large Rifle	2630	2430	2250	2070	1900	1740	2355	2020	1725	1460	1230	1035
|2| NEW	17012	7x61mm Sharpe & Hart Super	154	9.97	Soft Point	Large Rifle	3060	2720	2400	2100	1820	1580	3200	2520	1965	1505	1135	850
|2|	17013	7x64mm Brenneke	154	9.97	Soft Point	Large Rifle	2820	2610	2420	2230	2050	1870	2720	2335	1995	1695	1430	1200
|2|	17511	7.5x55mm Swiss	180	11.66	Boat-tail Soft Point	Large Rifle	2650	2450	2250	2060	1880	1720	2805	2390	2020	1700	1415	1180
|3|	17638	308 Norma Magnum	180	11.66	Dual Core	Large Magnum Rifle	3020	2820	2630	2440	2270	2090	3645	3175	2755	2385	2050	1750
|2|	17634	7.62x54Rmm Russian	180	11.66	Boat-tail Soft Point	Large Rifle	2580	2370	2180	2000	1820	1660	2650	2250	1900	1590	1325	1100
|2|	17637	7.62x54Rmm Russian	150	9.72	Soft Point	Large Rifle	2950	2700	2450	2220	2000	1800	2905	2420	2005	1645	1335	1075
|2|	17701	7.65x53mm Argentine	150	9.72	Soft Point	Large Rifle	2660	2380	2120	1880	1660	1460	2355	1895	1500	1175	915	705
|2|	17702	7.65x53mm Argentine	180	11.66	Soft Point	Large Rifle	2590	2390	2200	2010	1830	1670	2685	2280	1925	1615	1345	1115
|2|	17712	303 British	150	9.72	Soft Point	Large Rifle	2720	2440	2180	1930	1700	1500	2465	1985	1580	1240	965	745
|2|	17721	7.7x58mm Japanese	130	8.42	Soft Point	Large Rifle	2950	2530	2150	1800	1500	1260	2510	1850	1335	935	650	455
|2|	17722	7.7x58mm Japanese	180	11.66	Boat-tail Soft Point	Large Rifle	2500	2300	2100	1920	1750	1590	2490	2105	1770	1475	1225	1015
|2|	*18017	8x57mm JS Mauser	165	10.69	Prot'd Power Cavity	Large Rifle	2850	2520	2210	1930	1670	1440	2985	2330	1795	1360	1015	755
|3|	*18003	8x57mm JS Mauser	196	12.70	Soft Point Alaska	Large Rifle	2530	2200	1890	1620	1380	1200	2775	2100	1555	1140	830	625
|3|	19303	9.3x57mm Mauser	286	18.53	Soft Point Alaska	Large Rifle	2070	1810	1590	1390	1230	1110	2710	2090	1600	1220	955	780
|3|	19315	9.3x62mm Mauser	286	18.53	Soft Point Alaska	Large Rifle	2360	2090	1840	1610	1410	1240	3535	2770	2145	1645	1255	980
|3| NEW	19001	358 Norma Magnum	250	16.2	Soft Point	Large Magnum Rifle	2800	2510	2230	1970	1730	1510	4350	3480	2750	2145	1655	1265

*Only for use in barrels intended for .323 inch diameter bullets. Do not use in 8x57mm J Commission Rifles (M1888) or in sporting or other military arms of .318 inch bore diameter.

Norma Pistol and Revolver Ballistics (Approximate)   Usage Key: |3|=Self defense |4|=Target shooting, training, practice

Usage	Federal Load No.	Caliber	Bullet Wgt. in Grains	Grams	Bullet Style	Factory Primer	Velocity in Feet Per Second Muzzle	25 yds.	50 yds.	75 yds.	100 yds.	Energy in Foot/Pounds Muzzle	25 yds.	50 yds.	75 yds.	100 yds.	Mid-Range Trajectory 25 yds.	50 yds.	75 yds.	100 yds.	Test Barrel Length Inches
|3|, |4|	11001	10mm Auto	200	12.96	FMJ	Large Pistol	1120	1080	1040	1010	980	555	515	480	450	425	0.2	0.9	2.2	4.0	5
|3|	11002	10mm Auto	170	11.01	JHP	Large Pistol	1300	1210	1140	1090	1040	640	555	490	445	410	0.2	0.7	1.8	3.3	5

FEDERAL/NORMA BALLISTICS

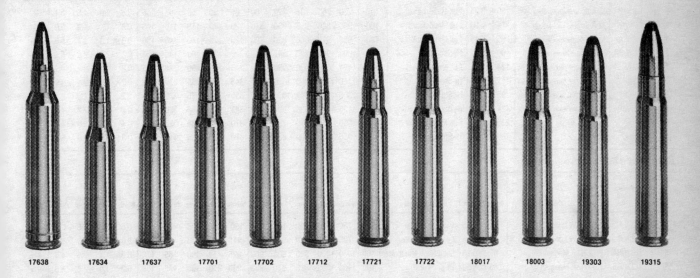

17638 17634 17637 17701 17702 17712 17721 17722 18017 18003 19303 19315

| Wind Drift in Inches 10 mph Crosswind | | | | | Height of Bullet Trajectory in Inches Above or Below Line of Sight if Zeroed at + Yards. Sights 1.5 Inches Above Bore Line. | | | | | | | | | | Test Barrel Length Inches | Federal Load No. |
| | | | | | Average Range | | | | Long Range | | | | | | | |
100 yds.	200 yds.	300 yds.	400 yds.	500 yds.	50 yds.	100 yds.	200 yds.	300 yds.	50 yds.	100 yds.	200 yds.	300 yds.	400 yds.	500 yds.		
0.9	4.0	9.7	18.6	31.6	−0.5	⊕	−1.2	− 3.2	−0.1	+0.6	⊕	− 4.3	−13.6	− 29.9	24	15701
1.8	7.7	19.2	37.6	63.6	−0.1	⊕	−4.9	−19.3	+1.2	+2.5	⊕	−11.9	−37.7	− 83.0	24	15604
1.0	4.3	10.1	18.8	30.7	+0.1	⊕	−6.0	−21.0	+1.6	+3.0	⊕	−12.0	−34.8	− 70.7	24	16531
1.6	6.8	16.2	30.3	49.0	+0.4	⊕	−8.9	−31.2	+2.6	+4.5	⊕	−17.8	−52.7	−108.4	24	16532
1.3	5.4	12.8	24.2	40.0	+0.1	⊕	−5.9	−21.3	+1.6	+3.0	⊕	−12.4	−36.8	− 76.4	24	16535
0.9	3.7	8.8	16.5	27.0	0	⊕	−4.8	−17.1	+1.2	+2.4	⊕	− 9.9	−29.0	− 59.3	24	16537
1.0	4.3	10.4	19.6	32.6	−0.2	⊕	−3.8	−14.3	+0.8	+1.9	⊕	− 8.6	−25.7	53.6	24	16558
1.1	4.7	11.3	21.4	35.5	−0.1	⊕	−4.7	−17.3	+1.1	+2.4	⊕	−10.3	−30.6	− 63.9	24	16552
0.8	3.2	7.5	13.9	22.8	−0.1	⊕	−4.1	−14.9	+0.9	+2.1	⊕	− 8.7	−25.1	− 50.9	24	17002
0.8	3.3	7.6	14.2	23.1	−0.1	⊕	−4.4	−15.8	+1.0	−2.2	⊕	− 9.2	−26.6	− 53.9	24	17005
1.1	4.5	10.8	20.5	34.5	−0.2	⊕	−3.2	−12.6	+0.6	+1.6	⊕	− 7.7	−23.4	− 49.5	24	17012
0.7	3.0	7.1	13.1	21.3	−0.2	⊕	−3.6	−13.2	+0.7	+1.8	⊕	− 7.8	−22.7	− 46.1	24	17013
0.8	3.4	8.0	14.9	24.3	−0.1	⊕	−4.3	−15.5	+1.0	+2.2	⊕	− 9.0	−26.1	− 52.9	24	17511
0.6	2.5	5.9	10.9	17.6	−0.2	⊕	−2.9	−10.8	+0.5	+1.4	⊕	− 6.5	−18.8	− 37.8	24	17638
0.9	3.6	8.4	15.6	25.4	0	⊕	−4.7	−16.8	+1.1	+2.4	⊕	− 9.8	−28.5	− 57.9	24	17634
0.8	3.5	8.2	15.4	25.3	−0.2	⊕	−3.3	−12.3	+0.6	+1.6	⊕	− 7.4	−21.7	− 44.6	24	17637
1.1	4.7	11.3	21.4	35.6	−0.1	⊕	−4.7	−17.2	+1.1	+2.3	⊕	−10.2	−30.3	− 63.2	24	17701
0.8	3.5	8.3	15.4	25.2	0	⊕	−4.6	−16.4	+1.1	+2.3	⊕	− 9.5	−27.6	− 56.0	24	17702
1.1	4.6	10.9	20.7	34.4	−0.1	⊕	−4.4	−16.1	+1.0	+2.2	⊕	− 9.6	−28.5	− 59.5	24	17712
1.4	6.2	15.1	29.4	50.1	−0.2	⊕	−4.0	−15.6	+0.8	+2.0	⊕	− 9.6	−30.1	− 65.8	24	17721
0.9	3.8	8.9	16.5	27.0		⊕	−5.1	−18.0	+1.3	+2.5	⊕	−10.4	−30.2	− 61.2	24	17722
1.2	5.0	12.1	23.1	38.8	−0.1	⊕	−4.0	−15.2	+0.9	+2.0	⊕	− 9.2	−27.8	− 58.8	24	18017
1.5	6.5	15.8	30.3	50.6	0	⊕	−5.7	−21.2	+1.5	−2.9	⊕	−12.6	−38.4	− 81.8	24	18003
1.7	7.3	17.4	32.4	52.3	+0.4	⊕	−9.2	−32.3	+2.7	+3.8	⊕	−18.6	−55.2	−113.8	24	19303
1.4	6.0	14.3	27.1	44.7	+0.1	⊕	−6.5	−23.3	+1.8	+3.3	⊕	−13.6	−40.5	− 84.5	24	19315
1.1	4.6	11.0	20.8	34.7	−0.1	⊕	−4.1	−15.2	+0.9	+2.0	⊕	− 9.1	−27.2	− 57.0	24	19001

These trajectory tables were calculated by computer using the best available data for each load. Trajectories are representative of the nominal behavior of each load at standard conditions (59°F temperature; barometric pressure of 29.53 inches; altitude at sea level). Shooters are cautioned that actual trajectories may differ due to variations in altitude, atmospheric conditions, guns, sights, and ammunition.

FEDERAL BALLISTICS

Automatic Pistol Ballistics (Approximate) Usage Key: 1=Varmints, predators, small game 2=Medium game 3=Self defense 4=Target shooting, training, practice

Usage	Federal Load No.	Caliber	Bullet Wgt. in Grains	Grams	Bullet Style	Factory Primer No.	Velocity in Feet Per Second Muzzle	25 yds.	50 yds.	75 yds.	100 yds.	Energy in Foot-Pounds Muzzle	25 yds.	50 yds.	75 yds.	100 yds.	Mid-Range Trajectory 25 yds.	50 yds.	75 yds.	100 yds.	Test Barrel Length Inches
3, 4	25AP	25 Auto (6.35mm Browning)	50	3.24	Full Metal Jacket	100	760	750	730	720	700	65	60	59	55	55	0.5	1.9	4.5	8.1	2
3, 4	32AP	32 Auto (7.65mm Browning)	71	4.60	Full Metal Jacket	100	905	880	855	830	810	129	120	115	110	105	0.3	1.4	3.2	5.9	4
3, 4	380AP	380 Auto (9x17mm Short)	95	6.15	Full Metal Jacket	100	955	910	865	830	790	190	175	160	145	130	0.3	1.3	3.1	5.8	3¾
3	380BP	380 Auto (9x17mm Short)	90	5.83	Hi-Shok JHP	100	1000	940	890	840	800	200	175	160	140	130	0.3	1.2	2.9	5.5	3¾
3, 4	9AP	9mm Luger (9x19mm Parabellum)	124	8.03	Full Metal Jacket	100	1120	1070	1030	990	960	345	315	290	270	255	0.2	0.9	2.2	4.1	4
3	9BP	9mm Luger (9x19mm Parabellum)	115	7.45	Hi-Shok JHP	100	1160	1100	1060	1020	990	345	310	285	270	250	0.2	0.9	2.1	3.8	4
3	9CP	9mm Luger (9x19mm Parabellum)	95	6.15	Hi-Shok JSP	100	1300	1190	1140	1050	1010	355	300	275	235	215	0.2	0.8	1.8	3.4	4
3	N9BP	9mm Luger (9x19mm Parabellum)	124	8.03	Nyclad Hollow Point	100	1120	1070	1030	990	960	345	315	290	270	255	0.2	0.9	2.2	4.1	4
3, 4	45A	45 Auto	230	14.90	Full Metal Jacket	150	850	830	810	790	770	370	350	335	320	305	0.4	1.6	3.6	6.6	5
3	45C	45 Auto	185	11.99	Hi-Shok JHP	150	950	920	900	880	860	370	350	335	315	300	0.3	1.3	2.9	5.3	5

Revolver Ballistics (Approximate)

Usage	Federal Load No.	Caliber	Bullet Wgt. in Grains	Grams	Bullet Style	Factory Primer No.	Velocity in Feet Per Second Muzzle	25 yds.	50 yds.	75 yds.	100 yds.	Energy in Foot/Pounds Muzzle	25 yds.	50 yds.	75 yds.	100 yds.	Mid-Range Trajectory 25 yds.	50 yds.	75 yds.	100 yds.	Test Barrel Length Inches
4	32LA	32 S&W Long	98	6.35	Lead Wadcutter	100	780	700	630	560	500	130	105	85	70	55	0.5	2.2	5.6	11.1	4
4	32LB	32 S&W Long	98	6.35	Lead Round Nose	100	705	690	670	650	640	115	105	98	95	90	0.6	2.3	5.3	9.6	4
3	32HRA	32 H&R Magnum	95	6.15	Lead Semi-Wadcutter	100	1030	1000	940	930	900	225	210	190	185	170	0.3	1.1	2.5	4.7	4½
3	32HRB	32 H&R Magnum	85	5.50	Hi-Shok JHP	100	1100	1050	1020	970	930	230	210	195	175	165	0.2	1.0	2.3	4.3	4½
3 NEW	9FA	9mm Federal	115	7.45	Hi-Shok JHP	100	1280	1200	1130	1080	1040	420	370	330	300	280	0.2	0.7	1.8	3.3	4-V
4	38B	38 Special	158	10.23	Lead Round Nose	100	755	740	723	710	690	200	190	183	175	170	0.5	2.0	4.6	8.3	4-V
4	N38B	38 Special	158	10.23	Nyclad Round Nose	100	755	740	723	710	690	200	190	183	175	170	0.5	2.0	4.6	8.3	4-V
3, 4	38C	38 Special	158	10.23	Lead Semi-Wadcutter	100	755	740	723	710	690	200	190	183	175	170	0.5	2.0	4.6	8.3	4-V
3	N38M	38 Special	125	8.10	Nyclad Hollow Point	100	825	780	730	690	650	190	170	150	130	115	0.4	1.8	4.3	8.1	2-V
1, 3	38E	38 Special (High Velocity +P)	125	8.10	Hi-Shok JHP	100	945	920	898	880	860	248	235	224	215	205	0.3	1.3	2.9	5.4	4-V
1, 3	38F	38 Special (High Velocity +P)	110	7.13	Hi-Shok JHP	100	995	960	926	900	870	242	225	210	195	185	0.3	1.2	2.7	5.0	4-V
1, 3	38G	38 Special (High Velocity +P)	158	10.23	Semi-Wadcutter HP	100	890	870	855	840	820	278	265	257	245	235	0.3	1.4	3.3	5.9	4-V
1, 3	N38G	38 Special (High Velocity +P)	158	10.23	Nyclad SWC-HP	100	890	870	855	840	820	270	265	257	245	235	0.3	1.4	3.3	5.9	4-V
3, 4	38H	38 Special (High Velocity +P)	158	10.23	Lead Semi-Wadcutter	100	890	870	855	840	820	270	265	257	245	235	0.3	1.4	3.3	5.9	4-V
1, 3	38J	38 Special (High Velocity +P)	125	8.10	Hi-Shok JSP	100	945	920	898	880	860	248	235	224	215	205	0.3	1.3	2.9	5.4	4-V
1, 3	N38N	38 Special (High Velocity +P)	125	8.10	Nyclad Hollow Point	100	945	920	898	880	860	248	235	224	215	205	0.3	1.3	2.9	5.4	4-V
2, 3	357A	357 Magnum	158	10.23	Hi-Shok JSP	100	1235	1160	1104	1060	1020	535	475	428	395	365	0.2	0.8	1.9	3.5	4-V
1, 3	357B	357 Magnum	125	8.10	Hi-Shok JHP	100	1450	1340	1240	1160	1100	583	495	427	370	335	0.1	0.6	1.5	2.8	4-V
4	357C	357 Magnum	158	10.23	Lead Semi-Wadcutter	100	1235	1160	1104	1060	1020	535	475	428	395	365	0.2	0.8	1.9	3.5	4-V
1, 3	357D	357 Magnum	110	7.13	Hi-Shok JHP	100	1295	1190	1094	1040	990	410	340	292	260	235	0.2	0.8	1.9	3.5	4-V
2, 3	357E	357 Magnum	158	10.23	Hi-Shok JHP	100	1235	1160	1104	1060	1020	535	475	428	395	365	0.2	0.8	1.9	3.5	4-V
2, 3	N357E	357 Magnum	158	10.23	Nyclad SWC-HP	100	1235	1160	1104	1060	1020	535	475	428	395	365	0.2	0.8	1.9	3.5	4-V
2	357G	357 Magnum	180	11.66	Hi-Shok JHP	100	1090	1030	980	930	890	475	425	385	350	320	0.2	1.0	2.4	4.5	4-V
1, 2, 3	41A	41 Rem. Magnum	210	13.60	Hi-Shok JHP	150	1300	1210	1130	1070	1030	790	680	595	540	495	0.2	0.7	1.8	3.3	4-V
1, 3	44SA	44 S&W Special	200	12.96	Semi-Wadcutter HP	150	900	860	830	800	770	360	330	305	285	260	0.3	1.4	3.4	6.3	6½-V
1, 2, 3	44A	44 Rem. Magnum	240	15.55	Hi-Shok JHP	150	1180	1130	1081	1050	1010	741	675	623	580	550	0.2	0.9	2.0	3.7	6½-V
1, 2	44B	44 Rem. Magnum	180	11.66	Hi-Shok JHP	150	1610	1480	1365	1270	1180	1035	875	750	640	555	0.1	0.5	1.2	2.3	6½-V
1, 3	45LCA	45 Colt	225	14.58	Semi-Wadcutter HP	150	900	880	860	840	820	405	385	369	355	340	0.3	1.4	3.2	5.8	5½

+P ammunition is loaded to a higher pressure. Use only in firearms so recommended by the gun manufacturer.   "V" indicates vented barrel to simulate service conditions.

Premium Hydro-Shok™ Pistol and Revolver Ballistics (Approximate) Usage Key: 3=Self defense

Usage	Federal Load No.	Caliber	Bullet Wgt. in Grains	Grams	Bullet Style	Factory Primer No.	Velocity in Feet Per Second Muzzle	25 yds.	50 yds.	75 yds.	100 yds.	Energy in Foot-Pounds Muzzle	25 yds.	50 yds.	75 yds.	100 yds.	Mid-Range Trajectory 25 yds.	50 yds.	75 yds.	100 yds.	Test Barrel Length Inches
3 NEW	P9HS1	9mm Luger (9x19mm Parabellum)	124	8.03	Hydra-Shok HP	100	1120	1070	1030	990	960	345	315	290	270	255	0.2	0.9	2.2	4.1	4
3 NEW	P9HS2	9mm Luger (9x19mm Parabellum)	147	9.52	Hydra-Shok HP	100	1050	1010	980	950	920	360	335	310	295	275	0.3	1.1	2.5	4.5	4
3 NEW	P45HS1	45 Auto	230	14.90	Hydra-Shok HP	150	850	830	810	790	770	370	350	335	320	305	0.4	1.6	3.6	6.6	5
3 NEW	P38HS1	38 Special (High Velocity +P)	129	8.36	Hydra-Shok HP	100	945	930	910	890	870	255	245	235	225	215	0.3	1.3	2.9	5.3	4-V
3 NEW	P357HS1	357 Magnum	158	10.23	Hydra-Shok HP	100	1235	1160	1104	1060	1020	535	475	428	395	365	0.2	0.8	1.9	3.5	4-V

+P ammunition is loaded to a higher pressure. Use only in firearms so recommended by the gun manufacturer.   "V" indicates vented barrel to simulate service conditions.

HORNADY BALLISTICS

RIFLE	MUZZLE VELOCITY	VELOCITY FEET PER SECOND					ENERGY FOOT - POUNDS						TRAJECTORY TABLES				
Caliber	Muzzle	100 yds.	200 yds.	300 yds.	400 yds.	500 yds.	Muzzle	100 yds.	200 yds.	300 yds.	400 yds.	500 yds.	100 yds.	200 yds.	300 yds.	400 yds.	500 yds.
222 Rem., 50 gr. SX	3140	2602	2123	1700	1350	1107	1094	752	500	321	302	136	+2.2	0.0	−10.0	−32.3	−73.8
222 Rem., 55 gr. SX	3020	2562	2147	1773	1451	1201	1114	801	563	384	257	176	+2.2	0.0	−9.9	−31.0	−68.7
223 Rem., 53 gr. HP	3330	2882	2477	2106	1710	1475	1305	978	722	522	369	356	+1.7	0.0	−7.4	−22.7	−49.1
223 Rem., 55 gr. SP	3240	2747	2304	1905	1554	1270	1282	921	648	443	295	197	+1.9	0.0	−8.5	−26.7	−59.6
223 Rem., 55 gr. FMJ	3240	2759	2326	1933	1587	1301	1282	929	660	456	307	207	+1.9	0.0	−8.4	−26.2	−57.9
223 Rem., 60 gr. SP	3150	2782	2442	2127	1837	1575	1322	1031	795	603	450	331	+1.6	0.0	−7.5	−22.5	−48.1
22-250 Rem., 53 gr. HP	3680	3185	2743	2341	1974	1646	1594	1194	886	645	459	319	+1.0	-0-	−5.7	−17.8	−38.8
22-250 Rem., 55 gr. SP	3680	3137	2656	2222	1832	1439	1654	1201	861	603	410	272	+1.1	-0-	−6.0	−19.2	−42.6
22-250 Rem., 55 gr. FMJ	3680	3137	2656	2222	1836	1439	1654	1201	861	603	410	273	+1.1	-0-	−6.0	−19.2	−42.6
22-250 Rem., 60 gr. SP	3600	3195	2826	2485	2169	1878	1727	1360	1064	823	627	470	+1.0	-0-	−5.4	−16.3	−34.8
220 Swift, 55 gr. SP	3650	3194	2772	2384	2035	1724	1627	1246	939	694	506	363	+1.0	-0-	−5.6	−17.4	−37.5
220 Swift, 60 gr. HP	3600	3199	2824	2475	2156	1868	1727	1364	1063	816	619	465	+1.0	-0-	−5.4	−16.3	−34.8
243 Win., 75 gr. HP	3400	2970	2578	2219	1890	1595	1926	1469	1107	820	595	425	+1.2	-0-	−6.5	−20.3	−43.8
243 Win., 80 gr. FMJ	3350	2955	2593	2259	1951	1670	1993	1551	1194	906	676	495	+1.2	-0-	−6.5	−19.9	−42.5
243 Win., 87 gr. SP	3300	2992	2705	2435	2181	1943	2104	1730	1414	1146	919	729	+1.2	-0-	−6.1	−18.0	−37.3
243 Win., 100 BTSP	2960	2728	2508	2299	2099	1910	1945	1653	1397	1174	979	810	+1.6	-0-	−7.2	−21.0	−42.8
6MM Rem., 100 BTSP	3100	2861	2634	2419	2231	2018	2134	1818	1541	1300	1088	904	+1.3	-0-	−6.5	−18.9	−38.5
257 Roberts, 100 SP (+P)	3000	2633	2295	1982	1697	1447	1998	1539	1169	872	639	465	+1.7	-0-	−8.5	−25.9	−55.5
257 Roberts, 117 gr. BTSP (+P)	2780	2587	2402	2225	2055	1893	2008	1739	1499	1286	1097	931	+1.7	-0-	−8.0	−23.2	−46.5
25-06 100 gr. SP	3230	2893	2580	2287	2014	1762	2316	1858	1478	1161	901	689	+1.6	-0-	−6.9	−20.5	−42.7
25-06 117 gr. BTSP	2990	2788	2595	2409	2232	2062	2323	2020	1750	1508	1295	1105	+1.6	-0-	−6.6	−19.4	−39.3
270 Win., 130 gr. SP	3060	2800	2560	2330	2110	1900	2700	2265	1890	1565	1285	1045	+1.8	-0-	−7.1	−20.6	−42.0
270 Win., 140 gr. BTSP	2940	2747	2562	2385	2214	2050	2688	2346	2041	1769	1524	1307	+1.6	-0-	−7.0	−20.2	−40.3
270 Win., 150 gr. SP	2850	2500	2180	1890	1620	1390	2705	2085	1585	1185	870	640	+2.0	-0-	−9.7	−29.2	−62.2
7 x 57 Mau., 139 gr. BTSP	2700	2504	2316	2137	1965	1802	2251	1936	1656	1410	1192	1002	+2.0	-0-	−8.5	−24.9	−50.3
7 x 57 Mau., 154 gr. SP	2600	2400	2208	2025	1852	1689	2312	1970	1668	1403	1173	976	+2.2	-0-	−9.5	−27.7	−55.8
7MM Rem. Mag., 139 gr. BTSP	3150	2933	2727	2530	2341	2160	3063	2656	2296	1976	1692	1440	+1.2	-0-	−6.1	−17.7	−35.5
7MM Rem. Mag., 154 gr. SP	3035	2814	2604	2404	2212	2029	3151	2708	2319	1977	1674	1408	+1.3	-0-	−6.7	−19.3	−39.3
7MM Rem. Mag., 162 gr. BTSP	2940	2757	2582	2413	2251	2094	3110	2735	2399	2095	1823	1578	+1.6	-0-	−6.7	−19.7	−39.3
7MM Rem. Mag., 175 gr. SP	2860	2650	2440	2240	2060	1880	3180	2720	2310	1960	1640	1370	+2.0	-0-	−7.9	−22.7	−45.8
30 M1 Carb., 110 gr. RN	1990	1570	1240	1040	920	840	965	600	375	260	210	175	-0-	−13.5	−49.9		
30 M1 Carb., 110 gr. FMJ	1990	1600	1280	1070	950	870	970	620	400	280	220	185	-0-	−7.2	−38.7		
30-30 Win., 150 gr. RN	2390	1973	1605	1303	1095	974	1902	1296	858	565	399	316	-0-	−8.2	−30.0		
30-30 Win., 170 gr. FP	2200	1895	1619	1381	1191	1064	1827	1355	989	720	535	425	-0-	−8.9	−31.1		
308 Win., 150 gr. SP	2820	2533	2263	2009	1774	1560	2648	2137	1705	1344	1048	810	+2.3	-0-	−9.1	−26.9	−55.7
308 Win., 150 gr. BTSP	2820	2560	2315	2084	1866	1644	2649	2183	1785	1447	1160	922	+2.0	-0-	−8.5	−25.2	−51.8
308 Win., 165 gr. SP	2700	2440	2194	1963	1748	1551	2670	2180	1763	1411	1119	881	+2.5	-0-	−9.7	−28.5	−58.8
308 Win., 165 gr. BTSP	2700	2496	2301	2115	1937	1770	2672	2283	1940	1639	1375	1148	+2.0	-0-	−8.7	−25.2	−51.0
308 Win., 168 gr. BTHP MATCH	2700	2524	2354	2191	2035	1885	2720	2377	2068	1791	1545	1326	+2.0	-0-	−8.4	−23.9	−48.0
308 Win., 180 gr. SP	2620	2393	2178	1974	1782	1604	2743	2288	1896	1557	1269	1028	+2.6	-0-	−9.9	−28.9	−58.8
30-06 150 gr. SP	2910	2617	2342	2083	1843	1622	2820	2281	1827	1445	1131	876	+2.1	-0-	−8.5	−25.0	−51.8
30-06 150 gr. BTSP	2910	2645	2395	2159	1937	1729	2821	2331	1911	1553	1250	996	+1.7	-0-	−8.0	−23.3	−48.1
30-06 150 gr. FMJ BT	2910	2705	2508	2320	2141	1969	2821	2438	2096	1793	1527	1292	+1.6	-0-	−7.2	−20.9	−42.3
30-06 165 gr. BTSP	2800	2591	2392	2202	2020	1848	2873	2460	2097	1777	1495	1252	+1.8	-0-	−8.0	−23.3	−47.0
30-06 168 gr. BTHP MATCH	2790	2620	2447	2280	2120	1966	2925	2561	2234	1940	1677	1442	+1.7	-0-	−7.7	−22.2	−44.3
30-06 180 gr. SP	2700	2488	2287	2098	1921	1754	2913	2203	1635	1192	859	625	+2.7	-0-	−11.3	−34.4	−73.7
300 Win. Mag., 180 gr.	2960	2745	2540	2344	2157	1979	3501	3011	2578	2196	1859	1565	+1.9	-0-	−7.3	−20.9	−41.9
300 Win. Mag., 190 BTSP	2900	2711	2529	2355	2187	2026	3549	3101	2699	2340	2018	1732	+1.6	-0-	−7.1		

All 24″ barrels except 30 M1 Carbine — 20″ barrel.

BARREL LENGTH	PISTOL	MUZZLE VELOCITY	VELOCITY FT. PER SECOND		ENERGY		
	Caliber	Muzzle	50 yds.	100 yds.	Muzzle	50 yds.	100 yds.
2″	25 Auto, 50 gr. FMJ RN	760	707	659	64	56	48
2″	25 Auto, 50 gr. JHP	760	707	659	64	56	48
3¾″	380 Auto, 90 gr. JHP	1000	902	823	200	163	135
3¾″	380 Auto, 100 gr. FMJ	950	875	810	200	170	146
4″	9MM Luger, 90 gr. JHP	1360	1112	978	370	247	191
4″	9MM Luger, 100 gr. FMJ	1220	1059	959	331	249	204
4″	9MM Luger, 115 JHP	1155	1047	971	341	280	241
4″	9MM Luger, 115 gr. FMJ	1155	1047	971	341	280	241
4″	9MM Luger, 124 gr. FMJ/RN	1110	1030	971	339	292	259
4″	9MM Luger, 124 gr. FMJ/FP	1110	1030	971	339	292	259
4″	38 Special, 110 gr. JHP	975	903	841	232	199	173
4″	38 Special, 125 gr. JHP	950	888	834	251	219	193
4″	38 Special, 125 gr. JFP	950	888	834	251	219	193
4″	38 Special, 140 gr. JHP	900	850	806	252	225	202
4″	38 Special, 158 gr. JHP	800	765	731	225	205	188
4″	38 Special, 158 gr. JFP	800	765	731	225	205	188
4″	38 Special, 148 gr. HBWC	710	634	566	166	132	105
4″	38 Special, 158 gr. LRN	755	723	692	200	183	168
4″	38 Special, 158 gr. SWC	755	723	692	200	183	168
4″	38 Special, 158 gr. SWC/HP	755	723	692	200	183	168
4″	357 Mag., 125 gr. JHP	1450	1240	1090	583	427	330

BARREL LENGTH	PISTOL	MUZZLE VELOCITY	VELOCITY FT. PER SECOND		ENERGY		
	Caliber	Muzzle	50 yds.	100 yds.	Muzzle	50 yds.	100 yds.
4″	357 Mag., 125 gr. JFP	1450	1240	1090	583	427	330
4″	357 Mag., 140 gr. JHP	1360	1195	1076	575	444	360
4″	357 Mag., 158 gr. JHP	1235	1104	1015	535	428	361
4″	357 Mag., 158 gr. JFP	1235	1104	1015	535	428	361
4″	357 Mag., 158 gr. SWC	1235	1104	1015	535	428	361
4″	357 Mag., 158 gr. SWC/HP	1235	1104	1015	535	428	361
5″	10MM Auto, 155 gr. JHP	1410	—	—	—	—	—
5″	10MM Auto, 170 gr. JHP	1320	—	—	—	—	—
5″	10MM Auto, 200 gr. FMJ-FP	1150	—	—	—	—	—
7½″	44 Rem. Mag., 180 gr. JHP	1610	1365	1175	1036	745	551
7½″	44 Rem. Mag., 200 gr. JHP	1500	1284	1128	999	732	565
7½″	44 Rem. Mag., 240 gr. JHP	1350	1188	1078	971	753	619
7½″	44 Rem. Mag., 240 gr. SWC	1000	935	879	533	466	412
7½″	44 Rem. Mag., 240 gr. SWC/HP	1000	935	879	533	466	412
5″	45 ACP, 185 gr. JHP	950	880	819	371	318	276
5″	45 ACP, 185 gr. JSWC (M)	950	707	650	244	205	174
5″	45 ACP, 200 gr. FMJ C/T (M)	1000	938	885	444	391	348
5″	45 ACP, 200 gr. SWC	800	733	671	284	239	200
5″	45 ACP, 230 gr. FMJ/RN	850	809	771	369	334	304
5″	45 ACP, 230 gr. FMJ/FP	850	809	771	369	334	304

V = Vented   M = Match

REMINGTON BALLISTICS

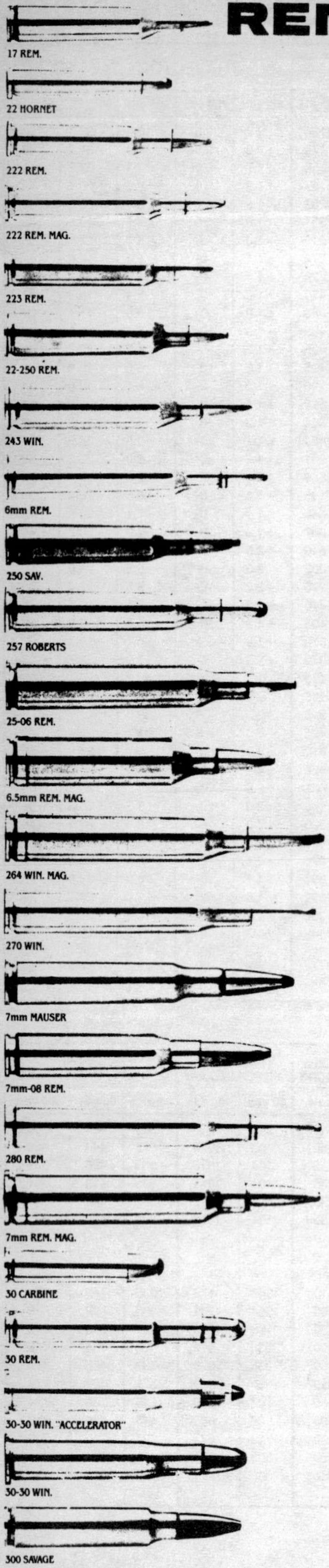

17 REM.
22 HORNET
222 REM.
222 REM. MAG.
223 REM.
22-250 REM.
243 WIN.
6mm REM.
250 SAV.
257 ROBERTS
25-06 REM.
6.5mm REM. MAG.
264 WIN. MAG.
270 WIN.
7mm MAUSER
7mm-08 REM.
280 REM.
7mm REM. MAG.
30 CARBINE
30 REM.
30-30 WIN. "ACCELERATOR"
30-30 WIN.
300 SAVAGE

Remington Ballistics

CALIBERS	REMINGTON Order No.	BULLET Wt.-Grs.	BULLET Style	Primer No.
17 REM.	R17REM	25*	Hollow Point Power-Lokt®	7½
22 HORNET	R22HN1	45*	Pointed Soft Point	6½
	R22HN2	45	Hollow Point	6½
222 REM.	R222R1	50	Pointed Soft Point	7½
	R222R3	50*	Hollow Point Power-Lokt	7½
	R222R4§	55	Metal Case	7½
222 REM. MAG.	R222M1	55*	Pointed Soft Point	7½
	R222M2§	55	Hollow Point Power-Lokt	7½
223 REM.	R223R1	55	Pointed Soft Point	7½
	R223R2	55*	Hollow Point Power-Lokt	7½
	R223R3	55	Metal Case	7½
	R223R4★	60	Hollow Point Match	7½
22-250 REM.	R22501	55*	Pointed Soft Point	9½
	R22502	55	Hollow Point Power-Lokt	9½
243 WIN.	R243W1	80	Pointed Soft Point	9½
	R243W2	80*	Hollow Point Power-Lokt	9½
	R243W3	100	Pointed Soft Point Core-Lokt®	9½
6mm REM.	R6MM1	80‡	Pointed Soft Point	9½
	R6MM2	80‡	Hollow Point Power-Lokt	9½
	R6MM4	100*	Pointed Soft Point Core-Lokt	9½
6mm BR REM.	R6MMBR★	100	Pointed Soft Point	7½
25-20 WIN.	R25202	86*	Soft Point	6½
250 SAV.	R250SV	100*	Pointed Soft Point	9½
257 ROBERTS	R257	117	Soft Point Core-Lokt	9½
	R257A	100*	Pointed Soft Point Core-Lokt	9½
25-06 REM.	R25061	87	Hollow Point Power-Lokt	9½
	R25062	100*	Pointed Soft Point Core-Lokt	9½
	R25063	120	Pointed Soft Point Core-Lokt	9½
6.5mm REM. MAG.	R65MM2§	120*	Pointed Soft Point Core-Lokt	9½M
264 WIN. MAG.	R264W2	140*	Pointed Soft Point Core-Lokt	9½M
270 WIN.	R270W1	100	Pointed Soft Point	9½
	R270W2	130*	Pointed Soft Point Core-Lokt	9½
	R270W3	130	Bronze Point	9½
	R270W4	150	Soft Point Core-Lokt	9½
7mm BR REM.	R7MMBR	140*	Pointed Soft Point	7½
7mm MAUSER (7x57)	R7MSR1	140*	Pointed Soft Point	9½
7mm-08 REM.	R7M081	140	Pointed Soft Point	9½
	R7M083	120*	Hollow Point	9½
280 REM.†	R280R3	140	Pointed Soft Point	9½
	R280R1	150	Pointed Soft Point Core-Lokt	9½
	R280R2	165	Soft Point Core-Lokt	9½
	R280R4	120*	Hollow Point	9½
7mm REM. MAG.	R7MM2	150	Pointed Soft Point Core-Lokt	9½M
	R7MM3	175	Pointed Soft Point Core-Lokt	9½M
	R7MM4	140*	Pointed Soft Point	9½M
30 CARBINE	R30CAR	110*	Soft Point	6½
30 REM.	R30REM	170*	Soft Point Core-Lokt	9½
30-30 WIN. ACCELERATOR®	R3030A	55*	Soft Point	9½
30-30 WIN.	R30301	150*	Soft Point Core-Lokt	9½
	R30302	170	Soft Point Core-Lokt	9½
	R30303	170	Hollow Point Core-Lokt	9½
300 SAVAGE	R30SV3	180*	Soft Point Core-Lokt®	9½
	R30SV2	150	Pointed Soft Point Core-Lokt	9½

†280 Rem. and 7mm Express™ Rem. are interchangeable.   *Illustrated (not shown actual size).
‡Interchangeable in 244 Rem.   §Subject to stock on hand.

REMINGTON BALLISTICS

VELOCITY FEET PER SECOND						ENERGY FOOT-POUNDS						TRAJECTORY** SHORT RANGE Bullet does not rise more than one inch above line of sight from muzzle to sighting-in range.						LONG RANGE Bullet does not rise more than three inches above line of sight from muzzle to sighting-in range.							BARREL LENGTH
Muzzle	100 Yds.	200 Yds.	300 Yds.	400 Yds.	500 Yds.	Muzzle	100 Yds.	200 Yds.	300 Yds.	400 Yds.	500 Yds.	50 Yds.	100 Yds.	150 Yds.	200 Yds.	250 Yds.	300 Yds.	100 Yds.	150 Yds.	200 Yds.	250 Yds.	300 Yds.	400 Yds.	500 Yds.	
4040	3284	2644	2086	1606	1235	906	599	388	242	143	85	0.1	0.5	0.0	-1.5	-4.2	-8.5	2.1	2.5	1.9	0.0	-3.4	-17.0	-44.3	24"
2690	2042	1502	1128	948	840	723	417	225	127	90	70	0.3	0.0	-2.4	-7.7	-16.9	-31.3	1.6	0.0	-4.5	-12.8	-26.4	-75.6	-163.4	24"
2690	2042	1502	1128	948	840	723	417	225	127	90	70	0.3	0.0	-2.4	-7.7	-16.9	-31.3	1.6	0.0	-4.5	-12.8	-26.4	-75.6	-163.4	
3140	2602	2123	1700	1350	1107	1094	752	500	321	202	136	0.5	0.9	0.0	-2.5	-6.9	-13.7	2.2	1.9	0.0	-3.8	-10.0	-32.3	-73.8	24"
3140	2635	2182	1777	1432	1172	1094	771	529	351	228	152	0.5	0.9	0.0	-2.4	-6.6	-13.1	2.1	1.8	0.0	-3.6	-9.5	-30.2	-68.1	
3020	2562	2147	1773	1451	1201	1114	801	563	384	257	176	0.6	1.0	0.0	-2.5	-7.0	-13.7	2.2	1.9	0.0	-3.8	-9.9	-31.0	-68.7	
3240	2748	2305	1906	1556	1272	1282	922	649	444	296	198	0.4	0.8	0.0	-2.2	-6.0	-11.8	1.9	1.6	0.0	-3.3	-8.5	-26.7	-59.5	24"
3240	2773	2352	1969	1627	1341	1282	939	675	473	323	220	0.4	0.8	0.0	-2.1	-5.8	-11.4	1.8	1.6	0.0	-3.2	-8.2	-25.5	-56.0	
3240	2747	2304	1905	1554	1270	1282	921	648	443	295	197	0.4	0.8	0.0	-2.2	-6.0	-11.8	1.9	1.6	0.0	-3.3	-8.5	-26.7	-59.6	24"
3240	2773	2352	1969	1627	1341	1282	939	675	473	323	220	0.4	0.8	0.0	-2.1	-5.8	-11.4	1.8	1.6	0.0	-3.2	-8.2	-25.5	-56.0	
3240	2759	2326	1933	1587	1301	1282	929	660	456	307	207	0.4	0.8	0.0	-2.1	-5.9	-11.6	1.9	1.6	0.0	-3.2	-8.4	-26.2	-57.9	
3100	2712	2355	2026	1726	1463	1280	979	739	547	397	285	0.5	0.8	0.0	-2.2	-6.0	-11.5	1.9	1.6	0.0	-3.2	-8.3	-25.1	-53.6	
3680	3137	2656	2222	1832	1493	1654	1201	861	603	410	272	0.2	0.5	0.0	-1.6	-4.4	-8.7	2.3	2.6	1.9	0.0	-3.4	-15.9	-38.9	24"
3680	3209	2785	2400	2046	1725	1654	1257	947	703	511	363	0.2	0.5	0.0	-1.5	-4.1	-8.0	2.1	2.5	1.8	0.0	-3.1	-14.1	-33.4	
3350	2955	2593	2259	1951	1670	1993	1551	1194	906	676	495	0.3	0.7	0.0	-1.8	-4.9	-9.4	2.6	2.9	2.1	0.0	-3.6	-16.2	-37.9	24"
3350	2955	2593	2259	1951	1670	1993	1551	1194	906	676	495	0.3	0.7	0.0	-1.8	-4.9	-9.4	2.6	2.9	2.1	0.0	-3.6	-16.2	-37.9	
2960	2697	2449	2215	1993	1786	1945	1615	1332	1089	882	708	0.5	0.9	0.0	-2.2	-5.8	-11.0	1.9	1.6	0.0	-3.1	-7.8	-22.6	-46.3	
3470	3064	2694	2352	2036	1747	2139	1667	1289	982	736	542	0.3	0.6	0.0	-1.6	-4.5	-8.7	2.4	2.7	1.9	0.0	-3.3	-14.9	-35.0	24"
3470	3064	2694	2352	2036	1747	2139	1667	1289	982	736	542	0.3	0.6	0.0	-1.6	-4.5	-8.7	2.4	2.7	1.9	0.0	-3.3	-14.9	-35.0	
3100	2829	2573	2332	2104	1889	2133	1777	1470	1207	983	792	0.4	0.8	0.0	-1.9	-5.2	-9.9	1.7	1.5	0.0	-2.8	-7.0	-20.4	-41.7	
2550	2310	2083	1870	1671	1491	1444	1185	963	776	620	494	0.3	0.0	-1.9	-5.6	-11.4	-19.3	2.8	2.3	0.0	-4.3	-10.9	-31.7	-65.1	15"
1460	1194	1030	931	858	797	407	272	203	165	141	121	0.0	-4.1	-14.4	-31.8	-57.3	-92.0	0.0	-8.2	-23.5	-47.0	-79.6	-175.9	-319.4	24"
2820	2504	2210	1936	1684	1461	1765	1392	1084	832	630	474	0.2	0.0	-1.6	-4.7	-9.6	-16.5	2.3	2.0	0.0	-3.7	-9.5	-28.3	-59.5	24"
2650	2291	1961	1663	1404	1199	1824	1363	999	718	512	373	0.3	0.0	-1.9	-5.8	-11.9	-20.7	2.9	2.4	0.0	-4.7	-12.0	-36.7	-79.2	24"
2980	2661	2363	2085	1827	1592	1972	1572	1240	965	741	563	0.1	0.0	-1.3	-4.0	-8.3	-14.3	2.0	1.7	0.0	-3.3	-8.3	-24.6	-51.4	
3440	2995	2591	2222	1884	1583	2286	1733	1297	954	686	484	0.3	0.6	0.0	-1.7	-4.8	-9.3	2.5	2.9	2.1	0.0	-3.6	-16.4	-39.1	24"
3230	2893	2580	2287	2014	1762	2316	1858	1478	1161	901	689	0.4	0.7	0.0	-1.9	-5.0	-9.7	1.6	1.4	0.0	-2.7	-6.9	-20.5	-42.7	
2990	2730	2484	2252	2032	1825	2382	1985	1644	1351	1100	887	0.5	0.8	0.0	-2.1	-5.6	-10.7	1.9	1.6	0.0	-3.0	-7.5	-22.0	-44.8	
3210	2905	2621	2353	2102	1867	2745	2248	1830	1475	1177	929	0.4	0.7	0.0	-1.8	-4.9	-9.5	2.7	3.0	2.1	0.0	-3.5	-15.5	-35.3	24"
3030	2782	2548	2326	2114	1914	2854	2406	2018	1682	1389	1139	0.5	0.8	0.0	-2.0	-5.4	-10.2	1.8	1.5	0.0	-2.9	-7.2	-20.8	-42.2	24"
3430	3021	2649	2305	1988	1699	2612	2027	1557	1179	877	641	0.3	0.6	0.0	-1.7	-4.6	-9.0	2.5	2.8	2.0	0.0	-3.4	-15.5	-36.4	24"
3060	2776	2510	2259	2022	1801	2702	2225	1818	1472	1180	936	0.5	0.8	0.0	-2.0	-5.5	-10.4	1.8	1.5	0.0	-2.9	-7.4	-21.6	-44.3	
3060	2802	2559	2329	2110	1904	2702	2267	1890	1565	1285	1046	0.4	0.8	0.0	-2.0	-5.3	-10.1	1.8	1.5	0.0	-2.8	-7.1	-20.6	-42.0	
2850	2504	2183	1886	1618	1385	2705	2087	1587	1185	872	639	0.7	1.0	0.0	-2.6	-7.1	-13.6	2.3	2.0	0.0	-3.8	-9.7	-29.2	-62.2	
2215	2012	1821	1643	1481	1336	1525	1259	1031	839	681	555	0.5	0.0	-2.7	-7.7	-15.4	-25.9	1.8	0.0	-4.1	-10.9	-20.6	-50.0	-95.2	15"
2660	2435	2221	2018	1827	1648	2199	1843	1533	1266	1037	844	0.2	0.0	-1.7	-5.0	-10.0	-17.0	2.5	2.0	0.0	-3.8	-9.6	-27.7	-56.3	24"
2860	2625	2402	2189	1988	1798	2542	2142	1793	1490	1228	1005	0.6	0.9	0.0	-2.3	-6.1	-11.6	2.1	1.7	0.0	-3.2	-8.1	-23.5	-47.7	24"
3000	2725	2467	2223	1992	1778	2398	1979	1621	1316	1058	842	0.5	0.8	0.0	-2.1	-5.7	-10.8	1.9	1.6	0.0	-3.0	-7.6	-22.3	-45.8	
3000	2758	2528	2309	2102	1905	2797	2363	1986	1657	1373	1128	0.5	0.8	0.0	-2.1	-5.5	-10.4	1.8	1.5	0.0	-2.9	-7.3	-21.1	-42.9	24"
2890	2624	2373	2135	1912	1705	2781	2293	1875	1518	1217	968	0.6	0.9	0.0	-2.3	-6.2	-11.8	2.1	1.7	0.0	-3.3	-8.3	-24.2	-49.7	
2820	2510	2220	1950	1701	1479	2913	2308	1805	1393	1060	801	0.2	0.0	-1.5	-4.6	-9.5	-16.4	2.3	1.9	0.0	-3.7	-9.4	-28.1	-58.8	
3150	2866	2599	2348	2110	1887	2643	2188	1800	1468	1186	949	0.4	0.7	0.0	-1.9	-5.1	-9.7	2.8	3.0	2.2	0.0	-3.6	-15.7	-35.6	
3110	2830	2568	2320	2085	1866	3221	2667	2196	1792	1448	1160	0.4	0.8	0.0	-1.9	-5.2	-9.9	1.7	1.5	0.0	-2.8	-7.0	-20.5	-42.1	24"
2860	2645	2440	2244	2057	1879	3178	2718	2313	1956	1644	1372	0.6	0.9	0.0	-2.3	-6.0	-11.3	2.0	1.7	0.0	-3.2	-7.9	-22.7	-45.8	
3175	2923	2684	2458	2243	2039	3133	2655	2240	1878	1564	1292	0.4	0.7	0.0	-1.8	-4.8	-9.1	2.6	2.9	2.0	0.0	-3.4	-14.5	-32.6	
1990	1567	1236	1035	923	842	967	600	373	262	208	173	0.9	0.0	-4.5	-13.5	-28.3	-49.9	0.0	-4.5	-13.5	-28.3	-49.9	-118.6	-228.2	20"
2120	1822	1555	1328	1153	1036	1696	1253	913	666	502	405	0.7	0.0	-3.3	-9.7	-19.6	-33.8	2.2	0.0	-5.3	-14.1	-27.2	-69.0	-136.9	24"
3400	2693	2085	1570	1187	986	1412	886	521	301	172	119	0.4	0.8	0.0	-2.4	-6.7	-13.8	2.0	1.8	0.0	-3.8	-10.2	-35.0	-84.4	24"
2390	1973	1605	1303	1095	974	1902	1296	858	565	399	316	0.5	0.0	-2.7	-8.2	-17.0	-30.0	1.8	0.0	-4.6	-12.5	-24.6	-65.3	-134.9	24"
2200	1895	1619	1381	1191	1061	1827	1355	989	720	535	425	0.6	0.0	-3.0	-8.9	-18.0	-31.1	2.0	0.0	-4.8	-13.0	-25.1	-63.6	-126.7	
2200	1895	1619	1381	1191	1061	1827	1355	989	720	535	425	0.6	0.0	-3.0	-8.9	-18.0	-31.1	2.0	0.0	-4.8	-13.0	-25.1	-63.6	-126.7	
2350	2025	1728	1467	1252	1098	2207	1639	1193	860	626	482	0.5	0.0	-2.6	-7.7	-15.6	-27.1	1.7	0.0	-4.2	-11.3	-21.9	-55.8	-112.0	24"
2630	2354	2095	1853	1631	1432	2303	1845	1462	1143	806	685	0.3	0.0	-1.8	-5.4	11.0	18.8	2.7	2.2	0.0	-4.2	-10.7	-31.5	-65.6	

**Inches above or below line of sight. Hold low for positive numbers, high for negative numbers.

Specifications are nominal. Ballistics figures established in test barrels. Individual rifles may vary from test-barrel specifications.

★New for 1989.

REMINGTON BALLISTICS

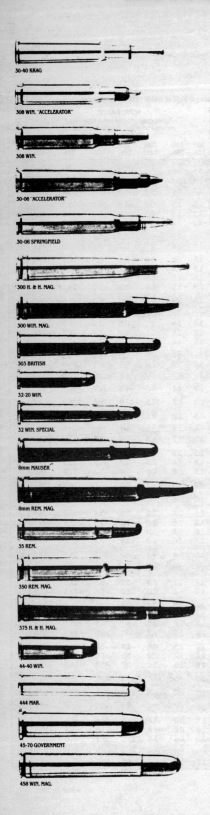

30-40 KRAG

308 WIN. "ACCELERATOR"

308 WIN.

30-06 "ACCELERATOR"

30-06 SPRINGFIELD

300 H. & H. MAG.

300 WIN. MAG.

303 BRITISH

32-20 WIN.

32 WIN. SPECIAL

8mm MAUSER

8mm REM. MAG.

35 REM.

350 REM. MAG.

375 H. & H. MAG.

44-40 WIN.

444 MAR.

45-70 GOVERNMENT

458 WIN. MAG.

Remington Ballistics

CALIBERS	REMINGTON Order No.	BULLET		
		Wt.-Grs.	Style	Primer No.
30-40 KRAG	R30402	180*	Pointed Soft Point Core-Lokt	9½
308 WIN. ACCELERATOR®	R308W5	55*	Pointed Soft Point	9½
308 WIN.	R308W1	150	Pointed Soft Point Core-Lokt	9½
	R308W6	165	Pointed Soft Point Core-Lokt	9½
	R308W2	180	Soft Point Core-Lokt	9½
	R308W3	180	Pointed Soft Point Core-Lokt	9½
	R308W7	168*	Boattail H.P. Match	9½
30-06 ACCELERATOR	R30069	55*	Pointed Soft Point	9½
30-06 SPRINGFIELD	R30061	125	Pointed Soft Point	9½
	R30062	150	Pointed Soft Point Core-Lokt	9½
	R30063	150	Bronze Point	9½
	R3006B	165*	Pointed Soft Point Core-Lokt	9½
	R30064	180	Soft Point Core-Lokt	9½
	R30065	180	Pointed Soft Point Core-Lokt	9½
	R30066	180	Bronze Point	9½
	R30067	220	Soft Point Core-Lokt	9½
	R3006C★	168	Boattail H.P. Match	9½
300 H&H MAG.	R300HH	180*	Pointed Soft Point Core-Lokt	9½M
300 WIN. MAG.	R300W1	150	Pointed Soft Point Core-Lokt	9½M
	R300W2	180*	Pointed Soft Point Core-Lokt	9½M
300 WBY. MAG.	R300WB1★	180	Pointed Soft Point Core-Lokt	9½M
	R300WB2★	220	Soft Point Core-Lokt	9½M
303 BRITISH	R303B1	180*	Soft Point Core-Lokt	9½
7.62x39mm	R762391★	125	Pointed Soft Point	7½
32-20 WIN.	R32201	100	Lead	6½
	R32202	100*	Soft Point	6½
32 WIN. SPECIAL	R32WS2	170*	Soft Point Core-Lokt	9½
8mm MAUSER	R8MSR	170*	Soft Point Core-Lokt	9½
8mm REM. MAG.	R8MM1	185*	Pointed Soft Point Core-Lokt	9½M
	R8MM2	220	Pointed Soft Point Core-Lokt	9½M
338 WIN. MAG.	R338W1	225*	Pointed Soft Point	9½M
	R338W2	250	Pointed Soft Point	9½M
35 REM.	R35R1	150	Pointed Soft Point Core-Lokt	9½
	R35R2	200*	Soft Point Core-Lokt	9½
350 REM. MAG.	R350M1	200*	Pointed Soft Point Core-Lokt	9½M
35 WHELEN	R35WH1	200	Pointed Soft Point	9½M
	R35WH2	250*	Soft Point	9½M
	R35WH3★	250	Pointed Soft Point	9½M
375 H&H MAG.	R375M1	270*	Soft Point	9½M
	R375M2	300	Metal Case	9½M
416 REM. MAG.	R416R1★	400	Solid	9½M
	R416R2★	400	Pointed Soft Point	9½M
44-40 WIN.	R4440W	200*	Soft Point	2½
44 REM. MAG.	R44MG2	240	Soft Point	2½
	R44MG3	240	Semi-Jacketed Hollow Point	2½
	R44MG6	210	Semi-Jacketed Hollow Point	2½
444 MAR.	R444M	240	Soft Point	9½
	R444M2	265*	Soft Point	9½
45-70 GOVERNMENT	R4570G	405*	Soft Point	9½
	R4570L	300	Jacketed Hollow Point	9½
458 WIN. MAG.	R458W1	500	Metal Case	9½M
	R458W2	500*	Soft Point	9½M

*Illustrated (not shown actual size).　　　　★New for 1989.

REMINGTON BALLISTICS

VELOCITY FEET PER SECOND — Muzzle, 100, 200, 300, 400, 500 Yds.
ENERGY FOOT-POUNDS — Muzzle, 100, 200, 300, 400, 500 Yds.
TRAJECTORY SHORT RANGE — Bullet does not rise more than one inch above line of sight from muzzle to sighting-in range. — 50, 100, 150, 200, 250, 300 Yds.
LONG RANGE — Bullet does not rise more than three inches above line of sight from muzzle to sighting-in range. — 100, 150, 200, 250, 300, 400, 500 Yds.

Velocity Muz.	100	200	300	400	500	Energy Muz.	100	200	300	400	500	Short 50	100	150	200	250	300	Long 100	150	200	250	300	400	500	Barrel
2430	2213	2007	1813	1632	1468	2360	1957	1610	1314	1064	861	0.4	0.0	-2.1	-6.2	-12.5	-21.1	1.4	0.0	-3.4	-8.9	-16.8	-40.9	-78.1	24"
3770	3215	2726	2286	1888	1541	1735	1262	907	638	435	290	0.2	0.5	0.0	-1.5	-4.2	-8.2	2.2	2.5	1.8	0.0	-3.2	-15.0	-36.7	24"
2820	2533	2263	2009	1774	1560	2648	2137	1705	1344	1048	810	0.2	0.0	-1.5	-4.5	-9.3	-15.9	2.3	1.9	0.0	-3.6	-9.1	-26.9	-55.7	
2700	2440	2194	1963	1748	1551	2670	2180	1763	1411	1119	881	0.2	0.0	-1.7	-5.0	-10.1	-17.2	2.5	2.1	0.0	-3.9	-9.7	-28.5	-58.8	
2620	2274	1955	1666	1414	1212	2743	2066	1527	1109	799	587	0.3	0.0	-2.0	-5.9	-12.1	-20.9	2.9	2.4	0.0	-4.7	-12.1	-36.9	-79.1	24"
2620	2393	2178	1974	1782	1604	2743	2288	1896	1557	1269	1028	0.2	0.0	-1.8	-5.2	-10.4	-17.7	2.6	2.1	0.0	-4.0	-9.9	-28.9	-58.8	
2680	2493	2314	2143	1979	1823	2678	2318	1998	1713	1460	1239	0.2	0.0	-1.6	-4.7	-9.4	-15.9	2.4	1.9	0.0	-3.5	-8.9	-25.3	-50.6	
4080	3485	2965	2502	2083	1709	2033	1483	1074	764	530	356	0.4	1.0	0.9	0.0	-1.9	-5.0	1.8	2.1	1.5	0.0	-2.7	-12.5	-30.5	24"
3140	2780	2447	2138	1853	1595	2736	2145	1662	1269	953	706	0.4	0.8	0.0	-2.1	-5.6	-10.7	1.8	1.5	0.0	-3.0	-7.7	-23.0	-48.5	
2910	2617	2342	2083	1843	1622	2820	2281	1827	1445	1131	876	0.6	0.9	0.0	-2.3	-6.3	-12.0	2.1	1.8	0.0	-3.3	-8.5	-25.0	-51.8	
2910	2656	2416	2189	1974	1773	2820	2349	1944	1596	1298	1047	0.6	0.9	0.0	-2.2	-6.0	-11.4	2.0	1.7	0.0	-3.2	-8.0	-23.3	-47.5	
2800	2534	2283	2047	1825	1621	2872	2352	1909	1534	1220	963	0.7	1.0	0.0	-2.5	-6.7	-12.7	2.3	1.9	0.0	-3.6	-9.0	-26.3	-54.1	
2700	2348	2023	1727	1466	1251	2913	2203	1635	1192	859	625	0.2	0.0	-1.8	-5.5	-11.2	-19.5	2.7	2.3	0.0	-4.4	-11.3	-34.4	-73.7	24"
2700	2469	2250	2042	1846	1663	2913	2436	2023	1666	1362	1105	0.2	0.0	-1.6	-4.8	-9.7	-16.5	2.4	2.0	0.0	-3.7	-9.3	-27.0	-54.9	
2700	2485	2280	2084	1899	1725	2913	2468	2077	1736	1441	1189	0.2	0.0	-1.6	-4.7	-9.6	-16.2	2.4	2.0	0.0	-3.6	-9.1	-26.2	-53.0	
2410	2130	1870	1632	1422	1246	2837	2216	1708	1301	988	758	0.4	0.0	-2.3	-6.8	-13.8	-23.6	1.5	0.0	-3.7	-9.9	-19.0	-47.4	-93.1	
2710	2522	2346	2169	2003	1845	2739	2372	2045	1754	1497	1270	0.7	1.0	0.0	-2.5	-6.6	-12.4	2.3	1.9	0.0	-3.5	-8.6	-24.7	-49.4	
2880	2640	2412	2196	1990	1798	3315	2785	2325	1927	1583	1292	0.6	0.9	0.0	-2.3	-6.0	-11.5	2.1	1.7	0.0	-3.2	-8.0	-23.3	-47.4	24"
3290	2951	2636	2342	2068	1813	3605	2900	2314	1827	1424	1095	0.3	0.7	0.0	-1.8	-4.8	-9.3	2.6	2.9	2.1	0.0	-3.5	-15.4	-35.5	24"
2960	2745	2540	2344	2157	1979	3501	3011	2578	2196	1859	1565	0.5	0.8	0.0	-2.1	-5.5	-10.4	1.9	1.6	0.0	-2.9	-7.3	-20.9	-41.9	
3200	2942	2698	2467	2248	2040	4092	3458	2909	2433	2019	1663	0.4	0.7	0.0	-1.8	-4.7	-9.0	2.6	2.8	2.0	0.0	-3.3	-14.4	-32.4	24"
2850	2541	2283	1984	1736	1512	3967	3155	2480	1922	1471	1117	0.6	1.0	0.0	-2.5	-6.7	-12.9	2.3	1.9	0.0	-3.6	-9.1	-27.2	-56.8	
2460	2124	1817	1542	1311	1137	2418	1803	1319	950	687	517	0.4	0.0	-2.3	-6.9	-14.1	-24.4	1.5	0.0	-3.8	-10.2	-19.8	-50.5	-101.5	24"
2365	2062	1783	1533	1320	1154	1552	1180	882	652	483	370	0.4	0.0	-2.5	-7.3	-14.3	-25.7	1.7	0.0	-4.8	-10.8	-20.7	-52.3	-104.0	24"
1210	1021	913	834	769	712	325	231	185	154	131	113	0.0	-6.3	-20.9	-44.9	-79.3	-125.1	0.0	-11.5	-32.3	-63.8	-106.3	-230.3	-413.3	24"
1210	1021	913	834	769	712	325	231	185	154	131	113	0.0	-6.3	-20.9	-44.9	-79.3	-125.1	0.0	-11.5	-32.3	-63.6	-106.3	-230.3	-413.3	
2250	1921	1626	1372	1175	1044	1911	1393	998	710	521	411	0.6	0.0	-2.9	-8.6	-17.6	-30.5	1.9	0.0	-4.7	-12.7	-24.7	-63.2	-126.9	24"
2360	1969	1622	1333	1123	997	2102	1463	993	671	476	375	0.5	0.0	-2.7	-8.2	-17.0	-29.8	1.8	0.0	-4.5	-12.4	-24.3	-63.8	-130.7	24"
3080	2761	2464	2186	1927	1688	3896	3131	2494	1963	1525	1170	0.5	0.8	0.0	-2.1	-5.6	-10.7	1.8	1.6	0.0	-3.0	-7.6	-22.5	-46.8	24"
2830	2581	2346	2123	1913	1716	3912	3254	2688	2201	1787	1438	0.6	1.0	0.0	-2.4	-6.4	-12.1	2.2	1.8	0.0	-3.4	-8.5	-24.7	-50.5	
2780	2572	2374	2184	2003	1832	3860	3305	2815	2383	2004	1676	0.6	1.0	0.0	-2.4	-6.3	-12.0	2.2	1.8	0.0	-3.3	-8.4	-24.0	-48.4	24"
2660	2456	2261	2075	1898	1731	3927	3348	2837	2389	1999	1663	0.2	0.0	-1.7	-4.9	-9.8	-16.6	2.4	2.0	0.0	-3.7	-9.3	-26.6	-53.6	
2300	1874	1506	1218	1039	934	1762	1169	755	494	359	291	0.6	0.0	-3.0	-9.2	-19.1	-33.9	2.0	0.0	-5.1	-14.1	-27.8	-74.0	-152.3	24"
2080	1698	1376	1140	1001	911	1921	1280	841	577	445	369	0.8	0.0	-3.8	-11.3	-23.5	-41.2	2.5	0.0	-6.3	-17.1	-33.6	-87.7	-176.4	
2710	2410	2130	1870	1631	1421	3261	2579	2014	1553	1181	897	0.2	0.0	-1.7	-5.1	-10.4	-17.9	2.6	2.1	0.0	-4.0	-10.3	-30.5	-64.0	20"
2675	2378	2100	1842	1606	1399	3177	2510	1958	1506	1145	869	0.2	0.0	-1.8	-5.3	-10.8	-18.5	2.6	2.2	0.0	-4.2	-10.6	-31.5	-65.9	
2400	2066	1761	1492	1269	1107	3197	2369	1722	1235	893	680	0.4	0.0	-2.5	-7.3	-15.0	-26.0	1.6	0.0	-4.0	-10.9	-21.0	-53.8	-108.2	24"
2400	2197	2005	1823	1652	1496	3197	2680	2230	1844	1515	1242	0.4	0.0	-2.2	-6.3	-12.6	-21.3	1.4	0.0	-3.4	-9.0	-17.0	-41.0	-77.8	
2690	2420	2166	1928	1707	1507	4337	3510	2812	2228	1747	1361	0.2	0.0	-1.7	-5.1	-10.3	-17.6	2.5	2.1	0.0	-3.9	-10.0	-29.4	-60.7	24"
2530	2171	1843	1551	1307	1126	4263	3139	2262	1602	1138	844	0.3	0.0	-2.2	-6.5	-13.5	-23.4	1.5	0.0	-3.6	-9.8	-19.1	-49.1	-99.5	
2400	2042	1718	1436	1212	1062	5115	3702	2620	1832	1305	1001	0.4	0.0	-2.5	-7.5	-15.5	-27.0	1.7	0.0	-4.2	-11.3	-21.9	-56.7	-115.1	24"
2400	2175	1962	1763	1579	1414	5115	4201	3419	2760	2214	1775	0.4	0.0	-2.2	-6.5	-13.0	-22.0	1.5	0.0	-3.5	-9.3	-17.6	-42.9	-82.2	
1190	1006	900	822	756	699	629	449	360	300	254	217	0.0	-6.5	-21.6	-46.3	-81.8	-129.1	0.0	-11.8	-33.3	-65.5	-109.5	-237.4	-426.2	24"
1760	1380	1114	970	878	806	1650	1015	661	501	411	346	0.0	-2.7	-10.0	-23.0	-43.0	-71.2	0.0	-5.9	-17.6	-36.3	-63.1	-145.5	-273.0	
1760	1380	1114	970	878	806	1650	1015	661	501	411	346	0.0	-2.7	-10.0	-23.0	-43.0	-71.2	0.0	-5.9	-17.6	-36.3	-63.1	-145.5	-273.0	20"
1920	1477	1155	982	880	802	1719	1017	622	450	361	300	0.0	-2.2	-8.3	-19.7	-37.6	-63.2	0.0	-5.1	-15.4	-32.1	-56.7	-134.0	-256.2	
2350	1815	1377	1087	941	846	2942	1755	1010	630	472	381	0.6	0.0	-3.2	-9.9	-21.3	-38.5	2.1	0.0	-5.6	-15.9	-32.1	-87.8	-182.7	24"
2120	1733	1405	1160	1012	920	2644	1768	1162	791	603	498	0.7	0.0	-3.6	-10.8	-22.5	-39.5	2.4	0.0	-6.0	-16.4	-32.2	-84.3	-170.2	
1330	1168	1055	977	918	869	1590	1227	1001	858	758	679	0.0	-4.7	-15.8	-34.0	-60.0	-94.5	0.0	-8.7	-24.6	-48.2	-80.3	-172.4	-305.9	24"
1810	1497	1244	1073	969	895	2182	1492	1031	767	625	533	0.0	-2.3	-8.5	-19.4	-35.9	-59.0	0.0	-5.0	-14.8	-30.1	-52.1	-119.5	—	
2040	1823	1623	1442	1237	1161	4620	3689	2924	2308	1839	1469	0.7	0.0	-3.3	-9.6	-19.2	-32.5	2.2	0.0	-5.2	-13.6	-25.8	-63.2	-121.7	24"
2040	1770	1527	1319	1157	1046	4712	3547	2640	1970	1516	1239	0.8	0.0	-3.5	-10.3	-20.8	-35.6	2.4	0.0	-5.6	-14.9	-28.5	-71.5	-140.4	

nches above or below line of sight. Hold low for positive numbers, high for negative numbers.   Specifications are nominal. Ballistics figures established in test barrels. Individual rifles may vary from test-barrel specifications.

WEATHERBY BALLISTICS

BULLETS			VELOCITY (in Feet per Second)						ENERGY (in Foot Pounds)						BULLET DROP (in Inches From Bore Line)			PATH OF BULLET (Above or below Line-of-sight) For riflescopes mounted 1.5" above bore		
Cartridge	Weight in Grains	Type	Muzzle	100 Yds.	200 Yds.	300 Yds.	400 Yds.	500 Yds.	Muzzle	100 Yds.	200 Yds.	300 Yds.	400 Yds.	500 Yds.	100 Yds.	200 Yds.	300 Yds.	100 Yds.	200 Yds.	300 Yds.
.224 WBY MAG	55	Pt-Ex	3650	3192	2780	2403	2057	1742	1627	1244	943	705	516	370	-1.4	-6.3	-15.6	2.8	3.6	0
.240 WBY MAG	87	Pt-Ex	3500	3202	2924	2663	2416	2183	2366	1980	1651	1370	1127	920	-1.5	-6.4	-15.4	2.6	3.4	0
	100	Pt-Ex	3395	3106	2835	2581	2339	2112	2559	2142	1785	1478	1215	990	-1.6	-6.8	-16.8	2.9	3.6	0
	100	Partition	3395	3069	2766	2483	2216	1966	2559	2091	1698	1368	1091	859	-1.6	-6.9	-16.8	3.0	3.8	0
.257 WBY MAG	87	Pt-Ex	3825	3456	3118	2805	2513	2239	2826	2308	1878	1520	1220	969	-1.3	-5.5	-13.2	2.1	2.9	0
	100	Pt-Ex	3555	3237	2941	2665	2404	2159	2806	2326	1920	1576	1283	1035	-1.5	-6.2	-15.1	2.6	3.3	0
	100	Partition	3555	3292	3044	2810	2589	2377	2806	2406	2058	1754	1488	1254	-1.5	-6.1	-14.5	2.4	3.1	0
	117	Semi Pt-Ex	3300	2882	2502	2152	1830	1547	2829	2158	1626	1203	870	621	-1.7	-7.7	-19.3	3.7	4.6	0
	117	Partition	3300	2998	2717	2452	2202	1967	2829	2335	1917	1561	1260	1005	-1.7	-7.3	-17.7	3.2	3.7	0
	120	Partition	3290	3074	2869	2673	2486	2306	2884	2518	2193	1904	1646	1416	-1.7	-7.0	-16.7	2.9	3.6	0
.270 WBY MAG	100	Pt-Ex	3760	3380	3033	2712	2412	2133	3139	2537	2042	1633	1292	1010	-1.3	-5.7	-13.9	2.3	3.0	0
	130	Pt-Ex	3375	3100	2842	2598	2366	2148	3287	2773	2330	1948	1616	1331	-1.6	-6.6	-16.4	2.9	3.6	0
	130	Partition	3375	3119	2878	2649	2432	2225	3287	2808	2390	2026	1707	1429	-1.6	-6.8	-16.2	2.8	3.6	0
	150	Partition	3245	3019	2803	2598	2402	2215	3507	3034	2617	2248	1922	1634	-1.7	-7.3	-17.3	3.0	3.8	0
	150	Partition	3245	3036	2837	2647	2465	2290	3507	3070	2681	2334	2023	1746	-1.7	-7.2	-17.1	3.0	3.7	0
7mm WBY MAG	139	Pt-Ex	3400	3138	2892	2659	2437	2226	3567	3039	2580	2181	1832	1529	-1.6	-6.7	-16.0	2.7	3.5	0
	140	Partition	3400	3163	2939	2726	2522	2328	3593	3110	2684	2309	1978	1684	-1.6	-6.6	-15.7	2.7	3.4	0
	150	Pt-Ex	3260	3023	2799	2586	2382	2189	3539	3044	2609	2227	1890	1595	-1.7	-7.2	-17.2	3.0	3.7	0
	154	Pt-Ex	3260	3023	2800	2586	2383	2189	3633	3125	2681	2287	1941	1638	-1.8	-7.3	-17.4	3.0	3.7	0
	160	Partition	3200	3004	2816	2637	2464	2297	3637	3205	2817	2469	2156	1875	-1.8	-7.4	-17.4	3.0	3.7	0
	175	Partition	3070	2879	2696	2520	2351	2189	3662	3220	2824	2467	2147	1861	-1.9	-8.0	-19.0	3.4	4.1	0
.300 WBY MAG	110	Pt-Ex	3900	3441	3028	2652	2305	1985	3714	2891	2239	1717	1297	962	-1.2	-5.4	-13.5	2.2	3.0	0
	150	Pt-Ex	3600	3297	3015	2751	2502	2266	4316	3621	3028	2520	2084	1709	-1.4	-6.0	-14.5	2.4	3.1	0
	150	Partition	3600	3307	3033	2776	2533	2295	4316	3642	3064	2566	2137	1766	-1.4	-6.0	-14.4	2.4	3.1	0
	165	Boat Tail	3450	3220	3003	2797	2599	2409	4360	3799	3303	2865	2475	2126	-1.5	-6.4	-15.2	2.5	3.2	0
	180	Pt-Ex	3300	3064	2841	2629	2426	2233	4352	3753	3226	2762	2352	1992	-1.7	-7.1	-16.8	2.9	3.6	0
	180	Partition	3300	3077	2865	2663	2470	2287	4352	3784	3280	2834	2438	2086	-1.7	-7.0	-16.6	2.9	3.6	0
	220	Semi Pt-Ex	2905	2498	2126	1787	1490	1250	4122	3047	2207	1560	1085	763	-2.3	-10.2	-25.8	5.3	6.5	0
.340 WBY MAG	200	Pt-Ex	3260	3011	2775	2552	2339	2137	4719	4025	3420	2892	2429	2027	-1.7	-7.3	-17.4	3.1	3.8	0
	210	Partition	3250	2991	2746	2515	2295	2086	4924	4170	3516	2948	2455	2029	-1.7	-7.4	-17.6	3.1	3.9	0
	250	Semi Pt-Ex	3000	2670	2363	2078	1812	1574	4995	3958	3100	2396	1823	1375	-2.1	-9.1	-22.4	4.8	5.8	0
	250	Partition	3000	2806	2621	2443	2272	2108	4995	4371	3812	3311	2864	2465	-2.0	-8.5	-19.9	3.6	4.3	0
.378 WBY MAG	270	Pt-Ex	3180	2976	2781	2594	2415	2243	6062	5308	4635	4034	3495	3015	-1.8	-7.5	-17.8	1.9	1.7	-5.8
	300	RN	2925	2576	2252	1952	1680	1439	5698	4419	3379	2538	1881	1379	-2.2	-9.7	-24.0	1.9	0	-8.7
.460 WBY MAG	500	RN	2700	2404	2128	1869	1635	1425	8092	6416	5026	3878	2969	2254	-2.6	-11.2	-27.4	2.3	0	-9.8
	500	FMJ	2700	2425	2166	1923	1700	1497	8092	6526	5210	4105	3209	2488	-2.5	-11.1	-26.9	2.2	0	-9.5

LEGEND: Pt-Ex=Pointed-expanding. Semi Pt-Ex=Semi pointed-expanding. RN=Round nose. FMJ=Full metal jacket.

NOTE: These tables were calculated by computer using a standard modern scientific technique to predict trajectories from the best available data for each cartridge. The figures shown are expected to be reasonably accurate of ammunition behavior under standard conditions. However, the shooter is cautioned that performance will vary because of variations in rifle, ammunition and atmospheric conditions.

BALLISTIC COEFFICIENTS used for these tables are as published by Hornady and Nosler ballistic data compiled using 26" barrels.

WINCHESTER BALLISTICS
CENTERFIRE PISTOL AND REVOLVER
Super-X®

Cartridge	Symbol	Bullet Wt. Grs.	Type	Velocity (fps)			Energy (ft.-lbs.)			Mid Range Traj. (in.)		Barrel Length Inches
				Muzzle	50 Yds.	100 Yds.	Muzzle	50 Yds.	100 Yds.	50 Yds.	100 Yds.	
25 Automatic (6.35mm) Expanding Point	X25AXP	45	XP**	815	729	655	66	53	42	1.8	7.7	2
25 Automatic (6.35mm) Full Metal Case	X25AP	50	FMC	760	707	659	64	56	48	2.0	8.7	2
30 Luger (7.65mm) Full Metal Case	X30LP	93	FMC	1220	1110	1040	305	255	225	0.9	3.5	4½
# 30 Carbine Hollow Soft Point	X30M1	110	HSP	1790	1601	1430	783	626	500	0.4	1.7	10
# 30 Carbine Full Metal Case	X30M2	110	FMC	1740	1552	1384	740	588	468	0.4	1.8	10
32 Smith & Wesson Lead Round Nose	X32SWP	85	Lead-RN	680	645	610	90	81	73	2.5	10.5	3
32 Smith & Wesson Long (Colt New Police) Lead Round Nose	X32SWLP	98	Lead-RN	705	670	635	115	98	88	2.3	10.5	4
32 Short Colt Lead Round Nose	X32SCP	80	Lead-RN	745	665	590	100	79	62	2.2	9.9	4
† 32 Long Colt Lead Round Nose	X32LCP	82	Lead-RN	755	715	675	105	93	83	2.0	8.7	4
32 Automatic Silvertip Hollow Point	X32ASHP	60	STHP	970	895	835	125	107	93	1.3	5.4	4
32 Automatic Full Metal Case	X32AP	71	FMC	905	855	810	129	115	97	1.4	5.8	4
38 Smith & Wesson Lead Round Nose	X38SWP	145	Lead-RN	685	650	620	150	135	125	2.4	10.0	4
380 Automatic Silvertip Hollow Point	X380ASHP	85	STHP	1000	921	860	189	160	140	1.2	5.1	3¾
380 Automatic Full Metal Case	X380AP	95	FMC	955	865	785	190	160	130	1.4	5.9	3¾
38 Special Silvertip Hollow Point	X38S9HP	110	STHP	945	894	850	218	195	176	1.3	5.4	4V
38 Special Lead Round Nose	X38S1P	158	Lead-RN	755	723	693	200	183	168	2.0	8.3	4V
38 Special Lead Semi-Wad Cutter	X38WCPSV	158	Lead-SWC	755	721	689	200	182	167	2.0	8.4	4V
† 38 Special Metal Point	X38S2P	158	Met. Pt.	755	723	693	200	183	168	2.0	8.3	4V
38 Special Silvertip Hollow Point + P	X38SSHP	95	STHP	1100	1002	932	255	212	183	1.0	4.3	4V
# 38 Special Jacketed Hollow Point + P	X38S6PH	110	JHP	995	926	871	242	210	185	1.2	5.1	4V
# 38 Special Jacketed Hollow Point + P	X38S7PH	125	JHP	945	898	858	248	224	204	1.3	5.4	4V
# 38 Special Silvertip Hollow Point + P	X38S8HP	125	STHP	945	898	858	248	224	204	1.3	5.4	4V
38 Special Lead Hollow Point + P	X38SPD	158	Lead-HP	890	855	823	278	257	238	1.4	6.0	4V
38 Special Lead Semi-Wad Cutter + P	X38WCP	158	Lead-SWC	890	855	823	278	257	238	1.4	6.0	4V
38 Special Match Lead Mid-Range (Clean Cutting) Match	X38SMRP	148	Lead-WC	710	634	566	166	132	105	2.4	10.8	4V
9mm Luger (Parabellum) Full Metal Case	X9LP	115	FMC	1155	1047	971	341	280	241	0.9	3.9	4
9mm Luger (Parabellum) Silvertip Hollow Point	X9MMSHP	115	STHP	1225	1095	1007	383	306	259	0.8	3.6	4
* 38 Super Automatic Silvertip Hollow Point + P	X38ASHP	125	STHP	1240	1130	1050	427	354	306	0.8	3.4	5
* 38 Super Automatic Full Metal Case + P	X38A1P	130	FMC	1215	1099	1017	426	348	298	0.8	3.6	5
† 38 Automatic (For all 38 Automatic Pistols) Full Metal Case	X38A2P	130	FMC	1040	980	925	310	275	245	1.0	4.7	4½
# 357 Magnum Jacketed Hollow Point	X3573P	110	JHP	1295	1095	975	410	292	232	0.8	3.5	4V
# 357 Magnum Jacketed Hollow Point	X3576P	125	JHP	1450	1240	1090	583	427	330	0.6	2.8	4V
# 357 Magnum Silvertip Hollow Point	X357SHP	145	STHP	1290	1155	1060	535	428	361	0.8	3.5	4V
357 Magnum Lead Semi-Wad Cutter	X3571P	158	Lead-SWC**	1235	1104	1015	535	428	361	0.8	3.5	4V
# 357 Magnum Jacketed Hollow Point	X3574P	158	JHP	1235	1104	1015	535	428	361	0.8	3.5	4V
# 357 Magnum Jacketed Soft Point	X3575P	158	JSP	1235	1104	1015	535	428	361	0.8	3.5	4V
New 10mm Automatic Silvertip Hollow Point	X10MMSTHP	175	STHP	1290	1141	1037	649	506	418	0.7	3.3	5½
# 41 Remington Magnum Silvertip Hollow Point	X41MSTHP	175	STHP	1250	1120	1029	607	488	412	0.8	3.4	4V
41 Remington Magnum Lead Semi-Wad Cutter	X41MP	210	Lead-SWC	965	898	842	434	376	331	1.3	5.4	4V
# 41 Remington Magnum Jacketed Soft Point	X41MJSP	210	JSP	1300	1162	1062	788	630	526	0.7	3.2	4V
# 41 Remington Magnum Jacketed Hollow Point	X41MHP2	210	JHP	1300	1162	1062	788	630	526	0.7	3.2	4V
# 44 Smith & Wesson Special Silvertip Hollow Point	X44STHPS2	200	STHP	900	860	822	360	328	300	1.4	5.9	6½
44 Smith & Wesson Special Lead Round Nose	X44SP	246	Lead-RN	755	725	695	310	285	265	2.0	8.3	6½
# 44 Remington Magnum Silvertip Hollow Point	X44MSTHP2	210	STHP	1250	1106	1010	729	570	475	0.8	3.5	4V
# 44 Remington Magnum Hollow Soft Point	X44MHSP2	240	HSP	1180	1081	1010	741	623	543	0.9	3.7	4V
44 Remington Magnum Lead Semi-Wad Cutter (Med. Vel.)	X44MWCP	240	Lead-SWC	1000	937	885	533	468	417	1.2	4.9	6½V
44 Remington Magnum Lead Semi-Wad Cutter (Gas Check)	X44MP	240	Lead-SWC	1350	1186	1069	971	749	608	0.7	3.1	4V
45 Automatic Silvertip Hollow Point	X45ASHP2	185	STHP	1000	938	888	411	362	324	1.2	4.9	5
45 Automatic Full Metal Case	X45A1P2	230	FMC	810	776	745	335	308	284	1.7	7.2	5
45 Automatic Super-Match Full Metal Case Semi-Wad Cutter	X45AWCP	185	FMC-SWC	770	707	650	244	205	174	2.0	8.7	5
# 45 Colt Silvertip Hollow Point	X45CSHP2	225	STHP	920	877	839	423	384	352	1.4	5.6	5½
45 Colt Lead Round Nose	X45CP2	255	Lead-RN	860	820	780	420	380	345	1.5	6.1	5½
# 45 Winchester Magnum Full Metal Case	X45WM	230	FMC	1400	1232	1107	1001	775	636	0.6	2.8	5
(Not for Arms Chambered for Standard 45 Automatic)												

CENTERFIRE BLANK CARTRIDGES

Cartridge	Symbol		Type									
32 Smith & Wesson Black Powder	32BL2P		Black Powder	—	—	—	—	—	—	—	—	—
† 38 Smith & Wesson Smokeless Powder	38BLP		Smokeless Powder	—	—	—	—	—	—	—	—	—
38 Special Smokeless Powder	38SBLP		Smokeless Powder	—	—	—	—	—	—	—	—	—

FMC-Full Metal Case ● JHP-Jacketed Hollow Point ● JSP-Jacketed Soft Point ● RN-Round Nose
Met. Pt.-Metal Point ● XP-Expanding Point ● WC-Wad Cutter ●
SWC-Semi Wad Cutter ● HSP-Hollow Soft Point ●
STHP-Silvertip Hollow Point ● HP-Hollow Point
**Lubaloy
*For use only in 38 Super Automatic Pistols.

+ P Ammunition with (+P) on the case head stamp is loaded to higher pressure. Use only in firearms designated for this cartridge and so recommended by the gun manufacturer.
V-Data is based on velocity obtained from 4" vented test barrels for revolver cartridges (38 Special, 357 Magnum, 41 Rem. Mag. and 44 Rem. Mag.)

Specifications are nominal. Test barrels are used to determine ballistics figures. Individual firearms may differ from test barrel statistics.
Specifications subject to change without notice.
Acceptable for use in rifles also.
† Obsolete in 1989.

WINCHESTER BALLISTICS
CENTERFIRE RIFLE

Super-X®

Cartridge	Symbol	Game Selector Guide	CXP Guide Number	Wt. Grs.	Bullet Type	Barrel Length (In.)	Velocity In Feet Per Second (fps)					
							Muzzle	100	200	300	400	500
218 Bee	X218B	V	1	46	HP	24	2760	2102	1550	1155	961	85*
22 Hornet	X22H1	V	1	45	SP	24	2690	2042	1502	1128	948	84*
22-250 Remington	X222501	V	1	55	PSP	24	3680	3137	2656	2222	1832	149*
222 Remington	X222R	V	1	50	PSP	24	3140	2602	2123	1700	1350	110*
222 Remington	X222R1	V	–	55	FMC	24	3020	2675	2355	2057	1783	153*
223 Remington	X223RH	V	1	53	HP	24	3330	2882	2477	2106	1770	147*
223 Remington	X223R	V	1	55	PSP	24	3240	2747	2304	1905	1554	127*
223 Remington	X223R1	V	–	55	FMC	24	3240	2877	2543	2232	1943	167*
223 Remington	X223R2	D	2	64	PP	24	3020	2621	2256	1920	1619	136*
225 Winchester	X2251	V	1	55	PSP	24	3570	3066	2616	2208	1838	151*
243 Winchester	X2431	V	1	80	PSP	24	3350	2955	2593	2259	1951	167*
243 Winchester	X2432	D,O/P	2	100	PP	24	2960	2697	2449	2215	1993	178*
6mm Remington	X6MMR1	V	1	80	PSP	24	3470	3064	2694	2352	2036	174*
6mm Remington	X6MMR2	D,O/P	2	100	PP	24	3100	2829	2573	2332	2104	188*
25-06 Remington	X25061	V	1	90	PEP	24	3440	3043	2680	2344	2034	174*
25-06 Remington	X25062	D,O/P	2	120	PEP	24	2990	2730	2484	2252	2032	182*
# 25-20 Winchester	X25202	V	1	86	SP	24	1460	1194	1030	931	858	79*
25-35 Winchester	X2535	D	2	117	SP	24	2230	1866	1545	1282	1097	98*
250 Savage	X2503	D,O/P	2	100	ST	24	2820	2467	2140	1839	1569	133*
257 Roberts + P	X257P2	D,O/P	2	100	ST	24	3000	2633	2295	1982	1697	144*
257 Roberts + P	X257P3	D,O/P	2	117	PP	24	2780	2411	2071	1761	1488	126*
264 Winchester Mag.	X2642	D,O/P	2	140	PP	24	3030	2782	2548	2326	2114	191*
270 Winchester	X2701	V	1	100	PSP	24	3430	3021	2649	2305	1988	169*
270 Winchester	X2705	D,O/P	2	130	PP	24	3060	2802	2559	2329	2110	190*
270 Winchester	X2703	D,O/P	2	130	ST	24	3060	2776	2510	2259	2022	180*
270 Winchester	X2704	D,M	3	150	PP	24	2850	2585	2336	2100	1879	167*
284 Winchester	X2842	D,O/P,M	2	150	PP	24	2860	2595	2344	2108	1886	168*
7mm Mauser (7 × 57)	X7MM1	D	2	145	PP	24	2690	2442	2206	1985	1777	158*
† 7mm Mauser (7 × 57)	X7MM	D	2	175	SP	24	2440	2137	1857	1603	1382	120*
7mm Remington Mag.	X7MMR1	D,O/P,M	2	150	PP	24	3110	2830	2568	2320	2085	186*
7mm Remington Mag.	X7MMR2	D,O/P,M	3	175	PP	24	2860	2645	2440	2244	2057	187*
# 30 Carbine	X30M1	V	1	110	HSP	20	1990	1567	1236	1035	923	84*
30-30 Winchester	X30301	D	2	150	HP	24	2390	2018	1684	1398	1177	103*
30-30 Winchester	X30306	D	2	150	PP	24	2390	2018	1684	1398	1177	103*
30-30 Winchester	X30302	D	2	150	ST	24	2390	2018	1684	1398	1177	103*
30-30 Winchester	X30303	D	2	170	PP	24	2200	1895	1619	1381	1191	106*
30-30 Winchester	X30304	D	2	170	ST	24	2200	1895	1619	1381	1191	106*
30-06 Springfield	X30062	V	1	125	PSP	24	3140	2780	2447	2138	1853	159*
30-06 Springfield	X30061	D,O/P	2	150	PP	24	2920	2580	2265	1972	1704	146*
30-06 Springfield	X30063	D,O/P	2	150	ST	24	2910	2617	2342	2083	1843	162*
30-06 Springfield	X30065	D,O/P,M	2	165	SP	24	2800	2573	2357	2151	1956	177*
30-06 Springfield	X30064	D,O/P,M	2	180	PP	24	2700	2348	2023	1727	1466	125*
30-06 Springfield	X30066	D,O/P,M,L	3	180	ST	24	2700	2469	2250	2042	1846	166*
30-06 Springfield	X30069	M,L	3	220	ST	24	2410	2192	1985	1791	1611	144*

† Obsolete in 1989.

	CXP Class	Examples
V-Varmint	1	Prairie dog, coyote, woodchuck
D-Deer	2	Antelope, deer, black bear
O/P-Open or Plains	3	Elk, moose
M-Medium Game	3D	All game in category 3 plus large dangerous game (i.e. Kodiak bear)
L-Large Game	4	Cape Buffalo, elephant
XL-Extra Large Game		

#Acceptable for use in pistols and revolvers also.

HSP-Hollow Soft Point, PEP-Positive Expanding Point, PSP-Pointed Soft Point®, FMC-Full Metal Case, SP-Soft Point, HP-Hollow Point, ST-Silvertip®, JHP-Jacket Hollow Point, PP-Power Point

Specifications are nominal. Test barrels are used to determine ballistics figures. Individual firearms may differ from these test barrels statistics. Specifications subject to change without notice.

WINCHESTER BALLISTICS
CENTERFIRE RIFLE

Energy In Foot Pounds (ft.-lbs.)						Trajectory, Short Range Yards		⊕				Trajectory, Long Range Yards		⊕				
Muzzle	100	200	300	400	500	50	100	150	200	250	300	100	150	200	250	300	400	500
778	451	245	136	94	74	0.3	0	-2.3	-7.2	-15.8	-29.4	1.5	0	-4.2	-12.0	-24.8	-71.4	-155.6
723	417	225	127	90	70	0.3	0	-2.4	-7.7	-16.9	-31.3	1.6	0	-4.5	-12.8	-26.4	-75.6	-163.4
1654	1201	861	603	410	272	0.2	0.5	0	-1.6	-4.4	-8.7	2.3	2.6	1.9	0	-3.4	-15.9	-38.9
1094	752	500	321	202	136	0.5	0.9	0	-2.5	-6.9	-13.7	2.2	1.9	0	-3.8	-10.0	-32.3	-73.8
1114	874	677	517	388	288	0.5	0.9	0	-2.2	-6.1	-11.7	2.0	1.7	0	-3.3	-8.3	-24.9	-52.5
1305	978	722	522	369	256	0.3	0.7	0	-1.9	-5.3	-10.3	1.7	1.4	0	-2.9	-7.4	-22.7	-49.1
1282	921	648	443	295	197	0.4	0.8	0	-2.2	-6.0	-11.8	1.9	1.6	0	-3.3	-8.5	-26.7	-59.6
1282	1011	790	608	461	344	0.4	0.7	0	-1.9	-5.1	-9.9	1.7	1.4	0	-2.8	-7.1	-21.2	-44.6
1296	977	723	524	373	264	0.6	0.9	0	-2.4	-6.5	-12.5	2.1	1.8	0	-3.5	-9.0	-27.4	-59.6
1556	1148	836	595	412	280	0.2	0.6	0	-1.7	-4.6	-9.0	2.4	2.8	2.0	0	-3.5	-16.3	-39.5
1993	1551	1194	906	676	495	0.3	0.7	0	-1.8	-4.9	-9.4	2.6	2.9	2.1	0	-3.6	-16.2	-37.9
1945	1615	1332	1089	882	708	0.5	0.9	0	-2.2	-5.8	-11.0	1.9	1.6	0	-3.1	-7.8	-22.6	-46.3
2139	1667	1289	982	736	542	0.3	0.6	0	-1.6	-4.5	-8.7	2.4	2.7	1.9	0	-3.3	-14.9	-35.0
2133	1777	1470	1207	983	792	0.4	0.8	0	-1.9	-5.2	-9.9	1.7	1.5	0	-2.8	-7.0	-20.4	-41.7
2364	1850	1435	1098	827	611	0.3	0.6	0	-1.7	-4.5	-8.8	2.4	2.7	2.0	0	-3.4	-15.0	-35.2
2382	1985	1644	1351	1100	887	0.5	0.8	0	-2.1	-5.6	-10.7	1.9	1.6	0	-3.0	-7.5	-22.0	-44.8
407	272	203	165	141	122	0	-4.1	-14.4	-31.8	-57.3	-92.0	0	-8.2	-23.5	-47.0	-79.6	-175.9	-319.4
1292	904	620	427	313	252	0.6	0	-3.1	-9.2	-19.0	-33.1	2.1	0	-5.1	-13.8	-27.0	-70.1	-142.0
1765	1351	1017	751	547	398	0.2	0	-1.6	-4.9	-10.0	-17.4	2.4	2.0	0	-3.9	-10.1	-30.5	-65.2
1998	1539	1169	872	639	465	0.5	0.9	0	-2.4	-4.9	-12.3	2.9	3.0	1.6	0	-6.4	-23.2	-51.2
2009	1511	1115	806	576	415	0.8	1.1	0	-2.9	-7.8	-15.1	2.6	2.2	0	-4.2	-10.8	-33.0	-70.0
2854	2406	2018	1682	1389	1139	0.5	0.8	0	-2.0	-5.4	-10.2	1.8	1.5	0	-2.9	-7.2	-20.8	-42.2
2612	2027	1557	1179	877	641	0.3	0.6	0	-1.7	-4.6	-9.0	2.5	2.8	2.0	0	-3.4	-15.5	-36.4
2702	2267	1890	1565	1285	1046	0.4	0.8	0	-2.0	-5.3	-10.1	1.8	1.5	0	-2.8	-7.1	-20.6	-42.0
2702	2225	1818	1472	1180	936	0.5	0.8	0	-2.0	-5.5	-10.4	1.8	1.5	0	-2.9	-7.4	-21.6	-44.3
2705	2226	1817	1468	1175	932	0.6	1.0	0	-2.4	-6.4	-12.2	2.2	1.8	0	-3.4	-8.6	-25.0	-51.4
2724	2243	1830	1480	1185	940	0.6	1.0	0	-2.4	-6.3	-12.1	2.1	1.8	0	-3.4	-8.5	-24.8	-51.0
2334	1920	1568	1268	1017	810	0.2	0	-1.7	-4.9	-10.0	-17.1	1.1	0	-2.7	-7.3	-13.8	-33.9	-65.1
2313	1774	1340	998	742	563	0.4	0	-2.3	-6.8	-13.8	-23.7	1.5	0	-3.7	-10.0	-19.1	-48.1	-95.4
3221	2667	2196	1792	1448	1160	0.4	0.8	0	-1.9	-5.2	-9.9	1.7	1.5	0	-2.8	-7.0	-20.5	-42.1
3178	2718	2313	1956	1644	1372	0.6	0.9	0	-2.3	-6.0	-11.3	2.0	1.7	0	-3.2	-7.9	-22.7	-45.8
967	600	373	262	208	173	0.9	0	-4.5	-13.5	-28.3	-49.9	0	-4.5	-13.5	-28.3	-49.9	-118.6	-228.2
1902	1356	944	651	461	357	0.5	0	-2.6	-7.7	-16.0	-27.9	1.7	0	-4.3	-11.6	-22.7	-59.1	-120.5
1902	1356	944	651	461	357	0.5	0	-2.6	-7.7	-16.0	-27.9	1.7	0	-4.3	-11.6	-22.7	-59.1	-120.5
1902	1356	944	651	461	357	0.5	0	-2.6	-7.7	-16.0	-27.9	1.7	0	-4.3	-11.6	-22.7	-59.1	-120.5
1827	1355	989	720	535	425	0.6	0	-3.0	-8.9	-18.0	-31.1	2.0	0	-4.8	-13.0	-25.1	-63.6	-126.7
1827	1355	989	720	535	425	0.6	0	-3.0	-8.9	-18.0	-31.1	2.0	0	-4.8	-13.0	-25.1	-63.6	-126.7
2736	2145	1662	1269	953	706	0.4	0.8	0	-2.1	-5.6	-10.7	1.8	1.5	0	-3.0	-7.7	-23.0	-48.5
2839	2217	1708	1295	967	716	0.6	1.0	0	-2.4	-6.6	-12.7	2.2	1.8	0	-3.5	-9.0	-27.0	-57.1
2820	2281	1827	1445	1131	876	0.6	0.9	0	-2.3	-6.3	-12.0	2.1	1.8	0	-3.3	-8.5	-25.0	-51.8
2873	2426	2036	1696	1402	1151	0.7	1.0	0	-2.5	-6.5	-12.2	2.2	1.9	0	-3.6	-8.4	-24.4	-49.6
2913	2203	1635	1192	859	625	0.2	0	-1.8	-5.5	-11.2	-19.5	2.7	2.3	0	-4.4	-11.3	-34.4	-73.7
2913	2436	2023	1666	1362	1105	0.2	0	-1.6	-4.8	-9.7	-16.5	2.4	2.0	0	-3.7	-9.3	-27.0	-54.9
2837	2347	1924	1567	1268	1024	0.4	0	-2.2	-6.4	-12.7	-21.6	1.5	0	-3.5	-9.1	-17.2	-41.8	-79.9

Trajectory Illustration

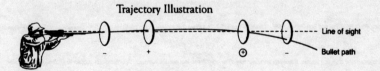

Line of sight — Bullet path

TRAJECTORY inches above (+) or below (−) line of sight. 0 = yardage at which rifle is sighted in.

WINCHESTER BALLISTICS CENTERFIRE RIFLE

Super-X®

Cartridge	Symbol	Game Selector Guide	CXP Guide Number	Wt. Grs.	Bullet Type	Barrel Length (In.)	Muzzle	100	200	300	400	500
30-40 Krag	X30401	D	2	180	PP	24	2430	2099	1795	1525	1298	1128
300 Winchester Mag.	X30WM1	D,O/P	2	150	PP	24	3290	2951	2636	2342	2068	1813
300 Winchester Mag.	X30WM2	O/P,M,L	3	180	PP	24	2960	2745	2540	2344	2157	1979
300 Winchester Mag.	X30WM3	M,L,XL	3D	220	ST	24	2680	2448	2228	2020	1823	1640
300 H. & H. Magnum	X300H2	O/P,M,L	3	180	ST	24	2880	2640	2412	2196	1991	1798
300 Savage	X3001	D,O/P	2	150	PP	24	2630	2311	2015	1743	1500	1295
300 Savage	X3003	D,O/P	2	150	ST	24	2630	2354	2095	1853	1631	1434
300 Savage	X3004	D	2	180	PP	24	2350	2025	1728	1467	1252	1098
303 Savage	X3032	D	2	190	ST	24	1890	1612	1372	1183	1055	970
303 British	X303B1	D	2	180	PP	24	2460	2233	2018	1816	1629	1459
307 Winchester	X3075	D	2	150	PP	24	2760	2321	1924	1575	1289	1091
308 Winchester	X3085	D,O/P	2	150	PP	24	2820	2488	2179	1893	1633	1405
308 Winchester	X3082	D,O/P	2	150	ST	24	2820	2533	2263	2009	1774	1560
308 Winchester	X3086	D,O/P,M	2	180	PP	24	2620	2274	1955	1666	1414	1212
308 Winchester	X3083	M,L	3	180	ST	24	2620	2393	2178	1974	1782	1604
32 Win. Special	X32WS2	D	2	170	PP	24	2250	1870	1537	1267	1082	971
32 Win. Special	X32WS3	D	2	170	ST	24	2250	1870	1537	1267	1082	971
# 32-20 Winchester	X32201	V	1	100	Lead	24	1210	1021	913	834	769	712
8mm Mauser (8 × 57)	X8MM	D	2	170	PP	24	2360	1969	1622	1333	1123	997
338 Winchester Mag.	X3381	D,O/P,M	3	200	PP	24	2960	2658	2375	2110	1862	1635
338 Winchester Mag.	X3383	M,L,XL	3D	225	SP	24	2780	2572	2374	2184	2003	1832
35 Remington	X35R1	D	2	200	PP	24	2020	1646	1335	1114	985	901
356 Winchester	X3561	D,M	2	200	PP	24	2460	2114	1797	1517	1284	1113
356 Winchester	X3563	M,L	3	250	PP	24	2160	1911	1682	1476	1299	1158
# 357 Magnum	X3575P	V,D	2	158	JSP	20	1830	1427	1138	980	883	809
358 Winchester	X3581	D,M	3	200	ST	24	2490	2171	1876	1610	1379	1194
375 Winchester	X375W	D,M	2	200	PP	24	2200	1841	1526	1268	1089	980
375 Winchester	X375W1	D,M	2	250	PP	24	1900	1647	1424	1239	1103	1011
375 H. & H. Magnum	X375H1	M,L,XL	3D	270	PP	24	2690	2420	2166	1928	1707	1507
375 H. & H. Magnum	X375H2	M,L,XL	3D	300	ST	24	2530	2268	2022	1793	1583	1397
375 H. & H. Magnum	X375H3	XL	4	300	FMC	24	2530	2171	1843	1551	1307	1126
# 38-40 Winchester	X3840	D	2	180	SP	24	1160	999	901	827	764	716
38-55 Winchester	X3855	D	2	255	SP	24	1320	1190	1091	1018	963	917
# 44 Remington Magnum	X44MHSP2	D	2	240	HSP	20	1760	1362	1094	953	861	787
# 44-40 Winchester	X4440	D	2	200	SP	24	1190	1006	900	822	756	699
45-70 Government	X4570H	D,M	2	300	JHP	24	1880	1650	1425	1235	1105	1010
458 Winchester Mag.	X4580	XL	4	500	FMC	24	2040	1823	1623	1442	1287	1161
458 Winchester Mag.	X4581	L,XL	3D	510	SP	24	2040	1770	1527	1319	1157	1048

† Obsolete in 1989.

	CXP Class	Examples
V-Varmint	1	Prairie dog, coyote, woodchuck
D-Deer	2	Antelope, deer, black bear
O/P-Open or Plains	3	Elk, moose
M-Medium Game	3D	All game in category 3 plus large dangerous game (i.e. Kodiak bear)
L-Large Game	4	Cape Buffalo, elephant
XL-Extra Large Game		

#Acceptable for use in pistols and revolvers also.
HSP-Hollow Soft Point, PEP-Positive Expanding Point, PSP-Pointed Soft Point®, FMC-Full Metal Case, SP-Soft Point, HP-Hollow Point, ST-Silvertip®, JHP-Jacket Hollow Point, PP-Power Point

Specifications are nominal. Test barrels are used to determine ballistics figures. Individual firearms may differ from these test barrels statistics. Specifications subject to change without notice.

WINCHESTER BALLISTICS CENTERFIRE RIFLE

Energy In Foot Pounds (ft.-lbs.)						Trajectory, Short Range Yards						Trajectory, Long Range Yards						
Muzzle	100	200	300	400	500	50	100	150	200	250	300	100	150	200	250	300	400	500
2360	1761	1288	929	673	508	0.4	0	−2.4	−7.1	−14.5	−25.0	1.6	0	−3.9	−10.5	−20.3	−51.7	−103.9
3605	2900	2314	1827	1424	1095	0.3	0.7	0	−1.8	−4.8	−9.3	2.6	2.9	2.1	0	−3.5	−15.4	−35.5
3501	3011	2578	2196	1859	1565	0.5	0.8	0	−2.1	−5.5	−10.4	1.9	1.6	0	−2.9	−7.3	−20.9	−41.9
3508	2927	2424	1993	1623	1314	0.2	0	−1.7	−4.9	−9.9	−16.9	2.5	2.0	0	−3.8	−9.5	−27.5	−56.1
3315	2785	2325	1927	1584	1292	0.6	0.9	0	−2.3	−6.0	−11.5	2.1	1.7	0	−3.2	−8.0	−23.3	−47.4
2303	1779	1352	1012	749	558	0.3	0	−1.9	−5.7	−11.6	−19.9	2.8	2.3	0	−4.5	−11.5	−34.4	−73.0
2303	1845	1462	1143	886	685	0.3	0	−1.8	−5.4	−11.0	−18.8	2.7	2.2	0	−4.2	−10.7	−31.5	−65.5
2207	1639	1193	860	626	482	0.5	0	−2.6	−7.7	−15.6	−27.1	1.7	0	−4.2	−11.3	−21.9	−55.8	−112.0
1507	1096	794	591	469	397	1.0	0	−4.3	−12.6	−25.5	−43.7	2.9	0	−6.8	−18.3	−35.1	−88.2	−172.5
2418	1993	1627	1318	1060	851	0.3	0	−2.1	−6.1	−12.2	−20.8	1.4	0	−3.3	−8.8	−16.6	−40.4	−77.4
2538	1795	1233	826	554	397	0.2	0	−1.9	−5.6	−11.8	−20.8	1.2	0	−3.2	−8.7	−17.1	−44.9	−92.2
2648	2061	1581	1193	888	657	0.2	0	−1.6	−4.8	−9.8	−16.9	2.4	2.0	0	−3.8	−9.8	−29.3	−62.0
2648	2137	1705	1344	1048	810	0.2	0	−1.5	−4.5	−9.3	−15.9	2.3	1.9	0	−3.6	−9.1	−26.9	−55.7
2743	2066	1527	1109	799	587	0.3	0	−2.0	−5.9	−12.1	−20.9	2.9	2.4	0	−4.7	−12.1	−36.9	−79.1
2743	2288	1896	1557	1269	1028	0.2	0	−1.8	−5.2	−10.4	−17.7	2.6	2.1	0	−4.0	−9.9	−28.9	−58.8
1911	1320	892	606	442	356	0.6	0	−3.1	−9.2	−19.0	−33.2	2.0	0	−5.1	−13.8	−27.1	−70.9	−144.3
1911	1320	892	606	442	356	0.6	0	−3.1	−9.2	−19.0	−33.2	2.0	0	−5.1	−13.8	−27.1	−70.9	−144.3
325	231	185	154	131	113	0	−6.3	−20.9	−44.9	−79.3	−125.1	0	−11.5	−32.3	−63.6	−106.3	−230.3	−413.3
2102	1463	993	671	476	375	0.5	0	−2.7	−8.2	−17.0	−29.8	1.8	0	−4.5	−12.4	−24.3	−63.8	−130.7
3890	3137	2505	1977	1539	1187	0.5	0.9	0	−2.3	−6.1	−11.6	2.0	1.7	0	−3.2	−8.2	−24.3	−50.4
3862	3306	2816	2384	2005	1677	1.2	1.3	0	−2.7	−7.1	−12.9	2.7	2.1	0	−3.6	−9.4	−25.0	−49.9
1812	1203	791	551	431	360	0.9	0	−4.1	−12.1	−25.1	−43.9	2.7	0	−6.7	−18.3	−35.8	−92.8	−185.5
2688	1985	1434	1022	732	550	0.4	0	−2.3	−7.0	−14.3	−24.7	1.6	0	−3.8	−10.4	−20.1	−51.2	−102.3
2591	2028	1571	1210	937	745	0.6	0	−3.0	−8.7	−17.4	−30.0	2.0	0	−4.7	−12.4	−23.7	−58.4	−112.9
1175	715	454	337	274	229	0	−2.4	−9.1	−21.0	−39.2	−64.3	0	−5.5	−16.2	−33.1	−57.0	−128.3	−235.8
2753	2093	1563	1151	844	633	0.4	0		−6.5	−13.3	−23.0	1.5	0	−3.6	−9.7	−18.6	−47.2	−94.1
2150	1506	1034	714	527	427	0.6		−3.2	−9.5	−19.5	−33.8	2.1	0	−5.2	−14.1	−27.4	−70.1	−138.1
2005	1506	1126	852	676	568	0.9		−4.1	−12.0	−24.0	−40.9	2.7	0	−6.5	−17.2	−32.7	−80.6	−154.1
4337	3510	2812	2228	1747	1361	0.2	0	−1.7	−5.1	−10.3	−17.6	2.5	2.1	0	−3.9	−10.0	−29.4	−60.7
4263	3426	2723	2141	1669	1300	0.3	0	−2.0	−5.9	−11.9	−20.3	2.9	2.4	0	−4.5	−11.5	−33.8	−70.1
4263	3139	2262	1602	1138	844	0.3	0	−2.2	−6.5	−13.5	−23.4	1.5	0	−3.6	−9.8	−19.1	−49.1	−99.5
538	399	324	273	233	201	0	−6.7	−22.2	−47.3	−83.2	−130.8	0	−12.1	−33.9	−66.4	−110.6	−238.3	−425.6
987	802	674	587	525	476	0	−4.7	−15.4	−32.7	−57.2	−89.3	0	−8.4	−23.4	−45.6	−75.2	−158.8	−277.4
1650	988	638	484	395	332	0	−2.7	−10.2	−23.6	−44.2	−73.3	0	−6.1	−18.1	−37.4	−65.1	−150.3	−282.5
629	449	360	300	254	217	0	−6.5	−21.6	−46.3	−81.8	−129.1	0	−11.8	−33.3	−65.5	−109.5	−237.4	−426.2
2355	1815	1355	1015	810	680	0	−2.4	−8.2	−17.6	−31.4	−51.5	0	−4.6	−12.8	−25.4	−44.3	−95.5	
4620	3689	2924	2308	1839	1496	0.7	0	−3.3	−9.6	−19.2	−32.5	2.2	0	−5.2	−13.6	−25.8	−63.2	−121.7
4712	3547	2640	1970	1516	1239	0.8	0	−3.5	−10.3	−20.8	−35.6	2.4	0	−5.6	−14.9	−28.5	−71.5	−140.4

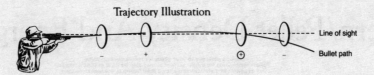

Trajectory Illustration

Line of sight
Bullet path

TRAJECTORY inches above (+) or below (−) line of sight. 0 = yardage at which rifle is sighted in.

WINCHESTER SUPREME CENTERFIRE RIFLE BALLISTICS

Cartridge	Symbol	Game Selector Guide	CXP Guide Number	Bullet Wt. (grs.)	Bullet Type	Barrel Length (In.)	Velocity In Feet Per Second (fps)					
							Muzzle	100	200	300	400	500
22-250 Remington	S22250R52	V	1	52	HPBT	24	3750	3268	2835	2442	2082	1755
243 Winchester	S243W100	D,O/P	2	100	SPBT	24	2960	2712	2477	2254	2042	1843
270 Winchester	S270W140	D,O/P	2	140	STBT	24	2960	2753	2554	2365	2183	2009
30-30 Winchester	S3030W150	D	2	150	ST	24	2390	2018	1684	1398	1177	1036
30-06 Springfield	S3006S165	D,O/P,M	2	165	STBT	24	2800	2597	2402	2216	2038	1869
30-06 Springfield	S3006S180	D,O/P,M,L	3	180	STBT	24	2700	2503	2314	2133	1960	1797
308 Winchester	S308W180	D,O/P,M	3	180	STBT	24	2610	2424	2245	2074	1911	1756
300 Winchester Mag.	S300WM190	O/P,M,L	3D	190	STBT	24	2885	2698	2519	2347	2181	2023

	CXP Class	Examples
V-Varmint		
D-Deer	1	Prairie dog, coyote, woodchuck
O/P-Open or Plains	2	Antelope, deer, black bear
M-Medium Game	3	Elk, moose
L-Large Game	3D	All game in category 3 plus large dangerous game (i.e. Kodiak bear)
XL-Extra Large Game	4	Cape Buffalo, elephant

Rimfire

RIMFIRE RIFLE AND PISTOL

Cartridge	Symbol	Bullet Wt/Grs	Bullet Type	Game Guide	RIFLE					PISTOL		
					Velocity (fps) Muzzle 100 yds		Energy (ft. lbs.) Muzzle 100 yds.		Nominal Mid-Range Trajectory 100 yds.	Barrel Length (in.)	Muzzle Velocity	Muzzle Energy (ft. lbs.)
Super-X High Velocity Cartridges — copperplated bullets												
22 Short	X22S	29	LRN*	P,S	1095	903	77	52	4.5	6	1010	66
22 Long Rifle	X22LR	40	LRN*	P,S,V,T,H	1255	1017	140	92	3.6	6	1060	100
22 Long Rifle	X22LR1	40	LRN*	P,S,V,T,H	1255	1017	140	92	3.6	6	1060	100
† 22 Long Rifle	X22LRBP	40	LRN*	P,S,V,T,H	1255	1017	140	92	3.6	6	1060	100
22 Long Rifle Hollow Point	X22LRH	37	LHP*	P,S,V	1280	1015	135	85	3.5	–	–	–
22 Long Rifle Hollow Point	X22LRH1	37	LHP*	P,S,V	1280	1015	135	85	3.5	–	–	–
Super-X 22 Winchester Magnum Cartridges — jacketed bullets												
22 Win Mag	X22WMR	40	JHP	P,S,V,H	1910	1326	324	156	1.7	6.5	1480	195
22 Win Mag	X22MR1	40	FMC	P,S,V,H	1910	1326	324	156	1.7	6.5	1480	195
Winchester Super Silhouette												
22 Long Rifle	XS22LR1	42	LTC	P,S,V,T,H	1220	1003	139	94	3.6	6/10	1025/1105	98/114
Winchester T22 Standard Velocity Cartridges												
22 Long Rifle Target	XT22LR	40	LRN	P,T	1150	976	117	85	4.0	6	950	80
Other Winchester Rimfire Cartridges												
22 Long Rifle, Wildcat	WW22LR	40	LRN	P,S,V,T,H	1255	1017	140	92	3.6	6	1060	100
22 Long Rifle, Shot	X22LRS	37	#12 Shot	V	–	–	–	–	–	–	–	–
22 Short Blank	22BL	Black Powder		–	–	–	–	–	–	–	–	–
22 Short C.B.	WW22CBS2	29	LRN	P,T	725	–	–	–	–	–	–	–

*Lubaloy coated
LRN — Lead Round Nose
LHP — Lead Hollow Point

JHP — Jacketed Hollow Point
FMC — Full Metal Case
LTC — Lead Truncated Cone

Game Guide
P — Plinking   S — Squirrel   V — Varmint   T — Target   H — Silhouette

Pattern/Pellet Density And Energy Guide

Look up distance to your game for recommended pellet.
Pellets appropriate for longer distances may also be used at shorter range.
Use of pellets at distances surpassing their listing is not recommended.

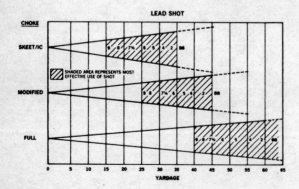

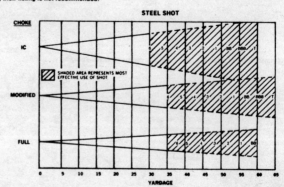

CONVERSION FACTORS

Common inch calibers converted to metric

.25 inch = 6.35mm
.256 inch = 6.5mm
.270 inch = 6.858mm
.280 inch = 7.11mm
.297 inch = 7.54mm
.300 inch = 7.62mm
.301 inch = 7.62mm
.303 inch = 7.696mm
.308 inch = 7.82mm
.311 inch = 7.899mm
.312 inch = 7.925mm
.380 inch = 9.65mm
.400 inch = 10.16mm
.402 inch = 10.21mm
.450 inch = 11.43mm
.455 inch = 11.557mm
.500 inch = 12.7mm
.550 inch = 13.97mm
.577 inch = 14.65mm
.600 inch = 15.24mm
.661 inch = 16.79mm

Pressure

1 kg per sq. cm = 14.223 lb. per sq. inch
1 kg per sq. cm = 0.0063493 tons per sq. inch
1 kg per sq. cm = 0.968 Atmospheres
1 Atmosphere = 14.7 lb. per sq. inch
1 Atmosphere = 0.00655 tons per sq. inch
1 ton per sq. inch = 152.0 Atmospheres
1 lb. per sq. inch = 0.0680 Atmospheres
1 Atmosphere = 1.03 kg per sq. cm
1 lb. per sq. inch = 0.070309 kg per sq. cm
1 ton per sq. inch = 157.49 kg per sq. cm

Energy

1 m.kg = 7.2331 foot lb.
1 foot lb. = 0.13825 m.kg

Velocity

1 meter per second = 3.2809 feet per second
1 foot per second = 0.30479 meters per second

Weight

1 gram = 15.432 grains
1 grain = 0.0648 grams
1 oz. = 28.349 grams

Linear

1 meter = 1.0936 yards
1 meter = 3.2808 feet
1 yard = 0.91438 meters
1 foot = 0.30479 meters
1 inch = 25.4mm
1/4 inch = 6.35mm
1/2 inch = 12.7mm
3/4 inch = 19.05mm
1/8 inch = 3.175mm
3/8 inch = 9.525mm
5/8 inch = 15.875mm
7/8 inch = 22.225mm
1/16 inch = 1.5875mm
3/16 inch = 4.7625mm
5/16 inch = 7.9375mm
7/16 inch = 11.1125mm
9/16 inch = 14.2875mm
11/16 inch = 17.4625mm
13/16 inch = 20.6375mm
15/16 inch = 23.8125mm

Reloading

FOR ADDRESSES AND PHONE
NUMBERS OF MANUFACTURERS AND
DISTRIBUTORS INCLUDED IN THIS
SECTION, SEE *DIRECTORY OF
MANUFACTURERS AND SUPPLIERS*

BUFFALO BULLET AMMUNITION

.45 Caliber
285 Grain
Hollow Point
Hollow Base

.45 Caliber
325 Grain
Hollow Point
Flat Base

.50 Caliber
385 Grain
Hollow Point
Hollow Base

.50 Caliber
410 Grain
Hollow Point
Hollow Base

.54 Caliber
425 Grain
Hollow Point
Hollow Base

.54 Caliber
435 Grain
Round Nose
Hollow Base

.54 Caliber
460 Grain
Round Nose
Flat Base

BUFFALO MAXI BULLETS

Buffalo's black powder bullets are cold formed in precision dies from pure lead, eliminating the air voids, sprue marks or parting lines that spoil consistent accuracy. Other features include increased barrel-to-bullet bearing surface, uniform lubrication, smaller base diameter for easy "thumb starting," hollow point for better expansion, double gas seals, plus a choice of hollow or flat base. Available in 45, 50 or 54 caLIBERS (see below). Prices range from $6.75 (285 grain) for a 20-bullet box to $9.00 (460 grain).

38 Special   357 Magnum   10mm   41 Magnum   41 Action Express   44 Special   44 Magnum   45 ACP   223 Rifle   308 Winchester

25 ACP   32 ACP   380   9mm   9mm Sub-sonic

BUFFALO BULLET CORE-SHOT

Core-Shot ammunition is custom-loaded with a pre-fragmented projectile containing a small lead core swaged over #12 shot. While maintaining the advantages of fragmented ammunition, Core-Shot also yields moderate penetration. Upon eruption of the thin copper jacket and core, hundreds of sub-particles are released into the target medium, creating a substantial wound channel. Sure-Shot is designed to expend all of the bullet's energy into the target medium without over-penetration. It also reduces hazardous ricochet action, an important safety factor. Core-Shot is available in the calibers pictured below. Prices range from $14.25 per 6-round pack to $19.25.

REMINGTON BULLETS

REMINGTON RIFLE BULLETS

Remington component rifle bullets bring the renown performance of "Core-Lokt", "Power-Lokt" and "Bronze Point" to reloaders.

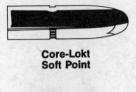

Core-Lokt Soft Point

Core-Lokt Pointed Soft Point

Power-Lokt Hollow Point

Bronze Point

"Core-Lokt" Pointed Soft Point and Soft Point bullets for controlled expansion and high weight retention—ideal for medium and big game.

"Power-Lokt" hollow points for pin point accuracy on targets, small game and varmints.

"Bronze Point" for flat trajectory and excellent accuracy at extended ranges.

Order No.	Caliber	Bullet weight	Bullet style	Boxes per case*	Case wt., lbs.
B1705	17 Cal	25 gr.	Hollow Point "Power-Lokt"	40	
B2240	22 Cal	50 gr.	Hollow Point "Power-Lokt"	40	
B2265	22 Cal	55 gr.	Hollow Point "Power-Lokt"	40	
B2430	6mm	80 gr.	Hollow Point "Power-Lokt"	24	
B2460	6mm	100 gr.	Pointed Soft Point "Core-Lokt"	24	
B2510	25 Cal	87 gr.	Hollow Point "Power-Lokt"	24	
B2540	25 Cal	120 gr.	Pointed Soft Point "Core-Lokt"	24	
B2720	270	130 gr.	Pointed Soft Point "Core-Lokt"	24	
B2730	270	130 gr.	"Bronze Point"	20	
B2830	7mm	150 gr.	Pointed Soft Point "Core-Lokt"	20	
B2850	7mm	175 gr.	Pointed Soft Point "Core-Lokt"	20	
B3020	30 Cal	150 gr.	"Bronze Point"	20	
B3030	30 Cal	150 gr.	Pointed Soft Point "Core-Lokt"	20	
B3060	30 Cal	180 gr.	"Bronze Point"	20	
B3080	30 Cal	180 gr.	Pointed Soft Point "Core-Lokt"	20	

*Packed 100 per box.

REMINGTON HANDGUN BULLETS

The Choice of Champions

Semi-Jacketed Hollow Point
Scalloped jacket delivers maximum expansion and stopping power, with controlled expansion even at high velocities.

Soft Point
Delivers deeper penetration than the semi-jacketed hollow point.

Metal Case
Helps ensure positive functioning in autoloaders.

Jacketed Hollow Point
Controlled expansion with no exposed lead to impair functioning in autoloaders.

Wadcutter
Solid lead for precision target shooting. Leave an easy-to-see hole in the target.

Lead Round Nose
A general purpose bullet and standard for law enforcement.

Order No.	Caliber	Bullet weight	Bullet style	Boxes per case*	Case wt., lbs.
B2525	25	50 gr.	Metal Case	40	
B3550	9mm	115 gr.	Jacketed Hollow Point	24	
B3552	9mm	124 gr.	Metal Case	24	
B3572	357	125 gr.	Semi-Jacketed Hollow Point	24	
B3576	357	158 gr.	Semi-Jacketed Hollow Point	20	
B3578	357	158 gr.	Lead	20	
B3810	38	95 gr.	Semi-Jacketed Hollow Point	24	
B3830D	38	148 gr.	Wadcutter	20*	
B4110	41 Mag	210 gr.	Soft Point	20	
B4120	41 Mag	210 gr.	Lead	20	
B4410	44 Mag	240 gr.	Soft Point	20	
B4420	44 Mag	240 gr.	Semi-Jacketed Hollow Point	20	
B4405	44 Mag	180 gr.	Semi-Jacketed Hollow Point	20	
B4520	45	185 gr.	Jacketed Hollow Point	20	
B4530	45	230 gr.	Metal Case	20	

*Packed 100 per box except B3830D, 500 per box.

SIERRA BULLETS

.22 Caliber Hornet (.223/5.66MM Diameter)
- 40 gr. Hornet Varminter #1100
- 45 gr. Hornet Varminter #1110

.22 Caliber Hornet (.224/5.69MM Diameter)
- 40 gr. Hornet Varminter #1200
- 45 gr. Hornet Varminter #1210

.22 Caliber (.224/5.69MM Diameter) High Velocity
- 40 gr. HP Varminter #1385
- 45 gr. SMP Varminter #1300
- 45 gr. SPT Varminter #1310
- 50 gr. SMP Varminter #1320
- 50 gr. SPT Varminter #1330
- 50 gr. Blitz Varminter #1340
- 52 gr. HPBT MatchKing #1410
- 53 gr. HP MatchKing #1400

- 55 gr. Blitz Varminter #1345
- 55 gr. SMP Varminter #1350
- 55 gr. FMJBT GameKing #1355
- 55 gr. SPT Varminter #1360
- 55 gr. SBT GameKing #1365
- 55 gr. HPBT GameKing #1390
- 60 gr. HP Varminter #1375
- 63 gr. SMP Varminter #1370
- 69 gr. HPBT MatchKing #1380

6MM .243 Caliber (.243/6.17MM Diameter)
- 60 gr. HP Varminter #1500
- 70 gr. HPBT MatchKing #1505
- 75 gr. HP Varminter #1510
- 85 gr. SPT Varminter #1520
- 85 gr. HPBT GameKing #1530

- 90 gr. FMJBT GameKing #1535
- 100 gr. SPT Pro-Hunter #1540
- 100 gr. SMP Pro-Hunter #1550
- 100 gr. SBT GameKing #1560

.25 Caliber (.257/6.53MM Diameter)
- 75 gr. HP Varminter #1600
- 87 gr. SPT Varminter #1610
- 90 gr. HPBT GameKing #1615
- 100 gr. SPT Pro-Hunter #1620
- 100 gr. SBT GameKing #1625
- 117 gr. SBT GameKing #1630
- 117 gr. SPT Pro-Hunter #1640
- 120 gr. HPBT GameKing #1650

6.5MM .264 Caliber (.264/6.71MM Diameter)

- 85 gr. HP Varminter #1700
- 100 gr. HP Varminter #1710
- 120 gr. SPT Pro-Hunter #1720
- NEW 120 gr. HPBT MatchKing #1725
- 140 gr. SBT GameKing #1730
- 140 gr. HPBT MatchKing #1740

.270 Caliber (.277/7.04MM Diameter)
- 90 gr. HP Varminter #1800
- 110 gr. SPT Pro-Hunter #1810
- 130 gr. SBT GameKing #1820
- 130 gr. SPT Pro-Hunter #1830
- 140 gr. HPBT GameKing #1835
- 140 gr. SBT GameKing #1845
- 150 gr. SBT GameKing #1840
- 150 gr. RN Pro-Hunter #1850

SIERRA BULLETS

7MM .284 Caliber (.284/7.21MM Diameter)

- 100 gr. HP Varminter #1895
- 120 gr. SPT Pro-Hunter #1900
- 140 gr. SBT GameKing #1905
- 140 gr. SPT Pro-Hunter #1910
- 150 gr. SBT GameKing #1913
- 150 gr. HPBT MatchKing #1915
- 160 gr. SBT GameKing #1920
- 160 gr. HPBT GameKing #1925
- 168 gr. HPBT MatchKing #1930
- 170 gr. RN Pro-Hunter #1950
- 175 gr. SBT GameKing #1940

.30 (30-30) Caliber (.308/7.82MM Diameter)

- 125 gr. HP Pro-Hunter #2020
- 150 gr. FN Pro-Hunter #2000 POWER JACKET
- 170 gr. FN Pro-Hunter #2010 POWER JACKET

.30 Caliber 7.62MM (.308/7.82MM Diameter)

- 110 gr. RN Pro-Hunter #2100
- 110 gr. FMJ Pro-Hunter #2105
- 110 gr. HP Varminter #2110
- 125 gr. SPT Pro-Hunter #2120
- 150 gr. FMJBT GameKing #2115
- 150 gr. SPT Pro-Hunter #2130
- 150 gr. SBT GameKing #2125
- 150 gr. HPBT MatchKing #2190
- 150 gr. RN Pro-Hunter #2135
- 165 gr. SBT GameKing #2145
- 165 gr. HPBT GameKing #2140
- 168 gr. HPBT MatchKing #2200
- 180 gr. SPT Pro-Hunter #2150
- 180 gr. SBT GameKing #2160
- 180 gr. HPBT MatchKing #2220
- 180 gr. RN Pro-Hunter #2170
- 190 gr. HPBT MatchKing #2210
- 200 gr. SBT GameKing #2165
- 200 gr. HPBT MatchKing #2230
- 220 gr. HPBT MatchKing #2240
- 220 gr. RN Pro-Hunter #2180

.303 Caliber 7.7MM (.311/7.90MM Diameter)

- 150 gr. SPT Pro-Hunter #2300
- 180 gr. SPT Pro-Hunter #2310

8MM (.323/8.20MM Diameter)

- 150 gr. SPT Pro-Hunter #2400
- 175 gr. SPT Pro-Hunter #2410
- 220 gr. SBT GameKing #2420

.338 Caliber (.338/8.59MM Diameter)

- 250 gr. SBT GameKing #2600

.35 Caliber (.358/9.09MM Diameter)

- 200 gr. RN Pro-Hunter #2800
- NEW 225 gr. SBT GameKing #2850

.375 Caliber (.375/9.53MM Diameter)

- 200 gr. FN Pro-Hunter #2900 POWER JACKET
- 300 gr. SBT GameKing #3000

.45 Caliber (45.70) (.458/11.63MM Diameter)

- 300 gr. HP Pro-Hunter #8900

SIERRA BULLETS

Single Shot Pistol Bullets

6MM .243 Dia. 80 gr. SPT Pro-Hunter #7150

7MM .284 Dia. 130 gr. SPT Pro-Hunter #7250

.30 cal. .308 Dia. 135 gr. SPT Pro-Hunter #7350

.25 Caliber (.251/6.38MM Diameter)

50 gr. FMJ Tournament Master #8000

.32 Caliber 7.65MM (.3127.92MM Diameter)

71 gr. FMJ Tournament Master #8010

.32 Mag. .3127.92MM Diameter

90 gr. JHC Sports Master #8030 POWER JACKET

9MM .355 Caliber (.355/9.02MM Diameter)

90 gr. JHP Sports Master #8100 POWER JACKET

95 gr. FMJ Tournament Master #8105

115 gr. JHP Sports Master #8110 POWER JACKET

115 gr. FMJ Tournament Master #8115

125 gr. FMJ Tournament Master #8120

130 gr. FMJ Tournament Master #8345

.38 Caliber (.357/9.07MM Diameter)

110 gr. JHC Blitz Sports Master #8300 POWER JACKET

125 gr. JSP Sports Master #8310

125 gr. JHC Sports Master #8320 POWER JACKET

140 gr. JHC Sports Master #8325 POWER JACKET

158 gr. JHC Sports Master #8360 POWER JACKET

158 gr. JSP Sports Master #8340

170 gr. JHC Sports Master #8365 POWER JACKET

170 gr. FMJ Match Tournament Master #8350

180 gr. FPJ Match Tournament Master #8370

10MM .400 Caliber (.400/10.16MM Diameter)

150 gr. JHP Sports Master #8430 POWER JACKET

180 gr. JHP Sports Master #8460 POWER JACKET

NEW 190 gr. FPJ Sports Master #8480

.41 Caliber (.410/10.41MM Diameter)

170 gr. JHC Sports Master #8500 POWER JACKET

210 gr. JHC Sports Master #8520 POWER JACKET

220 gr. FPJ Match Tournament Master #8530

.44 Magnum (.4295/10.91MM Diameter)

180 gr. JHC Sports Master #8600 POWER JACKET

210 gr. JHC Sports Master #8620 POWER JACKET

220 gr. FPJ Match Tournament Master #8605

240 gr. JHC Sports Master #8610 POWER JACKET

250 gr. FPJ Match Tournament Master #8615

NEW 300 gr. JSP Sports Master #8630

.45 Caliber (.4515/11.47MM Diameter)

185 gr. JHP Sports Master #8800 POWER JACKET

185 gr. FPJ Match Tournament Master #8810

200 gr. FPJ Match Tournament Master #8825

230 gr. FMJ Match Tournament Master #8815

240 gr. JHC Sports Master #8820 POWER JACKET

SPEER BULLETS

HANDGUN BULLETS—JACKETED

CALIBER & TYPE	25 TMJ	9mm JHP	32 JHP	9mm TMJ	9mm JHP	9mm TMJ	9mm JHP	9mm TMJ	9mm PSP	38 JHP	38 JSP	38 JHP	38 TMJ	38 JHP
WEIGHT (GRS.)	50	88	100	95	100	115	115	124	124	110	125	125	125	140
DIAMETER	.251"	.355"	.312"	.355"	.355"	.355"	.355"	.355"	.355"	.357"	.357"	.357"	.357"	.357"
USE	P	P,V	P,V	P	P,V	P,T,V	P,V	P,T,V	P,V	P,V	P,V	P,V	P,T	P,V
PART NUMBER	3982	4000	3981	4001	3983	3995*	3996	4004	3997	4007	4011	4013	4015	4203

NEW

	38 JHP-SWC	38 TMJ	38 JHP	38 JSP	38 JSP-WC	38 TMJ-Sil.	38 TMJ-Sil.	10mm TMJ	41 JHP-SWC	41 JSP-SWC	41 TMJ-Sil.	44 Mag.-JHP	44 JHP-SWC	44 JSP-SWC
	146	150	158	158	160	180	200	190	200	220	210	200	225	240
	.357"	.357"	.357"	.357"	.357"	.357"	.357"	.400"	.410"	.410"	.410"	.429"	.429"	.429"
	P,V	P,T,V	P,V,S	P,V,S	P,V,S	P,S	P,S	P,S,M	P,V,SG,S	P,V,S,D	S,T	P,V,SG,S	P,V,SG,S,D	P,V,SG,S,D
	4205	4207	4211	4217	4223	4229*	4231*	4403	4405	4417	4420	4425	4435	4447

	44 Mag.-JHP	44 Mag.-JSP	44 TMJ-Sil.	45 TMJ-Match	45 TMJ-Match	45 JHP	45 Mag.-JHP	45 TMJ	45 JHP
	240	240	240	185	200	200	225	230	260
	.429"	.429"	.429"	.451"	.451"	.451"	.451"	.451"	.451"
	P,V,SG,S,D	P,V,SG,S,D	P,V,S	P,T,M	P,T,M	P,V,SG	P,V,SG,S	P,T,S	P,V,S,D
	4453	4457	4459*	4473	4475	4477	4479	4480*	4481

HANDGUN BULLETS—LEAD

CALIBER & TYPE	32 HB-WC	9mm RN	38 BB-WC
WEIGHT (GRS.)	98	125	148
DIAMETER	.314"	.356"	.358"
USE	P,T,M	P,T	P,T
PART NUMBER	4600**	4601*	4605*

	38 HB-WC	38 SWC	38 HP-SWC	38 RN	44 SWC	45 SWC	45 RN	45 SWC
	148	158	158	158	240	200	230	250
	.358"	.358"	.358"	.358"	.430"	.452"	.452"	.452"
	P,T,M	P,T,V,SG	P,T,V,SG	P,T	P,T,V,SG,D	P,T,M	P,T	P,T,V,SG,D
	4617*	4623*	4627*	4647*	4660*	4677*	4690*	4683*

PLASTIC INDOOR AMMO

NOTE: Shown are 44 bullet and 44 case. 45 bullet is used with regular brass case.

		BULLETS	CASES
NO PER BOX		50	50
PART #	38 CAL.	8510	8515
	44 CAL.	8520	8525
	45 CAL.	8530	See Note

Abbreviation Guide:
JHP–Jacketed Hollow Point
TMJ™–Totally Metal Jacketed™
PSP–Plated Soft Point
JSP–Jacketed Soft Point
Sil.–Silhouette
WC–Wadcutter
SWC–Semi-Wadcutter
HB–Hollow Base
BB–Bevel Base
RN–Round Nose
P–Plinking; T–Target
V–Varmint; M–Match
SG–Small Game
S–Silhouette; D–Deer.
* Also available in 500-bullet Bulk-Pak.
** Available in bulk quantities only.

LEAD BALLS

WT. (GRS.)	64	80	120	128	133	138	141	144	177	182	224	230	278
DIAMETER	.350"	.375"	.433"	.440"	.445"	.451"	.454"	.457"	.490"	.495"	.530"	.535"	.570"
PART #	5110	5113	5127	5129	5131	5133	5135	5137	5139	5140	5142	5150	5180
GUN TYPE	Some 36 Pistols & Rifles	36 Sheriffs Revolver / 36 Leech & Rigdon Revolver / 36 Navy Revolver	45 Hawken / 45 Kentucky / 45 Percussion Pistols	45 Thompson Center Rifle Seneca Hawken	45 Kentucky (F&P) / 45 Mountain / 45 Yorkshire / 45 Michigan Carbine / 45 Morse Navy / 45 Huntsman	44 Revolvers / 44 Percussion Revolving Carb. / 44 Ballister Revolver	44 Percussion Revolving Carb.	Ruger New Old Army	50 Thompson Center Hawken	50 Douglas / 50 Sharon / 50 Morse Navy	54 Thompson Center Renegade	54 Douglas / 54 Sharon / 54 Mountain	58 Harpers Ferry Pistol / 58 Morse Navy

SPEER BULLETS

RIFLE BULLETS

BULLET CALIBER AND TYPE	22 Spire Soft Point	22 Spitzer Soft Point	22 Spire Soft Point	22 Spitzer Soft Point	22 Spitzer Soft Point	22 Hollow Point	22 Full Metal Jacket	22 Spitzer Soft Point	22 Spitzer S.P. w/ Cannelure	22 Semi-Spitzer Soft Point	6mm Hollow Point	6mm Spitzer Soft Point	6mm Spitzer Soft Point B.T.	6mm Full Metal Jacket
DIAMETER	.223"	.223"	.224"	.224"	.224"	.224"	.224"	.224"	.224"	.224"	.243"	.243"	.243"	.243"
WEIGHT (GRS.)	40	45	40	45	50	52	55	55	55	70	75	80	85	90
USE	V	V	V	V	V	V	V	V	V	HV	V	V	HV,LG	HV
PART NUMBER	1005	1011	1017	1023	1029	1035	1045	1047	1049	1053	1205	1211	1213	1215

CAL. & TYPE	270 Spitzer Soft Point B.T.	270 Spitzer Soft Point	7mm Hollow Point	7mm Spitzer Soft Point	7mm Spitzer Soft Point B.T.	7mm Spitzer Soft Point B.T.	7mm Spitzer Soft Point	7mm Match B.T.	7mm Spitzer Soft Point B.T.	7mm Spitzer Soft Point	7mm Mag-Tip Soft Point	7mm Mag-Tip Soft Point	30 Round Soft Point Plinker®	30 Hollow Point	30 Round Soft Point
DIA.	.277"	.277"	.284"	.284"	.284"	.284"	.284"	.284"	.284"	.284"	.284"	.284"	.308"	.308"	.308"
WT.	150	150	115	130	130	145	145	145	160	160	160	175	100	110	110
USE	BG	BG	V	HV,LG	HV,LG	BG	BG	M	BG	BG	BG	BG	V	V	V
PART #	1604	1605	1617	1623	1624	1628	1629	1631	1634	1635	1637	1641	1805	1835	1845

CAL. & TYPE	30 Mag-Tip Soft Point	30 Match B.T.	30 Spitzer Soft Point	303 Spitzer Soft Point	303 Round Soft Point	32 Flat Soft Point	8mm Spitzer Soft Point	8mm Semi-Spitzer Soft Point	8mm Spitzer Soft Point	338 Spitzer Soft Point	338 Semi-Spitzer Soft Point	35 Flat Soft Point	35 Flat Soft Point	35 Spitzer Soft Point	9.3mm Semi-Spitzer Soft Point
DIA.	.308"	.308"	.308"	.311"	.311"	.321"	.323"	.323"	.323"	.338"	.338"	.358"	.358"	.358"	.366"
WT.	180	190	200	150	180	170	150	170	200	200	275	180	220	250	270
USE	BG	M	BG	BG	BG	BG	BG	BG	BG	BG	BG	BG	BG	BG	BG
PART #	2059	2080	2211	2217	2223	2259	2277	2283	2285	2405	2411	2435	2439	2453	2459

V–Varmint; HV–Heavy Varmint (coyote); LG–Light Game (whitetail, antelope); BG–Big Game; M–Match. ⬤ Hot-Cor.

SPEER BULLETS

6mm Spitzer Soft Point	6mm Spitzer Soft Point B.T.	6mm Round Soft Point	6mm Spitzer Soft Point	25 Spitzer Soft Point	25 Spitzer Soft Point	25 Hollow Point	25 Spitzer Soft Point B.T.	25 Spitzer Soft Point	25 Spitzer Soft Point	6.5mm Spitzer Soft Point	6.5mm Spitzer Soft Point	270 Hollow Point	270 Spitzer Soft Point	270 Spitzer Soft Point B.T.	270 Spitzer Soft Point
.243"	.243"	.243"	.243"	.257"	.257"	.257"	.257"	.257"	.257"	.263"	.263"	.277"	.277"	.277"	.277"
90	100	105	105	87	100	100	100	120	120	120	140	100	100	130	130
HV,LG	LG	LG	LG	HV	HV,LG	HV	HV,LG	BG	BG	HV,LG	BG	V	V	BG	BG
1217	1220	1223	1229	1241	1405	1407	1408	1410	1411	1435	1441	1447	1453	1458	1459

30 Spire Soft Point	30 Hollow Point	30 Flat Soft Point	30 Flat Soft Point	30 Round Soft Point	30 Spitzer Soft Point B.T.	30 Spitzer Soft Point	30 Mag-Tip Soft Point	30 Round Soft Point	30 Spitzer Soft Point	30 Spitzer Soft Point B.T.	30 Match B.T.	30 Flat Soft Point	30 Round Soft Point	30 Spitzer Soft Point B.T.	30 Spitzer Soft Point
.308"	.308"	.308"	.308"	.308"	.308"	.308"	.308"	.308"	.308"	.308"	.308"	.308"	.308"	.308"	.308"
110	130	130	150	150	150	150	150	165	165	165	168	170	180	180	180
V	V	HV,LG	BG	BG	BG	BG	BG	BG	BG	BG	M	BG	BG	BG	BG
1855	2005	2007	2011	2017	2022	2023	2025	2029	2034	2035	2040	2041	2047	2052	2053

375 Semi-Spitzer Soft Point	45 Flat Soft Point
.375"	.458"
235	400
BG	BG
2471	2479

GRAND SLAM™

BULLET CALIBER AND TYPE	270 G.S. Soft Point	270 G.S. Soft Point	7mm G.S. Soft Point	7mm G.S. Soft Point	30 G.S. Soft Point	30 G.S. Soft Point	338 G.S. Soft Point	375 G.S. Soft Point
DIAMETER	.277"	.277"	.284"	.284"	.308"	.308"	.338"	.375"
WEIGHT (GRS.)	130	150	160	175	165	180	250	285
USE	BG	BG	BG	BG	BG	BG	BG	BG
PART NUMBER	1465	1608	1638	1643	2038	2063	2408	2473

REMINGTON CASES & PRIMERS

Remington brass cases with 5% more brass for extra strength in head section — annealed neck section for longer reloading life — primer pocket dimension controlled to .0005 inch to assure precise primer fit — heavier bridge and sidewalls — formed and machined to exacting tolerances for consistent powder capacity.

RIFLE CASES (UNPRIMED)	QTY. PER BOX	KLEANBORE® PRIMER NO.
17 REMINGTON • U17REM*	20	7 1/2
22 HORNET • U22HRN	50	6 1/2
222 REMINGTON • U222R	20	7 1/2
222 REMINGTON MAGNUM • U222MG	20	7 1/2
22-250 REMINGTON • U22250	20	9 1/2
223 REMINGTON • U223	20	7 1/2
6mm REMINGTON • U6MM	20	9 1/2
243 WINCHESTER • U243	20	9 1/2
250 SAVAGE • U250SV	20	9 1/2
25-06 REMINGTON • U2506	20	9 1/2
264 WINCHESTER MAGNUM • U264	20	9 1/2M
270 WINCHESTER • U270	20	9 1/2
280 REMINGTON • U280	20	9 1/2
7mm MAUSER • U7MSR	20	9 1/2
7mm-08 REMINGTON • U7MM08	20	9 1/2

RIFLE CASES (UNPRIMED)	QTY. PER BOX	KLEANBORE® PRIMER NO.
7mm REMINGTON MAGNUM • U7MMAG	20	9 1/2 M
7mmBR REMINGTON • U7MMBR	20	7 1/2
30 CARBINE • U30CAR	50	6 1/2
30-06 SPRINGFIELD • U3006	20	9 1/2
30-30 WINCHESTER • U3030	20	9 1/2
308 WINCHESTER • U308	20	9 1/2
300 WINCHESTER • U300W	20	9 1/2M
8mm REMINGTON MAGNUM • U8MMAG	20	9 1/2M
338 WINCHESTER MAGNUM • U338	20	9 1/2M
35 REMINGTON • U35REM	20	9 1/2
375 H&H MAGNUM • U375HH	20	9 1/2M
444 MARLIN • U444	20	9 1/2
458 WINCHESTER MAGNUM • U458	20	9 1/2M
45-70 GOVERNMENT • U4570	20	9 1/2

ALL UNPRIMED CASES PACKED 1000 IN A CASE.

* Designed for Remington No. 7 1/2 primer only. Substitutions not recommended. U number is unprimed.

WINCHESTER PRIMERS & UNPRIMED CASES

CENTERFIRE PRIMERS

Centerfire primers are recommended for use as follows:

SYMBOL	PRIMER	TYPE
WLR	#8½-120	Large Rifle
WLRM	#8½M-120	Large Rifle Magnum
WSR	#6½-116	Small Rifle
WSP	#1½-108	Small (Regular) Pistol
WSPM	#1½M-108	Small (Magnum) Pistol
WLP	#7-111	Large (Regular Pistol)

Large Rifle
220 Swift
22-250 Rem.
225 Winchester
243 Winchester
6mm Remington
250 Savage
25-06 Rem.
257 Roberts + P
264 Win. Mag.
270 Winchester
284 Winchester
7mm Mauser
7mm Rem. Mag.
30-30 Winchester
30-06 Springfield
30-40 Krag

300 Win. Mag.
300 H&H Mag.
300 Savage
303 British
307 Winchester
308 Winchester
32 Win. Special
32-20 Winchester
8mm Mauser
338 Win. Mag.
348 Winchester
35 Remington
356 Winchester
358 Winchester
375 Winchester
375 H&H Mag.
38-55 Winchester

45-70 Gov.
458 Win. Mag.
Small Rifle
218 Bee
22 Hornet
222 Remington
223 Remington
25-20 Winchester
256 Win. Mag.
30 Carbine
32-20 Winchester
Small (Reg.) Pistol
25 Automatic
32 Automatic
32 S&W
32 S&W Long

9mm Luger
38 S&W
38 Special
38 Automatic
380 Automatic
Small (Mag.) Pistol
357 Magnum
9mm Win. Mag.
357 Rem. Max.
Large (Reg.) Pistol
38-40 Winchester
41 Rem. Mag.
44 Rem. Mag.
44 S&W Special
45 Colt
45 Automatic
45 Win. Mag.

UNPRIMED BRASS CASES

UNPRIMED RIFLE SYMBOL	CALIBER	UNPRIMED RIFLE SYMBOL	CALIBER	UNPRIMED PISTOL/REVOLVER SYMBOL	CALIBER
U218	*218 Bee	U300H	300 H&H Mag.	U25A	*25 Auto.
U22H	*22 Hornet	U300	300 Savage	U256	*256 Win. Mag.
U22250	22-250 Rem.	U307	307 Win.	U32A	*32 Auto. (7.65mm Browning)
U22OS	220 Swift	U308	308 Win.		
U222R	222 Rem.	U303	303 British		
U223R	223 Rem.	U32W	32 Win. Special	U32SW	*32 S&W
U225	225 Win.	U3220	*32-20 Win.	U32SWL	*32 S&W Long (32 Colt New Police)
U243	243 Win.	U3240	32-40 Win.		
U6MMR	6mm Rem.	U8MM	8mm Mauser	U357	*357 Mag.
U2520	25-20 Win.	U338	338 Win. Mag.	U357MAX	*357 Rem. Max.
U256	*256 Win. Mag.	U348	348 Win.	U9MM	*9mm Luger (9mm Parabellum)
U250	250 Savage	U35R	35 Rem.		
U2506	25-06 Rem.	U356	356 Win.	U9MMWM	*9mm Win. Mag.
U257P	257 Roberts + P	U358	358 Win.	U38SW	*38 S&W (38 Colt New Police)
U264	264 Win. Mag.	U357H	375 H&H Mag.		
U270	270 Win.	U375W	375 Win.	U38SP	*38 Special
U284	284 Win.	U3840	38-40 Win.	U38A	*38 Auto (and 38 Super)
U7MM	7mm Mauser	U3855	*38-55 Win.		
U7MAG.	7mm Rem. Mag.	U4440	*44-40 Win.	U380A	*380 Auto (9mm Short-9mm Corto)
U30C	*30 Carbine	U44M	*44 Rem. Mag.		
U3030	30-30 Win.	U4570	*45-70 Govt.	U41	*41 Rem. Mag.
U3006	30-06 Springfield	U458	458 Win. Mag.	U44S	*44 S&W Special
U3040	30-40 Krag			U44M	*44 Rem. Mag.
U300WM	300 Win. Mag.			U45C	*45 Colt
				U45A	*45 Auto
				U45WM	*45 Win. Mag.

*50 cases per box—all others are 20 cases per box.

HODGDON POWDERS

PYRODEX
Replica Black Powder for Percussion Muzzleloaders and Black Powder Cartridge Arms

The first real improvement in propellants for muzzleloading weapons. Designed for use in percussion muzzleloading firearms, Pyrodex gives the shooter less fouling, exceptional accuracy, more shots per pound, and eliminates the need for cleaning between shots. It is officially sanctioned by the National Muzzleloading Rifle Association for use in competition. Available in three grades: "P," "RS," and "CTG." Pyrodex can be used in any firearm with impressive results.

RS PYRODEX® 1 LB. **$9.65**
P PYRODEX® 1 LB. **$9.65**
CTG PYRODEX® 1 LB. **$7.95**

VOLUME TO VOLUME COMPARISON CHART: BLACK POWDER TO PYRODEX

BLACK POWDER	PYRODEX	BLACK POWDER	PYRODEX
10 Gr.	8 Gr.	110 Gr.	88 Gr.
20 Gr.	16 Gr.	120 Gr.	96 Gr.
30 Gr.	24 Gr.	130 Gr.	104 Gr.
40 Gr.	32 Gr.	140 Gr.	112 Gr.
50 Gr.	40 Gr.	150 Gr.	120 Gr.
60 Gr.	48 Gr.	160 Gr.	128 Gr.
70 Gr.	56 Gr.	170 Gr.	136 Gr.
80 Gr.	64 Gr.	180 Gr.	144 Gr.
90 Gr.	72 Gr.	190 Gr.	152 Gr.
100 Gr.	80 Gr.	200 Gr.	160 Gr.

Pyrodex is bulkier than black powder resulting in up to 25% more shots per pound than with black.

EXAMPLE: If you use 70 Gr. Hodgdon Black Powder the same measure setting would give 56 Gr. Pyrodex, obtaining a ballistically similar load.

HODGDON MUZZLELOADING PRODUCTS

SPIT-PATCH $4.35
Non-fouling lube for rifle shooters. Improves accuracy and gives more shots between cleaning. Makes cleaning simple, deposits lube in bore while firing. Resists corrosion, dissolves fouling.

SPIT-BATH $3.25
For both rifle and pistol. Removes fouling, replaces moisture with light gun oil. Cleans between shots and for final cleanup after shoot. Prevents loss of accuracy. Kills all black powder odors.

SPIT-BALL $4.35
Non-fouling lube for pistol shooters. Stops chain firing in pistols. Dissolves fouling, makes cleaning simple. Improves accuracy and gives more shots between cleaning. Resists corrosion. Depsoits lube in bore while firing.

MINNE LUBE $3.05
Especially compounded to work in muzzleloading black powder guns, using the old time hollow base minnie-ball, or the new modern sabot type maxi-ball.

HODGDON SMOKELESS POWDER

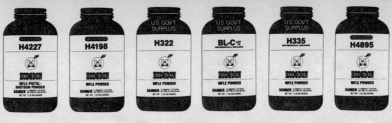

RIFLE POWDER

H4227 AND H4198
$14.98/lb.

H4227 is the fastest burning of the IMR series. Well adapted to Hornet, light bullets in 222 and all bullets in 357 and 44 Magnum pistols. Cuts leading with lead bullets. H4198 was developed especially for small and medium capacity cartridges.

H322
$14.98/lb.

A new extruded bench rest powder which has proved to be capable of producing fine accuracy in the 22 and 308 bench rest guns. This powder fills the gap between H4198 and BL-C(2). Performs best in small to medium capacity cases.

SPHERICAL BL-C®, Lot No. 2
$14.98/lb.

A highly popular favorite of the bench rest shooters. Best performance is in the 222, and in other cases smaller than 30/06.

SHOTGUN AND PISTOL POWDER

HP38
$13.65/lb.

A fast pistol powder for most pistol loading. Especially recommended for mid-range 38 specials.

TRAP 100
$12.80/lb.

Trap 100 is a spherical trap and light field load powder, also excellent for target loads in centerfire pistols. Mild recoil.

SPHERICAL H335®
$14.98/lb.

Similar to BL-C(2), H335 is popular for its performance in medium capacity cases, especially in 222 and 308 Winchester.

H4895®
$14.98/lb.

4895 may well be considered the most versatile of all propellants. It gives desirable performance in almost all cases from 222 Rem. to 458 Win. Reduced loads, to as low as $3/5$ of maximum, still give target accuracy.

SPHERICAL H380®
$14.98/lb.

This number fills a gap between 4320 and 4350. It is excellent in 22/250, 220 Swift, the 6mm's, 257 and 30/06.

#25 DATA MANUAL (544 pp.)
$14.95

HS-6 and HS-7
$13.65/lb.

HS-6 and HS-7 for Magnum field loads are unsurpassed, since they do not pack in the measure. They deliver uniform charges and are dense to allow sufficient wad column for best patterns.

H110
$14.65/lb.

A spherical powder made especially for the 30 M1 carbine. H110 also does very well in 357, 44 Spec., 44 Mag. or .410 ga. shotshell. Magnum primers are recommended for consistent ignition.

SPHERICAL H414®
$7.99/lb.

A new development in spherical powder. In many popular medium to medium-large calibers, pressure velocity relationship is better.

SPHERICAL H870®
$7.99/lb.

Very slow burning rate adaptable to overbore capacity Magnum cases such as 257, 264, 270 and 300 Mags with heavy bullets.

H4350
$14.98/lb.

This powder gives superb accuracy at optimum velocity for many large capacity metallic rifle cartridges.

H4831®
$14.98/lb.

The most popular of all powders. Outstanding performance with medium and heavy bullets in the 6mm's, 25/06, 270 and Magnum calibers.

H1000 EXTRUDED POWDER
$14.98

Fills the gap between H4831 and H870. Works especially well in overbore capacity cartridges (1,000-yard shooters take note).

IMR SMOKELESS POWDERS

SHOTSHELL POWDER

Hi-Skor 700-X Double-Base Shotshell Powder. Specifically designed for today's 12-gauge components. Developed to give optimum ballistics at minimum charge weight (means more reloads per pound of powder). 700-X is dense, easy to load, clean to handle, and loads uniformly.

PB Shotshell Powder. Produces exceptional 20- and 28-gauge skeet reloads; preferred by many in 12-gauge target loads, it gives 3-dram equivalent velocity at relatively low chamber pressures.

Hi-Skor 800-X Shotshell Powder. An excellent powder for 12-gauge field loads and 20- and 28-gauge loads.

SR-4756 Powder. Great all-around powder for target and field loads.

SR-7625 Powder. A fast growing "favorite" for reloading target as well as light and heavy field loads in 4 gauges. Excellent velocity-chamber pressure.

IMR-4227 Powder. Can be used effectively for reloading .410-gauge shotshell ammunition.

RIFLE POWDER

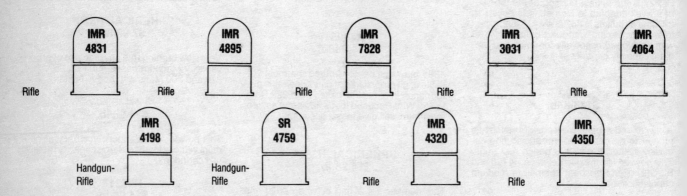

IMR-3031 Rifle Powder. Specifically recommended for medium-capacity cartridges.

IMR-4064 Rifle Powder. Has exceptionally uniform burning qualities when used in medium- and large-capacity cartridges.

IMR-4198. Made the Remington 222 cartridge famous. Developed for small- and medium-capacity cartridges.

IMR-4227 Rifle Powder. Fastest burning of the IMR Series. Specifically designed for the 22 Hornet class of cartridges.

SR-4759. Brought back by shooter demand. Available for cast bullet loads.

IMR-4320. Recommended for high-velocity cartridges.

IMR-4350 Rifle Powder. Gives unusually uniform results when loaded in Magnum cartridges. Slowest burning powder of the IMR series.

IMR-4831. Produced as a canister-grade handloading powder. Packaged in 1 lb. canister, 8 lb. caddy and 20 lb. kegs.

IMR-4895 Rifle Powder. The time-tested standard for caliber 30 military ammunition; slightly faster than IMR-4320. Loads uniformly in all powder measures. One of the country's favorite powders.

IMR-7828 Rifle Powder. The slowest-burning DuPont IMR cannister powder, intended for large capacity and magnum-type cases with heavy bullets.

PISTOL POWDER

PB Powder. Another powder for reloading a wide variety of centerfire handgun ammunition.

IMR-4227 Powder. Can be used effectively for reloading "Magnum" handgun ammunition.

"Hi-Skor" 700-X Powder. The same qualities that make it a superior powder contribute to its exellent performance in all the popular handguns.

SR-7625 Powder. For reloading a wide variety of centerfire handgun ammunition.

SR-4756, IMR-3031 and IMR-4198. Three more powders in a good selection—all clean burning and with uniform performance.

C-H RELOADING ACCESSORIES

ZINC BASE SWAGE DIE

- Maximum Energy
- 100% expansion, every time
- Zinc Base coats the bore with every shot
- Actually cleans the bore as you shoot
- No leading, even using maximum loads
- Perfect gas seal
- Use with any standard loading press
- Simple to use—one stroke of the handle and tap the finished bullet out.
- The perfect lubricating qualities of zinc combined with the perfect expansion

of pure lead produce outstanding, accurate bullets and will appreciably increase bore life.

No. 105-Z Zinc Base Swage Dies, 38/357 SWC
Shipping weight, 1 lb. **$29.95**
No. 105 Z1 Nose Punch, SWC, caliber 38/357 . . . . **4.00**
38/357 caliber Zinc Base Washer, per 1000 (shipping weight per M, 1 lb.) **23.20**

308 WINCHESTER AND 223 REMINGTON TAPER CRIMP DIE

- No longer necessary to have perfect trimmed cases
- Use as a separate die to form a perfect taper crimp each time
- Eliminates time-consuming trimming
- Produces Match Grade ammo
- Perfect feeding in semiauto rifles
- Load your ammo just like the factory does

Taper Crimp Die
Shipping weight 1 lb. **$17.00**

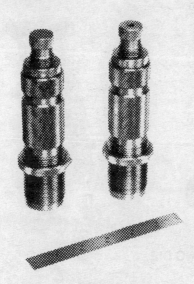

50 CALIBER BMG LOADING DIES

With **50 BMG Priming Accessories** the priming post and the shell holder can be used as is with any Hollywood tool. With the addition of the shell holder die, the priming can be accomplished with any existing loading tool with 7/8-inch top threads. The shell holder die screws into the top of the tool and the threaded shell holder is screwed into this. By adding the priming post you have a complete separate priming system.

Priming Post complete **$11.95**
Shell Holder Die 9.95
Shell Holder with lock ring 17.95

50 BMG DIE SET

C-H offers a die set for loading 50 caliber BMG. To give you an idea of the massive size of these dies they are shown with a 6-inch steel rule alongside a standard 308 Win. die and cartridge. They are threaded 1 1/2 × 12.

50 BMG Die set (full-length sizer and crimp seater) **$275.00**

DEBURRING/CHAMFERING TOOL

Standard size: Bevels both the inside and outside of the case mouth for easy bullet insertion. Hardened for long life. Extra sharp cutters. Fits 17 to 45 calibers.
Magnum size: For those who load 45 caliber and over, a Magnum Deburring Tool is available from C-H. Fits all cases from 45 to 60 caliber.

Standard Deburring Tool . . . . **$ 8.95**
Magnum Deburring Tool 14.95

C-H RELOADING TOOLS

Available for 38 Special/357, 45 ACP, 44 Mag. and 9mm Luger. Features reloading capability of 500 rounds per hour. Fully progressive loading. Powder measure cam allows you to "jog" the machine without dispensing powder. Simple powder measure emptying device included with each unit. Tungsten-carbide sizing die at no extra cost. Unit comes with your choice of powder bushing and seating stem (round nose, wadcutter or semi-wadcutter). Seating die cavity tapered for automatic alignment of the bullet. One 100-capacity primer tube, two 15-capacity case tubes and tube coupling also included at no extra cost **$699.00**

AUTO CHAMPION MARK V-a PROGRESSIVE RELOADING PRESS

MODEL 444 "H" PRESS

Offers 4-station versatility—two, three or four-piece die sets may be used. New casting design offers increased strength, and there is sufficient room for the longest magnum cases.

Model 444 4-Station "H" Press (includes 4 rams, 4 shell-holders, primer arm, and primer catcher **$158.00**
Same model but with one standard caliber die set **176.00**

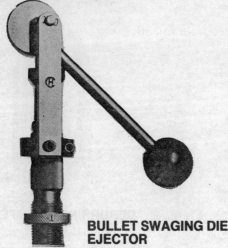

BULLET SWAGING DIE EJECTOR

A helpful accessory for use with the new C-H jacketed bullet swaging dies. The ejector attaches easily to the swaging die body with one screw. Can be used with either the core seating die or the swage die. Ejects the seated core or finished bullet with ease. No more tapping the top of the die.

Price **$24.65**

³/₄ JACKETED PISTOL BULLET SWAGING DIES

- Any bullet weight from 110 gr. to 250 gr. with same set of dies
- Can be used in any good ⁷/₈″ × 14 loading tool
- Absolutely no leading
- Complete no extras to buy
- Increased velocity
- Solid nose or hollow point
- Available in 38/357, 41 S & W, 44 Mag. and 45 Colt calibers

Price: **$44.45**

CANNELURE TOOL

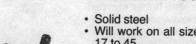

- Solid steel
- Will work on all sizes of bullets, from 17 to 45
- Completely adjustable for depth and height
- One set will process thousands of bullets
- Necessary for rolling in grooves on bullets prior to crimping
- Hardened cutting wheel, precision-machined throughout

Price: **$34.95**

C-H RELOADING ACCESSORIES

C-HAMPiON PRESS

Compound leverage press for all phases of reloading. Heavyweight (26#) C-Hampion comes complete with primer arms, $7/8 \times 14$ bushing for use with all reloading dies. Spent primers fall through back of press into waste basket. 'O' frame design will not spring under any conditions. Ideal press for swaging bullets. Top of frame bored $1^{1}/_{4} \times 18$ for use with special dies and shotshell dies.

C-Hampion Press $199.50

NO. 725 POWDER and BULLET SCALE

Chrome-plated, brass beam. Graduated in 10 gr., 1 gr. and 1/10th gr. increments. Convenient pouring spout on pan. Leveling screw on base. All metal construction. 360 gr. capacity.

Price. $35.95

NO. 301 CASE TRIMMER

This design features a unique clamp to lock case holder in position. Ensures perfect uniformity from 22 through 45 caliber whether rifle or pistol cases. Complete including hardened case holder.

No. 301 Case Trimmer $21.95
Extra case holders (hardened & hand-lapped). 3.50

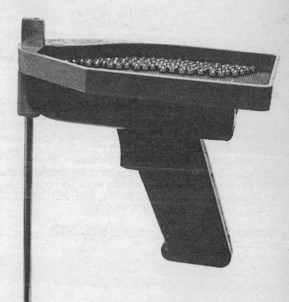

PRIMER TUBE FILLER

Fills a primer tube with 100 primers in seconds. Adjustable gate prevents upside-down primers from entering tube. Filler comes with three tubes and tube rack.

Model L (Large Primers). $39.95
Model S (Small Primers). 39.95

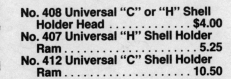

UNIVERSAL SHELL HOLDERS

Up to now, shell holders came in one piece—you needed as many shell holders as the calibers you wished to reload. With the C-H Universal Shell Holder all the reloader needs is the Shell Holder ram.

No. 408 Universal "C" or "H" Shell
    Holder Head $4.00
No. 407 Universal "H" Shell Holder
    Ram 5.25
No. 412 Universal "C" Shell Holder
    Ram 10.50

FORSTER/BONANZA RELOADING TOOLS

CASE TRIMMER

The Forster Case Trimmer trims all cases from 17 cal. to 458 Winchester. Its shell holder is a Brown & Sharpe type collet, which closes on the case rim without pulling the case back, thus insuring uniform case length (even when there is variation in rim diameter).

Case Trimmer (less collet and pilot) **$40.00**
Case Trimmer Pilot **1.98**
Case Trimmer Collet **6.80**

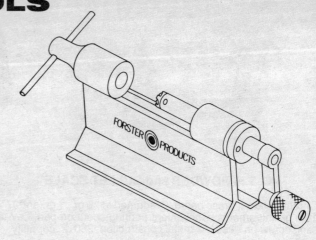

OUTSIDE NECK TURNER
(Shown on Forster Case Trimmer)

The Outside Neck Turner consists of a cutter head which carries an adjustable circular carbide cutter. The tool will turn any diameter between .170 and .375. The short pilot used in case trimming is replaced with an extra long, hardened and ground pilot of the desired caliber. As the wall of the neck passes progressively between the pilot and the cutter, the neck wall of the case is reduced to a uniform thickness. The rate of feed is controlled by rotating the feeder cam; a mechanical stop controls the length of the cut. Outside Neck Turners are available for following caliber sizes: 17, 224, 243, 257, 277, 263, 284, 308, 311, 323, 333, 338, 358 and 375.

Outside Neck Turner (complete w/one pilot) **$27.00**

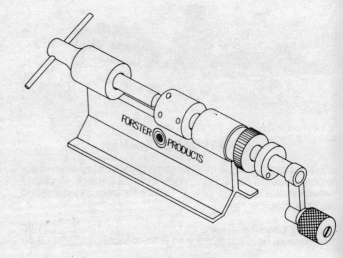

POWER CASE TRIMMER

Can be used with any standard drill press. Case length is controlled by the stop on drill press spindle. A line-up bar aligns the trimmer and drill press spindle. The threaded lever for opening and closing the Brown & Sharpe collet can be removed easily. The cutter shaft is made with a 1/4" shank and has four staggered cutting edges for chatterless trimming of cases.

Power Case Trimmer (less collet and pilot) **$40.00**

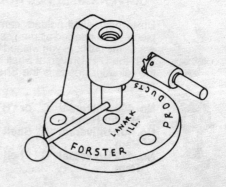

FORSTER/BONANZA RELOADING TOOLS

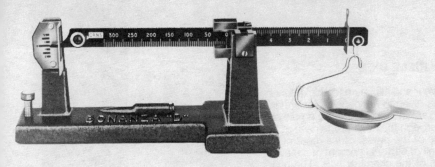

POWDER AND BULLET SCALE
MODEL "D"™ $44.00

330-grain capacity, tempered stainless steel right-hand poise, diamond-polished agate "V" bearings, non-glare white markings. Die cast aluminum base, strengthened beam at pivot points, powder pan for right or left pouring. Easy to read pointer and reference point. Guaranteed accurate to $1/10$ grain; sensitivity guaranteed to $1/20$ grain.

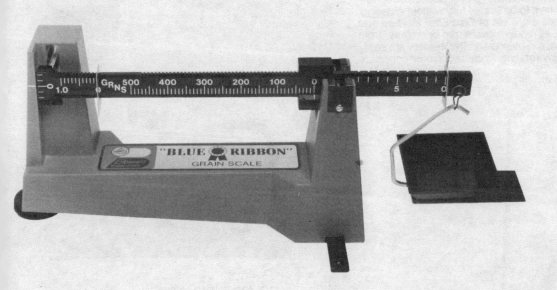

BLUE RIBBON GRAIN SCALE

511-grain capacity for ease of weighing powder. "Blue Ribbon" scales have three poises for better accuracy and convenience. White markings on non-glare enhance reading with less eye strain. Comparator scale and resting point locator lie in the same plane, which eliminates errors in reading due to parallax. Base has three point suspension, eliminating rocking. Guaranteed accurate to $1/10$ grain. Sensitivity to $1/20$ grain.

"Blue Ribbon"™ Magnetic Dampened Grain Scale $59.90

FORSTER/BONANZA RELOADING TOOLS

CO-AX® BENCH REST® RIFLE DIES

Bench Rest Rifle Dies are glass hard for long wear and minimum friction. Interiors are polished mirror smooth. Special attention is given to headspace, tapers and diameters so that brass will not be overworked when resized. Our sizing die has an elevated expander button which is drawn through the neck of the case at the moment of the greatest mechanical advantage of the press. Since most of the case neck is still in the die when expanding begins, better alignment of case and neck is obtained. **Bench Rest® Seating Die** is of the chamber type. The bullet is held in alignment in a close-fitting channel. The case is held in a tight-fitting chamber. Both bullet and case are held in alignment while the bullet is being seated. Cross-bolt lock ring included at no charge.

Bench Rest® Die Set $50.00
Full Length Sizer 22.00
Bench Rest Seating Die 29.00

PRIMER SEATER
with "E-Z-Just" Shellholder

The Bonanza Primer Seater is designed so that primers are seated Co-Axially (primer in line with primer pocket). Mechanical leverage allows primers to be seated fully without crushing. With the addition of one extra set of Disc Shell Holders and one extra Primer Unit, all modern cases, rim or rimless, from 222 up to 458 Magnum, can be primed. Shell holders are easily adjusted to any case by rotating to contact rim or cannelure of the case.

Primer Seater $46.50
Primer Tube 3.25

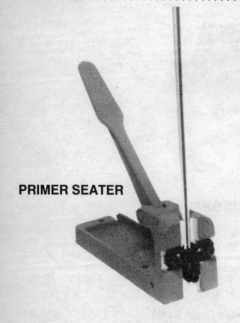

PRIMER SEATER

CO-AX® INDICATOR

Bullets will not leave a rifle barrel at a uniform angle unless they are started uniformly. The Co-Ax Indicator provides a reading of how closely the axis of the bullet corresponds to the axis of the cartridge case. The Indicator features a spring-loaded plunger to hold cartridges against a recessed, adjustable rod while the cartridge is supported in a "V" block. To operate, simply rotate the cartridge with the fingers; the degree of misalignment is transferred to an indicator which measures in one-thousandths.

Price: without dial $39.00
Indicator Dial 45.00

HORNADY

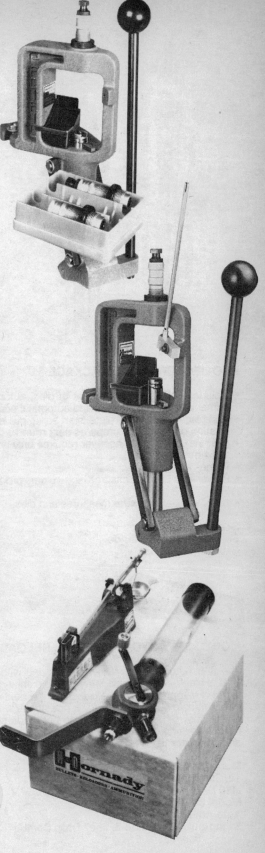

THE 00-7 PRESS PACKAGE
A reloading press complete with dies and shell holder

Expanded and improved to include Automatic Primer Feed. It sets you up to load any caliber in the list below and includes: Choice of a basic 00-7 complete with • Set of Durachrome Dies • Primer catcher • Removable head shell holder • Positive Priming System • Automatic Primer Feed.

00-7 Package (13 lbs.) **$148.65**
00-7 Package Series II Titanium Nitride (13 lbs.) 161.15

00-7 PRESS

* "Power-Pac" linkage multiplies lever-to-arm power.
* Frame of press angled 30° to one side, making the "O" area of press totally accessible.
* More mounting area for rock-solid attachment to bench.
* Special strontium-alloy frame provides greater stress, resistance. Won't spring under high pressures needed for full-length resizing.

00-7 Press (does not include dies or shell holder) **$106.00**
00-7 Automatic Primer Feed (complete with large and small primer tubes) 12.75

THE HANDLOADER'S ACCESSORY PACK I

Here's everything you need in one money-saving pack. It includes: • Deluxe powder measure • Powder scale • Two non-static powder funnels • Universal loading block • Primer turning plate • Case lube • Chamfering and deburring tool • 3 case neck brushes • Large and small primer pocket cleaners • Accessory handle. Plus one copy of the Hornady Handbook of Cartridge Reloading.

Handloader's Accessory Pack I No. 030300 . . . . **$150.00**

HORNADY

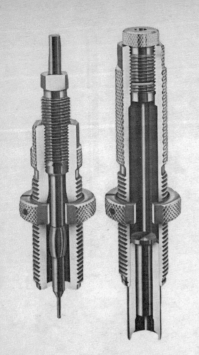

NEW DIMENSION RELOADING DIES

Features an Elliptical Expander that minimizes friction and reduces case neck stretch, plus the need for a tapered expander for "necking up" to the next larger caliber. Other recent design changes include a hardened steel decap pin that will not break, bend or crack even when depriming stubborn military cases. A bullet seater alignment sleeve guides the bullet and case neck into the die for in-line benchrest alignment. All New Dimension Reloading Dies include collar and collar lock to center expander precisely; one-piece expander spindle with tapered bottom for easy cartridge insertion; wrench flats on die body, Sure-Loc™ lock rings and collar lock for easy tightening; and built-in crimper.

New Dimension Reloading Dies:

Series I Two-die Rifle Set	$23.50
Series I Three-die Rifle Set	25.50
Series II Three-die Pistol Set (w/Titanium Nitride)	36.00
Series III Two-die Rifle Set	30.00
Series IV Custom Die Set	53.00

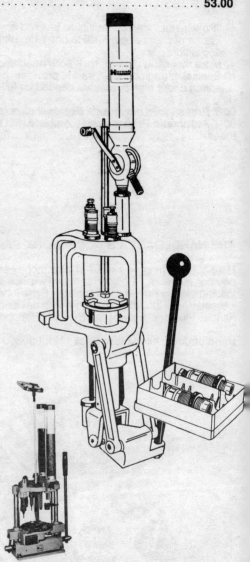

PRO-JECTOR PRESS PACKAGE

- Includes Pro-Jector Press, set of dies, automatic primer feed, brass kicker, primer catcher, shell plate, and automatic primer shut-off
- Just place case in shell plate, start bullet, pull lever and drop powder. Automatic rotation of shell plate prepares next round.
- Fast inexpensive changeover requires only shell plate and set of standard 7/8 × 14 threaded dies.
- Primes automatically.
- Power-Pac Linkage assures high-volume production even when full-length sizing.
- Uses standard powder measures and dies.

Series I	$342.50
Series II Titanium Nitride	355.00
Extra Shell Plates	21.50

MODEL 366 AUTO SHOTSHELL RELOADER

The 366 Auto features full-length resizing with each stroke, automatic primer feed, swing-out wad guide, three-stage crimping featuring Taper-Loc for factory tapered crimp, automatic advance to the next station and automatic ejection. The turntable holds 8 shells for 8 operations with each stroke. The primer tube filler is fast. The automatic charge bar loads shot and powder. Right- or left-hand operation; interchangeable charge bushings, die sets and Magnum dies and crimp starters for 6 point, 8 point and paper crimps.

Model 366 Auto Shotshell Reloader:

12, 20 or 28 Gauge	$450.00
.410 Bore	470.00
Model 366 Auto Die Set	90.00
Auto Advance	43.85
Swing-out Wad Guide & Shell Drop Combo	108.50

LYMAN BULLET SIZING EQUIPMENT

MAG 20 ELECTRIC FURNACE

The MAG 20 is a new furnace offering several advantages to cast bullet enthusiasts. It features a steel crucible of 20-pound capacity and incorporates a proven bottom-pour valve system and a fully adjustable mould guide. The improved design of the MAG 20 makes it equally convenient to use the bottom-pour valve, or a ladle. A new heating coil design reduces the likelihood of pour spout "freeze." Heat is controlled from "Off" to nominally 825° F by a calibrated thermostat which automatically increases temperature output when alloy is added to the crucible. A pre-heat shelf for moulds is attached to the back of the crucible. Availalbe for 100 V and 200 V systems.

Price: 110 V $227.95
220 V 235.00

UNIVERSAL DECAPPING DIE

Covers all calibers .22 through .45 (except .378 and .460 Weatherby). Can be used before cases are cleaned or lubricated. Requires no adjustment when changing calibers; fits all popular makes of $7/8 \times 14$ presses, single station or progressive, and is packaged with 10 replacement pins.

Universal Decapping Die $9.95

Deburring Tool
Lyman's deburring tool can be used for chamfering or deburring of cases up to 45 caliber. For precise bullet seating, use the pointed end of the tool to bevel the inside of new or trimmed cases. To remove burrs left by trimming, place the other end of the deburring tool over the mouth of the case and twist. The tool's centering pin will keep the case aligned . . **$11.50**

Mould Handles
These large hardwood handles are available in three sizes single-, double- and four-cavity.
Single-cavity handles (for small block, black powder and specialty moulds; 12 oz.) **$19.95**
Double-cavity handles (for two-cavity and large-block single-cavity moulds; 12 oz.) 19.95
Four-cavity handles (1 lb.) 22.95

Rifle Moulds
All Lyman rifle moulds are available in double cavity only, except those moulds where the size of the bullet necessitates a single cavity (12 oz.) **$45.95**

Hollow-Point Bullet Moulds
Hollow-point moulds are cut in single-cavity blocks only and require single-cavity handles (9 oz.) **$45.95**

Shotgun Slug Moulds
Available in 12 or 20 gauge; do not require rifling. Moulds are single cavity only, cut on the larger double-cavity block and require double-cavity handles (14 oz.) **$45.95**

Pistols Moulds
Cover all popular calibers and bullet designs in double-cavity blocks and, on a limited basis, four-cavity blocks.
Double-cavity mould block **$45.95**
Four-cavity mould block 75.95

Lead Casting Dipper
Dipper with cast-iron head. The spout is shaped for easy, accurate pouring that prevents air pockets in the finished bullet **$11.00**

Gas Checks
Gas checks are gilding metal caps which fit to the base of cast bullets. These caps protect the bullet base from the burning effect of hot powder gases and permit higher velocities. Easily seated during the bullet sizing operation. Only Lyman gas checks should be used with Lyman cast bullets.

22 through 35 caliber (per 1000) $20.95
375 through 45 caliber (per 1000) 22.95
Gas check seater 7.95

Lead Pot
Cast-iron pot allows bullet caster to any source of heat. Pot capacity is 8 pounds of alloy. The flat bottom prevents tipping **$11.00**

LYMAN RELOADING TOOLS
FOR RIFLE OR PISTOL CARTRIDGES

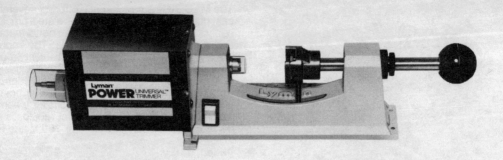

POWERED CASE TRIMMER

The new Lyman Power Trimmer is powered by a fan-cooled electric motor designed to withstand the severe demands of case trimming. The unit, which features the Universal® Chuckhead, allows cases to be positioned for trimming or removed with fingertip ease. The Power Trimmer package includes Nine Pilot Multi-Pack. In addition to two cutter heads, a pair of wire end brushes for cleaning primer pockets are included. Other features include safety guards, on-off rocker switch, heavy cast base with receptacles for nine pilots, and bolt holes for mounting on a work bench. Available for 110 V or 220 V systems.

Prices: 110 V Model $184.95
         220 V Model 189.95

ACCULINE OUTSIDE NECK TURNER
(not shown)

To obtain perfectly concentric case necks, Lyman's Outside Neck Turner assures reloaders of uniform neck wall thickness and outside neck diameter. The unit fits Lyman's Universal Trimmer and AccuTrimmer. In use, each case is run over a mandrel, which centers the case for the turning operation. The cutter is carefully adjusted to remove a minimum amount of brass. Rate of feed is adjustable and a mechanical stop controls length of cut. Mandrels are available for calibers from .17 to .375; cutter blade can be adjusted for any diameter from .195″ to .405″.

Outside Neck Turner w/extra blade, 6 mandrels . . . $27.95
Outside Neck Turner only 19.95
Individual Mandrels 4.00

LYMAN "ORANGE CRUSHER" RELOADING PRESS

The only press for rifle or pistol cartridges that offers the advantage of powerful compound leverage combined with a true magnum press opening. A unique handle design transfers power easily where you want it to the center of the ram. A 4½-inch press opening accommodates even the largest cartridges.

"Orange Crusher" Press:
With Priming Arm and Catcher $89.95

LYMAN RELOADING TOOLS

T-MAG TURRET RELOADING PRESS

With the T-Mag you can mount up to six different reloading dies on our turret. This means you can have all your dies set up, precisely mounted, locked in and ready to reload at all times. The T-Mag works with all $^7/_8 \times 14$ dies. The T-Mag turret with its quick-disconnect release system is held in rock-solid alignment by a $^3/_4$-inch steel stud.

Also featured is Lyman's Orange Crusher compound leverage system. It has a longer handle with a ball-type knob that mounts easily for right- or left-handed operation.

T-Mag Press w/Priming Arm & Catcher **$129.95**
    Extra Turret Head **31.00**

Now available: **EXPERT KIT** that includes T-MAG Press, Universal Case Trimmer and pilot Multi-Pak, Model 500 powder scale and Model 50 powder measure, plus accessories. Available in 9mm Luger, 38/357, 44 Mag., 45 ACP and 30-06 . . . . **$349.95.**

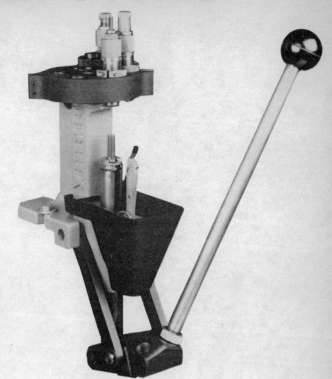

PISTOL ACCUMEASURE

Lyman's Pistol AccuMeasure uses changeable brass rotors pre-drilled to drop precise charges of ball and flake pistol propellants (the tool is not intended for use with long grain IMR-type powders). Most of the rotors are drilled with two cavities for maximum accuracy and consistency. The brass operating handle, which can be shifted for left or right hand operation, can be removed. The Pistol AccuMeasure can be mounted on all turret and single station presses; it can also be hand held with no loss of accuracy.

Pistol AccuMeasure **$19.95**
    With 3-rotor starter kit **29.95**

Now available: **PISTOL POWDER HANDLING KIT** that includes every tool (except reloading press) needed to produce high-quality ammunition **$119.95**
Also, a **ROTOR SELECTION SET** including 8 dual-cavity rotors and 4 single-cavity units. Enables reloaders to throw a variety of charges for all pistol calibers through 45 . . . . **$49.95**

LYMAN RELOADING TOOLS

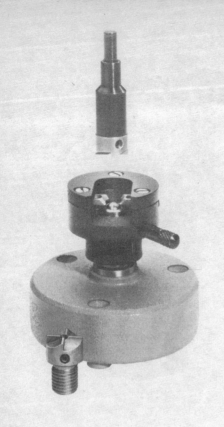

DRILL PRESS CASE TRIMMER

Intended for competitive shooters, varmint hunters, and other sportsmen who use large amounts of reloaded ammunition; this new drill press case trimmer consists of the Universal™ Chuckhead, a cutter shaft adapted for use in a drill press, and two quick-change cutter heads. Its two major advantages are speed and accuracy. An experienced operator can trim several hundred cases in a hour, and each will be trimmed to a precise length.

Price: **$41.95**

UNIVERSAL TRIMMER WITH NINE PILOT MULTI-PACK

This trimmer with patented chuckhead accepts all metallic rifle or pistol cases, regardless of rim thickness. To change calibers, simply change the case head pilot. Other features include coarse and fine cutter adjustments, an oil-impregnated bronze bearing, and a rugged cast base to assure precision alignment and years of service. Optional carbide cutter available. Trimmer Stop Ring includes 20 indicators as reference marks.

Trimmer less pilots **$60.95**
Extra pilot (state caliber) **2.95**
Replacement carbide cutter **39.95**
Trimmer Multi-Pack (incl. 9 pilots: 22, 24, 27, 28/7mm, 30, 9mm, 35, 44 and 45A **65.95**
Nine Pilot Multi-Pack **9.95**

ACCU TRIMMER

Lyman's new Accu Trimmer can be used for all rifle and pistol cases from 22 to 458 Winchester Magnum. Standard shell-holders are used to position the case, and the trimmer incorporates standard Lyman cutter heads and pilots. Mounting options include bolting to a bench, C-clamp or vise.

Accu Trimmer **$31.95**
  With 9-pilot multi-pak **36.95**

LYMAN RELOADING ACCESSORIES

PRIMER POCKET REAMER

Cleans and removes rough metal edges from a primer pocket. This tool is a must for military-type primers. Available in large or small see priming punch size in cartridge table.

Price $8.50

POWDER FUNNEL

This plastic powder funnel is designed to fill cases from 22 Hornet through 45-70 without inserts or adjustments.

Price $2.95

POWDER DRIBBLER

Assures full measure of accuracy; an ideal companion for any powder scale.

Price $9.95

NO. 55 POWDER MEASURE

This Powder Measure and dispensing device charges any number of cases with black or smokeless powder loads that are consistant within a fraction of a grain. The 2400-grain capacity plastic reservoir gives a clear view of the powder level. The reservoir is fabricated from blue-tinted polyvinyl-chloride plastic that resists chemical action of double base powders, and filters out light rays that would damage powders. An optional 7000-grain reservoir is available. The measure clamps securely to the loading bench, or mounts directly to any turret press by means of threaded drop tubes (supplied with measure). A knocker mounted on the side of the measure insures complete discharge of powder directly into the cartridge case. No funnel is required.

The unique three-slide micrometer adjustable cavity is the key to the unfailing accuracy of the 55 Powder Measure. Micrometer adjustments for both width and depth provide a dependable, consistent measure that minimizes cutting of coarse powder.

No. 55 Powder Measure $73.95
Optional 7000-grain capacity reservoir 9.95

THREE-SLIDE MICROMETER
ADJUSTABLE CAVITY

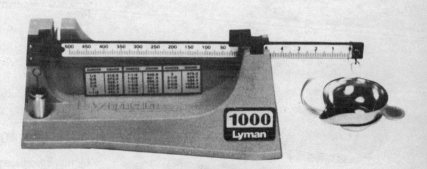

LYMAN M-1000 SCALE

Dial markings are white on jet black for easy reading. The pointer and dial are placed on the same plane to eliminate parallax error. Its high capacity of up to 1005 grains permits the heaviest charges and even bullets to be weighed. Features magnetic damping, one-tenth of a grain of sensitivity.

M-500 Scale $62.95
M-1000 Scale 84.95

LYMAN RELOADING ACCESSORIES

TURBO TUMBLERS

Lyman's Turbo Tumblers process cases twice as fast as old style tumblers. Their unique design allows the media to swirl around totally immersed cases in a high-speed, agitated motion that cleans and polishes interior and exterior surfaces simultaneously; it also allows inspection of cases without stopping the polishing operation. The Turbo 3200 cleans and polishes up to 1,000 .38 Special cartridge cases. The Turbo 1200 can handle the equivalent of over 300 .38 Specials or 100 .30-06 cartridges. The Turbo 600 cleans half the Model 1200 capacity.

Prices:

Turbo 600 (7 lbs.)	110V	....	**$116.95**
Turbo 1200 (10 lbs.)	110V	....	**146.95**
Turbo 2200 (12 lbs.)	110V	....	**169.95**
Turbo 3200 (13 lbs.)	110V	....	**219.95**

Turbo™ Tumbler Capacities

Model	Lyman Media	Number of .38 Special Cases	Nominal Capacity*
600	1 lb.	175	3 Pints
1200	2 lbs.	350	4 Quarts
2200	4 lbs.	750	1.5 Gallons
3200	5 lbs.	1000	2.2 Gallons

*Refer to product instructions for suggested operating procedures and weight guidelines for best results.

TURBO SIFTER & MEDIA (not shown)

Lyman's Turbo Sifter allows easy separation of cleaned and polished cases from the Turbo Tumbler media. Its diameter of 14″ allows the sifter to fit the mouth of most household buckets. Open grate bottom allows media to pass into recepticle while stopping the bases.
Price: **$7.95**

Turbo Media produces a "factory finish" and eliminates abrasive and wax films.
Prices:

1 lb. can	.... **$ 3.95**
2 lb. box	.... **6.95**
10 lb. box	.... **19.95**

RETRO-FIT AUTO-FLO MEDIA DRAINING SYSTEMS

Lyman introduces a major option for its Model 2200 and high-capacity Model 3200 Turbo Tumblers. Auto-Flo allows automatic, hands-off separation of media from cases following the cleaning-polishing process. Using the Turbo Tumbler's agitating motion, the media is expelled through a post (in the unit's bowl) into a drain pan. Draining of the media takes 2-3 minutes. The vibration of the cases in the near-empty bowl tends to loosen media from flash holes.
Prices:
RETRO-FIT (to Model 2200 Turbo Tumbler) **$59.95**
RETRO-FIT (to Model 3200 Turbo Tumbler) **69.95**

MEC RELOADING

ACCESSORY EQUIPMENT

SPINDEX CRIMP STARTER
(not shown)

Rotates automatically and realigns perfectly on the original crimp of the shell. This precision-built one-piece crimp starter is made of rugged Celcon and can be changed from 6 point to 8 point in a matter of seconds.

ACCESSORIES
301L 13X BH & Cap Accy.	$3.66
453P Wad Finger Ptlc.	1.10
634P Crimp St. Paper	1.25
8042 Magnum Container	5.20
15CA E-Z Pak Accy.	6.40

FOR THE MEC 600 JR.
741 Die Set (12, 16, 20, 28, .410) specify gauge	$46.69
741P-10 Die Set	52.27
73 Kit Versa MEC 700 Modification	13.13
ProCheck	4.00
63 Kit for 3″ shells (12 and 20 gauge)	5.76

FOR THE VERSAMEC 700
741 Die Set (10, 12, 16, 28, .410) specify gauge	$46.91

E-Z PRIME "V"
For 600 Jr. and
700 Versamec

E-Z PRIME "S"
For 650 and
Super 600

E-Z PRIME "S" AND "V"
AUTOMATIC PRIMER FEEDS

From carton to shell with security, these primer feeds provide safe, convenient primer positioning and increase rate of production. Reduce bench clutter, allowing more free area for wads and shells.
- Primers transfer directly from carton to reloader, tubes and tube fillers
- Positive mechanical feed (not dependent upon agitation of press)
- Visible supply
- Automatic. Eliminate hand motion
- Less susceptible to damage
- Adapt to all domestic and most foreign primers with adjustment of the cover
- May be purchased separately to replace tube-type primer feed or to update your present reloader

E-Z Prime "S" (for Super 600 and 650) or **E-Z Primer "V"** (for 600 Jr. and Versa MEC 700) **$33.94**

MEC SIZEMASTER 77
(not shown)

- Pro-check
- Adjusta-guide wad feed
- Wad pressure gauge
- Wad height gauge
- Extra capacity shot container
- Spindex crimp starter
- Cam-actuated crimping station
- Single-stage
- Precision shell holder
- Exclusive resizing chamber
- Automatic primer feed
- Positive repriming
- Charge bar window

Size Master 77 (includes Primer Feed)	$207.99
77 Die Set (12, 16, 20, 28 and .410)	78.08
77 10-gauge Die Set	91.63

MEC E-Z PAK

Here's how to pack shotshell reloads the easy way. As each shell is reloaded, they're placed in E-Z Pak, exactly as if they were being placed in the box. After each 25 shells, original box is slipped over E-Z Pak, which is then inverted, and removed. Available in all gauges.
Price: **$6.40**

MEC SHOTSHELL RELOADERS

MODEL 600 JR. MARK 5
$137.53

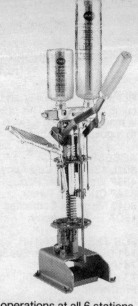

MODEL 8567 GRABBER
$392.20

This single-stage reloader features a cam-action crimp die to ensure that each shell returns to its original condition. MEC's 600 Jr. Mark 5 can load 8 to 10 boxes per hour and can be updated with the 285 CA primer feed. Press is adjustable for 3″ shells. Die sets are available in all gauges at **$52.29.**

This reloader features 12 different operations at all 6 stations, producing finished shells with each stroke of the handle. It includes a fully automatic primer feed and Auto-Cycle charging, plus MEC's exclusive 3-stage crimp. The "Power Ring" resizer ensures consistent, accurately sized shells without interrupting the reloading sequence. Simply put in the wads and shell casings, then remove the loaded shells with each pull of the handle. Optional kits to load 3″ shells and steel shot make this reloader tops in its field. Resizes high and low base shells. Available in 12, 16, 20, 28 gauge and .410 bore. No die sets are available.

MODEL 650
$273.39

SIZEMASTER
$207.99

Sizemaster's "Power Ring" collet resizer returns each base to factory specifications. This new generation resizing station handles brass or steel heads, both high and low base. An 8-fingered collet squeezes the base back to original dimensions, then opens up to release the shell easily. The E-Z Prime auto primer feed is standard equipment. Press is adjustable for 3″ shells and is available in 10, 12, 16, 20, 28 gauge and .410 bore. Die sets are available at: **$78.08.** In .410: **$91.63.**

HUSTLER (not shown)
$1022.44

This reloader works on 6 shells at once. A reloaded shell is completed with every stroke. The MEC 650 does not resize except as a separate operation. Automatic Primer feed is standard. Simply fill it with a full box of primers and it will do the rest. Reloader has 3 crimping stations: the first one starts the crimp, the second closes the crimp, and the third places a taper on the shell. Available in 12, 16, 20 and 28 gauge and .410 bore. No die sets are available.

The fastest and most precise reloader available, the Hustler features a powerful hydraulic system that operates on conventional 110-volt household current. Control is maintained by a foot pedal, leaving hands free to add wads and remove loaded shells. When the pedal is released, the press returns automatically to the top of the stroke. Available in 12, 16, 20, 28 gauge and .410 bore. No die sets are available.

MTM

CASE-GARD PISTOL AMMO WALLET
CASE-GARD 6, 12 AND 18

MTM offers 3 different models of varying capacity. All share common design features:
- Textured finish looks like leather, and provides good gripping surface, even when wet.
- Snap-lok latch protects contents from damage, even if unit is dropped.
- Integral hinge.
- Contents are protected from dust and moisture.
- Each round is carried securely in its own individual rattle-proof recess.
- Available in dark brown.

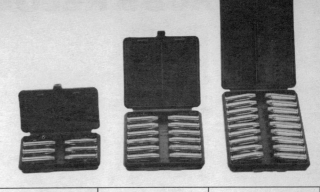

Capacity	380 Auto & 9mm	38 & 357 Mag	41 Mag	44 Mag	45 Auto
6 Round	W6-9/$3.09	W6-38/$3.09	W6-41/$3.09	W6-44/$2.83	W6-45/$3.09
12 Round	W12-9/$3.20	W12-38/$3.20	W12-41/$3.20	W12-44/$3.05	W12-45/$3.20
18 Round	18-9/$3.80	18-38/$3.80	18-41/$3.80	18-44/$3.60	18-45/$3.80

CASE-GARD AMMO WALLET
FOR 22's

Special **Case-Gard Ammo Wallet** carrier holds 30 rounds, 22 Longs or 22 Mags . . . a convenient way to carry ammo to the range or field. Design features are:
- Leather-like finish available in dark brown.
- Snap-lok latch protects case against inadvertent opening, even if dropped.
- Each round is carried securely in its own recess.
- Virtually indestructible hinge.

30-22M . . . . ea. **$3.40**

MTM HANDLOADER'S LOG

Space is provided for 1,000 entries covering date, range, group size or score, components, and conditions. Book is heavy-duty vinyl, reinforced 3-ring binder.

HL-74 . . . . **$9.41**
HL-50 (incl. 50 extra log sheets) 4.09

CASE-GARD 100 AMMO CARRIER
FOR SKEET AND TRAP

The **MTM™ Case-Gard®** 100-round shotshell case carries 100 rounds in 2 trays; or 50 rounds plus 2 boxes of factory ammo; or 50 rounds plus sandwiches and insulated liquid container; or 50 round with room left for fired hulls. Features include:
- Recessed top handle for easy storage.
- High-impact material supports 300 pounds, and will not warp, split, expand or contract.
- Dustproof and rainproof.
- Living hinge guaranteed 3 years.
- Available in deep forest green.

SF-100-12 (12 gauge) **$14.28**
SF-100-20 (20 gauge) 14.28

FUNNELS

MTM Benchrest Funnel Set is designed specifically for the bench-rest shooter. One fits 222 and 243 cases only; the other 7mm and 308 cases. Both can be used with pharmaceutical vials popular with bench-rest competitors for storage of pre-weighed charges. Funnel design prevents their rolling off the bench.

MTM Universal Funnel fits all calibers from 222 to 45.
UF-1 . . . . **$2.19**
Patented MTM Adapt 5-in-1 Funnel Kit includes funnel, adapters for 17 Rem., 222 Rem. and 30 through 45. Long drop tube facilitates loading of maximum charges: 222 to 45.
AF-5 . . . . **$3.96**

RCBS RELOADING TOOLS

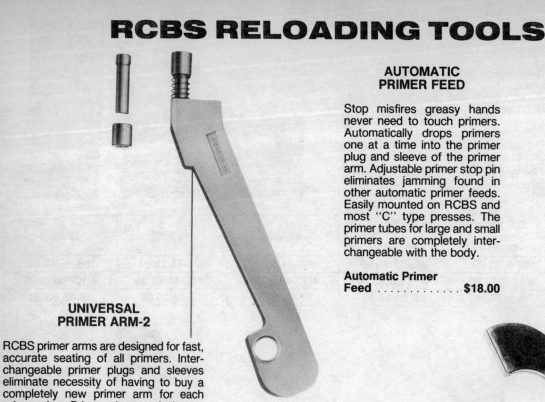

AUTOMATIC PRIMER FEED

Stop misfires greasy hands never need to touch primers. Automatically drops primers one at a time into the primer plug and sleeve of the primer arm. Adjustable primer stop pin eliminates jamming found in other automatic primer feeds. Easily mounted on RCBS and most "C" type presses. The primer tubes for large and small primers are completely interchangeable with the body.

**Automatic Primer
Feed** $18.00

UNIVERSAL PRIMER ARM-2

RCBS primer arms are designed for fast, accurate seating of all primers. Interchangeable primer plugs and sleeves eliminate necessity of having to buy a completely new primer arm for each primer size. Primer plugs and sleeves furnished for large and small primers. Body cast of rust-resistant zinc alloy. The Universal Primer Arm-2 is designed for use with RCBS Rock Chucker and J.R. as well as most "C" type presses.

Universal Primer Arm-2 . . . . . . $9.00
Plug and Sleeve (sm. or lg.) . . . 2.50

PRIMER TRAY

For fast, easy handling of primers and loading automatic primer feed tubes, place primers in this tray, shake tray horizontally, and primers will automatically position themselves anvil side up. Sturdy plastic case.

Primer Tray $2.40

AUTOMATIC PRIMING TOOL

Precision-engineered to provide fast, accurate and uniform seating of primers in one simple step. Single-stage leverage system is so sensitive it enables you actually to "feel" the primer being seated to the bottom of the primer pocket. This priming tool permits you to check visually each primer pocket before seating the primer, thus eliminating wasted motion or slowing down the reloading process.

Primers are released one at a time through the RCBS automatic primer feed, eliminating contamination caused by handling primers with oily fingers. Both primer rod assemblies furnished with this tool will handle all large and small American-made Boxer-type rifle and pistol primers.

Economy Features: If you already have RCBS automatic primer feed tubes and RCBS shell holders, they will fit this RCBS Priming Tool, thus eliminating the need to buy extras.

Berdan Primer Rod Assemblies: Optional Berdan Primer Rod Assemblies are available in three sizes and are interchangeable with the American Boxer-type Primer Rod Assemblies, furnished with the Priming Tool.

Priming Tool (less shell holder) $57.00

RCBS RELOADING TOOLS

ROCK CHUCKER "COMBO"

The Rock Chucker Press, with patented RCBS compound leverage system, delivers up to 200% more leverage than most presses for heavy-duty reloading of even the largest rifle and pistol cases. Rugged, Block "O" Frame prevents press from springing out of alignment even under the most strenuous operations. It case-forms as easily as most presses full-length size; it full-length sizes and makes bullets with equal ease. Shell holders snap into sturdy, all-purpose shell holder ram. Non-slip handle with convenient grip. Operates on downstroke for increased leverage. Standard 7/8-inch×14 thread.

Rock Chucker Press
   (Less dies) $129.00
Rock Chucker Combo, Rifle . . 154.70
Rock Chucker Combo,
   Pistol 156.80

Combos include interchangeable primer plugs and sleeves for seating large and small rifle and pistol primers, shell holder, and primer catcher.

PRIMER POCKET SWAGER COMBO

For fast, precision removal of primer pocket crimp from military cases. Leaves primer pocket perfectly rounded and with correct dimensions for seating of American Boxer-type primers. Will not leave oval-shaped primer pocket that reaming produces. Swager Head Assemblies furnished for large and small primer pockets no need to buy a complete unit for each primer size. For use with all presses with standard 7/8-inch×14 top thread, except RCBS "A-3" Press. The RCBS "A-2" Press requires the optional Case Stripper Washer.

Pocket Swager Combo $21.00

PRIMER POCKET BRUSH COMBO

A slight twist of this tool thoroughly cleans residue out of primer pockets. Interchangeable stainless steel brushes for large and small primer pockets attach easily to accessory handle.

Primer Pocket Brush Combo: $11.00

RCBS RELOADING TOOLS

RELOADING SCALE
MODEL 5-0-5

This 511-grain capacity scale has a three-poise system with widely spaced, deep beam notches to keep them in place. Two smaller poises on right side adjust from 0.1 to 10 grains, larger one on left side adjusts in full 10-grain steps. The first scale to use magnetic dampening to eliminate beam oscillation, the 5-0-5 also has a sturdy die-cast base with large leveling legs for stability. Self-aligning agate bearings support the hardened steel beam pivots for a guaranteed sensitivity to 0.1 grains.

Model 5-0-5	09071	1½ lbs.	$69.00

RELOADER SPECIAL-3

This RCBS Reloader Special-3 Press is the ideal setup to get started reloading your own rifle and pistol ammo from 12 gauge shotshells and the largest Magnums down to 22 Hornets. This press develops ample leverage and pressure to perform all reloading tasks including: (1) resizing cases their full length; (2) forming cases from one caliber into another; (3) making bullets. Rugged Block "O" Frame, designed by RCBS, prevents press from springing out of alignment even under tons of pressure. Frame is offset 30° for unobstructed front access, and is made of 48,000 psi aluminum alloy. Compound leverage system allows you to swage bullets, full-length resize cases, form 30-06 cases into other calibers. Counter-balanced handle prevents accidental drop. Extra-long ram-bearing surface minimizes wobble and side play. Standard ⁷/₈-inch-14 thread accepts all popular dies and reloading accessories.

Reloader Special
  (Less dies) . . . . $ 93.00
Reloader Special-3 Combo,
  Rifle 120.50
Reloader Special-3 Combo,
  Pistol 122.60

RELOADING SCALE
MODEL 10-10

Up to 1010 Grain Capacity
Normal capacity is 510 grains, which can be increased, without loss in sensitivity, by attaching the included extra weight.

  Features include micrometer poise for quick, precise weighing, special approach-to-weight indicator, easy-to-read graduations, magnetic dampener, agate bearings, anti-tip pan, and dust-proof lid snaps on to cover scale for storage. Sensitivity is guaranteed to 0.1 grains.

Model 10-10 Scale	09073	3 lbs.	$102.50

RCBS RELOADING TOOLS

SIDEWINDER CASE TUMBLER

This RCBS case tumbler cleans cases inside and out and was designed exclusively for handloaders. Instead of just vibrating, the tilted easy-access drum rotates for fast, thorough cleaning. Its built-in timer adjusts for automatic shut-offs from five minutes to 12 hours. A perforated cap doubles as a screen to separate either liquid or dry RCBS cleaning medium from cleaned cases. Capacity is up to 300 38 Special cases or 150 30-06 cases. Available in 120 or 240 volt models. An 8-ounce bottle of Liquid Case Cleaner is included.

Sidewinder Case Tumbler
120 V **$185.00**
240 V **195.50**

CASE TRIMMER PILOT
$2.60

PART NO.	PILOT CAL.	PART NO.	PILOT CAL.
09377	17	09387	33
09378	22	09388	34
09379	24	09389	35
09380	25	09390	36
09381	26	09391	37
09382	27	09392	40
09383	28	09393	41
09384	30	09394	44
09385	31	09395	45
09386	32	09396	.45-R

This tool is used to: (1) trim to standard length those cases which have stretched after repeated firings; (2) trim a quantity of cases to the same length for uniform bullet seating; (3) correct uneven case mouths.

CASE TRIMMER COLLET
$6.50

PART NO.	COLLET NO.	PART NO.	COLLET NO.
09371	1	09373	3
09372	2	09374	4

ROTARY CASE TRIMMER-2

Much like a miniature lathe, this Precisioneer® tool is the ideal way to trim stretched cases, shorten a quantity of them to the same exact length, or correct slightly uneven case mouths. This improved model has been redesigned for absolute case length control. Adjustments have been simplified and refined for near-perfect precision in trimming fired cases.

Case is locked into trimmer collet, the cutting blade is adjusted to desired case length, the handle is turned a few times, and it's done. You then bevel and deburr the trimmed case, and it's ready to reload.

The interchangeable collets are available for all popular calibers (17 to 45) and are designed to lock cases securely for accurate trimming. Special trimmer pilots come in 20 sizes to fit 17 to 45 caliber cases. Each is Precisioneered®, and locks into the cutter with set screw. This type of lock ensures perfect case alignment, both vertically and horizontally.

The cutting assembly features a lock ring so that any quantity of cases can be trimmed to the exact same length with a single adjustment. Cutter blades are made of hardened steel for prolonged service life. Case trimmer also has sockets for holding extra collets and pilots and holes for screwing base to bench.

Rotary Case Trimmer-2 . . . . **$49.50**
Kit **78.00**

RCBS RELOADING TOOLS

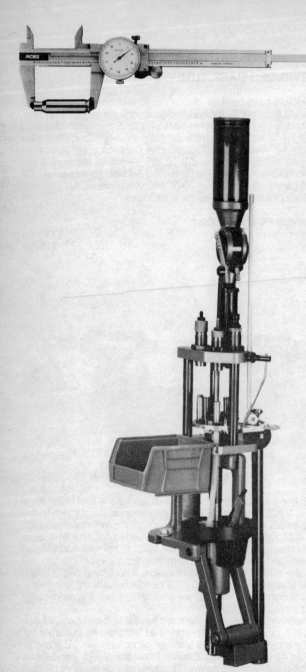

STAINLESS STEEL DIAL CALIPER

Features include easy-to-read dial, 6″ capacity, and measures four ways: outside, inside, depth and step. Dial graduations are in .001″; vernier measures are in millimeters. An ideal companion to RCBS Rotary Case Trimmer.
Stainless Steel Dial Caliper/Case Length Gauge . . **$58.00**

VIBRATORY CASE CLEANER

Large 3½-quart bowl cleans up to 550 .38 Special cases or 190 .30-06 cases at one time. Thermally protected 1/30 hp (2900 rpm) ball-bearing motor is available in 120 or 240 VAC. Steel case and thick ¼″ bowl ensure durability. Other features include removable lid (for fast inspection while motor is running) and 2 lb. package of Walnut shell Dry Media Case.
Vibratory Case Cleaner
120 VAC **$150.00**
240 VAC **160.00**

PIGGYBACK CONVERSION UNIT

A simple, inexpensive way to convert a single-stage press to a five-station, fully automatic progressive reloading tool (and back again). Mounts easily to RCBS Rock Chucker or RS-3 in less than 10 minutes. For pistol ammo and up to .223 caliber cartridges.
Piggyback Conversion Unit **$117.00**
Five Station Shell Plates **26.50**

REDDING RELOADING TOOLS

MODEL 721
"THE BOSS" PRESS

This "O" type reloading press features a rigid cast iron frame whose 36° offset provides the best visibility and access of comparable presses. Its "Smart" primer arm moves in and out of position automatically with ram travel. The priming arm is positioned at the bottom of ram travel for lowest leverage and best feel. Model 721 accepts all standard 7/8-14 threaded dies and universal shell holders.

Model 721 "The Boss" . . . . $ 89.95
    With Shellholder and 10A Dies 117.50

Now available: **Boss Pro-Pak Deluxe Reloading Kit.** Includes Boss Reloading Press, #2 Powder and Bullet Scale, Powder Trickler, Reloading Dies, and more $234.95

ULTRAMAG MODEL 700

Unlike other reloading presses that connect the linkage to the lower half of the press, the Ultramag's compound leverage system is connected at the top of the press frame. This allows the reloader to develop tons of pressure without the usual concern about press frame deflection. Huge frame opening will handle 50 × 3¼-inch Sharps with ease.

No. 700 Press, complete $192.00
No. 700K Kit, includes shell holder and one set of dies 219.50

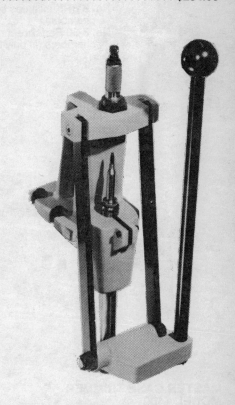

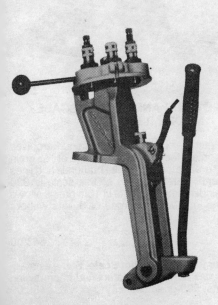

METALLIC TURRET RELOADING PRESS
MODEL 25

Extremely rugged, ideal for production reloading. No need to move shell, just rotate turret head to positive alignment. Ram accepts any standard snap-in shell holder. Includes primer arm for seating both small and large primers.

No. 25 Press, complete $219.95
No. 25K Kit, includes press, shell holder, and one set of dies 247.50
No. 19T Automatic Primer Feeder 16.95

REDDING RELOADING TOOLS

MATCH GRADE POWDER MEASURE MODEL 3BR

Designed for the most demanding reloaders—bench rest, silhouette and varmint shooters. The Model 3BR is unmatched for its precision and repeatability. Its special features include a powder baffle and zero backlash micrometer.

No. 3BR with Universal or Pistol Metering Chamber . . . . $ 98.00
No. 3 BRK includes both metering chambers 124.95
No. 3-30 Benchrest metering chambers (fit only 3BR) 28.50

MASTER POWDER MEASURE MODEL 3

Universal- or pistol-metering chambers interchange in seconds. Measures charges from 1/2 to 100 grains. Unit is fitted with lock ring for fast dump with large "clear" plastic reservoir. "See-thru" drop tube accepts all calibers from 22 to 600. Precision-fitted rotating drum is critically honed to prevent powder escape. Knife-edged powder chamber shears coarse-grained powders with ease, ensuring accurate charges.

No. 3 Master Powder Measure (specify Universal- or Pistol-Metering chamber) $79.95
No. 3K Kit Form, includes both Universal and Pistol chambers 98.00
No. 3-12 Universal or Pistol chamber 19.95

POWDER TRICKLER MODEL 5

Brings underweight charges up to accurate reading, adding powder to scale pan a granule or two at a time by rotating knob. Speeds weighing of each charge. Solid steel, low center of gravity. "Companion" height to all reloading scales; weighs a full pound.

No. 5 Powder Trickler $14.50

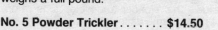

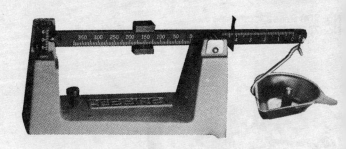

MASTER CASE TRIMMER MODEL 1400

This unit features a universal collet that accepts all rifle and pistol cases. The frame is solid cast iron with storage holes in the base for extra pilots. Both coarse and fine adjustments are provided for case length.

The case-neck cleaning brush and primer pocket cleaners attached to the frame of this tool make it a very handy addition to the reloading bench. Trimmer comes complete with:
- New speed cutter shaft
- Two pilots (22 and 30 cal.)
- Universal collet
- Two neck cleaning brushes (22 thru 30 cal.)
- Two primer pocket cleaners (large and small)

No. 1400 Master Case Trimmer complete $62.95
No. 1500 Pilots 2.50

STANDARD POWDER AND BULLET SCALE MODEL RS-1

For the beginner or veteran reloader. Only two counterpoises need to be moved to obtain the full capacity range of 1/10 grain to 380 grains. Clearly graduated with white numerals and lines on a black background. Total capacity of this scale is 380 grains. An over-and-under plate graduate in 10th grains allows checking of variations in powder charges or bullets without further adjustments.

Model No. RS-1 . . . . $48.00

Also available: **Master Powder & Bullet Scale.** Same as standard model, but includes a magnetic dampened beam swing for extra fast readings. 505-grain capacity $59.00

Reference

THE SHOOTER'S BOOKSHELF

An up-to-date listing of book titles, old and new, of interest to shooters and gun enthusiasts. Most of these books can be found at your local library, bookstore, or gun shop. If not available, contact the publisher. Names and addresses of leading publishers in the field are listed at the end of this section.

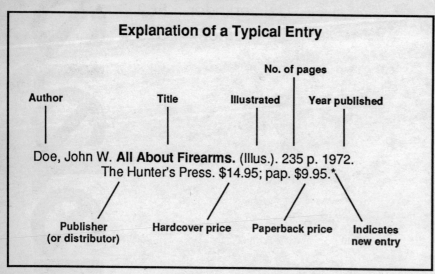

Explanation of a Typical Entry

- No. of pages
- Author
- Title
- Illustrated
- Year published

Doe, John W. **All About Firearms.** (Illus.). 235 p. 1972.
The Hunter's Press. $14.95; pap. $9.95.*

- Publisher (or distributor)
- Hardcover price
- Paperback price
- Indicates new entry

AIR GUNS
Churchill, Bob & Davies, Granville. **Modern Airweapon Shooting,** (Illus.), 1981. David & Charles. $25.95.

Walter, John. **The Airgun Book.** (Illus.). 128 p. 1988. Sterling. $29.95.*

AMMUNITION
Brown, Ronald. **Homemade Guns & Homemade Ammo.** 191 p. 1986. Loompanics. pap. text ed. $9.95.

Donnelly, John J. **Handloader's Manual of Cartridge Conversions.** (Illus.) 1056 p. 1987. Stoeger Pub. Co. pap. $24.95; spiral bound $29.95; hardcover $34.95.

Evaluation of Police Handgun Ammunition. (Law Enforcement Series) 1986. Gordon Press. $79.95 (lib. bdg.).

Geary, Don. **The Reloader's Bible: The Complete Guide to Making Ammunition at Home.** (Illus.) 256 p. 1986. Prentice-Hall. $17.95.

Goad, K.J. & Halsey, D. H. **Ammunition, Grenades & Mines.** 1982. Pergamon Press. $39.00; pap. $21.00.

Long, Duncan. **Combat Ammunition: Everything You Need to Know.** (Illus.). 136 p. 1986. Palladin Pr. text. ed. $19.95.

Parkerson, Codman. **A Brief History of Bullet Moulds.** Pioneer Press. $1.75.

Sears & Roebuck 1910 **Ammunition Catalog** (Illus.). pap. Sand Pond $2.00.

Stegen, Arthur E. **Biathlon.** (Illus.). 144 p. National Rifle Assn. $30.00.

Steindler, R. A. **Reloader's Guide.** 3rd ed. (Illus.). 1975. softbound. Stoeger. $9.95.

Trzoniec, Stanley W. **Handloader's Guide.** (Illus.). 256 p. pap. 1985. Stoeger. $11.95.

ARCHERY (see also Bow and Arrow)
Ascham, Roger. **Toxophilius, 1545.** Arber, Edward ed. 1971 Repr. of 1895 ed. Scholarly Press. $29.00.

Athletic Institute, ed. **Archery: A Sport for Everyone.** (Illus.). 96 p. 1984. Athletic Inst. pap. $7.95.

Barrett, Jean. **Archery.** 3rd ed. 1980. Scott, Foresman & Co. $6.95.

Bear, Fred. **Archer's Bible.** (Illus.). 1980. pap. Doubleday, $7.95.

Combs, Roger. **Archers Digest,** 4th ed. (Illus.) 256 p. 1986. DBI. pap. $12.95.

Cub Scouts Sports Archery. (Illus.). 32 p. 1985. BSA. pap. $0.95.

Glogan, Joseph. **Sportsman's Book of U.S. Records.** (Illus.). 1980. pap. text ed. NY Outdoor Guide. $4.95.

Haywood, Kathleen & Lewis, Catherine. **Archery: Steps to Success.** (Illus.). 1988. Leisure Press. Price not set.*

Henderson, Al. **Understanding Winning Archery.** Helgeland, G., ed. (Illus.). 114 p. 1983. Target Comm. pap. $8.95.

Johnson, Dewayne J. & Oliver, Robert A. **Archery.** 1980. pap. American Press. $3.95.

Kember-Smith, Jackson S. **Archery Today: Techniques & Philosophies in Action.** (Illus.). 160 p. 1988. David & Charles. $22.95.*

Klann, Margaret L. **Target Archery.** 1970. pap. Addison-W. $7.95.

Latham, J. D. ed. **Saracen Archery.** (Illus.). Albert Saifer, pub. $35.00.

Laubin, Reginald & Laubin, Gladys. **American Indian Archery.** (Illus.). 1980. University of Oklahoma Press. $18.95.

McKinney, Wayne C. & McKinney, Mike W. **Archery.** 5th ed. (Illus.). 176 p. 1985. Wm. C. Brown. Price on request.

Markham, Gervase. **The Art of Archerie.** facs. ed. 1968. Repr. of 1634 ed. George Shumway Publisher. $15.00.

Morisawa, Jackson S. **The Secret of the Target.** 144 p. 1988. Routledge, Chapman & Hall. pap. $14.95.*

Mosley, Walter M. **An Essay on Archery.** 1976. Charles River Books. $17.50.

Neade, William. **The Double Armed Man.** facs. ed. (Illus.). 1971. George Shumway Publisher. $10.00.

Odums, R.I. & Allen, D.G. **Career Guide to Officiating Archery & Riflery.** Tessman, Rita, ed. (Illus.) 150 p. 1986. Guideposts Pub. Dists. $12.95.

Thompson, J. Maurice. **The Witchery of Archery.** 1986. Fundingsland. pap. $8.95.*

Wood, William. **The Bowman's Glory, or, Archery Revived.** 1976. Charles River Books. $7.50

ARMS AND ARMOR (see also Firearms)
Albion, Robert G. **Introduction to Military History.** (Illus.). 1971. Repr. of 1929 ed. AMS Press. $29.00.

American Machines & Foundry Co. **Silencers: Patterns & Principles, Vol. 2.** (Illus.). 1972. pap. Paladin Enterprises. $12.95.

Beckett, Brian. **Weapons of Tomorrow.** 160 p. 1983. Plenum Pub. $14.95.

Berman, Vladimir. **Masterpieces of the Gunsmiths.** (Illus.). 144 p. 1981. State Mutual Books. $81.00.*

Bivens, John. **Art of the Fire-Lock, Twentieth Century: Being a Discourse Upon the Present and Past Practices of Stocking and Mounting the Sporting Fire-Lock Rifle Gun.** 1982. Shumway. $40.00.

Blair, Claude. **Arms, Armour & Base Metalwork.** (Illus.). 532 p. 1985. Sotheby Pubns. text ed. $85.00.

Constant, James N. **Fundamentals of Strategic Weapons.** 940 p. 1981. Sijthoff & Nordoff. $140.00.

Curtis, Anthony. **The Lyle Offical Arms & Armour Review.** 416 p. 1983. Apollo. $24.95.

—**Lyle Official Arms & Armour Review** (Illus.). 415 p. 1982. Apollo. $24.95.

Daniel, Larry J. & Gunter, Riley W. **Confederate Cannon Foundries.** Pioneer Press. ed. Pioneer Press. $17.95.

Diagram Group. **Weapons** (Illus.). 1980. St. Martin's Press. $27.50.

Dunnigan, James F. **How to Make War: A Comprehensive Guide to Modern Warfare.** (Illus.). 416 p. 1981. Morrow $14.50.

Dupuy, Trevor N. **The Evolution of Weapons & Warfare.** (Illus.). 360 p. 1984. Repr. of 1980 ed. Hero Bks. text ed. $19.95.

Ezell, Edward C. **Small Arms Today: Latest Reports on the World's Weapons & Ammunition.** 256 p. (Orig.). 1984. pap. Stackpole. $16.95.

Frost, H. Gordon. **Blades and Barrels: Six Centuries of Combination Weapons.** Walloon Press. $16.95. deluxe ed. $25.00; presentation ed. $50.00.

Funcken, Lilane & Funcken, Fred. **Arms & Uniforms: The Second World War,** vols. I, III & IV. 120 p. 1984. P-H. $17.95 (ea.).

Gordon, Don E. **Electronic Warfare: Element of Strategy & Multiplier of Combat Power.** (Illus.). 200 p. 1982. Pergamon Press. $24.00.

Gruzanski, C. V. **Spike and Chain.** Wehman Brothers, Inc. $7.50.

Guthman, William, ed. **Guns and Other Arms.** (Illus.). 1980. pap. Mayflower Books. $7.95.

Hamilton, T. M. **Firearms on the Frontier: Guns at Fort Michilimackinac 1715–1781.** Armour, David A., ed. (Illus.). 1976. pap. Mackinac Island State Park Commission. $3.00.

—**Colonial Frontier Guns.** 1987. Pioneer Press. $13.95.*

Hart, Harold H. **Weapons & Armor: A Pictorial Archive of Woodcuts & Engravings.** 1983. Peter Smith. $14.50.

Illustrations of United States Military Arms 1976–1903: And Their Inspector's Marks. 1987. Pioneer Press. $4.95.*

Jane's Infantry Weapons 1987–88. Hogg, Ian, ed. (Illus.). 1000 p. 1987. Janes Info Group. $150.00.*

Johnson, Thomas M. **Collecting the Edged Weapons of the Third Reich.** 4 vols. Bradach, Wilfrid, tr. (Illus.). T. M. Johnson. Vol. 1: $18.50; Vol. 2: $18.50. Vol. 3; $20.00; Vol. 4: $25.00.

Journal of the Arms and Armour Society. Vol. 1. (Illus.). 1970. George Shumway Publisher. $12.00.

Klare, Michael T. **American Arms Supermarket.** (Illus.). 336 p. 1985. pap. U. of Texas Pr. $12.95.

Kozan, S. **Manufacture of Armour and Helmets in Sixteenth Century Japan.** Albert Saifer, Publisher. $35.00.

Laking, Guy F. **A Record of European Armour and Arms Through Seven Centuries.** 5 vols. (Illus.). Repr. AMS Press. set $295.00.

Lenga. **Amazing Fact Book of Weapons.** 1987. Creative Editions. $15.55.*

McAulay, John D. **Carbines of the Civil War, 1861–1865.** 1981. Pioneer Press. $8.95.

Macksey, Kenneth. **Technology in War:** The Impact on Science of Weapon Development & Modern Battles. (Illus.) 224 p. 1986. Arco. $19.95.

Marchant-Smith, D. J. & Haslem, P. R. **Small Arms & Cannons.** (Brassey's Battlefield Weapons System & Technology: Vol. 5) 160 p. 1982. Pergamon. $16.95.

Matunas, Edward. **Handbook of Metallic Cartridge Reloading.** (Illus.) 272 p. 1981. New Century. $19.95.

Mowbray, E. Andrew, ed. **Arms-Armor: From the Atelier of Ernst Schmidt, Munich.** (Illus.) 1967. Mowbray Co. $15.00.

Owen, J. I. ed. **Infantry Weapons of the Armies of Africa, the Orient and Latin America.** 1980. pap. Pergamon Press. $29.00.

—**Infantry Weapons of the NATO Armies.** 2nd ed. 1980. pap. Pergamon Press. $28.75.

—**Infantry Weapons of the Warsaw Pact Armies.** 2nd ed. 1979. Pergamon Press. $28.50.

Peterson, Harold L. **The American Sword. 1775–1945.** (Illus.). 1983. Riling, Ray, Arms Books. $35.00.

Pierre, Andrew, J. **The Global Politics of Arms Sales.** 1981. Princeton University Press. $20.00; pap. $5.95.

Rossnow-Owen, Davis. **Vietnam Weapons Handbook.** (Illus.) 128 p. 1986. Sterling. pap. $7.99.

Royal United Service Institute for Defense Studies, ed. **International Weapon Developments: A Survey of Current Developments in Weapons Systems,** 4th ed. (Illus.). 1980. pap. Pergamon Press. $17.50.

Schuyler-Hartley-Graham Military Furnishers. **Illustrated Catalog Arms and Military Goods.** facs. ed. (Illus.). 1864. Flayderman, N. & Co. $9.50.

Smith, W. H. **Small Arms of the World: A Basic Manual of Small Arms,** 12th ed. 896 p. 1983. Stackpole. $49.95.

Suenega, M. **Pictorial History of Ancient Japanese Weapons, Armour & Artifacts.** (Illus.). 100 p. 1983. pap. Saifer. $12.95.

Tenesvary, Ferenc. **Arms & Armour.** (Illus.). 126 p. 1982. Int'l Spec. Books. $19.95.*

Truby, J. David. **Quiet Killers, Vol. 1.** (Illus.). 1972. pap. Paladin Enterprises. $8.00.

—**Quiet Killers II: Silencer Update** (Illus.). 1979. pap. Paladin Enterprises. $8.00.

Warry, John. **Warfare in the Classical World: An Illustrated Encyclopedia of Weapons, Warriors and Warfare in the Ancient Civilizations of Greece and Rome.** 1981. St. Martin. $19.95.

Whisker, James B. **Arms Makers of Pennsylvania.** (Illus.). 1988. Susquehanna U. Press. $60.00.

Wintringham, Thomas H. **Story of Weapons and Tactics.** facs. ed. 1943. Arno Press. $16.00.

Wright, James & Rossi, Peter. **Under the Gun: Weapons, Crime & Violence in America.** 360 p. 1983. Aldine de Gruyter Pub. $34.95.

Zaloga, Stephen J. & Grandsen, James. **The Eastern Front.** 96 p. 1983. Squad Sig. Pubns. $7.95.

ARTILLERY

Bidwell, Shefford, ed. **Brassey's Artillery of the World.** 2nd rev. ed. 1981. Pergamon Press. $59.50.

Foss, Christopher. **Artillery of the World.** 2nd ed. (Illus.). 1976. Scribner's. $8.95.

Foss, Christopher F., ed. **Jane's Armour & Artillery 1987–88** (Illus.). 1000 p. 1987 Janes Info Group. $152.50.

—**Jane's Armour & Artillery, 1988–89.** (Illus.). 800 p. 1988. Janes Info Group. $127.50.

Gander, Terry. **Artillery** (Modern Military Techniques Service). (Illus.). 48 p. (gr. 5 up) 1987. Lerner Publications. $9.95.

Macchiavelli, Nicolo. **The Arte of Warre (Certain Wales of the Orderying of Souldiours).** Whitehorne, P., tr. 1969. Repr. of 1562 ed. W. J. Johnson. $42.00.

Manucy, Albert. **Artillery through the Ages:** A Short Illus. History of Cannon Emphasizing Types Used in America. (Illus.) 96 p. 1985. Govt. Ptg. Off. pap. $2.75.

Rogers. H. B. **A History of Artillery.** (Illus.). 230 p. 1974. Lyle Stuart. $7.95.

Rogers, H. C. **A History of Artillery.** (Illus.). 1977. Citadel Press. pap. $4.95.

Simienowicz, Casimir. **The Great Art of Artillery.** 1976. Charles River Books. $20.00.

BALLISTICS

Farrar, C. L. & Leeming, D. W. **Military Ballistics: A Basic Manual.** 225 p. 1983. Pergamon Press. $17.25.

Krier, Herman & Summerfield, Martin, eds. **Interior Ballistics of Guns.** 385 p. 1979. AIAA. $69.00.

Laible, Roy C. **Ballistic Materials & Penetration Mechanics.** 1980. Elsevier. $97.50

Mann, Franklin W. **The Bullet's Flight to Target From Powder: The Ballistics of Small Arms.** 391 p. 1980. Wolfe Pub. Co. Repr. text ed. $22.50.

Mannes, Philip. **Tables of Bullet Performance.** Wolfe, Dave, ed. 407 p. (Orig.). 1980. pap. text ed. Wolfe Pub. Co. $17.50.

Wilber, Charles G. **Ballistic Science for the Law Enforcement Officer.** (Illus.). 1977. C. C. Thomas. $37.00.

—**Forensic Biology for the Law Enforcement Officer.** (Illus.). 1974. C. C. Thomas. $45.00.

Williams, M. **Practical Handgun Ballistics.** 1980. C. C. Thomas. $25.25.

Wolfe, Dave, ed. **The Art of Bullet Casting.** (Illus.). 258 p. pap. 1981. Wolfe Pub. Co. pap. $12.95.

—**Propellant Profiles.** (Illus.) 158 p. 1982. Wolfe Pub. Co. pap. text ed. $12.95.

BIRD DOGS

Falk, John R. **The Complete Guide to Bird Dog Training.** rev. ed. 1986. Winchester Press. $15.95.

Rafe, Stephen C. **Training Your Dog For Birdwork.** (Illus.). 96 p. 1987. Denlingers. pap. $16.95.

Stuart, Jack. **Bird Dogs and Upland Game Birds.** (Illus.). 1983. Denlingers. $24.95.

Waterman, Charles F. **Gun Dogs & Bird Guns: A Charley Waterman Reader.** (Illus.). 244 p. 1987. GSJ Press (South Hamilton, Mass.). text ed. $25.00.

BLACK POWDER GUNS (see also Firearms)

Bridges, Toby. **Advanced Muzzeloader's Guide.** (Illus.). 256 p. 1985. pap. Stoeger. $11.95.

Elliot, Brook. **Complete Smoothbore Hunter.** (Illus.) 240 p. 1986. New Century. $16.95.

Nonte, George C. Jr., **Black Powder Guide.** 2d ed. (Illus.). 256 p. pap. Stoeger Pub. Co. $11.95.

BOW AND ARROW (see also Archery)

Adams, Chuck. **Bowhunter's Digest.** 2nd ed. pap. 1981. DBI Books. $12.95.

Bear, Fred. **The Archer's Bible.** rev. ed. (Illus.). 1980. Doubleday. pap. $7.95.

Bowring, Dave. **Bowhunting for Whitetails: Your Best Methods for Taking North America's Favorite Deer.** (Illus.). 320 p. 1985. Stackpole. $24.95.

Helgeland, G. **Archery World's Complete Guide to Bow Hunting.** 1975. P-H. pap. $6.95.

Kinton, Tony. **The Beginning Bowhunter.** (Illus.). 128 p. 1985. ICS Books. pap. $9.95.

Maynard, Roger. **Advanced Bowhunting Guide.** (Illus.). 224 p. 1984. Stoeger Pub. Co. pap. $12.95.

Schuh, Dwight. **Bowhunting for Mule Deer.** 1986. Stoneydale Press Pub. $14.95. pap. $9.95.

—**Bowhunter's Encyclopedia: Practical, Easy-to-Find Answers to Your Bowhunting Questions.** (Illus.). 576 p. 1987. Stackpole. $39.95.*

Smyth, John & Barwick, Humphrey. **Bow vs. Gun.** 1976. Reprint. Charles River Books. $15.00

Thayer, Dixon. **Bow Hunting Basics: Fundamentals for Successful Hunting.** (Illus.). 32 p. 1985. Blue Sky. pap. $2.95.

Wise, Larry. **Tuning Your Compound Bow.** Helgeland, Glenn, ed. (Illus.). 132 p. 1985. Target Comm. pap. $6.95.

Wood, William. **The Bowman's Glory, or, Archery Revived.** 1976. Charles River Books. $7.50.

BOWHUNTING (see Bow and Arrow)

CARTRIDGES

Bartlett, W. A. & Gallatin, D. B. **B and G Cartridge Manual,** Pioneer Press. $2.00.

Datig, Fred A. **Cartridges for Collectors,** 3 vols. Borden, $10.95 ea.

Donnelly, John J. **Handloader's Manual of Cartridge Conversions.** (Illus.) 1056 p. 1987. Stoeger Pub. Co. pap. $29.95; spiral bound $29.95; hardcover $34.95.

Keith, Elmer. **Sixgun Cartridges & Loads.** 1985. Repr. of 1936 ed Gun Room. $19.95.

Manual of Pistol & Revolver Cartridges. 2 vols. 1987. Gordon Press. lib. bdg. $79.75.

Matthews, Charles. **Shoot Better With Centerfire Rifle Cartridges-Ballistics Tables.** (Illus.). 560 p. 1984. Matthews Inc. pap. $16.45.

Nonte, George. **The Home Guide to Cartridge Conversions.** rev. ed. Gun Room Press. $19.95.

Suydam, Charles R. **American Cartridge.** Borden. $12.95.

Thomas, Gough. **Shotguns and Cartridges for Game and Clays.** 3rd ed. (Illus.). 1976. Transatlantic Arts, Inc. $25.00.

COLLECTING (see Firearms—Collectors and Collecting)

COLT REVOLVERS

Bady, Donald B. **Colt Automatic Pistols,** rev. ed. 1973. Borden. $19.95.

Cochran, Keith. **Colt Peacemaker Ready-Reference Handbook.** (Illus.) 76 p. 1985. Cochran Pub. pap. $12.95.

—**Colt Peacemaker Encyclopedia.** (Illus.). 434 p. 1986. Cochran Pub. $59.95.

—**Colt Peacemaker Yearly Variations.** (Illus.). 96 p. 1987. Cochran Pub. $17.95. pap. $12.95.

The Colt Point Forty-Five Auto Pistol. 1986. Gordon Pr. $79.95.

The Colt .45 Exotic Weapons System. (Illus.). 88 p. 1984. Paladin Pr. pap. $15.00.

Graham, Ron, et al. **A Study of the Colt Single Action Army Revolver.** (Illus.) 523 p. 1985. Repr. of 1976 ed. Kopec Pubns. $69.95.

Moore, C. Kenneth. **Colt Revolvers & the U.S. Navy 1865–1888.** (Illus.). 144 p. 1986. Dorrance. $29.95.

Shumaker, P. L. **Colt's Variations of the Old Model Pocket Pistol.** 1957. Borden. $10.95.

Whittington, Robert D. III. **The Colt Whitneyville-Walker Pistol.** (Illus.). 96 p. 1984. Brownlee Books. $20.00.

CROSSBOWS

Benson, Ragnar. **Bull's-Eye Crossbows by Ragnar Benson.** (Illus.). 96 p. 1985. Paladin Press. pap. $10.00.

Combs, Roger, ed. **Crossbows.** (Illus.). 192 p. 1987. DBI. $10.95.

Payne-Gallwey, Ralph. **Cross-Bow, Medieval and Modern.** Saifer, Albert, Pub. $50.00.

Wilbur, C. Martin. **History of the Crossbow.** (Illus.). Repr. of 1936 ed. pap. Shorey. $2.95.

DECOYS (see also Duck Shooting)

Art, Brad & Kimball, Scott. **The Fish Decoy,** vol. II. 192 p. 1987. Aardvark WL. $60.00.*

Barber, Joel. **Wild Fowl Decoys.** (Illus.). pap. Dover. $8.95.

—**Wild Fowl Decoys.** (Illus.). Peter Smith. $13.50.

Berkey, Barry R., et al. **Pioneer Decoy Carvers: A Biography of Lemuel and Stephen Ward.** (Illus.). 1977. Tidewater. $17.50.

Bridenhagen, Keith. **Decoy Pattern Book.** (Illus.). 224 p. (Orig.). 1984. pap. Sterling. $9.95.

—**Realistic Decoys.** 224 p. 1985. Stoeger Pub. Co. pap. $14.95.

Bridenhagen, Keith & Spielman, Patrick. **Realistic Decoys: Carving, Texturing, Painting & Finishing.** (Illus.). 224 p. (Orig.). 1985. Sterling. pap. $14.95.

Carpenter, Pearl E. **The Duck Book One & Two:** Basics for Painting Wood-Carved Ducks & Birds. (Illus.) 1984. Shades Mother Nature wkbk. $12.75.

Chapell, Carl & Sullivan, Clark. **Wildlife Woodcarvers:** A Complete How-to-do-it Book for Carving & Painting Wildfowl. (Illus.) 216 p. 1986. Stackpole. $39.95.

Chitwood, Henry C., et al. **Connecticut Decoys.** (Illus.). 256 p. 1987. Schiffer. $45.00.

Connett, Eugene. **Duck Decoys.** 1980. Durrell. $12.50.

Coykendall, Ralf, Sr. **Duck Decoys & How To Rig Them.** Coykendall, Ralf, Jr., ed. (Illus.). 135 p. 1987. New Century. pap. $14.95.

Delph, John and Delph, Shirley. **Factory Decoys of Mason Stevens.** (Illus.). Schiffer. $35.00.

Earnest, Adele. **The Art of the Decoy: American Bird Carvings.** (Illus.). 1982. pap. Schiffer. $14.95.

Frank, Chas. W., Jr. **Wetland Heritage: The Louisiana Duck Decoy.** 192 p. 1985. Pelican. $49.95.

Hillman, Anthony. **Carving Famous Antique Bird Decoys: Patterns & Instructions for Reproducing 16 Masterpieces from Shelburne Museum.** 72 p. 1988. Dover. pap. $5.95.*

—**Carving Classic Swan & Goose Decoys.** 72 p. 1987. Dover. pap. $5.95.*

—**Miniature Duck Decoys for Woodcarvers.** 40 p. 1985. Dover. $4.95.

—**Painting Duck Decoys: 24 Full-Color Plates.** 56 p. 1985. Dover. pap. $4.95.

—**Painting Shorebird Decoys.** (Illus.). 40 p. 1987. Dover. pap. $4.95.*

Johnsgard, Paul A. ed. **The Bird Decoy: An American Art Form.** (Illus.). 1976. University of Nebraska Press. $17.95.

Luckey, Carl F. **Collecting Antique American Bird Decoys: An Identification and Value Guide.** (Illus.). 208 p. 1983. pap. Books Americana. $14.95.

Mackey, William J., Jr. **American Bird Decoys.** (Illus.). 256 p. 1987. Dutton. $22.50.

Mackey, William F., Jr. & Colio, Quinton. **American Bird Decoys.** (Illus.). 1979. Repr. of 1965 ed. Schiffer. $19.95.

Parmalee, Paul W. & Loomis, Forrest D. **Decoys and Decoy Carvers of Illinois.** 1969. pap. Northern Illinois University Press. $25.00.

Reiger, George. **Floaters & Stick-Ups.** 208 p. 1986. Godine. $45.00.

Schroeder, Roger. **How To Carve Wildfowl: Nine North American Masters Reveal the Carving and Painting Techniques That Win Them International Blue Ribbons.** 256 p. 1984. Stackpole. $39.95.

Shourds, Harry V. & Hillman, Anthony. **Carving Duck Decoys.** 1981. pap. Dover. $5.95.

Spielman, Patrick. **Making Wood Decoys.** 1982. Sterling. pap. $9.95.

Veasey, William. **Head Patterns.** (Illus.). 58 p. 1983. pap. Schiffer. $14.95.

—**Making Hunting Decoys.** (Illus.). 256 p. 1986. Schiffer. $45.00.

—**Miniature Decoy Patterns.** (Illus.). 58 p. 1983. pap. $14.95.

Veasey, William & Hull, Cary S. **Waterfowl Carving: Blue Ribbon Techniques.** (Illus.). 1982. Schiffer. $35.00.

Walsh, Clune, Jr. & Jackson, Lowell G., eds. **Waterfowl Decoys of Michigan and the Lake St. Clair Region.** (Illus.). 175 p. 1983. Gale. $50.00.

DEER HUNTING (see also Hunting)

Adams, Chuck. **Complete Guide to Bowhunting Deer.** 256 p. 1984. pap. DBI. $12.95.

Bowring, Dave. **Bowhunting for Whitetails: Your Best Methods for Taking North America's Favorite Deer.** 304 p. 1985. Stackpole. $24.95.

Cameron, Donald. **Among The Red Deer: The Stalking Portfolio of Henry Hope Creslock.** 1985. State Mutual Bks. $300.00.

Chalmers, Patrick R. **Deer-Stalking.** 256 p. 1985. State Mutual Bks. $60.00.

Conway, Bryant W. **Successful Hints on Hunting White Tail Deer.** 2nd ed. 1967. pap. Claitors. $3.98.

Cunningham, Marci. **The Deerhunter's Guide to Success: From the Woods to the Skillet.** 1985. Backwoods Bks. $3.50.

Dalrymple, Bryon W. **The Complete Book of Deer Hunting.** 256 p. pap. Stoeger. $9.95.

—**Deer Hunting with Dalrymple: A Lifetime of Lore on The Whitetail and Mule Deer.** 256 p. 1983. pap. Arco. $7.95.

Deer Hunter's Guide. (Illus.). 160 p. Nat'l Rifle Assn. $4.95.

Elman, Robert, ed. **All About Deer Hunting in America.** 1976. New Century. $16.95.

Fadala, Sam. **Successful Deer Hunting.** 288 p. 1983. pap. DBI Books. $12.95.

Guide to Deer Hunting in the Catskill Mountains. pap. Outdoor Pubns. $2.00.

Hayes, Tom. **How to Hunt the White Tail Deer.** A. S. Barnes, rev. ed. pap. $6.95.

Horner, Kent. **Art & Science of Whitetail Hunting: How to Interpret the Facts & Find the Deer.** (Illus.) 192 p. 1986. Stackpole. pap. $11.95.

Lapinski, Mike. **Whitetail Deer Hunting.** (Illus.). 64 p. 1988. Stoneydale Press. pap. $3.50.*

Laycock, George. **Deer Hunter's Bible.** rev. ed. (Illus.). 1971. pap. Doubleday. $6.95.

Nelson, Norm. **Mule Deer: How To Bring Home North America's Big Deer of the West.** (Illus.). 208 p. 1987. Stackpole. $16.95.

Ozoga, John J. **Whitetail Country.** Petrie, Chuck, ed. (Illus.). 157 p. 1988. Willow Creek Press. $39.00.*

Patridge, Ray. **The Deer Hunter Log Book.** 36 p. 1984. Bootstrap Pubns. softcover $6.95.

Sell, Francis E. **Art of Successful Deer Hunting.** 1980. pap. Willow Creek. $5.95.

Sisley, Nick. **Deer Hunting Across North America.** (Illus.). 1975. Freshet Press. $12.95.

Smith, Richard P. **Deer Hunting.** rev. ed. (Illus.). 1981. pap. Stackpole Books. $10.95.

Wegner, Robert. **Deer & Deer Hunting:** The Serious Hunter's Guide. 324 p. 1984. Stackpole. $24.95.

—**Deer & Deer Hunting.** Book 2. (Illus.). 400 p. 1987. Stackpole. $29.95.*

Wolff, Ed. **Taking Big Bucks: Solving the Whitetail Riddle.** (Illus.). 176 p. 1987. Stoneydale Pr. Pub. pap. $9.95.

Wooters, John. **Hunting Trophy Deer.** rev. ed. (Illus.). 265 p. 1983. pap. New Century. $13.95.

Zumbo, Jim & Elman, Robert. **All-American Deer Hunter's Guide.** (Illus.). 320 p. 1983. New Century. $29.95.

DUCK & GEESE SHOOTING (see also Decoys)

Cadieux, Charles L. **Successful Goose Hunting.** (Illus.). 240 p. 1986. Stone Wall Press. $24.95.

Hinman, Bob. **The Duck Hunter's Handbook.** (Illus.). 1976. softbound. Stoeger. $9.95.

Jordan, James M. & Alcorn, George T., eds. **The Wildfowler's Heritage.** (Illus.). 120 p. 1984. JCP Corp. Va. $46.50.

McGrath, Brian J. **Duck Calls & Other Game Calls.** (Illus.). 1988. Thos. B. Reel. $40.00.*

MacQuarrie, Gordon. **The Last Stories of the Old Duck Hunters.** (Illus.). 204 p. 1985. Willow Creek. $17.50.

—**Stories of the Old Duck Hunters & Other Drivel.** repr. of 1967 ed. Willow Creek. $17.50.

Milner, Robert, **Retriever Training for the Duck Hunter.** (Illus.) 150 p. 1985. Repr. of 1983 ed. Junction Press. $18.95.

Smith, Steve. **Hunting Ducks & Geese: Hard Facts, Good Bets and Serious Advice From a Duck Hunter You Can Trust.** 160 p. 1984. Stackpole. $14.95.

FALCONRY (see also Fowling)

Beebe, Frank L. **A Falconry Manual.** (Illus.). 128 p. 1983. pap. Hancock House. $12.95.

Bert, Edmund. **An Approved Treatise of Hawkes and Hawking Divided into Three Bookes.** 1968. Repr. of 1619 ed. W. J. Johnson. $45.00.

Fisher, Charles H. **Falconry Reminiscences.** 1972. Falcon Head Press. $15.00; deluxe ed. $45.00.

Fox, David G. **Garden of Eagles: The Life & Times of a Falconer.** (Illus.). 216 p. 1984. Merrimack Pub. Cir. $16.95.

Frederick II of Hohenstaufen. **The Art of Falconry.** Wood, Casey A. & Fyfe, F. Marjorie, eds. (Illus.). 1943. Stanford University Press. $60.00.

Freeman, Gage E. & Salvin, Francis H. **Falconry: Its Claims, History and Practice.** 1972. Falcon Head Press. $12.50; deluxe ed. $25.00.

Gryndall, William. **Hawking, Hunting, Fouling and Fishing;** Newly Corrected by W. Gryndall Faulkner. 1972. Repr. of 1596 ed. Walter J. Johnson, Inc. $25.00.

Harting, James E. **Bibliotheca Accipitraria, a Catalogue of Books Ancient and Modern Relating to Falconry.** 1977. Repr. of 1963 ed. Oak Knoll Books. $45.00.

Jameson, E. W. Jr. & Peeters, Hans J. **Introduction to Hawking.** 2nd ed. (Illus.). 1977. pap. E. W. Jameson, Jr. $8.85.

Lascelles, Gerald. **Art of Falconry.** (Illus.). Saifer. $12.50.

Latham, Simon. **Lathams Falconry, 2 pts.** 1977. Repr. of 1615 ed. Walter J. Johnson, Inc. $32.50.

Madden, D. H. **Chapter of Medieval History.** 1969. Repr. of 1924 ed. Kennikat. lib. bdg. $55.00.

Mellor, J. E. **Falconry Notes by Mellor.** 1972. Falcon Head Press. $15.00.

Mitchell, E. B. **Art & Practice of Falconry.** (Illus.). 303 p. Saifer. $26.00.

O'Brien, Dan. **Rites of Autumn: A Falconer's Journey Across the American West.** 1988. Atlantic Monthly. $17.95.*

Oswald, Allan. **The History & Practice of Falconry.** 128 p. 1981. State Mutual Book Svce. $12.50.

Phillott, D. C. & Harcourt, E. S., trs. from Persian Urdu. **Falconry—Two Treatises.** 1968. text ed. Falcon Head Press. $45.00.

Rowley, Sam R. **Discovering Falconry: A Comprehensive Guide to Contemporary Falconry.** (Illus.). 160 p. 1985. New Dawn. pap. $11.95.

Samson, Jack. **Modern Falconry: Your Illustrated Guide To The Art & Sport of Hunting With North American Hawks.** 160 p. 1984. Stackpole. pap. $13.95.

Schlegel, H. & Verster De Wulverhorst, J. A. **The World of Falconry.** 1980. Vendome Press. $60.00.

Schlegel, H. & Wulverhorst, A. H. **Traite De Fauconnerie: Treatise of Falconry.** Hanlon, Thomas, tr. (Illus.). 1973. Chasse Pubns. $32.50.

FIREARMS (see also Arms and Armor, Pistols, Revolvers, Rifles, Shotguns)

Anderson, Robert S., ed. **Gun Digest Hunting Annual,** 1988. 5th ed. (Illus.). 256 p. 1987. DBI. pap. $13.95.

Askins, Charles. **Askins on Pistols and Revolvers.** Bryant, Ted & Askins, Bill. eds., 1980. National Rifle Association, $25.00; pap. $8.95.

Automatic and Concealable Firearms: Design Book, 3 vols. 1986. Gordon Pr. $299.00 (lib. bdg.).

Barwick, Humphrey. **Concerning the Force and Effect of Manual Weapons of Fire.** 1974. Repr. of 1594 ed. W. J. Johnson. $20.00.

Berger, Robert J. **Know Your Broomhandle Mausers.** (Illus.). 96 p. 1985. Blacksmith Corp. pap. $6.95.

Bodio, Stephen. **Good Guns.** 128 p. 1986. N. Lyons Bks. $14.95.

Bridges, Toby. **Advanced Muzzleloader's Guide.** 256 p. 1985. Stoeger Pub. Co. pap. $11.95.

Brown, Ronald. **Homemade Guns & Homemade Ammo.** 191 p. 1986. Loompanics. pap. text ed. $12.00.

Browne, Bellmore H. **Guns and Gunning.** (Illus.). Repr. of 1908 ed. pap. Shorey. $4.95.

The Browning Hi-Power Exotic Weapons System. (Illus.). 72 p. 1985. Paladin Pr. pap. $15.00.

Cameron, Frank. **Micro Guns.** (Illus.). 48 p. 1982. Mosaic Press, OH. $24.00.

Clede, Bill. **Police Handgun Manual: How To Get Street-Smart Survival Habits.** (Illus.). 128 p. Stackpole. $13.95.

Combs, Roger. **Holsters and Other Gun Leather: Gun Digest Book.** 256 p. 1983. pap. DBI Books. $11.95.

Cromwell, Giles. **The Virginia Manufactory of Arms.** 1975. University Press of Virginia. $20.00.

Davis, John E. **Introduction to Tool Marks, Firearms and the Striagraph.** (Illus.). 1958. C. C. Thomas. $28.25.

Daw, George. **Gun Patents 1864.** 1982. Saifer. $25.00.

Donnelly, John. **Handloader's Manual of Cartridge Conversions.** (Illus.). 1056 p. 1987. Stoeger Pub. $34.95. sp. bd. $29.95. pap. $29.95.

Edsall, James. **Volcanic Firearms and Their Successors.** Pioneer Press. $2.50.

Erickson, Wayne R. & Pate, Charles E. **The Broomhandle Pistol: 1896–1936.** 300 p. E&P Enter. $49.95.

Ezell, Edward C. **Handguns of the World.** (Illus.). 1981. Stackpole Books, $39.95.

—**Small Arms Today: Latest Reports on the World's Weapons & Ammunition.** 256 p. (Orig.). 1984. pap. Stackpole. $16.95.

Farnum, John. **The Street Smart Gun Book.** Police Bookshelf. pap. $11.95.

Flayderman, Norm. **Flayderman's Guide to Antique American Firearms & Their Values,** 4th ed. (Illus.). 624 p. 1987. DBI. pap. $24.95.

Flores, Eliezer, ed. **How To Make Disposable Silencers,** Vol. II. (Illus.). 120 p. 1985. J.O. Flores. pap. $12.00.

Flynn, George & Gottlieb, Alan. **Guns for Women: The Complete Handgun Buying Guide for Women.** 108 p. 1988. Merril Pr. pap. $9.95.*

Gates, Elgin. **Gun Digest Book of Metallic Silhouette Shooting.** 2d ed. (Illus.). 256 p. 1988. DBI. pap. $12.95.*

George, John N. **English Pistols and Revolvers.** Albert Saifer, Pub. $20.00.

Grennell, Dean A. **ABC's of Reloading.** 4th ed. (Illus.). 1988. pap. DBI Books. $14.95.

—**Gun Digest Book of 9MM Handguns.** (Illus.) 256 p. 1986. DBI. pap. $12.95.

—**Handgun Digest.** (Illus.). 256 p. 1987. DBI. pap. $12.95.

Grennell, Dean & Clapp, Wiley M. **Gun Digest Book of Handgun Reloading.** (Illus.). 256 p. 1987. DBI. pap. $12.95.*

Gresham, Grits. **Grits on Guns.** (Illus.). 352 p. 1988. Cane River AK. $25.00.*

Hamilton, T. M. **Early Indian Trade Guns: 1625–1775.** (Contributions of the Museum of the Great Plains Ser.: No. 3). (Illus.). 1968. pap. Museum of the Great Plains Pubns. Dept. pap. $6.95.

Hatcher. **The Book of the Garand.** Gun Room Press. $17.95.

Hatcher, Julian S. **Hatcher's Notebook.** rev. ed. (Illus.). 1962. Stackpole Books. $24.95.

Hoffschmidt, Edward J. **Know Your Gun, Incl. Know Your .45 Auto Pistols; Know Your Walther P. .38 Pistols; Know Your Walther P. P. and P. P. K. Pistols; Know Your M1 Garand Rifles; Know Your Mauser Broomhandle Pistol; Know Your Anti-Tank Rifle.** 1976. Borden pap. $6.95. ea.

Hogg, Brig., fwrd. by **The Compleat Gunner.** (Illus.). 1976. Repr. Charles River Books. $10.50.

Home Workshop Silencers 1. 1980. pap. Paladin Enterprises. $12.00.

Huebner, Siegfried. **Silencers for Hand Firearms.** Schreier, Konrad & Lund, Peter C., eds. 1976. pap. Paladin Enterprises. $11.95.

Huntington, R. T. **Hall's Breechloaders: John H. Hall's Invention and Development of a Breechloading Rifle with Precision-Made Interchangeable Parts, and Its Introduction Into the United States Service.** (Illus.). 1972. pap. George Shumway Publisher. $22.50.

Jackson & Whitelaw. **European Hand Firearms.** 1978. Albert Saifer, Pub. $25.00.

James, Garry, ed. **Guns for Home Defense.** (Illus.). 1975. pap. Petersen Publishing. $3.95.

Kelly, Palo. **An American Tradition: Handguns.** (Illus.) 250 p. 1986. Tarantula Press. pap. $9.95.

Kelvin, Martin Dr. **Collecting Antique Firearms.** (Illus.). 224 p. 1988. David & Charles. $55.00.

Kennedy, Monty. **Checkering and Carving of Gunstocks.** rev. ed. (Illus.). 1952. Stackpole Books. $29.95.

King, Peter. **The Shooting Field: One Hundred Fifty Years with Holland & Holland.** (Illus.). 176 p. 1985. Blacksmith. $39.95.

Kukla, Robert J. **Gun Control.** 449 p. Nat'l Rifle Assn. pap. $4.95.

Larson, E. Dixon. **Remington Tips.** Pioneer Press. $4.95.

Lauber, George. **How to Build Your Own Flintlock Rifle or Pistol.** Seaton. Lionel tr. from Ger. (Illus.). 1976. pap. Jolex. $6.95.

—**How To Build Your Own Wheellock Rifle or Pistol.** Seaton, Lionel, tr. from Ger. (Illus.). 1976. pap. Jolex. $12.50.

Laycock, George. **Shotgunner's Bible.** (Illus.). 176 p. 1987. Doubleday. pap. $7.95.

Lenk, Torsten. **Flintlock: Its Origin & Development.** Saifer. $55.00.

Lewis, Jack. **Gun Digest Book of Modern Gun Values,** 6th ed. (Illus.). 448 p. 1987. DBI. pap. $15.95.

Leurs, Jack & Mitchell, Jack. **Combat Handgunnery.** (Illus.). 288 p. 1983. DBI. pap. $12.95.

Lindsay, Merrill. **Twenty Great American Guns.** (Illus.). 1976. Repr. pap. Arma Press. $1.75.

Long, Duncan. **Automatics: Fast Firepower, Tactical Superiority.** (Illus.). 144 p. 1986. Paladin Pr. pap. text ed. $14.95.

—**Firearms for Survival.** (Illus.). 144 p. 1987. Paladin Press. pap. $16.95.

Matunas, Edward A. **Metallic Cartridge Reloading.** 2d ed. (Illus.). 320 p. 1988. DBI. pap. $15.95.*

Miller, Martin. **Collector's Illustrated Guide to Firearms.** (Illus.). 1978. Mayflower Books. $24.95.

Murtz, Harold A. **Guns Illustrated.** 21st ed. (Illus.) 320 p. 1988. DBI. pap. $15.95.

Myatt, F. **An Illustrated Guide to Rifles and Automatic Weapons.** (Illus.). 1981. Arco. $9.95.

National Muzzle Loading Rifle Association. Muzzle Blasts: Early Years Plus Vol. I and II 1939–41. 1974. pap. George Shumway Publisher. $18.00.

Norton (R. W.) Art Gallery. **E. C. Prudhomme: Master Gun Engraver.** (Illus.). 1973. pap. Norton Art Gallery. $3.00.

NRA Gun Collectors Guide. 336 p. Nat'l Rifle Assn. $4.50.

Painter, Doug. **Hunting & Firearms Safety Primer.** 128 p. 1986. N. Lyons Bks. pap. $8.95.

Pollard, Hugh B. **The History of Firearms.** 1974. Burt Franklin, Pub. $29.50; pap. $8.95.

Price, Robert M. **Firearms Self-Defense: An Introductory Guide.** (Illus.). 1986. Gordon Press. lib. bdg. $79.95.

Reese, Michael, II. **Nineteen Hundred Luger—U.S. Test Trials.** 2nd rev. ed. Pioneer Press, ed. (Illus.). Pioneer Press. $4.95.

Reilly, Robert M. **United States Military Small Arms, 1816–1865.** 1983. Gun Room. $35.00.

Riling, Ray. **Guns and Shooting: A Bibliography.** (Illus.). 1981. Ray Riling. $75.00.

Riviere, Bill & Elman, Robert. **Gunner's Bible.** 3d rev. ed. (Illus.). 192 p. 1985. Doubleday. pap. $7.95.

The Ruger Exotic Weapons System. (Illus.). 96 p. (Orig.). 1984. pap. Paladin Pr. $15.00.

Rutherford, Ken. **Collecting Shotgun Cartridges.** (Illus.). 126 p. 1988. David & Charles. $45.00.

Sharpe, Phil. **Complete Guide to Handloading.** 230 p. 1988. Repr. of 1949 ed. Wolfe Pub. Co. $60.00.*

Shelsby, Earl, ed. **NRA Gunsmithing Guide:** Updated rev. ed. (Illus.). 336 p. (Orig.). 1980. pap. Nat'l Rifle Assn. $11.95.

Shooter's Bible 1989. Vol. 80. (Illus.). 576 p. 1988. Stoeger Pub. Co. $14.95.

Shooter's Bible 1990. Vol. 81. (Illus.). 576 p. 1989. Stoeger Pub. Co. $14.95.*

Smythe, John & Barwick, Humphrey. **Bow vs. Gun.** 1976. Repr. Charles River Books. $15.00.

Steindler, R. A. **Reloader's Guide.** (Illus.). 3rd ed. 1975. softbound. Stoeger. $9.95.

Steiner, Bradley. **The Death Dealer's Manual.** (Illus.). 120 p. 1982. pap. Paladin Press. $12.00.

Stockbridge, V. D. **Digest of U.S. Patents Relating to Breech-loading & Magazine Small Arms, 1836–1873.** (Illus.). 1963. N. Flayderman & Co. $12.50.

Sybertz, Gustav. **Technical Dictionary for Weaponry.** (Ger.-Eng.). 1969. French & European Pubns. Inc. pap. $24.95.

Taylor, Chuck. **The Combat Shotgun & Submachine Gun: A Special Weapons Analysis.** 176 p. 1985. Paladin Pr. pap. $16.95.

Thielen, Thomas W. **The Complete Guide to Gun Shows.** 1980. pap. Loompanics Unlimited. $6.95.

Thomas, Donald G. **Complete Book of Thompson Patents.** 1985. Gun Room. pap. $15.95.

Thompson, Leroy & Smeets, Rene. **Great Combat Handguns.** (Illus.). 224 p. 1987. Sterling. $29.95.*

Thompson Submachine Gun. 1986. Gordon Press. lib. bdg. $79.95.

Traister, John E. **How To Buy and Sell Used Guns.** (Illus.). 1982. softbound. Stoeger. $10.95.

—**Gunsmithing at Home.** (Illus.). 256 p. pap. (Orig.). 1985. Stoeger. $12.95.

—**Professional Care & Finishing of Gun Stocks.** (Illus.). 208 p. 1985. TAB Bks. pap. $15.95.

Trzoniec, Stanley. **Handloader's Guide.** 256 p. 1985. Stoeger Pub. Co. pap. $12.95.

Van Rensselaer, S. **American Firearms.** (Illus.). 1948. pap. Century House. pap. $15.00.

Waite, Malden & Ernst, Bernard. **Trapdoor Springfield.** 1985. Gun Room. $29.95.

Walsh, J. H. **The Modern Sportsman's Gun & Rifle.** Vol I & II. (Illus.). 536 p. 1986. Wolfe Pub. Co. Price on request.

Walter, John. **The Luger Book.** (Illus.). 288 p. 1987. Sterling. $45.00.

Warner, Ken, ed. **Handloader's Digest.** 11th ed. 1987. DBI Books. $15.95.

—**Gun Digest 1989.** 43d ed. (Illus.). B. West. $42.00.*

West, Bill. **Winchester Encyclopedia.** (Illus.). B. West. $15.00.

—**Winchester Lever-Action Handbook.** (Illus.). B. West. $25.00.

—**The Winchester Single Shot.** (Illus.). B. West. $19.00.

—**Winchesters, Cartridges, & History.** (Illus.). B. West. $42.00.*

Weston, Paul B. **The New Handbook of Handgunning.** (Illus.). 1980. C. C. Thomas $14.25.

Williams, John J. **Survival Guns and Ammo.** (Illus.). 1979. pap. Consumertronics. pap. $15.00.

Williams, Mason. **The Law Enforcement Book of Weapons, Ammunition & Training Procedures: Handguns, Rifles and Shotguns.** (Illus.). 1977. C. C. Thomas. $61.25.

Wirnsberger, Gerhard. **Standard Directory of Proof Marks.** Steindler, R. A. tr. from Ger. (Illus.). 1976. pap. Jolex. $9.95.

Withers, John. **Precision Handloading.** 224 p. 1985. Stoeger Pub. Co. pap. $11.95.

Wood, J. B. **Gun Digest Book of Firearm Assembly-Disassembly: Law Enforcement Weapons, Pt. VI** (Illus.). 1981. pap. DBI Books. $12.95.

Zellman, Aaron & Neuens, Michael L. **Consumer's Guide to Handguns.** (Illus.). 208 p. 1986. Stackpole. pap. $16.95.

Zhuk, A. B. **Revolvers & Pistols.** 304 p. 1987. State Mutual Bks. $40.00.

FIREARMS—CATALOGS

Barnes, Frank L. **Cartridges of the World,** 5th ed. (Illus.). 416 p. 1985. DBI. pap. $16.95.

Remington Gun Catalog 1877. Pioneer Press. $1.50.

Saxon, K. **The Weaponeer: An Encyclopedia of Weapons.** 1986. Gordon Press. lib. bdg. $79.95.

Sears & Roebuck c1910 Ammunition Catalog. (Illus.). pap. Sand Pond. $2.00.

Tarassuk, Leonid, ed. **Antique European and American Firearms at the Hermitage Museum.** (Illus., Eng. & Rus.). 1976. Arma Press. ltd. ed. $40.00.

Tinkham, Sandra S., ed. **Catalog of Tools, Hardware, Firearms, and Vehicles.** 1979. Chadwyck-Healey. pap. $40.00.

United States Cartridge Co.-Lowell, Mass. 1891 Catalog. (Illus.). Sand Pond. $3.50.

Wahl, Paul. **Gun Trader's Guide,** 13th ed. 464 p. 1989. Stoeger Pub. Co. pap. $14.95.*

Walmer, Max, et al, eds. **The Illustrated Directory of Modern American Weapons.** (Illus.). 480 p. 1986. P-H. pap. $14.95.

West, Bill. **Remington Arms Catalogues, 1877–1899.** 1st ed. (Illus.). 1971. B. West. $10.00.

Winchester Shotshell Catalog 1897. (Illus.). pap. Sand Pond. $1.50.

FIREARMS—COLLECTORS AND COLLECTING

Chapel, Charles E. **The Gun Collector's Handbook of Values.** 14th ed. (Illus.). 523 p. 1983. Putnam Pub. Group. $19.95.

—**Gun Collector's Handbook of Values.** 1984. Putnam Pub. Gp. pap. $11.95.

Dicarpegna, N. **Firearms in the Princes Odescalchi Collection in Rome.** (Illus.). 1976. Repr. of 1969 ed. Arma Press. $20.00.

Dixie Gun Works Antique Arms Catalog. Pioneer Press. $2.00.

Flayderman, Norm. **Flayderman's Guide to Antique American Firearms and Their Values.** 4th ed. (Illus.). 1987. pap. DBI Books. $22.95.

Frith, James & Andrews, Ronald. **Antique Pistols Collection 1400-1860.** Saifer. $25.00.

Gusler, Wallace B. & Lavin, James D. **Decorated Firearms 1540-1870, from the Collection of Clay P. Bedford.** 1977. University Press of Virginia. $25.00.

Madaus, H. Michael. **The Warner Collector's Guide to American Long Arms.** 1981. pap. Warner Books. $9.95.

Quertermous, Russel & Quertermous, Steve. **Modern Guns, Identification and Values.** 7th ed. 1988. pap. Collector Books., $12.95.

Serven, James. **Rare and Valuable Antique Arms.** 1976. Pioneer Press. $4.95.

Shumaker, P. L. **Colt's Variations of the Old Model Pocket Pistol.** 1957. Borden. $10.95.

Stevenson, Jan. **Modern Sporting Guns.** 1988. Doubleday. $19.95.

Traister, John E. **How To Buy and Sell Used Guns.** (Illus.). 1982. softbound. Stoeger. $10.95.

Wahl, Paul. **Gun Trader's Guide.** 13th ed. (Illus.). Stoeger. $14.95.

Wilson, R. L. **Colt—Christie's Rare and Historic Firearms Auction Catalogue.** (Illus.). 1981. Arma Press. $25.00.

FIREARMS—HISTORY

Ayalon, David. **Gunpowder and Firearms in the Mamluk Kingdom: A Challenge to Medieval Society.** 2nd ed. 1978. Biblio Distribution Centre. $25.00.

Barnes, Duncan. **History of Winchester Firearms 1866-1980.** 5th ed. rev. (Illus.). 256 p. New Century. $18.95.

Batchelor, John & Walter, John. **Handgun: From Matchlock to Laser-Sited Weapon.** (Illus.). 160 p. 1988. Sterling. $19.95.*

Blanch, H. J. A. **A Century of Guns: A Sketch of the Leading Types of Sporting and Military Small Arms.** (Illus.). 1977. Repr. of 1909 ed. Charles River Books. $25.00.

Brown, M. L. **Firearms in Colonial America: The Impact of History and Technology 1492-1792.** 1980. Smithsonian Institution Press. $55.00.

Buchele, W. & Shumway, G. **Recreating the American Long Rifle.** Orig. Title: **Recreating the Kentucky Rifle.** (Illus.). 1973. George Shumway Publisher. pap. $27.50.

Fuller, Claude E. **Breech-Loader in the Service 1816-1917.** (Illus.). 1965. Flayderman, N. & Co. $14.50.

Garavaglia, Louis A. & Worman, Charles G. **Firearms of the American West, 1803-1865.** (Illus.). 1983. U of NM Press. $35.00.

—**Firearms of the American West, 1866-1894.** (Illus.). 423 p. 1983. U. of N. Mex. Press. $40.00.

Gusler, Wallace B. & Lavin, James D. **Decorated Firearms, 1540-1870 from the Collection of Clay P. Bedford.** 1977. (Colonial Williamburg Foundation). University Press of Virginia. $25.00.

Hackley, F. W. et al. **History of Modern U.S. Military Small Arms Ammunition: Vol. 2, 1940-1945.** Gun Room Press. $35.00.

Hamilton, T. M. ed. **Indian Trade Guns.** 1983. Pioneer Press. $10.95.

Helmer, William J. **The Gun That Made the Twenties Roar.** Gun Room Press. $17.95.

Hetrick, Calvin. **The Bedford County Rifle and Its Makers.** (Illus.). 1975. pap. George Shumway Publisher. (OP). pap. $7.50.

Holme, N. & Kirby, E. L. **Medal Rolls: Twenty-Third Foot Royal Welch Fusiliers, Napoleonic Period.** 1979. S. J. Durst. $45.00.

Hutslar, Donald A. **Gunsmiths of Ohio: 18th and 19th Centuries.** Vol. I. (Illus.). casebound. George Shumway Publisher. $40.00.

Kennett, Lee & Anderson, James L. **The Gun in America: The Origins of a National Dilemma.** (Illus., Orig). 1975. Greenwood Press. lib. bdg. $38.95.

Lindsay, Merrill. **The New England Gun: The First 200 Years.** (Illus.). 1976. Arma Press. pap. $12.50.

Nonte, George C., Jr. **Black Powder Guide.** 2nd ed. (Illus.). pap. Stoeger, $11.95.

North & North. **Simeon North: First Official Pistol Maker of the United States.** Repr. Gun Room Press. $12.95.

Peterson, Harold. **Historical Treasury of American Guns.** Benjamin Co. pap. $2.95.

Pollard, Hugh B. **History of Firearms.** (Illus.). 1974. B. Franklin. $29.50; pap. $8.95.

Reese, Michael II. **Nineteen-hundred Luger-U.S. Test Trials.** 2nd rev. ed. (Illus.). pap. Pioneer Press. $4.95.

Remington Arms & History, vols. 1 and 2. B. West. $42.00 ea.

Rosebush, Waldo E. **American Firearms and the Changing Frontier.** 1962. pap. Eastern Washington State Historical Society. $4.50.

Sawyer, C. W. **Firearms in American History 1600-1800.** Repr. of 1886 ed. Saifer. $25.00.*

Schreier, Konrad F., Jr. **Remington Rolling Block Firearms.** (Illus.). Pioneer Press. pap. $6.95.

Sellers, Frank M. **Sharps Firearms.** (Illus.). 1982. Sellers Pubns. $39.95.

Shelton, Lawrence P. **California Gunsmiths.** (Illus.). 302 p. 1977. George Shumway Publisher. casebound. $29.95.

Tonso, William R. **Gun & Society: The Social and Existential Roots of the American Attachment to Firearms.** 1982. U Press of America. pap. $16.75 lib bdg. $35.00.

West, Bill. **Marlin and Ballard, Arms and History, 1861-1978.** (Illus.). 1978. B. West. $42.00.

—**Savage & Stevens, Arms and History, 1849-1971.** (Illus.). 1971. B. West. $48.00.

FIREARMS—IDENTIFICATION

Baer, Larry L. **The Parker Gun.** Gun Room. $29.95.

Brophy, Williams S. **The Krag Rifle.** Gun Room. $29.95.

—**L.C. Smith Shotguns.** Gun Room. $29.95.

Garton, George. **Colt's SAA Post-War Models.** Gun Room. $21.95.

Madaus, H. Michael. **The Warner Collector's Guide to American Long Arms.** 1981. Warner Books. pap. $9.95.

Nelson, Thomas B. & Lockhaven, Hans B. **The World's Submachine Guns: Developments from 1915 to 1963.** Vol. I rev. ed. 1980. TBN Ent. $29.95.

Ruth, Larry. **M-1 Carbine.** pap. Gun Room. $17.95.

Small Arms Training: Sten Machine Carbine, Vol. I. 1983. pap. Ide House $0.95.

Wilber, Charles G. **Ballistic Science for the Law Enforcement Officer.** (Illus.). 1977. C. C. Thomas. $37.00.

FIREARMS—INDUSTRY AND TRADE

Grancsay, Stephen V. & Lindsay, Merrill. **Illustrated British Firearms Patents 1718-1853.** limited ed. (Illus.). Arma Press. $75.00.

Hartzler, Daniel D. **Arms Makers of Maryland.** 1975. George Shumway Publisher. $40.00.

Kirkland, Turner. **Southern Derringers of the Mississippi Valley.** Pioneer Press. $2.00.

Noel-Baker, Phillip. **The Private Manufacture of Armaments.** 1971. pap. Dover. $7.95.

Russell, Carl P. **Guns on the Early Frontiers: A History of Firearms from Colonial Times through the Years of the Western Fur Trade.** 1980. University of Nebraska Press. $27.95. pap. $10.95.

Stiefel, Ludwig, ed. **Gun Propulsion Technology.** 500 p. 1988. AJAA. $79.00.

Stockholm International Peace Research Institute (SIPRI). **The Arms Trade Registers.** 1975. MIT Press. $18.00.

West, Bill. **Browning Arms and History, 1842-1973.** (Illus.). 1972. B. West. $42.00.

FIREARMS—LAWS AND REGULATIONS

Cook, Phillip J. & Lambert, Richard D., eds. **Gun Control.** 1981. American Academy of Political and Social Science. pap. $7.95.

Foster, Carol D., et al. **Gun Control: Restricting Rights or Protecting People?** 104 p. 1987. Info Aids. pap. $16.95.

Garrison, William L. **Women's Views on Guns & Self-Defense.** 114 p. (Orig). 1983. pap. Second Amend. $5.50.

Gottlieb, Alan. **The Rights of Gun Owners.** 216 p. 1986. Gordon Press. lib. bdg. $79.95.

—**Gun Rights Fact Book.** 168 p. 1988. Merril Pr. $3.95.

Gun Control. 1976. pap. American Enterprise Institute for Public Policy Research. $6.00.

Halbrook, Stephen P. **That Every Man Be Armed: An Evolution of a Constitutional Right.** 240 p. 1984. U of N Mex. pap. $11.95.

Hardy, David T. **Origins & Development of the 2nd Amendment.** 96 p. 1986. Blacksmith Corp. $11.95.

Hill, J. B. **Weapons Law.** 96 p. 1988. Pergamon. pap. $12.50.*

Kates, Don B., ed. **Firearms & Violence: Issues of Public Policy.** 475 p. 1983. pap. Pacific Inst. Pub. $15.95.

Kennett, Lee & Anderson, James L. **The Gun in America.** (Illus.). text ed. pap. Greenwood Press. lib. bdg. $38.95.

Krema, Vaclav. **Identification and Registration of Firearms.** (Illus.). 1971. C. C. Thomas. $25.25.

Kruschke, Earl R. **The Right To Keep and Bear Arms.** 230 p. 1985. C.C. Thomas. $27.00.

Kukla, Robert J. **Gun Control: A Written Record of Efforts to Eliminate the Private Possession of Firearms in America.** Orig. Title: Other Side of Gun Control. 1973. Stackpole Books. pap. $9.95.

Leddy, Edward B. **Magnum Force Lobby: The NRA Fights Gun Control.** 1987. U. Pr. of Amer. $28.50.

Lester, David. **Gun Control: Issues & Answers.** 146 p. 1984. C. Thomas. pap. $16.25.

The Right To Keep & Bear Arms: A Presentation of Both Sides. 1986. Gordon Pr. $79.95 (lib. bdg).

Stewart, Alva W. **Gun Control: Its Pros & Cons. A Checklist.** 12 p. 1986. Vance Biblios. $3.75.

Whisker, James B. **The Citizen Soldier and U.S. Military Policy.** 1979. North River Press. $10.00.

Zimring, Franklin E. & Hawkins, Gordon. **The Citizen's Guide to Gun Control.** 224 p. 1987. Macmillan. $17.95.

FOWLING (see also Decoys, Duck & Geese Shooting, Falconry)

Bauer, Erwin A. **Duck Hunter's Bible.** pap. Doubleday. $6.95.

Bell, Bob. **Hunting the Long Tailed Bird.** (Illus.). 1975. Freshet Press. $14.95.

Churchill, James. **Field Dressing Small Game & Fowl: The Illustrated Guide to Dressing 20 Birds & Mammals.** (Illus.). 112 p. 1987. Stackpole. pap. $10.95.*

Dalrymple, Byron W. **Bird Hunting with Dalrymple: The Rewards of Shotgunning Across North America.** (Illus.) 288 p. 1987. Stackpole. $24.95.

Elliot, Charles. **Turkey Hunting With Charlie Elliot.** 288 p. Arco. pap. $8.95.

Gryndall, William. **Hawking, Hunting, Fowling and Fishing; Newly Corrected by W. Gryndall Faulkner.** 1972. Repr. of 1596 ed. W. J. Johnson. $25.00.

Smith, Steve. **Hunting Ducks & Geese: Hard Facts, Good Bets and Serious Advice From a Duck Hunter You Can Trust.** 160 p. 1984. Stackpole. $14.95.

Woolmer, Frank. **Grouse & Grouse Hunting.** (Illus.). 192 p. Repr. of 1970 ed. N. Lyons Bks. $18.95.

Zutz, Don. **Modern Waterfowl Guns & Gunning.** 288 p. 1985. Stoeger Pub. Co. pap. $11.95.

GAME AND GAME BIRDS (see also Duck & Geese Hunting, Fowling, Hunting)

Beasom, Sam L. & Roberson, Sheila F., eds. **Game Harvest Management.** (Illus.). 300 p. 1985. CK Wildlife Res. $20.00; pap. $15.00.

Billmeyer, Patricia. **The Encyclopedia of Wild Game and Fish Cleaning and Cooking.** Yeshaby Pubs. $3.95.

Blair, Gerry. **Predator Caller's Companion.** 1981. Winchester Press. $18.95.

Candy, Robert. **Getting The Most From Your Game & Fish.** (Illus.). 278 p. (Orig). 1984. pap. A. C. Hood Pub. $12.95.

Grooms, Steve. **Modern Pheasant Hunting.** (Illus.). 224 p. 1984. pap. Stackpole. $10.95.

Hagerbaumer, David. **Selected American Game Birds.** 1972. Caxton. $30.00.

Harbour, Dave. **Advanced Wild Turkey Hunting & World Records.** (Illus.). 264 p. 1983. New Century. $19.95.

McDaniel, John M. **Spring Turkey Hunting:** The Serious Hunter's Guide. (Illus.) 224 p. 1986. Stackpole. $21.95.

Marchington, John **The Natural History of Game.** (Illus.) 256 p. 1984. Longwood Publ. Gp. $27.00.

Nesbitt, W. H., ed. **Eighteenth Boone & Crockett Big Game Awards.** (Illus.). 306 p. 1984. Boone & Crockett. $25.00.

Nesbitt, W. H. & Wright, Phillip L., eds. **Records at North American Big Game.** 8th ed. 412 p. 1981, Boone & Crockett. $195.00.

Robbins, Charles T., ed. **Wildlife Feeding and Nutrition.** 1983. Academic Press. $45.00.

Sherwood, Morgan. **Big Game in Alaska.** 1981. Yale University Press. $36.00.

Smith, Steve. **Hunting Upland Game Birds: What the Wingshooter Needs to Know about the Birds, the Guns & the New Clay Games.** (Illus.). 160 p. 1987. Stackpole. $16.95.*

Stuart, Jack. **Bird Dogs & Upland Game Birds.** (Illus.). 1983. Denlinger. $24.95.

GAME AND GAME BIRDS—NORTH AMERICA

Bent, Arthur C. **Life Histories of North American Wild Fowl.** 685 p. 1987. Dover. pap. $12.95.

Boddington, Craig. **Campfires & Game Trails: Hunting North American Big Game.** (Illus.). 256 p. 1985. New Century. $19.95.

Foster. **New England Grouse Shooting.** 1983. Willow Creek. $45.00.

Johnsgaard, Paul. **North American Game Birds of Upland & Shoreline.** (Illus.). 231 p. 1975. U. of Nebraska Pr. pap. $8.95.

Leopold, A. Starker, et al. **North American Game Birds and Mammals.** (Illus.). 208 p. 1984. pap. Scribner. $14.95.

Nesbitt, W. H. & Wright, Phillip L., eds. **Records of North American Big Game.** 8th ed. 1981. Boone & Crockett Club. $29.50.

Phillips, John C. **American Game Mammals and Birds: A Catalog of Books, Sports, Natural History and Conservation. 1582–1925.** 1978. Repr. of 1930 ed. Ayer Co. Pubns. lib. bdg. $49.50

Sanderson, Glen C., ed. **Management of Migratory Shore & Upland Game Birds in North America.** 1980. pap. University of Nebraska Press. $10.95.

Tinsley, Russell, ed. **All About Small-Game Hunting in America.** 1976. Winchester Press. $16.95.

Walsh, Roy. **Gunning the Chesapeake: Duck & Goose Shooting on the Eastern Shore.** 130 p. 1960. Cornell Maritime. $14.95

GAME & FISH COOKERY (see also Outdoor Cookery)

Barbour, Judy. **Elegant Elk: Delicious Deer.** 3rd ed. (Illus.). 196 p. 1983 reprint of 1978 ed. Peters Studio. $13.95.

Billmeyer, Patricia. **The Encyclopedia of Wild Game and Fish Cleaning and Cooking.** 3 vols. Yesnaby Pubs. pap. $3.95 ea.

Cameron, Angus & Jones, Judith. **The L. L. Bean Game & Fish Cookbook.** 1983. Random. $21.95.

Canino, Thomas L. **Mountain Man Cookbook: Venison & Other Recipes.** 85 p. 1985. TLC Enterprises. pap. $7.95.

Chicken and Game Hen Menus. 1983. Silver. $18.60.

Cone, Joan. **Fish and Game Cooking.** 1981. pap. EPM Publications. $5.95.

De Gouy, Louis V. **The Derrydak Game Cookbook,** Vol. I. repr. of 1937 ed. 308 p. 1987. Willow Creek Pr. $25.00.

Del Guidice, Paula J. **Microwave Game & Fish Cookbook.** (Illus.). 160 p. 1985. Stackpole. pap. $12.95.

Dempsey, Jim (compiled by). **Wild Game Cookbook.** (Illus.). 156 p. 1987. UCS Press. pap. $8.95.*

D'Ermo, Dominique. **Dominique's Famous Fish, Game & Meat Recipes.** 1981. pap. Acropolis. $8.95.

Fadala, Sam. **Complete Guide to Game Care & Cookery.** 288 p. DBI. pap. $12.95.*

French, Jack. **Pioneer Heritage Wild Game Cookbook.** (Illus.). 416 p. 1987. Realco Pub. pap. $14.95.

Gaida, Urban & Marchello, Martin. **Going Wild: A Guide to Field Dressing, Butchering, Sausage-Making & Cooking Wild Game & Fish.** (Illus.). 240 p. 1987. Watab Mktg. pap. $16.95.*

Goolsby, Sam. **Great Southern Wild Game Cookbook.** 193 p. 1980. Pelican. $14.95.

Gorton, Audrey A. **Venison Book: How to Dress, Cut Up and Cook Your Deer.** 1957. pap. Greene. $4.95.

Gray, Rebecca & Reeve, Cintra. **Gray's Wild Game Cookbook: A Menu Cookbook.** (Illus.). 220 p. 1983. Grays Sporting. $25.00.

Hargreaves, Barbara, ed. **The Sporting Wife: A Guide to Game & Fish Cooking.** (Illus.). 336 p. 1988. David & Charles. pap. $15.95.*

Hibler, Jane. **Fair Game: A Hunter's Cookbook.** Lawrence, Betsy, ed. 1983. pap. Chalmers. $5.95.

Holmes, Ferne. **Easy Recipes for Wild Game & Fish.** (Illus.). 160 p. 1988. Golden West Pubns. pap. $6.50.*

Hull, Raymond & Sleight, Jack. **Home Book of Smoke Cooking Meat, Fish & Game.** (Illus.). 160 p. 1971. Stackpole. $10.95.

Humphreys, Angela. **Game Cookery.** (Illus.) 144 p. 1986. David & Charles. $24.95.

Hunting & Fishing Library: Dressing & Cooking Wild Game. (Illus.). 160 p. 1987. P-H. pap. $12.95.*

Jaxson, Jay. **Wild Country All Game & Fish Recipes.** (Illus.). 81 p. 1982. pap. Jackson G. B. $7.95.

Johnson, L. W., ed. **Wild Game Cookbook: A Remington Sportsmen's Library Bk.** pap. Benjamin Co. $3.95.

Knight, Jacqueline E. **The Hunter's Game Cookbook.** (Illus.). 1978. Winchester Press. $12.95.

Lamagna, Joseph. **Wild Game Cookbook for Beginner and Expert.** J. Lamagna. $6.95.

Mabbutt, Bill & Mabbutt, Anita: **North American Wild Game Cookbook.** 216 p. 1982. NC Book Exp. $9.95.

Mabbutt, Bill, et al. **North American Game Fish Cookbook.** 192 p. 1983. NC Bk. pap. $9.95.

MacIlquham, Frances. **Complete Fish & Game Cookery of North America.** (Illus.). 304 p. 1983. Winchester Press. $29.95.

Manion, Timothy E. **The Game & Fish Menu Cookbook.** (Illus.). 320 p. 1987. Weidenfeld. pap. $10.95.

—**Wild Game & Country Cooking.** 200 p. 1983. Manion Outdoors Co. 5 p. bd. $9.95.

Morris, Dan & Morris, Inez. **The Complete Fish Cookbook.** 1989. Stoeger Pub. Co. pap. $10.95.*

Oakland, Ann. **Buffalo at Steak.** 32 p. 1983. pap. One Percent. $3.95.

Obern, Jane & Waldron, Valerie, eds. **NAHC Wild Game Cookbook.** 192 p. 1987. N. Am. Hunt Club. pap. $14.95.

Pederson, Rolf. **Our Wild Harvest: Sowing, Reaping, Cooking, Eating.** (Illus.). 174 p. 1982. Rolf's Gallery. pap. $9.95.

Rojas-Lombardi, Felipe. **Game Cookery.** 1973. Livingston, dura. $3.95.

—**Game Cookery.** (Illus.). 1973. plastic bdg. Harrowood Books. $3.95.

Rywell, Martin. **Wild Game Cook Book.** 1952. pap. Buck Hill. $6.75.

Sagstetter, Brad. **The Venison Handbook.** (Illus.). 80 p. 1981. Larksdale. $5.95.

Smith, Capt. James A. **Dress 'Em Out.** (Illus.). 256 p. pap. (Orig.). Stoeger. $12.95.

Smith, John A. **Wild Game Cookbook.** 64 p. 1986. Dover. pap. $4.95.

Steindler, Geraldine. **Game Cookbook.** New Revised Edition. 1985. softbound. Stoeger. $12.95.

Turkey & Duck Menus. 1985. (Pub. by Time-Life) Silver. $18.60.

Upland Game Birds, Vol. I. (Illus.). 174 p. pap. Rolf's Gallery. $9.95.

Vail, Mike & Miller, Bill, eds. **NAHC Wild Game Cookbook.** (Illus.). 192 p. 1987. N. Amer. Hunt Club. pap. $14.95.*

Wary, Carol. **Wild Game Cookery: The Hunter's Home Companion.** (Illus.). 1984. pap. (Orig.). Countryman. $12.95.

Willard, John. **Game Is Good Eating.** 4th rev. ed. (Illus.). 111 p. repr. of 1954 ed. J.A. Willard. $7.95.

Wongrey, Jan. **Southern Wildfowl and Wildgame Cookbook.** 1976. Sandlapper Store. $7.95.

Zumbo, Jim & Zumbo, Lois. **The Venison Cookbook.** (Illus.) 208 p. 1986. P-H. $17.95.

GUNPOWDER (see Black Powder Guns, Ammunition)

GUNS (see Firearms, Pistols, Revolvers, Rifles, Shotguns)

GUNSMITHING

Angier, R. H. **Firearms Blueing and Browning.** 1936. Stackpole Books. $12.95.

Bish, Tommy L. **Home Gunsmithing Digest,** 3rd ed. 256 p. 1984. pap. DBI. $12.95.

Demeritt, Dwight B., Jr. **Maine Made Guns and Their Makers.** (Illus.). Maine State Museum Pubns. $22.00.

Dubino, Andrew D. **Gunsmithing with Simple Hand Tools: How to Repair, Improve & Add a Touch of Class to the Guns You Own.** (Illus.). 224 p. 1987. Stackpole. $19.95.*

Dunlap, Roy F. **Gunsmithing.** 1963. Stackpole Books. $29.95.

Fry, Franklin. **Gunsmithing Fundamentals: A Guide for Professional Results.** (Illus.). 176 p. 1988. TAB Books. pap. $10.95.*

Hartzler, Daniel D. **Arms Makers of Maryland.** (Illus.). 1977. George Shumway Publisher. $40.00.

Hutslar, Donald A. **Gunsmiths of Ohio: 18th and 19th Centuries.** Vol. 1. (Illus.). 1973. George Shumway Publisher. $40.00.

Mills, Desmond & Barnes, Mike. **Amateur Gunsmithing.** 1987. Longwood Pub. Group. $35.00.

Mitchell, Jack. **Gun Digest Book of Pistolsmithing.** 1980. pap. DBI Books. $12.95.

—**Gun Digest Book of Riflesmithing.** 256 p. 1982. pap. DBI Books. $12.95.

Norton Art Gallery. **Artistry in Arms: The Art of Gunsmithing and Gun Engraving.** (Illus.). 1971. pap. Norton Art Gallery. $2.50.

NRA Gunsmithing Guide. 336 p. Natl Rifle Assn. $9.95.

Sellers, Frank M. **American Gunsmiths: A Source Book.** 1983. Gun Room. $39.95.

Shelsby, Earl, ed. **NRA Gunsmithing Guide: Updated.** rev. ed. (Illus.). 336 p. 1980. pap. Natl. Rifle Assn. $11.95.

Shelton, Lawrence P. **California Gunsmiths.** (Illus.). 1977. George Shumway Publisher. $29.65.

Stelle & Harrison. **The Gunsmith's Manual: A Complete Handbook for the American Gunsmith.** (Illus.). Repr. of 1883 ed. Gun Room Press. $15.00.

Stiefel, Ludwig, ed. **Gun Propulsion Technology,** AAS 109. 500 p. 1988. AIAA. $79.50.*

Traister, John. **Gunsmithing at Home.** (Illus.). 256 p. pap. (Orig.). Stoeger. $12.95.

Vickery, W. F. **Advanced Gunsmithing.** 422 p. 1988. Repr. of 1940 ed. Wolfe Pub. Co. $42.00.*

Walker, Ralph. **Shotgun Gunsmithing: Gun Digest Book.** 256 p. 1983. pap. DBI. $12.95.

HAWKEN RIFLES

Baird, John D. **Fifteen Years in the Hawken Lode.** (Illus.). Gun Room Press. $17.95.

—**Hawken Rifles. The Mountain Man's Choice.** Gun Room Press. $17.95.

HUNTING (see also Bird Dogs, Decoys, Deer Hunting, Duck & Geese Shooting, Fowling, Hunting Dogs)

Acerrano, Anthony J. **The Practical Hunter's Handbook.** (Illus.). 1978. pap. Winchester Press. $13.95.

Bashline, L. James. ed. **The Eastern Trail.** (Illus.). 1972. Freshet Press. $8.95.

Bland, Dwain. **Turkey Hunter's Digest.** (Illus.) 256 p. 1986. DBI. pap. $12.95.

Brister, Bob. **Shotgunning: The Art and the Science.** 1976. Winchester Press. $17.95.

Burnham, Murry & Tinsley, Russell. **Murry Burnham's Hunting Secrets.** (Illus.). 244 p. 1983. New Century. $17.95.

Cadieux, Charles L. **Goose Hunting.** 208 p. 1983. Stoeger. $9.95.

Camp, Doug. **Turkey Hunting: Spring & Fall.** (Illus.). 176 p. 1983. pap. Outdoor Skills. $12.95.

Capossela, Jim. **How to Turn Your Fishing-Hunting Experiences Into Cash: Twenty-Five Ways to Earn Cash from Your Hobbies.** 1982. pap. Northeast Sportsmans. $3.50.

Carlisle, G. L. **Grouse & Gun.** (Illus.). 184 p. 1988. David & Charles. $24.95.*

Coon, Carlton. **The Hunting Peoples.** 423 p. 1987. N Lyons Bks. $15.95.

Douglas, James. **The Sporting Gun.** (Illus.). 240 p. 1983. David & Charles. $29.95.

Elliott, William. **Carolina Sports by Land and Water: Incidents of Devil-Fishing. Wild-Cat, Deer and Bear Hunting.** (Illus.). 1978. Repr. of 1859 ed. Attic Press. $12.50.

Ellsberg, Bob. **Bob Ellsberg's 1988 Hunting & Fisherman's Planning Yearbook.** (Illus.). 192 p. 1987. Outdoor Enterprises. pap. $12.95.

Elman, Robert. **The Hunter's Field Guide to the Game Birds and Animals of North America.** 1982. Knopf. $15.95.

—**One Thousand One Hunting Tips.** rev. ed. 1983. pap. New Century. $14.95.

Fears, J. Wayne. **Successful Turkey Hunting.** 92 p. 1984. Target Comm. pap. $5.95.

Fergus, Charles, et al. **Rabbit Hunting.** 1985. Allegheny. pap. $7.95.

Field & Stream. **Field and Stream Reader.** facs. ed. 1946. Ayer Co. Pub. $21.50.

Geer, Galen. **Meat On The Table: Modern Small-Game Hunting.** (Illus.). 216 p. 1985. Paladin Pr. $16.95.

Grinnell, George B. & Sheldon, Charles, eds. **Hunting and Conservation.** 1970. Repr. of 1925 ed. Arno. $33.00.

Gryndall, William. **Hawking, Hunting, Fouling and Fishing: Newly Corrected by W. Gryndall** Faulkener. 1972. Repr. of 1596 ed. W. J. Johnson. $25.00.

Hagel, Bob. **Game Loads and Practical Ballistics for the American Hunter.** (Illus.). 1978. Knopf. $14.95.

—**Guns, Loads & Hunting Tips.** Wolfe, Dave, ed. (Illus.) 536 p. 1986. Wolfe Pub. Co. $19.50.

Hammond, Samuel H. **Wild Northern Scenes or Sporting Adventures with Rifle and Rod.** (Illus.). 1979. Repr. of 1857 ed. Harbor Hill Books. $12.50.

Harbour, Dave. **Advanced Wild Turkey Hunting & World Records.** (Illus.). 264 p. 1983. New Century. $19.95.

Henckel, Mark. **Hunter's Guide to Montana.** (Illus.). 224 p. 1985. Falcon Pr. MT. pap. $9.95.

Hill, Gene. **A Hunter's Fireside Book: Tales of Dogs, Ducks, Birds and Guns.** (Illus.). 1972. Winchester Press. $14.95.

—**Mostly Tailfeathers.** 1975. Winchester Press. $14.95.

Hill, Gene & Smith, Steve. **Outdoor Yarns & Outright Lies.** 168 p. 1983. Stackpole. $16.95.

James, David & Stephens, Wilson, eds. **In Praise of Hunting.** (Illus.). 1961. Devin-Adair Co. $16.00.

Janes, Edward C. **Ringneck! Pheasants and Pheasant Hunting.** (Illus.). 1975. Crown. $8.95.

Johnson, et al. **Outdoor Tips.** pap. Benjamin Co. $2.95.

Keith, Elmer. **Keith's Rifles for Large Game.** (Illus.). 424 p. 1987. Repr. of 1946 ed. Wolfe Pub. Co. $54.00.*

Lindner, Kurt. **The Second Hunting Book of Wolfgang Birkner.** (Illus.). 1976. Ltd. ed. Arma Press. $175.00.

Liu, Allan J. **The American Sporting Collector's Handbook.** (Illus.). pap. Stoeger. $5.95.

McClane, A. J., ed. **McClane's Great Fishing & Hunting Lodges of North America.** 176 p. 1984. HR&W. $29.95.

McIntyre, Thomas. **The Way of the Hunter: The Art & Spirit of Modern Hunting.** 256 p. 1988. Dutton. $18.95.*

Madden, D. H. **Chapter of Mediaeval History.** 1969. Repr. of 1924 ed. Kennikat Press. $26.50.

Madden, Dodgson H. **Diary of Master William Silence: A Study of Shakespeare and Elizabethan Sport.** 1970. Repr. of 1897. ed. Haskell Booksellers. $51.95.

Merrill, Wm. & Rees, Clair. **Hunter's Bible,** rev. ed. (Illus.) 192 p. 1986. Doubleday. pap. $7.95.

Meyer, Jerry. **Bear Hunting.** 224 p. 1983. Stackpole. $16.95.

Money, Albert W. **Pigeon Shooting.** Gould, A. C., ed. (Illus.). 109 p. 1987. Repr. of 1896 ed. Gunnerman Pr. $19.95.

NRA Guidebook for Hunters. 144 p. Nat'l Rifle Assn. $5.00.

O'Connor, Jack. **The Shotgun Book.** 2d rev. ed. 1978. Knopf. pap. $13.95.

Ortega y Gasset, Jose. **Meditations on Hunting.** 144 p. 1986. Scribner. pap. $7.95.

Ottman, Jim. **Hunting on Horseback.** (Illus.). 151 p. 1987. Paladin Press. $16.95.

Painter, Doug. **Hunting & Firearms Safety Primer.** 128 p. 1986. N. Lyons Bks. pap. $8.95.

Pyle, Wilf E. **Hunting Predators for Hides & Profit.** 224 p. Stoeger Pub. Co. pap. $11.95.

Pyle, Wilf E. **Small Game & Varmint Hunting.** (Illus.). 1989. Stoeger Pub. Co. $14.95.*

Ricketts, Mitchell S. **Bobcat Trapper's Guide.** (Illus.). 116 p. 1987. Elk River Pr. pap. $10.95.

Schwenk, Sigrid, et al. eds. **Multum et Multa: Beitraege zur Literatur, Geschichte und Kultur der Jagd.** (Illus.). 1971. De Gruyter. $48.00.

Shelsby, Earl & Gilford, James eds. **Basic Hunter's Guide,** rev. ed. (Illus.). 280 p. 1982. pap. Nat'l Rifle Assn. $14.95.

Shooter's Bible 1989. Vol. 80. (Illus.). 576 p. 1988. Stoeger Pub. Co. pap. $14.95.

Shooter's Bible 1990, vol. 81. (Illus.). 576 p. 1989. Stoeger Pub. Co. pap. $14.95.*

Smith, James A. **Dress 'Em Out.** (Illus.). 1982. pap. Stoeger. $12.95.

Smith, Steve. **More & Better Pheasant Hunting.** (Illus.). 192 p. 1987. New Century. $15.95.

Stehsel, Donald L. **Hunting the California Black Bear.** (Illus.). pap. Donald Stehsel. $7.00.

Strong, Norman. **The Art of Hunting.** (Illus.). 160 p. 1985. Prentice-Hall. $17.95.

Walrod, Dennis. **More Than a Trophy.** (Illus.). 256 p. 1983. pap. Stackpole. $12.95.

—**Grouse Hunter's Guide.** 192 p. 1985. Stackpole. $16.95.

Washburn, O. A. **General Red.** (Illus.). Jenkins. $5.50.

Waterman, C. F. **The Hunter's World.** (Illus.). 250 p. 1983. reprint of 1973 ed. New Century. $29.95.

Whelen, Townsend. **The Hunting Rifle.** 464 p. 1984. Repr. of 1924 ed. Wolfe Pub. Co. $39.00.

Whitney. **The Coonhunter's Handbook.** Holt & Co. $11.95.

Wolff, Ed. **Elk Hunting in the Northern Rockies.** 164 p. 1984. pap. Stoneydale Pr. Pub. $14.95.

Young, Ralph. W. **Grizzlies Don't Come Easy.** (Illus.). 1981. Winchester Press. $15.95.

—**My Lost Wilderness.** (Illus.). 196 p. 1984. New Century. $15.95.

Zumbo, Jim. **Hunting America's Mule Deer.** 1981. Winchester Press. $17.95.

HUNTING—DICTIONARIES

Frevert, W. **Woerterbuch der Jaegerei.** 4th ed. (Ger.) 1975. French & European Pubns. Inc. $24.95.

Kehrein, Franz. **Woerterbuch der Weidmannssprache.** (Ger.) 1969. French & European Pubns. Inc. $110.00.

Kirchoff, Anne. **Woerterbuch der Jagel. (Ger., Eng. & Fr. Dictionary of Hunting.)** 1976. French & European Pubns. Inc. $75.00.

Sparano, Vin T. **The Sportsman's Dictionary of Fishing & Hunting Lingo.** (Illus.) 1987. McKay. $12.45.

Wisconsin Hunting Encyclopedia. 1976. pap. Wisconsin Sportsman. $2.95.

HUNTING—HISTORY

Greene, Robert. **The Third and Last Part of Conny-Catching.** 1923. Arden Library. $12.50.

Petersen, Eugene T. **Hunters' Heritage: A History of Hunting in Michigan.** Lowe, Kenneth S. ed. (Illus.). 1979. Michigan United Conservation Clubs. $4.65.

Rick, John W. **Prehistoric Hunters of the High Andes.** (Studies in Archaeology Ser.). 1980. Academic Press. $29.95.

Speth, John D. **Bison Kills and Bone Counts: Decision Making by Ancient Hunters.** 272 p. 1983. pap. U of Chicago $9.00.

Spiess, Arthur E. **Reindeer and Caribou Hunters: An Archaeological Study.** (Studies in Archaeology Ser.). 1979. Academic Press. $24.95.

HUNTING—AFRICA

Buckley, William. **Big Game Hunting in Central Africa.** (Illus.). 320 p. 1988. St. Martin. $15.95.*

Capstick, Peter H. **Death in the Long Grass.** (Illus.). 1978. St. Martin's Press. $15.95.

—**Death in the Dark Continent.** (Illus.). 320 p. 1983. St. Martin. $14.95.

Cloudsley-Thompson, J. L. **Animal Twilight, Man and Game in Eastern Africa.** (Illus.). 1967. Dufour Editions, Inc. $13.95.

Findlay, Frederick R. N. & Croonwright-Schreiner, S. C. **Big Game Shooting and Travel in Southeast Africa: Account of Shooting Trips in the Cheringoma and Gorongoza Divisions of Portuguese South-East Africa and in Zululand.** Repr. of 1903 ed. Arno. $44.25.

Foran, Robert. **Kill or Be Killed: The Rambling Reminiscences of an Amateur Hunter.** (Illus.). 400 p. 1988. St. Martin. $15.95.*

Gilmore, Parker. **Days and Nights by the Desert.** Repr. of 1888 ed. Arno. $22.50.

Hemingway, Ernest. **Green Hills of Africa.** 1935. Scribner's. pap. $9.95.

Holub, Emil. **Seven Years in South Africa.** 2 vols. 1881. Set. Scholarly Press. $49.00.

Lechter, Owen. **Big Game Hunting in North-Eastern Rhodesia.** (Illus.). 272 p. 1987. St. Martin. $15.95.*

Lyell, Denis D. **Memories of an African Hunter.** (Illus.). 288 p. 1987. St. Martin. $15.95.

—**African Adventures: Letters from Famous Big-Game Hunters.** (Illus.). 304 p. St. Martin. $15.95.

MacQueen, Peter. **In Wildest Africa.** 1909. Scholarly Press. $29.00.

Mellon, James. **African Hunter.** (Illus.). 522 p. 1988. Safari Press. $100.00.

Selous, Frederick. **Hunter's Wanderings in Africa.** 526 p. 1986. repr. of 1920 ed. Wolfe Pub. Co. $47.00.

Stigand, Chauncey H. **Hunting the Elephant in Africa.** (Illus.) 400 p. 1985. St. Martin. $14.95.

White, S. E. **Lions in the Path.** (Illus.). 352 p. 1987. Repr. of 1926 ed. Wolfe Pub. Co. $25.00.

—**African Campfires.** (Illus.). 456 p. 1987. Repr. of 1910 ed. Wolfe Pub. Co. $25.00.*

HUNTING—ALASKA

Batin, Christopher M. **Hunting in Alaska.** (Illus.). 416 p. 1987. Alaska Angler. pap. $24.95.*

Keim, Charles J. **Alaska Game Trails with a Master Guide.** pap. Alaska Northwest. $8.95.

Schetzle, Harold. **Alaska Wilderness Hunter.** (Illus.). 224 p. 1987. Great Northwest. $19.95.

HUNTING—GREAT BRITAIN

Jeffries, Richard. **The Gamekeeper at Home and the Amateur Poacher.** 1978. pap. Oxford University Press. $6.95.

Martin, Brian. **The Great Shoots: Britain's Premier Sporting Estates.** (Illus.). 240 p. 1988. David & Charles. $34.95.*

Thomas, William B. **Hunting England: A Survey of the Sport and of its Chief Grounds.** 1978. Repr. of 1936 ed. R. West. $30.00.

Watson, J. N. **British and Irish Hunts and Huntsmen: Vols. I & II.** (Illus.). 1981. David and Charles. $90.00.

HUNTING—NORTH AMERICA

Dalrymple, Byron W. **Bird Hunting with Dalrymple: The Rewards of Shotgunning Across North America.** (Illus.). 288 p. 1987. Stackpole. $24.95.

Irwin, R. Stephen. **Hunters of the Buffalo.** (Illus.). 52 p. 1984. Hancock House. pap. $3.95.

Leopold, Luna. B., ed. **Round River: From the Journals of Aldo Leopold.** (Illus.). 1972. pap. Oxford University Press. $3.95.

Selous, F. C. **Hunting Trips in North America.** (Illus.). 528 p. 1988. Repr. of 1907 ed. Wolfe Pub. Co. $52.00.*

HUNTING—U.S.

Abbott, Henry. **Birch Bark Books of Henry Abbott: Sporting Adventures and Nature Observations in the Adirondacks in the Early 1900s).** Illus., Repr. of 1914 & 1932 eds.). 1980. Harbor Hill Books. $22.50.

Baily's Hunting Directory. 1978–79. (Illus.). 1978. J. A. Allen. $25.00.

Baker, Ron. **The American Hunting Myth.** 287 p. 1985. Vantage. $10.95.

Barsness, John. **Hunting the Great Plains.** 164 p. 1979. pap. Mountain Press. $6.95.

Burk, R. L. **Mule Deer Hunting.** (Illus.). 64 p. 1988. Stoneydale Press. pap. $3.50.*

Cory, Charles B. **Hunting and Fishing in Florida, Including a Key to the Water Birds.** 1970. Repr. of 1896 ed. Ayer Co. Pubs. $19.00.

Dahl, Ruby W., et al. **Lander: One-Shot Antelope Hunt.** 129 p. 1986. $19.95; leather bound lmtd. ed. $50.00.

Elman, Robert, ed. **All About Deer Hunting in America 1976.** New Century. $16.95.

Gilchrist, Duncan. **Antelope Hunting.** (Illus.). 64 p. 1988. Stoneydale Press. pap. $3.50.*

—**Moose Hunting.** (Illus.). 64 p. 1988. Stoneydale Press. pap. $3.50.*

—**Mountain Goat Hunting.** (Illus.). 64 p. 1988. Stoneydale press. pap. $3.50.*

Hirsch, Bob. **Outdoors in Arizona: A Guide to Fishing & Hunting.** 192 p. 1986. Arizona Highway. pap. $12.95.

Huggler, Tom. **Hunt Michigan: How to, Where to, When to.** (Illus.). 1985. Mich. United Conserv. pap. $12.95.

Johnson, John A. **Oregon Hunting Guide.** (Illus.). 176 p. 1988. Stoneydale Press. pap. $12.95.*

Kozickey, Edward L. **Hunting Preserves for Sport or Profit.** 250 p. 1987. CK Wildlife Res. $24.95.

Lapinski, Mike, et al. **All About Elk.** Miller, Bill, ed. 253 p. 1987. N Amer. Hunt Club. text ed. $15.95.

Lowenstein, Bill. **Hunting in Michigan: The Early 80's.** Arnold, David A., ed. 1981. pap. Michigan Natural Resources Michigan. $6.95.

Mitchell, John G. **The Hunt.** 1980. Knopf $12.45.

—**The Hunt.** 1981. pap. Penguin. $4.95.

Pennaz, Steve, ed. **North American Hunting Adventures.** (Illus.). 208 p. 1988. Amer. Hunt Club. $19.95.*

Roosevelt, Theodore. **Outdoor Pastimes of an American Hunter.** 1970. Repr. of 1905 ed. Arno Press. $29.00.

—**Ranch Life and the Hunting-Trail.** 1985. Repr. of 1901 ed. Hippocrene. pap. $8.95.

—**Theodore Roosevelt's America.** Wiley, Farida, ed. (Illus.). 1955. Devin-Adair Co. $14.95.

—**Wilderness Hunter.** 1970. Repr. of 1900 ed. Irvington, Price not set.

Sandoz, Mari. **The Buffalo-Hunters: The Story of the Hide Men.** 1978. pap. University of Nebraska Press. $7.95.

Tome, Philip. **Pioneer Life or Thirty Years a Hunter: Being Scenes and Adventures in the Life of Philip Tome.** (Illus.). 1971. Repr. of 1854 ed. Gulf Pubns. $20.00.

Wootters, John. **A Guide to Hunting in Texas.** 1979. pap. Pacesetter Press. $9.95.

Zumbo, Jim. **Hunt Elk.** 256 p. 1985. New Century. $17.95.

HUNTING DOGS (see also Bird Dogs)

Bernard, Art. **Dog Days.** 1969. Caxton. $5.95.

Duffey, David M. **Hunting Dog Know-How** (Illus.). 1983. Winchester Press. pap. $10.95.

Erlandson, Keith. **Gundog Training.** (Illus.). 224 p. 1988. David & Charles. $29.95.*

Hartley, Oliver. **Hunting Dogs.** pap. A. R. Harding Pub. $4.00.

Irving, Joe. **Training Spaniels.** (Illus.). 1980. David & Charles. $18.95.

—**Gun Dogs: Their Learning Chain.** 231 p. 1983. State Mutual Bks. $35.00.

Lent, Patricia A. **Sport with Terriers.** (Illus.). 1973. Arner Publications. $13.95.

Petrie, Chuck, ed. **Just Dogs: A Photographic & Literary Tribute to the Great Hunting Breeds.** (Illus.). 160 p. 1988. Willow Creek Press. $35.00.*

Robinson, Jerome. **Training the Hunting Retriever.** (Illus.). 233 p. 1987. B. Robinson. $18.95.

Roebuck, Kenneth C. **Gun-Dog Training Spaniels and Retrievers.** 1982. Stackpole. $14.95.

—**Gun-Dog Training Pointing Dogs.** 192 p. 1983. Stackpole. $14.95.

Salmon, H. M. **Gazehounds and Coursing.** (Illus.). 1977. North Star Press. $18.50.

Tarrant, Bill. **Best Way to Train Your Gun Dog: The Dalmar Smith Method.** 1977. David McKay Co. $11.95.

Waterman, Charles F. **Gun Dogs & Bird Guns: A Charley Waterman Reader.** (Illus.). 244 p. 1987. GSJ Press. text ed. $25.00.

Wehle, Robert G. **Wing and Shot.** 1964. Country Press NY. $25.00.

Whitney, Leon F. & Underwood, Acil B. **Coon Hunter's Handbook.** 1952. Holt, Rinehart & Winston. $11.95.

HUNTING STORIES

Hill, Gene. **Hill Country: Stories About Hunting and Fishing and Dogs and Such.** (Illus.). 198. Dutton. $15.95.

McManus, Patrick. **They Shoot Canoes, Don't They?** 1981. Holt, Rinehart & Winston. $12.95.

MacQuarrie. Gordon. **The Last Stories of the Old Duck Hunters.** 1985. pap. Willow Creek Press. $17.50.

—**More Stories of the Old Duck Hunters.** 1983. Willow Creek. $17.50.

—**Stories of the Old Duck Hunters & Other Drivel.** 228 p. 1985. repr. of 1967 ed. Willow Creek. $17.50.

Sassoon, Siegfried. **Memoirs of a Fox-Hunting Man.** 320 p. 1960. pap. Faber & Faber. $6.95.

Smith, Steve. **Picking Your Shots & Other Stories of Dogs & Birds & Guns & Days Afield.** (Illus.). 160 p. 1986. Stackpole. $16.95.

Sobol, Donald. **Encyclopedia Brown's Book of the Wacky Outdoors.** (gr. 5 up). 1988. Bantam. pap. $2.50.

Sparano, Vin., ed. **Hunting Tales,** Vol. II. 256 p. 1987. Beaufort Bks. NY. $18.95.

Willow Creek Press Editors. **Wingshooter's Autumn.** (Illus.). 256 p. 1986. Willow Creek Press. $65.00.

HUNTING WITH BOW AND ARROW
(see Bow and Arrow)

KNIVES

Berner, Douglas C. **Survival Knife Reference Guide.** (Illus.) 207 p. 1986. Bee Tree. pap. $12.95.

Brewster, Melvyn & Hoyem, George. **Remington Bullet Knives.** (Illus.). 60 p. 1985. Armory Pubns. pap. $9.95.

Erhardt, Roy & Ferrell, J. **Encyclopedia of Pocket Knives: Book One and Book Two Price Guide.** rev. ed. (Illus.). 1977. Heart of America Press. $6.95.

Goins, John E. **Pocketknives—Markings, Manufacturers & Dealers.** 2d ed. 280 p. 1982. pap. Knife World. $8.95.

Hardin, Albert N., Jr. & Hedden, Robert W. **Light but Efficient: A Study of the M1880 Hunting and M1890 Intrenching Knives and Scabbards.** (Illus.). 1973. Albert N. Hardin. $7.95.

Hughes, B. R. **Modern Hand-Made Knives.** Pioneer Press. $9.95.

Latham, Sid. **Knives and Knifemakers.** (Illus.). 1974. pap. Macmillan. $13.50.

Levine, Bernard R. **Levine's Guide to Knife Values.** (Illus.). 480 p. 1985. DBI. pap. $19.95.

Lewis, Jack. **Gun Digest Book of Knives.** 3d ed. (Illus.). 256 p. 1988. DBI. pap. $12.95.*

McCreight, Tim. **Custom Knifemaking: 10 Projects from a Master Craftsman.** (Illus.). 234 p. 1985. Stackpole. pap. $14.95.

Parker, James, ed. **The Official Price Guide to Knives,** 9th ed. 1988. Ballantine. pap. $12.95.*

Paul, Don. **Everybody's Knife Bible.** (Illus.). 128 p. 1987. Pathfinder. pap. $9.95.

Peterson, Harold L. **American Knives.** 1980. Gun Room. $17.95.

Sanchez, John. **Blade Master: Advanced Survival Skills for the Knife Fighter.** (Illus.). 96 p 1982. pap. Paladin Press. $10.00.

Stephens, Frederick J. **Fighting Knives.** (Illus.). 144 p. 1985. Arco. pap. $11.95.

Tappan, Mel. ed. **A Guide to Handmade Knives and the Official Directory of the Knifemaker's Guild.** (Illus.). 1977. Janus Press. $9.95.

Warner, Ken. **Practical Book of Knives.** (Illus.). 1976. softbound. Stoeger. $10.95.

Watson, Jim. **Sharpening & Knife Making.** (Illus.). 150 p. 1987. Schiffer. $12.95.

NATURAL HISTORY—OUTDOOR BOOKS

Barrus, Clara, ed. **The Heart of Burrough's Journals.** 1979. Repr. of 1928 ed. Arden Lib. $30.00.

Bedichek, Roy. **Adventures with a Texas Naturalist.** (Illus.). 1961. pap. University of Texas Press. $9.95.

Errington, Paul L. **The Red Gods Call.** (Illus.). 1973. Iowa State University Press. $9.50.

Fuller, Raymond T. **Now That We Have to Walk: Exploring the Out-of-Doors.** facsimile ed. Repr. of 1943 ed. Ayer Co. $19.00.

Godfrey, Michael A. **A Sierra Club Naturalist's Guide to the Piedmont of Eastern North America.** (Illus.). 432 p. 1980. pap. Sierra. $9.95.

Jefferies, Richard. **Old House at Coate.** 1948. Arno Press. $18.00.

Kieran, John F. **Nature Notes.** facs. ed. 1941. Arno Press. $16.50.

Leopold, Aldo. **Sand County Almanac: With Other Essays on Conservation from Round River.** (Illus.). 1966. Oxford University Press. $17.95.

Olson, Sigurd F. **Listening Point.** (Illus.). 1958. Knopf. $13.45.

—**Sigurd Olson's Wilderness Days.** (Illus.). 1972. Knopf. $29.45.

Pearson, Haydn S. **Sea Flavor.** facs. ed. 1948. Arno Press. $17.00.

Rowlands, John J. **Cache Lake County.** 1959. W. W. Norton & Co. $12.95.

Sharp, Dallas L. **Face of the Fields.** facs. ed. 1911. Ayer Co. Pubns. $17.00.

—**Sanctuary! Sanctuary!** facs. ed. 1926. Ayer Co. Pubns. $12.00.

Sharp, William. **Where the Forest Murmurs.** 1906. Ayer Co. Pubns. $21.50.

Shepard, Odell. **Harvest of a Quiet Eye: A Book of Digressions.** facs. ed. Repr. of 1927 ed. Ayer Co. Pubns. $21.50.

Wiley, Farida, ed. **John Burroughs' America.** (Illus.). Devin-Adair Co. $10.50; pap. $9.95.

ORDNANCE (see also Ballistics)

Colby, C. B. **Civil War Weapons: Small Arms and Artillery of the Blue and Gray.** (Illus.). 1962. Coward, McCann & Geoghegan. $6.99.

Derby, Harry L. **The Hand Cannons of Imperial Japan.** Reidy, John and Welge, Albert, eds., 1981. Derby Publishing Co. $37.95.

Marchant-Smith, D. J. & Haslem, P. R. **Small Arms and Cannons.** 1982. Pergamon Press. pap. $16.95.

Norton, Robert. **The Gunner, Shewing the Whole Practise of Artillerie.** 1973. Repr. of 1628 ed. W. J. Johnson. $70.00.

ORIENTATION

Burton, Maurice. **The Sixth Sense of Animals.** (Illus.). 192 p. 1973. Taplinger. $7.95.

Henley, B. M. **Orienteering.** (Illus.). 1976. Charles River Books. $6.95.

Kals, W. S. **Land Navigation Handbook: The Sierra Club Guide to Map & Compass.** (Illus.). 288 p. 1983. pap. Sierra. $8.95.

Lynn, R. **Attention, Arousal & The Orientation Reaction.** 1966. ed. pap. Pergamon. $14.25.

Ratliff, Donald E. **Map Compass and Campfire.** (Illus.). 1970. Binford & Mort Pubs. pap. $3.95.

Vassilevsky, B. **Where is the North?** 1977. pap. Imported Pubns. $3.95.

Watson, J. D. **Orienteering.** (Illus.). 1975. Charles River Books. pap. $2.50.

OUTDOOR COOKERY (see also Game Cookery)

Anderson, Beverly M. & Hamilton, Donna M. **The New High Altitude Cookbook.** (Illus.). 1980. Random House. $17.95.

Antell, Steven. **Backpacker's Recipe Book.** (Illus.). 1980. pap. Pruett. $7.95.

Banks, James E. **Alfred Packer's Wilderness Cookbook.** (Illus.). 1969. Filter Press. $7.00. pap. $1.50.

Barker, Harriett. **The One-Burner Gourmet.** rev. ed. 1981. pap. Contemporary Books. $10.95.

Bock, Richard. **Camper Cookery.** 1977. pap. Lorenz Press. $5.95.

Brent, Carol D., ed. **Barbecue: The Fine Art of Charcoal, Gas and Hibachi Outdoor Cooking.** (Illus.). 1971. Doubleday. (OP).

Braun, Robert L. **Wilderness Recipie.** 96 p. 1988. Todd & Honeywell. $8.95.*

Bunnelle, Hasse. **Food for Knapsackers: And Other Trail Travelers.** 1971. pap. Sierra Club Books. $4.95.

Bunnelle, Hasse & Sarvis, Shirley. **Cooking for Camp and Trail.** 1972. pap. Sierra Club. $7.95.

Drew, Edwin P. **The Complete Light-Pack Camping and Trail-Food Cookbook.** 1977. pap. McGraw-Hill. $4.95.

Fleming, June. **The Well-Fed Backpacker.** (Illus.). 1981. pap. Random House. $4.95.

Heffron, Lauren. **Cycle Food: A Guide to Satisfying Your Inner Tube.** (Illus.). 96 p. 1983. pap. Ten Speed Press. $4.95.

Hemingway, Joan & Maricich, Connie. **The Picnic Gourmet.** (Illus.). 1978. pap. Random House. $10.95.

Holm, Don. **Old-Fashioned Dutch Oven Cookbook.** 1969. pap. Caxton Printers. $5.95.

Hughes, Stella. **Chuck Wagon Cookin'.** 1974. pap. University of Arizona Press. $9.95.

Krenzel, Kathleen & Heckendorf, Robyn. **The Sporting Life Gourmet.** (Illus.). 74 p. 1980. R. Louis Pub. $9.95.

McElfresh, Beth. **Chuck Wagon Cookbook.** pap. Swallow Press. 72 p. 1960. $4.95.

McHugh, Gretchen. **The Hungry Hiker's Book of Good Cooking.** (Illus.). 1982. Alfred A. Knopf. $17.50. pap. $11.95.

Macmillan, Diane D. **The Portable Feast.** rev. ed. (Illus.). 1984. 101 Productions. pap. $7.95.

Mendenhall, Ruth D. **Backpack Cookery.** (Illus.). 1974. pap. La Siesta. $1.95.

Miller, Dorcas S. **The New Healthy Trail Food Book.** rev. ed. (Illus.). 1980. pap. Globe Pequot. $4.95.

Nagy, Jean. **Brown Bagging It: A Guide to Fresh Food Cooking in the Wilderness.** 1976 pap. Marty-Nagy Bookworks. $2.50.

Outdoor Cooking. (Illus.). 176 p. 1983. Time Life. $14.95.

Picnic and Outdoor Menus. 1984. Silver. $18.60.

Prater, Yvonne & Mendenhall, Ruth D. **Gorp, Glop and Glue Stew: Favorite Foods from 165 Outdoor Experts.** (Illus.). 1981. pap. Mountaineers. $9.95.

Raup, Lucy G. **Camper's Cookbook.** 1967. pap. C. E. Tuttle. $3.75.

Schultz, Philip S. **Cooking with Fire and Smoke.** 273 p. 1986. S&S. $17.95.

Tarr, Yvonne Y. **The Complete Outdoor Cookbook.** (Illus.). 1973. Times Books. $8.95.

Thomas, Dian. **Roughing It Easy: A Unique Ideabook on Camping and Cooking.** (Illus.). 1974. pap. Brigham Young University Press. pap. $6.95.

Wary, Carol & Wary, William. **Fish & Fowl Cookery: The Outdoorsman's Home Companion.** 224 p. 1987. Countryman. pap. $10.95.

Woodall's Campsite Cookbook. Woodall. pap. $4.95.

Woodruff, Leroy L. **Cooking the Dutch Oven Way.** (Illus.). 1980. pap. ICS Books. $10.95.

OUTDOOR LIFE

Acerrano, Anthony. **The Outdoorsman's Emergency Manual.** 1976. 352 p. softbound. Stoeger. $9.95.

Anderson, Steve. **The Orienteering Book.** (Illus.). 1980. pap. Anderson World. $3.95.

Angier, Bradford. **How to Stay Alive in the Woods.** Orig. Title: **Living off the Country.** 1962. pap. Macmillan. $5.95.

Brown, Vinson. **Reading the Outdoors at Night.** (Illus.). 1982. pap. Stackpole Books. $9.95.

Camazine, Scott. **The Naturalist's Year: Twenty-Six Outdoor Explorations.** 1987. Wiley. pap. $14.95.

Douglas & McIntyre. **Outdoor Safety & Survival.** (Illus.). 154 p. 1986. Salem Hse Pub. $4.95.

Eastman, P. F. **Advanced First Aid for All Outdoors.** 1976. pap. Cornell Maritime Press. $6.00.

Fear, Gene. **Fundamentals of Outdoor Enjoyment.** (Illus.). 1976. pap. Survival Ed. Assoc. $5.00.

Grow, Laurence. **The Old House Book of Outdoor Living Places.** (Illus.). 1981. Warner Books. $15.00; pap. $8.95.

Hamper, Stanley R. **Wilderness Survival.** 3rd ed. 1975. Repr. of 1963 ed. Peddlers Wagon. $1.79.

Hanley, Wayne. **A Life Outdoors: A Curmudgeon Looks at the Natural World.** (Illus.). 1980. Stephen Greene Press. pap. $5.95.

Hickin, Norman. **Beachcombing for Beginners.** 1976. pap. Wilshire Book Co. $2.00.

Johnson, et al. **Outdoor Tips: A Remington Sportsman's Library Book.** pap. Benjamin Co. $2.95.

Kodet, E. Russell & Angier, Bradford. **Being Your Own Wilderness Doctor.** (Illus.). 1975. Stackpole Books. $8.95.

Lund, Duane R. Nature's **Bounty for Your Table.** 1982. Adventure Pubns. $7.95.

Maguire, Jack. **Outdoor Spaces.** 1987. H. Holt. $19.95.

Mills, Robert & Haines, Olin, eds. **National Outdoor Guides Directory.** (Illus.). 434 p. 1987. Professional Guides Pub. $12.95.*

Olsen, Larry D. **Outdoor Survival Skills.** rev. ed. 1973. Brigham Young University Press. $7.95.

Olson, Sigurd F. **Olson's Wilderness Days.** (Illus.). 1972. Knopf. $29.45.

Outdoor Living Skills Instructor's Manual. 1979. pap. American Camping Association. $6.50.

Owings, Loren C., ed. **Environmental Values, 1860–1972: A Guide to Information Sources.** 1976. Gale Research Co. $68.00.

Patmore, J. Allan. **Land and Leisure in England and Wales.** 1971. Fairleigh Dickinson. $27.50.

Paul, Don, ed. **Great Livin' in Grubby Times.** 140 p. 1986. Pathfinder HL. pap. $12.95.

—**Green Beret's Guide to Outdoor Survival.** (Illus.). 134 p. 1986. Pathfinder HL. pap. $12.95.

Platten, David. **The Outdoor Survival Handbook.** David & Charles. $15.95.

Rae, William E., ed. **A Treasury of Outdoor Life.** (Illus.). 520 p. 1983. Stackpole. $24.95.

Rafferty, Milton D. **The Ozarks Outdoors:** A Guide for Fishermen, Hunters & Tourists. (Illus.) 408 p. 1985. U of Okla. Press. $24.95.

Rawick, George P. **From Sundown to Sunup.** 1972. pap. Greenwood Press. pap. $8.95.

Risk, Paul H. **Outdoor Safety and Survival.** 300 p. 1983. Macmillan. Write for info.

Roberts, Harry. **Keeping Warm and Dry.** (Illus.). 1982. pap. Stone Wall Press. $7.95.

Russell, Andy. **Trail of a Wilderness Wanderer.** 336 p. 1988. N. Lyons Bks. $12.95.*

Rutstrum, Calvin. **Once Upon a Wilderness.** (Illus.). 1973. Macmillan. $10.95.

Shepherd, Laurie. **A Dreamer's Log Cabin: A Woman's Walden.** (Illus.). 1981. Dembner Books. $8.95.

Van De Smissen, Betty, et al. **Leader's Guide to Nature-Oriented Activities.** 3rd ed. (Illus.). 1977. pap. Iowa State University Press. $12.95.

Wood, Dave. **Wisconsin Life Trip.** 1982. Adventure Pubns. $5.95.

Wurman, Richard S. et al. **The Nature of Recreation: A Handbook in Honor of Frederick Law Olmstead.** 1972. pap. MIT Press. $6.95.

PISTOL SHOOTING

Antal, Laslo. **Competitive Pistol Shooting.** 190 p. 1982. State Mutual Bks. $30.00.

Duncan, Mark. **On Target with Mark Duncan:** An Illustrated Pocket Guide to Handgun Accuracy. (Illus.) 52 p. 1984. Duncan Gun. pap. $4.95.

Given, T. **Survival Shooting: Handguns & Shotguns.** 1986. Gordon Pr. $79.95 (lib. bdg.).

Himmelwright, A. **Pistol & Revolver Shooting.** (Illus.). 496 p. Repr. of 1928 ed. Wolfe Pub. Co. Price not set.*

Mason, James D. **Combat Handgun Shooting.** (Illus.). 286 p. 1980. C. C. Thomas. $31.50.

Taylor, C. **The Complete Book of Combat Handgunning.** 1986. Gordon Press. $79.95 (lib. bdg.).

PISTOLS

American Historical Founcation Staff, ed. **M1911A1 Automatic Pistol:Proud American Legend.** (Illus.). 1985. Am. Hist. Found. pap. $8.95.

Antaris, Leonardo. **Astra Automatic Pistols.** 260 p. 1988. Firac Pub. Co. $40.00.*

Askins, Charles. **Askins on Pistols and Revolvers.** Bryant, Ted & Askins, Bill, eds. 1980. National Rifle Association. $25.00; pap. $8.95.

Blackmore, Howard L. **English Pistols.** (Illus.) 64 p. 1985. Sterling. $17.95.

Buxton, Warren H. **The P-38 Pistol,** Vol. 2. 1940–1945. (Illus.). 256 p. 1985. Ucross Bks. $45.50.

Datig, Fred A. **Luger Pistol.** rev. ed. Borden, $16.95.

Dyke, S. E. **Thoughts on the American Flintlock Pistol.** (Illus.). 1974. George Shumway Publisher. $7.50.

Erickson, Wayne & Pate, Charles E. **The Broomhandle Pistol, 1896 to 1936.** 300 p. 1985. E&P Enter. $49.95.

Gould, A. C. **Modern American Pistols & Revolvers.** (Illus.). 244 p. 1987. Repr. of 1888 ed. Wolfe Pub. Co. $37.00.

Hoffschmidt, E. J. **Know Your Forty-Five Caliber Auto Pistols.** (Illus.). 1973. pap. Blacksmith Corp. $5.95.

—**Know Your Walther PP and PPK Pistols.** (Illus.). 1975. pap. Blacksmith Corp. $5.95.

—**Know Your Walther P. 38 Pistols.** (Illus.). pap. 1974. Blacksmith Corp. $5.95.

Hogg, Ian. **Military Pistols & Revolvers.** (Illus.). 128 p. 1988. Sterling. $24.95.*

Horlacher, R., ed. **The Famous Automatic Pistols of Europe.** Seaton, L. & Steindler, R. A. trs. from Ger. (Illus.). 1976. pap. Jolex. $6.95.

Kirkland, Turner. **Southern Derringers of the Mississippi Valley.** Pioneer Press. $2.00.

Klay, Frank. **The Sammuel E. Dyke Collection of Kentucky Pistols.** 1980. Gun Room Press. $2.00.

Landskron, Jerry. **Remington Rolling Block Pistols.** (Illus.). 1981. Rolling Block Press. $34.95; deluxe ed. $39.95.

Long, Duncan. **Assault Pistols, Rifle & Submachine Guns.** 1986. Gordon Pr. $79.95 (lib. bdg.).

Manual of Pistol & Revolver Cartridges, Vols 1 & 2. 1987. Gordon Pr. lib. bdg. $79.75.

Mitchell, Jack. **The Gun Digest of Pistolsmithing.** 1980. pap. DBI Books. $12.95.

Myatt, F. **An Illustrated Guide to Pistols and Revolvers.** 1981. Arco. $9.95.

Nonte, George C. Jr. **Pistol Guide.** (Illus.). 1980. Stoeger. $11.95.

—**Pistolsmithing.** (Illus.). 1974. Stackpole. $27.95.

North & North. **Simeon North: First Official Pistol Maker of the United States.** Repr. Gun Room Press. $12.95.

The Parabellum Automatic Pistol. 1986. Gordon Pr. $79.95 (lib. bdg.).

Reese. Michael. **Collector's Guide to Luger Values.** 1972. pap. Pelican. $1.95.

The Ruger Pistol Exotic Weapon System. 1986. Gordon Pr. $79.95 (lib. bdg.).

Seaton, Lionel, tr. **Famous Auto Pistols and Revolvers, Vol. II.** (Illus.). 1971. Jolex. $6.95.

Van Der Mark, Kist & Van Der Sloot, Puype. **Dutch Muskets and Pistols.** (Illus.). 1974. George Shumway Publisher. $35.00.

Walther P-38 Auto Pistol Caliber 9mm Parabellum. 1986. Gordon Pr. lib. bdg. $79.95.

Whittington, Robert D. **German Pistols and Holsters, 1943–45: Military-Police-NSDAP.** (Illus.). Gun Room Press. $17.95.

Whittington, Robert D. III. **The Colt Whitneyville-Walker Pistol.** 96 p. 1984. Brownlee Books. $20.00.

Williams, Mason. **The Sporting Use of the Handgun.** (Illus.). 1979. C. C. Thomas. $16.25.

Wood, J. B. **Gun Digest Book of Firearms Assembly-Disassembly. Pt. 1: Automatic Pistols.** (Illus.). 1979. pap. DBI Books. $12.95.

—**Beretta Automatic Pistols: The Collector's & Shooter's Comprehensive Guide.** (Illus.). 192 p. 1985. Stackpole. $19.95.

RELOADING (see also Firearms, Rifles, Shotguns)

Donnelly, John J. **Handloader's Manual of Cartridge Conversions.** (Illus.) 1056 p. 1987. Stoeger Pub. Co. pap. $29.95; spiral bound $29.95; hardcover $34.95.

Matunas, Edward. **Handbook of Metallic Cartridge Reloading.** (Illus.). 1981. Winchester Press. $15.95.

Steindler, R. A. **Reloader's Guide.** 3rd ed. (Illus.). 1975. softbound. Stoeger, $9.95.

REVOLVERS (see also Colt Revolvers)

Askins, Charles. **Askins on Pistols and Revolvers.** Bryant, Ted & Askins, Bill, eds. 1980. National Rifle Association. $25.00; pap. $8.95.

Dougan, John C. **Know Your Ruger Single Action Revolvers: 1953–1963.** Amber, John T., ed. 1981. Blacksmith Corp. $35.00.

Gould, A. C. **Modern American Pistols & Revolvers.** (Illus.). 244 p. 1987. Repr. of 1888 ed. Wolfe Pub. Co. $37.00.*

Hogg, Ian V. **Revolvers.** (Illus.). 1984. Stackpole. $14.95.

—**Military Pistols & Revolvers.** (Illus.). 128 p. 1988. Sterling. $24.95.*

Munnell, J. C. **A Blacksmith Guide to Ruger Rimfire Revolvers.** (Illus.). 56 p. 1982. pap. Blacksmith Corp. $7.50.

Myatt, F. **An Illustrated Guide to Pistols & Revolvers.** 160 p. 1981. Arco. (Illus.). 1980. Stoeger. $9.95.

Nonte, George C. Jr. **Revolver Guide.** (Illus.). 1980. Stoeger. $10.95.

Ross, H. W. **A Blacksmith Guide to Ruger Flattops & Super Blackhawks.** (Illus.). 96 p. 1982. pap. Blacksmith Corp. $9.95.

Seaton, Lionel, tr. **Famous Auto Pistols and Revolvers, Vol. II.** (Illus.). 1979. Jolex. $6.95.

Williams, Mason. **The Sporting Use of the Handgun.** (Illus.). 1979. C. C. Thomas. $16.25.

Wood, J. B. **Gun Digest Book of Firearms Assembly-Disassembly: Part II: Revolvers.** (Illus.). 320 p. 1979. pap. DBI. $12.95.

RIFLES (see also Firearms, Hawken Rifles, Sharps Rifles, Winchester Rifles)

Bridges, Toby. **Custom Muzzleloading Rifles: An Illustrated Guide to Building or Buying a Handcrafted Muzzleloader.** (Illus.) 224 p. 1986. Stackpole. pap. $16.95.

Buchele, William and Shumway, George. **Recreating the American Longrifle.** Orig. Title: Recreating the Kentucky Rifle. (Illus.). 1973. pap. George Shumway Publisher. $27.50.

Clayton, Joseph D. **The Ruger Number One Rifle.** (Illus.). 212 p. 1982. Blacksmith Corp. $39.95.

Colvin & Viall. **The Manufacture of Model 1903 Springfield Service Rifle.** 392 p. 1984. repr. of 1917 ed. Wolfe Pub. Co. $19.50.

Davis, Henry. **A Forgotten Heritage: The Story of the Early American Rifle.** 1976. Repr. of 1941 ed. Gun Room Press $9.95.

DeHaas, Frank. **Bolt Action Rifle.** rev. ed. 448 p. 1984. DBI. pap. $14.95.

Ezell, Edw. C. **The Great Rifle Controversy: Search for The Ultimate Infantry Weapon From World War II Through Vietnam & Beyond.** 352 p. 1984. Stackpole. $29.95.

—**The AK47 Story: Evolution of the Kalishnokov Weapons.** (Illus.). 256 p. 1986. Stackpole. pap. $12.95.

Fadala, Sam. **Rifleman's Bible.** (Illus.). 192 p. 1987. Doubleday. pap. $7.95.

Fadala, Sam. **The Book of the Twenty-Two.** (Illus.). 1989. Stoeger Pub. Co. $14.95.*

Fremantle, J. F. **The Book of the Rifle.** (Illus.). 576 p. 1985. repr. of 1901 ed. Wolfe Pub. Co. $54.00.

Grant James J. **More Single Shot Rifles.** (Illus.). Gun Room Press. $25.00.

—**Single-Shot Rifles.** Gun Room Press. $25.00.

—**Still More Single Shot Rifles.** 1979. Pioneer Press. $17.50.

Grissom, Ken. **Buckskins & Black Powder: A Mountain Man's Guide to Muzzle Loading.** (Illus.). 224 p. New Century. $15.95.

Hanson. **The Plains Rifle.** Gun Room Press. $19.95.

Hoffschmidt, E. J. **Know Your M-1 Garand Rifles.** 1976. pap. Blacksmith Corp. $5.95.

Hoyem, George. **The History & Development of Small Arms: British Sporting Rifle,** vol. 3. 236 p. 1985. Armory Pubns. $39.50.

Huddleston, Joe D. **Colonial Riflemen in the American Revolution.** (Illus.). 1978. George Shumway Publisher. $20.00.

James, Edsall. **The Golden Age of Single Shot Rifles.** Pioneer Press. $2.75.*

Keith, Elmer. **Big Game Rifles & Cartridges.** 176 p. 1985. repr. of 1936 ed. Gun Room. $19.95.

—**Big Game Rifles & Cartridges.** (Illus.). 176 p. 1984. Deluxe ed. Wolfe Pub. Co. $30.00.

Kindig, Joe, Jr. **Thoughts on the Kentucky Rifle in Its Golden Age.** annotated 2nd ed. (Illus.). 1982. George Shumway Publisher. $75.00.

Kirton, Jonathan G. **British Falling Block Breechloading Rifles From 1865.** (Illus.). 250 p. 1985. Armory Pubns. $39.95.

Klinger, Bernd., ed. **Rifle Shooting As a Sport.** 1981. A. S. Barnes. $15.00.

Lewis, Jack. **The Hunting Rifle: A Gun Digest Book.** 356 p. 1983. pap. DBI. $12.95.

Long, Duncan. **Assault Pistols, Rifles & Submachine Guns.** (Illus.). 152 p. 1986. Paladin Pr. text ed. $19.95.

—**The Mini-14: The Plinker, Hunter, Assault & Everything Else Rifle.** (Illus.).120 p. 1987. Paladin Pr. pap. text ed. $10.00.

McAulay, John D. **Carbines of the Civil War, 1861–1865.** 1981. Pioneer Press. $8.95.

Mallory, Franklin B. & Olson, Ludwig. **The Krag Rifle Story.** 1980. Springfield Research Service. $20.00.

Matthews, Charles W. **Shoot Better With Centerfire Rifle Cartridges-Ballistic Tables.** (Illus.). 560 p. 1984. Matthews Inc. pap. $16.45.

Myatt, F. **An Illustrated Guide to Rifles and Automatic Weapons.** (Illus.). 1981. Arco. $9.95.

O'Connor, Jack, **The Rifle Book.** 3rd ed. (Illus.). 1978. Knopf. $13.95; pap. $13.95.

Otteson, Stuart. **The Bolt Action.** 2 vols. rev. ed. 1984. Wolfe Pub. Co. cased set $39.00.

—**Benchrest Actions & Triggers.** Wolfe, Dave, ed. 61 p. 1983. Wolfe Pub. Co. pap. $8.50.

Page, Warren. **The Accurate Rifle.** (Illus.). 1975. softbound. Stoeger. $9.95.

Rywell, Martin. **American Antique Rifles.** Pioneer Press. $2.00.

Sharpe, Philip. **The Rifle in America.** (Illus.). 726 p. 1987. Repr. of 1938 ed. Wolfe Pub. Co. $59.00.

Shelsby, Earl, ed. **NRA Gunsmithing Guide.** Updated rev. ed. (Illus.). 336 p. (Orig.). 1980. pap. Nat'l Rifle Assn. $11.95.

Shumway, George. **Pennsylvania Longrifles of Note.** (Illus.). 1977. pap. George Shumway Publisher. $7.50.

—**Rifles of Colonial America.** 2 vols. incl. Vol. 1; Vol. 2. (Illus.). 1980. casebound. George Shumway Publisher. ea. $49.50.

Steindler, R. A. **Rifle Guide.** 1978. softbound. Stoeger. $9.95.

Taylor, C. **African Rifles and Cartridges.** Gun Room Press. $21.95.

—**The Fighting Rifles.** 1986. Gordon Pr. $79.95 (lib. bdg.).*

Tryon, T. B. **The Complete Rehabilitation of the Flintlock Rifle.** 1987. Pioneer Press. $5.95.

U.S. Rifle Caliber .30 Model 1903. Pioneer Press. $2.00.

U.S. Rifle Model 1866 Springfield. Pioneer Press. $1.75.

U.S. Rifle Model 1870 Remington. Pioneer Press. $1.75.

Walsh, J. H. **The Modern Sportsman's Gun & Rifle.** Vol. I & II. (Illus.). 536 p. 1986. Wolfe Pub. Co. price on request.

Whelen, Townsend. **The Hunting Rifle.** 464 p. 1984. Repr. of 1924 ed. Wolfe Pub. Co. $39.00.

White, S. E. **The Long Rifle.** (Illus.). 544 p. 1987. Repr. of 1930 ed. Wolfe Pub. Co. $25.00.

Wood, J. B. **Gun Digest Book of Firearms Assembly/Disassembly. Pt. III: Rimfire Rifles.** (Illus.). 1980. pap. DBI Books. $12.95.

—**Gun Digest Book of Firearms Assembly/Disassembly. Part IV: Centerfire Rifles.** (Illus.). 1979. pap. $12.95.

Workman, William E. **Know Your Ruger 10-22 Carbine.** (Illus.) 96 p. 1986. Blacksmith Corp. pap. $9.95.

SHARPS RIFLES

Manual of Arms for the Sharps Rifle. Pioneer Press. $1.50.

Rywell, Martin. **Sharps Rifle: The Gun That Shaped American Destiny.** Pioneer Press. $5.00.

SHOOTING (see also Firearms, Trap & Skeet Shooting)

Berger, Robert J. **Know Your Broomhandle Mauser.** (Illus.) 96 p. 1985. Blacksmith Corp. pap. $6.95.

Bogardus, A. H. **Field, Cover & Trap Shooting.** (Illus.). 500 p. 1987. Repr. of 1878 ed. Wolfe Pub. Co. $43.00.

Bowles, Bruce. **The Orvis Wing Shooting Handbook.** 96 p. 1985. N Lyons Bks. pap. $8.95.

Brister, Bob. **Shotgunning: The Art and the Science.** (Illus.). 1976. Winchester Press. $17.95.

Crossman, Jim. **Olympic Shooting.** (Illus.). 144 p. Natl Rifle Assn. $12.95.

Day, J. Wentworth. **The Modern Shooter.** 1976. Repr. of 1952 ed. Charles River Books. $15.00.

Farrow, W. M. **How I Became a Crack Shot With Hints to Beginners.** (Illus.). 204 p. Wolfe Pub. Co. $16.50.

Hagel, Bob. **Guns, Loads & Hunting Tips.** Wolfe, Dave, ed. (Illus.). 536 p. 1986. Wolfe Pub. Co. $19.50.

Humphreys, John. **Learning To Shoot.** (Illus.). 192 p. 1985. David & Charles. $20.95.

Jarrett, William S., ed. **Shooter's Bible 1989.** 80th ed. (Illus.). 576 p. 1988. Stoeger Pub. Co. $14.95.

—**Shooter's Bible 1990.** (Illus.). 576 p. 1989. Stoeger Pub. Co. $14.95.*

King, Peter. **The Shooting Field: 150 Years With Holland & Holland.** (Illus.). 176 p. 1985. Blacksmith. $39.95.

Klinger, Bernd, ed. **Rifle Shooting as a Sport.** (Illus.). 186 p. 1981. A. S. Barnes. $15.00.

Lind, Ernie. **Complete Book of Trick and Fancy Shooting.** (Illus.). 1977. pap. Citadel Press. $3.95.

McGivern, Ed. **Fast and Fancy Revolver Shooting.** New Century. $15.95.

Marchington, John. **Shooting: A Complete Guide for Beginners.** (Illus.). 1982. pap. Faber & Faber. $6.95.

Merkley, Jay P. **Marksmanship with Rifles: A Basic Guide.** (Illus.). pap. American Press. $3.95.

Rees, Clair. **Be An Expert Shot: With Rifle, Handgun, or Shotgun.** (Illus.). 192 p. 1984. New Century. $19.95.

Reynolds, Mike & Barnes, Mike. **Shooting Made Easy.** (Illus.) 144 p. 1986. Longwood Pub. Gp. $19.95.

Riling, Ray. **Guns and Shooting: A Bibliography.** (Illus.). 1981. Ray Riling. $75.00.

Ruffer, J. E. **Good Shooting.** (Illus.). 1980. David & Charles. $22.50.

Set Your Sights: A Guide to Handgun Basics. (Illus.). 1982. Outdoor Empire. $1.95.

Slabor, Stephen, et al. **Shooting Guide for Beginners.** (Illus.). 144 p. 1986. Allegheny. pap. $7.95.

Weston, Paul B. **Combat Shooting for Police.** 2nd ed. (Illus.). 1978. C. C. Thomas. $16.25.

Willock, Colin. **Duck Shooting.** (Illus.). 144 p. 1981. Andre Deutsch. $18.95.

Yochem, Barbara. **Barbara Yochem's Inner Shooting.** 1981. By By Productions. $6.95; pap. $3.95.

SHOTGUNS

Anderson, Robert S., ed. **Reloading for Shotgunners,** 2d ed. (Illus.). 256 p. 1985. pap. DBI. $12.95.

Askins, Charles. **The American Shotgun.** (Illus.). 336 p. 1987. Repr. of 1910 ed. Wolfe Pub. Co. $39.00.

Bowlen, Bruce. **The Orvis Wing Shooting Handbook.** 96 p. 1985. N. Lyons Bks. pap. $8.95.

Brockway, William R. **Recreating the Double Barrel Muzzleloading Shotgun.** (Illus.). 1985. Shumway. $27.50; pap. $27.50.

Elliott, Robert W. & Cobb, Jim. **Lefevre: Guns of Lasting Fame.** 174 p. 1987. R. W. Elliott. $29.95.

Grozik, Richard S. **Game Gun.** (Illus.) 160 p. 1986. Willow Creek. $39.00.

Hastings, Macdonald. **The Shotgun: A Social History.** 1981. David & Charles. $34.95.

Hinman, Bob. **The Golden Age of Shotgunning,** 2nd ed. Wolfe, Dave, ed. (Illus.). 175 p. Wolfe Pub. Co. $17.95.

Lewis, Jack & Mitchell, Jack. **Shotgun Digest.** 2nd ed. 1980. pap. DBI Books. $12.95.

O'Connor, Jack. **The Shotgun Book,** 2nd ed. rev. (Illus.). 1978. Knopf. pap. $13.95.

Robinson, Roger H. **The Police Shotgun Manual.** (Illus.). 1973. C. C. Thomas. $21.75.

Skillen, Charles R. **Combat Shotgun Training.** (Illus.). 1982. C. C. Thomas. $29.50.

Swearengen, Thomas F. **World's Fighting Shotguns.** 1978. TBN Ent. $29.95.

Thomas, Gough. **Shotguns and Cartridges for Game and Clays.** 3rd ed. (Illus.). 1976. Transatlantic Arts, Inc. $25.00.

Zutz, Don. **The Double Shotgun,** rev. ed. 304 p. (Illus.). 1985. New Century. $19.95.

SURVIVAL (see also Outdoor Life)

Angier, Bradford. **How to Stay Alive in the Woods.** Orig. Title: **Living Off the Country.** 1962. pap. Macmillan. $5.95.

Benson, Ragnar. **Live Off the Land in The City and Country.** (Illus.). 1981. Paladin Enterprises. $16.95.

Canadian Government. **Never Say Die: The Canadian Air Force Survival Manual.** (Illus.). 208 p. 1979. Paladin Pr. pap. $8.00.

Clayton, Bruce D. **Life After Doomsday: A Survivalist Guide to Nuclear War and Other Disasters.** (Illus.). 1981. pap. Dial Press. $14.95.

Dennis, Lawrence. **Operational Thinking for Survival.** 1969. R. Myles. $5.95.

Dept. of the Air Force. **Survival: Air Force Manual 64–5.** (Illus.). 1976. pap. Paladin Enterprises. $8.00.

Fear, Daniel E., ed. **Surviving the Unexpected: A Curriculum Guide for Wilderness Survival and Survival from Natural and Man Made Disasters.** (Illus.). rev. ed. 1974. Survival Education Association. $5.00.

Fear, Eugene H. **Surviving the Unexpected Wilderness Emergency.** 6th ed. (Illus.). 1979. pap. Survival Education Association. $6.00.

Freeman, Daniel B. **Speaking of Survival.** (Illus.). pap. Oxford University Press. $6.95.

Olsen, Larry D. **Outdoor Survival Skills.** 4th rev. ed. 1973. Brigham Young University Press. $7.95.

—**Outdoor Survival Skills.** 1984. pap. Pocket Books. $3.95.

Read, Piers Paul. **Alive: The Story of the Andes Survivors.** (Illus.). 1975. pap. Avon. pap. $4.95.

Survival Improvised Weapons. 1986. Gordon Press. $79.95 (lib. bdg.).

Thygerson, Alton L. **Disaster Survival Handbook.** (Illus.). 1979. pap. Brigham Young University Press. $7.95.

Wiseman, John. **Survive Safely Anywhere:** The SAS Survival Manual. (Illus.) 1986. Crown. $29.95.

TAXIDERMY

Farnham, Albert B. **Home Taxidermy for Pleasure and Profit.** (Illus.). pap. A. R. Harding Publishing. $4.00.

Grantz, Gerald J. **Home Book of Taxidermy and Tanning.** (Illus.). 1985. Stackpole. pap. $9.95.

Metcalf, John C. **Taxidermy: A Computer Manual.** (Illus.). 166 p. 1981. pap. Biblio Dist. $15.00.

Moyer, John W. **Practical Taxidermy.** 2nd ed. 1984. Wiley. pap. $12.95.

Pray, Leon L. **Taxidermy.** (Illus.). 1943. Macmillan. $11.95.

Smith, Capt. James A. **Dress 'Em Out,** (Illus.). 1982. softbound. Stoeger. $12.95.

Tinsley, Russell. **Taxidermy Guide.** 2nd ed. (Illus.). 1977. softbound. Stoeger. $9.95.

TRAP AND SKEET SHOOTING

Blatt, Art. **Gun Digest Book of Trap & Skeet Shooting.** 256 p. 1984. pap. DBI. $12.95.

Campbell, Robert, ed. **Trapshooting with D. Lee Braun and the Remington Pros.** pap. Benjamin Co. $5.95.

—**Skeet Shooting with D. Lee Braun:** A Remington Sportsman's Library Book. Benjamin Co. $4.95.

Cradock, Chris. **Manual of Clayshooting.** (Illus.) 192 p. 1986. David & Charles. $30.95.

National Skeet Shooting Association Record Annual. 320 p. Natl. Skeet Shoot. Assn. $9.00.

TRAPPING

Bateman, James A. **Animal Traps & Trapping.** (Illus.). 388 p. 1988. David & Charles. $32.95.*

Errington, Paul L. **Muskrats and Marsh Management.** (Illus.). 1978. University of Nebraska Press. pap. $4.50.

Geary, Steven. **Fur Trapping in North America.** (Illus.). 384 p. 1985. Stackpole. pap. $10.95.

Get Set To Trap. (Illus.). 1982. Outdoor Empire. $1.95.

Gilsvik, Bob. **The Modern Trapline: Methods and Materials.** 1980. Chilton Book Co. $12.50.

Harding, A. R. **Deadfalls and Snares.** (Illus.). pap. A. R. Harding Publishing. $4.00.

—**Fox Trapping.** (Illus.). pap. A. R. Harding Publishing. $4.00.

—**Mink Trapping.** (Illus.). pap. A. R. Harding Publishing. $4.00.

—**Trappers' Handbook.** 1975. pap. A. R. Harding Publishing. $2.00.

—**Trapping as a Profession.** 1975. pap. A. R. Harding Publishing. $2.00.

—**Wolf & Coyote Trapping.** (Illus.) 252 p. A. R. Harding Pub. pap. $4.00.

Jamison, Rick. **Trapper's Handbook.** 224 p. 1983. pap. DBI. $12.95.

Kreps, E. **Science of Trappings.** (Illus.). pap. A. R. Harding Publishing. $4.00.

Lindsey, Neil M. **Tales of A Wilderness Trapper.** 1973. pap. A. R. Harding Publishing. $2.00.

Lynch, V. E. **Trails to Successful Trapping.** pap. A. R. Harding Publishing. $4.00.

McCracken, Harold & Van Cleve, Harry. **Trapping.** (Illus.). 1974. A. S. Barnes. $8.95.

Martin, Dale. **The Trapper's Bible: Traps, Snares & Pathguards.** (Illus.). 72 p. 1987. Paladin Press. $8.00.

Mascall, Leonard. **A Booke of Fishing with Hooke and Line.** 1973. Repr. of 1590 ed. Walter J. Johnson. $25.00.

Montgomery, David. **Mountain Man Crafts & Skills.** (Illus.). 1981. Horizon Utah. $12.95.

Musgrove, Bill & Blair, Gerry. **Fur Trapping.** (Illus.). 1984. New Century. $12.95.

Russell, Andy. **Trails of a Wilderness Wanderer.** 1975. Knopf. $15.45.

Sandoz, Mari. **The Beaver Men: Spearheads of Empire.** (Illus.). 1978. pap. University of Nebraska Press. $7.50.

The Trapper's Companion. (Illus.). pap. A. R. Harding Publishing. $3.00.

Walters, Keith. **The Book of the Free Trapper.** 1981. Pioneer Press. $7.95.

Woodcock, E. N. **Fifty Years a Hunter and Trapper.** pap. A. R. Harding Publishing. $4.00.

WINCHESTER RIFLES

Fadala, Sam. **Winchester's 30-30, Model 94:** The Rifle America Loves. (Illus.) 224 p. 1986. Stackpole. $24.95.

Madis, George. **The Winchester Model Twelve.** (Illus.). 1982. Art & Ref. $19.95.

—**The Winchester Book.** 3rd ed. (Illus.). 1979. Art & Reference House. $45.00.

—**The Winchester Handbook.** (Illus.). 1981. Art & Reference House. $19.50.

Twesten, Gary. **Winchester 1894 Carbine: A 90-Year History of the Variations of the Winchester Carbine 1894–1984.** (Illus.). 1984. G. Twesten. $20.00; pap. $20.00.

—**Winchester Model 1892 Carbine.** 1985. G. Tuesten. Pap. $10.00.

West, Bill. **Winchester Encyclopedia.** (Illus.). B. West. $15.00.

—**Winchester Lever-Action Handbook.** (Illus.). B. West. $25.00.

—**Winchester Single Shot.** (Illus.). B. West. $19.00.

—**Winchesters, Cartridges and History.** (Illus.). B. West. $42.00.

Williamson, Snooky. **The Winchester Lever Legacy.** (Illus.). 650 p. 1988. Buffalo Press Pubns. $59.95.*

Winchester—Complete Volume I: All Early Winchester Arms 1849–1919. (Illus.) 1981. B. West. $42.00

Winchester—Complete Volume II: All Winchester Arms 1920–1982. 1981. B. West. $42.00.

Names and Addresses of Leading Gun Book Publishers

ARCO PUBLISHING INC.
(see Prentice-Hall Inc.)

ARMORY PUBLICATIONS
P.O. Box 44372
Tacoma, Washington 98444

BLACKSMITH CORP.
P.O. Box 424
Southport, Ct. 06490

DAVID & CHARLES INC.
P.O. Box 57
Pomfret, Vermont 05053

DBI BOOKS, INC.
4092 Commercial Avenue
Northbrook, Illinois 60062

DENLINGER'S PUBLISHERS LTD.
P.O. Box 76
Fairfax, Virginia 22030

E & P ENTERPRISES
P.O. Box 2116
San Antonio, Texas 78297-2116

GUN ROOM PRESS
127 Raritan Avenue
Highland Park, N.J. 08904

HOUSE OF COLLECTIBLES
1904 Premier Row
Orlando, Florida 32809

JANE'S PUBLISHING INC.
c/o International Thomson Organisation Inc.
135 W. 50 Street
New York, N.Y. 10020

ALFRED A. KNOPF, INC.
201 E. 50 Street
New York, N.Y. 10022

LONGWOOD PUBLISHING GROUP INC.
51 Washington Street
Dover, New Hampshire 03820

NATIONAL RIFLE ASSOCIATION
1600 Rhode Island Avenue NW
Washington, D.C. 20036

NEW CENTURY PUBLICATIONS, INC.
220 Old New Brunswick Road
Piscataway, N.J. 08854
(also handles titles published under Winchester
Press imprint)

PALADIN PRESS
P.O. Box 1307
Boulder, Colorado 80306

PRENTICE-HALL
Englewood Cliffs, N.J. 07632

ROLLING BLOCK PRESS
P.O. Box 5357
Buena Park, California 90622

ALBERT SAIFER, PUBLISHERS
P.O. Box 239
West Orange, N.J. 07052

SAIGA PUBLISHING CO. LTD.
(see under Longwood Pub. Group Inc.)

GEORGE SHUMWAY PUBLISHERS
RD 7, P.O. Box 388B
York, Pennsylvania 17402

STACKPOLE BOOKS
P.O. Box 1831
Harrisburg, Pennsylvania 17105

STEIN & DAY
Scarborough House
Briarcliff Manor, N.Y. 10510

STERLING PUBLISHING CO., INC.
2 Park Avenue
New York, N.Y. 10016

STOEGER PUBLISHING COMPANY
55 Ruta Court
South Hackensack, N.J. 07606

TAB BOOKS INC.
Blue Ridge Summit
Pennsylvania 17214

TARGET COMMUNICATIONS CORP.
7626 West Donges Bay Road
P.O. Box 188
Mequon, Wisconsin 53092

WILLOW CREEK PRESS
Div. of Wisconsin Sportsman
P.O. Box 2266
Oshkosh, Wisconsin 54903

WOLFE PUBLISHING COMPANY, INC.
P.O. Box 3030
Prescott, Arizona 86302

Directory of Manufacturers and Suppliers

Action Arms, Ltd. (handguns, rifles, scopes)
P.O. Box 9573
Philadelphia, Pennsylvania 19124
(215) 744-0100

Aimpoint (sights, mounts)
203 Elden Street, Suite 302
Herndon, Virginia 22070
(703) 471-6828

American Arms (handguns, shotguns)
715 E. Armour Road
N. Kansas City, Missouri 64116
(816) 474-3161

American Derringer Corp. (handguns)
127 North Lacy Drive
Waco, Texas 76705
(817) 799-9111

American Military Arms Corp. (Iver Johnson pistols, rifles)
2202 Redmond Road
Jacksonville, Arkansas 72076
(501) 982-1633

Anschutz (handguns, rifles)
Available through Precision Sales International

Arcadia Machine & Tool Inc. (AMT handguns)
6226 Santos Diaz Street
Irwindale, California 91702
(818) 334-6629

Armes de Chasse (Chapuis and Merkel shotguns)
P.O. Box 827
Chadds Ford, Pennsylvania 19317
(215) 388-1146

Armsport, Inc. (shotguns, black powder, scopes)
3590 NW 49th Street
Miami, Florida 33142
(305) 635-7850

A-Square Co., Inc. (rifles)
Route 4, Simmons Road
Madison, Indiana 47250
(812) 273-3633

Astra (handguns)
Available through Interarms

Bausch & Lomb (scopes)
See Bushnell (Division of)

Beeman Precision Arms, Inc. (imported handguns, rifles, scopes)
3440-SBL Airway Drive
Santa Rosa, California 95403-2040
(707) 578-7900

Benelli (shotguns)
Available through Heckler & Koch

Beretta U.S.A. Corp. (handguns, shotguns)
17601 Indian Head Highway
Accokeek, Maryland 20607
(301) 283-2191
See also under Uberti, USA

Bernardelli (handguns, shotguns)
Available through Quality Arms (shotguns) and Magnum Research (handguns)

Bersa (handguns)
Available through Outdoor Sports Headquarters

Blaser USA, Inc. (rifles)
c/o Autumn Sales, Inc.
1320 Lake Street
Fort Worth, Texas 76102
(817) 335-1634

Bonanza (reloading tools)
See Forster Products

Brno (handguns, rifles)
Available through Saki International

Browning (handguns, rifles, shotguns)
Route One
Morgan, Utah 84050
(801) 543-3200

B-Square Company (mounts)
P.O. Box 11281
Fort Worth, Texas 76110
(817) 923-0964

Maynard P. Buehler, Inc. (mounts)
17 Orinda Highway
Orinda, California 94563
(415) 254-3201

Buffalo Bullet Co., Inc. (ammunition)
7352 Whittier Avenue
Whittier, California 90602
(213) 696-5738

Burris Company, Inc. (scopes, sights, mounts)
331 East Eighth Street, P.O. Box 1747
Greeley, Colorado 80632
(303) 356-1670

Bushnell (scopes)
Division of Bausch & Lomb
300 North Lone Hill Avenue
San Dimas, California 91773
(714) 592-8000

CCI (ammunition, primers)
Available through Omark Industries, Inc.

C-H Tool & Die Corp. (reloading)
106 N. Harding St., P.O. Box L
Owen, Wisconsin 54460
(715) 229-2146

CVA (black powder guns)
5988 Peachtree Corners East
Norcross, Georgia 30071
(404) 449-4687

Chapuis (shotguns)
Available through Armes de Chasse

Charter Arms Corp. (handguns)
430 Sniffens Lane
Stratford, Connecticut 06497
(203) 377-8080

Churchill (rifles, shotguns)
Available through Ellett Brothers, Inc.

Classic Doubles (shotguns)
1982 Innerbelt Business Center
St. Louis, Missouri 63114
(314) 423-6191

Classic Rifles Co. (rifles)
P.O. Box 321
Rodgers Lane
Charleroi, Pennsylvania 15022
(412) 483-6358

Colt Industries Firearms Division (handguns)
Talcott Road, Box 1868
Hartford, Connecticut 06101
(203) 236-6311

Coonan Arms, Inc. (handguns)
830 Hampden Ave.
St. Paul, Minnesota 55114
(612) 646-6672

Dakota (handguns, rifles)
Available through E.M.F. Co., Inc.

Charles Daly (shotguns)
Available through Outdoor Sports Headquarters Inc.

Davis Industries (handguns)
15150 Sierra Bonita Lane
Chino, California 91710
(714) 597-4726

Detonics (handguns)
See under New Detonics Manufacturing Corp.

Dixie Gun Works (black powder guns)
Reelfoot Avenue, P.O. Box 130
Union City, Tennessee 38261
(901) 885-0561

Ellett Brothers, Inc. (Churchill rifles, shotguns)
P.O. Drawer G
Chapin, South Carolina 29036
(800) 845-3711

E.M.F. Company, Inc. (Dakota handguns, rifles, black powder)
1900 East Warner Avenue 1-D
Santa Ana, California 92705
(714) 261-6611

Erma (handguns)
Available through Precision Sales (target guns only), Beeman (PO8 model) and American Arms

Euroarms of America Inc. (black powder guns)
1501 Lenoir Drive, P.O. Box 3277
Winchester, Virginia 22601
(703) 662-1863

Excam (Targa and Tanarmi pistols, shotguns)
4480 E. 11th Avenue
Hialeah, Florida 33013
(305) 681-4661-2

Federal Cartridge Corporation (Federal/Norma ammunition, bullets, primers, cases)
900 Ehlen Drive
Anoka, Minnesota 55303-7503
(612) 422-2840

Ferlib (shotguns)
Available through W. L. Moore & Co.

FIE Corporation (pistols, black powder guns, Franchi shotguns)
4530 Northwest 135th Street
Opa-Locka, Florida 33054
(305) 685-5966

Forster Products (Bonanza and Forster reloading)
82 East Lanark Avenue
Lanark, Illinois 61046
(815) 493-6360

Franchi (shotguns)
Available through FIE Corp.

Freedom Arms (handguns)
One Freedom Lane, P.O. Box 1776
Freedom, Wyoming 83120
(307) 883-2468

Galaxy Imports, Ltd., Inc. (Laurona shotguns)
P.O. Box 3361
Victoria, Texas 77903
(512) 573-GUNS

Garbi (shotguns)
Available through W. L. Moore & Co.

Glock, Inc. (handguns)
6000 Highlands Parkway
Smyrna, Georgia 30082
(404) 432-1202

Gonic Arms (black powder rifles)
134 Flagg Road
Gonic, New Hampshire 03867
(603) 332-8457

Gun South Inc. (Steyr, Steyr Mannlicher rifles)
108 Morrow Ave., P.O. Box 129
Trussville, Alabama 35173
(205) 655-8299

Hammerli (handguns)
Available through Beeman Precision Arms

Heckler & Koch (handguns, rifles, Benelli shotguns)
21480 Pacific Boulevard
Sterling, Virginia 22170-8903
(703) 450-1900

Heym America, Inc. (rifles)
1426 East Tillman Road
Fort Wayne, Indiana 46816
(219) 447-5772

Hodgdon Powder Co., Inc. (gunpowder)
6231 Robinson, P.O. Box 2932
Shawnee Mission, Kansas 66201
(913) 362-9455

J.B. Holden Co. (scope mounts)
295 West Pearl, P.O. Box 320
Plymouth, Michigan 48170
(313) 455-4850

Hopkins & Allen Arms (black powder guns)
3 Ethel Avenue, P.O. Box 217
Hawthorne, New Jersey 07507
(201) 427-1165

Hornady Manufacturing Company (reloading, ammunition)
P.O. Box 1848
Grand Island, Nebraska 68802-1848
(308) 382-1390

Howa (rifles)
Available through Interarms

IMR Powder Company (gunpowder)
R.D. 5, Box 247E
Plattsburgh, New York 12901
(518) 561-9530

Interarms (handguns, shotguns and rifles, including Astra, Howa, Mark X, Rossi, Star, Walther, Whitworth)
10 Prince Street
Alexandria, Virginia 22313
(703) 548-1400

Ithaca Acquisition Corp. (shotguns)
123 Lake Street
Ithaca, New York 14850
(607) 273-0200

Iver Johnson/AMAC (handguns, rifles)
Available through American Military Arms Corp.

Paul Jaeger, Inc. (Schmidt & Bender scopes, mounts)
P.O. Box 449
1 Madison Ave.
Grand Junction, Tennessee 38039
(901) 764-6909

K.D.F. Inc. (rifles)
2485 Highway 46 North
Seguin, Texas 78155
(512) 379-8141

Kassnar Imports (handguns, scopes, Omega shotguns)
P.O. Box 6097
Harrisburg, Pennsylvania 17112
(717) 652-6101

Kimber (rifles, scopes)
9039 S.E. Jannsen Road
Clackamas, Oregon 97015
(503) 656-1704

Krico (rifles)
Available through Beeman Precision Arms

Krieghoff International Inc. (shotguns)
Boschstrasse 22
D-7900 Ulm, West Germany
731/42017

L.A.R. Manufacturing, Inc. (Grizzly handguns)
4133 West Farm Road
West Jordan, Utah 84084
(801) 255-7106

Laurona (shotguns)
Available through Galaxy Imports

Leupold & Stevens, Inc. (scopes, mounts)
P.O. Box 688
Beaverton, Oregon 97005
(503) 646-9171

Llama (handguns)
Available through Stoeger Industries

Lyman Products Corp. (black powder guns, sights, scopes, reloading tools)
Route 147
Middlefield, Connecticut 06455
(203) 349-3421

M.O.A. Corp. (handguns)
7996 Brookville-Salem Road
Brookville, Ohio 45309
(513) 833-5559

MTM Case Gard Co. (reloading tools)
3370 Obco Court
Dayton, Ohio 45414
(513) 890-7461

Magnum Research Inc. (Desert Eagle handguns, Bernardelli and Victory Arms handguns, Bernardelli shotguns)
P.O. Box 32221
Minneapolis, Minnesota 55432
(612) 574-1868

Mark X (rifles)
Available through Interarms

Marlin Firearms Company (rifles, shotguns)
100 Kenna Drive
North Haven, Connecticut 06473
(203) 239-5621

McMillan & Co., Inc. (rifles)
21438 7th Avenue, Suite E
Phoenix, Arizona 85027
(602) 582-9627

MEC Inc. (reloading tools)
℅ Mayville Engineering Co.
715 South Street
Mayville, Wisconsin 53050
(414) 387-4500

Merit Corporation (sights, optical aids)
Box 9044
Schenectady, New York 12309
(518) 346-1420

Merkel (shotguns)
Available through Armes de Chasse

Millett Sights (sights and mounts)
16131 Gothard Street
Huntington Beach, California 92647
(714) 847-5575

Mitchell Arms (handguns)
3411 Lake Center Dr.
Santa Ana, California 92704
(714) 957-5711

Modern Muzzle Loaders Inc. (black powder guns)
Highway 136 East, P.O. Box 130
Lancaster, Missouri 63548
(816) 457-2125

William L. Moore & Co. (Garbi, Ferlib and
Piotti shotguns)
31360 Via Colinas, No. 109
Westlake Village, California 91361
(818) 889-4160

O.F. Mossberg & Sons, Inc. (shotguns)
7 Grasso Avenue
North Haven, Connecticut 06473
(203) 288-6491

Navy Arms Company, Inc. (shotguns, black powder
guns, replicas)
689 Bergen Boulevard
Ridgefield, New Jersey 07657
(201) 945-2500

New Detonics Manufacturing Corp. (handguns)
13456 Southeast 27th Place
Bellevue, Washington 98005
(206) 747-2100

Norma (ammunition, gunpowder, reloading cases)
Available through Federal Cartridge Corp.

North American Arms (handguns)
1800 North 300 West
P.O. Box 707
Spanish Fork, Utah 84660
(801) 798-7401 or (800) 821-5783

Olin/Winchester (ammunition, primers, cases)
East Alton, Illinois 62024
(618) 258-2000
Shotguns now available Classic Doubles

Omark Industries, Inc. (CCI ammunition; shotguns
available through Classic Doubles; RCBS reloading
tools, Speer bullets, Weaver mount rings)
Box 856
Lewiston, Idaho 83501
(208) 746-2351

Omega (shotguns)
Available through Kassnar Imports

Outdoor Sports Headquarters, Inc. (Bersa handguns,
Charles Daly shotguns)
P.O. Box 1327
967 Watertower Lane
Dayton, Ohio 45449
(513) 865-5855

Parker-Hale (rifles, shotguns)
Available through Precision Sports

Parker Reproduction (shotguns)
124 River Road
Middlesex, New Jersey 08846
(201) 469-0100

Pentax (scopes)
35 Inverness Drive East
Englewood, Colorado 80112
(303) 799-8000

Perazzi U.S.A. (shotguns)
1207 S. Shamrock Ave.
Monrovia, California 91016
(818) 303-0068

Piotti (shotguns)
Available through W.L. Moore & Co.

Precision Sales International (Anschutz pistols, rifles;
Erma pistols)
P.O. Box 1776
Westfield, Massachusetts 01086
(413) 562-5055

Precision Sports (Parker-Hale rifles, shotguns)
P.O. Box 708, Kellogg Road
Cortland, New York 13045
(607) 756-2851 or (800) 847-6787

Quality Arms (Bernardelli shotguns)
P.O. Box 19477
Houston, Texas 77224
(713) 870-8377

Raven Arms (handguns)
1300 Bixby Drive
Industry, California 91745
(818) 961-2511

RCBS, Inc. (reloading tools)
See Omark Industries, Inc.

Redding Reloading Equipment (reloading tools)
1089 Starr Road
Cortland, New York 13045
(607) 753-3331

Redfield (sights, scopes)
5800 East Jewell Avenue
Denver, Colorado 80224
(303) 757-6411

Remington Arms Company, Inc. (handguns, rifles,
shotguns, ammunition, primers)
1007 Market Street
Wilmington, Delaware 19898
(302) 773-5291

Rossi (handguns, rifles, shotguns)
Available through Interarms

Ruger (handguns, rifles, shotguns, black powder
guns)
See Sturm, Ruger & Company, Inc.

Saki International (Brno handguns, rifles)
19800 Center Ridge Road
P.O. Box 16189
Rocky River, Ohio 44116
(216) 331-3533

Sako (rifles, actions, scope mounts)
Available through Stoeger Industries

Sauer (rifles)
Available through Sigarms, Inc.

Savage Arms (rifles, shotguns)
Springdale Road
Westfield, Massachusetts 01085
(413) 562-2361

Schmidt and Bender (scopes)
Available through Paul Jaeger, Inc.

Shilo Sharps Arms Co., Inc. (black powder rifles)
P.O. Box 279, Industrial Park
Big Timber, Montana 59011
(406) 932-4454

Sierra Bullets (bullets)
10532 S. Painter Avenue
Santa Fe Springs, California 90670
(213) 941-0251 or (800) 223-8799

Sigarms Inc. (handguns, Sauer rifles)
470 Spring Park Place, Unit 900
Herndon, Virginia 22070
(703) 481-6660

Sig-Sauer (handguns)
Available through Sigarms Inc.

Simmons Outdoor Corp. (scopes)
14205 SW 119th Ave.
Miami, Florida 33186
(305) 252-0477

SKB Shotguns (shotguns)
c/o Ernie Simmons Enterprises
719 Highland Avenue
Lancaster, Pennsylvania 17603
(717) 664-4040

Smith & Wesson (handguns)
2100 Roosevelt Avenue
Springfield, Massachusetts 01102-2208
(413) 781-8300

Southern Gun Distributors (Tanarmi and Targa
handguns)
13490 N.W. 45th Avenue
Opa-Locka (Miami), Florida 33054-0025
(305) 685-8451

Speer (bullets)
See Omark Industries, Inc.

Springfield Armory (handguns, scopes)
420 West Main Street
Geneseo, Illinois 61254
(309) 944-5631

Star (handguns)
Available through Interarms

Steyr (handguns, paramilitary)
Available through Gun South Inc.

Steyr Mannlicher (rifles)
Available through Gun South Inc.

Stoeger Industries (Sako rifles, Llama handguns,
Stoeger shotguns, Tikka and Valmet rifles, shotguns;
scopes, mounts, actions)
55 Ruta Court
South Hackensack, New Jersey 07606
(201) 440-2700

Sturm, Ruger and Company, Inc. (Ruger handguns,
rifles, shotguns)
Lacey Place
Southport, Connecticut 06490
(203) 259-7843

Swarovski American (scopes)
1 Kenney Drive
Cranston, Rhode Island 02920
(401) 463-3000

Tanarmi and Targa (pistols)
Available through Southern Gun Distributors

Tasco (scopes)
7600 N.W. 26th Street
Miami, Florida 33122
(305) 591-3670

Taurus International, Inc. (Taurus handguns)
4563 Southwest 71st Avenue
Miami, Florida 33155
(305) 662-2529

Thompson/Center Arms (handguns, rifles, black
powder guns)
Farmington Road, P.O. Box 2426
Rochester, New Hampshire 03867
(603) 332-2394

Tikka (rifles)
Available through Stoeger Industries

Traditions, Inc. (black powder guns)
P.O. Box 235
Deep River, Connecticut 06417
(203) 526-9555

Uberti USA, Inc. (handguns, black powder rifles and
revolvers)
41 Church Street
New Milford, Connecticut 06776
(203) 355-8827

Ultra Light Arms Company (rifles)
214 Price Street, P.O. Box 1270
Granville, West Virginia 26534
(304) 599-5687

U.S. Repeating Arms Co. (Winchester rifles,
shotguns)
275 Winchester Avenue
New Haven, Connecticut 06511
(203) 789-5000

Valmet, Inc. (rifles, shotguns)
Available through Stoeger Industries

Varner Sporting Arms (rifles)
1004F Cobb Parkway, N.E.
Marietta, Georgia 30062
(404) 422-5468

Victory Arms (handguns)
Available through Magnum Research

Walther (handguns, rifles)
Available through Interarms

Weatherby, Inc. (rifles, shotguns, scopes,
ammunition)
2781 Firestone Boulevard
South Gate, California 90280
(213) 569-7186

Weaver (mount rings)
% Omark Industries
Route 2, Box 39
Onalaska, Wisconsin 54650
(800) 635-7656

Dan Wesson Arms, Inc. (handguns)
293 Main Street
Monson, Massachusetts 01057
(413) 267-4081

Whitworth (rifles)
Available through Interarms

Wildey Inc. (handguns)
P.O. Box 475
Brookfield, Connecticut 06804
(203) 355-9000

Williams Gun Sight Co. (sights, scopes, mounts)
7389 Lapeer Road, P.O. Box 329
Davison, Michigan 48423
(313) 653-2131

Winchester (ammunition, primers, cases)
See Olin/Winchester

Winchester (domestic rifles, shotguns)
See U.S. Repeating Arms Co.

Winslow Arms Co. (rifles)
P.O. Box 783
Camden, South Carolina 29020
(803) 432-2938

Zeiss Optical, Inc. (scopes)
1015 Commerce Street
Petersburg, Virginia 23803
(804) 861-0033

GUNFINDER

To help you find the model of your choice, the following list includes each gun found in the catalog section of **Shooter's Bible 1990**. A supplemental listing of **Discontinued Models** and the **Caliberfinder** follow immediately after this section.

BLACK POWDER GUNS
MUSKETS AND RIFLES

CVA

Squirrel	350
Blazer	350
St. Louis Hawken	350
Hunter Hawken	351
Hawken	351
Kentucky	351
Pennsylvania Long	353
Express Double Barrel	353
Double Barrel Carbine	352
Ozark Mountain	352
Frontier Carbine	353

Dixie

Second Model Brown Bess	357
Kentuckian Flintlock/Perc.	357
Hawken	358
Tennessee Mountain	358
Tennessee Squirrel	358
Pennsylvania	358
Mississippi Rifle	359
Winchester '73 Carbine	359
Wesson	359
1862 Three-Band Enfield	360
1858 Two-Band Enfield	360
1863 Springfield Civil War	360
Tryon Creedmoor	359

Euroarms

Magnum Cape	362
London Armory Company 3-Band	363
Cook & Brother Confederate Carbine	362
London Armory Company (two-band)	387
London Armory Company Enfield (3-Band & Musketoon)	363

Gonic

Model GA-87 (458 Express)	365

Lyman

Great Plains	366
Trade	366

Modern Muzzleloading

Knight MK-85	367

Navy Arms

Parker-Hale Whitworth Military Target	373
Parker-Hale 451 Volunteer	373
Ithaca/Navy Hawken	373
#2 Creedmoor Target	374
Rolling Block Buffalo	374
Country Boy	374
1853 Enfield	375
1858 Enfield	375
1861 Enfield Musketoon	375
1863 Springfield	376
Mississippi Model 1841	376
Rigby-Style Target	376
Henry Military	377
Iron Frame Henry	377
Henry Trapper	377
Henry Carbine	377

Shiloh Sharps

Model 1874 Business	379
Model 1874 Military	379
Model 1874 Carbine	379
Model 1874 Sporting #1	380
Model 1874 Sporting #3	380
Model 1863 Sporting	380

Thompson/Center

White Mountain Carbine	382
Pennsylvania Hunter	382
Hawken	382
New Englander	381
Renegade	383
Renegade Hunter	383
Cherokee	383

Traditions

Frontier Scout	384
Hunter	384
Hawken	384
Hawken Woodsman	385
Pennsylvania	385
Pioneer	385
Trophy	385
Trapper	386
Frontier	386

A. Uberti

1858 New Army Target Revolving Carbine	387
Santa Fe Hawken	387

PISTOLS

CVA

Hawken	349
Kentucky	349
Colonial	349
Philadelphia Derringer	349
Siber	349

Dixie

Screw Barrel Derringer	355
French Charleville Flint	355
"Hideout" Derringer	355
Lincoln Derringer	355
Pennsylvania	356
Abilene Derringer	355
LePage Perc.	356
Queen Anne	356
Pedersoli English Dueling	356

Lyman

Plains Pistol	366

Navy Arms

LePage Flintlock	371
LePage Percussion	371
LePage Double Cased Set	371
Kentucky	372
Harper's Ferry	372
Elgin Cutlass	372

Thompson/Center

Patriot	381

Traditions

Trapper	386

REVOLVERS

Armsport

Models 5133/5136/5138/5120/5139/5140	344
Models 5145/5152/5153/5154	345

CVA

1861 Colt Navy	347
1851 Colt Navy	347
Colt Sheriff's Model	347
1860 Colt Army	347
1858 Remington Army	346
Colt Walker	346
New Model Pocket Remington	346
Wells Fargo Model Colt	348
Remington Bison	348
Third Model Colt Dragoon	348
Colt Pocket Police	348

Dixie

1860 Army	354
Navy Revolver	354
Spiller & Burr	354
Walker	355
Third Model Dragoon	355

EMF

Sheriff's Model 1851	361
Model 1860 Army	361
Model 1862 Police	361
Model 1851 Steel Navy	361
Second Model 44 Dragoon	361

Euroarms

Rogers & Spencer (Model 1005)	364
Rogers & Spencer Army (Model 1006)	364
Rogers & Spencer (Model 1007)	364
New Model Army (Model 1020)	364
Remington 1858 New Model Army (Models 1025 & 1040)	364
Schneider & Glassick 1851 Navy Confederate	365
Schneider & Glassick 1851 Navy	365

Navy Arms

Lemat	368
Colt Walker 1847	368
1862 Police	367
Reb Model 1860	369
Colt Army 1860	369
1851 Navy Yank	369
Rogers & Spencer Navy	368
Stainless Steel 1858 Remington	370
Target Model Remington	370
Deluxe 1858 Remington-Style	370
Remington New Model Army	370
Army 60 Sheriff's	370

A. Uberti

1st, 2nd & 3rd Model Dragoons	387
1861 Navy	388
1858 New Army 44	387
Walker	388
1851 Navy	388
1862 Pocket Navy	388

RIFLES
CENTERFIRE, AUTOLOADING & SLIDE ACTION

CENTERFIRE, BOLT ACTION

DISCONTINUED MODELS

The following models, all of which appeared in the 1989 edition of Shooter's Bible, have been discontinued by their manufacturers and/or distributors and therefore do not appear in this year's edition.

BLACK POWDER

ARMSPORT
Tryon Trailblazer
Model 5110 Kentucky rifle
Model 5115 rifle/shotgun
Models 5101 thru 5104 (Hawken)
Models 5124 & 5125 (Double Barrel shotgun)

CVA
Blazer II rifle
Missouri Ranger
Hawken rifle (replaced by Hunter Hawken)

EUROARMS
Schneider & Glassick 1851 Navy Sheriff
(Model 1080) revolver
Remington 1858 New Model Army Target
(Model 1045)
Hawken rifle (Model 2210A)

HOPKINS & ALLEN
Kentucky pistol (Model 10)
Boot Pistol (Model 13)
Brush rifle (Model 345)
Underhammer rifle (Model 32)
Pennsylvania Hawken rifle (Model 29)

MICHIGAN ARMS
Wolverine
Silverwolf
Friendship Special Match

NAVY ARMS
Henry Carbine Engraved

TRADITIONS
Sheandoah rifle

HANDGUNS

CHARTER ARMS
Undercover

F.I.E.
Model A27BW "The Best" (25 ACP pistol)

KIMBER
Predator Bolt Action pistol

LLAMA
Super Comanche V .357 Magnum

NEW ENGLAND
Double Action revolvers

RUGER
Model P210 Double Action pistol

SMITH & WESSON
Model 67 revolver
Model 439
Model 459
Model 469
Model 639

RIFLES

ANSCHUTZ
Model 1422D Custom
Model 64MS Featherweight
Model 2000 MK

BEEMAN
Beeman/FWB 2000
Beeman/Krico Models 320, 340, 420, 600, 640, 700

BLAZER
Ultimate Bolt Action

CHURCHILL
Regent Bolt Action

IVER JOHNSON
U.S. Carbine Model 22

MARLIN
Model 25 MB Midget Magnum

MAUSER
Model 66

PARKER-HALE
Model 1000 Standard

REMINGTON
Model 700 Gun Kit

SAUER
Model 200 (American & European)

TIKKA
Model M65

WINSLOW
Model Grade Crown

SHOTGUNS

BROWNING
Model B-80 Hunting (12 ga.) & Upland Special

CHURCHILL
Regent Trap & Skeet
Regent VII models

CHARLES DALY
Gas Automatic
Over-Under Diamond Trap & Skeet

F.I.E.
Over-Under 12 & 20 gauge

GAMBA
Principessa side-by-side
Oxford side-by-side

LEBEAU-COURALLY
Box Lock side-by-side
Sidelock H&H

MOSSBERG
Model 712 Slugster
Model 712A

NEW ENGLAND FIREARMS
"Pardner" Single Barrel
Turkey
Waterfowl Single Barrel
Handi-Gun 2-Barrel rifle
Shotgun System

REMINGTON
Model 870 Field Grade

ROSSI
Overland

ROTTWEIL
American Skeet

SAVAGE & STEVENS
Model 67/67-R
Model 68-RXG

STEVENS & FOX
Model BSE
Model 311

SOVEREIGN
Side-by-Side
Folding Single Barrel
Over-Under

CALIBERFINDER

How to use this guide: To find a 22LR handgun, look under that heading below. You'll find several models of that description, including Beretta Model 21. Turn next to the **Gunfinder** section and locate the heading for **Beretta** (pistols, in this case). Beretta's **Model 21,** as indicated, appears on p. 103.

BLACK POWDER

HANDGUNS

31
CVA Pocket Remington, Wells Fargo Model Colt, Vest Pocket Derringer

36
Armsport Models 5133, 5134, 5135
CVA Models 1851 & 1861 Colt Navy Revolvers, Sheriff's Model
Dixie Navy Revolver, Spiller & Burr Revolver
EMF 1851 Sheriff's Model, 1851 Steel Navy, Model 1862 Police
Euroarms Schneider & Glassick 1851 Navy & Navy Sheriff, Schneider & Glassick 1851 Navy Confederate Revolver
Navy Arms 1862 Police Revolver, Reb Model 1860, Army 1860 Sheriff's Model, ''Yank'' Revolver
Traditions Trapper Pistol
A. Uberti 1851 Navy, 1861 Navy, 1862 Pocket Navy

38
Dixie Pedersoli Navy Target Pistol

41
Dixie Abilene & Lincoln Derringers

44
Armsport Models 5138, 5120, 5134, 5136, 5145, 5152, 5135, 5136
CVA 1861 Colt Navy, 1860 Colt Army Revolvers, Colt Walker, Third Model Colt Dragoon, Remington Bison, 1858 Remington Army Steel Frame Revolver (also Brass Frame)
Dixie Walker Revolver, Pennsylvania Pistol, Third Model Dragoon, Wyatt Earp Revolver
EMF Model 1860 Army, Second Model 44 Dragoon
Euroarms Rogers & Spencer Models 1005 & 1006, Remington 1858 New Model Army (and Target)
Navy Arms Colt Walker 1847, Reb Model 1860 Revolver, Colt Army 1860 Revolver, Rogers & Spencer Navy Revolver, Target Model Remington Revolver, Army 60 Sheriff's Model, Stainless Steel 1858 Remington, Remington New Model Army, LeMat Revolvers, 1851 Navy Yank Revolver, Deluxe 1858 Remington-Style Revolver
Uberti 1st Model Dragoon, 1858 New Army, Walker

45
CVA Colonial, Philadelphia Derringer, Siber
Dixie Pedersoli English Dueling Pistol
Navy Arms LePage Percussion & Flint Pistols, Moore & Patrick English Pistols, Double Cased LePage Pistols
Thompson/Center Patriot
Traditions Trapper Pistol

50
CVA Kentucky Pistol, Hawken Pistol
Lyman Plains Pistol
Traditions Trapper

56
Navy Arms Harper's Ferry Pistol

RIFLES (Black Powder)

32
CVA Squirrel
Dixie Tennessee Squirrel
Navy Arms Country Boy
Thompson/Center Cherokee

36
CVA Squirrel
Navy Arms Country Boy
Traditions Trapper, Frontier Scout

44
Navy Arms Henry Carbine, Iron Frame
Uberti 1858 New Army Target Revolving Carbine

44-40
Dixie Winchester '73 Carbine
Navy Arms Henry Carbine, Henry Trapper, Military, Iron Frame

45
Dixie Kentuckian, Hawken, Pedersoli Waadtlander, Tryon Creedmoor
Modern Muzzleloading Knight MK-85
Navy Arms Country Boy
Thompson/Center Cougar, Hawken, Cherokee
Traditions Frontier, Frontier Scout, Hawken, Pennsylvania, Kentucky Scout, Trapper

451
Navy Arms Rigby-Style Target Rifle, Parker-Hale Whitworth Military Target, Parker-Hale 451 Volunteer

45-70
Navy Arms Rolling Block Buffalo rifle, #2 Creedmoor Target
Shiloh Sharps Model 1874

45-90
Shiloh Sharps Model 1874 Sporting #1 & #3; Business/Carbine

45-120
Shiloh Sharps Model 1874 Sporting #1 & #3, Business

458
Gonic Model GA-87

50
CVA Frontier, Blazer, Kentucky, Pennsylvania Long Rifle, Hunter Hawken, Express Double

Rifle & Carbine, Over-Under Carbine, Ozark Mountain
Dixie Hawken, Tennessee Mountain, Wesson
Lyman Great Plains, Trade Rifle
Modern Muzzleloading Knight MK-85
Navy Arms Country Boy, Ithaca-Navy Hawken
Thompson/Center Renegade, Renegade Hunter, Cougar Hawken, Hawken, New Englander, Pennsylvania Hunter, White Mountain Carbine
Traditions Frontier Scout, Hunter, Hawken, Frontier, Pennsylvania, Hawken Woodsman, Trapper, Pioneer, Trophy
Uberti Santa Fe Hawken

50-70
Shiloh Sharps Model 1874 Business, Sporting #1 & #3, Military

50-90
Shiloh Sharps Model 1874 Business, Sporting #1 & #3

50-140
Shiloh Sharps Model 1874 Business, Sporting #1 & #3

54
CVA St. Louis Hawken, Hawken Mountain, Hunter Hawken, Ozark Mountain
Dixie Hawken
Lyman Great Plains, Trade Rifle
Modern Muzzleloading Knight MK-85
Navy Arms Ithaca, Navy Hawken
Shiloh Sharps Model 1863 Sporting
Thompson/Center Renegade, Renegade Hunter, Hawken, New Englander
Traditions Hunter, Hawken, Hawken Woodsman, Pioneer, Trophy
Uberti Sante Fe Hawken

56
Thompson/Center Renegade

58
Dixie Hawken, Mississippi, 1863 Springfield Civil War Musket, 1862 Three-Band Enfield Rifle Musket, 1858 Two-Band Enfield rifle
Euroarms Model 2260 London Armory Company Enfield Rifled Musket, Models 2270 and 2280 London Armory Company Enfield Rifled Muskets, Model 2300 Cook & Brother Confederate Carbine
Navy Arms 1863 Springfield, Mississippi Model 1841
Traditions Hawken

74
Dixie Second Model Brown Bess Musket

75
Navy Arms Second Model Brown Bess Musket

557
Navy Arms 1853 Enfield Rifle Musket, 1858 Enfield, 1861 Enfield Musketoon

SHOTGUNS (Black Powder)

CVA Trapper (12 ga.)
Euroarms Model 2295 Magnum Cape (single barrel)
Navy Arms Model T&T, Flintlock, Fowler (12 ga.)
Thompson/Center New Englander

HANDGUNS

22LR

American Arms Models PK & PX
Anschutz Exemplar
Astra Constable
Beeman Unique 69 Target, Model PO8, Model 150 Free Pistol, Model 152 Electronic, Beeman/Hammerli Model 208 Target & Model 215 Target
Beretta Model 21
Bernardelli Model PO10 Standard, Model 69, AMR, USA
Bersa Model 226
Browning Buck Mark 22
Charter Arms Pathfinder, Off-Duty
Dakota Model 1873, Dakota Target, 1894 Bisley
Davis Model D-22
Erma ESP 85A Sporting Pistol, Model 772 Match Revolver, Match 777 Sporting Revolver
F.I.E. Arminius, Titan II, Cowboy
Freedom Arms FA-S
Iver Johnson Pocket Model
Llama Automatic (Small Frame)
Mitchell Arms SA Army Model (revolvers)
North American Arms Mini-Revolvers
Rossi Model 511
Ruger New Model Single-Six, Mark II Pistols
Smith & Wesson Models 17, 34, 63, 41, 422
Springfield Armory Model 1911-A2 SASS
Tanarmi Model TA76M
Targa Model GT22T
Taurus Model 94
Thompson/Center Contender
A. Uberti DA Automatics (Models PP, P-38, TPH, GSP Match, GSP Jr., UIT-BV), 1871 Rolling Block Target Pistol
Walther Model P-38, Model TPH-DA, Models OSP & GSP, Model FP (Free Pistol), Model U.I.T.-BV

22 Rimfire Magnum

American Derringer Model 1
AMT 22 Automag II
Dakota Model 1873
North American Mini-Revolvers
Ruger Government Target Model
Uberti 1871 Rolling Block Target Pistol, 1873 Stallion Quick Draw
Dan Wesson 22 Rimfire Magnum

22 Short

Beeman Unique 2000-U, Beeman/Hammerli Model 232 Rapid Fire
Beretta Model 950 BS
F.I.E. Arminius DA
North American Arms Mini-Revolvers

22 Hornet

American Derringer Model 1
MOA Maximum
Thompson/Center Contender

22 Win. Mag.

F.I.E. Arminius
Freedom Arms FA-S
North American Mini-Revolvers

Tanarmi Model TA76M
Thompson/Center Contender

223 Remington

Remington Model XP-100
Springfield Armory Model 1911-A2 SASS
Thompson/Center Contender

223 Rem. Comm. Auto

American Derringer Model 1
Thompson/Center Contender

6mm BR

Remington XP-100 Long-Range Custom

25 Auto

Beretta Model 21, Model 950BS
Davis Model D-22 Derringer
F.I.E. Titan 25
Iver Johnson Pocket
Kassnar Model PSP-25
Raven Arms Model P-25

250 Savage

Remington XP-100 Long-Range Custom

7mm BR

Remington Model XP-100
Springfield Armory Model 1911-A2 SASS

7mm-08

Remington Model XP-100 Long-Range Custom

7-30 Water

Thompson/Center Contender

30 Carbine

Ruger Model BN-31
Thompson/Center Contender

30 Mauser (7.62 Tokarev)

American Derringer Model 1

30-30 Win.

American Derringer Model 1
Thompson/Center Contender

32 Mag.

American Derringer Models 1, 3 & 7
Charter Arms Police Bulldog, Bonnie & Clyde

32 Auto

Davis Models D-22 and P-32
F.I.E. Super Titan II
Llama Auto (Small Frame)

32 H&R

Charter Arms Police Undercover
Ruger New Model Single-Six SSM
Thompson/Center Contender

32 S&W Long

American Derringer Model 7
F.I.E. Arminius
Ruger New Model Single-Six SSM
Smith & Wesson Model 31
Taurus Model 73
Walther Model GSP-C

32 S&W Wadcutter

Erma ESP 85A Sporting Pistol, Model 773 Match Revolver

32-20

American Derringer Model 1
Dakota Model 1873

35 Remington

Remington Model XP-100
Thompson/Center Contender

357 Mag.

American Derringer Models 1, 6
Astra 357 Mag.
Beeman Korth
Charter Arms Bulldog Tracker, Police Bulldog
Colt King Cobra, Python
Coonan Arms Model B
Dakota Target, 1894 Bisley, 1875 Outlaw, Model 1873, Model 1813 Premier SA, Custom Engraved SA
Erma Model 777 Sporting Revolver
F.I.E. Arminius
L.A.R. Grizzly Mark I
Llama Comanche III
Magnum Research Desert Eagle
Mitchell Arms SA Army revolvers
Rossi Model 971
Ruger Model GP-100, New Model Bisley, Blackhawk SA
Smith & Wesson Models 13, 19, 27, 65, 66, 586
Springfield Armory Model 1911-A2 SASS
Taurus Models 65, 66, 669
Thompson/Center Contender
Uberti 1875 Remington Army Outlaw, 1871 Rolling Block Target pistol, 1873 Cattleman Quick Draw
Dan Wesson 357 Mag., 357 Super Mag.

357 Maximum

American Derringer Model 1
Thompson/Center Contender

358 Winchester

MOA Maximum
Springfield Armory Model 1911-All SASS

38 Special

American Derringer 1, 3, 7, 11
Charter Arms Police Undercover, Police Bulldog, Off-Duty, Undercover 38 Special, Bonnie & Clyde
F.I.E. Derringer D-86, Titan Tiger, Arminius
Rossi Models 68, M88, M951, 971
Ruger Model SP101
Smith & Wesson Models 649, Lady Smith
Taurus Models 66, 80, 82, 86, 669
Uberti 1873 Cattleman Quick Draw
Dan Wesson 38 Special

380 Auto

American Arms Models EP & ZC
American Derringer Models 1 and 7
Astra Constable
Beeman Model Mini-PO8
Beretta Models 84, 85, 86
Bernardelli Models AMR, USA
Bersa Model 383 DA
Browning Model BDA-380
Colt Government Model, Mustang, Mustang Plus II, Mustang Pocket Lite 380
F.I.E. Titan II, Super Titan II
Heckler & Koch Model P7K3
Llama Automatic (Small Frame)

Sig Sauer Model 230
Targa Model GT380XE
Taurus Model PT 58
Walther Model PPK

38 Super

American Derringer Model 7
Colt Combat Commander, Government Model
Sig Sauer Model 220
Springfield Armory Model 1911-A1 Standard,
   Omega
Victory Arms Model MC5

38 S&W

American Derringer Model 7
Smith & Wesson Models 10, 13, 15, 36, 38, 49,
   52, 60, 64, 65

9mm Federal

American Derringer Model 1

9mm Luger

American Derringer Model 1
Colt Combat Commander
Heckler & Koch Model P7
Smith & Wesson Model 5900 & 6900 Series
Thompson/Center Contender

9mm Parabellum

Action Arms Models AT-88S, AT-88P, AT-88H
American Arms Model TT
American Derringer Semmerling LM-4
Astra Model A-90
Beretta Model 92F
Bernardelli Model P018
Brno Model CZ75
Browning 9mm Hi-Power
F.I.E. Model TZ75
Glock Models 17, 17L Competition, 19
Heckler & Koch Model P7M8 & P7M13
Kassnar Model 941 Jericho
Llama Automatics (Compact Frame), Model M-82,
   M-87 Comp
Ruger Model P-85
Sig Sauer Models 220, 225, 226
Smith & Wesson Third Generation Pistols (Model
   3900 Series)
Springfield Armory Model 1911-A1 Standard,
   Model P9 DA
Star Models BKM, BM, 30M & 30 PK
Tanarmi Models BTA90B & BTA90C
Taurus Models PT92 & PT99
Victory Arms Model MC5
Walther Models P-38, P-88DA, P-5DA
Wildey Pistols

10mm

Colt Delta Elite
Springfield Armory Omega
Victory Arms Model MC5

41 Action Express

Action Arms Models AT-88S, AT-88P, AT-88H
American Derringer Model 1
F.I.E. Model TZ75
Kassnar Model 941 Jericho
Tanarmi Model TA90B
Victory Arms Model MC5

41 Mag.

American Derringer Model 1
Magnum Research Desert Eagle
Ruger New Model Bisley, Redhawk, Blackhawk
   SA
Smith & Wesson Models 57, 657
Dan Wesson 41 Mag Revolvers

.410

American Derringer Models 1, 4, 6

44 Magnum

American Derringer Model 1
Astra Model 44
Llama Super Comanche IV
Magnum Research Desert Eagle
Mitchell Arms SA Army Model Revolvers
Ruger Redhawk, New Model Bisley, Blackhawk
   SA, Super Blackhawk, Super Redhawk DA
Smith & Wesson Model 29
Springfield Armory Model 1911-A2
Thompson/Center Contender
Dan Wesson 44 Mag. Revolvers

44 Special

American Derringer Models 1 and 7
Charter Arms Bulldog Pug, New Police Bulldog
Uberti 1873 Cattleman Quick Draw

44-40

American Derringer Model 1
Dakota Models 1873, 1875 Outlaw, 1894 Bisley,
   Custom Engraved SP
A. Uberti 1873 Cattleman Quick Draw, 1875
   Remington Army Outlaw

45 Auto

American Derringer Models 1, 6, Semmerling
   LM-4
Astra Model A-90
Colt Combat Commander, Lightweight
   Commander, Gold Cup National Match, Officer's
   ACP
Detonics Combat Master
L.A.R. Grizzly Mark I
Llama Automatics (Large and Compact Frames)
Sig Sauer Model 220
Smith & Wesson Third Generation (Model 4500
   Series)
Springfield Armory Model 1911-A1 Standard,
   Defender, Commander, Omega
Star Model PD
Victory Arms Model MC5

45 Colt

American Derringer Models 1, 4, 6
Astra Model 45
Dakota Target, Models 1873, 1875, 1894 Bisley,
   1873 Premier SA, Custom Engraved SA
Mitchell Arms SA Army Model Revolvers
Ruger New Model Bisley
Smith & Wesson Model 25
Thompson/Center Contender
Uberti 1873 Cattleman Quick Draw, 1875
   Remington Army Outlaw

45 Win. Mag.

American Derringer Model 1
L.A.R. Grizzly Mark I
Wildey Pistols

454 Casull

Freedom Arms Casull Model FA-454AS

RIFLES

CENTERFIRE BOLT ACTION

Standard Calibers

17 Rem.

Kimber Model 84

Remington Model 700 BDL
Sako Hunter, Varmint, Deluxe
Ultra Light Model 20
Winslow Varmint

220 Swift

Ruger Model M-77V Varmint

22 PPC

Sako Varmint, BR, Hunter, Deluxe

222 Rem.

Brno Models ZKK 600, 601, 602
Churchill Highlander
Kimber Model 84
Remington Model 700 BDL
Sako Varmint, Hunter, Deluxe, Carbine
Steyr-Mannlicher Model SL
Ultra Light Model 20
Winslow Varmint

223 Rem.

Brno Model ZKK601
Browning A-Bolt
Heckler & Koch Models 630
Howa Trophy Sporting, Varmint
Kimber Model 84
Mark X Mini
Remington Models 700 BDL, Seven, Sportsman
   78
Ruger M-77 Mark II
Sako Fiberclass, Hunter, Varmint, Deluxe, LS
Savage Model 110E
Steyr-Mannlicher Model SL
Tikka New Generation Rifles
Ultra Light Model 20
Weatherby Vanguard Classic I, Weatherguard
Winchester Models 70 Featherweight, Sporter,
   Lightweight, Super Express, Varmint
Winslow Varmint

22-250

Blaser Model R84
Browning Short Action A-Bolt
Dakota 76 SA
Howa Trophy, Sporting, Varmint
Mark X American Field Mauser System
McMillan Classic Sporter SA
Parker-Hale Models M81, 1200, 2100, 1100 LWT
Remington Model 700 ADL Deluxe, Model 700
   BDL
Ruger Models M-77RL, M-77RSI International, M-
   77V Varmint
Sako Deluxe, Varmint, Carbine, Hunter,
   Fiberclass, LS
Savage Model 110E
Steyr-Mannlicher Model L
Ultra Light Model 20
Weatherby Deluxe
Winchester Model 70 Featherweight, Lightweight,
   VGX Sporter & Super Express, Varmint
Winslow Classic

224

Weatherby Mark V Lazermark, Deluxe

240

Weatherby Mark V Lazermark, Deluxe, Ultramark,
   Fibermark, Euromark

243 Win.

Beeman/Krico Models 600, 700
Blaser Model R84
Brno Model ZKK 601
Churchill Highlander
Dakota Model 76 SA

Heym Model SR20
Howa Trophy Sporting, Model 1500 Series (barreled actions)
K.D.F. Model 225 Mauser
Mark X American Field Mauser System
McMillan Classic Sporter SA
Parker-Hale Models M81, 1200, 1100, LWT, 2100, M87
Remington Models 700 BDL, LS & FS, 78, 7400, 7600, 700 Mountain, 700 ADL Deluxe, Model Seven
Ruger Models RS, RSI International
Sako Carbine, Varmint, Fiberclass, Hunter, Deluxe, LS
Sauer Models 90 Supreme & Lux
Savage Models 110E
Steyr-Mannlicher Models L, SSG Marksman
Tikka New Generation Rifles
Ultra Light Model 20
Weatherby Vanguard Classic I, Classic II, Weatherguard
Winchester Models 70 Featherweight, Lightweight, Varmint, Sporter & Super Express, Ranger Youth
Winslow Basic

6mm Rem.

Blaser Model R84
McMillan Classic Sporter SA, Benchrest
Parker-Hale Models 81, 1100 LWT, 1200, 2100
Remington Model Seven, Model 700 BDL
Ruger Model M-77 Varmint
Ultra Light Model 20
Steyr-Mannlicher Model L

250-3000 Savage

Dakota Model 76 SA
Ruger Model M-77RSI International
Ultra Light Model 20

257

Ultra Light Model 20
Weatherby Mark V Lazermark, Deluxe, Fibermark, Euromark

6 PPC

Sako Varmint, BR/Varmint, Hunter, Deluxe

25-06

Blaser Model R84
Browning A-Bolt
Churchill Highlander
K.D.F. Model 225 Mauser
Mark X American Field Mauser System
McMillan Classic Sporter LA
Remington Model 700 ADL, BDL
Ruger Models M-77V Varmint, 77RS
Sako Fiberclass, Hunter, Carbine, Deluxe, LS
Sauer Models 90 Supreme & Lux
Steyr-Mannlicher Model M

257 Roberts

Browning A-Bolt Short Action
Dakota Arms Model 76 Classic
Winslow Basic

270 Win.

Beeman/Krico Model 720
Blaser Models R84
Brno Model ZKK 600
Browning A-Bolt
Churchill Highlander
Dakota Arms Model 76 Classic
Heym Model SR20

Howa Trophy Sporting, Lightning, Model 1500 Series (barreled action)
Kimber Big Game
Mark X LTW, American Field Mauser System, LTW Sporter
McMillan Classic Sporter LA, Alaskan, Titanium Mountain
Parker-Hale Models M81, 1100, 1200, 2100
Remington Models 78, 700 LS, FS & RS, 7400, 7600, 700 ADL & BDL, 700 Mountain
Ruger Model M77 RS, RL Ultralight, 77RSI International
Sako Deluxe, Carbine, Fiberclass, Hunter, LS
Sauer Model 90 Supreme & Lux, Stutzen
Savage Model 110E
Steyr-Mannlicher Model M
Tikka New Generation Rifles
Weatherby Models Mark V Lazermark, Deluxe, Fibermark, Vanguard Classic I & II, VGX, Weatherguard Euromark
Winchester Models 70 Lightweight, Featherweight, Ranger, Winlite, Sporter & Super Express
Winslow Basic

280 Rem.

Blaser Model R 84
Browning A-Bolt
Dakota Arms Model 76 Classic
Kimber Big Game
McMillan Classic Sporter LA, Alaskan
Remington Models 700 RS, 7400, 7600, 700 BDL
Winchester Models 70 Featherweight, Winlite, Lightweight
Winslow Basic

284 Win.

McMillan Classic Sporter SA
Ultra Light Model 20
Winslow Basic

7mm-08

Browning A-Bolt Short Action
Dakota Model 76 SA
McMillan Classic Sporter SA
Remington Model Seven, Model 700 Mountain, Model Seven "FS", Model 700 BDL
Sako Hunter, Deluxe, LS, Varmint
Ultra Light Model 20

30-06

Beeman/Krico Model 700, 720
Blaser Model R 84
Brno Model ZKK 600
Browning A-Bolt
Churchill Highlander
Dakota Arms Model 76 Classic
Heckler & Koch Model 940
Heym Model SR20
Howa Trophy Sporting, Lightning, Model 1500 Series (barreled action)
K.D.F. Model 225 Mauser
Kimber Big Game
Mark X American Field Mauser System, LTW Sporter
McMillan Classic Sporter LA, Alaskan
Parker-Hale Models M81 Classic, 1100 Lightweight, 1200 Super, 2100 Midland, M87
Remington Models 78, 700 LS, FS & RS, BDL, 7400, 7600, Model 700 Mountain, Model 700 ADL
Ruger Model M-77RS, 77RL Ultra Light, 77RSI International
Sako Carbine, Fiberclass, Hunter, Deluxe, LS
Sauer Model 90 Supreme & Lux, Stutzen
Savage Model 110E

Steyr-Mannlicher Model M
Tikka New Generation Rifles
Weatherby Fibermark, Lazermark, Euromark, Deluxe
Winchester Models 70 Featherweight, Winlite, Lightweight, Sporter & Super Express
Winslow Basic

30-06 Carbine

Remington Models 7400, 7600

300 Savage

Ultra Light Model 20

308 Win.

Beeman/Krico Models 600, 640
Brno Model ZKK 601
Browning A-Bolt Short Action
Churchill Highlander
Dakota Model 76 SA
Heckler & Koch Models HK PSG-1, 770
Heym Model SR20
Howa Trophy Sporting, Model 1500 Series (barreled action)
K.D.F. Model 225 Mauser
Krieghoff Ulm & Teck
Mark X American Field Mauser System
McMillan Classic Sporter SA, National Match, Benchrest
Parker-Hale Models M81, 1100, 1200, 2100, M87
Remington Models Seven, 700 Mountain, 7400, 7600, 700 ADL & BDL
Ruger Models M-77RS, 77RSI International, 77V Varmint
Sako Carbine, Varmint, Fiberclass, Hunter, Deluxe, LS
Sauer Models 90 Supreme & Lux
Savage Model 110E
Steyr-Mannlicher Models L, SSG Marksman & Match UIT
Ultra Light Model 20
Weatherby Vanguard Classic I, Weatherguard
Winchester Model 70 Lightweight, Featherweight (short action)
Winslow Basic

35 Whelen

Remington Models 700 BDL & CL, 7400, 7600

358 Win.

Ultra Light Model 20
Winslow Basic

MAGNUM CALIBERS

222 Rem. Mag.

Kimber Model 84 Sporter
Steyr-Mannlicher Model SL

257 Weatherby

Blaser Model R84
K.D.F. Model 225 Mauser
Steyr-Mannlicher Model S
Winslow Basic

264 Win. Mag.

Blaser Model R84
Steyr-Mannlicher Model S
Winchester Model 70 Sporter & Super express

270 Weatherby Mag.

K.D.F. Model 225 Mauser
Winchester Model 70 Sporter & Super Express

270 Win. Mag.

Sako Carbine

7mm Rem. Mag.

Blaser Model R84
Browning A-Bolt
Churchill Highlander
Dakota Arms Model 76 Classic
Heym Model SR20
Howa Lightning, Model 1500 Series (barreled action)
K.D.F. Model 225 Mauser
Kimber Big Game
Mark X American Field Mauser System, LTW Sporter
McMillan Classic Sporter LA, Alaskan
Remington Models 700 LS & FS, 700 ADL & BDL
Parker-Hale Model M81 Classic
Ruger Models M-77RS, 77RL
Sako Fiberclass, Hunter, Carbine, Deluxe, LS
Sauer Model 90 Supreme & Lux
Savage Model 110E
Steyr-Mannlicher Model S
Weatherby Mark V Fibermark, Euromark, Deluxe, Lazermark, Vanguard VGX, Classic II
Winchester Model 70 Winlite, Sporter & Super Express

8mm Rem. Mag.

Remington Model 700 Safari

338 Win. Mag.

Blaser Model R84
Browning A-Bolt
Dakota Arms Model 76 Safari, Classic
Heym Model SR20
McMillan Classic Sporter MA, Safari
Kimber Big Game
Ruger Model M-77RS
Sako Safari Grade, Hunter, Carbine, Deluxe, LS, Fiberclass
Tikka New Generation Rifles
Weatherby Vanguard VGX, Classic II
Winchester Model 70 Winlite, Sporter & Super Express
Winslow Basic

340 Weatherby

McMillan Classic Sporter MA

340 Win. Mag.

McMillan Safari
Weatherby Mark V Lazermark, Euromark, Fibermark, Deluxe

375 H&H

Blaser Model R84
Brno Model ZKK 602
Browning A-Bolt
Dakota Arms Model 76 Safari, Classic
Heym Model SR20
K.D.F. Model 225 Mauser
Kimber Big Game
Krieghoff Ulm & Teck
McMillan Classic Sporter MA, Safari
Parker-Hale Model M81 Safari
Remington Model 700 Safari
Sako Safari Grade, Carbine, Fiberclass, Hunter, LS, Deluxe
Sauer Model 90 Supreme & Lux
Steyr-Mannlicher Models S & S/T
Whitworth Safari Grade Express
Winchester Model 70 Super Express (standard)
Winslow Basic

378 Win. Mag.

McMillan Safari
Weatherby Mark V Lazermark, Euromark, Deluxe

416 Rem. Mag.

Remington Model 700 Safari
Weatherby Mark V Euromark, Deluxe, Lazermark

416 Rigby

Dakota Arms African Grade 76
McMillan Safari

458 Win. Mag.

Brno Model ZKK 602
Dakota Arms Model 76 Safari, Classic
Krieghoff Ulm & Teck
McMillan Safari
Remington Model 700 Safari
Ruger No. 1 Tropical
Sauer Model S90 Safari
Steyr-Mannlicher Model S/T
Whitworth Safari Grade Express
Winchester Model 70 Super Express Walnut Magnum
Winslow Basic

460 Win. Mag.

Weatherby Lazermark, Euromark, Deluxe

CENTERFIRE LEVER ACTION

218 Bee

Browning Model 65

22 Magnum

A. Uberti Model 1866, Model 1871, Model 1873 Carbine

222 Rem./223 Rem.

Browning Models 81 BLR, 1885

22-250

Browning Models 81 BLR, 1885

243 Win.

Browning Model 81 BLR
Ruger Model No. 1RSI International
Savage Model 99-C

257 Roberts

Browning Model 81 BLR

270

Browning Model 1885
Ruger Model No. 1RSI International

284 Win.

Browning Model 81 BLR

7mm-08

Browning Model 81 BLR

307 Win.

Winchester Model 94 Standard, Big Bore Walnut

308 Win.

Browning Model 81BLR
Savage Model 99-C

30-30 Win.

Marlin Models 336CS, 336 Lightweight, 30AS
Winchester Models 94 Standard, Big Bore Walnut

30-06

Browning Model 1885
Ruger Model No. 1 International

32-20 Win.

Marlin Model 1894 Classic

35 Rem.

Marlin Model 336CS

356 Win.

Winchester Model 94 Standard, Big Bore Walnut

357 Mag.

Marlin Model 1894CS
Rossi Puma (Model M92)
Uberti Models 1871, 1875 Army SA

358 Win.

Browning Model 81BLR

375 Win.

Marlin Model 336CS

38 Special

Marlin Model 1894CS
Rossi Puma (Model M92)
A. Uberti 1866 Sporting, 1873 Carbine

41 Mag.

Marlin Model 1894S

44 Special

Marlin Model 1894S

44 Rem. Mag.

Browning Model 92
Marlin Model 1894S
Winchester Model 94 Walnut Trapper

444 Marlin

Marlin Model 444SS

44-40

Uberti Models 1886, 1875 Army SA, 1873 Carbine, Buckhorn Carbine

45 Colt

Browning Model 1885
Marlin Model 1894S
Uberti Model 1875 Army SA, 1873 Carbine
Winchester Model 94 Walnut Trapper

45-70 Government

Marlin Model 1895SS

7mm Rem. Mag.

Browning Model 1885

SINGLE SHOT

22S,L,LR

Iver Johnson L'il Champ
Varner Favorite Hunter Model
Walther Running Boar, Model GX-1, UIT Match, Model KK/MS

22 BR Rem.

Remington Model 40XB-BR

22 Hornet

Thompson/Center Hunter

22 PPC

Sako Varmint

220 Swift

Ruger No. 1 Special Varminter, Standard

222 Rem.

Remington Models 40-XB, 40XB-BR

223

Remington Model 40XB-BR
Ruger No. 1 Standard
Thompson/Center Hunter

22-250 Rem.

Blaser Model K 77A
Remington Model 40-XB
Ruger No. 1 Standard, Special Varminter
Thompson/Center Hunter

243 Win.

Blaser Model K 77A
Ruger No. 1 Light Sporter, Standard
Thompson/Center Hunter

25-06

Remington Model 40-XB
Ruger No. 1V Special Varminter, No. 1B Standard

6mm BR Rem.

Remington Model 40XB-BR

6mm Rem.

Remington Model 40XB-BR
Ruger No. 1 Special Varminter, Standard

6 PPC

Sako Varmint

257 Roberts

Ruger No. 1 Standard

270 Win.

Blaser Model K 77A
Ruger No. 1 Light Sporter, Standard, RSI International
Thompson/Center Hunter

280 Rem.

Blaser Model K 77A
Ruger No. 1 Standard

30-06

Blaser Model K 77A
Remington Model 40XB
Ruger No. 1 Light Sporter, Standard, RSI International
Thompson/Center Hunter

300 Win. Mag.

Blaser Model K 77A
Browning BAR Magnum
Remington Model 40-XB
Ruger No. 1 Medium Sporter, No. 1S Medium Sporter, Standard

308 Win.

Remington Model 40-XB
Thompson/Center Hunter

7mm Rem. Mag.

Blaser Model K 77A
Browning BAR Magnum

Remington Model 40-XB

Remington Model 40-XB
Ruger No. 1 Standard
Thompson/Center Hunter

300 Weatherby Mag.

Blaser Model K 77A
Ruger No. 1 Standard

338 Win. Mag.

Browning BAR Magnum
Ruger No. 1 Medium Sporter, Standard

375 H&H

Ruger No. 1 Tropical

458 Win. Mag.

Ruger No. 1 Tropical

AUTOLOADING

22 Win. Mag.

Heckler & Koch Model 300 Varmint

222 Rem.

Thompson/Center Contender

223 Rem.

Ruger Mini-14, Mini-14 Ranch
Valmet Hunter
Thompson/Center Contender

243 Win.

Browning BAR Standard
Valmet Hunter

30-06

Browning BAR Standard, Big game Series
Valmet Hunter

30-30 Win.

Thompson/Center Contender

300 Win. Mag.

Browning BAR Standard

308 Win.

Browning BAR Standard
Valmet Hunter

35 Rem.

Thompson/Center Contender

44 Mag.

Thompson/Center Contender

45 Auto

Marlin Model 45

9mm

Marlin Model 9 Camp

RIMFIRE BOLT ACTION

22S,L,LR

Anschutz Match 54 & Match 64 Sporters, Models 64MS, 54, 18MS, 1907, 1910, 1911, 1913, 1808, Model 1700, Achiever
Beeman/Weihrauch Models HW60 Smallbore, HW660 Match
Beeman/FWB Model 2600
Beeman/Krico Models 320, 340, Sporter
Browning Model A-Bolt 22, A-Bolt Stalker
K.D.F. Model 201

Kimber Model 82

Kimber Model 82
Marlin Models 15, 25N, 880, 881
Remington Models 40-XR, 40-XC, 541-T, 581-S, 552 BDL, 572 BDL
Rossi Gallery Rifles
Ruger Model 77/22RS

22 Hornet

Beeman/Krico Model 400

22 WMR

Marlin Models 25MN, 882, 883

22 Mag.

K.D.F. Model 201

222 Rem.

Beeman/Weihrauch Model HW 60J-ST

RIMFIRE AUTOLOADING

22S,L,LR

Anschutz Model 525
Browning Model 22 (Grades I & VI)
Iver Johnson Targetmaster
Marlin Models 70P, 70HC, 75C, 60, 995
Remington Model 572 BDL Fieldmaster
Ruger Model 10/22
Weatherby Mark XXII

RIMFIRE LEVER ACTION

22S,L,LR

Browning Model BL-22 (Grades I & II)
Iver Johnson Wagonmaster
Marlin Models 39TD, Golden 39AS
Winchester Model 9422

444 Marlin

Marlin Model 444SS

DOUBLE RIFLES

308

Krieghoff Models Ulm & Teck

30-06

Krieghoff Models Ulm & Teck

300 Win. Mag.

Krieghoff Models Ulm & Teck

375 H&H

Heym Model 88 Safari
Krieghoff Models Ulm & Teck

458 Win.

Heym Model 88 Safari
Krieghoff Models Ulm & Teck

470 N.E.

Heym Model 88 Safari

500 N.E.

Heym Model 88 Safari

RIFLE/SHOTGUN COMBOS

22 Mag./12 ga.

Heym Model 22S

22 Hornet/12 ga.

Heym Model 22S

| 222 Rem./12 ga. |

Churchill Regent
Heym Model 22S
Savage Model 24-F

| 222 Rem. Mag./12 ga. |

Heym Model 22S

| 223 Rem./12 ga. |

Churchill Regent
Savage Model 24-F

| 243 Win./12 ga. |

Heym Model 22S

| 270 Win./12 ga. |

Churchill Regent

| 308 Win./12 ga. |

Churchill Regent

| 30-06/12 ga. |

Churchill Regent

| 30-30/12 ga. |

Savage Model 24F

INDEX

NOTES